D0152529

PROCEDURAL ELEMENTS FOR COMPUTER GRAPHICS

PROCEDURAL ELEMENTS FOR COMPUTER GRAPHICS

Second Edition

David F. Rogers
Professor of Aerospace Engineering
United States Naval Academy, Annapolis, Md.

Boston, Massachusetts
Burr Ridge, Illinois Dubuque, Iowa Madison, Wisconsin
New York, New York San Francisco, California St. Louis, Missouri

WITHDRAWN

LIBRARY
OF
MOUNT SAINT MARY'S
COLLEGE
EMMITSBURG, MARYLAND

WCB/McGraw-Hill

*A Division of The **McGraw·Hill** Companies*

Copyright © 1998 by The McGraw-Hill Companies, Inc. All rights reserved. Previous edition(s) © 1985. Printed in the United States of America. Except as permitted under the United States Copyright Act of 1976, no part of this publication may be reproduced or distributed in any form or by any means, or stored in a data base or retrieval system, without the prior written permission of the publisher.

This book is printed on acid-free paper.

1 2 3 4 5 6 7 8 9 0 QPF/QPF 9 0 9 8 7

ISBN 0-07-053548-5

Editorial director: *Kevin Kane*
Publisher: *Tom Casson*
Executive editor: *Elizabeth A. Jones*
Senior developmental editor: *Kelley Butcher*
Marketing manager: *John Wannemacher*
Project manager: *Kari Geltemeyer*
Production supervisor: *Heather D. Burbridge*
Senior designer: *Laurie J. Entringer*
Compositor: *NAR Associates*
Printer: *Quebecor Printing Book Group/Fairfield*

Cover illustration credits:

Front Cover: Image created by Peter Kipfer and François Sillion using a hierarchical radiosity lighting simulation developed in the iMAGIS project GRAVIR/IMAG-INRIA (Grenoble, France) in consultation with the author (Annapolis, MD). The entire project was accomplished electronically from initial concept to final images. The image incorporates the simple block structure from the first edition to illustrate the vast improvements in rendering capability. There are 287 initial surfaces in 157 clusters. Adaptive subdivision resulted in 1,861,974 links. Image Copyright © 1997 François Sillion, Peter Kipfer and David F. Rogers. All rights reserved.

Back cover: The image shows an adaptively subdivided coarse mesh, created with a factor of 30 increase in the error metric, superimposed over the front cover image. Image Copyright © 1997 François Sillion, Peter Kipfer and David F. Rogers. All rights reserved.

Library of Congress Cataloging-in-Publication Data

Rogers, David F.
    Procedural elements for computer graphics / David F. Rogers - -
2nd ed.
        p.   cm.
    Includes bibliographical references and index.
    ISBN 0-07-053548-5
    1. Computer graphics. I. Title.
    T385.R63   1998
    006.6 - - dc21   97-13301

http://www.mhhe.com

*This one is for my wife
and best friend
Nancy A. (Nuttall) Rogers
without whom this book
and all the others
would not have been possible.*

CONTENTS

PREFACE

In the preface to the first edition I wrote "Computer graphics is now a mature discipline." Little did I or anyone else anticipate the developments of the last dozen years. Then, ray tracing was an active research topic — now there are freely available programs for personal computers; radiosity was just on the horizon — today commercially rendering systems commonly use this technique; texture was a software application — today hardware texture acceleration is common place; color image quantization algorithms were certainly available in the computer graphics community, but today downloading an image from the World Wide Web depends on color image quantization. The list goes on. Computer graphics is thoroughly integrated into our daily lives, across fields as diverse as advertising, entertainment, medicine, education, science, engineering, navigation, etc. In fact, most computer programs, including the most popular operating systems, have a graphical user interface.

The present volume represents a major rewrite of the first edition. As a result, it is nearly twice the size of the original volume. Major new additions include a discussion of graphical user interfaces, an expanded discussion of line, circle and ellipse drawing and image compression algorithms. New clipping algorithms for lines and polygons are presented. In particular, the Liang–Barsky and Nicholl–Lee–Nicholl clipping algorithms are now discussed along with the classical Cohen–Sutherland, midpoint, Cyrus–Beck and Sutherland–Hodgman clipping algorithms.

The chapter on visible surface algorithms now includes sections on the Appel, haloed line and A-buffer algorithms, along with discussions of the binary space partitioning (BSP), octree and marching cubes algorithms. The discussion of the visible surface ray tracing algorithm is considerably expanded.

The rendering chapter is significantly enhanced. It now includes expanded discussions of physically based illumination models, transparency, shadows and textures. More recent advances in ray tracing, for example, cone, beam, pencil and stochastic ray tracing, are included along with a detailed discussion of the fundamentals of radiosity. The section on color is expanded to include uniform color spaces and a more detailed discussion of gamma correction. Sections on color image quantization and color reproduction for print media are included.

The book is suitable for use by professional programmers, engineers and scientists. A course in computer graphics at either the senior undergraduate or first year graduate level that emphasizes rendering techniques will benefit from the book. Combining it with its companion volume, *Mathematical Elements for Computer Graphics*, allows increasing the scope of the course to include manipulative transformations and curves and surfaces. The book retains the detailed worked examples from the first edition as well as presenting new ones — a total of 90 worked examples. An adequate background is provided by college level mathematics and knowledge of a higher-level programming language.

No computer graphics book is complete without algorithms. There are three types of algorithms presented in the book. The first is a narrative description often presented in list form; the second is a detailed procedural description of the algorithm, while the third is a more formal presentation using pseudocode. Although many books now present algorithms in C, I resisted this temptation. I believe that actually implementing an algorithm yields better understanding and appreciation of the nuances of the algorithm which no book can cover. Furthermore, as the algorithm is implemented additional efficiencies specific to the implementation language frequently suggest themselves. For those algorithms presented in pseudocode, the actual implementation is relatively straightforward.

No book is ever written without the assistance of many individuals. Thanks are expressed to my colleagues who read various parts of the manuscript. John Dill and his students read all of Chapter 3 on clipping and made many valuable comments. Paul Heckbert read both the sections on color image quantization and textures. Both sections are much the better for his comments. Maureen Stone lent her expertise on color reproduction. Eric Haines commented extensively on the ray tracing sections. I particularly enjoyed the ensuing discussions. John Wallace read the section on radiosity and set me straight on one or two key points. However, any errors are mine alone.

Special thanks are due my colleagues François Sillion and Peter Kipfer at the iMAGIS project in Grenoble, France, who created the cover image to an impossibly short deadline using hierarchical radiosity software developed under the direction of François Sillion and George Drettakis. You enthusiastically made all the changes that I requested! It was great working with you.

My editor of more than two and a half decades, B.J.Clark, has now left for other pastures. Without his initial faith in a young academic who wanted to do a book on computer graphics, and his gentle encouragement over the years, none of this would have happened. Thanks are due Fred Eckardt and his crew at Fine Line Illustrations for their efforts in creating the line art. They even trusted me with the original files. The production crew at McGraw-Hill — Kari Geltemeyer, Laurie Entringer and Heather Burbridge — did an outstanding job.

Last, but certainly not least, a very special thanks is due my wife Nancy for not only her long term patience with my need to write, but especially for the outstanding job of copy editing, proof reading and typesetting. I think you now qualify as a TeXpert.

David F. Rogers

PREFACE TO THE FIRST EDITION

Computer graphics is now a mature discipline. Both hardware and software are available that facilitate the production of graphical images as diverse as line drawings and realistic renderings of natural objects. A decade ago the hardware and software to generate these graphical images cost hundreds of thousands of dollars. Today, excellent facilities are available for expenditures in the tens of thousands of dollars and lower performance, but in many cases adequate facilities are available for tens of hundreds of dollars. The use of computer graphics to enhance information transfer and understanding is endemic in almost all scientific and engineering disciplines. Today, no scientist or engineer should be without a basic understanding of the underlying principles of computer graphics. Computer graphics is also making deep inroads into the business, medical, advertising, and entertainment industries. The presence in the boardroom of presentation slides prepared using computer graphics facilities as well as more commonplace business applications is considered the norm. Three-dimensional reconstructions using data obtained from CAT scans is becoming commonplace in medical applications. Television as well as other advertising media are now making frequent use of computer graphics and computer animation. The entertainment industry has embraced computer graphics with applications as diverse as video games and full-length feature films. Even art is not immune, as evidenced by some of the photos included in this book.

It is almost a decade now since the appearance of the companion volume to this book, *Mathematical Elements for Computer Graphics*. During that time significant strides in raster scan graphics have been made. The present volume concentrates on these aspects of computer graphics. The book starts with an introduction to computer graphics hardware with an emphasis on the conceptual understanding of cathode ray tube displays and of interactive devices. The following chapters look at raster scan graphics including line and circle drawing, polygon filling, and antialiasing algorithms; two- and three-dimensional clipping including clipping to arbitrary convex volumes; hidden-line and hidden-surface algorithms including ray tracing; and finally, rendering, the *art* of making realistic pictures, including local and global illumination models, texture, shadows, transparency, and color effects. The book continues the presentation technique of its predecessor. Each thorough topic discussion is followed by presentation of a detailed algorithm or a worked example, and where appropriate both.

The material in the book can be used in its entirety for a semester-long first formal course in computer graphics at either the senior undergraduate or graduate level with an emphasis on raster scan graphics. If a first course in computer graphics based on the material in the companion volume *Mathematical Elements for Computer Graphics* is presented, then the material in this book is ideal for a second course. This is the way it is used by the author. If broader material coverage in a single-semester course is desired, then the two volumes can be used together. Suggested topic coverage is: Chapter 1 of both volumes, followed by Chapters 2 and 3 with selected topics from Chapter 4 of *Mathematical Elements for Computer Graphics*, then selected topics from Chapter 2 (e.g., 2-1 to 2-5, 2-7, 2-15 to 2-19, 2-22, 2-23, 2-28), Chapter 3 (e.g., 3-1, 3-2, 3-4 to 3-6, 3-9, 3-11, 3-15, 3-16), Chapter 4 (e.g., 4-1, part of 4-2 for backplane culling, 4-3, 4-4, 4-7, 4-9, 4-11, 4-13), and Chapter 5 (e.g., 5-1 to 5-3, 5-5, 5-6, 5-14) of the present volume. The book is also designed to be useful to professional programmers, engineers, and scientists. Further, the detailed algorithms and worked examples make it particularly suitable for self-study at any level. Sufficient background is provided by college level mathematics and a knowledge of a higher-level programming language. Some knowledge of data structures is useful but not necessary.

There are two types of algorithms presented in the book. The first is a detailed procedural description of the algorithm, presented in narrative style. The second is more formal and uses an algorithmic 'language' for presentation. Because of the wide appeal of computer graphics, the choice of an algorithmic presentation language was especially difficult. A number of colleagues were questioned as to their preference. No consensus developed. Computer science faculty generally preferred PASCAL but with a strong sprinkling of C. Industrial colleagues generally preferred FORTRAN for compatibility with existing software. The author personally prefers BASIC because of its ease of use. Consequently, detailed algorithms are presented in pseudocode. The pseudocode used is based on extensive experience teaching computer graphics to classes that do not enjoy knowledge of a common programming language. The pseudocode is easily converted to any of the common computer languages. An appendix discusses the pseudocode used. The pseudocode algorithms presented in the book have all been either directly implemented from the pseudocode or the pseudocode has been derived from an operating program in one or more of the common programming languages. Implementations range from BASIC on an Apple IIe to PL1 on an IBM 4300 with a number of variations in between. A suit of demonstration programs in available from the author.

A word about the production of the book may be of interest. The book was computer typeset using the TEX typesetting system at TYX Corporation of Reston, Virginia. The manuscript was coded directly from handwritten copy. Galleys and two sets of page proofs were produced on a laser printer for editing and page makeup. Final reproduction copy ready for art insertion was produced on a phototypesetter. The patience and assistance of Jim Gauthier and Mark Hoffman at TYX while the limits of the system were explored and solutions to all the myriad small problems found is gratefully acknowledged. The outstanding job done by Louise Bohrer and Beth Lessels in coding the handwritten manuscript is gratefully acknowledged. The usually fine McGraw-Hill copyediting was supervised by David Damstra and Sylvia Warren.

No book is ever written without the assistance of many individuals. The book is based on material prepared for use in a graduate level course given at the Johns Hopkins University Applied Physics Laboratory Center beginning in 1978. Thanks are due the many students in this and other courses from whom I have learned so much. Thanks are due Turner Whitted who read the original outline and made valuable suggestions. Thanks are expressed to my colleagues Pete Atherton, Brian Barsky, Ed Catmull, Rob Cook, John Dill, Steve Hansen, Bob Lewand, Gary Meyer, Alvy Ray Smith, Dave Warn, and Kevin Weiler, all of whom read one or more chapters or sections, usually in handwritten manuscript form, red pencil in hand. Their many suggestions and comments served to make this a better book. Thanks are extended to my colleagues Linda Rybak and Linda Adlum who read the entire manuscript and checked the examples. Thanks are due three of my students: Bill Meier who implemented the Roberts algorithm, Gary Boughan who originally suggested the test for convexity discussed in Sec. 3-7, and Norman Schmidt who originally suggested the polygon splitting technique discussed in Sec. 3-8. Thanks are due Mark Meyerson who implemented the splitting algorithms and assured that the technique was mathematically well founded. The work of Lee Billow and John Metcalf who prepared all the line drawings is especially appreciated.

Special thanks are due Steve Satterfield who read and commented on all 800 handwritten manuscript pages. Need more be said!

Special thanks are also due my eldest son Stephen who implemented all of the hidden surface algorithms in Chapter 4 as well as a number of other algorithms throughout the book. Our many vigorous discussions served to clarify a number of key points.

Finally, a very special note of appreciation is extended to my wife Nancy and to my other two children, Karen and Ransom, who watched their husband and father disappear into his office almost every weeknight and every weekend for a year and a half with never a protest. That is support! Thanks.

David F. Rogers

INTRODUCTION TO
COMPUTER GRAPHICS

Today computers and computer graphics are an integral part of daily life for many people. Computer graphics is in daily use in the fields of science, engineering, medicine, entertainment, advertising, the graphic arts, the fine arts, business, education and training to mention only a few. Today, learning to program involves at least an exposure to two- and in most cases three-dimensional computer graphics. Even the way we access our computer systems is in most cases now graphically based. As an illustration of the growth in computer graphics, consider that in the early 1970s SIGGRAPH, the annual conference of the Association of Computing Machinery's (ACM) Special Interest Group on GRAPHics, involved a few hundred people. Today, the annual conference draws tens of thousands of participants.

1–1   Overview of Computer Graphics

Computer graphics is a complex and diversified technology. To begin to understand the technology, it is necessary to subdivide it into manageable parts. This can be accomplished by considering that the end product of computer graphics is a picture. The picture may, of course, be used for a large variety of purposes; e.g., it may be an engineering drawing, an exploded parts illustration for a service manual, a business graph, an architectural rendering for a proposed construction or design project, an advertising illustration, an image for a medical procedure or a single frame for an animated movie. The picture is the fundamental cohesive concept in computer graphics. We must therefore consider how:

Pictures are represented in computer graphics

Pictures are prepared for presentation

Previously prepared pictures are presented

Interaction with the picture is accomplished

Here 'picture' is used in its broadest sense, to mean any collection of lines, points, text, etc. displayed on a graphics device.

Representing Pictures

Although many algorithms accept picture data as polygons or edges, each polygon or edge can in turn be represented by points. Points, then, are the fundamental building blocks of picture representation. Of equal fundamental importance is the algorithm, which explains how to organize these points. To illustrate this, consider a unit square in the first quadrant. The unit square can be represented by its four corner points (see Fig. 1–1):

$$P_1(0,0) \qquad P_2(1,0) \qquad P_3(1,1) \qquad P_4(0,1)$$

An associated algorithmic description might be

$$\text{Connect } P_1 P_2 P_3 P_4 P_1 \text{ in sequence}$$

The unit square can also be described by its four edges

$$E_1 \equiv P_1 P_2 \quad E_2 \equiv P_2 P_3 \quad E_3 \equiv P_3 P_4 \quad E_4 \equiv P_4 P_1$$

Here, the algorithmic description is

$$\text{Connect } E_1 E_2 E_3 E_4 \text{ in sequence}$$

Finally, either the points or edges can be used to describe the unit square as a single polygon, e.g.

$$S_1 = P_1 P_2 P_3 P_4 P_1 \qquad \text{or} \qquad S_1 = E_1 E_2 E_3 E_4$$

The fundamental building blocks, i.e., points, can be represented as either pairs or triplets of numbers, depending on whether the data are two- or three-dimensional. Thus, (x_1, y_1) or (x_1, y_1, z_1) represent a point in either two- or three-dimensional space. Two points represent a line or edge, and a collection of three or more points a polygon. The representation of curved lines is usually accomplished by approximating them by connected short straight line segments.

The representation of textual material is quite complex, involving in many cases curved lines or dot matrices. Fundamentally, textual material is again represented by collections of lines and points and an organizing algorithm. Unless the user is concerned with pattern recognition, the design of special character fonts or the design of graphic hardware, he or she need not be concerned with these details.

Preparing Pictures for Presentation

Pictures ultimately consist of points and a drawing algorithm to display them. This information is generally stored in a file before it is used to present the

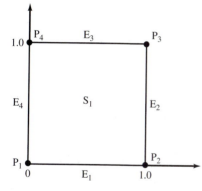

Figure 1–1   Picture data descriptions.

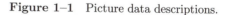

picture; this file is called a data base. Very complex pictures require very complex data bases, which require a complex algorithm to access them. These complex data bases contain data organized in various ways, e.g., ring structures, B-tree structures, quadtree structures, etc., generally referred to as a data structure. The data base itself may contain pointers, substructures and other nongraphic data. The design of these data bases and the algorithms which access them is an ongoing topic of research, a topic which is clearly beyond the scope of this text. However, many computer graphics applications involve much simpler pictures, for which the user can readily invent simple data structures which can be easily accessed. The simplest is, of course, a lineal list. Surprisingly, this simplest of data structures is quite adequate for many reasonably complex pictures.

Because points are the basic building blocks of a graphic data base, the fundamental operations for manipulating these points are of interest. There are three fundamental operations when treating a point as a (geometric) graphic entity: move the beam, pen, cursor, plotting head (hereafter called the cursor) invisibly to the point; draw a visible line to a point from an initial point; or display a dot at that point. Fundamentally there are two ways to specify the position of a point: absolute coordinates, or relative (incremental) coordinates. In relative, or incremental, coordinates, the position of a point is defined by giving the displacement of the point with respect to the previous point. All computer graphics software is based on these fundamental operations.

Presenting Previously Prepared Pictures

The data used to prepare the picture for presentation is rarely the same as that used to present the picture. The data used to present the picture is frequently called a display file. The display file represents some portion, view or scene of the picture represented by the total data base. The displayed picture is usually formed by rotating, translating, scaling and performing various projections on the data. These basic orientation or viewing preparations are generally performed using a 4×4 transformation matrix, operating on the data represented in homogeneous coordinates (see [Roge90a]).

Hidden line or hidden surface removal (see Chapter 4), shading, transparency, texture or color effects (see Chapter 5) may be added before final presentation of the picture. If the picture represented by the entire data base is not to be presented, the appropriate portion must be selected. This is a process called clipping. Clipping may be two- or three-dimensional, as appropriate. In some cases, the clipping window, or volume, may have holes in it or may be irregularly shaped. Clipping to standard two- and three-dimensional regions is frequently implemented in hardware. A complete discussion of these effects is given in Chapter 3.

Two important concepts associated with presenting a picture are windows and viewports. Windowing is the process of extracting a portion of a data base by clipping the data base to the boundaries of the window. For large data bases, performance of the windowing or the clipping operation in software generally is sufficiently time consuming that real-time interactive graphics is not possible. Again, sophisticated graphics devices perform this function in special-purpose hardware or microcode. Clipping involves determining which lines or portions of lines in the picture lie outside the window. Those lines or portions of lines are then discarded and not displayed; i.e., they are not passed on to the display device.

In two dimensions, a window is specified by values for the left, right, bottom and top edges of a rectangle. The window edge values are specified in user or world coordinates, i.e., the coordinates in which the data base is specified. Floating point numbers are usually used.

Clipping is easiest if the edges of the rectangle are parallel to the coordinate axes. Such a window is called a regular clipping window. Irregular windows are

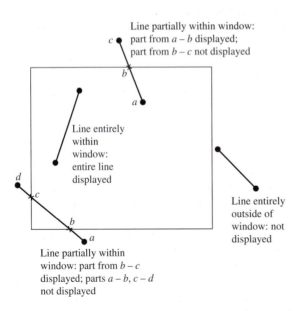
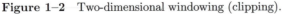

Figure 1–2 Two-dimensional windowing (clipping).

also of interest for many applications (see Chapter 3). Two-dimensional clipping is represented in Fig. 1–2. Lines are retained, deleted or partially deleted, depending on whether they are completely or partially within or without the window. In three dimensions, a regular window or clipping volume consists of a rectangular parallelepiped (a box) or, for perspective views, a frustum of vision. A typical frustum of vision is shown in Fig. 1–3. In Fig. 1–3 the near (hither) boundary is at N, the far (yon) boundary at F and the sides at SL, SR, ST and SB.

A viewport is an area of the display device on which the window data is presented. A two-dimensional regular viewport is specified by giving the left, right, bottom and top edges of a rectangle. Viewport values may be given in actual physical device coordinates. When specified in actual physical device coordinates, they are frequently given using integers. Viewport coordinates may be normalized to some arbitrary range, e.g., $0 \le x \le 1.0$, $0 \le y \le 1.0$, and specified by floating point numbers. The contents of a single window may be displayed in multiple viewports on a single display device, as shown in Fig. 1–4. Keeping the proportions of the window and viewport(s) the same prevents distortion. The mapping of windowed (clipped) data onto a viewport involves translation and scaling (see [Roge90a]).

An additional requirement for most pictures is the presentation of alphanumeric or character data. There are, in general, two methods of generating characters — software and hardware. If characters are generated in software using lines, they are treated in the same manner as any other picture element. In fact, this is necessary if they are to be clipped and then transformed along with other picture elements. However, many graphics devices have hardware character generators. When hardware character generators are used, the actual characters are generated just prior to being drawn. Up until this point they are treated

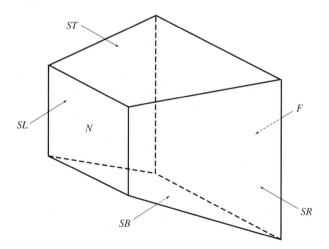

Figure 1–3   Three-dimensional frustum of vision.

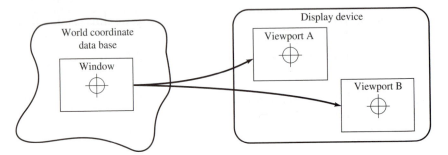

Figure 1–4   Multiple viewports displaying a single window.

as character codes. Hardware character generation yields significant efficiencies. However, it is less flexible than software character generation, because it does not allow for clipping or general transformation; e.g., usually only limited rotations and sizes are possible.

Before discussing how we interact with the picture, we first look at some fundamentals of cathode ray tubes and how they are used in computer graphics, and discuss some of the physical output devices that are used in computer graphics.

1–2   Raster Refresh Graphics Displays

Although storage tube and calligraphic line drawing refresh graphics displays, sometimes called random line scan displays, are still occasionally used in computer graphics,[†] the raster refresh graphics display is the predominant graphics display. On both the storage tube and the calligraphic line drawing refresh display, a straight line can be drawn directly from any addressable point to any other addressable point. In contrast, the raster CRT graphics display is a point plotting device. A raster graphics device can be considered a matrix of discrete cells, each of which can be made bright. It is not possible, except in special cases, to directly draw a straight line from one addressable point, or pixel, in the matrix to another.[‡] The line can only be approximated by a series of dots (pixels) close to the path of the line (see Chapter 2). Figure 1–5a illustrates the basic concept. Only in the special cases of completely horizontal, vertical or for square pixels 45° lines, does a straight line of dots or pixels result. This is shown in Fig. 1–5b. All other lines appear as a series of stair steps; this is called aliasing, or the 'jaggies' (see Chapter 2).

[†] See [Roge90a] for a description.

[‡] When a pixel is addressed or identified by its lower left corner, it occupies a finite area to the right and above this point. Addressing starts at $0, 0$. This means that the pixels in an $n \times n$ raster are addressed in the range 0 to $n - 1$. For example, the top and right-most lines in Fig. 1–5 do not represent addressable *pixel* locations.

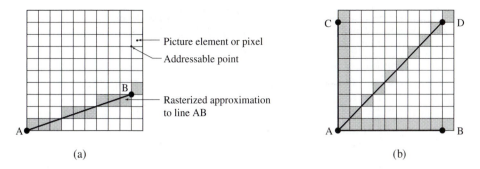

Figure 1–5 Rasterization. (a) General line; (b) special cases.

Frame Buffers

The most common method of implementing a raster CRT graphics device uses a frame buffer. A frame buffer is a large, contiguous piece of computer memory. At a minimum, there is one memory bit for each pixel (picture element) in the raster; this amount of memory is called a bit plane. A 1024×1024 element square raster requires 2^{20} ($2^{10} = 1024$; $2^{20} = 1024 \times 1024$) or 1,048,576 memory bits in a single bit plane. The picture is built up in the frame buffer one bit at a time. Because a memory bit has only two states (binary 0 or 1), a single bit plane yields a black-and-white (monochrome) display. Because the frame buffer is a digital device, while the raster CRT is an analog device, conversion from a digital representation to an analog signal must take place when information is read from the frame buffer and displayed on the raster CRT graphics device. This is accomplished by a digital-to-analog converter (DAC). Each pixel in the frame buffer must be accessed and converted before it is visible on the raster CRT. A schematic diagram of a single-bit-plane, black-and-white frame buffer, raster CRT graphics device is shown in Fig. 1–6.

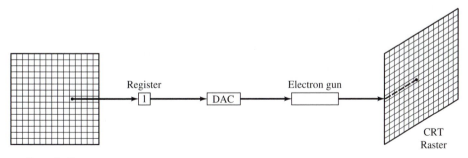

Figure 1–6 A single-bit-plane black-and-white frame buffer raster CRT graphics device.

Color or gray levels are incorporated into a frame buffer raster graphics device by using additional bit planes. Figure 1–7 schematically shows an N-bit-plane gray level frame buffer. The intensity of each pixel on the CRT is controlled by a corresponding pixel location in each of the N bit planes. The binary value (0 or 1) from each of the N bit planes is loaded into corresponding positions in a register. The resulting binary number is interpreted as an intensity level between 0 (dark) and $2^N - 1$ (full intensity). This is converted into an analog voltage between 0 and the maximum voltage of the electron gun by the DAC. A total of 2^N intensity levels are possible. Figure 1–7 illustrates a system with 3 bit planes for a total of 8 (2^3) intensity levels. Each bit plane requires the full complement of memory for a given raster resolution; e.g., a 3-bit-plane frame buffer for a 1024×1024 raster requires $3,145,728$ ($3 \times 1024 \times 1024$) memory bits.

An increase in the number of available intensity levels is achieved for a modest increase in required memory by using a lookup table; this is shown schematically in Fig. 1–8. Upon reading the bit planes in the frame buffer, the resulting number is used as an index into the lookup table. The lookup table must contain 2^N entries. Each entry in the lookup table is W bits wide. W may be greater than N. When this occurs, 2^W intensities are available; but only 2^N different intensities are available at one time. To get additional intensities, the lookup table must be changed (reloaded).

Because there are three primary colors, a simple color frame buffer is implemented with three bit planes, one for each primary color. Each bit plane drives an individual color gun for each of the three primary colors used in color video. These three primaries (red, green and blue) are combined at the CRT to yield

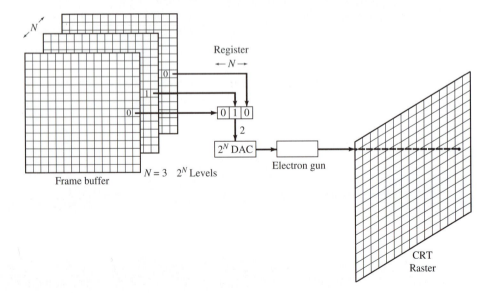

Figure 1–7   An N-bit-plane gray level frame buffer.

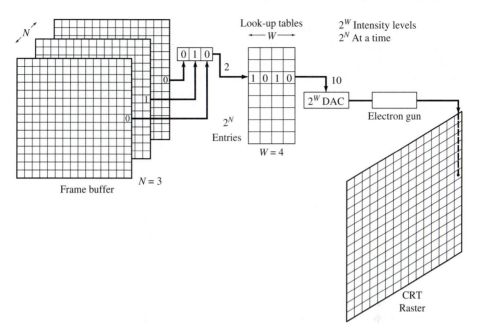

Figure 1–8 An N-bit-plane gray level frame buffer, with a W-bit-wide lookup table.

eight colors, as shown in Table 1–1. A simple color raster frame buffer is shown schematically in Fig. 1–9.

Additional bit planes can be used for each of the three color guns. A schematic of a multiple-bit-plane color frame buffer, with 8 bit planes per color, i.e., a 24-bit-plane frame buffer, is shown in Fig. 1–10. Each group of bit planes drives an 8-bit DAC. Each group generates 256 (2^8) shades or intensities of red, green or blue. These are combined into $16,777,216 \left[(2^8)^3 = 2^{24}\right]$ possible colors. This is a 'full' color frame buffer.

The full color frame buffer can be further expanded by using the groups of bit planes as indices to color lookup tables. This is shown schematically in Fig. 1–11.

Table 1–1 Simple 3-bit plane frame buffer color combinations

	Red	Green	Blue
Black	0	0	0
Red	1	0	0
Green	0	1	0
Blue	0	0	1
Yellow	1	1	0
Cyan	0	1	1
Magenta	1	0	1
White	1	1	1

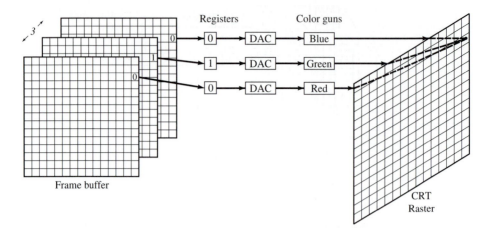

Figure 1–9 Simple color frame buffer.

For N bit planes/color, with W-bit-wide color lookup tables, $(2^3)^N$ colors from a palette of $(2^3)^W$ possible colors can be shown at any one time. For example, for a 24-bit-plane ($N = 8$) frame buffer with three 10-bit-wide ($W = 10$) color lookup tables, 16,777,216 (2^{24}) colors from a palette of 1,073,741,824 (2^{30}) colors, i.e., about 17 million colors from a palette of a little more than 1 billion, can be obtained. Although three separate lookup tables are schematically shown in Fig. 1–11, for small numbers of physical bit planes (up to about 12) it is more advantageous if the lookup tables are implemented contiguously with $(2^3)^N$ table entries.

Because of the large number of pixels in a raster scan graphics device, achieving real-time performance and acceptable refresh or frame rates is not straightforward. For example, if pixels are accessed individually with an average access time of 200 nanoseconds (200×10^{-9} second), then it requires 0.0614 second to access all the pixels in a 640×480 frame buffer. This is equivalent to a refresh rate of 16 frames (pictures)/second, well below the required minimum refresh rate of 30 frames/second. A 1024×1024 frame buffer contains slightly more than 1 million bits (1 megabit) and, at 200 nanoseconds average access time, requires 0.21 second to access all the pixels. This is 5 frames/second. A 4096×4096 frame buffer contains 16.78 million bits per memory plane! At a 200-nanosecond access time per pixel, it requires 0.3 second to access all the pixels. To achieve a refresh rate of 30 frames/second, a 4096×4096 raster requires an average effective access rate of 2 nanoseconds/pixel. Recall that light travels two *feet* in this small time period. Real-time performance with raster scan devices is achieved by accessing pixels in groups of 16, 32, 64 or more simultaneously, as well as other hardware optimizations.

One distinct and important advantage of a raster CRT device is solid area representation. This is shown in Fig. 1–12. Here, a representation of the solid figure bounded by the lines L1, L2, L3, L4 is achieved by setting all the pixels

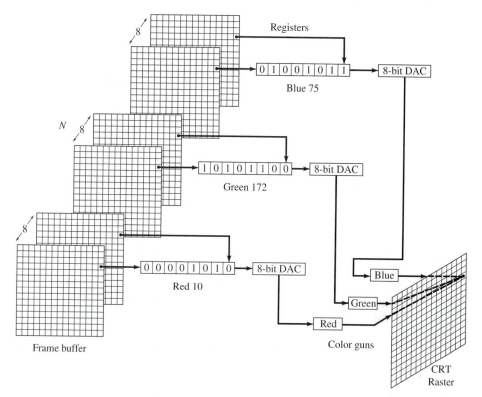

Figure 1–10 A 24-bit-plane color frame buffer.

within the bounding polygon to the appropriate code in the frame buffer. This is called solid area scan conversion. Algorithms for scan conversion are discussed in Chapter 2.

1–3   Cathode Ray Tube Basics

A frame buffer as described in Sec. 1–2 is not itself a display device; it is simply used to assemble and hold a digital representation of the picture. The most common display device used with a frame buffer is a video monitor. An understanding of raster displays, and to some extent line drawing refresh displays, requires a basic understanding of CRTs and video display techniques.

The CRT used in video monitors is shown schematically in Fig. 1–13. A cathode (negatively charged) is heated until electrons 'boil' off in a diverging cloud (electrons repel each other because they have the same charge). These electrons are attracted to a highly charged positive anode. This is the phosphor coating on the inside of the face of the large end of the CRT. If allowed to continue uninterrupted, the electrons simply flood the entire face of the CRT with a bright glow. However, the cloud of electrons is focused into a narrow, precisely

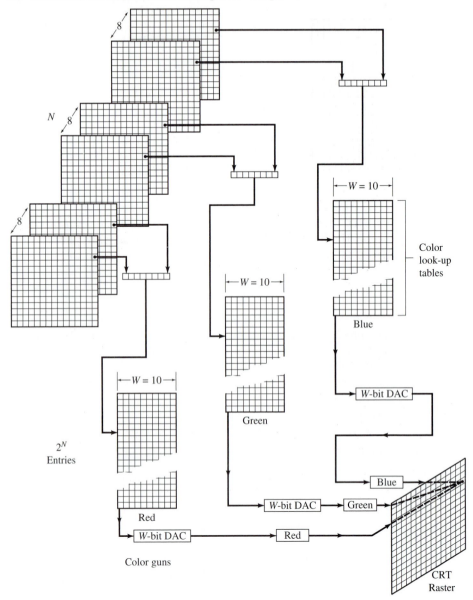

Figure 1–11   A 24-bit-plane color frame buffer, with 10-bit-wide lookup tables.

collimated beam with an electron lens. At this point, the focused electron beam produces a single bright spot at the center of the CRT. The electron beam is deflected or positioned to the left or right of the center, and/or above or below the center by means of horizontal and vertical deflection amplifiers.

It is at this point that line drawing displays, both storage and refresh, and raster scan displays differ. In a line drawing display, the electron beam may be

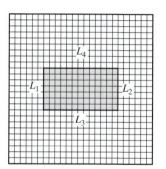

Figure 1–12   Solid figures with a raster graphics device.

deflected directly from any arbitrary position to any other arbitrary position on the face of the CRT (anode). A perfectly straight line results. In contrast, in a raster scan display the beam is deflected in a set, rigidly controlled pattern; this pattern comprises the video picture.

Color CRT Raster Scan Monitors

In a color raster scan CRT or color monitor there are three electron guns, one for each of the three primary colors, red, green and blue (see Sec. 5–19). The electron guns are frequently arranged in a triangular pattern corresponding to a similar triangular pattern of red, green and blue phosphor dots on the face of the CRT (see Fig. 1–14). The electron guns and the corresponding red, green and blue phosphor dots may also be arranged in a line. To ensure that the individual electron guns excite the correct phosphor dots (e.g., the red gun excites only the red phosphor dot), a perforated metal grid is placed between the electron guns and the face of the CRT. This is the shadow mask of the standard shadow mask color CRT. The perforations in the shadow mask are arranged in the same triangular or linear pattern as the phosphor dots. The distance between perforations is called the pitch. The color guns are arranged so that the individual beams converge and intersect at the shadow mask (see Fig. 1–15). Upon passing through

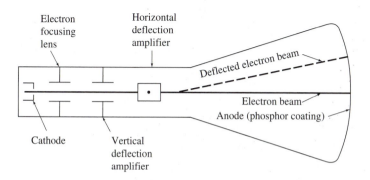

Figure 1–13   Cathode ray tube.

the hole in the shadow mask, the red beam, for example, is prevented or masked from intersecting either the green or blue phosphor dot; it can only intersect the red phosphor dot. By varying the strength of the electron beam for each individual primary color, different shades (intensities) are obtained. These primary color shades are combined into a large number of colors for each pixel. For a high-resolution display, there are usually two to three color triads for each pixel.

1–4 Video Basics

The process of converting the rasterized picture stored in a frame buffer to the rigid display pattern of video is called scan conversion (see also Chapter 2, Secs. 2–15 to 2–25). The scanning pattern and the frequency of repetition are based on both visual perception and electronic principles. The human visual perception system requires a finite amount of time to resolve the elements of a picture. If individual images are presented at a rate greater than the time required for the visual system to resolve individual images, one image persists while the next is being presented. This persistence of vision is used to achieve flicker-fusion. The result is perceived as a continuous presentation. A number of factors affect flicker, including image brightness and the particular CRT screen phosphor used. Experience indicates that a practical minimum picture presentation, or update rate, is 25 frames/second, provided the minimum refresh or repetition rate is twice this, i.e., 50 frames/second. This is actually what is done with movie film. With movie film 24 frames/second are presented, but the presentation of each frame is interrupted so that it is presented twice for an effective repetition rate of 48 frames/second. Thus, for film the update rate is 24 and the refresh rate is 48. The same effect is achieved in video using a technique called interlacing.

American Standard Video

Video is a raster scan technique. The American standard video system uses a total of 525 horizontal lines, with a frame or viewing aspect ratio of 4:3; i.e., the viewing area is three-quarters as high as it is wide. The repetition, or frame rate,

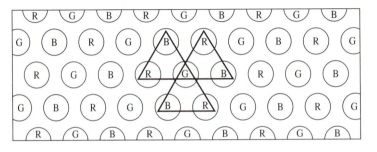

Figure 1–14 Phosphor dot pattern for a shadow mask CRT.

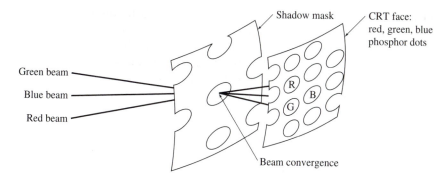

Figure 1–15   Color CRT electron gun and shadow mask arrangement.

is 30 frames/second. However, each frame is divided into two fields, each containing one-half of the picture. The two fields are interlaced or interwoven, and they are presented alternatively every other ¹/₆₀ second. One field contains all the odd-numbered scan lines (1, 3, 5, . . .), and the other has the even-numbered scan lines (2, 4, 6, . . .). The scanning pattern begins at the upper left corner of the screen, with the odd field. Each line in the field is scanned or presented from the left to the right. As the electron beam moves across the screen from left to right, it also moves vertically downward but at a much slower rate. Thus, the 'horizontal' scan line is in fact slightly slanted. When the beam reaches the right edge of the screen, it is made invisible and rapidly returned to the left edge. This is the horizontal retrace, which usually requires approximately 17 percent of the time allowed for one scan line. The process is then repeated with the next odd scan line. Because half of 525 is 262¹/₂ lines, the beam is at the bottom center of the screen when the odd scan line field is complete (see Figs. 1–16 and 1–17). The beam is then quickly returned to the top center of the screen. This is the odd field vertical retrace. The time required for the vertical retrace is equivalent to that for 21 lines. The even scan line field is then presented. The even scan line field ends in the lower right hand corner. The even field vertical retrace returns the beam to the upper left hand corner, and the entire sequence is repeated. Thus, two fields are presented for each frame, i.e., 60 fields per second. Because the eye perceives the field repetition rate, this technique significantly reduces flicker.

Although the American standard video system calls for 525 lines, only 483 lines are actually visible, because a time equivalent to 21 lines is required to accomplish the vertical retrace for each field.[†] During this time, the electron beam is invisible, or blanked. The time available for each scan line is calculated for a frame repetition rate of 30 as

1/30 second/frame × 1/525 frame/scan lines = 63¹/₂ microseconds/scan line

---

[†]Many raster scan graphics devices use this time for processing other information.

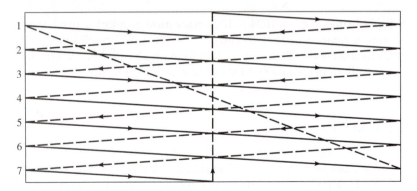

Figure 1–16 Schematic of a seven-line interlaced scan line pattern. The odd field begins with line 1. The horizontal retrace is shown dashed.

Because approximately $10\,1/2$ microseconds is required for horizontal retrace, the visible portion of each scan line must be completed in 53 microseconds. With a normal video aspect ratio of 4:3, there are 644 pixels on each scan line. The time available to access and display a pixel is thus

53 microseconds/scan line $\times$ 1/644 scan line/pixels = 82 nanoseconds

Equivalent results are obtained for the 625-line 25-frame repetition rate used in Great Britain and in most of Europe.

The interlaced technique described here is not required when presenting a video picture. However, this noninterlaced (progressive scan) picture is not compatible with a standard television set. In fact, most high quality raster scan graphics devices present a noninterlaced picture. To prevent flicker, noninterlaced displays require a repetition rate of at least 60 frames/second. This, of course, reduces the available pixel access and display time by a factor of 2. Higher scan line and pixel-per-line resolutions also decrease the available pixel

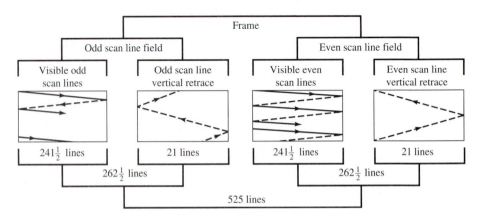

Figure 1–17 A 525-line standard frame schematic.

access and display time, e.g., a 1024×1024 resolution requires a pixel access and display time a quarter of that required by a 512×512 resolution — approximately 25 nanoseconds. Thus, a very fast frame buffer memory, a very fast frame buffer controller, an equally fast DAC and a very high bandwidth monitor are required.

High Definition Television

A recent standard for high definition television (HDTV), or the advanced television system (ATV), has been approved. The standard supports 60 Hz interlaced and noninterlaced high resolution displays, as shown in Table 1-2. It also changes the standard aspect ratio (width to height) to 16:9, compared with the 4:3 ratio of the current NTSC television standard. The video compression algorithm is based on the Motion Picture Expert Group (MPEG) MPEG-2 Main Profile. The standard also incorporates an improved Dolby AC-3 audio compression encoding.

1–5   Flat Panel Displays

Although today the CRT is unrivaled as the computer graphics display of choice, it is bulky, heavy, fragile and currently limited in size to about 50 inches diagonally, although projection systems are considerably larger. For these as well as other reasons, flat panel displays are becoming of increasing importance. All flat panel displays are raster refresh displays.

Flat panel displays are broadly divided into those based on active (light-emitting) and passive (light-modulating) technologies. Among the active technologies are flat CRTs, plasma-gas discharge, electroluminescent (EL) and vacuum fluorescent displays. Liquid crystal (LC) and light-emitting diodes (LED) are representative of the passive technologies.

Of the active flat panel display technologies, plasma-gas discharge and electroluminescent-based displays are currently most suitable for the relatively large sizes and high resolutions required by computer graphics applications. Except for applications with special requirements, e.g., avionics where light emitting diode-based displays have certain advantages, liquid crystal based displays are the most suitable of the passive technologies.

Flat CRT

As shown in Fig. 1–18, a flat CRT is obtained by initially projecting the electron beam parallel to the screen and then reflecting it through $90°$. Reflecting the electron beam significantly reduces the depth of the CRT bottle and, consequently, of the display. The flat CRT has all the performance advantages of the conventional CRT. Currently, flat CRTs are only available in relatively small sizes. The length of the 'neck' may limit their utility in larger sizes. The utility of vacuum fluorescent displays is also currently size-limited.

Table 1–2   ATV System Scanning Formats

Vertical	Horizontal	Aspect Ratio	Scan Rate
1080	1920	16:9	60I, 30P, 24P
720	1280	16:9	60P, 30P, 24P
480	704	16:9	60I, 60P, 30P, 24P
480	640	4:3	60I, 60P, 30P, 24P

Plasma Display

Plasma-gas discharge, electroluminescent and liquid crystal displays have several operating characteristics in common. Each consists of a matrix of individual pixel locations on a raster. Each pixel must contain some mechanism, or material, activated by application of either a voltage or a current, that either emits light or modulates incident light. The required voltage or current is supplied to the pixel using an individual electronic switching device, e.g., a thin film transistor, diode or metal-insulator-metal nonlinear resistor, located at each pixel. Displays using this technology are called active matrix displays.

An alternate, and more common, technique that significantly reduces the number of switches or drivers uses row–column addressing of the raster. This technique requires that the display material have a switching threshold. Only when the switching threshold is exceeded does emission or modification of light occur. Part of the voltage or current required to activate an individual pixel is applied through the appropriate row, and the other part through the appropriate column. The individual row or column voltage or current supplied is below the switching threshold; together, it is above the switching threshold. Consequently, unwanted pixels along either the row or column are not activated. Only the desired pixel at the intersection of the row and column receives enough voltage or current to exceed the switching threshold and hence is activated.

When using row–column addressing, bistable pixel memory is highly desirable. With bistable memory, once it is activated a pixel remains activated until explicitly turned off. Bistable pixel memory eliminates the necessity of

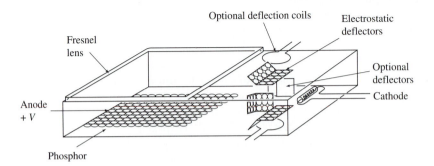

Figure 1–18   Flat CRT schematic.

constantly refreshing pixels. Consequently, no external memory is required to refresh the display. In addition, the display controller is simplified.

The basic technology of a plasma or gas discharge display is quite simple. Essentially, the display consists of a matrix of cells (the raster) in a glass envelope. Each cell is filled with a gas (usually neon, or a neon/argon mixture) at low pressure (below atmospheric). When a sufficiently high voltage is applied, the gas dissociates, i.e., electrons are stripped from the atoms. The dissociated gas is called a plasma, hence the name plasma display. When the electrons recombine, energy is released in the form of photons; and the gas glows with the characteristic bright orange-red hue. A typical color plasma display is shown in Fig. 1–19.

Plasma displays can be AC or DC, or combined AC/DC activated. AC, DC and hybrid AC/DC activated plasma displays are shown schematically in Figs. 1–20a, 1–20b and 1–20c, respectively. The DC activated display is simpler than the AC display. It consists of a dielectric spacer plate, which contains the gas cavities sandwiched between plates containing the row–column conductors. The electric field is applied directly to the gas. A DC activated plasma display requires continuous refreshing.

In the AC activated plasma display, a dielectric layer is placed between the conductors and the gas. Thus, the only coupling between the gas and the conductors is capacitive. Hence, an AC voltage is required to dissociate the gas. AC activated plasma displays have bistable memory; thus, the necessity to continuously refresh the display is eliminated. Bistable memory is obtained by using a low AC keep alive voltage. The characteristic capacitive coupling provides enough voltage to maintain the activity in the conducting pixels, but not enough to activate nonconducting pixels.

A hybrid AC/DC plasma display (see Fig. 1–20c) uses DC voltage to 'prime' the gas and make it more easily activated by the AC voltage. The principal advantage of the hybrid AC/DC plasma display is reduced driver circuitry. Large size plasma displays are available, as are high resolution (100 pixels/inch) displays. Gray scale and color systems are also available, as illustrated by Fig. 1–19.

Figure 1–19   Typical large color plasma display. (Courtesy of Fujitsu Limited).

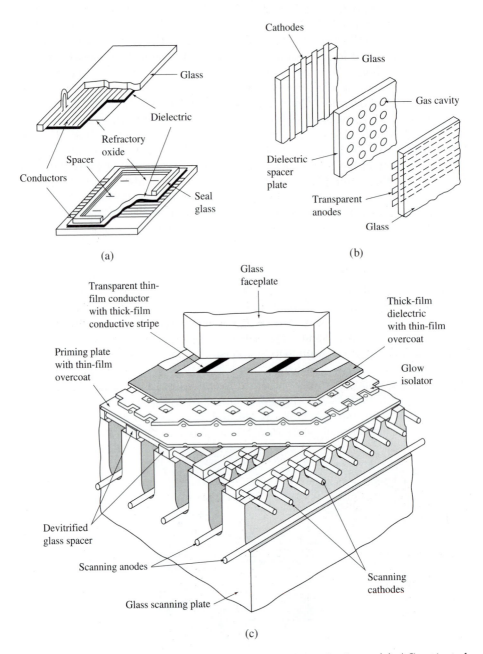

Figure 1–20 Basic structure of gas discharge-plasma displays. (a) AC activated; (b) DC activated; (c) AC/DC activated.

Electroluminescent Display

In an electroluminescent display, a phosphorescent material emits light when excited by either an AC or DC electric field. Because the phosphorescent material is typically zinc sulfide doped with manganese, electroluminescent displays typically have a yellow color. Pixel addressing uses the row–column technique previously discussed for plasma displays. When the applied voltage exceeds the switching threshold, the manganese dopant electrons are excited. When an excited atom returns to a lower energy state, it emits a photon which causes the characteristic yellow color. Good 'gray' scale is obtainable, because the luminescence varies with the voltage and frequency of the applied electric field. By using alternate dopants, other colors are obtained. Consequently, using multiple phosphorescent layers yields a color display. The phosphorescent material is deposited macroscopically either as a powder yielding a thick film, or as molecular scale particles yielding a thin film. An AC or DC excited thin film electroluminescent display is most frequently used in computer graphics applications. The basic structure of an electroluminescent display is shown in Fig. 1–21. Reasonable-sized displays with reasonable resolutions are currently available.

Liquid Crystal Display

While plasma and electroluminescent displays are examples of active flat panel technologies, the liquid crystal display is an example of a passive technology. A typical display is shown in Fig. 1–22. A liquid crystal display either transmits or reflects incident light. The polarizing characteristics of certain organic compounds are used to modify the characteristics of the incident light.

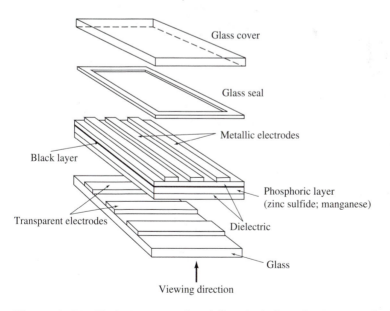

Figure 1–21 Basic structure of an AC excited electroluminescent display.

Figure 1–22 Color liquid crystal display (LCD). (Courtesy of NEC Technologies, Inc., © 1997 NEC Technologies, Inc., reproduced with permission).

The basic principles of polarized light are shown in Fig. 1–23. In Fig. 1–23a, noncoherent light is passed through the first (left) polarizer. The resulting transmitted light is polarized in the xy plane. Since the polarizing axis of the second polarizer is also aligned with the xy plane, the light continues through the second polarizer. In Fig. 1–23b, the polarizing axis of the second polarizer is rotated 90° to that of the first. Consequently, the plane polarized light that passed through the first polarizer is absorbed by the second.

Certain organic compounds which exist in the mesophase are stable at temperatures between the liquid and solid phases, hence the name liquid crystal.

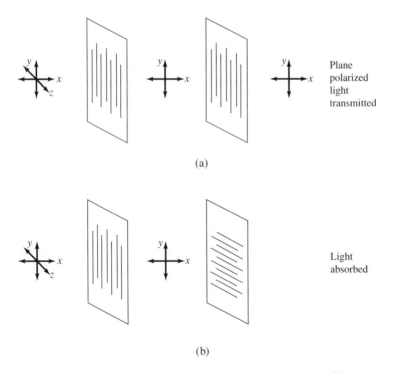

Figure 1–23 Polarization of light. (a) Light transmitted; (b) light absorbed.

Liquid crystals exhibit three types of mesophase: smectic, nematic and choles-
teric. In the nematic phase, the long axis of the liquid crystal molecules align
parallel to each other. The alignment direction is sensitive to temperature, surface tension, pressure and, most important for display technology, electric and
magnetic fields. The optical characteristics of the liquid crystal are also sensitive
to these effects.

The key to one type of liquid crystal display technology is the creation of
a twisted nematic crystal sandwich, in which the alignment axis of the crystals
rotates or twists through 90° from one face of the sandwich to the other. The
basic structure of a reflective twisted nematic liquid crystal display is shown in
Fig. 1–24. The two plates at the top and bottom of the liquid crystal sandwich
are grooved. The top plate is grooved in one direction and the bottom at ninety
degrees to that direction. The liquid crystals adjacent to the plate surface align
with the grooves, as shown in Fig. 1–24.

The display contains two plane polarizers, one on each side of the sandwich
and aligned at 90° to each other. With a display pixel in its off or twisted state,
light entering the display is plane polarized by the first polarizer, passes through

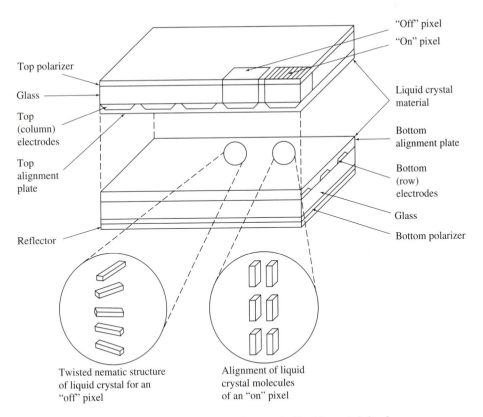

Figure 1–24   Basic structure of a twisted nematic liquid crystal display.

the liquid crystal sandwich (where it is twisted through 90°), passes through the second polarizer and is reflected back out the display. The pixel appears light.

Turning the pixel on by applying an electric field to the liquid crystal sandwich causes the crystal to untwist. Now light entering the display is plane polarized by the first polarizer, passes through the liquid crystal sandwich where it is *not* twisted and hence is absorbed by the second polarizer. The pixel appears dark. Twisted nematic liquid crystal displays require constant refreshing.

A bistable liquid crystal display using smectic liquid crystals is also possible. Two stable orientations of the smectic liquid crystal molecules have different optical properties, e.g., absorption. This difference in optical properties produces an optical contrast. A voltage pulse causes the molecules to change state. Bistable liquid crystal displays do not require refreshing.

Color liquid crystal displays use colored filters or phosphors with twisted-nematic technology or use guest–host (dye) technology. Guest–host liquid crystal displays combine dichroic-dye guest molecules with the host liquid crystal molecules. The spectral characteristics of different guest molecules are used to produce different colors. Here, the application of an electric field realigns the orientation of both the guest and host molecules, to allow transmission of light.

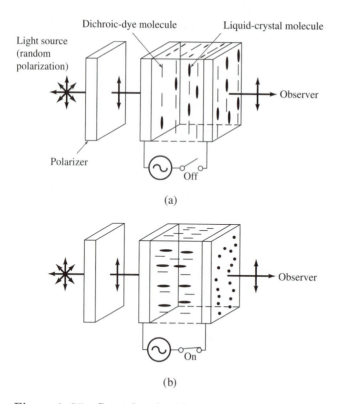

Figure 1–25   Guest–host liquid crystal display dye and molecules aligned to (a) block transmission and (b) allow transmission.

A typical guest–host transmissive liquid crystal display is shown schematically in Fig. 1–25. Note that only a single polarizer is required. Reflective guest–host liquid crystal displays are also possible. Liquid crystal displays are either row–column addressed or contain active matrix elements, e.g., individual transistors or diodes at each pixel.

1–6   Hardcopy Output Devices

There is a large selection of hardcopy output devices, for example electrostatic, ink jet, pen and ink, thermal and dye sublimation plotter/printers; laser printers; phototypesetters, etc. Here we discuss only a few of the more common devices.

Electrostatic Plotters

An electrostatic plotter is a raster scan device (see Sec. 1–2). Basically, it operates by depositing small particles of toner onto electrostatically charged areas of a special paper. Figure 1–26 shows the general scheme employed.

In more detail, a specially coated medium that will hold an electrostatic charge is passed over a writing head, which contains one or more rows of small writing nibs or styli. Higher densities require multiple rows of styli. As the medium is passed over the styli, an individual dot of negative electrostatic charge is deposited by each stylus. The medium is then passed over a toner applicator, where positively charged particles of liquid toner are attracted to the negatively

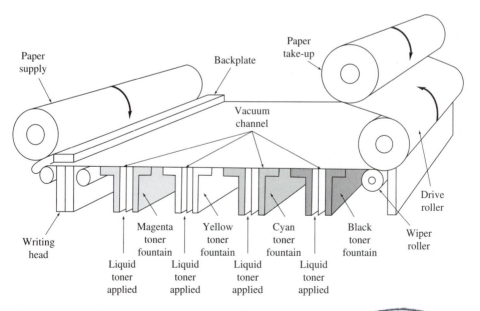

Figure 1–26   Conceptual description of a multiple-pass color electrostatic plotter.

LIBRARY OF MOUNT ST. MARY'S COLLEGE EMMITSBURG, MARYLAND

charged dots on the medium, making them visible. The carbon toner particles are subsequently dried and fixed to the medium to make them permanent. Available plotting media include opaque and translucent vellum paper, and clear and matte polyester films.

Electrostatic plotters are available in large widths, and the length of the plot is limited only by the length of the media roll. The resolution of an electrostatic plotter is given by the number of styli or dots per inch (dpi). Accuracy is defined in a somewhat different way. Assuming that the direction of media movement can be reversed, accuracy is defined as the error that occurs in the position of two dots, made by the same stylus on two successive passes of the medium.

An electrostatic plotter is a raster device, consequently aliasing occurs (see Sec. 2–16). High resolution devices attempt to minimize the effects of aliasing by overlapping the individual dots. Figure 1–27 shows typical dot patterns. Typical dot overlap is 30 to 50 percent. Since an electrostatic plotter is a raster scan device, picture elements, e.g., lines and polygons, must be rasterized and the picture organized into raster scan order: top to bottom, left to right. Although preparation of the picture in raster format can be accomplished by the host computer, it poses significant computational requirements. Furthermore, communication of the rasterized picture to the plotter at sufficient speed to fully utilize the plotter's capability requires a high speed interface. Consequently, many electrostatic plotters use special purpose controllers to perform these functions [BenD86]. A typical electrostatic plotter and output is shown in Fig. 1–28.

Color electrostatic plotters are available. The three subtractive primary colors (cyan, magenta and yellow (CMY), see Sec. 5–19) and black are applied to the medium in either a single pass or in four successive passes. If the colors are applied in a single pass, separate rows of nibs are used for each of the colors. If the colors are applied in successive passes, the medium is rewound between application of each color. Color shading of filled polygons is accomplished using dither and patterning (see Sec. 2–17). The number of available colors depends on both the size of the pattern used, e.g., 2×2, 3×3 or 4×4, and the resolution of the plotter.

Ink Jet Plotters

Ink jet printers are raster scan devices. They are particularly suited for generating low cost color output. The basic idea is to shoot tiny droplets of ink onto

 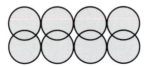 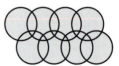

Figure 1–27 Dot patterns. (a) Nonoverlapping; (b) overlapping y only; (c) overlapping x and y.

(a)

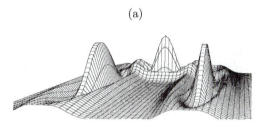

(b)

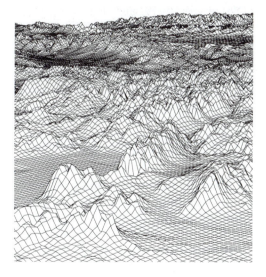

(c)

Figure 1–28 Electrostatic plotter. (Courtesy of Hewlett Packard). Typical output. (a) Plotter; (b) low resolution 100 dpi; (c) high resolution 400 dpi. (Courtesy of Versatec Corp.).

a medium. There are basically two types of ink jet printers, continuous flow and drop-on-demand.

The continuous flow ink jet produces a stream of droplets by spraying ink out of a nozzle. The stream of ink from the nozzle is broken up into droplets by ultrasonic waves. If ink is desired on the medium, selected droplets are electrostatically charged. Deflection plates are used to then direct the droplet onto the medium. If not, the droplet is deflected into a gutter, from which the ink is returned to the reservoir. Paper and transparency film are typical media. This system is shown schematically in Fig. 1–29a.

Drop-on-demand technology, as its name implies, fires ink at the medium only if a dot is required at a particular location. Here, ink from a reservoir is supplied to a nozzle under pressure. The ink is fired on demand by applying an electric voltage to a piezoelectric crystal as the head makes a pass across the medium. When a voltage is applied, the piezoelectric crystal expands, decreasing the volume of the ink chamber. This causes a drop of ink to squirt out of the nozzle. Release of the voltage causes the piezoelectric crystal to contract, decreasing the volume of the reservoir and sucking the ink back into the nozzle. A typical arrangement is shown schematically in Fig. 1–29b.

The resolution of ink jet printers is determined by the size of the droplet, and hence by the size of the nozzle. Because of the extremely small nozzle size required, nozzle clogging, ink contamination and air bubbles in the ink can be significant problems.

Color ink jet printers typically use four nozzles, three for the subtractive primary colors cyan, magenta and yellow, and one for black. One of the advantages of color ink jet technology is its ability to blend colors. Because liquid droplets of ink are used in a single pass across the medium, the droplets blend together before drying. This gives ink jet colors a depth and vibrancy not found in most other reflective technologies. Again, patterning and dither, including multiply dot size techniques, are used to produce several thousand colors (see Sec. 2–17 and [Kubo84]).

Thermal Plotters

There are basically two thermal printing or plotting techniques, direct thermal transfer and indirect thermal transfer. The direct thermal transfer technique uses a temperature sensitive paper that changes color when heated. The image is formed by print head elements that selectively heat dots on the paper as the head moves across it. Either dot matrix print heads or full row nib heads, similar to those in electrostatic plotters, are used. The chief and most serious limitation of the direct thermal transfer technique is the special paper that unfortunately fades with time.

The indirect thermal transfer technique uses a thin film or paper ribbon coated with a wax-based ink. Heating elements which are usually located behind the ribbon melt the wax coating. The pigmented ink is then rolled onto the paper. Either dot matrix print heads that move across the medium or a full

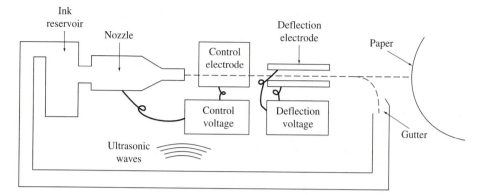

(a)

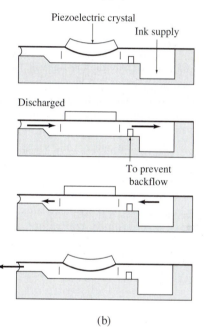

(b)

Figure 1–29 Schematics of various ink jet printer technologies. (a) Continuous; (b) drop-on-demand.

row of nib heads are used. Figure 1–30 schematically illustrates this technique. The medium is ordinary paper. Color is obtained by using multicolored ribbons. Typically, seven colors are obtained directly by combining the CMY primaries from the ribbon, plus black. Patterning and dither are used to expand the color palette (see Sec. 2–17 and [Kubo84]). Since the inks are not absorbed by the paper, quite brilliant colors are obtained. Indirect thermal transfer inks have excellent longevity.

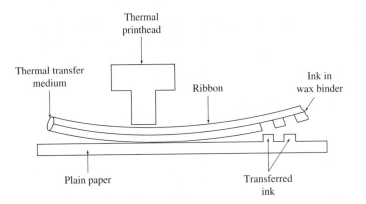

Figure 1–30   Indirect thermal transfer technique.

Dye Sublimation Printers

Dye sublimation printers currently provide the highest quality color printer output. Dye sublimation is sometimes called dye diffusion, dye transfer or sublimable dye technology. Dye sublimation printing is continuous tone in contrast to, e.g., thermal wax transfer, which depends upon halftoning to generate large numbers of colors. The plastic dye sublimation transfer ribbon, which contains the three or four color dyes (cyan, magenta, yellow and black, CMYK), lies between the print head containing the heating elements and the paper. Heating the dye on the dye sublimation transfer ribbon to various temperatures causes varying amounts of dye to change from a solid to a gas and diffuse (sublimate) onto the paper or the resin coating of a transparency. Consequently, varying intensity levels are produced. By carefully controlling the temperature, precise amounts of each of the primary colored dyes are transferred. The amount and duration of the heat, and hence the amount of dye transferred and absorbed by the medium, is also used to vary the intensity and saturation of the dot. The dyes combine on a single pixel and diffuse to adjacent pixels to yield the desired continuous tone color, rather than depending upon halftoning and the eyes ability as an integrator to yield the impression of continuous tone. In addition, because halftoning is not required, the apparent resolution of the device is increased in comparison to devices that depend upon halftoning. Dye sublimation yields the best results when used for continuous tone (natural) images. Unless special image processing software is used, lines and characters may be fuzzy, have tails or even disappear. In addition, images rendered onto a transparency may appear washed out and undersaturated. Fundamentally, this is because dyes are transparent and represent a subtractive color system. As light passes through the dye it absorbs the color of the dye. With an opaque medium there are two chances to absorb the color; once when the light is incident upon the medium and once after it has been reflected from the medium. With transparent media, the color is absorbed only once as the light passes through the medium. The majority of dye sublimation printers are four color printers: cyan, magenta, yellow and black. Although not a severe limitation, it does somewhat constrain the number of possible colors. Varying the dot size significantly increases the number of possible colors (see Sec. 2–17). Using more colors, e.g., cyan, magenta, yellow, black, light and medium cyan, and light and medium magenta, with a fixed dot size, also significantly increases the number of possible colors. An example of a dye sublimation printer is shown in Fig. 1–31.

Pen and Ink Plotters

Digital pen and ink plotters are of three basic types, flatbed, drum and pinch roller. The basic mechanisms are shown schematically in Fig. 1–32.

In a moving-arm flatbed plotter (see Fig. 1–32a) the medium is fixed in position on the bed of the plotter. Two-dimensional motion of the plotting head is obtained by movement of an arm suspended across the width of the plotter bed. This provides motion in one direction. Motion in the second direction is obtained by moving the plotting head along the suspended arm.

A moving head flatbed plotter (see Fig. 1–32b) uses a plotting tool carriage suspended above the bed by magnetic forces that are counterbalanced by an air bearing. This arrangement provides nearly frictionless movement. Movement of the head in two dimensions is controlled electromagnetically, using the Sawyer motor principle.

Large flatbed plotters usually fix the medium to the plotter bed using vacuum. Large flatbed plotters have resolutions and plotting speeds as high as 0.0004 inch and 3600 inch/minute, respectively. Flatbed plotters are available in sizes from $8\frac{1}{2} \times 11$ inches up to several tens of feet in length and width. A large variety of plotting media can be used, e.g., paper, vellum, Mylar, photographic

Figure 1–31 Dye sublimation printer.(Courtesy of Iris Graphics, Inc., a scitex company).

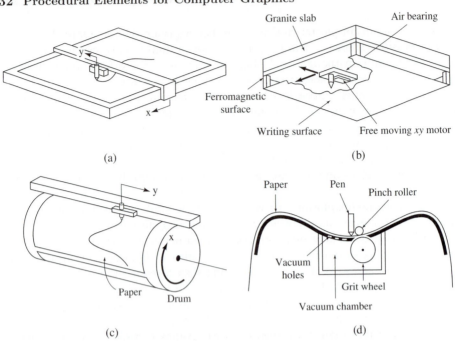

Figure 1–32 Schematic diagrams of pen and ink plotter types. (a) Flatbed — moving arm; (b) flatbed — moving head; (c) drum; (d) pinch roller.

film, scribe coat, sheet metal and cloth. Combined with this large variety of media is an accompanying variety of plotting tools, including ballpoint, felt tip and wet ink pens; photographic and laser light beams; engraving tools, scribe and cloth cutters and laser cutting beams. As the wide variety of available media and tools suggests, flatbed plotters are used in a wide variety of applications. In addition to traditional pen and ink plots, large flatbed plotters are used to generate masks for printed circuit boards and integrated circuits. Here, the plotting medium is photographic film, and the plotting tool is a light beam. Adaptations of flatbed plotters are also used to cut out men's and ladies' apparel and even sailboat sails. Here, the medium is an appropriate cloth and the plotting tool a knife or laser cutting beam.

Smaller, lower cost flatbed plotters are less versatile, have lower resolutions and lower plotting speeds. They also typically use an electrostatic hold-down system for the media, which are generally limited to paper, vellum and transparency film.

Drum plotters (see Fig. 1–32c) are mechanically more complex than flatbed plotters. Here, the plotting head moves along a fixed arm to provide one dimension. The medium itself is rolled back and forth under the fixed arm to provide the second dimension.

The medium is fixed to the drum using either a vacuum or tensioned supply and takeup rollers. Media types are limited to those that are easily rolled.

Typically, the drum plotter medium is either paper or vellum. Only the width of the medium is fixed. The length of a plot is limited only by the length of the medium roll. Although resolutions are similar to those for flatbed plotters (0.0005 inch), plotting speeds are typically considerably lower.

The pinch roller plotter is a hybrid of the flatbed and drum plotters. The drawing medium is held at each edge between a pinch wheel and the plotting surface (see Fig. 1–32d). The plotting surface is cylindrical. As the pinch wheel rotates, the medium moves back and forth under a fixed arm on which the plotting head moves. These plotters use either cut or roll stock, which is usually limited to paper, vellum or transparency film. A pinch roll plotter is shown in Fig. 1–33.

Most pen and ink plotters operate in an incremental mode driven by stepping motors. The plotting tool moves across the plotting surface in a series of small steps. The number of movement directions is limited to eight, horizontal, vertical and diagonal, as shown in Fig. 1–34. This results in lines other than those in the directions shown in Fig. 1–34, appearing as a series of stair steps. This stair-step, or jaggies, effect is a manifestation of a fundamental phenomenon called aliasing (see Sec. 2–16). The algorithm usually chosen to select the one of eight movement directions that most nearly approximates the direction of the line is Bresenham's algorithm (see Sec. 2–3). Although Bresenham's algorithm is most often associated with raster scan displays, it was originally developed for digital incremental plotters. True motion directions are obtained by using

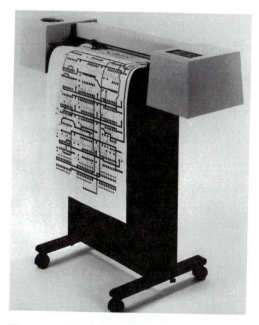

Figure 1–33 Pinch roll plotter. (Courtesy of Hewlett Packard).

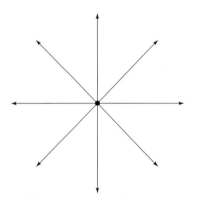

Figure 1–34   Eight directions of movement for
incremental plotters.

servomotors to drive the plotting head. In this case, a feedback servocircuit constantly modulates both drive motors simultaneously to yield smooth lines.

Although speed is important in a plotter, the acceleration of the plotting head is generally more important for overall throughput. Fundamentally, this is because the typical drawing is made up of short straight line segments. Consequently, the plotter must start and stop between segments. High acceleration allows the plotter to attain full speed more quickly. Many plotter controllers are also equipped with look-ahead software, designed to prevent the plotter from unnecessarily stopping, e.g., when a series of short connected straight line segments is used to represent a curve.

Pen and ink plotters produce the highest quality line drawing output of any graphics device. An example is shown in Fig. 1–35.

Laser Printers

Although originally designed for printing and typographic applications, laser printers are used extensively for computer graphics output. This is particularly true in publishing, where systems for combining print and graphics on the same output page are important (see for example [Adob85]). These systems are capable of combining near-typeset-quality text, line art and halftone pictures on a single page. Figure 1–36 shows a typical example.

A laser printer is a raster scan device. The basic process, shown schematically in Fig. 1–37, is similar to xerography. The print engine contains a drum that is coated with a photoconductive material. The drum is scanned by either a gas or semiconductor diode laser. As the drum rotates, the coating is electrically charged. The drum remains charged until struck by the highly coherent light from the laser. The laser light selectively discharges areas (dots) on the drum to form a negative image, i.e., the charge is removed from dots that do *not* appear in the final image.[†] Positioning of the laser beam on the drum is accomplished

---

[†] This description is for what is called a write-black print engine. Write-white engines reverse the process.

Figure 1–35   Typical output from a digital incremental plotter.

using a rotating polygonal mirror. A black plastic-based powder, called toner, is attracted to the remaining charged areas on the drum. The image on the drum is then transferred to the oppositely precharged paper. Finally, the toner is fused to the paper, using heat and pressure to form the permanent image.

Laser printers are currently available with resolutions from 300×300 dpi up to 1200×1200 dpi, with a 600×600 dpi resolution typical. Although extensively used for desktop publishing, the resolution of typical laser printers is only now approaching that of good quality phototypesetters (1200 to 5000 dpi).[†] Current laser printers typically use a single dot size. Using variable dot size, or micropositioning, allows increased flexibility in generating halftone images (see Sec. 2–17). Although laser printers typically produce correspondence-sized pages, they are available in larger widths that produce, for example, D-size (22×44 inch) and E-size (34×44 inch) drawings.

Laser printing is a continuous process. Once printing of a page starts, it must continue at a constant speed. Because of the high resolution, very high continuous data rates are required. For example, a 600×600 dpi printer producing a $7\frac{1}{2} \times 10\frac{1}{2}$ inch printed area, on an $8\frac{1}{2} \times 11$ inch page at 8 pages/minute, requires a sustained data rate to the laser print engine of 4 megabits/second. Because of these high data rates, the laser printer, like the electrostatic plotter, uses a separate controller, including on-board memory. The general scheme is shown in Fig. 1–38. Here, the host computer provides a description of the page using a higher-level page description language (see, for example, [Adob85]). The image processor-controller takes care of generating individual font characters, lines or half tone patterns, and sending the required bit (dot) stream to the print engine.

Figure 1–39 shows a typical laser printer. Figure 1–40 shows examples of typical laser printer generated line drawings and halftones.

[†]This book, including much of the line art, was set on a 2400 dpi phototypesetter.

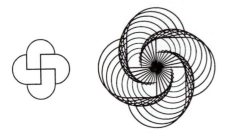
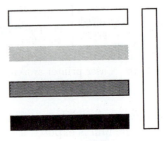

The picture (top left) was made with the rlineto command and the arc command. Then by scaling and rotating the picture we can make other interesting and different designs.

By defining a variable called box, we can print it in many different ways. Using the stroke, the setgray, and the fill commands, we can print the same box in many other shades and positions.

Figure 1–36   Laser printer-generated page showing a combination of text, line art and halftone picture. (Courtesy of QMS, Inc.)

Color Film Cameras

With the advent of high quality color raster displays, coupled with full color frame buffers (see Sec. 1–9) capable of displaying over 16 million colors, the need arose for a technique for preserving these results. Currently, the only available techniques are based on color photographic film. In computer graphics, the most frequently used device is a color camera.

Conceptually, a color camera, shown schematically in Fig. 1–41, is quite simple. The technique is called field sequential recording. A small (5 inch diameter) precision flat-faced monochrome (white) CRT is used. First, a red photographic filter is placed in the optical path from a camera to the CRT. Then, only the red intensity signal for the picture is fed to the CRT. The film is exposed; the CRT is erased, the red filter removed and a green filter rotated into position.

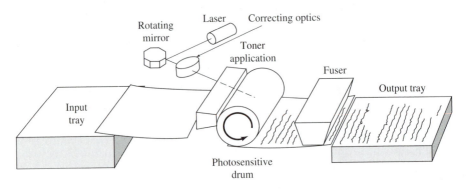

Figure 1–37   Schematic of a laser print engine.

Figure 1–38 Laser printer system schematic.

Then, only the green intensity signal for the picture is fed to the CRT. Without advancing, the film is exposed a second time. Finally, the process is repeated for the blue component of the picture. This triply exposed film now contains the complete picture.

The quality of the CRT is critical to the success of the technique. A flat-faced CRT is used, rather than the curved CRT used in most monitors, to eliminate distortions. The glass used in the CRT must also be of high quality, free of bubbles, striations and other defects. To allow nearly equal response to all three signals (RGB), a broadband phosphor is used. The phosphor layer must be free of blemishes and patterns, fine grained and smoothly textured. The CRT beam spot size must be as small as practical for increased resolution, and the electromagnetic focusing system must be of highest quality.

With care, practical resolutions of 3000 to 5000 dpi per side on a 5 inch monitor are possible. Note that resolution and addressability are not the same. Resolution measures the number of separately distinguishable spots, whereas addressability measures the number of distinct positions at which the electron beam can be placed. Because of the characteristics of the eye, a picture made with higher addressability than resolvability will look better, even though the points are not resolved.

1–7   Logical Interactive Devices

Before discussing physical interactive devices, it is useful to discuss the functional capabilities of interactive graphics devices. The functional capabilities are

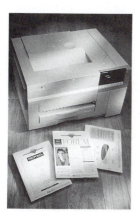

Figure 1–39 Laser printer. (Courtesy of Hewlett Packard Co.).

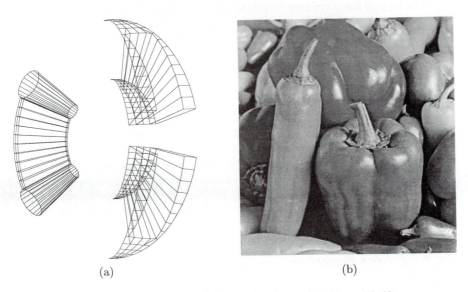

(a)   (b)

Figure 1–40   Laser printer output. (a) Line drawing; (b) patterned halftone.

generally considered to be of four or five logical types. The logical interaction devices, as opposed to the physical devices discussed in the next section, are a locator, a valuator, a button and a pick. A fifth functional capability, called keyboard, is frequently included, because of the general availability of the alphanumeric keyboard. In fact, a keyboard can conceptually and functionally be considered as a collection of buttons.

The Locator Function

The locator function provides coordinate information in either two or three dimensions. Generally, the coordinate numbers returned are in normalized coordinates and may be either relative or absolute.

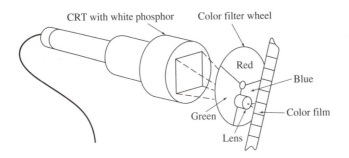

Figure 1–41   Schematic of a color camera.

The locator function may be either direct or indirect. It may also be discrete or continuous. With direct implementations, the user indicates the coordinate directly, e.g., using his or her finger with a touch pad. Alternatively, he or she may directly type coordinate numbers using an alphanumeric keyboard. Indirect implementations require the user to coordinate the location or movement of an on-screen cursor with the position of a mouse, tablet stylus, joystick, etc.

Discrete implementations accept coordinate information as discrete, sometimes fixed, increments. For example, each press of a cursor key may increment a coordinate by a fixed amount. Continuous implementations correlate cursor movement (coordinate updates) with smooth hand motion. When an on-screen cursor is used to indicate the position and movement, the control-to-hand ratio, i.e., the rate at which the control is moved compared to the rate at which the screen cursor moves, becomes important. This ratio may be programmed to increase with increasing speed of control (hand motion) and decrease with decreasing speed of control.

The Valuator Function

The valuator function provides a single value. Generally this value is presented as a real number. Valuators may be bound or unbound. A bound valuator has mechanical or programmed stops within a fixed range. An unbounded valuator continuously increases or decreases, i.e., an unbounded valuator has a theoretical infinite range. In practice, physical valuators are numerically bound. Programming yields incremental or absolute values within the dynamic range of the computer. Screen feedback is required for interactive use. The control to display ratio may be varied to yield gross or fine incremental adjustment of the value.

The Button or Choice Function

The button function is used to select and activate events or procedures which control the interactive flow or change the underlying task paradigm. It generally provides only binary (on or off) digital information. Again, an alphanumeric keyboard can be considered as a collection of buttons.

The Pick Function

The pick function identifies or selects objects or elements of objects within the displayed picture. It is a direct action function. Feedback in the form of blinking, change of color or style of presentation of the picked entity, e.g., a solid line, which becomes dashed, is required for effective use.

1–8   Physical Interactive Devices

Physical interactive devices include tablets, light pens, joysticks, mice, control dials, function switches or buttons, data gloves, touch screens and, of course, the common alphanumeric keyboard, to name only a few. Because of increased incidence of repetitive motion syndrome, ergonomic keyboards are becoming popular. A typical ergonomic keyboard is shown in Fig. 1–42. These physical devices are used to implement the logical interactive devices discussed in the previous section.

Tablets

The tablet is the most common locator device. A typical tablet is shown in Fig. 1–43. Tablets may either be used in conjunction with a CRT graphics display or stand alone. In the latter case, they are frequently referred to as digitizers. The tablet itself consists of a flat surface and a pen-like stylus (or puck), which is used to indicate a location on the tablet surface. Usually the proximity of the stylus to the tablet surface is also sensed. When used in conjunction with a CRT display, feedback from the CRT face is provided by means of a small tracking symbol called a cursor, which follows the movement of the stylus on the tablet surface. When used as a stand-alone digitizer, feedback is provided by digital readouts.

Tablets typically provide two-dimensional coordinate information. The values returned are in tablet coordinates. Software converts the tablet coordinates to user or world coordinates. Typical resolution and accuracy is 0.01 to 0.001 inch.

A number of different principles have been used to implement tablets. The original RAND tablet (see [Davi64]) used an orthogonal matrix of individual wires beneath the tablet surface. Each wire was individually coded such that the stylus acting as a receiver picked up a unique digital code at each intersection. Decoding yielded the x, y coordinates of the stylus. The obvious limitations on the resolution of such a matrix-encoded tablet were the density of the wires and the receiver's ability to resolve a unique code. The accuracy was limited by the linearity of the individual wires, as well as the parallelism of the wires in the two orthogonal directions.

Figure 1–42   An ergonomic alphanumeric keyboard. (Courtesy of Kinesis Corp.).

Figure 1–43 Typical tablet with wireless pens. (Courtesy of CalComp).

Another interesting early implementation for a tablet used sound waves. A stylus was used to create a spark, which generated a sound wave. The sound wave moved outward from the stylus on the surface of the tablet in a circular wave front. Two sensitive ribbon microphones were mounted on adjacent sides of the tablet. Thus, they were at right angles. By accurately measuring the time that it took the sound wave to travel from the stylus to the microphones, the coordinate distances were determined.

The most popular tablet implementation is based on a magnetic principle. In this tablet implementation, strain wave pulses travel through a grid of wires beneath the tablet surface. Appropriate counters and a stylus containing a pick-up are used to determine the time it takes for alternate pulses parallel to the x and y coordinate axes to travel from the edge of the tablet to the stylus. These times are readily converted into x, y coordinates.

Touch Panels

A locator device similar to a tablet is the touch panel. In a typical low-cost touch panel, light emitters are mounted on two adjacent edges, with companion light detectors mounted in the opposite edges. Anything, e.g., a finger, interrupting the two orthogonal light beams yields an x, y coordinate pair. Capacitive touch panels can be directly imbedded in the face of a CRT. Currently, resolutions up to 1024 touch points are available. Because of its relatively low resolution, the touch panel is most useful for gross pointing operations.

Control Dials

Locator devices such as the joystick, trackball and mouse are frequently implemented using sensitive variable resistors or potentiometers as part of a voltage divider. Control dials, which are valuators, are similarly implemented. The accuracy is dependent on the quality of the potentiometer, typically 0.1 to 10 percent of full throw. Although resolution of the potentiometer is basically infinite, use in a digital system requires analog-to-digital (A/D) conversion. Typically, the resolution of the A/D converter ranges from 8 to 14 bits, i.e., from 1 part in 2^8 (256) to 1 part in 2^{14} (16384). Valuators are also implemented with digital shaft encoders, which, of course, provide a direct digital output for each incremental rotation of the shaft.

Perhaps the simplest of the valuators is the control dial. Control dials, shown in Fig. 1–44, are essentially sensitive rotating potentiometers, or accurate digital shaft encoders. They generally are used in groups, and are particularly useful for activating rotation, translation, scaling or zoom functions.

Joystick

A typical locator is the joystick, shown in Fig. 1–45. A movable joystick is generally implemented with two valuators, either potentiometers or digital shaft encoders, mounted in the base. The valuators provide results proportional to the movement of the shaft. A third dimension is readily incorporated into a joystick, e.g., by using a third valuator to sense rotation of the shaft. A tracking symbol is normally used for feedback. Joysticks are also implemented using forces. Here, the joystick itself does not move, except minutely. The strain in the joystick shaft is measured in two orthogonal directions and converted to cursor movement.

Trackball

The trackball shown in Fig. 1–46 is similar to the joystick. It is frequently seen in radar installations, e.g., in air traffic control. Here, a spherical ball is

Figure 1–44   Control dials. (Courtesy of Evans & Sutherland Computer Corp.).

Figure 1–45 Joystick. (Courtesy of Measurement Systems, Inc.).

mounted in a base with only a portion projecting above the surface. The ball is free to rotate in any direction. Two valuators, either potentiometers or shaft encoders, mounted in the base sense the rotation of the ball and provide results proportional to its relative position. In addition to feedback from the normal tracking symbol, users obtain tactile feedback from the rotation rate or angular momentum of the ball. Trackballs are frequently equipped with buttons in order that they can be substituted for a mouse, and are more ergonomically acceptable than mice.

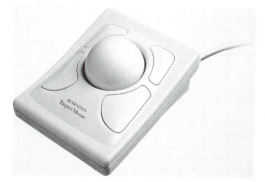

Figure 1–46 Trackball with four programmable buttons. (Courtesy of Kensington Microware Ltd.).

Mouse

The joystick has a fixed location with a fixed origin. The mouse and trackball, on the other hand, have only a relative origin. A typical mouse consists of an upside-down trackball mounted in a small, lightweight box. As the mouse is moved across a surface, the ball rotates and drives the shafts of two valuators, either potentiometers or digital shaft encoders. The cumulative movement of the shafts provides x, y coordinates. A typical mouse is shown in Fig. 1–47. The mouse can be picked up, moved and set back down in a different orientation. In this case the coordinate system in which data is generated, i.e., the mouse, is changed, but not the data coordinate system itself. Under these circumstances, the tracking symbol used for feedback does not move when the mouse is not moving on the contact surface. The mouse suffers from inaccuracies due to slippage. Mice that work on both optical and magnetic principles are available. These implementations eliminate the inaccuracies due to slippage. An optical mouse uses a 'mouse pad' with orthogonally oriented embedded light reflecting strips. The mouse contains both a small light source and a small photoelectric cell. As the mouse is moved across the pad the number of light pulses in both directions is counted. These numbers are then converted into x, y coordinates.

Function Switches

Buttons or function switches, shown in Fig. 1–48, are either toggle or push-button switches. They may be either continuously closed/continuously open or momentary-contact switches. The most convenient type of function switch incorporates both capabilities. Software-controlled lights, indicating which switches or buttons are active, are usually provided. Buttons and switches are frequently incorporated into other devices. For example, the stylus of a tablet usually has a switch in the tip activated by pushing down on the stylus. A mouse or trackball typically incorporates one or more buttons.

Figure 1–47   A mouse with four programmable buttons. (Courtesy of Kensington Microware, Ltd.).

Figure 1–48 Function switches. (Courtesy of Adage, Inc.).

Light Pen

The light pen is the only true pick device. The pen, shown schematically in Fig. 1–49, contains a sensitive photoelectric cell and associated circuitry. Because the basic information provided by the light pen is timing, it depends on the picture being repeatedly produced in a predictable manner. The use of a light pen is limited to refresh displays, either line drawing or raster scan.

On a calligraphic line drawing refresh display (see Sec. 1–2), if the light pen is activated and placed over an area of the CRT which is subsequently written on, the change in intensity sends a signal to the display controller, which identifies

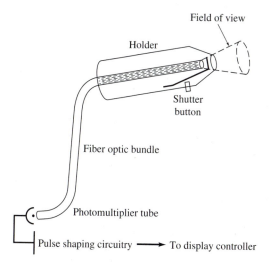

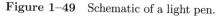

Figure 1–49 Schematic of a light pen.

the appropriate segment of the picture. A light pen can also be used as a locator on a line drawing refresh device by using a tracking symbol.

Because in a raster scan display the picture is generated in a fixed sequence, the light pen is used to determine the horizontal scan line (y coordinate) and the position on the scan line (x coordinate). Again, this allows the particular line segment, object or subpicture to be determined. The actual process is somewhat complicated if an interlace scheme is used (see Sec. 1–4). This description also indicates that, on a raster scan device, a light pen can be used as a locator rather than as a pick device. Figure 1–50 shows a light pen used to simulate a logical button.

Spaceball

One direct three-dimensional interaction device is the Spaceball (see Fig. 1–51). The sphere contains strain gages. As the user pushes or pulls on the sphere, the output of the strain gages is converted into three-dimensional translations and rotations. For example, if the user attempts to rotate the sphere about the vertical axis by twisting it, the result is a rotation of the image about the corresponding axis even though the sphere itself does not move.

Data Glove

The data glove records three-dimensional hand and finger positions, and hence hand and finger motions. In the original VPL Data Glove, each finger joint has a short length of fiber optic cable attached. At one end of the fiber optic cable is a small light-emitting diode (LED); at the other end is a phototransistor. A small

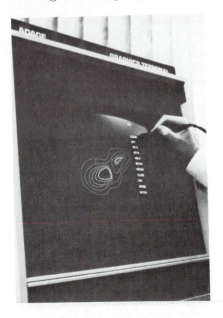

Figure 1–50 A light pen used to simulate a logical button function via menu picking. (Courtesy of Adage, Inc.).

Figure 1–51 Spaceball. (Courtesy of Spacetec IMC Corp.).

portion of the cable is roughened. When the cable is flexed by movement of the finger, some of the light is lost; hence less light is received by the phototransistor. The intensity of the received light is interpreted as the position of the finger joint. In addition, a separate system senses the gross position of the glove.

More recent data gloves use electro-mechanical rather than electro-optical sensing techniques. In particular, pressure sensors are imbedded in the glove finger joints. The sensor converts the small pressure generated by bending the finger into an electrical signal. The strength of the signal is again interpreted as the position of the finger joint. Again, the gross hand position is determined independently. An example of a data glove is shown in Fig. 1–52.

Simulation of Alternate Devices

Although physical devices are available to implement all the logical interactive devices, an individual graphics device may not have the appropriate physical devices available. Thus, simulation of the logical interactive devices is required. An example is shown in Fig. 1–50, where a light pen is being used to simulate a logical button function by picking light buttons from a menu.

The tablet is one of the most versatile of the physical devices. It can be used as a digitizer to provide absolute x, y coordinate information. In addition, it can

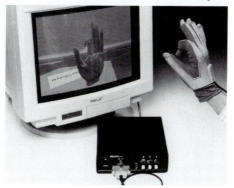

Figure 1–52 A data glove. (Courtesy of Nissho Electronics Corp.).

readily be used to simulate all the logical interactive functions. This is shown in Fig. 1–53. The tablet itself is a locator (a in Fig. 1–53). The button function can be implemented by using a tracking symbol. The tracking symbol is positioned at or near menu buttons using the tablet stylus. The tablet coordinates are compared with the known x, y coordinates of the menu buttons. If a match is obtained, then that button is activated (b in Fig. 1–53). A keyboard can be implemented in a similar manner (c in Fig. 1–53).

A single valuator is usually implemented in combination with a button. The particular function for evaluation is selected by a button, usually in a menu. The valuator is then simulated by a 'number line' or 'sliderbar' (d in Fig. 1–53). Moving the tracking symbol along the line generates x and y coordinates, one of which is interpreted as a percentage of the valuator's range.

The pick function can be implemented using a locator by defining the relative x and y coordinates of a small 'hit window.' The hit window is then made the tracking symbol, and the stylus is used to position it. The x, y coordinates of each of the line segments, objects or subpictures of interest are then compared with those of the current location of the hit window. If a match is obtained, that entity is picked. Implemented in software, this can be slow for complex pictures.

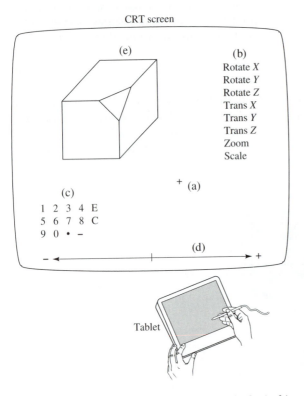

Figure 1–53 A tablet used to simulate the logical interactive functions. (a) Locator; (b) button; (c) keyboard; (d) valuator; (e) pick.

Implemented in hardware, there is no noticeable delay. Although a light pen or a mouse cannot be used as a digitizer, like the tablet they can also be used to simulate all the logical interactive functions.

1–9 Data Generation Devices

There is an increasing interest and need to convert data, either textual or graphical, from hardcopy to digital form. Digitizing large amounts of data a single point at a time is both time consuming and error prone. Consequently, digital scanning devices are used. Flexible two-dimensional material, e.g., printed documents, and monochrome or color photographs or similar material, can be scanned on either a drum or flatbed scanner. More rigid two-dimensional material requires a flatbed scanner.

Scanners

A schematic of a drum scanner is shown in Fig. 1-54. Here, the flexible material is wrapped around a drum. A deflection system scans (moves) a laser beam across the drum. The reflected beam is captured by a light detection system. Using suitable filters, the red, green and blue components of the reflected light are captured on successive scans. A single scan line is scanned three times before the drum is incrementally rotated.

Typically eight or ten (or more) bits of information are retained for each of the red, green and blue components of the light. The most significant bits of the captured data are quite accurate. However, the least significant bits are less accurate. Consequently, the highest quality systems capture more bits than necessary and discard the least significant bit or two.

Flat bed scanners work on a similar principle. Flat bed scanners may be either moving head or moving table. The more common type uses a moving

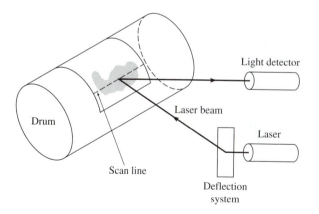

Figure 1–54 Schematic of a drum scanner.

head. However, the principle is the same. Here either single or multiple rows (typically three) of CCDs (Charged Coupled Devices) are used for detection. Multiple-pass devices use a single row of CCDs, while single-pass devices use multiple rows. A strong light shines on the surface to be scanned. The light reflected from the surface, after passing through appropriate filters, is detected by the CCDs and converted to binary information. Again, typical precision is either eight or ten bits of information, with the better devices capturing more bits than necessary and discarding the least significant bit or two. Current systems that are intended to scan opaque material have typical optical resolutions up to approximately 1200 dpi. Systems designed to scan transparent material, e.g., slides, have optical resolutions up to approximately 2700 dpi. The resulting image files are quite large.

Three-dimensional Digitizers

Three-dimensional digitizers can be categorized as either contact or noncontact. A typical contact digitizer is shown in Fig. 1-55. By precisely knowing the length of each of the arms and carefully keeping track of the rotations of each of the joints as the digitizer point is moved allows calculation of the location of the digitizer point in a relative coordinate system.

Noncontact three-dimensional digitizer or locator systems use sound, optical tracking or electromagnetic coupling to determine position. Typically, the volume of the space in which the systems work is limited to on the order of 10 cubic feet. By positioning receivers at known locations within or on the edges of the system volume and using either single or multiple transmitters, the radii of several spheres centered on the known receiver locations are obtained. Determination of the location of the transmitter is then a matter of solving the associated geometry (see Figs. 1–56 and 1–57).

Figure 1–55   A contact three-dimensional digitizer. (Courtesy of Immersion Corp.).

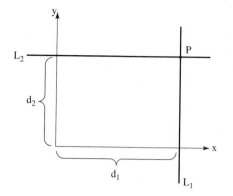

Figure 1–56 Geometry for two-dimensional digitizing.

Motion Capture

The principles underlying three-dimensional motion capture are fundamentally the same as those governing two-dimensional digitizing (see Sec. 1–8), i.e., the distance from a fixed point in space is required. In the case of two-dimensional digitizing, the mathematics is somewhat simplified by determining the distance of a line parallel to a known line in the two-dimensional plane. Hence, only two distances are required, as shown in Fig. 1–56. Here, $x = d_1$ and $y = d_2$.

Figure 1–57 shows a two-dimensional analog for three-dimensional motion capture. Here, the centers C_1, C_2 and C_3 are known receiver positions. By some means, the distances to a point in the two-dimensional plane are known — for example, by timing a signal pulse emitted by a sender, or by a disturbance in a magnetic field, or by visually triangulating a known spot on the object from a video image. Thus, the centers and distances (radii) define circles in the two-dimensional plane and spheres in three-space. Figure 1–57 shows that intersection of only two circles yields ambiguous results, e.g., the circles centered at C_1 and C_2, with radii r_1 and r_2, intersect at two points labelled A and B in Fig. 1–57. The ambiguity is resolved by using a third circle centered at C_3, with radius r_3 to select point B.[†] In the three-dimensional case, a fourth point is required to resolve any ambiguity.

Three-dimensional motion capture systems are used in biomechanical and biomedical studies, e.g., in gait analysis; in sports, e.g., in analysis of the motion of an athlete in swinging a baseball bat; in character animation, where the

---

[†] Each of the circles is governed by an equation of the form $(x - h)^2 + (y - k)^2 = r^2$. Writing this equation for each of the circles initially yields a set of three nonlinear equations for x and y. Rather than solve these equations directly, it is best to obtain linear equations by translating the center of one of the circles to the origin. The equation of this circle is now of the form $x^2 + y^2 = r_i^2$ and can be used to eliminate the nonlinear terms from the other two. The resulting pair of equations is then solved simultaneously for the correct intersection point. (See also [Roge80c].)

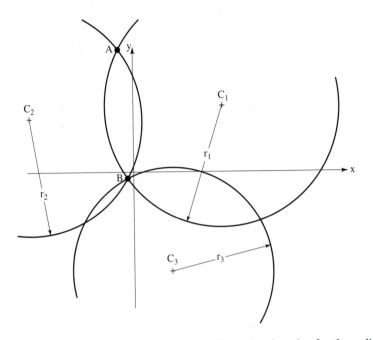

Figure 1–57   Geometry for the two-dimensional analog for three-dimensional motion capture.

motion of a live person is translated into the motion of an animated cartoon character; and in virtual reality systems. Systems may be either connected or disconnected. In connected systems, data is transmitted from the subjects body to the support computer system via a cable tail. In disconnected systems, data is transmitted wirelessly. Color Plate 1 shows a three-dimensional motion capture system that requires no physical connection between the object and the receiver. Here, sensors are mounted at key points of the subject's body; and a pulsed DC magnetic field is used to determine the position of each sensor. Signals from each sensor, as well as from other body mounted devices, e.g., a data glove, are sent via wires to a small 'fanny pack', from whence they are transmitted wirelessly to a receiver. A support computer then determines the position and generates appropriate transformation matrices.

1–10   Graphical User Interfaces

Today the large majority of individuals involved even peripherally in computers are familiar with graphical user interfaces (GUIs), either through a window operating system or through a web browser. Although a computer system may have multiple interactive devices, typically visual representations of position, valuator, button and pick functions accessed using a single interactive device are used to control the system or a specific application running on the system. User interface design is both an art and a science. The details are well beyond the scope of this text. Three of the key principles are consistency, testing and submergence of the designers ego, i.e., listen to the user. Perhaps *some* of the underlying principles of all user interface design are best illustrated by a command line interface, i.e., a nongraphical user interface.[†]

For a command line interface, the alphanumeric keyboard is the interactive device. A properly designed keyboard interface is easy to learn, fast and efficient. Production environments frequently use keyboard command line interfaces.

Unless a numeric value is specifically required, a keyboard interface should accept alphabetic words for inputs. Numbered lists of responses are unacceptable. The fundamental reason is that the user thinks in terms of words and phrases, *not* numbered items on a list. For example, if the desired action is to rotate an object, the user thinks rotate and *not* item 3 on the option list.

Not all individuals are touch typists. Consequently, the number of characters required to initiate a command should be kept to a minimum. However, individuals who are touch typists should not be placed at a disadvantage (annoyed) by the use of odd sequences of characters. One solution is to allow full words as input and then *truncate* those words to the minimum number of characters necessary to uniquely define the command. For example, the rotate command is truncated to the first two characters, i.e., ro. Acceptable truncation that yields unique character sequences is indicated by parentheses, e.g., (ro)tate. Numeric input must be accepted in free format; i.e., decimal points are *not* required for floating point numbers. For example, 30 and 30. are equivalent.

A command menu should be provided. The question of how and when it is provided is important. It should be displayed once upon initial execution of the program and upon request thereafter. It should *not* be redisplayed after each command is accepted. Doing so is both annoying to the frequent user and time consuming. The command menu should occupy a single screen. Appropriate command menus should be provided at all levels within the program that accept commands. In lieu of continuous display of the command menu, after the first instance, a single command line is used. The command line consists of a single word or character, e.g., ? or Option? or Command? But what about the infrequent user who needs help?

There are as many ways of requesting a command or help menu (screen) as there are programmers, e.g., typing h or help or ? or ?? or menu or whatever! Discovering the appropriate command is often rather interesting. You can always make it a menu item, but who is going to remember that? And how do you get the menu to display if it is not always displayed? A simple solution is to accept any of them or a simple carriage return. Why? Because a frustrated user will almost always eventually hit some kind of key. Implementation is simple. If, in parsing the command input, a legal input is not found, then the command menu (help screen) appropriate to that level is displayed. Commands should also be case insensitive.

[†]To some extent, these comments represent the author's bias. To understand some of these biases, note that the author is a high speed touch typist and dislikes mice and windows-style interfaces as being too slow and cumbersome.

The efficiency of the interface is increased by a concept called 'command stacking'. The concept is best illustrated by an example. Consider a program to manipulate objects in three-space. For rotation in three dimensions, the rotate command might require the specification of the axis of rotation (x, y, z or general) and the rotation angle in degrees. The top level command processor accepts the rotate command and invokes a lower level command processor that asks for and accepts the axis and angle inputs. Command stacking allows the familiar user to type

```
ro x 30
```

where here the command responses are separated by spaces. The top level command processor parses the input string, determines if the first command, ro, is acceptable and, if acceptable, passes the remaining commands to lower-level command processors. If not acceptable, it displays the menu. Command stacking allows the familiar user to accomplish multiple manipulations with little input and minimal waiting, meanwhile allowing the occasional user access to the same capabilities. With command stacking

```
sc o 2
ro x 30
Ro y -45
dr
```

scales the current object by a factor of 2 using overall scaling, rotates about the x-axis by 30°, rotates about the y-axis by $-45°$ and draws the result on the $z = 0$ plane using an orthographic projection. Notice that the commands have all been truncated: (sc)ale, (o)verall, (ro)tate, (Ro)tate, (x)-axis, (y)-axis and (dr)aw. Note also that (ro)tate and (Ro)tate are equivalent.

Finally, a user interface should be consistent at all levels. However, "consistency for consistencies sake is the hobgoblin of small minds", as Emerson said. The user interface should also adhere to the 'principle of least astonishment'. The principle of least astonishment, simply stated, is that when a response to a command can be implemented in multiple ways, the choice is made on the basis of 'what response will least astonish the user'. However, the least astonishing response is frequently a matter of opinion.

There are a number of fundamental elements that are used to construct graphical user interfaces. We briefly discuss some of the more common elements.

Cursors

The principle use of a cursor is to indicate location on the screen, i.e., it is used as a locator. However, the shape of the cursor can also be used to indicate not only location but the operation available, by clicking a 'mouse' button, for example the circle with a tail surrounding a plus sign to indicate magnification, or the hour glass or watch used to indicate a 'wait state' while the application is processing a request. Such cursors are iconic in nature, i.e., they are symbols used to convey complex information. Although a cursor is normally a small symbol, it can be expanded to full or nearly full screen/window size to aid in accomplishing interactive tasks. For example, if a simple upright cross or plus sign + is used to indicate position, expanding it to full screen/window size is effective in aligning elements of the image. Several cursor shapes are shown in Fig. 1–58.

Radio Buttons

Radio buttons are used to visually implement the choice or button function. The items in the list should be mutually exclusive. Alternatively, the buttons can be used to indicate an on/off status for a particular feature. In this case it is not necessary that the items be mutually exclusive. Figure 1–59 shows a simple example of the latter use.

The 'color' of the surrounding 'box', and the size of the buttons and accompanying text, should be sufficient for the user to easily identify and select the buttons. The button itself should change 'color' when selected.

Valuators

The valuator function is frequently implemented as either a fixed length slider bar or a dial pointer, as shown in Fig. 1–60. Figure 1–60a shows a simple line with an arrow, indicating where along the line the selected value lies. Additional feedback is provided by a numerical value shown under the arrow. Figure 1–60b uses a dial with a pointer. Again, additional feedback is provided by a numerical value. The user grabs the indicator and moves it, typically by moving the 'mouse' with a button pressed. Releasing the button freezes the value. An alternative visual implementation is to use a type-in box separately, or in conjunction with either a slider bar or dial, as shown in Figs. 1–60a and 1–60b. A valuator, implemented as an up and down counter, is shown in Fig. 1–60c. Here the user clicks on the plus sign to increase the value, and on the minus sign to decrease the value. An up and down counter eliminates the necessity to use a keyboard for input of precise numbers. These representations work well for fixed interval valuators.

For infinite valuators, e.g., infinite rotation, fixed length slider bars are not satisfactory. Furthermore, although useful, dials take up valuable screen space.

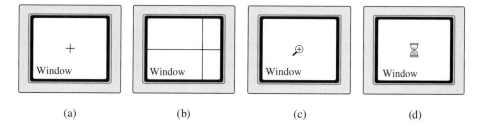

(a)   (b)   (c)   (d)

Figure 1–58 Cursor shapes. (a) Simple plus; (b) expanded plus for alignment; (c) magnification icon; (d) hour glass icon indicating wait.

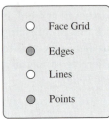

Figure 1–59 Radio buttons used to select display features. A dark gray button indicates that the feature is on.

In the context of three-dimensional manipulation of objects, the author has used an invisible slider bar along with a three button mouse to both save screen space and to seamlessly implement variable control to display ratios. First the operation, e.g., rotation, translation, scaling, etc., is selected from a menu using a pick function. The cursor icon is changed to indicate that manipulation is active. The screen is divided vertically in the center. The color of the cursor changes as it moves from left of center to right of center. The color indicates the direction of application of the operation. A small 'dead band' at the center of the screen, where the cursor is a third color, indicates to the user that the direction of application is changing. For example, if the cursor is to the left of center, rotation is negative, if to the right, rotation is positive. Only the horizontal location of the cursor is used. Consequently, the cursor can be at any vertical position on the screen. The speed of rotation is proportional to the distance from the center of the screen. The constant of proportionality is user modifiable. The axis of motion is selected by using one of the three mouse buttons, e.g., left $-x$, middle $-y$ and right $-z$. Releasing the 'mouse' button terminates the action. The system is easy to learn. It also allows precise positioning of objects. Pressing multiple 'mouse' buttons results in simultaneous motion on multiple axes. Figure 1–60d illustrates the concept.

Scroll Bars

Scroll bars are specialized sliders usually used to indicate and/or move to a position within a document or other entity. A typical example is shown in Fig. 1–61. Generally they are implemented without a numerical indicator. The arrows indicate the direction of motion. Clicking on an arrow moves the user through the document in the indicated direction. The position icon also moves to show the relative position within the document. Grabbing the position icon and holding the 'mouse' button down while dragging the mouse quickly moves the user through the document. Clicking within the scroll bar but not on the arrow or the position icon moves through the document in steps.

Grids

Grids are used to provide guidance in constructing objects. They are implemented as background lines or dots at each grid intersection. Snap-to grids,

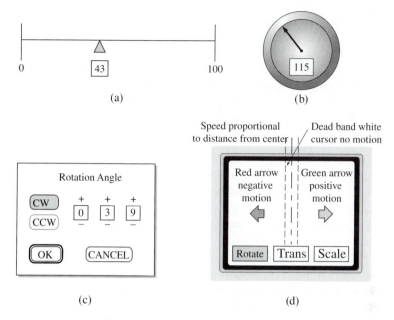

(a) (b)

Speed proportional   Dead band white
to distance from center   cursor no motion

Red arrow   Green arrow
negative   positive
motion   motion

Rotation Angle

CW   +   +   +
      0   3   9
CCW   –   –   –

OK   CANCEL

Rotate Trans Scale

(c) (d)

Figure 1–60 Valuator visual interfaces. (a) Simple fixed interval slider bar; (b) control dial; (c) up and down value counters; (d) infinite slider bar with variable control ratio.

usually implemented in world coordinates, force construction entities to lie on the grid. Snapping to a grid location is accomplished by rounding the value to that of the nearest grid point.

Dialog Boxes

Dialog boxes are used when multiple inputs are required to specify the desired action. A dialog box may incorporate a number of different interactive tools, e.g.,

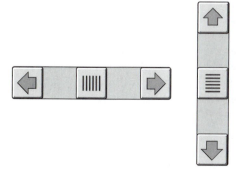

Figure 1–61 Scroll bars.

radio buttons, valuators, type in boxes, etc. A typical dialog box used to specify a type is shown in Fig. 1–62. Mutually exclusive selections should be prevented. For example, under alignment, type cannot be both centered and justified at the same time. Under Font, Size, Leading and Kerning, the arrows at the right of the box indicate the existence of a pop-up menu from which items are to be selected. The dialog box stays on the screen until specifically closed by the user, either by canceling the box or accepting the specified data. A preview of the requested action is frequently provided, along with an accept function for permanently applying the data.

Menus

Point and click menus are ubiquitous in graphical user interfaces. Menus can be organized alphabetically, by grouping similar topics or actions together, by dynamically inserting the last used command onto the bottom (or top) of a menu stack, by frequency of use or hierarchically. Hierarchical menus come in many flavors: pull down, pull up, pull out, pop-up and tear off, as shown in Fig. 1–63. Considering both words and symbols as specialized forms of icons, then menus are composed of icons. Figure 1–63a shows a typical pull down menu originating from the upper menu bar that uses words as icons. Figure 1–63b shows a pull out menu where symbols are used as icons, e.g., the circle with the tail is used to indicate a magnifying glass. The plus sign inside the magnifying glass indicates an increase in size, while the minus sign indicates a decrease in size. Figure 1–63c shows both a pull up and a tear off menu, as indicated by the dashed line at the top of the pull up menu. By pointing and clicking on the dashed line, the menu is

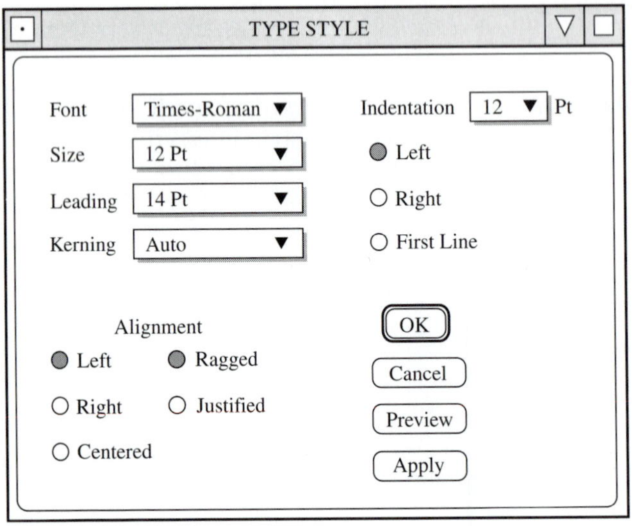

Figure 1–62 Dialog box.

detached from the lower menu bar. By holding down the 'mouse' button, it can be moved to any location on the screen. Releasing the mouse button places the menu at that location and keeps it visible (open) until specifically closed. Tear off menus are useful when several sequential operations are to be performed from a single or small group of menus. Figure 1–63d shows a series of hierarchical menus. The right arrowhead indicates that a submenu is available. The user recursively points at the main menu item, slides the 'mouse' to the right, typically while keeping the button depressed. Upon reaching an arrowhead, the appropriate submenu appears. Figure 1–63e shows a pop-up menu. Pop-up menus appear at the cursor location when specific buttons on the 'mouse' are pressed. They typically disappear when the button(s) are released.

Icons

Icons provide a pictorial representation of a concept, object or action. Carefully designed icons can be both language and culture independent. However, doing so is *not* easy. Making icons culturally independent is particularly difficult. Carefully designed icons can occupy less screen space than equivalent text. However, this is not necessarily true. Icons may also require more processing power than equivalent text. In designing icons, the goals are to make them easy

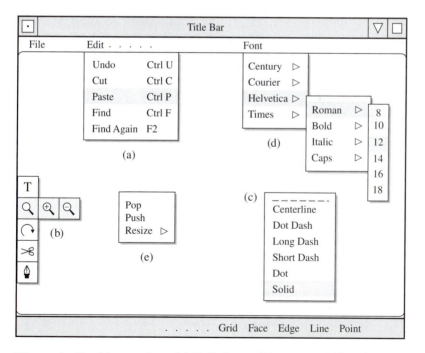

Figure 1–63   Menu styles. (a) Pull down; (b) pull out; (c) pull up and tear off, indicated by the dashed line; (d) hierarchical; (e) pop-up.

to remember, easily recognized and easily discriminated especially from other icons *at typical screen viewing sizes.* Typical icons are shown in Fig. 1–64.

Frequently, some metaphor is used in designing icons. The desktop metaphor is typical. Figure 1–64c is frequently used to represent a directory, i.e., a folder in the desktop metaphor. The folder icon is an action icon, because clicking on the folder causes it to appear to open and transfers the user to the directory. The name of the directory is typically printed either on the folder itself or, more frequently, directly under the folder. Similarly, the eraser icon (Fig. 1–64e) is an action icon. Figures 1–64g and 1–64h are two possible icons for rotation. Figure 1–64g is simple but lacks an indication of the rotation direction. Figure 1–64h seeks to indicate rotation by showing the before and after effects of the action.

Three-dimensional action icons are particularly difficult to design and implement. An example, designed to show rotation about three orthogonal axes, is shown in Fig. 1–65. Although one of the better icons for this purpose, notice that rotation about some arbitrary axis in space is not implemented. Sometimes words as icons are better.

Sketching

There are numerous methods for generating and modifying images, in particular line drawings. The end points of a line are specified by typing the end point coordinates, by positioning end point coordinates using a locator device and a screen cursor, or by rubber banding. Rubber banding is shown in Fig. 1–66. The initial end point is laid down by clicking the locator button at some position on the screen. While holding the locator button down or after releasing it, depending on the programmed paradigm, a line is drawn from the initial end point to the current location of the cursor, as if one end of a rubber 'band' was fixed at the initial end point and the other attached to the cursor. Either

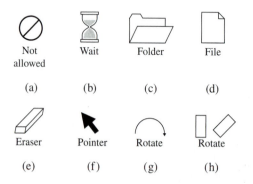

Not allowed   Wait   Folder   File

(a)   (b)   (c)   (d)

Eraser   Pointer   Rotate   Rotate

(e)   (f)   (g)   (h)

Figure 1–64 Typical icons. (a) Operation not allowed; (b) wait, operation in progress; (c) folder desktop metaphor for a directory; (d) desktop metaphor for a computer file; (e) the action of the eraser to delete/remove whatever it touches; (f) a pointer icon; (g) a simple rotation icon; (h) a before and after action rotation icon.

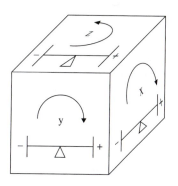

Figure 1–65 A three-dimensional rotation icon.

releasing the locator button or again clicking the locator button defines the final end point of the line.

Constraints can be imposed upon the direction of line generation, e.g., the generated line can be constrained to be horizontal, vertical, in a particular direction or perpendicular to a particular line or entity.

A series of connected straight line segments, i.e., a polyline, is generated by successively clicking the locator device at different screen locations. After the first click a line segment is generated between each successive click. The end of the polyline is indicated by either double clicking, by clicking a different button or combination of buttons or by deselecting the polyline element (icon) from a menu.

Rubber banding is also used to locally modify objects. For example, the roof of the simple house-shaped polygon shown in Fig. 1–67a is modified by first picking the vertex that defines the peak and then dragging the vertex while simultaneously showing the changes, i.e., the roof is 'rubber banded'. The vertex controlling the roof is frequently called a *handle*. More sophisticated applications include designing the shape of a Bézier or B-spline curve or surface (see [Roge90b]) by rubber banding the polygonal vertices that define the curve or surface, as shown by Rogers [Roge77, 80a, 80b, 82a, 82b, 83, 90b]. Here, the polygon vertex is the *handle*. Figure 1–67b illustrates the concept.

Rectangles, circles and ellipses are also 'rubberbanded'. One typical use of a rubberband rectangle is to define an area to be cropped from an image, or

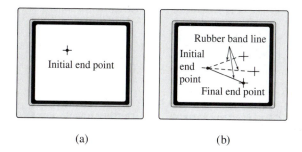

(a) (b)

Figure 1–66 Rubber banding. (a) Initial end point laid down; (b) final end point and rubber banded lines.

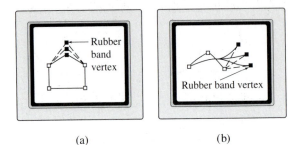

(a)　　　　　　　　　　(b)

Figure 1–67　More complex rubber banding. □ inactive handle, ■ active handle.
(a) House roof; (b) Bézier curve.

to define an area of an image that is to be 'blown up' in size. Rubber band circles and ellipses are, for example, used in design programs. Here, for example, the center of the circle is first indicated by clicking (button down) the locator device; a circle is then generated, with the radius given by the distance between the center and the current position of the locator device. Clicking again defines the circle. Ellipses are generated by using the sides of a rubberband rectangle to specify the major and minor axes of the ellipse. The center of the ellipse is at the center of the rubberbanded rectangle. Circles are also implemented as a special case of ellipses where the rectangle is a square.

Dragging, sometimes referred to as click and drag, is used to position objects. Generally, it is implemented such that placing the cursor over the object to be dragged and clicking (button down) on the object allows the object to be moved to a new location by moving the cursor. Releasing the button places the object and detaches it from the cursor. Subsequent movement of the cursor has no effect on the object.

Starting a new line that is to begin at the end of a previous line, or at the vertex of an object, is difficult. One technique is to zoom in on the end point or vertex. However, a less time consuming technique is to implement a zone of attraction (frequently called gravity fields) around the end point of the line, vertex or other entity, as shown in Fig. 1–68. If the cursor is anywhere within the

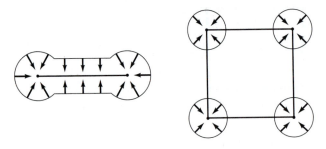

Figure 1–68　Zones of attraction (gravity fields).

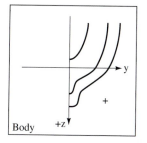

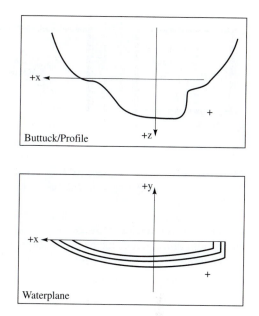

Figure 1–69   Three-dimensional object modification constrained to two dimensions.

zone of attraction, the entity being created, e.g., a line, snaps to the attraction entity, e.g., the end point of a line.

3-D Interaction

Three-dimensional interaction is more difficult than two-dimensional interaction. Consequently, the design of three-dimensional interactive metaphors is also difficult. Three-dimensional interaction either takes place in multiple two-dimensional views or directly in three dimensions The principal issues are mapping two-dimensional interactive devices to three dimensions, visualizing depth relationships and placing and picking in three dimensions.

Three-dimensional modification of an object is simplified if interaction takes place in multiple two-dimensional views and in the context of the particular application, as shown in Fig. 1–69. The cursor moves freely among the three views and is constrained to act in only the two directions shown in each view. In the naval architecture application shown in Fig. 1–69, appropriate handles are used to manipulate the ships curves. Incorporating a three-dimensional view in a fourth 'viewport' which can be manipulated, e.g., rotated, translated or scaled in three dimensions (see Fig. 1–65 and the associated discussion), is also useful.

Modification of an object in the three-dimensional view is accomplished by picking appropriate handles. Although left and right stereo views are useful for increased depth perception (see [Hodg85, 92]), direct picking of a handle in three dimensions is both time consuming and frustrating [Roge80a]. Three-dimensional picking is most conveniently accomplished in screen space, using

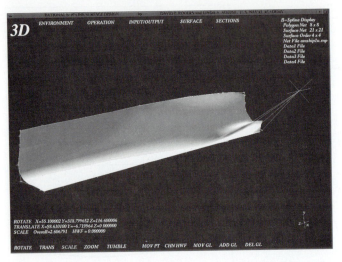

Figure 1–70   Direct three-dimensional object modification using a two-dimensional hit window.

the two-dimensional projection of the handle and a 'hit window' [Roge80a, 83b]. The hit window is a small movable square used as the visible cursor. If the handle falls within the hit window, then a pick has occurred. An example is shown in Fig. 1–70.

Summary

The elements discussed here are some of the many used in constructing the 'look and feel' of a graphical user interface. A graphical user interface should be designed for a specific application and for an anticipated general user, without unduly penalizing either the less or more experienced user. This is no small task. See, for example, Brown and Cunningham [Brow89] and *Macintosh Human Interface Guidelines* [Appl87] for additional details.

RASTER SCAN GRAPHICS

Raster scan graphics devices require special procedures to generate the display, to draw straight lines or curves and to fill polygons to give the impression of solid areas. This chapter examines these procedures.

2–1 Line Drawing Algorithms

Because a cathode ray tube (CRT) raster display is considered a matrix of discrete finite area cells (pixels), each of which can be made bright, it is not possible to directly draw a straight line from one point to another. The process of determining which pixels provide the best approximation to the desired line is properly known as rasterization. When combined with the process of generating the picture in scan line order, it is known as scan conversion. For horizontal, vertical and 45° lines, the choice of raster elements is obvious; for any other orientation, the choice is more difficult. This is shown in Fig. 2–1.

Before discussing specific line drawing algorithms, it is useful to consider the general requirements for such algorithms, i.e., what are the desirable characteristics for these lines. The primary design criteria are that straight lines appear as straight lines, and that they start and end accurately. In addition, displayed lines should have constant brightness along their length, independent of the line length and orientation. Finally, the lines should be drawn rapidly. As with most design criteria, not all can be completely satisfied. The very nature of a raster display precludes the generation of a completely straight line except for special cases, nor is it possible for a line to precisely begin and end at specified locations. However, with reasonable display resolution acceptable approximations are possible.

Only for horizontal, vertical and 45° lines is the brightness constant along the length. For all other orientations, the rasterization yields uneven brightness. This is shown in Fig. 2–1. Even for the special cases, the brightness is orientation dependent; e.g., note that the effective spacing between pixels for the 45°

65

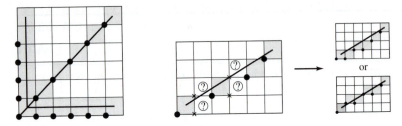

Figure 2–1 Rasterization of straight lines.

line is greater than for the vertical and horizontal lines. This makes vertical and horizontal lines appear brighter than the 45° line. Providing equal brightness along lines of varying length and orientation requires the calculation of a square root, and it assumes multiple brightness levels are available. This slows down the calculation. The compromise generally made is to calculate only an approximate line length, reduce the calculations to a minimum, preferably using integer arithmetic, and use incremental methods to simplify the calculations.

Additional design considerations for line drawing algorithms include: end point order, i.e., rasterizing the line $P_2 P_1$, which yields the same results as rasterizing the line $P_1 P_2$; end point shape, i.e., controlling the shape of the ends of the rasterized line, e.g., square, round, beveled, mitered, etc., so that lines join precisely and pleasingly; using the characteristics of multiple bit plane displays to control the intensity of the line as a function of slope and orientation; generating lines of greater than one pixel width, i.e., so-called thick lines (see [Bres90]); antialiasing thick lines to improve their appearance; insuring that end pixels are not written twice in a series of connected short straight line segments, i.e., for so called polylines. Here, only simple line drawing algorithms are considered.

2–2 Digital Differential Analyzer

One technique for obtaining a rasterized straight line is to solve the governing differential equation for a straight line, i.e.

$$\frac{dy}{dx} = \text{constant} \qquad \text{or} \qquad \frac{\Delta y}{\Delta x} = \frac{y_2 - y_1}{x_2 - x_1}$$

The solution of the finite difference approximation is

$$y_{i+1} = y_i + \Delta y$$

$$y_{i+1} = y_i + \frac{y_2 - y_1}{x_2 - x_1} \Delta x \qquad\qquad (2-1)$$

where x_1, y_1 and x_2, y_2 are the end points of the required straight line, and y_i is the initial value for any given step along the line. In fact, Eq. $(2-1)$ represents a recursion relation for successive values of y along the required line. Used to rasterize a line, it is called a digital differential analyzer (DDA).[†] For a simple DDA, either Δx or Δy, whichever is larger, is chosen as one raster unit. A simple algorithm which works in all quadrants is:

digital differential analyzer *(DDA) routine for rasterizing a line*

the line end points are (x_1, y_1) *and* (x_2, y_2), *assumed not equal*

Integer *is the integer function. Note: Many Integer functions are floor functions; i.e., Integer*$(-8.5) = -9$ *rather than* -8. *The algorithm assumes this is the case.*

Sign *returns* -1, 0, 1 *for arguments* < 0, $= 0$, > 0, *respectively*

    approximate the line length

    if abs$(x_2 - x_1) \geq$ abs$(y_2 - y_1)$ **then**

        Length $=$ abs$(x_2 - x_1)$

    else

        Length $=$ abs$(y_2 - y_1)$

    end if

    select the larger of Δx *or* Δy *to be one raster unit*

    $\Delta x = (x_2 - x_1)/$Length

    $\Delta y = (y_2 - y_1)/$Length

    round the values rather than truncate, so that center pixel addressing is handled correctly

    x $=$ x$_1$ $+$ 0.5

    y $=$ y$_1$ $+$ 0.5

    begin main loop

    i $= 1$

    while (i $\leq$ Length)

        setpixel (**Integer**(x), **Integer**(y))

        x $=$ x $+ \Delta$x

        y $=$ y $+ \Delta$y

        i $=$ i $+ 1$

    end while

finish

An example illustrates the algorithm.

Example 2–1   Simple DDA First Quadrant

Consider the line from (0, 0) to (5, 5). Use the simple DDA to rasterize this line. Evaluating the steps in the algorithm yields

---

[†]A digital differential analyzer is a mechanical device for integrating differential equations by simultaneously incrementing x and y in small steps proportional to dx and dy.

initial calculation

$x_1 = 0$
$y_1 = 0$
$x_2 = 5$
$y_2 = 5$
Length $= 5$
$\Delta x = 1$
$\Delta y = 1$
$x = 0.5$
$y = 0.5$

Incrementing through the main loop yields

i	setpixel	x	y
		0.5	0.5
1	$(0,0)$		
		1.5	1.5
2	$(1,1)$		
		2.5	2.5
3	$(2,2)$		
		3.5	3.5
4	$(3,3)$		
		4.5	4.5
5	$(4,4)$		
		5.5	5.5

The results are shown in Fig. 2–2. Note that the selected pixels are equally spaced along the line. The appearance of the line is quite acceptable. The end point at $(0,0)$ is apparently exact. However, the pixel corresponding to the end point at $(5,5)$ is not activated; thus the line appears to be too short. If i is initialized to zero instead of to one, as shown, the pixel at location $(5,5)$ is activated. However, this can lead to undesirable results. If the address of a pixel is given by the integer coordinates of the center of the pixel, then activating the pixel at location $(5,5)$ when a series of successive line segments is drawn, i.e., a polyline, activates the pixel at location $(5,5)$ twice: once at the end of a line segment, and again at the beginning of the successive line segment. The result is either a brighter pixel or, perhaps, a pixel of a different or odd color.

The next example illustrates results for the DDA in the third quadrant.

Example 2–2   Simple DDA in the Third Quadrant

Consider the line from $(0,0)$ to $(-8, -4)$ in the third quadrant. Evaluating the algorithm yields

initial calculations

$x_1 = 0$
$y_1 = 0$

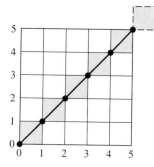

Figure 2–2 Results for a simple DDA in the first quadrant.

$$x_2 = -8$$
$$y_2 = -4$$
$$\text{Length} = 8$$
$$\Delta x = -1$$
$$\Delta y = -0.5$$
$$x = -0.5$$
$$y = -0.5$$

Incrementing through the main loop, assuming a floor integer function, yields

i	setpixel	x	y
		0.5	0.5
1	$(0,0)$		
		-0.5	0
2	$(-1,0)$		
		-1.5	-0.5
3	$(-2,-1)$		
		-2.5	-1.0
4	$(-3,-1)$		
		-3.5	-1.5
5	$(-4,-2)$		
		-4.5	-2.0
6	$(-5,-2)$		
		-5.5	-2.5
7	$(-6,-3)$		
		-6.5	-3.0
8	$(-7,-3)$		
		-7.5	-3.5

The results are shown in Fig. 2–3.

Although the results shown in Fig. 2–3 appear quite acceptable, considering the additional lines from $(0,0)$ to $(-8,4)$ and $(8,-4)$ shows that the rasterized line lies to one side of the actual line. Furthermore, if a true integer function rather than the assumed floor function is used, the results are different. Thus, either a more complicated algorithm which runs slower must be used, or position accuracy must be compromised. In addition, the algorithm suffers from the fact

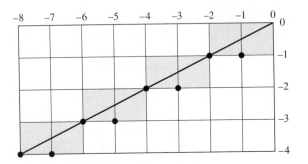

Figure 2–3   Results for a simple DDA in the third quadrant.

that it uses floating point arithmetic. A more suitable algorithm is given in the next section.

2–3   Bresenham's Algorithm

Although developed originally for use with digital plotters, Bresenham's algorithm [Bres65] is equally suited for use with CRT raster devices. The algorithm seeks to select the optimum raster locations that represent a straight line. To accomplish this, the algorithm always increments by one unit in either x or y, depending on the slope of the line. The increment in the other variable, either zero or one, is determined by examining the distance between the actual line and the nearest grid locations. This distance is called the error.

The algorithm is cleverly constructed so that only the sign of the error term need be examined. This is illustrated in Fig. 2–4 for a line in the first octant, i.e., for a line with a slope between zero and one. From Fig. 2–4 note that, if the slope of the required line through $(0,0)$ is greater than $1/2$, then its intercept

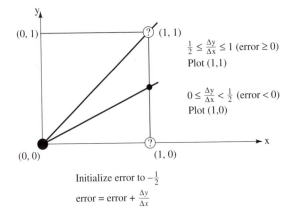

Figure 2–4   Basis of Bresenham's algorithm.

with the line $x = 1$ is closer to the line $y = 1$ than to the line $y = 0$. Hence, the raster point at $(1, 1)$ better represents the path of the line than that at $(1, 0)$. If the slope is less than $1/2$ the opposite is true. For a slope of precisely $1/2$, there is no clear choice. Here the algorithm chooses the raster point at $(1, 0)$.

Not all lines pass precisely through a raster point. This is illustrated in Fig. 2–5, where a line of slope $3/8$ initially passes through the raster point at $(0, 0)$ and subsequently crosses three pixels. Also illustrated is the calculation of the error in representing the line by discrete pixels. Because it is desirable to check only the sign of the error term, it is initialized to $-1/2$. Thus, if the slope of the line is greater than or equal to $1/2$, its value at the next raster point one unit away, $(1, 0)$, is determined by adding the slope of the line to the error term, that is

$$e = e + m$$

where m is the slope. In this case, with e initialized to $-1/2$

$$e = -\frac{1}{2} + \frac{3}{8} = -\frac{1}{8}$$

e is negative, therefore the line passes below the middle of the pixel. Hence, the pixel at the same horizontal level better approximates the location of the line; and y is not incremented. Again, incrementing the error term by the slope yields

$$e = -\frac{1}{8} + \frac{3}{8} = \frac{1}{4}$$

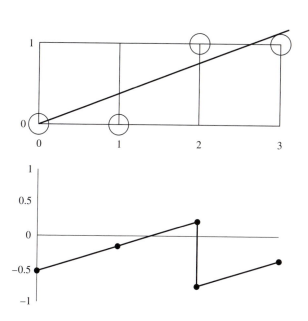

Figure 2–5 Error term in Bresenham's algorithm.

at the next raster point $(2, 0)$. Here e is positive, which shows that the line passes above the midpoint. The raster element at the next higher vertical location $(2, 1)$ better approximates the position of the line; hence y is incremented by one unit. Before considering the next pixel, it is necessary to reinitialize the error term. This is accomplished by subtracting 1 from it, thus

$$e = \frac{1}{4} - 1 = -\frac{3}{4}$$

Notice that the intercept of the vertical line at $x = 2$ and the desired line is $-\frac{1}{4}$ with respect to the line $y = 1$. Reinitializing to $-\frac{1}{2}$ relative to zero for the error term yields, as above, $-\frac{3}{4}$. Continuing to the next raster unit yields

$$e = -\frac{3}{4} + \frac{3}{8} = -\frac{3}{8}$$

e is negative, thus the y value is not incremented. From the previous discussion, it is easy to see that the error term is a measure of the y intercept of the desired line at each raster element referenced to $-\frac{1}{2}$.

Bresenham's algorithm for the first octant, i.e., for $0 \leq \Delta y \leq \Delta x$, is:

Bresenham's line rasterization algorithm for the first octant

the line end points are (x_1, y_1) *and* (x_2, y_2), *assumed not equal*
Integer *is the integer function*
x, y, Δx, Δy *are assumed integer; e is real*

   initialize variables

   x = x₁
   y = y₁
   Δx = x₂ − x₁
   Δy = y₂ − y₁
   m = Δy/Δx

   initialize e to compensate for a nonzero intercept

   e = m − 1/2

   begin the main loop

   for i = 1 **to** Δx
        setpixel (x, y)
        while (e > 0)
             y = y + 1
             e = e − 1
        end while
        x = x + 1
        e = e + m
   next i
finish

A flowchart is given in Fig. 2–6. Example 2–3 applies Bresenham's algorithm to the line from $(0,0)$ to $(5,5)$.

Example 2–3   Bresenham's Algorithm

Consider the line from $(0,0)$ to $(5,5)$. Rasterizing the line with the Bresenham algorithm yields

initial calculations

$$x = 0$$
$$y = 0$$
$$\Delta x = 5$$
$$\Delta y = 5$$
$$m = 1$$
$$e = 1 - 1/2 = 1/2$$

Incrementing through the main loop yields

i	setpixel	e	x	y
		$\frac{1}{2}$	0	0
1	$(0,0)$			
		$-\frac{1}{2}$	0	1
		$\frac{1}{2}$	1	1
2	$(1,1)$			
		$-\frac{1}{2}$	1	2
		$\frac{1}{2}$	2	2
3	$(2,2)$			
		$-\frac{1}{2}$	2	3
		$\frac{1}{2}$	3	3
4	$(3,3)$			
		$-\frac{1}{2}$	3	4
		$\frac{1}{2}$	4	4
5	$(4,4)$			
		$-\frac{1}{2}$	4	5
		$\frac{1}{2}$	5	5

The results are shown in Fig. 2–7 and are as expected. Note that the raster unit at $(5,5)$ is not activated. This raster unit can be activated by changing the **for-next** loop to 0 **to** Δx. The first raster unit at $(0,0)$ can be eliminated by moving the **setpixel** statement to just before **next** i.

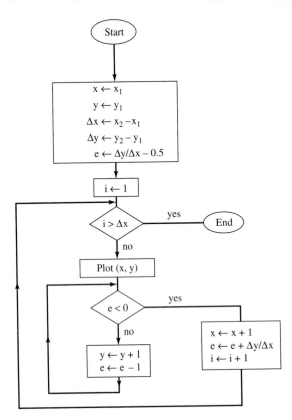

Figure 2–6 Flowchart for Bresenham's algorithm.

Integer Bresenham's Algorithm

Bresenham's algorithm as presented above requires the use of floating point arithmetic to calculate the slope of the line and to evaluate the error term. The speed of the algorithm is increased by using integer arithmetic.[†] Because only the sign of the error term is important, the simple transformation $\bar{e} = 2e\Delta x$ of the error term in the previous algorithm yields an integer algorithm [Spro82]. This allows the algorithm to be efficiently implemented in hardware or firmware. The integer algorithm for the first octant, i.e., for $0 \le \Delta y \le \Delta x$ is

> **Bresenham's integer algorithm** *for the first octant*
>
> *the line end points are* $(x_1,\ y_1)$ *and* $(x_2,\ y_2)$, *assumed not equal*
> *all variables are assumed integer*

[†]According to Jack Bresenham, the original impetus for an integer algorithm was the fact that the rather simple computer available in the plotter was *only* capable of integer arithmetic.

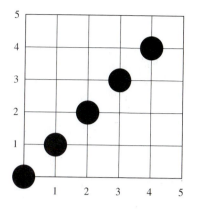

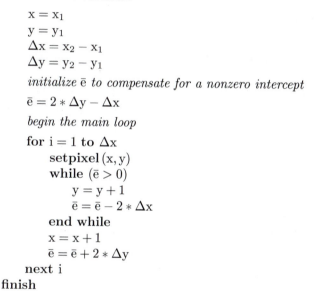

Figure 2–7 Results for the Bresenham algorithm in the first octant.

initialize variables

$x = x_1$
$y = y_1$
$\Delta x = x_2 - x_1$
$\Delta y = y_2 - y_1$

initialize ē to compensate for a nonzero intercept

$\bar{e} = 2 * \Delta y - \Delta x$

begin the main loop

for $i = 1$ **to** Δx
    setpixel (x, y)
    while $(\bar{e} > 0)$
        $y = y + 1$
        $\bar{e} = \bar{e} - 2 * \Delta x$
    end while
    $x = x + 1$
    $\bar{e} = \bar{e} + 2 * \Delta y$
  next i
finish

The flowchart in Fig. 2–6 is applicable, with appropriate changes in the calculation of the error term.

General Bresenham's Algorithm

A full implementation of Bresenham's algorithm requires modification for lines lying in the other octants. These can easily be developed by considering the quadrant in which the line lies, and the line's slope. When the absolute magnitude of the slope of the line is greater than 1, y is incremented by 1 and Bresenham's error criterion is used to determine when to increment x. Whether x or y is incremented by ± 1 depends on the quadrant. This is illustrated in Fig. 2–8. The general algorithm can be stated as

LIBRARY
OF
MOUNT ST. MARY'S
COLLEGE
EMMITSBURG, MARYLAND

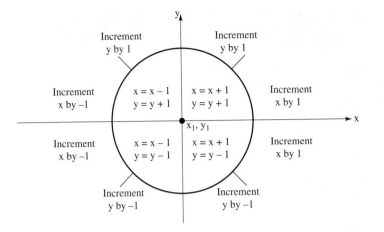

Figure 2–8 Conditions for general Bresenham's algorithm.

generalized integer Bresenham's algorithm *for all quadrants*
the line end points are (x_1, y_1) *and* (x_2, y_2), *assumed not equal*
all variables are assumed integer
the **Sign** *function returns* $-1, 0, 1$ *as its argument is* $< 0, = 0, or > 0$

initialize variables

$x = x_1$
$y = y_1$
$\Delta x = \text{abs}(x_2 - x)$
$\Delta y = \text{abs}(y_2 - y_1)$
$s_1 = \textbf{Sign}(x_2 - x_1)$
$s_2 = \textbf{Sign}(y_2 - y_1)$

interchange Δx *and* Δy, *depending on the slope of the line*

if $\Delta y > \Delta x$ **then**
      Temp = Δx
      $\Delta x = \Delta y$
      $\Delta y = $ Temp
      Interchange $= 1$
else
      Interchange $= 0$
end if

initialize the error term to compensate for a nonzero intercept

$\bar{e} = 2 * \Delta y - \Delta x$

main loop

for $i = 1$ **to** Δx
      setpixel (x, y)

> while ($\bar{e} > 0$)
>> if Interchange $= 1$ then
>>> $x = x + s_1$
>>
>> else
>>> $y = y + s_2$
>>
>> end if
>> $\bar{e} = \bar{e} - 2 * \Delta x$
>
> end while
> if Interchange $= 1$ then
>> $y = y + s_2$
>
> else
>> $x = x + s_1$
>
> end if
> $\bar{e} = \bar{e} + 2 * \Delta y$

next i
finish

Example 2–4   Generalized Bresenham's algorithm

To illustrate the general Bresenham algorithm, consider the line from $(0,0)$ to $(-8, -4)$. This line was previously considered in Ex. 2–2 using a simple DDA algorithm.

initial calculations

$x = 0$
$y = 0$
$\Delta x = 8$
$\Delta y = 4$
$s_1 = -1$
$s_2 = -1$
Interchange $= 0$
$\bar{e} = 0$

Incrementing through the main loop yields

i	setpixel	$\bar{e}$	x	y
		0	0	0
1	$(0,0)$			
		8	-1	0
2	$(-1,-1)$			
		-8	-1	-1
		0	-2	-1
3	$(-2,-1)$			
		8	-3	-1
4	$(-3,-1)$			
		-8	-3	-2
		0	-4	-2

i	setpixel	$\bar{e}$	x	y
5	$(-4, -2)$			
		8	-5	-2
6	$(-5, -2)$			
		-8	-5	-3
		0	-6	-3
7	$(-6, -3)$			
		8	-7	-3
8	$(-7, -4)$			
		-8	-7	-4
		0	-8	-4

The results are shown in Fig. 2–9. Comparison with Fig. 2–3 shows that the results are different.

Faster Line Rasterization Algorithms

While Bresenham's algorithm is the standard, faster algorithms are possible. For example, Bresenham's algorithm can be modified to rasterize the line from both ends simultaneously, thus effectively doubling the speed [Rokn90; Wyvi90]. Wu [Wu87; Wyvi90] developed a double-step algorithm and achieved a significant speed increase. Fundamentally, Wu's algorithm selects the next *two* pixels that best represent the line. In the first octant, analysis shows that there are only four possible patterns for the next two pixels that best represent the line. Again, the proper choice is reduced to a simple binary decision. Wyvill [Wyvi90] further increased the speed of this algorithm by using symmetry to plot the line from both ends. The resulting algorithm is between three and four times faster than the original Bresenham algorithm [Rokn90]. Gill [Gill94] investigated N-Step line algorithms and applied the results to develop a quad-step algorithm for microprocessor implementation. The algorithms are faster and produce exactly the same rasterization as Bresenham's algorithm.

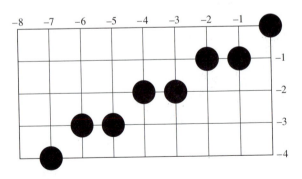

Figure 2–9 Results for Bresenham's general algorithm in the third quadrant.

2–4   Circle Generation—Bresenham's Algorithm

In addition to rasterizing straight lines, it is necessary to rasterize other more complicated functions. Considerable attention has been given to conic sections, i.e., circles, ellipses, parabolas, hyperbolas (see [Pitt67; Jord73; Bels76; Ramo76; Vana84, 85; Fiel86]). The circle has, of course, received the greatest attention. (See also [Horn76; Badl77; Doro79; Suen79].) One of the most efficient and easiest to derive of the circle algorithms is due to Bresenham [Bres77]. To begin, note that only one octant of the circle need be generated. The other parts are obtained by successive reflections. This is illustrated in Fig. 2–10. If the first octant (0 to 45° ccw) is generated, the second octant is obtained by reflection through the line $y = x$ to yield the first quadrant. The results in the first quadrant are reflected through the line $x = 0$ to obtain those in the second quadrant. The combined results in the upper semicircle are reflected through the line $y = 0$ to complete the circle. Figure 2–10 gives the appropriate two-dimensional reflection matrices.

To derive Bresenham's circle generation algorithm, consider the first quadrant of an origin-centered circle. Notice that if the algorithm begins at $x = 0$, $y = R$, then for clockwise generation of the circle y is a monotonically decreasing function of x in the first quadrant (see Fig. 2–11). Similarly, if the algorithm begins at $y = 0$, $x = R$, then for counterclockwise generation of the circle x is a monotonically decreasing function of y. Here, clockwise generation starting at $x = 0$, $y = R$ is chosen. The center of the circle and the starting point are both assumed located precisely at pixel elements.

Assuming clockwise generation of the circle, then for any given point on the circle there are only three possible selections for the next pixel which best represents the circle: horizontally to the right, diagonally downward to the right and

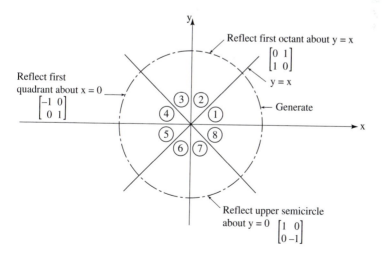

Figure 2–10   Generation of a complete circle from the first octant.

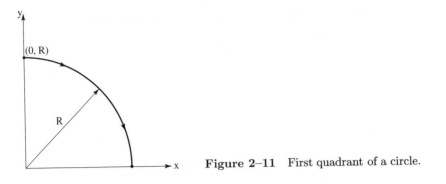

Figure 2–11   First quadrant of a circle.

vertically downward. These are labeled m_H, m_D, m_V, respectively, in Fig. 2–12. The algorithm chooses the pixel which minimizes the square of the distance between one of these pixels and the true circle, i.e., the minimum of

$$m_H = |(x_i + 1)^2 + (y_i)^2 - R^2|$$
$$m_D = |(x_i + 1)^2 + (y_i - 1)^2 - R^2|$$
$$m_V = |(x_i)^2 + (y_i - 1)^2 - R^2|$$

The calculations are simplified by noting that there are only five possible types of intersections of the circle and the raster grid in the vicinity of the point (x_i, y_i). These are shown in Fig. 2–13.

The difference between the square of the distance from the center of the circle to the diagonal pixel at $(x_i + 1, y_i - 1)$ and the distance to a point on the circle R^2 is

$$\Delta_i = (x_i + 1)^2 + (y_i - 1)^2 - R^2$$

As with the Bresenham line rasterizing algorithm, it is desirable to use only the sign of an error term rather than the magnitude, to select the appropriate pixel which best represents the actual circle.

If $\Delta_i < 0$, then the diagonal point $(x_i + 1, y_i - 1)$ is inside the actual circle, i.e., case 1 or 2 in Fig. 2–13. It is clear that either the pixel at $(x_i + 1, y_i)$, i.e., m_H, or that at $(x_i + 1, y_i - 1)$, i.e., m_D, must be chosen. To decide which, first consider case 1 by examining the difference between the squares of the distance from the actual circle to the pixel at m_H and the distance from the actual circle to the pixel at m_D, i.e.,

$$\delta = |(x_i + 1)^2 + (y_i)^2 - R^2| - |(x_i + 1)^2 + (y_i - 1)^2 - R^2|$$

If $\delta < 0$, then the distance from the actual circle to the diagonal pixel, m_D, is greater than that to the horizontal pixel, m_H. Conversely, if $\delta > 0$, then the distance to the horizontal pixel, m_H, is greater; thus, if

$$\delta \leq 0 \qquad \text{choose } m_H \text{ at } (x_i + 1, y_i)$$
$$\delta > 0 \qquad \text{choose } m_D \text{ at } (x_i + 1, y_i - 1)$$

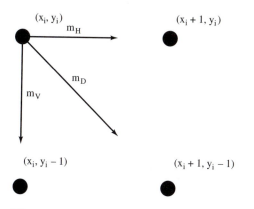

Figure 2–12   First quadrant pixel selections.

The horizontal move is selected when $\delta = 0$, i.e., when the distances are equal. The work involved in evaluating δ is reduced by noting that for case 1

$$(x_i + 1)^2 + (y_i)^2 - R^2 \geq 0$$
$$(x_i + 1)^2 + (y_i - 1)^2 - R^2 < 0$$

because the diagonal pixel at $(x_i + 1, y_i - 1)$ is always inside the circle, and the horizontal pixel at $(x_i + 1, y_i)$ is always outside the circle. Thus, δ can be evaluated as

$$\delta = (x_i + 1)^2 + (y_i)^2 - R^2 + (x_i + 1)^2 + (y_i - 1)^2 - R^2$$

Completing the square for the $(y_i)^2$ term by adding and subtracting $-2y_i + 1$ yields

$$\delta = 2\big[(x_i + 1)^2 + (y_i - 1)^2 - R^2\big] + 2y_i - 1$$

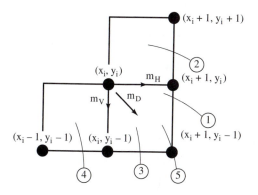

Figure 2–13   Intersection of a circle and the raster grid.

Using the definition for Δ_i gives

$$\delta = 2(\Delta_i + y_i) - 1$$

which is considerably simpler than the previous result.

In considering case 2 of Fig. 2–13, note that, because y is a monotonically decreasing function, the horizontal pixel at (x_i+1, y_i) must be chosen. Examining the components of δ shows that

$$(x_i + 1)^2 + (y_i)^2 - R^2 < 0$$
$$(x_i + 1)^2 + (y_i - 1)^2 - R^2 < 0$$

because the horizontal pixel at (x_i+1, y_i) and the diagonal pixel at (x_i+1, y_i-1) both lie inside the actual circle for case 2. Hence, $\delta < 0$; and the correct pixel at $(x_i + 1, y_i)$ is selected, using the same criteria as in case 1.

If $\Delta_i > 0$, then the diagonal point $(x_i + 1, y_i - 1)$ is outside the actual circle, i.e., case 3 or 4 in Fig. 2–13. Here, it is clear that either the pixel at $(x_i + 1, y_i - 1)$, i.e., m_D, or that at $(x_i, y_i - 1)$, i.e., m_V, must be chosen. Again, the decision criteria is obtained by first considering case 3 and examining the difference between the squares of the distance from the actual circle to the diagonal pixel at m_D, and the distance from the actual circle to the pixel at m_V, that is

$$\delta' = |(x_i + 1)^2 + (y_i - 1)^2 - R^2| - |(x_i)^2 + (y_i - 1)^2 - R^2|$$

If $\delta' < 0$, then the distance from the actual circle to the vertical pixel at $(x_i, y_i - 1)$ is larger and the diagonal move m_D to the pixel at $(x_i + 1, y_i - 1)$ is chosen. Conversely, if $\delta' > 0$, then the distance from the actual circle to the diagonal pixel is greater, and the vertical move to the pixel at $(x_i, y_i - 1)$ is chosen. Thus, if

$$\delta' \le 0 \qquad \text{choose } m_D \text{ at } (x_i + 1, y_i - 1)$$
$$\delta' > 0 \qquad \text{choose } m_V \text{ at } (x_i, y_i - 1)$$

Here, the diagonal move is selected when $\delta' = 0$, that is, when the distances are equal.

Again, examination of the components of δ' shows that

$$(x_i + 1)^2 + (y_i - 1)^2 - R^2 \ge 0$$
$$(x_i)^2 + (y_i - 1)^2 - R^2 < 0$$

because the diagonal pixel at $(x_i + 1, y_i - 1)$ is outside the actual circle, while the vertical pixel at $(x_i, y_i - 1)$ is inside the actual circle for case 3. This allows δ' to be written as

$$\delta' = (x_i + 1)^2 + (y_i - 1)^2 - R^2 + (x_i)^2 + (y_i - 1)^2 - R^2$$

Completing the square for the $(x_i)^2$ term by adding and subtracting $2x_i + 1$ yields

$$\delta' = 2\big[(x_i + 1)^2 + (y_i - 1)^2 - R^2\big] - 2x_i - 1$$

Using the definition of Δ_i then yields

$$\delta' = 2(\Delta_i - x_i) - 1$$

Now considering case 4, again note that, because y is a monotonically decreasing function as x monotonically increases, the vertical pixel at $(x_i, y_i - 1)$ must be selected. Examining the components of δ' for case 4 shows that

$$(x_i + 1)^2 + (y_i - 1)^2 - R^2 > 0$$
$$(x_i)^2 + (y_i - 1)^2 - R^2 > 0$$

because both the vertical and diagonal pixels are outside the actual circle. Hence, $\delta' > 0$; and the correct choice of m_V is selected using the same criteria developed for case 3.

It remains only to examine case 5 of Fig. 2–13, which occurs when the diagonal pixel at $(x_i + 1, y_i - 1)$ lies on the actual circle, i.e., for $\Delta_i = 0$. Examining the components of δ shows that

$$(x_i + 1)^2 + (y_i)^2 - R^2 > 0$$
$$(x_i + 1)^2 + (y_i - 1)^2 - R^2 = 0$$

Hence, $\delta > 0$; and the diagonal pixel at $(x_i + 1, y_i - 1)$ is selected. Similarly, the components of δ' are

$$(x_i + 1)^2 + (y_i - 1)^2 - R^2 = 0$$
$$(x_i)^2 + (y_i - 1)^2 - R^2 < 0$$

and $\delta' < 0$, which is the condition for selecting the correct diagonal move to $(x_i + 1, y_i - 1)$. Thus, the case of $\Delta_i = 0$ is satisfied by the same criteria used for $\Delta_i < 0$ or for $\Delta_i > 0$.

Summarizing these results yields

$\Delta_i < 0$		
$\delta \le 0$	choose the pixel at $(x_i + 1, y_i)$	$\longrightarrow \quad m_H$
$\delta > 0$	choose the pixel at $(x_i + 1, y_i - 1)$	$\longrightarrow \quad m_D$

$\Delta_i > 0$		
$\delta' \le 0$	choose the pixel at $(x_i + 1, y_i - 1)$	$\longrightarrow \quad m_D$
$\delta' > 0$	choose the pixel at $(x_i, y_i - 1)$	$\longrightarrow \quad m_V$
$\Delta_i = 0$	choose the pixel at $(x_i + 1, y_i - 1)$	$\longrightarrow \quad m_D$

Simple recursion relationships which yield an incremental implementation of the algorithm are easily developed. First, consider the horizontal movement, m_H, to the pixel at $(x_i + 1, y_i)$. Call this next pixel location $(i + 1)$. The coordinates of the new pixel and the value of Δ_i are then

$$x_{i+1} = x_i + 1$$
$$y_{i+1} = y_i$$
$$\Delta_{i+1} = (x_{i+1} + 1)^2 + (y_{i+1} - 1)^2 - R^2$$
$$= (x_{i+1})^2 + 2x_{i+1} + 1 + (y_i - 1)^2 - R^2$$
$$= (x_i + 1)^2 + (y_i - 1)^2 - R^2 + 2x_{i+1} + 1$$
$$= \Delta_i + 2x_{i+1} + 1$$

Similarly, the coordinates of the new pixel and the value of Δ_i for the move m_D to $(x_i + 1, y_i - 1)$ are

$$x_{i+1} = x_i + 1$$
$$y_{i+1} = y_i - 1$$
$$\Delta_{i+1} = \Delta_i + 2x_{i+1} - 2y_{i+1} + 2$$

Those for the move m_V to $(x_i, y_i - 1)$ are

$$x_{i+1} = x_i$$
$$y_{i+1} = y_i - 1$$
$$\Delta_{i+1} = \Delta_i - 2y_{i+1} + 1$$

A pseudocode implementation of the Bresenham circle algorithm is given below.

Bresenham's incremental circle algorithm *for the first quadrant*
all variables are assumed integer
    initialize the variables
      $x_i = 0$
      $y_i = R$
      $\Delta_i = 2(1 - R)$
      Limit $= 0$
      while $y_i \geq$ Limit
          call setpixel (x_i, y_i)
          determine if case 1 or 2, 4 or 5, or 3
          if $\Delta_i < 0$ **then**
              $\delta = 2\Delta_i + 2y_i - 1$
              determine whether case 1 or 2
              if $\delta \leq 0$ **then**
                  call mh(x_i, y_i, Δ_i)

```
            else
                call md(x_i, y_i, Δ_i)
            end if
        else if Δ_i > 0 then
            δ' = 2Δ_i − 2x_i − 1

            determine whether case 4 or 5
            if δ' ≤ 0 then
                call md(x_i, y_i, Δ_i)
            else
                call mv(x_i, y_i, Δ_i)
            end if
        else if Δ_i = 0 then
            call md(x_i, y_i, Δ_i)
        end if
    end while
finish
```

move horizontally

subroutine mh(x_i, y_i, Δ_i)
    $x_i = x_i + 1$
    $\Delta_i = \Delta_i + 2x_i + 1$
end sub

move diagonally

subroutine md(x_i, y_i, Δ_i)
    $x_i = x_i + 1$
    $y_i = y_i - 1$
    $\Delta_i = \Delta_i + 2x_i - 2y_i + 2$
end sub

move vertically

subroutine mv(x_i, y_i, Δ_i)
    $y_i = y_i - 1$
    $\Delta_i = \Delta_i - 2y_i + 1$
end sub

The limit variable is set to zero to terminate the algorithm at the horizontal axis. This yields the circle in the first quadrant. If only a single octant is desired, then setting Limit = Integer$(R/\sqrt{2})$ yields the second octant (see Fig. 2–10). Reflection about $y = x$ then yields the first quadrant. A flowchart is given in Fig. 2–14.

Example 2–5   Bresenham's Circle Algorithm

To illustrate the circle generation algorithm, consider the origin-centered circle of radius 8. Only the first quadrant is generated.

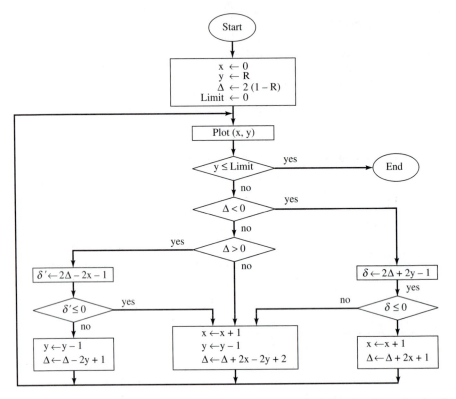

Figure 2–14   Flowchart for Bresenham's incremental circle algorithm in the first quadrant.

initial calculations

$$x_i = 0$$
$$y_i = 8$$
$$\Delta_i = 2(1 - 8) = -14$$
$$\text{Limit} = 0$$

Incrementing through the main loop yields

  $y_i > \text{Limit}$
  continue
  setpixel $(0, 8)$
  $\Delta_i < 0$
    $\delta = 2(-14) + 2(8) - 1 = -13$
    $\delta < 0$
    call mh$(0, 8, -14)$
    $x = 0 + 1 = 1$
    $\Delta_i = -14 + 2(1) + 1 = -11$
  $y_i > \text{Limit}$
  continue

setpixel $(1, 8)$
$\Delta_i < 0$
$\quad \delta = 2(-11) + 2(8) - 1 = -7$
$\quad \delta < 0$
$\quad$ **call** mh(1,8,−11)
$\quad x = 1 + 1 = 2$
$\quad \Delta_i = -11 + 2(2) + 1 = -6$
$y_i > $ Limit
continue
setpixel $(2, , 8)$

$\cdot$
$\cdot$
$\cdot$

continue

The details of each successive pass through the algorithm are summarized below. The list of pixels selected by the algorithm is $(0, 8)$, $(1, 8)$, $(2, 8)$, $(3, 7)$, $(4, 7)$, $(5, 6)$, $(6, 5)$, $(7, 4)$, $(7, 3)$, $(8, 2)$, $(8, 1)$, $(8, 0)$.

setpixel	Δ_i	δ	δ'	x	y
	−14			0	8
$(0, 8)$					
	−11	−13		1	8
$(1, 8)$					
	−6	−7		2	8
$(2, 8)$					
	−12	3		3	7
$(3, 7)$					
	−3	−11		4	7
$(4, 7)$					
	−3	7		5	6
$(5, 6)$					
	1	5		6	5
$(6, 5)$					
	9		−11	7	4
$(7, 4)$					
	4		3	7	3
$(7, 3)$					
	18		−7	8	2
$(8, 2)$					
	17		19	8	1
$(8, 1)$					
	18		17	8	0
$(8, 0)$					
	complete				

The results are shown in Fig. 2–15 along with the actual circle. The algorithm is easily generalized for other quadrants or for circular arcs.

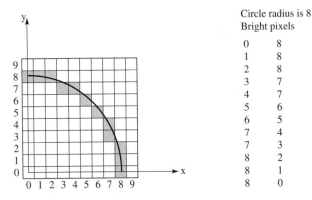

Figure 2–15   Results for Bresenham's incremental circle generation algorithm.

2–5   Ellipse Generation

Rasterization of the other closed conic section, the ellipse, is also of considerable importance.[†] Techniques for rasterizing the ellipse are discussed by Pitteway [Pitt67], Maxwell and Baker [Maxw79], Van Aken [VanA84], Kappel [Kapp85], Field [Fiel86], McIlroy [McIl92] and Fellner and Helmberg [Fell93]. Bresenham discusses several important rasterization details [Bres90]. Da Silva [DaSi89] increases the efficiency of the midpoint ellipse algorithm by using first partial differences. He also corrects a pixel selection problem that occurs when the algorithm switches from region 1 to region 2 (discussed later in this section) and a truncation problem for thin vertical ellipses. Finally, he considers the case of a rotated origin-centered ellipse. Wu and Rokne [Wu89a] develop a double-step algorithm that selects the next *two* pixels that best represent the ellipse and show that there are only four possible patterns. Again, the proper choice or pattern is reduced to a simple binary decision.

Recalling that a circle is a special case of an ellipse, extension of Bresenham's circle rasterization algorithm is straightforward. However, van Aken [Vana84] shows that the extension of Bresenham's circle algorithm to ellipses does not guarantee minimum linear error between the actual ellipse and the selected pixels. Van Aken [Vana84], building on earlier work by Pitteway [Pitt67, 77] and Horn [Horn76], presents an alternative technique for ellipses called the midpoint algorithm. Kappel [Kapp85] suggests several improvements to the algorithm. The algorithm is also applicable to line and circle rasterization (see Probs. 2–4 and 2–6). The van Aken ellipse algorithm guarantees that the maximum linear error between the ellipse and a selected pixel is one-half.

Consider the nonparametric representation of an origin-centered axis-aligned ellipse given by

---

[†]One technique for drawing 'circles' on raster devices with nonsquare pixels is to actually draw an ellipse.

$$\frac{x^2}{a^2} + \frac{y^2}{b^2} = 1$$

where a is the semimajor axis (abscissa) and b is the semiminor axis (ordinate). It is convenient to rewrite this equation by multiplying through by a^2b^2. Thus, the equation of the ellipse becomes

$$f(x,y) = b^2x^2 + a^2y^2 - a^2b^2 = 0$$

Notice that the ellipse intersects the x-axis at $x = a$ and the y-axis at $y = b$.

Only the portion of the ellipse in the first quadrant is considered here; results in the other quadrants are obtained by suitable reflections. Results for nonorigin-centered ellipses are obtained by suitable translations. Once again, as for the Bresenham circle rasterization algorithm, the midpoint ellipse algorithm depends on the ellipse in the first quadrant being a monotonically increasing or decreasing function of x and y.

The point on the ellipse where the slope is negative one, i.e., $dy/dx = -1$, divides the ellipse into two regions, as shown in Fig. 2–16. When rasterizing the ellipse in region 1, where $dy/dx < -1$, increments in Δx are more advantageous when selecting a pixel; in region 2, increments in Δy are more advantageous (see Figs. 2–17a and 2–17b). In Fig. 2–17 the current selected pixel, (x_i, y_i), is shaded. Again as in the Bresenham algorithms, it is desirable to use only the sign of a test function or error term in selecting the next location. An integer algorithm is also desirable. Note that for variety the direction of generation is reversed compared to that for the Bresenham circle generation algorithm, i.e., counterclockwise from the x-axis compared to clockwise from the y-axis.

In the Bresenham circle algorithm, the distance between the ellipse and the two nearest candidate pixels, e.g., those at $(x_i - 1, y_i + 1)$ and $(x_i, y_i + 1)$, is used to select the appropriate pixel. The pixel with the smallest distance is selected. In the midpoint algorithm the distance between the ellipse and the center of the span between the two candidate pixels is used, i.e., $f(x, y)$ is evaluated at a single point, e.g., $(x_i - \frac{1}{2}, y_i + 1)$.

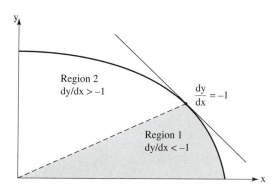

Figure 2–16 Division of the ellipse into two regions.

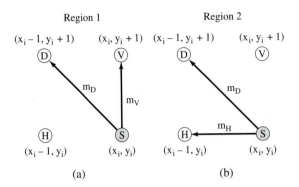

Figure 2–17   Pixel selection. (a) Region 1; (b) region 2.

Referring to Fig. 2–18a in region 1, where $dy/dx < -1$, if the ellipse passes to the right of or above the midpoint between pixels D and V pixel V is selected, and if to the left, pixel D is selected. Figure 2–18b shows that in region 2, where $dy/dx > -1$, if the ellipse passes above the midpoint between pixels H and D, pixel D is selected, while if the ellipse passes below the midpoint, pixel H is selected. From Fig. 2–18, it is clear that the magnitude of the maximum linear error is half the distance between the pixels, i.e., $0 \le |e| \le 1/2$. Alternatively, if e is assumed positive to the right of the midpoint of the span, $-1/2 \le e \le 1/2$.

Following van Aken, define a decision variable, d_i, as twice the value of $f(x, y)$ at the midpoint of the appropriate span, i.e., at $(x_i - 1/2, y_i + 1)$ in region 1, and at $(x_i - 1, y_i + 1/2)$ in region 2. Considering region 1 first

$$d_{1_i} = 2f\left(x_i - \frac{1}{2}, y_i + 1\right)$$

$$= 2\left[b^2\left(x_i - \frac{1}{2}\right)^2 + a^2(y_i + 1)^2 - a^2b^2\right]$$

$$= b^2\left(2x_i^2 - 2x_i + \frac{1}{2}\right) + a^2(2y_i^2 + 4y_i + 2) - 2a^2b^2$$

If the ellipse passes through the midpoint of the span, then $d_{1_i} = 0$. However, the ellipse is more likely to pass either to the right or left of the midpoint of the span at some location $(x_i - 1/2 + e_1, y_i + 1)$. Because this location is a point on the ellipse, $f(x, y) = 0$. Substituting $(x_i - 1/2 + e_1, y_i + 1)$ into $f(x, y) = 0$ yields

$$f\left(x_i - \frac{1}{2} + e_1, y_i + 1\right) = b^2\left(x_i - \frac{1}{2} + e_1\right) + a^2(y_i + 1) - a^2b^2 = 0$$

$$= f\left(x_i - \frac{1}{2}, y_i + 1\right) + 2b^2e_1\left(x_i - \frac{1}{2}\right) + b^2e_1^2 = 0$$

Substituting $d_{1_i}/2 = f(x_i - 1/2, y_i + 1)$ yields

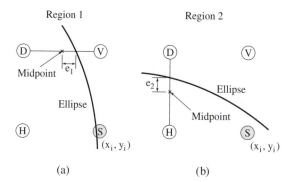

Region 1   Region 2

(a)   (b)

Figure 2–18 Error criteria for an ellipse. (a) Region 1; (b) region 2.

$$d_{1_i} = -4b^2 e_1 \left(x_i - \frac{1}{2} \right) - 2b^2 e_1^2$$
$$= -2b^2 e_1 [(2x_i - 1) + e_1]$$

Note that the sign of d_{1_i} is opposite that of e_1, provided $x_i > (1-e_1)/2$. Because $-1/2 \le e_1 \le 1/2$, this condition is satisfied for $x_i > 3/4$. For integer values of x_i, $x_i > 3/4$ corresponds to $x_i > 0$. Thus, if $d_{1_i} < 0$, then $e_1 > 0$ and the pixel at $(x_i, y_i + 1)$, i.e., V, is chosen. If $d_{1_i} > 0$, then $e_1 < 0$ and the pixel at $(x_i - 1, y_i + 1)$, i.e., D, is chosen. If $d_{1_i} = 0$, the algorithm chooses the diagonal pixel, D.

Turning now to region 2, d_i is

$$d_{2_i} = 2f\left(x_i - 1, y_i + \frac{1}{2} \right)$$
$$= 2\left[b^2 (x_i - 1)^2 + a^2 \left(y_i + \frac{1}{2} \right)^2 - a^2 b^2 \right]$$
$$= b^2 (2x_i^2 - 4x_i + 2) + a^2 \left(2y_i^2 + 2y_i + \frac{1}{2} \right) - 2a^2 b^2$$

If $d_{2_i} = 0$, the ellipse passes through the midpoint of the vertical span between pixels H and D (see Fig. 2–18b). Here e_2 is positive vertically upward from the midpoint of the span, and negative vertically downward. Evaluating the function $f(x, y) = 0$ at $(x_i - 1, y_i + 1/2 + e_2)$ and substituting for $d_{2_i}/2 = f(x_i - 1, y_i + 1/2)$ yields

$$d_{2_i} = -4a^2 e_2 \left(y_i + \frac{1}{2} \right) - 2a^2 e_2^2$$
$$= -2a^2 e_2 [(2y_i + 1) + e_2]$$

Consequently, since $-1/2 \le e_2 \le 1/2$, the sign of d_{2_i} is opposite that of e_2 provided $y_i > -1/2$, or for integer values of y_i for $y_i > 0$. Thus, if $d_{2_i} < 0$, then $e_2 > 0$ and pixel D is chosen. For $d_{2_i} > 0$, $e_2 < 0$ and pixel H is chosen (see Fig. 2–18b). If $d_{2_i} = 0$, the algorithm chooses the horizontal pixel H.

To complete the algorithm, criteria are required to determine when to switch from region 1 to region 2 and for how to start and stop the algorithm. The dividing point between region 1 and region 2 occurs for $dy/dx = -1$. Differentiating the equation for the ellipse yields

$$df(x, y) = d(b^2x^2 + a^2y^2 - a^2b^2) = 2b^2xdx + 2a^2ydy = 0$$

or
$$\frac{dy}{dx} = -\frac{b^2}{a^2}\frac{x}{y}$$

Since a, b, x are all positive or zero, and $y > 0$, $dy/dx < -1$ when $b^2x < a^2y$. In region 1, x is evaluated at the midpoint of the span, i.e., at $x_i - \frac{1}{2}$, and y at $y_i + 1$. Thus, the condition for switching from region 1 to region 2 is $b^2(x_i - \frac{1}{2}) \le a^2(y_i + 1)$.

The algorithm is started at $x = a$, $y = 0$ or

$$f(x, y) = b^2x^2 + a^2y^2 - a^2b^2 = a^2b^2 - a^2b^2 = 0$$

and stopped when $x \le 0$. An initial algorithm is

Naive midpoint ellipse algorithm for the first quadrant

initialize the variables
x = Integer(a + 1/2)
y = 0
while b*b*(x − 1/2) > a*a*(y + 1)   *start in region 1*
        call setpixel (x, y)
        d1 = b*b*(2*x*x − 2*x + 1/2) + a*a*(2*y*y + 4*y + 2) − 2*a*a*b*b
        if d1 < 0 then
                y = y + 1   *move vertically*
        else
                x = x − 1   *move diagonally*
                y = y + 1
        end if
end while

initialize the decision variable in region 2
d2 = b*b*(2*x*x − 4*x + 2) + a*a*(2*y*y + 2*y + 1/2) − 2*a*a*b*b

while x ≥ 0   *switch to region 2*
        call setpixel (x, y)
        if d2 < 0 then
                x = x − 1   *move diagonally*
                y = y + 1
        else
                x = x − 1   *move horizontally*

```
        end if
        d2 = b*b*(2*x*x−4*x+2)+a*a*(2*y*y+2*y+1/2)−2*a*a*b*b
    end while
finish
```

The algorithm is made more efficient by incrementally calculating new values of d_{1_i} and d_{2_i}. At a new pixel location

$$d_{1_{i+1}} = 2f\left(x_{i+1} - \frac{1}{2}, y_{i+1} + 1\right)$$

$$= b^2\left(2x_{i+1}^2 - 2x_{i+1} + \frac{1}{2}\right) + a^2(2y_{i+1}^2 + 4y_{i+1} + 2) - 2a^2b^2$$

and

$$d_{2_{i+1}} = 2f\left(x_{i+1} - 1, y_{i+1} + \frac{1}{2}\right)$$

$$= b^2(2x_{i+1}^2 - 4x_{i+1} + 2) + a^2\left(2y_{i+1}^2 + 2y_{i+1} + \frac{1}{2}\right) - 2a^2b^2$$

For a diagonal move, $x_{i+1} = x_i - 1$, $y_{i+1} = y_i + 1$. Thus, after substitution

$$d_{1_{i+1}} = b^2\left[2(x_i^2 - 2x_i + 1) - 2x_i + 2 + \frac{1}{2}\right]$$
$$+ a^2[2(y_i^2 + 2y_i + 1) + 4y_i + 4 + 2] - 2a^2b^2$$

Recalling $f(x_i - 1/2, y_i + 1)$ yields

$$d_{1_{i+1}} = 2f\left(x_i - \frac{1}{2}, y_i + 1\right) + a^2(4y_i + 6) - 4b^2(x_i - 1)$$
$$= d_{1_i} + 4a^2y_{i+1} - 4b^2x_{i+1} + 2a^2$$

Similarly, for $d_{2_{i+1}}$

$$d_{2_{i+1}} = b^2\left[2(x_i^2 - 4x_i + 2) - 4x_i + 6\right]$$
$$+ a^2\left[2(y_i^2 + 2y_i + 1) + 2(y_i + 1) + \frac{1}{2}\right] - 2a^2b^2$$

Recalling $f(x_i - 1/2, y_i + 1)$ yields

$$d_{2_{i+1}} = d_{2_i} + 4a^2y_{i+1} - 4b^2x_{i+1} + 2b^2$$

For a horizontal move, $x_{i+1} = x_i - 1$, $y_{i+1} = y_i$ and

$$d_{2_{i+1}} = d_{2_i} - 4b^2x_{i+1} + 2b^2$$

For a vertical move, $x_{i+1} = x_i$, $y_{i+1} = y_i + 1$ and

$$d_{1_{i+1}} = d_{1_i} - 4a^2 y_{i+1} + 2a^2$$

Using these results, a more efficient algorithm is:

Efficient midpoint ellipse algorithm for the first quadrant

> *initialize the variables*
>
> x = **Integer**(a + 1/2)
> y = 0
> *define temporary variables*
> taa = a ∗ a
> t2aa = 2 ∗ taa
> t4aa = 2 ∗ t2aa
>
> tbb = b ∗ b
> t2bb = 2 ∗ tbb
> t4bb = 2 ∗ t2bb
>
> t2abb = a ∗ t2bb
>
> t2bbx = t2bb ∗ x
> tx = x
>
> *initialize the decision variable in region 1*
> d1 = t2bbx ∗ (x − 1) + tbb/2 + t2aa ∗ (1 − tbb)
>
> **while** t2bb ∗ tx > t2aa ∗ y   *start in region 1*
>   **call setpixel** (x, y)
>   **if** d1 < 0 **then**
>   y = y + 1   *move vertically*
>   d1 = d1 + t4aa ∗ y + t2aa
>   tx = x − 1
>   **else**
>   x = x − 1   *move diagonally*
>   y = y + 1
>   d1 = d1 − t4bb ∗ x + t4aa ∗ y + t2aa
>   tx = x
>   **end if**
> **end while**
>
> *initialize the decision variable in region 2*
> d2 = t2bb ∗ (x ∗ x + 1) − t4bb ∗ x + t2aa ∗ (y ∗ y + y − tbb) + taa/2
>
> **while** x >= 0
>   **call setpixel** (x, y)
>   **if** d2 < 0 **then**
>   x = x − 1   *move diagonally*

$$y = y + 1$$
$$d2 = d2 + t4aa * y - t4bb * x + t2bb$$
    else
$$x = x - 1 \qquad move\ horizontally$$
$$d2 = d2 - t4bb * x + t2bb$$
    end if
  end while
finish

2–6   General Function Rasterization

It is tempting to consider algorithms for rasterization of general polynomial functions, e.g., cubic and quartic polynomials. Jordan et al. [Jord73] and Van Aken and Novak [VanA85] consider such algorithms. Unfortunately, these algorithms fail for general polynomials, especially those of degree higher than two [Bels76; Ramo76]. The fundamental reason for this failure is that, except for limited regions, the general polynomial function of degree three or greater is neither monotonically decreasing nor increasing in x and y. Consequently, the function can cross or loop back on itself, or curve back to pass less than a pixel distance from itself. Figure 2–19, where the arrows indicate the direction of rasterization, illustrates the basic difficulty.

In Fig. 2–19a if the function is evaluated at (x_{i+1}, y_{i+1}), then point 2 on the function may be selected instead of point 1. The partial derivatives at point 2, used to determine the next pixel on the rasterized curve, now 'point to' the pixels at (x_i, y_i) or (x_{i+1}, y_i) rather than the pixel at (x_{i+2}, y_{i+2}). Consequently, the pixel at (x_{i+2}, y_{i+2}) is never activated, and the curve is incorrectly rasterized.

Figure 2–19b, where the two lines might be the two branches of a 'narrow' hyperbola, illustrates that similar difficulties occur for some second-degree general polynomials. For example, if rasterization is proceeding along the branch labeled 1 and evaluation of the function at (x_{i+1}, y_{i+2}) yields a point on the

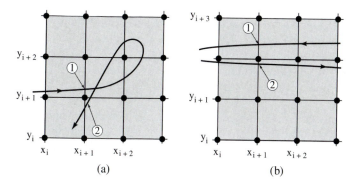

(a)   (b)

Figure 2–19   General polynomial function difficulties. (a) Loop; (b) close passage.

branch labeled 2, then again the partial derivatives used to determine the 'direction' of the function are inappropriate. The result is that large portions of the function are missed.

The curve rasterization technique described here and in the previous sections is frequently referred to as 'curve tracing'. An alternate technique is to examine each individual pixel in the raster to determine if the curve crosses that pixel. If the curve crosses the pixel, the pixel is activated; if not, it is ignored. It is obvious that the large majority of pixels are ignored; hence the algorithm is both expensive and inefficient. Successful algorithms of this type attempt to limit the number of pixels examined. Such algorithms are frequently referred to as recursive space subdivision algorithms.

The success of the recursive space subdivision algorithms depends upon subdividing boxes in either two or three dimensions.[†] The fundamental concept is shown in Fig. 2–20. The box defined by corners (x_i, y_i) and $(x_i + \Delta x, y_i + \Delta y)$ is examined. If the curve $f(x, y) = 0$ passes through the box and the box is larger than pixel size, the box is subdivided, as shown by the dashed lines. If the curve does not pass through the box, it is rendered at the background color or ignored. The algorithm is applied recursively to each of the subdivided boxes labeled in Fig. 2–20 as 2a, 2b, 2c and 2d. For the sample box in Fig. 2–20, the subdivided boxes labeled 2c and 2d are rendered at the background color or ignored. The boxes labeled 2a and 2b are either further subdivided or, if pixel size, rendered with the attributes assigned to the implicit curve, $f(x, y) = 0$.

The efficiency and accuracy of the recursive space subdivision algorithms depends upon the test used to determine if the implicit function, $f(x, y) = 0$, crosses a particular box. Since implicit curves can be multiple valued or multiply connected, and can have singular points where they are self-intersecting or where they split into multiple branches, the crossing test must be carefully crafted. The most successful algorithms (see, for example, the papers by Taubin [Taub94a,b]) are based on interval arithmetic (see [Moor79; Duff92]).

Computationally successful algorithms do not use a definitive yes–no test but rather a less computationally expensive no–maybe test to increase the speed of the algorithm.

Fundamentally, a no–maybe test excludes most, but not all, entities not satisfying a particular condition using a computationally inexpensive test. the remaining entities must eventually be excluded by using computationally more expensive and definitive yes–no tests. The result is a computationally more efficient and faster, complete algorithm.

The recursive space subdivision techniques are easily extended to three dimensions, where they are used to rasterize surfaces and the intersections of surfaces (see [Taub94b]).

For functions that are not monotonically increasing or decreasing and that do not have singular points over the desired range, the safest rasterization technique is to calculate a sufficient number of points on the function for adequate

---

[†]The Warnock hidden surface algorithm was one of the first of these algorithms (see Sec. 4–4).

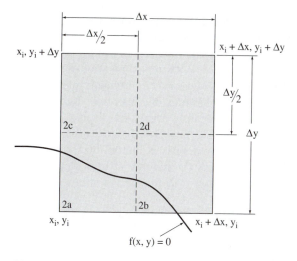

Figure 2–20 Recursive space subdivision.

representation, and then to use one of the straight line rasterization algorithms to connect them in proper sequence. Where possible, a parametric representation of the function is used to calculate the points. With proper parameterization, a parametric representation yields more closely spaced points where the function's curvature is large, and more widely spaced points where the curvature is low. The result is a better representation of the function.

2–7 Scan Conversion—Generation of the Display

In order to display the rasterized image using video techniques, it is necessary to organize the picture into the precise pattern required by the graphics display (see Sec. 1–4). This is the process called scan conversion. In contrast to the display list for a random scan or line drawing display, which contains only information about lines or characters, here the display list must contain information about every pixel on the screen. Furthermore, it is necessary that this information be organized and presented at appropriate frame rates in scan line order, that is, from the top to the bottom and from left to right. Three ways of accomplishing this are real-time scan conversion, run-length encoding and frame buffer memory. Real time scan conversion is most frequently used in vehicle simulators. Run-length encoding is generally used to 'store' images, or to transmit images (or text). Frame buffer memory is commonly used for image display in workstations and personal computers with graphics capability.

Real-time Scan Conversion

In real-time or on-the-fly scan conversion, the picture is randomly represented in terms of visual attributes and geometric properties. Typical visual attributes are color, shade and intensity, while x, y coordinates, slopes and text are typical geometric properties. These geometric properties are ordered in y. The processor scans through this information and calculates the intensity of every pixel on the screen during the presentation of each frame. With real-time scan conversion, large amounts of memory are unnecessary. Memory requirements are usually limited to that necessary to hold the display list plus one scan line. In addition, because picture information is held in a randomly organized display list, it is easy to add or delete information from the list. This greatly facilitates dynamic presentations. However, the complexity of the display is limited by the speed of the display processor. This usually means that the number of lines or polygons in the picture, the number of intersections on a scan line or the number of gray scales or colors is limited.

The simplest implementation for real-time scan conversion processes the entire display list to obtain the intersections (if any) of each line in the display list, with a particular scan line each time a scan line is displayed. For typical display rates, the short time available (less than 63.5 μsec) precludes using this technique for complex images.

For illustrative purposes, we restrict the current discussion to images containing only lines. Other image entities are handled in a similar fashion. Because, in general, not every line in a picture intersects every scan line, the amount of work required is reduced by maintaining an active edge list. The active edge list contains only those lines in the picture which intersect the scan line. The active edge list is developed and maintained using a number of techniques. All of the techniques first sort the lines by the largest value of y.

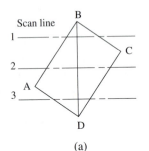

(a)

Scan line	1	2	3	1	2	3	1	2	3
	BC ← b	BC	BC	BA ← b	BA ← b	BA	BD ← b	BD ← b	BD ← b
	BA	BA ← b	BA	BC	BC	BC ← b	BA	BA	BA
	BD ← e	BD	BD ← b	BD ← e	BD	BD	BC ← e	BC	BC
	CD	CD ← e	CD	CD	CD ← e	CD	CD	CD ← e	CD
	AD	AD	AD ← e	AD	AD	AD ← e	AD	AD	AD ← e
		(b)			(c)			(d)	

Figure 2–21   A simple active edge list.

A Simple Active Edge List Using Pointers

A particularly simple technique for developing and maintaining the active edge list uses two floating pointers into the y sorted list. A *begin* pointer is used to indicate the beginning of the active edge list, and an *end* pointer is used to indicate the end of the active edge list. A simple line drawing, along with three typical scan lines, is shown in Fig. 2–21a. Figure 2–21b shows a typical sorted list of the lines in the figure. The begin pointer is initially set at the beginning of the list, i.e., at BC. The end pointer is set at the last line in the list that begins *above* the scan line under consideration, i.e., at BD. As the scan moves down the picture, the end pointer is moved down to include those new lines which now start on or above the current scan line. At the same time, the begin pointer is moved down to eliminate lines which end above the current scan line. This is illustrated in Fig. 2–21b for the scan lines labeled 2 and 3 in Fig. 2–21a. Figures 2–21c and 2–21d illustrate a problem with this simple algorithm. The sort order of the lines which begin at the same y value influences the size of the active edge list. For example, in Fig. 2–21d the line BC never drops off the active edge list. Thus, more information than necessary is processed.

A Sorted Active Edge List

These and similar problems can be eliminated at the expense of additional data structure. In addition, the calculation of the intersection of each line in the image with individual scan lines can be simplified. First, a y-bucket sort of all the lines in the picture is performed. A y-bucket sort,[†] illustrated in Fig. 2–22b, simply creates a storage location, or bucket, for each scan line. If, for example, there are 1024 scan lines, then 1024 buckets are used. As the lines in the display list are examined, information about each line is placed in the bucket corresponding to the largest y value of the line. For simple monochrome (black-and-white) line drawings, only the x intercept on the bucket scan line, Δx (the change in the x intercept from scan line to scan line), and Δy (the number of scan lines crossed by the line) are recorded. For simple images, most of the y buckets are empty.

The active edge list for the current scan line is formed by adding information from the y bucket corresponding to that scan line. The x intercepts are sorted into scan line order, and the active edge list is scan-converted. After the active edge list is scan-converted, Δy for each line on the active edge list is decremented by one. If $\Delta y < 0$, the line is deleted from the active edge list. Finally, the x intercepts for the new scan line are obtained by adding Δx to the previous values for each line on the active edge list. The process is repeated for all scan lines. The active edge list for scan lines 3, 5 and 7 for the simple line drawing of Fig. 2–22a is given in Fig. 2–22c.

If a fixed y-bucket size is used, a fixed amount of storage is available for intersections on each scan line. Thus, the maximum number of intersections

---

[†]A bucket sort is a form of radix sort with the radix equal to the number of buckets (scan lines). See Knuth [Knut73].

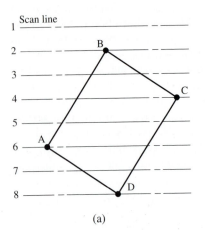

(a)

y-bucket

1   null

2   $x_{BA}, \Delta x_{BA}, \Delta y_{BA},$
    $x_{BC}, \Delta x_{BC}, \Delta y_{BC}$

3   null

4   $x_{CD}, \Delta x_{CD}, \Delta y_{CD}$

5   null

6   $x_{AD}, \Delta x_{AD}, \Delta y_{AD}$

7   null

8   null

(b)

Active Edge List

Scan line 3: $x_{BA} + \Delta x_{BA}, \Delta x_{BA},$
$\Delta y_{BA} - 1, x_{BC} + \Delta x_{BC},$
$\Delta x_{BC}, \Delta y_{BC} - 1$

Scan line 5: $x_{BA} + 3\Delta x_{BA}, \Delta x_{BA},$
$\Delta y_{BA} - 3, x_{CD} + \Delta x_{CD},$
$\Delta x_{CD}, \Delta y_{CD} - 1$

Scan line 7: $x_{CD}, 3\Delta x_{CD}, \Delta x_{CD},$
$\Delta y_{CD} - 3, x_{AC} + \Delta x_{AD},$
$\Delta x_{AD}, \Delta y_{AD} - 1$

(c)

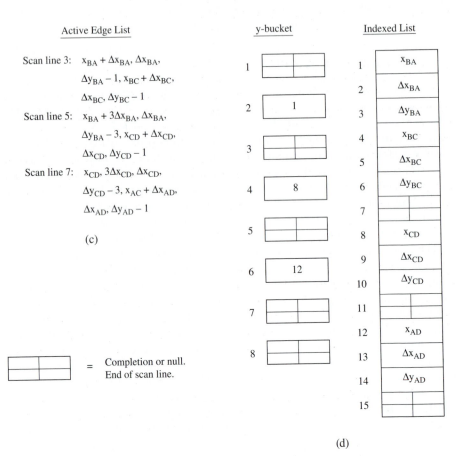

= Completion or null. End of scan line.

(d)

Figure 2–22 A y-bucket sort, active edge list and sequential indexed data structure.

on any given scan line is predetermined; and the complexity of the picture is limited. One technique for avoiding this limit is to use a sequential indexed list for the data structure. In this case, each y bucket contains only a pointer to the location in the data structure of the information for the first line originating on that scan line. The sequential indexed list and the data structure for Fig. 2–22a are shown in Fig. 2–22d. For the particular data structure shown, it is assumed that data for a given scan line are accessed in groups of three, until a null or completion is indicated.

The technique for determining line intersections with individual scan lines yields acceptable results for vertical and near vertical lines. However, for nearly horizontal lines very few intersection points are calculated. This yields an unacceptable line representation. A simple solution is to determine the intersections on two successive scan lines and activate all the pixels between the intersections. This is shown in Fig. 2–23. For horizontal line segments, the end points are used.

An Active Edge List Using a Linked List

Because the entire picture is processed for each frame, real-time scan conversion lends itself to highly interactive graphics. When a y-bucket sort is used, lines are added to or deleted from the display list by simply adding or deleting them from the appropriate y bucket and the associated data structure. This is easiest for fixed-length y buckets, as shown in Fig. 2–22b. In order to conveniently add and delete lines to the display, a linked list data structure is used. This is shown in Fig. 2–24. Note that in the linked list shown in Fig. 2–24b the end of each data group and the location of the next data group on that scan line, e.g., item 4, as well as the completion of the link, are required. If the line BD is now added to the figure, the linked list is modified as shown in Fig. 2–24d. The information about the line BD is added at the end of the data list. The display processor is directed to this location by the modified link instruction at location 8. If the line BC is now deleted from the figure, the linked list is modified as shown in Fig. 2–24f. Here, notice that the link instruction at location 4 is modified to jump around the locations containing information about the line BC.

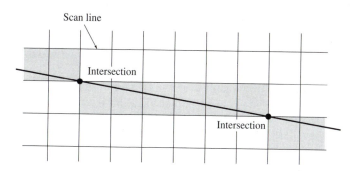

Figure 2–23 A simple scan conversion technique for nearly horizontal lines.

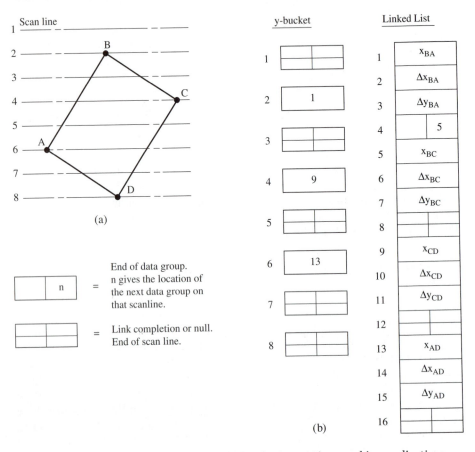

(a)

(b)

Figure 2–24 A y-bucket sort and linked list for interactive graphics applications.

Updating the Linked List

This simple example illustrates the basic concepts for modifying a linked list for interactive graphics applications. However, it does not illustrate all the required features. For example, it is obvious that, as illustrated, the length of the list grows continuously, unless the 'lost' locations (5 to 8 in Fig. 2–24f) are reused or the list is compressed.

This process is sometimes referred to as 'garbage collection'. One 'garbage collection' technique uses a push down stack, i.e., a first in last out stack (FILO). Briefly, the push down stack is initialized by pushing the first address of the linked list onto the stack. Before scan line information is placed into the linked list, the next available location in the list is popped (obtained) from the top of the stack. After all the information from that y bucket is inserted into the linked list, a terminator flag is placed in the next location and the address of the following location is pushed onto the stack.

A fragment of pseudocode for additions to the linked list is:

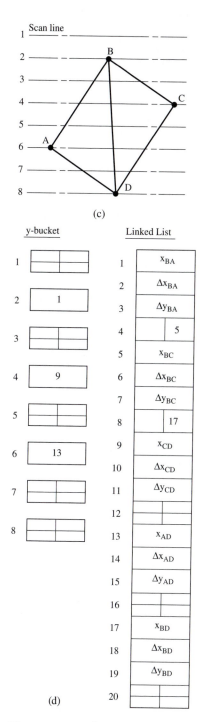

(c)

(d)

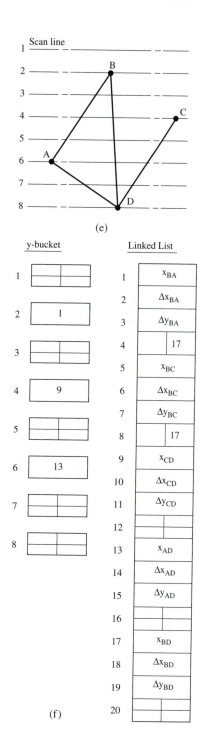

(e)

(f)

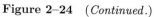

Figure 2–24 (*Continued.*)

get pointer into the linked list from the scan line y bucket
using pointer, follow linked list to the terminator flag
Pop next available link address from the stack
change terminator flag to the new link address
insert the new data
add terminator flag
then
if the stack is empty
 Push the next address onto the stack
end if

Deletions from the list are a bit more complex. Basically, the initial pointer to the linked list is obtained from the appropriate y bucket and followed, to identify the information to be deleted. Provided the data to be deleted is not the last item for that y bucket, the link address of the previous item is replaced with the link address for the deleted item; otherwise it is changed to a terminator flag.

A pseudocode fragment for deletions from the linked list is:

get pointer into the linked list from the scan line y bucket
if (data to be deleted is the first item) **then**
 Push y bucket pointer onto stack
 if (forward link address) <> terminator flag **then**
  change y bucket pointer to the forward link address
 end if
else
 Push previous link address onto stack
 if next link item is <> terminator flag **then**
  change previous link address to the next link address
 else
  change link address to terminator flag
 end if
end if

For further discussion of linked lists and data structures see, for example, Knuth [Knut73] or Standish [Stan80].

2–8 Image Compression

Two typical techniques for image compression are run-length encoding and area image compression. Both take advantage of image coherence.

Run-length Encoding

Run-length encoding seeks to take advantage of the fact that large areas of the picture have the same intensity or color. In its simplest form, run-length encoding specifies only the number of successive pixels on a given scan line with a given intensity. Figure 2–25a shows a simple monochrome (black-and-white) line drawing on a 30 × 30 raster and the associated encoding for scan lines 1, 15 and 30. The encoded data is to be considered in groups of two. The first number is the number of successive pixels on that scan line with a given intensity, i.e., the count, and the second is the intensity

Run Length	Intensity

Thus, in Fig. 2–25a scan line 1 has 30 pixels of zero intensity, i.e., white or the background intensity. The complete picture is encoded with 208 numbers.

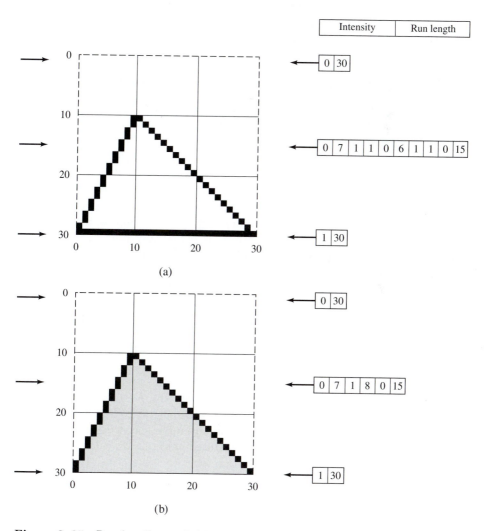

Figure 2–25 Run-length encoded image.

Pixel-by-pixel storage, i.e., one piece of information for each pixel (a bit map), requires 900 intensity values for the 30×30 raster of Fig. 2–25a. The data compression using run-length encoding in this case is 1:4.33, or 0.231.

Solid figures are easily handled with run-length encoding. This is shown in Fig. 2–25b, along with the encoding for scan lines 1, 15 and 30. Of particular interest is scan line 15. For Fig. 2–25b the entire picture is encoded, using 136 numbers for a data compression of 1:6.62, or 0.151. Images with solid figures encode with fewer pieces of information than line or wire frame drawings, because two edges are covered with one pair of intensity-length values.

This simple run-length encoding scheme is easily extended to include color. For color, the intensity of each of the red, green and blue color guns is given, preceded by the number of successive pixels for that color on that scan line, e.g.

Run Length	Red Intensity	Green Intensity	Blue Intensity

For a simple color display in which each individual color gun is either completely off (0) or fully on (1), the encoding for scan line 15 of Fig. 2–25b, with a yellow triangle on a blue background, is (see Table 1–1)

15	0	0	1	7	1	1	0	8	0	0	1

Data compression for run-length encoded pictures can approach 1:10. This is significant because it saves storage space for computer-generated animated sequences or film. It also saves transmission time for wire photos, facsimile and Internet images, where run-length encoding is extensively used. For example, consider the storage requirements for a $1024 \times 1280 \times 24$ resolution picture for a 30-second animated film sequence at video rates (30 frames per second). The storage requirement is

$$(1024 \times 1280 \times 24 \times 30 \times 30)/(8 \text{ bits/byte} = 3456 \text{ megabytes}$$

Even a modest run-length encoding data compression of 4:1 significantly reduces the storage requirement.

Run-length encoding has disadvantages. Since the run lengths are stored sequentially, adding or deleting lines or text from the picture is difficult and time-consuming. There is overhead involved with both encoding and decoding the picture. Finally, the storage requirement can approach twice that for pixel-by-pixel storage for short runs. This is illustrated in Fig. 2–26, where the picture consists of alternate black and white vertical lines one pixel wide. Here the run-length encoding is

repeated 15 times. Thus, a total of 1800 values must be stored for the run-length

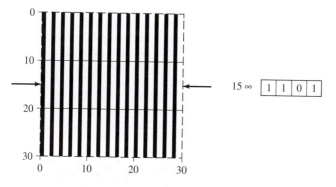

Figure 2–26   Run-length encoding limits for short runs.

encoded picture, in contrast to 900 for pixel-by-pixel storage. This is a 'negative' data compression of 2.

Good run-length encoding schemes identify situations that result in negative data compression and adaptively switch to pixel-by-pixel storage. A simple adaptive run-length encoding scheme (see [Glas91]) uses the sign of the number of encoded pixels to switch between run-length encoding and pixel-by-pixel storage. Specifically, if the sign of the count is negative, then pixel-by-pixel data follows; otherwise run-length encoded data follows. In both cases the magnitude of the count indicates the number of pixel intensities, or triplets of rgb intensities, that follow. For example

−3	1	0	0	1	0	1	0	0	1	6	1	2	6

defines three pixels with rgb values of $(1, 0, 0)$, $(0, 1, 0)$, $(1, 0, 0)$, followed by six pixels with rgb values of $(1, 2, 6)$.

Laws [Laws75], Hartke et al. [Hart78] and Peterson et al. [Pete86] discuss efficient implementation of run-length encoding schemes.

Area Image Compression

Run-length encoding attempts to take advantage of the scan line coherence of an image, i.e., the tendency of the next pixel on a scan line to have the same characteristics as the current pixel. Scan line coherence fundamentally treats the image as one-dimensional.

Area image compression techniques attempt to take advantage of area coherence, i.e., the tendency of pixels in adjacent areas to have the same characteristics. Area coherence fundamentally treats the image as two-dimensional.

While a Warnock style nondeterministic, divide and conquer algorithm (see Sec. 4–4) is possible, it is generally more convenient to consider the image in fixed-size pixel blocks taken in 'scan line' order. Although pixel blocks can be of any reasonable size, e.g., 2×2, 4×4, 8×8, 16×16, 32×32, etc., we concentrate here on 8×8 pixel blocks.

```
139  144  149  153  155  155  155  155        160  160  160  160  160  255  255  255
144  151  153  156  159  156  156  156        160  160  160  160  160  255  255  255
150  155  160  163  158  155  156  156        160  160  160  160  160  255  255  255
159  161  162  160  160  159  159  159        255  255  255  255  255    2    2    2
159  160  161  162  162  155  155  155        255  255  255  255  255    2    2    2
161  161  161  161  160  157  157  157        255  255  255  255  255    2    2    2
162  162  161  163  162  157  157  157        255  255  255  255  255    2    2    2
162  162  161  161  163  158  158  158        255  255  255  255  255    2    2    2
```

(a)   (b)

Figure 2–27   8 × 8 pixel blocks. (a) Monochrome continuous tone natural image; (b) monochrome simple, computer generated image.

Shown in Fig. 2–27 are the intensity values for two 8 × 8 pixel blocks taken from two different images. The 8 × 8 pixel block shown in Fig. 2–27a is from a monochrome, continuous tone, natural image with 256 gray (intensity) levels. The 8×8 pixel block shown in Fig. 2–27b is from a simple monochrome, computer generated image with 256 gray levels.

First we determine the average intensity value in each 8 × 8 block by adding all the intensity values, dividing by 64 and truncating to obtain an integer number. For the continuous tone image of Fig. 2–27a the average is 157. for the simple computer generated image of Fig. 2–27b the average is 173. The average intensity is then subtracted from each pixel intensity to yield the differential image results shown in Fig. 2–28, where the first element is the average intensity. Saving the average intensity increases the storage requirement; but as we shall see, it adds additional capability.

The run-length encoding scheme discussed in the previous section is now applied to each row of the differential images. For the differential image of Fig. 2–28a the result is shown in Fig. 2–29a, and for that in Fig. 2–28b the result is seen in Fig. 2–29b.

```
157                                           173
-18  -13  -8  -4  -2  -2  -2  -2        -13  -13  -13  -13  -13    82    82    82
-13   -6  -4  -1   2  -1  -1  -1        -13  -13  -13  -13  -13    82    82    82
 -7   -2   3   6   1  -2  -1  -1        -13  -13  -13  -13  -13    82    82    82
  2    4   5   3   3   2   2   2         82   82   82   82   82  -171  -171  -171
  2    3   4   5   5  -2  -2  -2         82   82   82   82   82  -171  -171  -171
  4    4   4   4   3   0   0   0         82   82   82   82   82  -171  -171  -171
  5    5   4   6   5   0   0   0         82   82   82   82   82  -171  -171  -171
  5    5   4   4   6   1   1   1         82   82   82   82   82  -171  -171  -171
```

(a)   (b)

Figure 2–28   Differential images for 8 × 8 pixel blocks. (a) Monochrome continuous tone natural image of Fig. 2–27a; (b) monochrome simple computer generated image of Fig. 2–27b.

157

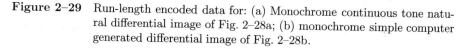

```
-4  -18  -13  -8  -4   4  -2
-5  -13   -6  -4  -1   2   3  -1
-8   -7   -2   3   6   1  -2  -1  -1
-5    2    4   5   3   3   3   2
-5    2    3   4   5   5   3  -2  -2
 4    4   -1   3   3   0
-5    5    5   4   6   5   3   0
-5    5    5   4   4   6   3   1
```

(a)

173

```
5  -13   3    82
5  -13   3    82
5  -13   3    82
5   82   3  -171
5   82   3  -171
5   82   3  -171
5   82   3  -171
5   82   3  -171
```

(b)

Figure 2–29 Run-length encoded data for: (a) Monochrome continuous tone natural differential image of Fig. 2–28a; (b) monochrome simple computer generated differential image of Fig. 2–28b.

Examining Fig. 2–29a shows that 64 pieces of information are now required to store the 8 × 8 pixel block. Consequently, no data compression is achieved. However, for the differential image of Fig. 2–28b, run-length encoding reduces the required number of pieces of information to 33, for a data compression factor of 0.515, as shown in Fig. 2–29b.

Alternate run-length encoding schemes can be used on the basic 8 × 8 pixel block. For example, the pixel block can be subdivided into 2 × 2 subpixel blocks to take further advantage of area coherence, as shown in Fig. 2–30a. Each 2 × 2 subpixel block is then run-length encoded in a zigzag pattern, as shown in the upper left subpixel block in Fig. 2–30a When applied to the differential image of Fig. 2–28a, 78 pieces of information are required for a compression factor of 1.22, i.e., a negative compression! Applying the same algorithm to the differential image of Fig. 2–28b yields a compression factor of 0.843.

An alternate zigzag run-length encoding pattern encompasses the entire 8×8 pixel block, as shown in Fig. 2–30b. Applying this zigzag pattern to the differential image of Fig. 2–28a requires 67 pieces of information for a negative compression factor of 1.05, and to Fig. 2–28b requires 32 pieces of information for a compression factor of 0.5. This zigzag run-length encoding pattern is used in the JPEG (Joint Photographic Expert Group) standard (see [Nels92]). Clearly, the amount of data compression depends heavily upon the character of the image and the encoding scheme.

If the user is viewing a large library of images in order to find a particular image, or if the user is remotely viewing an image, incremental image transmission or generation becomes important. Frequently, the user needs to see only a crude approximation of an image to decide to reject it or to view it in progressively finer detail. In addition, for complex images the user may be interested in examining only a portion of the image in fine detail. It is for this reason that we saved the average intensity of the 8 × 8 pixel block and created the differential image.

Continuing to work with an 8 × 8 pixel block, we develop a hierarchical representation of the image. After determining and storing the average intensity of the 8 × 8 pixel block, the pixel block is subdivided into four 4 × 4 pixel

157

−18	−13	−8	−4	−2	−2	−2	−2
−13	−6	−4	−1	2	−1	−1	−1
−7	−2	3	6	1	−2	−1	−1
2	4	5	3	3	2	2	2
2	3	4	5	5	−2	−2	−2
4	4	4	4	3	0	0	0
5	5	4	6	5	0	0	0
5	5	4	4	6	1	1	1

(a)

173

−13	−13	−13	−13	−13	82	82	82
−13	−13	−13	−13	−13	82	82	82
−13	−13	−13	−13	−13	82	82	82
82	82	82	82	82	−171	−171	−171
82	82	82	82	82	−171	−171	−171
82	82	82	82	82	−171	−171	−171
82	82	82	82	82	−171	−171	−171
82	82	82	82	82	−171	−171	−171

(b)

Figure 2–30 Zigzag run-length encoding schemes. (a) 2 × 2; (b) 8 × 8.

```
157                                      173
153  156  161  158                       183  189  255      65
144  152  156  155                       160  160  207     255
156  161  158  157                       207  207  168     128
160  161  158  156                       255  255  128       2
162  161  160  157                       255  255  128       2
 -4  -18  -13   -8   -4    4   -2           5  -13    3      82
 -5  -13   -6   -4   -1    2    3   -1       5  -13    3      82
 -8   -7   -2    3    6    1   -2   -1  -1   5  -13    3      82
 -5    2    4    5    3    3    3    2       5   82    3    -171
 -5    2    3    4    5    5    3   -2  -2   5   82    3    -171
  4    4   -1    3    3    0                 5   82    3    -171
 -5    5    5    4    6    5    3    0       5   82    3    -171
 -5    5    5    4    4    6    3    1       5   82    3    -171

              (a)                                     (b)
```

Figure 2–31   8×8 pixel blocks encoded for incremental transmission. (a) Monochrome continuous tone natural image; (b) monochrome simple computer generated image.

blocks. The average intensity of each 4×4 pixel block is calculated and stored in clockwise order, beginning with the upper left corner of the 8×8 pixel block. Each of these 4×4 pixel blocks is further subdivided into 2×2 pixel blocks, the average intensity determined and stored in clockwise order beginning with the upper left corner of the 4×4 pixel block. Finally, the pixel-by-pixel run-length encoded differential image, based on the average intensity value of the 8×8 pixel block (see Fig. 2–28), is determined and stored. The technique is similar to that of the mipmaps used in texture generation (see Sec. 5–12). The results are shown in Figs. 2–31a and 2–31b. Examination of Fig. 2–31a shows that negative data compression with a factor of 1.31 results for the natural image of Fig. 2–27a. For the computer generated image of Fig. 2–27b, the data compression factor is now 0.828 instead of 0.515. However, if the image is viewed using the average intensities of the 8×8 pixel blocks, rather than the intensities of each individual pixel, the transmission compression factor is 0.0152 for a 1024×1024 image (16k/1024k), and 0.25 if viewed using the average intensities of the 2×2 pixel blocks (256k/1024k).

2–9   Displaying Lines, Characters and Polygons

Displaying lines, characters and polygons are some of the essential elements of a raster graphics display.

Line Display

Recalling the discussion of frame buffers in Chapter 1 (see Sec. 1–2), conceptually a frame buffer can be considered as a simple drawing surface. Assuming that the frame buffer is a simple line drawing display, the frame buffer is first cleared or set to the background intensity or color. The line is then rasterized, using, for example, either the Bresenham or the DDA algorithm; and the appropriate pixels are written to the frame buffer. When the picture or frame is complete, the display controller reads the frame buffer in scan line order and passes the result to the video monitor.

Selective erase of lines can be implemented by again using the rasterizing algorithm to write the appropriate pixels to the frame buffer in the background intensity or color. This eliminates the line. However, Fig. 2–32 illustrates a problem with this technique. If the erased line crosses another line, then a hole is left in the line. Figure 2–32a shows two intersecting lines. If the horizontal line at $y = 5$ is erased by writing the background intensity or color to the frame buffer, a hole in the remaining line at pixel $(5, 5)$ results. It is not difficult to detect these holes and fill them; it is only necessary to determine the intersection of the deleted line with all other lines in the picture. For a complex picture, this is time-consuming.

Boxing or minimax tests are used to reduce the work required. This technique is shown in Fig. 2–33. Only lines which pass through the dashed box formed from the minimum and maximum values of x and y for the line segment ab can possibly intersect ab. The tests for each line segment are then

> **minimax or boxing test**
> > **if** Xlinemax < Xboxmin **or**
> > Xlinemin > Xboxmax **or**
> > Ylinemax < Yboxmin **or**
> > Ylinemin > Yboxmax
> > **then**
> > > no intersection
> > **else**
> > > calculate intersection

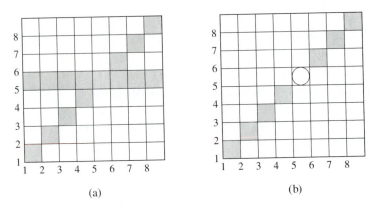

Figure 2–32 Selective erase of lines in a frame buffer.

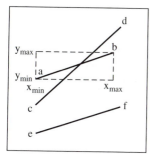

Figure 2–33   Boxing or minimax tests.

end if
finish

Boxing or minimax tests are fundamental to many computer graphics algorithms.

Character Display

Alphanumeric characters are written to the frame buffer using a mask. A character mask is a small raster which contains the relative locations of the pixels used to represent the character (see Fig. 2–34a). Special symbols unique to a particular application, e.g., resistors, capacitors or mathematical symbols, can also be represented with a character mask. The mask itself simply contains binary values indicating whether or not a particular pixel in the mask is used to represent the character or symbol shape. For simple black-and-white displays, a 1 normally indicates that a pixel is used in the representation, and a 0 indicates that it is not. For color displays additional bits are used to provide multiple color shades directly or as indices to a color lookup table.

The character is inserted into the frame buffer by indicating the location in the frame buffer (x_0, y_0) of the origin of the mask. Then each pixel in the mask is displaced by the amount (x_0, y_0). A simple algorithm to accomplish this for a binary mask is:

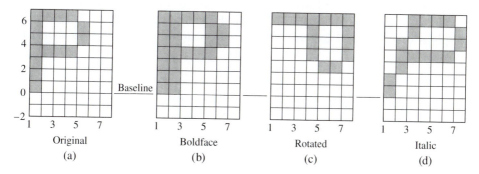

Figure 2–34   Transformed character masks. (a) Original; (b) bold face; (c) rotated; (d) italic.

Mask insertion *into the frame buffer*

Xmin, Xmax, Ymin, Ymax *are the limits of the mask*

x_0, y_0 *is the location in the frame buffer*

    for j = Ymin **to** Ymax − 1
        for i = Xmin **to** Xmax − 1
            if Mask(i, j) <> 0 **then**
                write Mask(i, j) to the frame buffer at $(x_0 + i,\ y_0 + j)$
            end if
        next i
    next j
finish

A character in the frame buffer is erased by rewriting it to the frame buffer using the background intensity or color.

The character mask can be modified as it is written to the frame buffer to produce alternate character styles or orientations. Some simple modifications are shown in Fig. 2–34. Figure 2–34a shows the original character mask. By writing the mask to two successive frame buffer locations, x_0 and $x_0 + 1$, a bold-faced character is obtained. This is shown in Fig. 2–34b. The character can be rotated, as shown in Fig. 2–34c, or skewed to give the appearance of italics, as shown in Fig. 2–34d.

Solid Area Scan Conversion

So far the discussion has been concerned with the presentation of lines on a raster scan device. However, one of the unique characteristics of a raster scan device is the ability to present solid areas. The generation of solid areas from simple edge or vertex descriptions is called solid area scan conversion, polygon filling or contour filling. Several techniques are used to fill a contour. They generally divide into two broad categories: scan conversion and seed fill.

Scan conversion techniques attempt to determine, in scan line order, whether or not a point is inside a polygon or contour. The algorithms generally proceed from the 'top' of the polygon or contour to the 'bottom.' These scan conversion techniques are equally applicable to line drawing displays. With line drawing displays they are used for cross-hatching or shading of contours, as shown in Fig. 2–35.

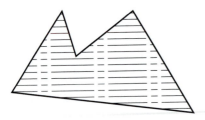

Figure 2–35   Contour cross-hatching or shading.

Seed fill techniques assume that some point inside the closed contour is known. The algorithms then proceed to search for points adjacent to the seed point that are inside the contour. If the adjacent point is not inside the contour, then a boundary of the contour has been found. If the adjacent point is inside the contour, then it becomes a new seed point and the search continues recursively. Seed fill algorithms are only applicable to raster devices.

2–10   Polygon Filling

Many closed contours are simple polygons. If the contour is composed of curved lines, it can be approximated by a suitable polygon or polygons. The simplest method of filling a polygon is to examine every pixel in the raster to see if it is inside the polygon. Since most pixels are not inside the polygon, this technique is wasteful. The amount of work is reduced by computing the bounding box for the polygon. The bounding box is the smallest rectangle that contains the polygon. Only those points inside the bounding box are examined. This is shown in Fig. 2–36. A bounding box test is similar to the minimax test discussed in Sec. 2–9. Using a bounding box for the polygon shown in Fig. 2–36a significantly reduces the number of pixels examined. However, for the polygon shown in Fig. 2-36b, the reduction is considerably smaller.

Scan-converting Polygons

A more efficient technique than the inside test can be developed by noting that, except at boundary edges, adjacent pixels are likely to have the same characteristics. This property is referred to as spatial coherence. For a raster scan graphics device, adjacent pixels on a scan line are likely to have the same characteristics. This is scan line coherence.

The characteristics of pixels on a given scan line change only where a polygon edge intersects the scan line. These intersections divide the scan line into regions.

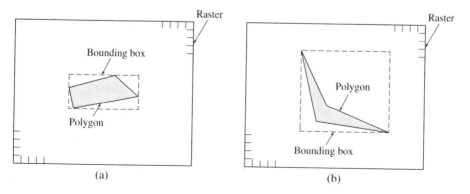

(a)   (b)

Figure 2–36   Polygon bounding box.

For the simple polygon shown in Fig. 2–37, the scan line labeled 2 intersects the polygon at $x = 1$ and $x = 8$. These intersections divide the scan line into three regions:

$x < 1$	outside the polygon
$1 \le x \le 8$	inside the polygon
$x > 8$	outside the polygon

Similarly, the scan line labeled 4 is divided into five regions:

$x < 1$	outside the polygon
$1 \le x \le 4$	inside the polygon
$4 < x < 6$	outside the polygon
$6 \le x \le 8$	inside the polygon
$x > 8$	outside the polygon

The intersections for scan line 4 are not necessarily determined in left-to-right order. For example, if the polygon is specified by the vertex list $P_1P_2P_3P_4P_5$ and the edge list by successive pairs of vertices, P_1P_2, P_2P_3, P_3P_4, P_4P_5, P_5P_1, then the intersections of the edges with scan line 4 are determined as 8, 6, 4, 1. They must then be sorted into ascending order in x, i.e., 1, 4, 6, 8.

In determining the intensity, color or shade of the pixels on a scan line, the sorted intersections are considered in pairs. For each interval formed by a pair of intersections, the intensity or color is that of the polygon. For intervals between pairs of intersections, the intensity or color is that of the background. Of course, from the beginning of the scan line until the first intersection, and from the last intersection to the end of the scan line, the intensity or color is that specified for the background. For the polygon in Fig. 2–37, the pixels from 0 to 1, 4 to 6 and 8 to 10 on scan line 4 are set at the background color, while those from 1 to 4 and 6 to 8 are set at the polygon intensity or color.

Determining exactly which pixels are to be activated requires some care. Consider the simple rectangular polygon shown in Fig. 2–38. Coordinates of the rectangle are $(1, 1)$, $(5, 1)$, $(5, 4)$, $(1, 4)$. Scan lines 1 to 4 have intersections

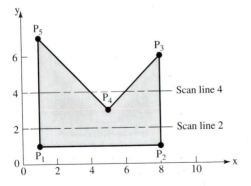

Figure 2–37 Solid area scan conversion.

with the polygon edges at $x = 1$ and 5. Recalling that a pixel is addressed by its center, then for each of the scan lines the pixels with x coordinates of 1, 2, 3, 4 and 5 are activated. The result is shown in Fig. 2–38a. Note that the area covered by the activated pixels is 20 units, while the true area of the rectangle is 12 units. Furthermore, if a new rectangle with coordinates of $(5, 1)$, $(10, 1)$, $(10, 4)$, $(5, 4)$ abuts the original rectangle, the pixels forming the left-hand edge overwrite those of the right edge of the original rectangle. If the two rectangles are different colors and the pixels are activated using **xor** mode, strange colors result.

Modification of the scan line coordinate system and the activation test corrects this problem. This is shown in Fig. 2–38b. The scan lines are considered to pass through the top edge of the row of pixels, i.e., at the half interval, as shown in Fig. 2–38b. The test for activation is modified to consider whether the right edge of the pixel at the right intersection is within the interval. However, the pixels are still addressed by the center coordinates. This technique yields the correct result, as shown in Fig. 2–38b.

In effect the half scan line right edge technique ignores the top and right edges of the polygon in the interest of properly handling adjacent polygons. Occasionally this results in artifacts, for example an unactivated pixel which results in a 'hole' between adjacent polygons. These artifacts are yet another manifestation of the aliasing that results from digitizing what is essentially a continuous analog signal with infinite frequency (see Sec. 2–16).

Horizontal edges cannot intersect a scan line and are thus ignored. This does not mean that horizontal edges are not formed. They are formed by the bottom and top edges of the rows of pixels. This is also illustrated in Fig. 2–38. Figure 2–38b illustrates that the modified scan line coordinate system yields the correct top and bottom edge for the polygon.

An additional difficulty occurs when a scan line intersects the polygon precisely at a vertex. Figure 2–39 illustrates this problem. Using the half scan line

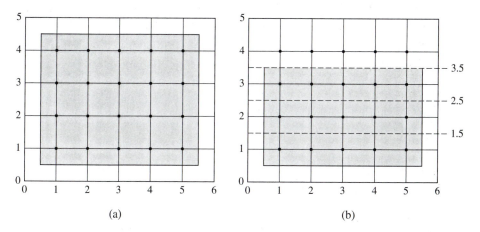

(a)   (b)

Figure 2–38   Scan line coordinate systems.

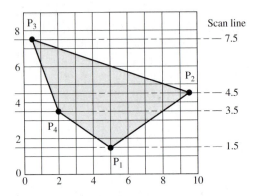

Figure 2–39   Scan line intersection singularities.

convention, the scan line at $y = 3.5$ intersects the polygon at 2, 2 and 8. This is an odd number of intersections. Hence, extracting the pixels in pairs yields an incorrect result; i.e., the pixels at $(0, 3)$ and $(1, 3)$ are set at the background color, the pixel at $(2, 3)$ at the polygon color, those from $(3, 3)$ to $(7, 3)$ at the background color and those at $(8, 3)$ and $(9, 3)$ at the polygon color. Observation suggests that at a scan line–polygon vertex intersection only one intersection should be counted. For the scan line at $y = 3.5$, this gives the correct result. However, examining the scan line at $y = 1.5$, which has two intersections at $(5, 1)$, shows that this technique is incorrect. For this scan line, extracting the pixels in pairs yields the correct result; i.e., only the pixel at $(5, 1)$ is set to the polygon color. If only one intersection is counted at the vertex, then the pixels from $(0, 1)$ to $(4, 1)$ are set at the background color, and those from $(5, 1)$ to $(9, 1)$ are set at the polygon color.

The correct result is obtained by counting two intersections when the scan line–polygon vertex intersections occur at local maxima or minima of the polygon, and only one if not. Whether the vertex under consideration is a local polygon maximum or minimum can be determined by examining the end points of the two edges meeting at the vertex. If the y values of these edges are both greater than the vertex being considered, then the vertex is a local minimum. If both are less than the vertex being considered, then the vertex is a local maximum. If one is greater and one less, then the vertex is neither a local minimum nor a local maximum. In Fig. 2–39, P_1 is a local minimum, P_3 a local maximum and P_2 and P_4 are neither local maxima nor minima. Hence, two scan line intersections are counted at P_1 and P_3 and only one at P_2 and P_4.

2–11   A Simple Parity Scan Conversion Algorithm

A simple polygon scan conversion algorithm that takes advantage of the fact that scan line polygon intersections occur in pairs uses a flag called a parity bit, to determine whether a particular pixel on a scan line is inside or outside the polygon. At the beginning of the scan line, the parity bit is set to zero to indicate that the scan line is outside the polygon. At the first intersection of the scan line and the polygon the parity bit is flipped to one, indicating that the scan line is now inside the polygon. At the next intersection, the parity bit is flipped back to zero to indicate the scan line has passed out of the polygon. When the parity bit is zero, pixels on the scan line are set to the background color; when the parity bit is one, pixels are set to the polygon color. Figure 2–40 illustrates the parity for two scan lines for a simple concave polygon. Using the half scan line convention, intersections for scan line 2, calculated at $y = 2.5$, are $x = 1, 8$. For scan line 4, calculated at $y = 4.5$, the intersections are $x = 1, 3.5, 6.5, 8$. At each intersection the parity changes, as shown below the polygon in Fig. 2–40. The pseudocode subroutine here implements a simple parity scan conversion algorithm.

A simple parity polygon scan conversion algorithm

sub Paritysc(y, left, right, numint, stack)

prior to calling paritysc, the intersections on a scan line are sorted into scanline order and pushed onto a stack. paritysc is then called for each scan line

    y   =   *the current scan line value*

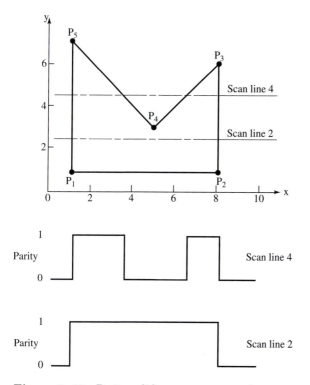

Figure 2–40   Parity solid area scan conversion.

```
left       =   the starting value for the left most pixel
right      =   the ending value for the right most pixel
numint     =   the number of intersections on the scan line
stack      =   contains the intersections sorted in scan line order
x          =   the current pixel on the scan line
```

Pop *is a function that removes intersection values from a stack*

initialize the variables
```
i = 1
parity = 0
oldparity = parity
oldxi = left − 1
x = left
```
Pop stack(xi)   *get the first intersection value*
for x *in the range* left ≤ x ≤ right *on the scan line*
while x ≤ right

    for each intersection on the scan line
    while i ≤ numint

        notice the rounding so that the right side of the pixel is checked
        xi = oldxi   *takes care of duplicate intersection values*
        if x ≥ int(xi + 0.5) **or** xi = oldxi **then**
            oldparity = parity
            parity = parity + 1
            if parity > 1 **then** parity = 0
            oldxi = xi
            i = i + 1
            Pop stack(xi)   *get the next intersection value*
        end if
        if parity = 1 **and** x + 0.5 ≤ xi **then**
            call setpixel (x, y, red, green, blue)
        end if
        x = x + 1
        if x ≥ right **then** i = i + 1
    end while
    x = x + 1
end while
end sub
```

The results of scan conversion of the polygons in Figs. 2–27 and 2–39 are shown in Figs. 2–41a and 2–41b, respectively. Notice that, as expected, the scan converted polygon lies to the left and below the actual polygon. This is a consequence of the decision to use center pixel addressing, and to bias the scan conversion algorithm to neglect the right and top edges of the polygon.
```

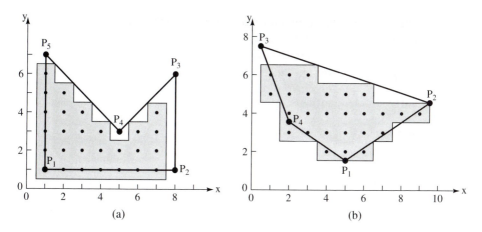

Figure 2–41   Parity scan converted polygons.

However, recalling from algebraic geometry (see, e.g., O'Rourke [ORou94]) that the area of an arbitrary convex or concave polygon with n counterclockwise-specified vertices is

$$A_p = \frac{1}{2} \sum_{i=1}^{n} (x_i y_{i+1} - y_i x_{i+1})$$

shows that the error in the area of the scan converted polygons is acceptable. Specifically, the actual area of the polygon in Fig. 2–41a is 26.5; and the scan converted area is 27, or a 1.9% error. Similarly, the actual area of the polygon in Fig. 2–41b is 24.75, and the scan converted area is 26 for an error of 5%. The error decreases with increasing resolution of the display.

All the scan conversion algorithms are very sensitive to the placement of $<$, $=$ or $>$ signs. For example, replacing the $\geq$ sign with a simple $>$ sign in the simple parity scan conversion algorithm significantly changes the results. Specifically, if the line

if x $\geq$ int(xi + 0.5) or xi = oldxi then

is replaced with

if x $>$ int(xi + 0.5) or xi = oldxi then

the pixels $(1, 1)$, $(1, 2)$, $(1, 3)$, $(1, 4)$, $(1, 5)$, $(1, 6)$ and $(6, 3)$ in Fig. 2–41a are not activated. The scan converted area is now 20 instead of 27, or an error of 24.5%. Similarly pixels $(1, 6)$, $(1, 5)$, $(4, 2)$ and $(2, 3)$ are not activated in Fig. 2–41b, increasing the area error to 11%.

2–12   Ordered Edge List Polygon Scan Conversion

Alternate techniques for efficiently scan-converting solid area polygons are the so-called ordered edge list algorithms. They depend upon sorting the polygon edge-scan line intersections into scan line order. The efficiency of the algorithms depend on the efficiency of the sorting.

A Simple Ordered Edge List Algorithm

A particularly simple algorithm is

A simple ordered edge list algorithm:

Prepare the data:

Determine for each polygon edge the intersections with the half interval scan lines. A Bresenham or DDA algorithm can be used for this. Horizontal edges are ignored. Store each intersection $(x, y+1/2)$ in a list.

Sort the list by scan line and increasing x on the scan line; i.e., (x_1, y_1) precedes (x_2, y_2) if $y_1 > y_2$ or $y_1 = y_2$ and $x_1 \leq x_2$.

Scan-convert the data:

Extract pairs of elements from the sorted list (x_1, y_1) and (x_2, y_2). The structure of the list ensures that $y = y_1 = y_2$ and $x_1 \leq x_2$. Activate pixels on the scan line y for integer values of x such that $x_1 \leq x + 1/2 \leq x_2$.

Example 2–8   Simple Ordered Edge List

Consider the polygon shown in Fig. 2–37. The polygon vertices are $P_1(1,1)$, $P_2(8,1)$, $P_3(8,6)$, $P_4(5,3)$ and $P_5(1,7)$. Intersections with the half interval scan lines are

scan line 1.5:   (8, 1.5), (1, 1.5)
scan line 2.5:   (8, 2.5), (1, 2.5)
scan line 3.5:   (8, 3.5), (5.5, 3.5), (4.5, 3.5), (1, 3.5)
scan line 4.5:   (8, 4.5), (6.5, 4.5), (3.5, 4.5), (1, 4.5)
scan line 5.5:   (8, 5.5), (7.5, 5.5), (2.5, 5.5), (1, 5.5)
scan line 6.5:   (1.5, 6.5), (1, 6.5)
scan line 7.5:   none

The complete list sorted in scan line order from the top to the bottom and then from left to right is

(1, 6.5), (1.5, 6.5), (1, 5.5), (2.5, 5.5), (7.5, 5.5), (8, 5.5), (1, 4.5),
(3.5, 4.5), (6.5, 4.5), (8, 4.5), (1, 3.5), (4.5, 3.5), (5.5, 3.5), (8, 3.5)
(1, 2.5), (8, 2.5), (1, 1.5), (8, 1.5)

Extracting pairs of intersections from the list and applying the algorithm given above yields the pixel activation list

$(1, 6)$

$(1, 5), (2, 5), (7, 5)$

$(1, 4), (2, 4), (3, 4), (6, 4), (7, 4)$

$(1, 3), (2, 3), (3, 3), (4, 3), (5, 3), (6, 3), (7, 3)$

$(1, 2,,) (2, 2), (3, 2), (4, 2), (5, 2), (6, 2), (7, 2)$

$(1, 1), (2, 1), (3, 1), (4, 1), (5, 1), (6, 1), (7, 1)$

The result is shown in Fig. 2–42. Notice that both vertical edges and the bottom edge are given correctly, and that the scan-converted area is biased to the left and downward, as expected. Also notice that the scan conversion is *not* the same as for the simple parity algorithm (see Fig. 2–41a). This does not mean that one algorithm is better than the other, only that they are different.

More Efficient Ordered Edge List Algorithms

The simple algorithm given in the previous section generates a large list which must be sorted. Making the sort more efficient improves the algorithm. This is accomplished by separating the vertical scan line sort in y from the horizontal scan line sort in x by using a y bucket sort, as previously discussed in Sec. 2–7. In particular, the algorithm is now:

A more efficient ordered edge list algorithm:

Prepare the data:

Determine for each polygon edge the intersections with the half interval scan lines, i.e., at $y + \frac{1}{2}$. A Bresenham or DDA algorithm can be used for this. Ignore horizontal edges. Place the x coordinate of the intersection in the bucket corresponding to y.

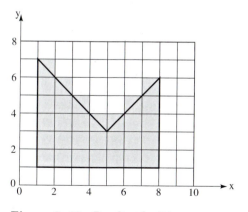

Figure 2–42   Results of solid area scan conversion of Fig. 2–37.

As each scan line is addressed, i.e., for each y bucket, sort the list of x intersections into increasing order; i.e., x_1 precedes x_2 if $x_1 \leq x_2$.

Scan-convert the data:

For each scan line, extract pairs of intersections from the x-sorted list. Activate pixels on the scan line y corresponding to that bucket for integer values of x such that $x_1 \leq x + \frac{1}{2} \leq x_2$.

This algorithm first sorts into scan line order with the y bucket sort, and then into order on the scan line. Thus, scan conversion begins prior to completion of the full sorting process. Also, with this algorithm it is easier to add or delete information from the display list, because it is only necessary to add or delete information from the appropriate y buckets. Hence, only the individual scan lines affected by the change need be resorted. An example further illustrates the algorithm.

Example 2–9   A More Efficient Ordered Edge List

Reconsider the polygon shown in Fig. 2–37 and discussed in Ex. 2–8. First, y buckets for scan lines 0 to 8 are established as shown in Fig. 2–43. The intersections obtained by considering each edge in turn, counterclockwise from P_1, are also shown in the buckets in Fig. 2–43a, unsorted in x. The intersections were calculated using the half scan line technique. For illustrative purposes, they are also shown sorted in Fig. 2–43b. In practice, a small scan line buffer such as is shown in Fig. 2–43c can be used to contain the x-sorted intersection values. This allows more efficient additions to, or deletions from, the intersection list. They can simply be added to the end of each y bucket list, because the x sort does not take place until an individual scan line is moved to the scan line buffer. Hence, a completely sorted y bucket list does not need to be maintained.

Extracting pairs of intersections from the x-sorted list and applying the algorithm above yields the pixel activation list for each scan line. The result is the same as in Ex. 2–8 and is shown in Fig. 2–42.

Although this second algorithm simplifies the sorting task, it either limits the number of intersections on a given scan line or requires the allocation of large amounts of storage, much of which may not be used. By using a linked list, this problem is overcome at the expense of additional data structure. The precalculation of the intersection of each scan line with each polygon edge is time-consuming. It also requires the storage of considerable data. By introducing an active edge list, as previously discussed for real-time scan conversion (see Sec. 2–7), data storage is further reduced and scan line intersections can be calculated incrementally. The resulting algorithm is:

An ordered edge list algorithm using an active edge list:

Prepare the data:

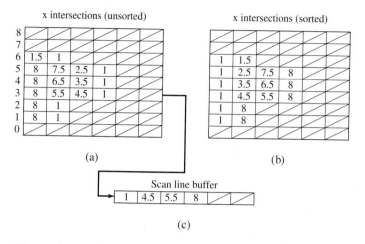

x intersections (unsorted)

x intersections (sorted)

(a)

(b)

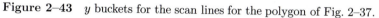

Scan line buffer

(c)

Figure 2–43 y buckets for the scan lines for the polygon of Fig. 2–37.

For each polygon edge, determine using the half interval scan lines, i.e., $y + \frac{1}{2}$, the highest scan lines intersected by the edge.

Place the polygon edge in the y bucket corresponding to the scan line.

Store the initial x intersection value, the number of scan lines crossed by the polygon edge, Δy, and the x increment, Δx, from scan line to scan line in a linked list.

Scan-convert the data:

For each scan line, examine the corresponding y bucket for any new edges; add any new edges to the active edge list.

Sort the x intercepts from the active edge list into increasing order, i.e., x_1 precedes x_2 if $x_1 \le x_2$.

Extract pairs of intersections from the sorted x list. Activate pixels on the scan line y for integer values of x such that $x_1 \le x + \frac{1}{2} \le x_2$. For each edge on the active edge list, decrement Δy by 1. If $\Delta y < 0$, drop the edge from the active edge list. Calculate the new x intercept, $x_{\text{new}} = x_{\text{old}} + \Delta x$.

Advance to the next scan line.

This algorithm assumes that all data has been previously converted to a polygonal representation. Heckbert [Heck90a] presents code for a similar algorithm. Whitted [Whit81] gives a more general algorithm which removes this restriction.

Example 2–10 Ordered Edge List with an Active Edge List

Again consider the simple polygon shown in Fig. 2–37. Examining the list of polygon edges shows that scan line 5 is the highest scan line intersected by edges P_2P_3 and P_3P_4, and scan line 6 is the highest intersected by edges P_4P_5 and P_5P_1. The structure of the linked list containing data for the nine y buckets corresponding to the nine scan lines (0 to 8) of Fig. 2–37 is shown conceptually in Fig. 2–44a.

Notice that most of the buckets are empty. A practical implementation is shown in Fig. 2–44b. Here, the y bucket list is a one-dimensional array, one element for each scan line. The array element corresponding to each scan line bucket contains only a simple pointer into the data array used for the linked list, which is also shown in Fig. 2–44b.

The linked list is implemented as an $n \times 4$ array. For each array index n, the four elements contain the x intersection for a polygon edge, with the highest scan line crossed by that edge; the increment, Δx, from scan line to scan line for that polygon edge; the number of scan lines crossed by the polygon edge, Δy; and the link pointer to the list address for data for the next polygon edge beginning on that scan line. This is shown in Fig. 2–44b. Note that the y bucket for scan line 5 contains the link pointer 1, which corresponds to the first address in the linked data list. The first three columns in the linked data list contain data about the edge P_2P_3. The number in the fourth column is the link pointer to the next data address.

The active edge list is implemented as an $n \times 3$ stack array. The contents of the active edge list are shown for all nine scan lines in Fig. 2–44c. The scan lines (y buckets) are examined sequentially from the top of the picture starting with scan line 8. Since the y buckets for scan lines 8 and 7 are empty, the active edge list is also empty. Scan line 6 adds two elements to the active edge list, and scan line 5 two more. At scan line 2, Δy for edges P_3P_4 and P_4P_5 becomes less than zero; hence, these edges are dropped from the active edge list. Similarly, edges P_2P_3 and P_5P_1 are dropped at scan line 0. Finally, note that at scan line 0 the y bucket is empty, that the active edge list is empty and that there are no further y buckets. Hence, the algorithm is complete.

For each scan line, the x intersections of the active edges for that scan line are extracted from the active edge list, sorted into increasing x order and placed in a span buffer implemented as a $1 \times n$ array. From the span buffer, the intersections are extracted in pairs. The active pixel list is then determined using the earlier algorithm. The combined pixel list for all the scan lines is the same as in the previous examples. Again, the result is shown in Fig. 2–37.

2–13 The Edge Fill Algorithm

The ordered edge list algorithm is very powerful. Each pixel in the display is visited only once, hence the input/output requirements are minimized. The end points of each group or span of active pixels are calculated before output. This allows the use of a shading algorithm along the span to obtain fully shaded pictures. Since the algorithm is independent of the input/output details, it is device independent. The algorithm's main disadvantage is the expense associated

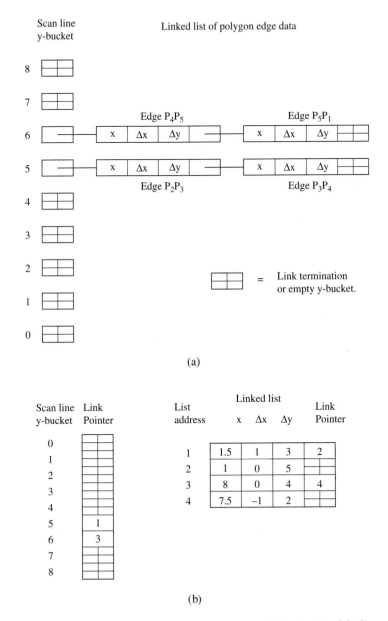

Figure 2–44 Linked list for the polygon of Fig. 2–37. (a) Conceptual structure; (b) implemented as a one-dimensional array; (c) active edge lists.

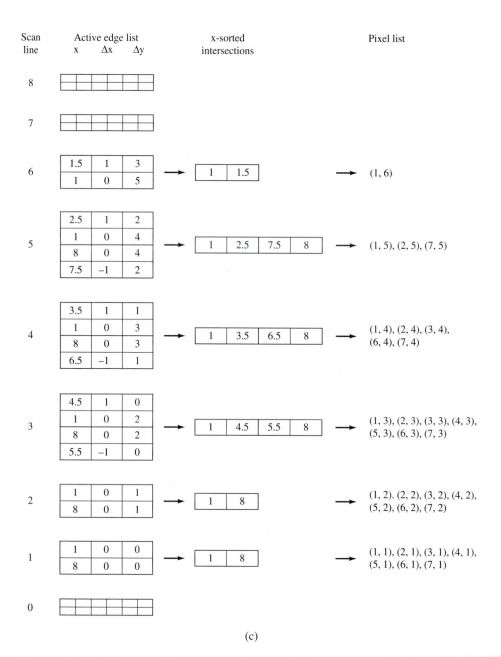

(c)

Figure 2–44 (*Continued.*)

with maintaining and sorting the various lists. An alternate solid area scan conversion technique, called the edge fill algorithm [Ackl80], eliminates most of these lists. The edge fill algorithm is very simple.

Edge fill algorithm

For each scan line intersecting a polygon edge at (x_1, y_1) complement all pixels whose midpoints lie to the right of (x_1, y_1), i.e., for (x, y_1), $x + \frac{1}{2} > x_1$.

The half scan line convention is used to calculate the scan line–edge intersections. The algorithm is applied to each polygon edge individually. The order in which the polygon edges are considered is unimportant. Figure 2–45 shows the various stages in scan-converting the solid area of the example polygon of Fig. 2–37. Notice that the activated pixels are the same as those for the simple parity algorithm (see Sec. 2–11) but are not the same as for the ordered edge list algorithm. In particular, the edge fill algorithm does not activate pixels at $(5, 3)$, $(6, 4)$, $(7, 5)$; i.e., the edge $P_3 P_4$ is rasterized differently. The difference is in the way pixels that are exactly half inside and half outside the polygon are handled. The ordered edge list algorithm always activates these pixels. The edge fill algorithm activates them only if the inside of the polygon lies to the left of the center of the pixel.

The algorithm is most conveniently used with a frame buffer. This allows the polygon edges to be considered in completely arbitrary order. As each edge is considered, the appropriate pixels in the frame buffer corresponding to an

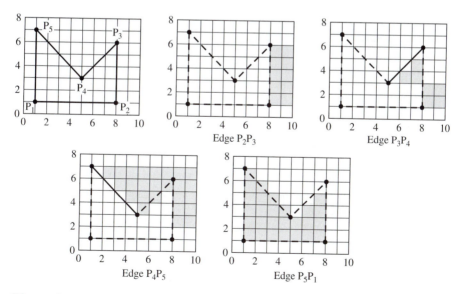

Figure 2–45 Edge fill algorithm.

edge-scan line intersection are addressed. After all edges are considered, the frame buffer is transferred to the display device in scan line order. Figure 2–45 illustrates the main disadvantages of the algorithm; i.e., for complex pictures each individual pixel is addressed many times. Hence, the algorithm is limited by input/output considerations.

The number of pixels addressed by the edge fill algorithm is reduced by introducing a fence [Dunl83]; this is the fence fill algorithm. The basic idea is illustrated in Fig. 2–46, again using the example polygon of Fig. 2–37. In particular, the fence fill algorithm is:

> The fence fill algorithm:
>
> > For each scan line intersecting a polygon edge:
> >
> > > If the intersection is to the left of the fence, complement all pixels having a midpoint to the right of the intersection of the scan line and the edge, and to the left of the fence.
> > >
> > > If the intersection is to the right of the fence, complement all pixels having a midpoint to the left of or on the intersection of the scan line and the edge, and to the right of the fence.

The half scan line conversion is used. A convenient fence location is usually one of the polygon vertices. Again, the algorithm is most conveniently used with a frame buffer. The disadvantage of both the edge fill and fence fill algorithms is the number of pixels addressed more than once. This disadvantage is eliminated

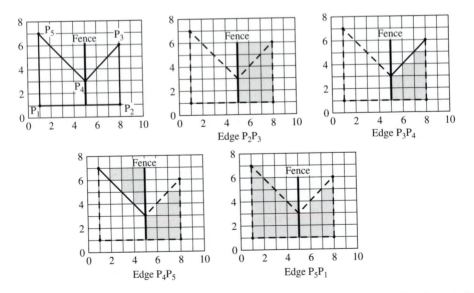

Figure 2–46 Fence fill algorithm.

by a modification called the edge flag algorithm [Ackl81]. The edge fill, fence fill and edge flag algorithms are not limited to simple polygons.

2–14   The Edge Flag Algorithm

The edge flag algorithm [Ackl81] is a two-step process. The first step is to outline the contour. This establishes pairs of span-bounding pixels on each scan line. The second step is to fill between these bounding pixels. The algorithm is more explicitly stated as:

> The edge flag algorithm:
>
> > Contour outline:
> >
> > > Using the half scan line convention for each edge intersecting the scan line, set the leftmost pixel whose midpoint lies to the right of the intersection, i.e., for $x + \frac{1}{2} > x_{\text{intersection}}$, to the boundary value.
> >
> > Fill:
> >
> > > For each scan line intersecting the polygon
> > >   Inside = FALSE
> > >   **for** x = 0 (left) to x = x$_{\text{max}}$ (right)
> > >   **if** the pixel at x is set to the boundary value **then**
> > >   negate Inside
> > >   **end if**
> > >   **if** Inside = TRUE **then**
> > >   set the pixel at x to the polygon value
> > >   **else**
> > >   reset the pixel at x to the background value
> > >   **end if**
> > >   **next** x

Example 2–11   Edge Flag Algorithm

Consider the application of the edge flag algorithm to the example polygon of Fig. 2–34. First the contour is outlined. The result is shown in Fig. 2–42a. Pixels at $(1,1)$, $(1,2)$, $(1,3)$, $(1,4)$, $(1,5)$, $(1,6)$, $(2,6)$, $(3,5)$, $(4,4)$, $(5,3)$, $(6,3)$, $(7,4)$, $(8,4)$, $(8,3)$, $(8,2)$, $(8,1)$ are activated.

The polygon is then filled. To illustrate this the scan line at 3 is extracted and shown in Fig. 2–47b. Pixels at $x = 1$, 5, 6, and 8 on this scan line are activated to outline the contour. Applying the fill algorithm yields

Initially

Inside = FALSE

For $x = 0$ The pixel is not set to the boundary value and Inside = FALSE. Therefore, no action is taken.

For $x = 1$	The pixel is set to the boundary value, Inside is negated to TRUE. Inside = TRUE, so the pixel is set to the polygon value.
For $x = 2, 3, 4$	The pixel is not set to the boundary value. Inside = TRUE, so the pixel is set to the polygon value.
For $x = 5$	The pixel is set to the boundary value, Inside is negated to FALSE. Inside = FALSE, so the pixel is set to the background value.
For $x = 6$	The pixel is set to the boundary value, Inside is negated to TRUE. Inside = TRUE, so the pixel is set to the polygon value.
For $x = 7$	The pixel is not set to the boundary value. Inside = TRUE, so the pixel is set to the polygon value.
For $x = 8$	The pixel is set to the boundary value, Inside is negated to FALSE. Inside = FALSE, so the pixel is set to the background.

The result is shown in Fig. 2–47c. The final result for the complete polygon is the same as for the edge fill algorithm as it is shown in Fig. 2–45.

The edge flag algorithm visits each pixel only once. Hence, the input/output requirements are considerably less than for the edge fill or fence fill algorithms. When used with a frame buffer, none of these algorithms requires building, maintaining and sorting edge lists. Implemented in software, the ordered edge list and the edge flag algorithms execute at about the same speed [Whit81]. However, the edge flag algorithm is suitable for hardware or firmware implementation,

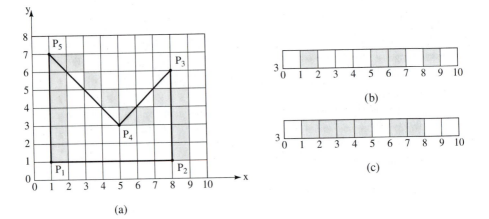

(a)

(b)

(c)

Figure 2–47 Edge flag algorithm.

where it executes one to two orders of magnitude faster than the ordered edge list algorithm [Ackl81].

2–15   Seed Fill Algorithms

The algorithms discussed in the previous sections fill the polygon in scan line order. A different approach is used in the seed fill algorithms. The seed fill algorithms assume that at least one pixel interior to a polygon or region is known. The algorithm then attempts to find and color or fill all other pixels interior to the region. Regions may be either interior- or boundary-defined. If a region is interior-defined, then all the pixels in the interior of the region are one color or value, and all the pixels exterior to the region are another, as shown in Fig. 2–48. If a region is boundary-defined, then all the pixels on the region boundary are a unique value or color, as shown in Fig. 2–49. None of the pixels interior to the region can have this unique value. However, pixels exterior to the boundary can have the boundary value. Algorithms that fill interior-defined regions are referred to as flood fill algorithms, and those that fill boundary-defined regions are known as boundary fill algorithms. The discussion in this section concentrates on boundary fill algorithms. However, the companion flood fill algorithms are developed in an analogous manner.

Interior- or boundary-defined regions are either 4-connected or 8-connected. If a region is 4-connected, then every pixel in the region can be reached by a combination of moves in only four directions: left, right, up, down. For an 8-connected region, every pixel in the region is reached by a combination of moves in the two horizontal, two vertical and four diagonal directions. An 8-connected algorithm fills a 4-connected region, but a 4-connected algorithm does not fill an 8-connected region. Simple examples of 4-, and 8-connected interior-defined regions are shown in Fig. 2–50. Although each of the subregions of the 8-connected region shown in Fig. 2–50b is 4-connected, passage from one subregion to the other requires an 8-connected algorithm. However, if each of the subregions is a separate 4-connected region, each to be filled with a separate color or value, then use of an 8-connected algorithm causes both regions to be incorrectly filled with a single color or value.

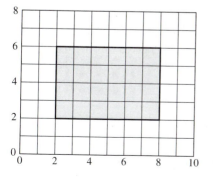

Figure 2–48   Interior-defined region.

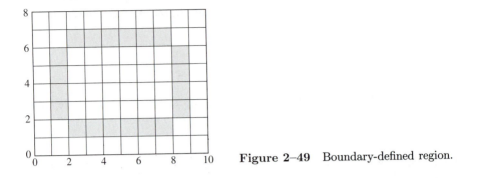

Figure 2–49 Boundary-defined region.

Figure 2–51 redefines the 8-connected region of Fig. 2–50 as a boundary-defined region. Figure 2–51 illustrates that when a region is 8-connected, where the two subregions touch at the corners, the boundary is 4-connected. It also illustrates that for 4-connected regions, the boundary is 8-connected. The discussion in Secs. 2–24 and 2–25 concentrates on 4-connected algorithms. The equivalent 8-connected algorithms are easily obtained by attempting to fill in eight, rather than four, directions.

A Simple Seed Fill Algorithm

A simple seed fill algorithm for a boundary-defined region can be developed using a stack. A stack is simply an array, or other storage space, into which values are sequentially placed, or from which they are sequentially removed. As new values are added to or pushed onto the stack, all previously stored values are pushed down one level. As values are removed or popped from the stack, previously stored values float or pop up one level. Such a stack is referred to as a first in, last out (FILO), or push-down, stack. A simple seed fill algorithm is then:

Simple seed fill algorithm using a stack:

Push the seed pixel onto the stack

while the stack is not empty

Pop a pixel from the stack

Set the pixel to the required value

For each of the 4-connected pixels adjacent to the current pixel, check if it is a boundary pixel, or if it has already been set to the

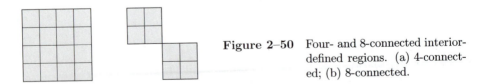

Figure 2–50 Four- and 8-connected interior-defined regions. (a) 4-connected; (b) 8-connected.

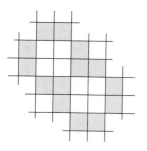

Figure 2–51   Four- and 8-connected boundary-defined regions.

required value. In either case, ignore it. Otherwise, push it onto the stack.

The algorithm can be modified for 8-connected regions by looking at the 8-connected pixels rather than only the 4-connected pixels. A more formal statement of the algorithm, assuming the existence of a seed pixel and a boundary-defined region, is

simple seed fill algorithm *for 4-connected boundary-defined regions*

Seed(x, y) *is the seed pixel*
Push *is a function for placing a pixel on the stack*
Pop *is a function for removing a pixel from the stack*
Pixel(x, y) = Seed(x, y)
initialize stack
Push Pixel(x, y)
while (stack not empty)

    get a pixel from the stack
    Pop Pixel(x, y)
    if Pixel(x, y) $<>$ New value **then**
        Pixel(x, y) = New value
    end if

    examine the surrounding pixels to see if they should be placed onto the stack
    if (Pixel(x + 1, y) $<>$ New value **and**
        Pixel(x + 1, y) $<>$ Boundary value) **then**
        Push Pixel(x + 1, y)
    end if
    if (Pixel(x, y + 1) $<>$ New value **and**
        Pixel(x, y + 1) $<>$ Boundary value) **then**
        Push Pixel(x, y + 1)
    end if
    if (Pixel(x − 1, y) $<>$ New value **and**
        Pixel(x − 1, y) $<>$ Boundary value) **then**
        Push Pixel(x − 1, y)

> **end if**
> **if** (Pixel(x, y − 1) < > New value **and**
>   Pixel(x, y − 1) < > Boundary value) **then**
>   **Push** Pixel(x, y − 1)
> **end if**
> **end while**

The algorithm examines the 4-connected pixels and pushes them onto the stack counterclockwise beginning with the pixel to the right of the current pixel.

Example 2–12   Simple Seed Fill Algorithm

As an example of the application of the algorithm consider the boundary-defined polygonal region defined by the vertices $(1,1)$, $(8,1)$ $(8,4)$, $(6,6)$, and $(1,6)$ as shown in Fig. 2–52. The seed pixel is at $(4,3)$. The algorithm fills the polygon pixel by pixel as shown by the line in Fig. 2–52 with the arrows. The numbers in each pixel give the stack location of the pixel as the algorithm proceeds. Notice that some pixels contain more than one number. This indicates that the pixel is pushed onto the stack more than once. When the algorithm reaches pixel $(5,5)$ the stack is 23 levels deep and contains the pixels $(7,4)$, $(7,3)$, $(7,2)$, $(7,1)$, $(6,2)$, $(6,3)$, $(5,6)$, $(6,4)$, $(5,5)$, $(4,4)$, $(3,4)$, $(3,5)$, $(2,4)$, $(2,3)$, $(2,2)$, $(3,2)$, $(5,1)$, $(3,2)$, $(5,2)$, $(3,3)$, $(4,4)$, $(5,3)$.

Because all of the pixels surrounding that at $(5,5)$ contain either boundary values or new values, none are pushed onto the stack. Hence, pixel $(7,4)$ is popped off of the stack, and the algorithm fills the column $(7,4)$, $(7,3)$, $(7,2)$, $(7,1)$. When pixel $(7,1)$ is reached, again the surrounding pixels either already contain the new value or are boundary pixels. Because the polygon is completely filled at this point, popping pixels from the stack until it is empty causes no additional pixels to be filled. When the stack is empty, the algorithm is complete.

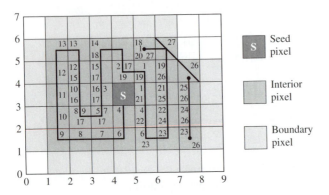

Figure 2–52   Seed fill using a simple stack algorithm.

The polygon in Example 2–12 is a simple open region. The algorithm also properly fills regions containing holes. This is illustrated in the next example.

Example 2–13   Simple Seed Fill Algorithm for Polygon with a Hole

As an example of the application of the algorithm to a polygonal boundary-defined region containing a hole, consider Fig. 2–53. Here, the exterior polygon vertices are the same as in the previous example, i.e., $(1, 1)$, $(8, 1)$, $(8, 4)$, $(6, 6)$, and $(1, 6)$. The interior hole is defined by $(3, 2)$, $(6, 2)$, $(6, 4)$, $(3, 4)$. The seed pixel is at $(4, 4)$. Because of the interior hole, the algorithm fills the polygon along a quite different path than in Ex. 2–12. This new path is shown by the arrowed line in Fig. 2–53. Again, the numbers in each pixel give the stack location as the algorithm proceeds. When the algorithm reaches pixel $(3, 1)$ all the 4-connected surrounding pixels either contain the new value or are boundary pixels. Hence, no pixels are pushed onto the stack. At this point the stack is 14 levels deep. It contains the pixels $(7, 1)$, $(7, 2)$, $(7, 3)$, $(6, 5)$, $(7, 4)$, $(6, 5)$, $(3, 1)$, $(1, 2)$, $(1, 3)$, $(1, 4)$, $(2, 5)$, $(3, 5)$, $(4, 5)$, $(5, 4)$.

After popping the pixel $(7, 1)$ from the stack, the algorithm fills the column $(7, 1)$, $(7, 2)$, $(7, 3)$, $(7, 4)$ without pushing any additional pixels onto the stack. At pixel $(7, 4)$, again all 4-connected surrounding pixels contain either the new value or are boundary pixels. Returning to the stack, the algorithm finds no new pixels until that at $(6, 5)$. Filling the pixel at $(6, 5)$ completes the polygon fill. The algorithm completes processing of the stack without further filling. When the stack is empty, the algorithm is complete.

A Scan Line Seed Fill Algorithm

Both of the examples in Sec. 2–15 show that the stack can become quite large. They also show that the stack frequently contains duplicate or unnecessary information. An algorithm which minimizes stack size attempts to seed only one pixel in any uninterrupted scan line span [Smit79]. This is called a scan line seed fill algorithm. An uninterrupted span is a group of contiguous pixels on a single scan line. Here, a heuristic approach is used to develop the algorithm. A more theoretical approach, based on graph theory, is also possible [Shan80].

The scan line seed fill algorithm is applicable to boundary-defined regions. The 4-connected boundary-defined region may be either convex or concave, and it may contain one or more holes. The region exterior to and adjacent to the boundary-defined region may not contain pixels with a value or color corresponding to the one used to fill the region or polygon. Conceptually, the algorithm works in four steps.

Scan line seed fill algorithm:

A seed pixel on a span is popped from a stack containing the seed pixel.

The span containing the seed pixel is filled to the right and left of the seed pixel along a scan line, until a boundary is found.

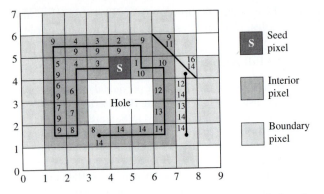

Figure 2–53 Seed fill of a region containing a hole using a simple stack algorithm.

The algorithm remembers the extreme left and the extreme right pixels in the span as $Xleft$ and $Xright$.

In the range of $Xleft \leq x \leq Xright$, the scan lines immediately above and immediately below the current scan line are examined to see if they completely contain either boundary pixels or previously filled pixels. If these scan lines do not contain either boundary or previously filled pixels, then in the range $Xleft \leq x \leq Xright$ the extreme right pixel in each span is marked as a seed pixel and pushed onto the stack.

The algorithm is initialized by pushing a single seed pixel onto the stack and is complete when the stack is empty. The algorithm jumps holes and indentations in the region boundary, as shown in Fig. 2–54 and in Ex. 2–14. A more complete statement of the algorithm is given in this pseudocode implementation:

scan line seed fill algorithm

Seed(x, y) *is the seed pixel*
Pop *is a function for removing a pixel from the stack*
Push *is a function for placing a pixel on the stack*

    initialize stack

    Push Seed(x, y)
    while (stack not empty)

        get the seed pixel and set it to the new value

        Pop Pixel(x, y)
        Pixel(x, y) = Fill value

        save the x coordinate of the seed pixel

        Savex = x

        fill the span to the right of the seed pixel

        x = x + 1

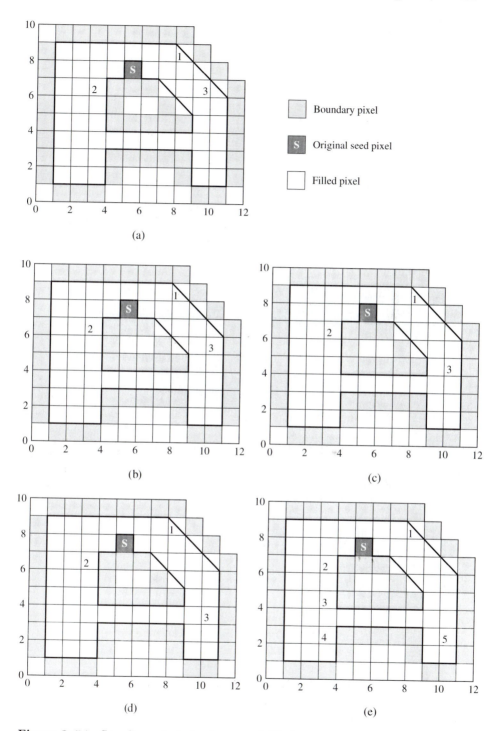

Figure 2–54 Scan-line-oriented polygon seed fill algorithm.

```
    while Pixel(x, y) < > Boundary value
        Pixel(x, y) = Fill value
        x = x + 1
    end while
```

save the extreme right pixel

```
    Xright = x − 1
```

reset the x coordinate to the value for the seed pixel

```
    x = Savex
```

fill the span to the left of the seed pixel

```
    x = x − 1
    while Pixel(x, y) < > Boundary value
        Pixel(x, y) = Fill value
        x = x − 1
    end while
```

save the extreme left pixel

```
    Xleft = x + 1
```

reset the x coordinate to the value for the seed pixel

```
    x = Savex
```

*check that the scan line above is neither a polygon boundary nor
    has been previously completely filled; if not, seed the scan line*

start at the left edge of the scan line subspan

```
    x = Xleft
    y = y + 1
    while x ≤ Xright
```

seed the scan line above

```
        Pflag = 0
        while (Pixel(x, y) <> Boundary value and
            Pixel(x, y) <> Fill value and x < Xright)
                if Pflag = 0 then Pflag = 1
                x = x + 1
        end while
```

push the extreme right pixel onto the stack

```
        if Pflag = 1 then
            if (x = Xright and Pixel(x, y) <> Boundary value
                and Pixel(x, y) <> Fill value then
                    Push Pixel(x, y)
            else
                    Push Pixel(x − 1, y)
            end if
            Pflag = 0
        end if
```

continue checking in case the span is interrupted

Xenter = x

while ((Pixel(x, y) = Boundary value or Pixel(x, y)
 = Fill value) **and** x < Xright)

   x = x + 1

end while

make sure that the pixel coordinate is incremented

if x = Xenter **then** x = x + 1

end while

*Check that the scan line below is not a polygon boundary
nor has been previously completely filled.*

*this algorithm is exactly the same as that for checking the scan
line above except that $y = y - 1$ is subsitituted for $y = y + 1$*

end while

finish

Here the function **Pop** gets the x, y coordinates of a pixel from the stack, and the function **Push** places them on the stack.

Example 2–14   Scan Line Seed Fill

Consider the application of the preceding algorithm to the boundary-defined polygonal region shown in Fig. 2–54. The algorithm is initialized by pushing the polygon seed pixel, labeled Seed $(5, 7)$ in Fig. 2–54a, onto the stack. This pixel is initially popped from the stack as the span seed. The span containing the seed is then filled to the right and to the left. The span limits are $Xright = 9$ and $Xleft = 1$. The scan line above is then examined. It is neither a boundary pixel nor has it been previously filled. The extreme right-hand pixel in the range $1 \leq x \leq 9$ is $(8, 8)$. This pixel, labeled 1 in Fig. 2–54a, is pushed onto the stack. The scan line below is examined and is determined to be neither a boundary pixel nor a previously filled pixel. Within the range $Xleft \leq x \leq Xright$ there are two subspans. The left subspan is seeded with the pixel $(3, 6)$, labeled 2 in Fig. 2–54a, which is pushed onto the stack. The right subspan is seeded with the pixel $(9, 6)$, which is also pushed onto the stack. Notice that this pixel $(9, 6)$ is not the extreme right pixel in the span. However, it is the extreme right pixel in the range $Xleft \leq x \leq Xright$, i.e., in the range $1 \leq x \leq 9$. One pass through the algorithm is now complete.

The algorithm continues by popping the top pixel from the stack. Here, the algorithm fills spans on the right side of the polygon on successively lower scan lines. The results are shown in Figs. 2–54b to 2–54d. The seed for scan line 3, shown in Fig. 2–54d, is pixel $(10, 3)$. Filling the span to the right and left yields $Xleft = 1$ and $Xright = 10$. Examining the scan line above yields the seed pixel $(3, 4)$ in the left subspan, which is pushed onto the stack. The right subspan is already filled. Examining the scan line below yields the seed pixel $(3, 2)$ for the left subspan and $(10, 2)$ for the right subspan. These pixels are also pushed onto the stack. The maximum stack depth occurs at this scan line.

From here, the algorithm continues to completion with only one additional point of interest. After filling the 4-connected polygonal subregions seeded with the pixels labeled 5, 4 and 3 in Fig. 2–54e, the pixel labeled 2 is popped from the stack. Here, the algorithm finds that all pixels on the seed scan line, on the scan line above and on the scan line below are already filled. Thus, no additional pixels are pushed onto the stack. The algorithm then pops the pixel labeled 1 as the seed pixel and fills the scan line. Again, no additional pixels are pushed onto the stack. The stack is now empty, the polygon is filled and the algorithm is complete.

In comparison with the seed fill algorithm of Sec. 2–15, the maximum stack depth in Ex. 2–14 is five. Other techniques for polygon or region seed fill are discussed by Pavlidis [Pavl82], Heckbert [Heck90b] and Fiskin [Fisk85, 90].

2–16   Fundamentals of Antialiasing

To provide effective antialiasing, it is necessary to understand the causes of aliasing itself. Fundamentally, the appearance of aliasing effects is due to the fact that lines, polygon edges, color boundaries, etc., are continuous, whereas a raster device is discrete. To present the line, polygon edge, etc., on the raster display device, it must be sampled at discrete locations. This can have surprising results; for example, consider a signal as shown in Fig. 2–55a. A second signal of lower frequency is given in Fig. 2–55c. If both signals are sampled or rasterized at the same rate, as shown by the small crosses, then the reconstructed signals are identical; this is illustrated in Figs. 2–55b and 2–55d. Figure 2–55d is called an alias of the sample in Fig. 2–55b, and hence of the signal in Fig. 2–55a. Here, the high-frequency signal (Fig. 2–55a) is undersampled. In order to prevent aliasing, a signal must be sampled at a rate at least twice the highest frequency in the

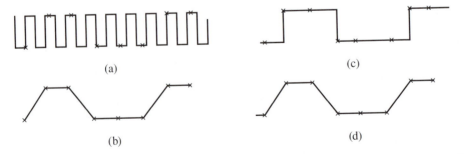

(a)

(c)

(b)

(d)

Figure 2–55   Sampling and aliasing. (a) High frequency signal; (b) reconstruction of the signal in (a) when sampled at the × locations; (c) low frequency signal; (d) reconstruction of the signal in (c) when sampled at the × locations. (d) is an alias of (b).

signal. In signal analysis, this rate is called the Nyquist limit, or frequency. In terms of the period of the signal (period ∝ 1/frequency) the sample interval must be less than half the period. Undersampling causes highly periodic images to be rendered incorrectly. For example, a picket fence or venetian blind might appear as a few broad stripes, rather than many individual smaller stripes.

The previous sections and this discussion illustrate two of three general manifestations of aliasing in computer generated images: jagged edges, and incorrectly rendered fine detail, or texture. The third manifestation occurs for very small objects. If an object is smaller than the size of a pixel, or does not cover the point within a pixel at which the pixel attributes are evaluated, it will not be included in the resulting picture. Alternatively, if the small object covers the point at which the pixel attributes are calculated, it can overly influence those attributes. The left-hand pixel in Fig. 2–56 shows this. If the center of the pixel is used to determine the attributes, then the entire pixel exhibits those of the small object. The right-hand pixels in Fig. 2–56 illustrate objects that are ignored or lost, because none of the objects covers the pixel center. Notice that long, thin objects can also be ignored. These effects are particularly noticeable in animation sequences. Figure 2–57 shows a small triangle in three frames of an animation sequence. If pixel attributes are determined at the pixel center, then in the first frame the object is not visible, in the second it is visible and in the third it is again invisible. In the animation sequence, the small object flashes on and off (scintillates).

Fundamentally, there are two methods of antialiasing. The first is to increase the sample rate. This is accomplished by increasing the resolution of the raster; finer detail is thus included. However, there is a limit to the ability of CRT raster scan devices to display very fine rasters. This limit suggests that the raster be calculated at higher resolution and displayed at lower resolution, using some type of averaging to obtain the pixel attributes at the lower resolution (see [Crow81]). This techniques is called supersampling or postfiltering.

The second method of antialiasing is to treat a pixel as a finite area rather than as a point. First some heuristic techniques are discussed followed by the mathematical foundations. Treating a pixel as a finite area is equivalent to prefiltering the image [Crow81].

Supersampling

In supersampling, or postfiltering, a pseudoraster of higher resolution than the physical raster is superimposed on the physical raster. The image is then rasterized at the higher resolution of the pseudoraster, and groups of subpixels are

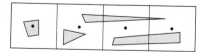

Figure 2–56   Aliasing effects for small objects.

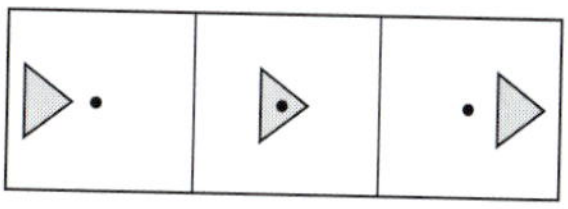

Figure 2–57   Aliasing effects in animation.

averaged to obtain the attributes of individual physical pixels. In general, there are three entities of interest: lines, edges of polygons or surfaces and interiors of polygons or surfaces.

Straight Lines

First, consider straight lines. By dividing each physical pixel into $n \times n$ subpixels and rasterizing the line within the physical pixel, using, for example, the Bresenham algorithm (see Secs. 2–3 to 2–5), we can count the number of activated subpixels. Figure 2–58, where the dashed lines indicate subpixels, illustrates the concept. The intensity of the physical pixel is then made proportional to the ratio of the number of activated subpixels to the total number of possible activated subpixels in a physical pixel. Here, the maximum number of rasterized subpixels on an $n \times n$ pseudoraster is n. Thus, the maximum number of intensities for the line is $n + 1$, including zero. The intensity of the physical pixel of the antialiased line is

$$I_{\text{line}} = \frac{s}{n} I_{\text{max}}$$

where s is the number of rasterized subpixels, and I_{max} is the maximum number of intensities supported by the system.

An alternate technique for antialiasing lines is to consider the line as having finite width, as shown in Fig. 2–59. Here, the line is represented as a rectangle of one physical pixel width. Counting the number of subpixel centers within the rectangle, for each physical pixel compared to $n^2 + 1$ possible intensities, determines the intensity of the physical pixel, i.e.

$$I_{\text{line}} = \frac{s}{n^2} I_{\text{max}}$$

Notice that in contrast to the previous technique, where only $n + 1$ intensities result for n^2 subpixels, here a total of $n^2 + 1$ intensities are possible.

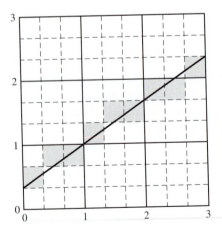

Figure 2–58 Aliasing thin straight lines.

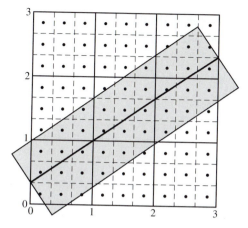

Figure 2–59   Antialiasing finite width straight lines.

For color it is necessary to antialias with respect to the background color. A linear interpolation is commonly used. If (r, g, b) represents a color triplet, then the antialiased pixel color is

$$(r,\ g,\ b)_{\text{pixel}} = (I)(r,\ g,\ b)_{\text{line}} + (1 - I)(r,\ g,\ b)_{\text{background}}$$

In order to determine s, it is necessary to count the number of subpixels that lie within the finite width rectangle representing the line. This requirement is an example of the so-called point-in-the-polygon problem (see Sec. 4–4). Here, a particularly simple technique called the substitution test is used.

Figure 2–60 shows an interior physical pixel along the line, i.e., not at either end of the line. The rectangular strip representing the line is one physical pixel wide, with the line passing through its center. The line lies in the first octant, with slope $0 \le m \le 1$. The square physical pixel is subdivided into nine square subpixels. The centers of the subpixels are marked by $+$ signs.

Because this is an interior physical pixel, the line passes through the pixel. Thus, it is only necessary to determine if the subpixel centers lie between the edges of the rectangular strip, i.e., between the upper and lower edges. (The ends of the line require that the ends of the rectangle also be examined.) For an interior pixel, determining whether the center of a subpixel lies within the rectangular strip is accomplished by using test functions developed from the equations of the lines forming the edges.

The equation of the line itself is

$$y = mx + y_1$$

where y_1 is the intercept of the line, with the left edge of the physical pixel at (x_i, y_i). Because the upper and lower edges are parallel to the line, they have the same slope. The y intercepts are obtained by considering the right triangles shown dashed in Fig. 2–60. The length of the perpendicular from the line to the edge is $1/2$. The perpendicular intercepts the edge a distance $m/2$ from the left edge of the physical pixel, thus

$$\ell = \frac{1}{2}\sqrt{m^2 + 1}$$

The equation of the lower edge is

$$y = mx + y_1 - \ell = mx + y_1 - \frac{1}{2}\sqrt{m^2 - 1}$$

and by symmetry the equation of the upper edge is

$$y = mx + y_1 - \ell = mx + y_1 + \frac{1}{2}\sqrt{m^2 - 1}$$

The test functions are then

$$\text{TF}_L = y - y_1 - mx + \frac{1}{2}\sqrt{m^2 - 1}$$

$$\text{TF}_U = y - y_1 - mx - \frac{1}{2}\sqrt{m^2 - 1}$$

where here, x and y are the coordinates of the point to be tested.

Looking along the edges in Fig. 2–60 from left to right, if the test function is positive, the point lies to the left of the line, and if negative to the right of the line. If the test function is zero, the point lies on the line. Thus, if a point is inside the rectangular strip, $\text{TF}_U \le 0$ and $\text{TF}_L \ge 0$. Notice that if a point is on the line it is assumed to be within the rectangular strip.

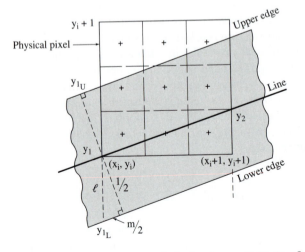

Figure 2–60 Counting subpixels when antialiasing finite width straight lines.

The simple pseudocode algorithm **pxlcnt** counts the number of subpixel centers within the rectangular strip for a given physical pixel. Notice that it takes advantage of the known spacing and location of the subpixel centers within the physical pixel.

Algorithm to count subpixel centers within a physical pixel for antialiasing lines

assumes the pixel is square and divided into n^2 subpixels
assumes the slope of the line is $0 \leq m \leq 1$

n *is the number of divisions on each edge of the physical pixel*
m *is the slope of the line*
x *is the x coordinate of the subpixel center*
y *is the y coordinate of the subpixel center*
y_1 *is the intercept at x_i relative to y_i*

sub pxlcnt$(y_1,n,m,hits)$

   these next four quantities, included here for completeness,
     should be calculated in the calling routine
     outside the calling loop for efficiency

   constant $= \left(\text{sqr}(m*m+1)\right)/2$
   increment $= 1/n$
   xstart $=$ increment$/2$
   xstop $= 1 -$ xstart
   ystart $= y_1 - 3*$increment
   ystop $= y_1 + 1 -$ increment
   hits $= 0$

   count the interior subpixel centers

   for y $=$ ystart **to** ystop **step** increment
      yconst $=$ y $- y_1$
      for x $=$ xstart **to** xstop **step** increment
         temp $=$ yconst $- m*x$
         tfu $=$ temp $-$ constant
         tfl $=$ temp $+$ constant

         change this next statement to **if** tfu $<> 0$ **and** tfl $<> 0$
            and Sign(tfu) $<>$ **Sign**(tfl) **then**
         if a subpixel center lying on an edge is to be excluded

         if Sign(tfu) $<>$ **Sign**(tfl) **then**
            hits $=$ hits $+ 1$
         end if
      next x
   next y
end sub

Horizontal or near horizontal (or vertical or near vertical) lines create special problems. Consider a point on the edge of the rectangular strip to be *outside*, i.e., use $TF_U < 0$ and $TF_L > 0$ as the test. Then for $y_1 = 0$, $m = 0$ three subpixel centers are inside the rectangular strip, while for $y_1 = 0^+$, $m = 0$ six subpixel centers are inside; and for $y_1 = 1/3^+$, $m = 0$, nine subpixel centers are inside the strip. Thus, the intensity of the pixel representing the line changes abruptly for minor changes in the y intercept of the line. (Basically, we have aliasing within our aliasing scheme.) This is particularly annoying for nearly horizontal lines and in animation sequences. Klassen [Klas93] and Schilling [Schi91] discuss efficient techniques for handling these difficulties.

Visually, antialiasing blurs the edges of polygons or lines considered as polygons and uses the excellent integration capabilities of the eye–brain combination to create the appearance of a smooth(er) edge or line. This characteristic of the visual system suggests using even wider rectangles to represent a line. However,

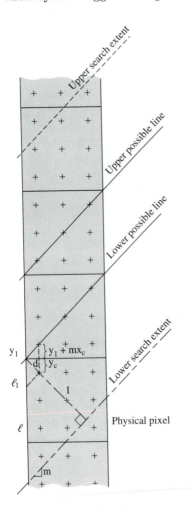

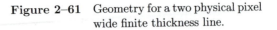

Figure 2–61   Geometry for a two physical pixel wide finite thickness line.

simply counting subpixel centers covered by the wider line is not sufficient. The contributions of each subpixel must be weighted based on some metric, for example linearly based on the distance of the subpixel center from the line. Such a 'metric' results in a triangular weighting function.

Figure 2–61 shows a line represented by a two-physical-pixel wide rectangular strip. Again, the line lies in the first octant, with slope $0 \le m \le 1$. In addition to counting the number of subpixel centers within the rectangular strip, it is now necessary to determine the perpendicular distance from the line to the subpixel center.

For a two-pixel-wide rectangular strip, the extent of the search area is

$$\frac{1}{2n} \le x \le 1 - \frac{1}{2n}$$

$$y_1 - \left(1 - \frac{1}{2n}\right) \le y \le y_1 + \left(2 + \frac{1}{2n}\right)$$

The length ℓ is now

$$\ell = \sqrt{m^2 + 1}$$

and the equations of the upper and lower edges become

$$y_U = mx + y_1 + \ell = mx + y_1 + \sqrt{m^2 + 1}$$

$$y_L = mx + y_1 - \ell = mx + y_1 - \sqrt{m^2 + 1}$$

with test functions

$$tfu = (y_U - y_1) - mx - \ell = (y - y_1) - mx - \sqrt{m^2 + 1}$$

$$tfl = (y_L - y_1) - mx + \ell = (y - y_1) - mx + \sqrt{m^2 + 1}$$

Referring to Fig. 2–26 and using similar triangles yields the perpendicular distance, d, from the line to a subpixel center

$$d = \frac{\ell_1}{\ell} = \frac{y_1 - y_c + mx_c}{\sqrt{m^2 + 1}}$$

where x_c, y_c are the coordinates of the center of a subpixel.

The triangular weighting function is

$$w = \frac{1 - fd}{3n^2} \qquad 0 \le f \le 1$$

where f modulates the weight of the extreme subpixels. For example, if $f = 0$, all subpixels are equally weighted; but if $f = 1$, pixels near the edges of the rectangular strip make little or no contribution. This weighting function has the additional benefit of decreasing the relative intensity of horizontal (and vertical in the more general implementation) lines, relative to the intensity of diagonal lines.

The previous subpixel counting algorithm is easily modified both to count the larger number of subpixels and to calculate the weighting function. The result is

Algorithm to count subpixel centers within a two physical pixel wide rectangular strip for antialiasing lines

assumes pixels are square and divided into n^2 subpixels
assumes the slope of the line is $0 \leq m \leq 1$

n *is the number of divisions on each edge of the physical pixel*
m *is the slope of the line*
x *is the x coordinate of the subpixel center*
y *is the y coordinate of the subpixel center*
y_1 *is the intercept at x_i relative to y_i*

sub bpxlcnt(y_1,n,m,hits)

> *these next four quantities, included here for completeness,*
> *should be calculated in the calling routine*
> *outside the calling loop for efficiency*

> constant = sqr(m $*$ m + 1))
> rconstant = 1/constant
> increment = 1/n
> halfincrement = increment/2
> ystart = y_1 − 1 − halfincrement
> ystop = y_1 + 2 + halfincrement
> xstart = halfincrement
> xstop = 1 − start
> hits = 0

> *count the interior subpixel centers*

> for y = ystart to ystop + 1 step increment
>> yconst = y − y_1
>> for x = xstart to xstop step increment
>>> temp = yconst − m $*$ x
>>> tfu = temp − constant
>>> tfl = temp + constant

>>> *change this next statement to* if tfu <> 0 and tfl <> 0
>>>> and Sign(tfu) <> Sign(tfl) then
>>> *if a subpixel center lying on an edge is to be excluded*

>>> if Sign(tfu) <> Sign(tfl) then
>>>> d = (y_1 − y + m $*$ x) $*$ rconstant
>>>> if d < 0 then
>>>>> hits = hits + (1 + fd)
>>>> else
>>>>> hits = hits + (1 − fd)

```
            end if
          end if
       next x
    next y
 end sub
```

With color, the linear blending function given previously is used. A further enhancement is to use the information from the subpixel count for the adjacent physical pixels, to modulate their color or intensity with the background.

Polygon Interiors

Now consider supersampling applied to the interior of a polygon. Two types of averaging are generally used, uniform and weighted. Figure 2–62a shows a uniform average of the surrounding pixels for pseudoresolutions of two and four times the physical resolution. Again, each display pixel is divided into subpixels to form the higher resolution pseudoraster. Pixel attributes are determined at the center of each subpixel and are uniformly averaged to obtain the attributes for the display pixel.

Somewhat better results are obtained by considering a larger number of subpixels and weighting their influence when calculating the display pixel attributes. Figure 2–62b shows weighted averages suggested by Crow [Crow81] for pseudoresolutions of two and four times the physical resolution. For these weighted averages, a pseudoresolution increase of a factor of two considers a weighted average of nine subpixels when calculating the attributes of a physical pixel. A pseudoresolution increase by a factor of four considers the weighted average of 49 subpixels when calculating the attributes of a physical pixel. Notice that for these weighted averages, sometimes called Bartlett filters, the contribution of a pixel decreases linearly in the x and y directions, but parabolically in the diagonal direction.

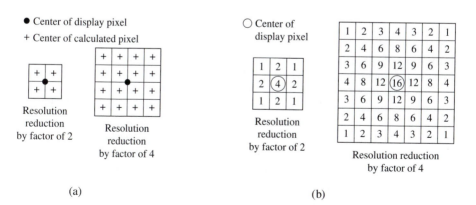

Figure 2–62 Pixel averaging. (a) Uniform; (b) weighted (numbers indicate the relative weights).

(a)   (b)

Figure 2–63 High-resolution images displayed at a 256 × 256 pixel resolution.
(a) Reduced from 512 × 512; (b) reduced from 1024 × 1024, using
uniform averaging. (Courtesy of Frank Crow).

Figure 2–63 shows a complex scene displayed at a resolution of 256 × 256
pixels. Figure 2–63a was calculated at a resolution of 512 × 512, and Fig. 2–63b
at 1024 × 1024. Uniform averaging was used to obtain the displayed resolution
of 256 × 256 pixels. Figures 2–64a and 2–64b show the same scene calculated at
resolutions of 512 × 512 and 1024 × 1024, respectively, and displayed at 256 × 256
using the weighted averages of Fig. 2–62b.

Simple Area Antialiasing

In the line rasterization, polygon fill and postfiltering algorithms discussed previously, the intensity or color of a pixel is determined by the intensity or color
of a single point within the pixel area. Such techniques assume that the pixel is
a mathematical point rather than a finite area. For example, recalling Fig. 2–4
and the Bresenham algorithm, the intensity of pixels is determined by the location of the single point of intersection of the line and the pixel boundary. In
the polygon solid area scan conversion techniques discussed previously, the determination of whether or not a pixel was inside or outside the polygon was
based on the location of the center of the pixel. If inside, the entire pixel area
was activated; if outside, the entire pixel area was ignored. For simple bilevel
displays, i.e., black or white, polygon color or background color, this technique
is necessary. The result is the characteristic stair step, or jagged, polygon edge
or line. Fundamentally, the stair step effect is due to undersampling the line or
polygon edge to make it conform to the discrete pixels of the display, as discussed
previously. In the antialiasing techniques discussed previously, the contribution
of a subpixel to the attributes of the physical pixel is based on the location of
its center. This simply postpones the aliasing effect to a lower level.

For multiple intensities, i.e., gray scales or multiple color shades, the appearance of the edge or line is improved by blurring. A simple heuristic approach

(a)   (b)

Figure 2–64   High-resolution images displayed at a 256 × 256 pixel resolution.
(a) Reduced from 512 × 512; (b) reduced from 1024 × 1024, using
weighted averaging. (Courtesy of Frank Crow).

is to let the intensity of a pixel along a polygon edge be proportional to the
area of the pixel inside the polygon. Figure 2–65 illustrates this simple form
of antialiasing. A single polygon edge with slope $5/8$ is shown. The inside of
the polygon is to the right. In Fig. 2–65a, the polygon edge is rasterized using
a standard Bresenham algorithm with only two intensity levels. The edge exhibits the characteristic jagged, or stair step, pattern. In Fig. 2–65b, the area
of the pixel inside the polygon is used to select one of eight (0 to 7) intensity
levels. Notice that some pixels that are totally black in Fig. 2–65a are white in
Fig. 2–65b, because less than $1/8$ the pixel area is inside the polygon.

A simple modification of Bresenham's algorithm by Pitteway and Watkins
[Pitt80] yields an approximation to the pixel area inside the polygon. This
approximation can be used to modulate the intensity. When a line of slope m
$(0 \leq m \leq 1)$ crosses a pixel, either one or two pixels may be involved, as shown
in Fig. 2–66. If only one pixel is crossed (Fig. 2–66a), then the area to the right
and below the line is $y_i + m / 2$. If two pixels must be considered (Fig. 2–66b), the

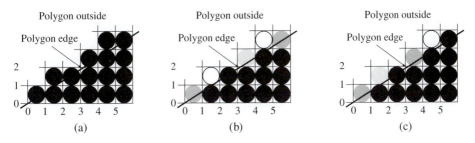

Figure 2–65   Simple antialiased polygon edge.   (a) No antialiasing; (b) intensity
proportional to area inside polygon; (c) modified Bresenham.

area for the lower pixel is $1 - (1 - y_i)^2/2m$ and for the upper $(y_i - 1 + m)^2/2m$. For a line in the first octant with slope $0 \le m \le 1$, the area of the upper pixel is sufficiently small that it can be ignored by the simple heuristic approach described above, e.g., pixel $(1, 1)$ in Fig. 2–65b. However, combining this area with that of the lower pixel more realistically represents the polygon edge. The combined area for the two pixels is given by $y_i + m/2$.

If the quantity $w = 1 - m$ is added to the error term in Bresenham's original algorithm, i.e., introduce the transformation $\bar{e} = e + w$, then $0 \le \bar{e} \le 1$. Now the error term $\bar{e}$ is a measure of the area of the pixel inside the polygon, i.e., of $y_i + m/2$. With these modifications, the initial value of the error term is $1/2$. With this addition, the algorithm given in Fig. 2–6 always yields an intensity of one-half the maximum for the first pixel. By relocating the setpxl statement, a more realistic value is obtained for this first pixel. The intensity can be obtained directly, rather than as a decimal fraction of the maximum, by multiplying the slope (m), the weighting factor w, and the error term $\bar{e}$ by the maximum number of available intensity levels, I. The modified algorithm is then

modified Bresenham algorithm with antialiasing

the line is from $((x_1, y_1))$ to (x_2, y_2)
I *is the number of available intensity levels*
all variables are assumed integer

> *initialize the variables*

> $x = x_1$
> $y = y_1$
> $\Delta x = x_2 - x_1$
> $\Delta y = y_2 - y_1$
> $m = (I * \Delta y)/\Delta x$
> $w = I - m$
> $\bar{e} = I/2$

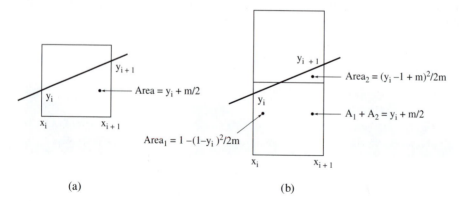

(a)   (b)

Figure 2–66 Bresenham's algorithm with area antialiasing.

```
        setpixel (x, y, m/2)
        while (x < x₂)
            if ē < w then
                x = x + 1
                ē = ē + m
            else
                x = x + 1
                y = y + 1
                ē = ē - w
            end if
            setpixel (x, y, ē)
        end while
    finish
```

The intensity for the first pixel assumes that the line starts at a pixel address. A flowchart is given in Fig. 2–67. Figure 2–65c illustrates the results for a line with slope $m = {}^5\!/_8$ and eight intensity levels. The algorithm is extended to the other octants in a manner similar to that for the fundamental Bresenham algorithm (see Sec. 2–3).

An alternate technique approximates the area of a pixel inside a polygon edge by subdividing pixels intersected by the edge, and counting the number of subpixel centers that are inside the polygon. Optimally, the number of subpixels equals the number of available intensities. For color, the number of subpixels equals the maximum number of intensities for each of the red, green and blue (or cyan, magenta and yellow) primary colors. The number of subpixel centers inside the polygon for a given physical pixel is determined using a modification of the pxlcnt routine discussed previously. For a monochrome display, the intensity of the physical pixel is then

$$I = \frac{s}{n^2} I_{\max}$$

where s is the number of subpixel centers inside the polygon and n^2 is the number of subpixels. For color

$$I(r, g, b) = \frac{s}{n^2} I(r, g, b)_{\text{polygon}} + \left(1 - \frac{s}{n^2}\right) I(r, g, b)_{\text{background}}$$

The technique approximates the prefiltering of the edges using the convolution of the edge with a box filter.

Figure 2–68 shows a polygon edge with slope $m = {}^5\!/_8$. The inside of the polygon is to the right. Each physical pixel intersected by the edge is subdivided into 16 subpixels on a 4 × 4 grid. The pixel labeled a has 9 subpixel centers inside the polygon, while the pixel labeled b has all of its subpixel centers inside the polygon. The pixel a is rendered at $9\!/_{16}$ of full intensity and pixel b at full intensity. Pixels e and f have 4 and 13 subpixels inside the polygon, and are rendered with intensities of $1\!/_4$ and $13\!/_{16}$, respectively.

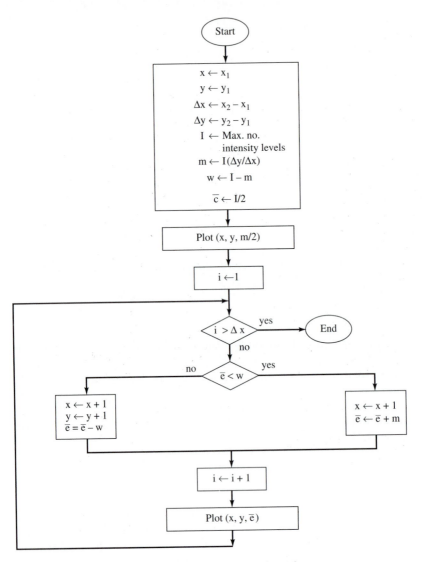

Figure 2–67 Area antialiasing Bresenham's algorithm.

The Convolution Integral and Antialiasing

Extension of the simple antialiasing methods discussed in the previous section requires use of a mathematical technique called the convolution integral. For antialiasing, the signal, i.e., the picture, is convolved with a convolution kernel. The result is used to determine the pixel attributes. The convolution integral is given by

$$c(\xi) = \int_{-\infty}^{\infty} h(\xi - x)y(x)dx$$

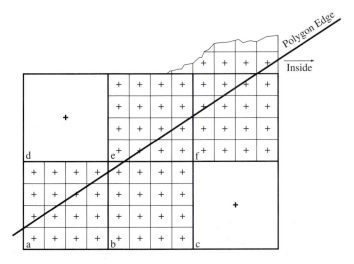

Figure 2–68   Approximate area antialiasing using subdivision.

where $h(\xi - x)$ is the convolution kernel or function

$y(x)$ is the function being convolved

$c(\xi)$ is the convolution of $h(\xi - x)$ and $y(x)$

It is extremely difficult to visualize the physical meaning of the convolution integral from the mathematical definition. However, a simple graphical analysis makes it clear (see [Brig74]).

Consider the convolution of the function $y(x) = x$, $0 \le x \le 1$, a 45° line segment, with a simple box or square convolution kernel, $h(x) = 1$, $0 \le x \le 1$. The graphical representation of the convolution kernel is shown in Fig. 2–69a. The convolution kernel is reflected about the ordinate to yield $h(-x)$, as shown in Fig. 2–69b. The reflected kernel is then translated to the right by an amount ξ to form $h(\xi - x)$, see Fig. 2–69c. This reflected, translated function is then multiplied together with the function being convolved $y(x)$ (see Fig. 2–69d) for various values of ξ, as shown in Fig. 2–69e. The area under the combined curves (functions) is the value of the convolution integral $c(\xi)$, which is also shown in Fig. 2–69e. Notice that for this case the convolution integral is nonzero only in the range $0 \le x \le 2$. Thus, determining the convolution integral is equivalent to reflecting the convolution kernel, sliding it past the function, multiplying the two functions together and determining the area under the combined curves.

Mathematically, the convolution kernel is

$$h(x) = 1 \qquad 0 \le x \le 1$$

Reflecting yields

$$h(-x) = 1 \qquad -1 \le x \le 0$$

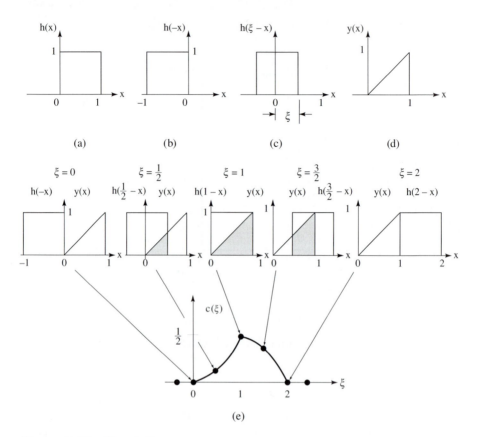

Figure 2–69 Convolution.

Translating by ξ gives

$$h(\xi - x) = 1 \qquad \xi - 1 \le x \le \xi$$

Because both the convolution kernel and the function $y(x)$ being convolved are nonzero for finite ranges, the limits on the convolution integral are also finite. How are those limits determined? Figure 2–69 clearly illustrates that the lower limit is the maximum of the minimum values for which both functions are nonzero, and the upper limit is the minimum of the maximum values for which both functions are nonzero. Thus

$$c(\xi) = \int_{-\infty}^{\infty} h(\xi - x)y(x)dx = \int_{0}^{\xi} h(\xi - x)y(x)dx \qquad 0 \le \xi \le 1$$

$$= \int_{\xi-1}^{2} h(\xi - x)y(x)dx \qquad 1 \le \xi \le 2$$

Substituting for $h(\xi - x)$ and $y(x)$ yields

$$c(\xi) = \int_0^\xi (1)(x)dx = \left. \frac{x^2}{2} \right]_0^\xi = \frac{\xi^2}{2} \qquad 0 \le \xi \le 1$$

$$= \int_{\xi-2}^1 (1)(x)dx = \left. \frac{x^2}{x} \right]_{\xi-1}^2 = \frac{\xi}{2}(2-\xi) \qquad 1 \le \xi \le 2$$

which are both parabolic functions, as shown in Fig. 2–69e. If the slope of the line is m rather than 1, then the results generalize to $m\xi^2/2$ and $m\xi/2(2-\xi)$.

To see how this technique relates to antialiasing, recall the heuristic intensity modulation technique using the area of the pixel inside the polygon to determine the pixel intensity as discussed previously. Examining the convolution function $c(\xi)$ given above shows that for $m \le 1$ the value of the convolution function at the right-hand edge of the pixel, i.e., at $x = \xi = 1$, is the area of the pixel inside the polygon, i.e., $m/2$ (see Fig. 2–50a, with $y_i = 0$). For $m > 1$, the value of the convolution integral gives the summation of the areas inside the polygon for the two pixels crossed (see Fig. 2–50b, with $y_i = 0$). The result is easily generalized for $y_i \ne 0$. Thus, the three previous algorithms (the heuristic area modulation algorithm, the modified Bresenham algorithm and the subpixel counting algorithm) are equivalent to the convolution of the edge functions, i.e., the straight line $y = mx + b$, with a box function or convolution kernel evaluated at the right-hand edge of the pixel.

The convolution operation is frequently called filtering, where the convolution kernel is the filter function. The simple area technique discussed earlier prefilters the image. Prefiltering adjusts the pixel attributes of the computed resolution before displaying the image.

Filter Functions

The previous discussion of convolution is one-dimensional. Computer graphics images are two-dimensional. The theory easily extends to two dimensions but becomes computationally more expensive. Generally, approximations to the theoretical results are used.

Although a simple two-dimensional box filter, or convolution kernel, yields acceptable results, triangular, Gaussian and B-spline filters yield better results. Simple box, pyramidal, conical and two-dimensional Gaussian convolution kernels, or filter functions, have been investigated (see [Crow81; Feib80; Warn80; Gupt81]). Figure 2–70a illustrates several theoretical two-dimensional filters, or convolution kernels. Although each filter is shown covering a 3×3 pixel area of the image, filters covering 5×5, 7×7, 9×9, etc. areas are possible. The effect of using filters that cover a larger area is to blur the image more. Figure 2–70b illustrates the corresponding discretized approximations to the theoretical filters. These are obtained by determining the value of the filter at the center of each of the pixels. The intensity at each pixel within the filter is multiplied by the

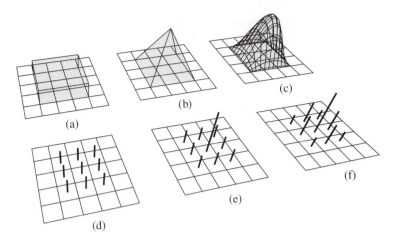

Figure 2–70   Two-dimensional filter functions. (a) Simple box filter; (b) pyramidal filter; (c) second-degree B-spline used as a filter; (d) discretized box filter; (e) discretized pyramidal filter; (f) discretized B-spline filter.

'weight' for that pixel; the values are summed and then divided by the number of pixels 'covered' by the filter function times the maximum weight. The division can be avoided by normalizing the weights so that the maximum value is one. This 'weighted average' intensity is then used to render the pixel at the center of the filter.

Figure 2–71 shows the same scene as Figs. 2–63 and 2–64 computed at a resolution of 256 × 256 pixels, prefiltered with a simple box filter and displayed at a resolution of 256 × 256. Note the decrease in 'aliasing artifacts' compared to Figs. 2–63 and 2–64.

Figure 2–71   Prefiltered antialiased image at a resolution of 256 × 256 pixels. (Courtesy of Frank Crow).

Simple convolution filters are not always effective for small polygons of area less than a pixel, or for long, thin polygons. However, antialiasing can be implemented using clipping (see Chapter 3 and [Crow81]). The edges of the pixel area form the clipping window; each individual polygon is clipped against the edges of the window. The remaining polygonal area, compared to the pixel area, is used to modulate the pixel intensity. If multiple small polygons are present within a pixel, then the average, either uniform or weighted, of their attributes is used to modulate the pixel attributes. An example is shown in Fig. 2–72.

A number of additional antialiasing techniques are discussed throughout the rest of the text, for example, shadows (Sec. 5–11), textures (Sec. 5–12), ray tracing (Secs. 4–20 and 5–16) and radiosity (Sec. 5–17).

2–17 Halftoning

Antialiasing is a technique using multiple intensity levels to obtain increased visual resolution. Halftoning, on the other hand, is a technique for using a minimum number of intensity levels to obtain increased visual resolution, i.e., gray scaling, or multiple intensity levels. The halftoning technique is quite old. It was originally used in the weaving of silk pictures and other textiles. Modern halftone printing was invented by Stephen Hargon in 1880. With this technique, a wide range of photographic gray scales is available using a strictly bilevel display medium: black ink on white paper. Halftone printing is a screen or cellular process (see [Koda82]). The size of the cell varies, depending on the fineness of the screen and length of exposure. Because of the low paper quality, screens with 50 to 90 dots per inch are used for newspaper photographs. The higher quality paper used in books and magazines allows the use of screens with 100 to 300 dots per inch. The success of the halftone process depends on the human visual system being an integrator; i.e., it blends or smooths discrete information.

Patterning

The visual resolution of computer generated images can be increased using a technique called patterning. In contrast to halftone printing, which uses variable

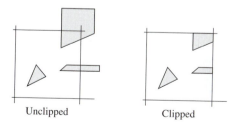

Unclipped   Clipped

Figure 2–72 Antialiasing using clipping.

cell sizes, patterning, which can be considered a form of clustered dot ordered dithering, generally uses fixed cell sizes. For a display of fixed resolution, several pixels are combined to yield a pattern cell. Thus, spatial resolution is traded for improved visual resolution. Figure 2–73a illustrates one possible group of patterns for a bilevel black-and-white display. Four pixels are used for each cell. This arrangement yields five possible intensity or gray levels (0 to 4). For a bilevel display, in general the number of possible intensities is one more than the number of pixels in a cell. For square cells, the number of intensities is $2^n + 1$, where n is the size of the square.

Care must be taken in selecting the patterns; otherwise, unwanted small-scale structure or contouring is introduced. For example, neither of the patterns shown in Figs. 2–73b or 2–73c should be used. For a large constant-intensity area, Fig. 2–73b results in unwanted horizontal lines and Fig. 2–73c in unwanted vertical lines appearing in the image. The number of intensity levels available is increased by increasing the cell size. Patterns for a 3×3 pixel cell are shown in Fig. 2–74. These patterns yield ten (0 to 9) intensity levels. Pattern cells need not be square. A 3×2 pixel cell yielding seven (0 to 6) intensity levels is shown in Fig. 2–75.

In general, to avoid introducing unwanted artifacts into the image, patterns should not be symmetrical. Patterns should represent a growth sequence, i.e., any pixel turned on when representing a lower intensity must also be turned on for all higher intensities. Patterns should also grow outward from the center of the cell, to give the effect of increasing dot size as the intensity increases. Because many output devices, specifically laser printers and film, do not render isolated dots or pixels well, pixels should be adjacent to each other. Notice that the patterns shown in Figs. 2–73a and 2–74 follow these rules; notice also that these patterns form a 45° angle with the horizontal. This angle corresponds to the 'screen angle' for traditional photographic halftoning. The patterning halftoning technique with variable screen angles is used in PostScript [Adob85]. Knuth [Knut87b] has experimented with patterns to produce fonts for digital halftoning.

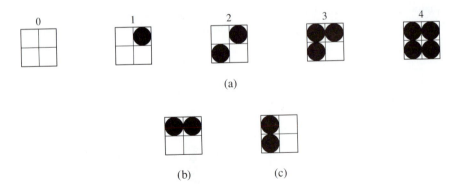

Figure 2–73 2×2 bilevel pattern cells.

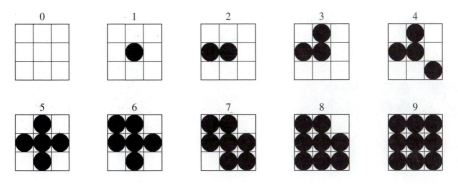

Figure 2–74 3×3 bilevel pattern cells.

If multiple dot sizes are available, additional intensity levels can be obtained. Figure 2–76 shows patterns for a 2×2 pixel cell with two dot sizes; this yields nine intensity levels. A similar 3×3 pixel cell with two dot sizes yields 27 intensity levels. If more than 1 bit per pixel is available, additional intensity levels are also possible. For a 2×2 pixel pattern cell, 2 bits per pixel yields 13 intensity levels, as shown in Fig. 2–77. More bits per pixel or larger cell patterns yield corresponding increases in available intensity levels [Pirs83].

Halftone cell patterns can be considered as matrices. For example, the simple 2×2 patterns shown in Fig. 2–73 are represented by the matrix

$$[P_2] = \begin{bmatrix} 3 & 1 \\ 2 & 4 \end{bmatrix}$$

Similarly, the 3×3 patterns in Fig. 2–74 are represented by the matrix

$$[P_3] = \begin{bmatrix} 6 & 3 & 9 \\ 2 & 1 & 5 \\ 8 & 7 & 4 \end{bmatrix}$$

Figure 2–75 3×2 bilevel pattern cells.

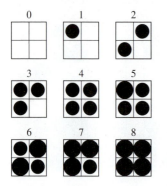

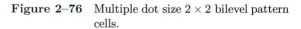

Figure 2–76 Multiple dot size 2×2 bilevel pattern cells.

If the intensity, I, of the pixel to be displayed equals or exceeds the value in the pattern matrix, then the corresponding pixel at that location in the pattern cell is activated.

The actual image to be displayed seldom is stored with a maximum intensity equal to that in the pattern matrix. Consequently, it is advantageous to normalize the entries in the pattern matrices to the range zero to one. For a square pattern matrix, the normalized matrix $[\widehat{P}_n]$ is

$$[\widehat{P}_n] = \frac{1}{n^2 + 1} [P_n]$$

For example, the normalized $[\widehat{P}_2]$ matrix is

$$[\widehat{P}_2] = \frac{1}{n^2 + 1} [P_2] = \frac{1}{5} [P_2] = \begin{bmatrix} 0.6 & 0.2 \\ 0.4 & 0.8 \end{bmatrix}$$

and the normalized $[\widehat{P}_3]$ matrix is

$$[\widehat{P}_3] = \frac{1}{n^2 + 1} [P_3] = \frac{1}{10} [P_3] = \begin{bmatrix} 0.6 & 0.3 & 0.9 \\ 0.2 & 0.1 & 0.5 \\ 0.8 & 0.7 & 0.4 \end{bmatrix}$$

If the image to be displayed has a maximum intensity of $I_{\max}$, then the normalized pattern matrix, $[\widehat{P}_n]$, is converted to the display pattern matrix, $[P_{n_D}]$, by multiplying each entry by $I_{\max}$ and taking the integer value, i.e.

$$[P_{n_D}] = \mathrm{Int}\left(I_{\max} [\widehat{P}_n]\right)$$

For example, if $I_{\max} = 255$ then

$$[P_{2_D}] = \mathrm{Int}\left(255 \begin{bmatrix} 0.6 & 0.2 \\ 0.4 & 0.8 \end{bmatrix}\right) = \begin{bmatrix} 153 & 51 \\ 102 & 204 \end{bmatrix}$$

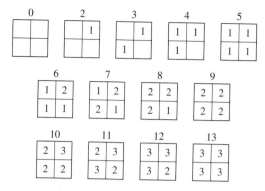

Figure 2–77 Two bits per pixel 2 × 2 pattern cells.

and
$$[P_{3_D}] = \text{Int}\left(255\begin{bmatrix}0.6 & 0.3 & 0.9\\0.2 & 0.1 & 0.5\\0.8 & 0.7 & 0.4\end{bmatrix}\right) = \begin{bmatrix}153 & 76 & 229\\51 & 25 & 127\\204 & 178 & 102\end{bmatrix}$$

An interesting question is how many intensity levels are required to adequately represent a continuous tone (photographic) image in a book like this? With 4, 8 and 16 intensity levels, contouring will be quite evident; but it almost disappears for 64 (or 2^n, with $n = 6$) intensity levels. To eliminate the remaining effects of contouring requires $n = 8$, or 256 intensity levels. To display an image at an effective resolution of 300 dpi (dots per inch) with 256 intensity levels using an 8 × 8 pattern thus requires a physical device resolution of 2400 dpi. Reducing the number of intensity levels to 64 ($n = 6$) requires a physical device resolution of 1800 dpi.

Thresholding and Error Distribution

Patterning results in the loss of spatial resolution. This is acceptable if the image is of lower resolution than the display. Techniques for improving visual resolution while maintaining spatial resolution have also been developed (see [Jerv76]). The simplest is to use a fixed threshold for each pixel. If the image intensity exceeds some threshold value the pixel is white, otherwise it is black, i.e.

if I(x, y) > T then White else Black

where I(x, y) is the intensity of the image at pixel (x, y), White corresponds to the maximum display intensity, and Black corresponds to the minimum display intensity. The threshold is usually set at approximately half the maximum display intensity. Figure 2–78b shows results for the photograph of Fig. 2–78a, with T = 150. For each pixel location, the intensity of the original photograph was quantized in the range 0 to 255, i.e., 8 bits. A matrix representation of simple thresholding uses a 1×1 matrix, $[T]$, where T is in the range of $0 \leq \widehat{T} \leq 1$ for the normalized matrix $[\widehat{T}]$ and in the range $0 \leq T \leq I_{\max}$ for the display matrix.

Figure 2–78b illustrates that a simple thresholding technique results in the loss of considerable fine detail. This is particularly noticeable in the hair and facial features. The fine detail is lost because of the relative large errors in displayed intensity for each pixel.

A technique developed by Floyd and Steinberg [Floy75] distributes the error in the displayed pixel intensity to surrounding pixels. Error diffusion algorithms are examples of dispersed dot algorithms. The Floyd–Steinberg error diffusion algorithm distributes the error to the right along the current scan line, and to adjacent pixels on the scan line below (or above) the current scan line. Specifically, $7/16$ of the error is distributed to the pixel to the right on the current scan line, $3/16$ to the pixel to the left on the scan line below (or above), $5/16$ to the pixel directly below (or above) and $1/16$ to the pixel to the right and on the scan line below (or above) the current pixel, as shown in Fig. 2–79a. The corresponding error distribution matrix, assuming a left to right, top to bottom scan line order, is

$$\frac{1}{16} \begin{bmatrix} 0 & 0 & 0 \\ 0 & * & 7 \\ 3 & 5 & 1 \end{bmatrix}$$

where the $*$ indicates the current pixel and 0 indicates that none of the error is distributed to the scan line above nor to the pixel to the left of the current pixel.

With the threshold midway between the maximum and minimum display intensities, T = (Black + White)/2, the Floyd–Steinberg error diffusion algorithm is

Floyd–Steinberg error distribution algorithm

Xmin, Xmax, Ymin, Ymax *are the raster limits for each scan line —
top to bottom*

    T = (Black + White)/2

    for y = Ymax to Ymin step -1

        for each pixel on a scan line–left to right

        for x = Xmin to Xmax

            determine pixel display value for threshold T
            and calculate error

            if I(x, y) < T then

                Pixel(x, y) = Black

                Error = I(x, y) − Black

            else

                Pixel(x, y) = White

                Error = I(x, y) − White

            end if

            display pixel

            setpixel (x, y, Pixel(x, y))

            distribute error to neighboring pixels

(a)

(b)

(c)

Figure 2–78   Bilevel display
techniques. (a)
Original photo-
graph; (b) simple
thresholding; (c)
ordered dither
with 8 × 8 dither
matrix. (Courte-
sy of J.F. Jarvis,
Bell Laborato-
ries).

$$I(x+1, y) = I(x+1, y) + 7*Error/16$$
$$I(x+1, y-1) = I(x+1, y-1) + Error/16$$
$$I(x, y-1) = I(x, y-1) + 5*Error/16$$
$$I(x-1, y-1) = I(x-1, y-1) + 3*Error/16$$

       next x

    next y

  finish

A simplification of the algorithm can be cleverly constructed such that the error is always distributed downward and to the right. Hence, if the image is computed in scan line order, no backtracking is necessary. In particular, the simplified Floyd–Steinberg algorithm distributes the error $3/8$ to the right, $3/8$ downward and $1/4$ diagonally downward and to the right. This error diffusion scheme is shown in Fig. 2–79b. The pseudocode algorithm given earlier is easily modified for the simplified algorithm. Distributing the error to neighboring pixels improves the detail in the image, because it preserves the information inherent in the image.

In addition to the Floyd–Steinberg algorithm, Jarvis et al. [Jarv76], Stucki [Stuc81] and Knuth [Knut87a] present single-pass error diffusion algorithms. In comparisons of digital halftoning techniques (see [Schu91; Gots93]) the Jarvis et al. minimized average error diffusion algorithm performed especially well, particularly for animated sequences of images. The Jarvis et al. error diffusion matrix is

$$\frac{1}{48}
\begin{bmatrix}
0 & 0 & 0 & 0 & 0 \\
0 & 0 & 0 & 0 & 0 \\
0 & 0 & * & 7 & 5 \\
3 & 5 & 7 & 5 & 3 \\
1 & 3 & 5 & 3 & 1
\end{bmatrix}$$

where again the $*$ represents the current pixel and 0 indicates a pixel which receives no contribution. The Jarvis et al. matrix attempts to minimize the intensity error between the source and displayed images. It also provides some

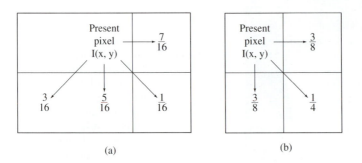

(a) (b)

Figure 2–79 Error distribution for Floyd–Steinberg algorithm. (a) Original algorithm; (b) simplified algorithm.

edge enhancement. Boundary pixels require special handling. Jarvis and colleagues set the error diffusion values to zero for a region two pixels wide at the top and at each size of the image. Multiple passes of iterative error diffusion algorithms are also used (see, for example, Wu [Wu94]).

Because of the fixed left-to-right order of the raster scan, error diffusion algorithms have a tendency to introduce repeating patterns into the image. The effect of these repeating patterns is reduced by 'breaking' the rigid scan line order. Ulichney [Ulic87] suggests using a serpentine pattern, i.e., generating a scan line left to right and the following scan line right to left recursively. Alternate image generation patterns, e.g., Peano curves (a type of fractal, see [Witt82]) are also used with good results. Velho and Gomes [Velh91] extend the technique to Hilbert curves.

The line diffusion algorithm by Zhang [Zhan96] processes the image along lines perpendicular to a diagonal of the image, e.g., along lines perpendicular to the diagonal from the upper left corner to the lower right corner of the image. The algorithm randomly distributes the error, using the concept of pixel classes introduced by Knuth in the dot diffusion algorithm [Knut87a]. The error is distributed to the pixel to the right, downward and diagonally downward and to the right, as in the simplified Floyd–Steinberg algorithm (see Fig. 2–78b). The line diffusion algorithm is easily paralyzed; the paralyzed algorithm takes the form of a neural network (see [Lipp87]). The algorithm also has an efficient sequential implementation. Results for the line diffusion algorithm are comparable to those for the Floyd–Steinberg error diffusion algorithm, as shown in Fig. 2–80.

Ordered dither

The ordered dither technique for bilevel displays also increases the visual resolution without reducing the spatial resolution, by introducing a random error into the image. This random error is added to the image intensity of each pixel before comparison with the selected threshold value. Adding a completely random error does not yield an optimum result. However, an optimum additive error pattern, which minimizes pattern texture effects, exists [Baye73]. Because the error pattern is smaller than image size, it is tiled across the image, i.e., added to the image in a repeating checkerboard pattern. This technique is a form of dispersed dot-ordered dither. In contrast to output devices like laser printers or film, CRTs are capable of adequately rendering single pixels. Thus, dispersed dot-ordered dither is the technique of choice.

The smallest ordered dither pattern or matrix is normally 2×2. An optimum 2×2 matrix, originally given by Limb [Limb69], is

$$[D_2] = \begin{bmatrix} 0 & 2 \\ 3 & 1 \end{bmatrix}$$

Larger dither patterns, 4×4, 8×8, etc., are obtained using the recursion relation (see [Jarv76])

$$[D_n] = \begin{bmatrix} 4D_{n/2} & 4D_{n/2} + 2U_{n/2} \\ 4D_{n/2} + 3U_{n/2} & 4D_{n/2} + U_{n/2} \end{bmatrix} \qquad n \geq 4$$

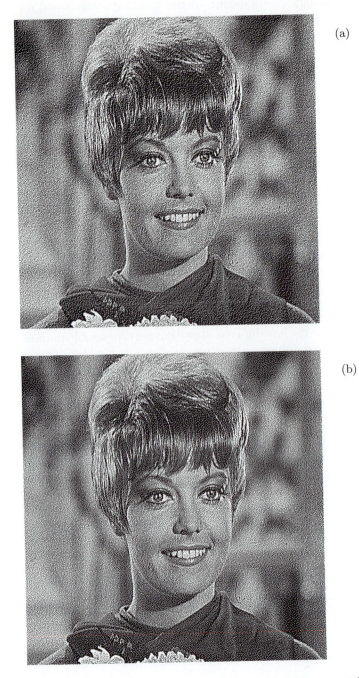

(a)

(b)

Figure 2–80   Halftone image of Zelda.   (a) Diffusion with edge enhancement; (b) Floyd–Steinberg error diffusion with edge enhancement. (Courtesy of Yuefeng Zhang).

where n is the matrix size and

$$[U_n] = \begin{bmatrix} 1 & 1 & \cdots & 1 \\ 1 & 1 & & \\ \vdots & & & \\ 1 & & & \end{bmatrix}$$

For example, the 4×4 dither matrix is

$$[D_4] = \begin{bmatrix} 0 & 8 & 2 & 10 \\ 12 & 4 & 14 & 6 \\ 3 & 11 & 1 & 9 \\ 15 & 7 & 13 & 5 \end{bmatrix}$$

As these two additional examples show, n^2 intensities are reproduced from a dither matrix, D_n. Furthermore, the image does not lose spatial resolution as n is increased. Normalized ordered dither matrices, $[\widehat{D}_n]$, are obtained by dividing by $n^2 - 1$. For a given maximum image intensity, $I_{\max}$, the display dither matrix is $I_{\max}[\widehat{D}_n]$. The ordered dither algorithm is

Ordered dither algorithm

Xmin, Xmax, Ymin, Ymax *are the raster limits for each scan line —*
  top to bottom
Mod *is a function that returns the modulo value of its arguments*

  for y = Ymax **to** Ymin **step** − 1
   for each pixel on a scan line–left to right
   for x = Xmin **to** Xmax
    determine position in dither matrix
    i = (x **Mod** n) + 1
    j = (y **Mod** n) + 1
    determine pixel display value
    if I(x, y) < D(i, j) **then**
     Pixel(x, y) = Black
    else
     Pixel(x, y) = White
    end if
    display pixel
    setpixel (x, y, Pixel(x, y))
   next x
  next y
 finish

Figure 2–78c shows the image in the original photograph of Fig. 2–78a processed with an 8×8 ordered dither matrix. The 8×8 dither matrix effectively introduces 64 intensity levels. Figure 2–78c shows that considerable fine detail is restored. Notice also that ordered dither results in reduced contrast.

If the resolution of the display is larger than the resolution of the image, then the quality of the displayed image is improved using interpolation to increase the resolution of the image to the resolution of the display and using ordered dither on the result. Jarvis et al. [Jarv76]) suggest the interpolation scheme

$$I_{x,y} = S_{x',y'}$$

$$I_{x+1,y} = \frac{1}{2}(S_{x',y'} + S_{x'+1,y'})$$

$$I_{x,y+1} = \frac{1}{2}(S_{x',y'} + S_{x',y'+1})$$

$$I_{x+1,y+1} = \frac{1}{4}(S_{x',y'} + S_{x'+1,y'} + S_{x',y'+1} + S_{x'+1,y'+1})$$

where (x', y') and (x, y) are pixel locations in the image and on the display, respectively, $x = 2x'$, $y = 2y'$ and $S_{x',y'}$ and $I_{x,y}$ represent the intensity of the image and display, respectively.

Additional details of dispersed dot-ordered dither are given in the standard reference work on digital halftoning by Ulichney [Ulic87]. Ulichney also discusses rotated dither patterns, the addition of random 'noise' (blue or white noise) to dither algorithms and the use of sharpening filters. Ostromoukhov et al. [Ostr94] also discuss rotated dispersed dot dither.

The previous discussion of halftoning assumes a bilevel (black and white) display medium. Halftoning is also used for multiply intensity monochrome (gray level) or color display images and mediums. The basic principles do not change. In the case of color images and display mediums, the algorithms are applied individually and simultaneously to each color component.

Kubo [Kubo84] applied patterning techniques to the display of color images. He used a 4×4 pattern cell for each of four colors (cyan, magenta, yellow and black) to achieve 4096 colors or shades on an ink jet printer. He rotated the pattern cell 90° about the center for each of the colors, i.e., if black is at 0°, then cyan is rotated 90°, magenta 180° and yellow 270° with respect to the black pattern. With black represented by the cell matrix[†]

$$\text{if} \quad \text{Black} = \begin{bmatrix} 0 & 8 & 2 & 11 \\ 12 & 4 & 15 & 5 \\ 3 & 9 & 1 & 10 \\ 14 & 7 & 13 & 6 \end{bmatrix} \quad \text{then} \quad \text{Cyan} = \begin{bmatrix} 14 & 3 & 12 & 0 \\ 7 & 9 & 4 & 8 \\ 13 & 1 & 15 & 2 \\ 6 & 10 & 5 & 11 \end{bmatrix}$$

and similarly

[†]Kubo used a somewhat different cell matrix.

$$\text{Magenta} = \begin{bmatrix} 6 & 13 & 7 & 14 \\ 10 & 1 & 9 & 3 \\ 5 & 15 & 4 & 12 \\ 11 & 2 & 8 & 0 \end{bmatrix} \qquad \text{Yellow} = \begin{bmatrix} 11 & 5 & 10 & 6 \\ 2 & 15 & 1 & 13 \\ 8 & 4 & 9 & 7 \\ 0 & 12 & 3 & 14 \end{bmatrix}$$

Kubo also experimented with preset 'random' patterns.

Heckbert [Heck82] used the simplified Floyd–Steinberg error diffusion algorithm to improve the quality of quantized color images. Thomas and Bogart [Thom91] give a multiple intensity version of the Floyd–Steinberg algorithm. For multiple intensity displays, it is important to insure that the propagated image intensity at any location x, y does not exceed the maximum allowable display intensity. If the maximum allowable display intensity is exceeded, then the value is reduced (clamped) to the maximum allowable value.

Thomas and Bogart [Thom91] also give a multiple intensity version of the ordered dither algorithm. If the multiple intensity display medium has $\ell + 1$ available intensities, then the inner loop of the ordered dither algorithm becomes

determine pixel display value

if $I(x, y) - \textbf{Integer}\left(\dfrac{I_{\max}}{\ell} \textbf{Integer}\left(\dfrac{I(x, y)}{I_{\max}} \ell \right) \right) < D(i, j)$ **then**

$\qquad Pixel(x, y) = \textbf{Integer}\left(\dfrac{I(x, y)}{I_{\max}} \ell \right)$

else

$\qquad Pixel(x, y) = \textbf{Integer}\left(\dfrac{I(x, y)}{I_{\max}} \ell \right) + 1$

end if

where $I(x, y)$ is the intensity of the image pixel at x, y, $I_{\max}$ is the maximum available display medium intensity and $P(x, y)$ is the intensity of the display pixel.

Well et al. [Well91] use nonlinear color dithering techniques based on the characteristics of the human visual system to improve image quality. They specifically investigated the case of 24 bit (8 bits of red, green and blue, respectively) images dithered to 12 bits (4 bits of red, green and blue, respectively). For the case of vectors, they found that aligning the dither matrix with the vector direction improved the results, especially when antialiasing the vectors (see Secs. 2–27 and 2–28).

CLIPPING

Clipping is the process of extracting a portion of a data base or identifying elements of a scene or picture inside or outside a specified region, called the clipping region. Clipping is fundamental to several aspects of computer graphics. In addition to its more typical use in selecting only the specific information required to display a particular scene or view from a larger environment, Chapter 2 showed that it is useful for antialiasing. Succeeding chapters show that clipping is useful in visible line, visible surface, shadow and texture algorithms, as well. Although beyond the scope of this text, the algorithms and concepts discussed here can be used to implement advanced clipping algorithms that clip polygonal volumes against polygonal volumes. Such algorithms are used to perform the Boolean operations required for simple solid modelers, e.g., the intersection and union of simple cubical and quadric volumes. Clipping is also useful for copying, moving or deleting a portion of a scene or picture, e.g., the classical 'cut and paste' operation in a 'windowing' system.

Clipping algorithms are two- or three-dimensional, and are for regular or irregular regions or volumes. Clipping algorithms are implemented in hardware or software. When implemented in software, complex clipping algorithms are often slower than required for real-time applications. For this reason, both two- and three-dimensional clipping algorithms are frequently implemented in hardware or firmware. These implementations are usually confined to regular clipping regions or volumes. However, very-large-scale integrated (VLSI) circuits are used for more general implementations, which operate at real-time speeds [Clar82] for both regular and irregular clipping regions or volumes.

3–1   Two-dimensional Clipping

Figure 3–1 shows a two-dimensional scene and a regular clipping window. It is defined by left (L), right (R), top (T) and bottom (B) two-dimensional edges. A regular clipping window is rectangular, with its edges aligned with those of the object space or display device. The purpose of a clipping algorithm is to determine which points, lines or portions of lines lie within the clipping window. These points, lines or portions of lines are retained for display; all others are discarded.

Because large numbers of points or lines must be clipped for a typical scene or picture, the efficiency of clipping algorithms is of particular interest. In many cases, the large majority of points or lines are either completely interior to or completely exterior to the clipping window. Therefore, it is important to be able to quickly accept a line like ab or a point like p, or reject a line like ij or a point like q in Fig. 3–1.

A Simple Visibility Algorithm

Points are interior to the clipping window provided that

$$x_L \leq x \leq x_R \qquad \text{and} \qquad y_B \leq y \leq y_T$$

The equal sign indicates that points on the window boundary are included within the window.

Lines are interior to the clipping window and hence visible if both end points are interior to the window, e.g., line ab in Fig. 3–1. However, if both end points of a line are exterior to the window, the line is not necessarily completely exterior to the window, e.g., line gh in Fig. 3–1. If both end points of a line are completely to the right of, completely to the left of, completely above or completely below the window, then the line is completely exterior to the window and hence invisible. This test eliminates all the lines labeled ij in Fig. 3–1. It does not eliminate either line gh, which is partially visible, or line kl, which is totally invisible.

If a and b are the end points of a line, then an algorithm for identifying completely visible and most invisible lines is:

> **simple visibility algorithm**
> a *and* b *are the end points of the line, with components* x *and* y
>> *for each line*
>> Visibility = True
>> *check for totally invisible lines*
>> *if both end points are left, right, above or below the window, the line is trivially invisible*
>> if $x_a < x_L$ and $x_b < x_L$ then Visibility = False
>> if $x_a > x_R$ and $x_b > x_R$ then Visibility = False
>> if $y_a > y_T$ and $y_b > y_T$ then Visibility = False
>> if $y_a < y_B$ and $y_b < y_B$ then Visibility = False
>> if Visibility <> False **then**   *avoid the totally visible calculation*
>>> *check if the line is totally visible*
>>> *if any coordinate of either end point is outside the window, then the line is not totally visible*

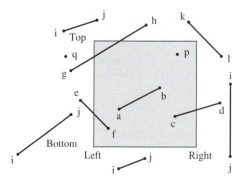

Figure 3–1   Two-dimensional clipping window.

> **if** $x_a < x_L$ **or** $x_a > x_R$ **then** Visibility = Partial
> **if** $x_b < x_L$ **or** $x_b > x_R$ **then** Visibility = Partial
> **if** $y_a < y_B$ **or** $y_a > y_T$ **then** Visibility = Partial
> **if** $y_b < y_B$ **or** $y_b > y_T$ **then** Visibility = Partial
> **end if**
>
> **if** Visibility = Partial **then**
>
> > *the line is partially visible or diagonally crosses a corner invisibly*
> > *determine the intersections and the visibility of the line*
>
> **end if**
>
> **if** Visibility = True **then**
>
> > *line is totally visible — draw line*
>
> **end if**
>
> *line is invisible*
>
> *next line*
>
> **finish**

Here, x_L, x_R, y_T, y_B are the x and y coordinates, respectively, of the left, right, top and bottom of the window edges. The order in which the tests for visibility or invisibility are performed is immaterial. Some lines require all four tests before being accepted as totally visible, or trivially rejected as totally invisible. Other lines require only one test. It is also immaterial whether the test for totally visible or totally invisible lines is performed first. However, the line–window edge intersection calculation is computationally expensive and should be performed last.

End Point Codes

The tests for totally visible lines and the region tests given above for totally invisible lines are formalized using a technique due to Dan Cohen and Ivan Sutherland. The technique uses a 4 bit (digit) code to indicate which of nine regions contains the end point of a line. The 4 bit codes are shown in Fig. 3–2. The rightmost bit is the first bit. The bits are set to 1, based on the following scheme:

First-bit set   —   if the end point is to the left of the window
Second-bit set —   if the end point is to the right of the window
Third-bit set   —   if the end point is below the window
Fourth-bit set —   if the end point is above the window

Otherwise, the bit is set to zero. From this it is obvious that, if both end point codes are *zero*, then both ends of the line lie inside the window; and the line is visible. The end point codes are also used to trivially reject totally invisible lines. Consider the truth table for the logical **and** operator:

True and False   →   False   1 and 0   →   0

                          False = 0

False and True   →   False   0 and 1   →   0

                             →

False and False   →   False   0 and 0   →   0

                           True = 1

True and True   →   True   1 and 1   →   1

If the bit-by-bit logical **and** of the two end point codes is *not zero*, then the line is totally invisible and is trivially rejected. The several examples shown in Table 3–1 help to clarify these statements. Notice in Table 3–1 that, when the logical **and** is not zero, the line is in fact totally invisible. However, when the logical **and** is zero, the line may be totally or partially visible, or in fact totally invisible. It is for this reason that it is necessary to check both end point codes separately to determine total visibility.

    End point code checking is easily implemented when bit manipulation routines are available. One possible software implementation that does *not* use bit manipulation routines is:

end point code algorithm

P_1 *and* P_2 *are the end points of the line*

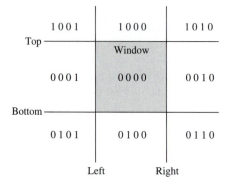

Figure 3–2   Codes for line end point regions.

Table 3–1   End Point Codes

Line (see Fig. 3–1)	End point codes (see Fig. 3–2)		Logical and	Comments
ab	0000	0000	0000	Totally visible
ij	0010	0110	0010	Totally invisible
ij	1001	1000	1000	Totally invisible
ij	0101	0001	0001	Totally invisible
ij	0100	0100	0100	Totally invisible
cd	0000	0010	0000	Partially visible
ef	0001	0000	0000	Partially visible
gh	0001	1000	0000	Partially visible
kl	1000	0010	0000	Totally invisible

x_L, x_R, y_T, y_B *are the left, right, top and bottom window coordinates*
 calculate the end point codes
 put the codes for each end into 1 × 4 arrays called P1code
  and P2code
 first end point: P_1
  if $x_1 < x_L$ **then** P1code(4) = 1 **else** P1code(4) = 0
  if $x_1 > x_R$ **then** P1code(3) = 1 **else** P1code(3) = 0
  if $y_1 < y_B$ **then** P1code(2) = 1 **else** P1code(2) = 0
  if $y_1 > y_T$ **then** P1code(1) = 1 **else** P1code(1) = 0
 second end point: P_2
  if $x_2 < x_L$ **then** P2code(4) = 1 **else** P2code(4) = 0
  if $x_2 > x_R$ **then** P2code(3) = 1 **else** P2code(3) = 0
  if $y_2 < y_B$ **then** P2code(2) = 1 **else** P2code(2) = 0
  if $y_2 > y_T$ **then** P2code(1) = 1 **else** P2code(1) = 0
finish

If totally visible and trivially invisible lines are determined first, then only potentially partially visible lines, for which the logical **and** of the end point codes is zero, are passed to the line intersection routine. This routine must also, of course, properly identify totally invisible lines that are passed to it.

The intersection between two lines can be determined either parametrically or nonparametrically. Explicitly, the equation of the infinite line through $P_1(x_1, y_1)$ and $P_2(x_2, y_2)$ is

$$y = m(x - x_1) + y_1 \qquad \text{or} \qquad y = m(x - x_2) + y_2$$

where
$$m = \frac{y_2 - y_1}{x_2 - x_1}$$

is the slope of the line. The intersections with the window edges are given by

Left:	$x_L, y = m(x_L - x_1) + y_1$	$m \neq \infty$
Right:	$x_R, y = m(x_R - x_1) + y_1$	$m \neq \infty$
Top:	$y_T, x = x_1 + (1/m)(y_T - y_1)$	$m \neq 0$
Bottom:	$y_B, x = x_1 + (1/m)(y_B - y_1)$	$m \neq 0$

Example 3–1 illustrates the explicit method for calculating the intersection values with the window edges.

Example 3–1   Explicit Line–Window Intersections

Consider the clipping window and the lines shown in Fig. 3–3. For the line from $P_1(3/2, 1/6)$ to $P_2(1/2, 3/2)$ the slope is

$$m = \frac{y_2 - y_1}{x_2 - x_1} = \frac{3/2 - 1/6}{1/2 - (-3/2)} = \frac{2}{3}$$

and the intersections with the window edge are

Left: $x = -1$ $y = \quad 2/3\,[-1 - (-3/2)] + 1/6$
                            $= \quad 1/2$

Right: $x = \quad 1$ $y = \quad 2/3\,[1 - (-3/2)] + 1/6$
                            $= \quad 11/6$

Top: $y = \quad 1$ $x = -3/2 \; + \; 3/2\,[1 \; - \; 1/6]$
                            $= -1/4$

Bottom: $y = -1$ $x = -3/2 \; + \; 3/2\,[-1 \; - \; 1/6]$
                            $= -13/4$

Notice that the intersection with the right edge occurs beyond the end of the line at P_2''.

Similarly, for the line from $P_3(-3/2, -1)$ to $P_4(3/2, 2)$

$$m = \frac{y_2 - y_1}{x_2 - x_1} = \frac{2 - (-1)}{3/2 - (-3/2)} = 1$$

and

Left: $x = -1$ $y = \quad (1)[-1 - (-3/2)] + (-1)$
                            $= -1/2$

Right: $x = \quad 1$ $y = \quad (1)[1 - (-3/2)] + (-1)$
                            $= \quad 3/2$

Top: $y = \quad 1$ $x = -3/2 \; + \; (1)[1 \; - \; (-1)]$
                            $= \quad 1/2$

Bottom: $y = -1$ $x = -3/2 \; + \; (1)[-1 \; - \; (-1)]$
                            $= -3/2$

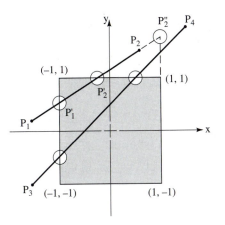

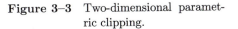

Figure 3–3   Two-dimensional parametric clipping.

In developing the structure of an efficient clipping algorithm, some special cases must be considered. If the slope of the line is infinite, it is parallel to the left and right edges; and only the top and bottom edges need be checked for intersections. Similarly, if the slope is zero, the line is parallel to the top and bottom edges; and only the left and right edges need be checked for intersections. Finally, if either end point code is zero, one end point is interior to the window; and only one intersection can occur. Rogers [Roge85] used these facts to develop an efficient explicit clipping algorithm.

3–2   Cohen–Sutherland Subdivision Line Clipping Algorithm

A clipping algorithm developed by Dan Cohen and Ivan Sutherland uses the end point codes to trivially accept or reject a line segment. If the line segment cannot be trivially accepted or rejected, then the Cohen–Sutherland algorithm divides the line at a window edge. The algorithm does not check to see if the intersection point is within the window, but rather attempts to accept or reject the two resulting segments using the line end point codes for the segments. Recalling line P_1P_2 of Fig. 3–3 immediately reveals a difficulty with this simple technique. If P_1P_2 is clipped against the left edge of the window, the two new segments are P_1P_1' and $P_1'P_2$. The end point codes for both these segments indicate that they both may be partially visible. Hence, neither can be rejected as invisible or accepted as visible. The key to the Cohen–Sutherland algorithm is always knowing that one of the end points is outside the window. Thus, the segment from this end point to the intersection point can always be rejected as invisible. The algorithm then proceeds with the remainder of the line. In effect this replaces the original end point with the intersection point. Simply stated, the Cohen–Sutherland algorithm is:

For each window edge:

For the line $P_1 P_2$, determine if the line is totally visible or can be trivially rejected as invisible.

If P_1 is outside the window, continue; otherwise, swap P_1 and P_2.

Replace P_1 with the intersection of $P_1 P_2$ and the window edge.

Example 3–2 further illustrates the algorithm.

Example 3–2   Cohen–Sutherland Clipping

Again consider the line $P_1 P_2$ clipped against the window shown in Fig. 3–3. The end point codes for $P_1(-3/2, 1/6)$ and $P_2(1/2, 3/2)$ are (0001) and (1000), respectively. The end point codes are not simultaneously zero, and the logical **and** of the end point codes is zero. Consequently, the line is neither totally visible nor trivially invisible. Comparing the first bits of the end point codes, the line crosses the left edge; and P_1 is outside the window.

The intersection with the left edge ($x = -1$) of the window is $P_1'(-1, 1/2)$. Replace P_1 with P_1' to yield the new line, $P_1(-1, 1/2)$ to $P_2(1/2, 3/2)$.

The end point codes for P_1 and P_2 are now (0000) and (1000), respectively. The line is neither totally visible nor trivially invisible.

Comparing the second bits, the line does not cross the right edge; skip to the bottom edge.

The end point codes for P_1 and P_2 are still (0000) and (1000), respectively. The line is neither totally visible nor trivially invisible.

Comparing the third bits, the line does not cross the bottom edge. Skip to the top edge.

The end point codes for P_1 and P_2 are still (0000) and (1000), respectively. The line is neither totally visible nor trivially invisible.

Comparing the fourth bits, the line crosses the top edge. P_1 is not outside. Swap P_1 and P_2 to yield the new line, $P_1(1/2, 3/2)$ to $P_2(-1, 1/2)$.

The intersection with the top edge ($y = 1$) of the window is $P_1'(-1/4, 1)$. Replace P_1 with P_1' to yield the new line, $P_1(-1/4, 1)$ to $P_2(-1, 1/2)$.

The end point codes for P_1 and P_2 are (0000) and (0000), respectively. The line is totally visible.

The procedure is complete.

Draw the line ($P_1' P_2'$ in Fig. 3–3).

The original Cohen–Sutherland algorithm is simple, elegant and efficient as originally implemented (see [Newm73, 79]). Duvanenko extensively studied the algorithm and, after optimization and recoding, improved the performance by between 50 and 80% [Duva90a, 90b, 93]. The improvements are based on the following observations:

> The slope of a clipped line is the same as the unclipped line; therefore, calculate the slope and inverse slope only once outside the main loop.

> If P_1 is not outside the window, P_1 and P_2 are swapped along with the end point codes. Thus, the intersection of the line and the window edge becomes the new P_1; P_2 remains unchanged. Therefore, only the end point code for P_1 needs to be recalculated.

> Examining Fig. 3–2 shows that, between any two of the nine regions, at most two bits need to be compared when determining if a line is trivially visible or invisible. Furthermore, if a partially visible line is already subdivided at a particular edge, it is not necessary to compare the bits for that edge when determining if the line crosses a different edge. Thus, it is only necessary to compare a single bit to determine if the line crosses a different edge. This addition to the code is particularly advantageous for the trivially invisible test.

The pseudocode implementation of the algorithm given below incorporates some, but for simplicity not all, of these optimizations. The remainder are left as an exercise for the student. Because the same concept is repeatedly applied, subroutine modules are used.

Cohen–Sutherland two-dimensional clipping algorithm

Window is a 1×4 array containing the edges x_L, x_R, y_B, y_T, respectively
P_1 and P_2 are the line end points with components P_1x, P_1y, P_2x, P_2y
P1code and P2code are 1×4 arrays containing the end point codes
Iflag classifies the slope; -1 vertical, 0 horizontal, $+1$ other

    call Endpoint(P_1, Window; P1code)
    call Endpoint(P_2, Window; P2code)
    call Sum(P1code; Sum1)
    call Sum(P2code; Sum2)
    call Visible(P1code, P2code, Sum1, Sum2; Vflag)

    find the trivially visible and invisible lines immediately and exit

    if Vflag = yes **then**   draw line and exit
    if Vflag = no **then**   exit without drawing line

    the line is partially visible
    calculate the slope which does not change as the line is clipped

    Iflag = 1   *initialize Iflag*

    check for vertical and horizontal lines

    if $P_2x = P_1x$ **then**
        Iflag = -1 *vertical line*
    else if $P_2y = P_1y$ **then**
        Iflag = 0   *horizontal line*

```
        else
              Slope = (P₂y − P₁y)/(P₂x − P₁x)        calculate slope
        end if
        clip a partially visible line
        while Vflag = partial
              for each window edge
              for i = 1 to 4
                    check to see if the line crosses the edge
                    if P1code(5 − i) <> P2code(5 − i) then
                          if P₁ is inside, swap the end points, Pcodes and Sums
                          if P1code(5 − i) = 0 then
                                Temp = P₁
                                P₁ = P₂
                                P₂ = Temp
                                Tempcode = P1code
                                P1code = P2code
                                P2code = Tempcode
                                Tempsum = Sum1
                                Sum1 = Sum2
                                Sum2 = Tempsum
                          end if
                          find intersections with the window edges
                          select the appropriate intersection routine
                          check for a vertical line
                          if Iflag <> −1 and  i ≤ 2 then        left and right edges
                                P₁y = Slope * (Window(i) − P₁x) + P₁y
                                P₁x = Window(i)
                                call Endpoint(P₁, Window; P1code)
                                call Sum(P1code; Sum1)
                          end if
                          if Iflag <> 0 and i > 2 then          bottom and top edges
                                if Iflag <> −1 then        not vertical line
                                      P₁x = (1/Slope) * (Window(i) − P₁y) + P₁x
                                end if
                                P₁y = Window(i)      if vertical line P₁x is unchanged
                                call Endpoint(P₁, Window; P1code)
                                call Sum(P1code; Sum1)
                          end if
                          call Visible(P1code, P2code, Sum1, Sum2; Vflag)
                          if Vflag = yes then   draw line and exit
                          if Vflag = no then   exit without drawing line
                    end if
              next i
        end while
finish
```

subroutine module to determine the visibility of a line segment

subroutine Visible(P1code, P2code, Sum1, Sum2; Vflag)

P1code *and* P2code *are* 1×4 *arrays containing the end point codes*
Sum1 *and* Sum2 *are the sums of the elements of the end point codes*
Vflag *is a flag set to no, partial, yes as the line segment is totally invisible, partially visible, or totally visible*

   assume the line is partially visible

   Vflag = partial

   check if the line is totally visible

   if Sum1 = 0 **and** Sum2 = 0 **then**
      Vflag = yes
   else

      check if the line is trivially invisible

      call Logical(P1code, P2code; Inter)
      if Inter <> 0 **then** Vflag = no
   end if

   the line may be partially visible

return

subroutine module to calculate the end point codes

subroutine Endpoint(P, Window; Pcode)

P_x, P_y *are the x and y components of the point* P
Window *is a* 1×4 *array containing the edges* x_L, x_R, y_B, y_T, *respectively*
Pcode *is a* 1×4 *array containing the end point code*

   determine the end point codes

   if $P_x < x_L$ **then** Pcode(4) = 1 **else** Pcode(4) = 0
   if $P_x > x_R$ **then** Pcode(3) = 1 **else** Pcode(3) = 0
   if $P_y < y_B$ **then** Pcode(2) = 1 **else** Pcode(2) = 0
   if $P_y > y_T$ **then** Pcode(1) = 1 **else** Pcode(1) = 0

return

subroutine to calculate the sum of the endpoint codes

subroutine Sum(Pcode; Sum)

Pcode *is a* 1×4 *array containing the end point code*
Sum *is the element-by-element sum of* Pcode

   calculate the sum

   Sum = 0
   for i = 1 **to** 4
      Sum = Sum + Pcode(i)
   next i

return

subroutine module to find the logical intersection

subroutine Logical(P1code, P2code; Inter)

P1code *and* P2code *are* 1×4 *arrays containing the end point codes*
Inter *is the sum of the bits for the logical intersection*

>   Inter $= 0$
>   **for** i $= 1$ **to** 4
>   Inter $=$ Inter $+$ Integer$((\text{P1code}(i) + \text{P2code}(i))/2)$
>   **next** i

return

Duvanenko, Gyurcsik and Robbins [Duva93] also show that three comparisons, rather than the four comparisons used previously, are sufficient to implement the trivially visible test. Rather than compare the end points to the window edges, the end points are compared to each other and to the window edges. The algorithm is

> **Duvanenko et al.'s trivial visible algorithm for the left and right edges.**
>
> *A similar algorithm is required for the bottom and top edges.*
> $P_1 x$ *and* $P_2 x$ *are the line end point* x *components*
> x_L, x_R *are the left and right window edges*
>
> >   **if** $P_1 x < P_2 x$ **then**
> >   **if** $P_1 x < x_L$ **then return** *not trivially visible*
> >   **if** $P_2 x > x_R$ **then return** *not trivially visible*
> >   **else**
> >   **if** $P_2 x < x_L$ **then return** *not trivially visible*
> >   **if** $P_1 x > x_R$ **then return** *not trivially visible*
> >   **end if**
> >
> >   *if get here then trivially visible*
> **finish**

Duvanenko, Gyurcsik and Robbins [Duva93] also show that two comparisons are optimal for determining if a line is trivially invisible. Their algorithm reverses the order of the two comparisons for the right edge of the window, i.e.

> **Duvanenko et al.'s trivial invisible algorithm for the left and right edges.**
>
> *A similar algorithm is required for the bottom and top edges.*
> $P_1 x$ *and* $P_2 x$ *are the line end point* x *components*
> x_L, x_R *are the left and right window edges*
>
> >   **if** $P_1 x < x_L$ **then**
> >   **if** $P_2 x < x_L$ **then return** *trivially invisible*
> >   **else**
> >   **if** $P_2 x > x_R$ **then**

$$\text{if } P_1x > x_R \text{ then return } \textit{trivially invisible}$$
        end if
     end if
  finish

They claim, on average, that this algorithm is more efficient than first comparing P_1x with x_R, followed by P_2x.

3–3   Midpoint Subdivision Algorithm

The Cohen–Sutherland algorithm requires the calculation of the intersection of the line with the window edge. This direct calculation is avoided by performing a binary search for the intersection by always dividing the line at its midpoint. The algorithm, which is a special case of the Cohen–Sutherland algorithm, was proposed by Sproull and Sutherland [Spro68] for implementation in hardware. Implementation in hardware is fast and efficient, because a parallel architecture is used and hardware addition and division by 2 are very fast. In hardware, division by 2 is accomplished by shifting each bit to the right. For example, the 4-bit binary representation of decimal 6 is 0110. Shifting each bit to the right by one yields 0011 which is decimal $3 = {}^6\!/_2$. Although originally designed for hardware implementation, the algorithm can be efficiently implemented in software provided the software system allows bit shifting.

The algorithm uses the line end point codes and associated tests to immediately identify totally visible lines, e.g., line a in Fig. 3–4, and trivially invisible lines, e.g., line b in Fig. 3–4. Lines which cannot be immediately identified using these tests, e.g., lines c to g in Fig. 3–4, are subdivided into two equal parts. The tests are then applied to each half until the intersection with the window edge is found or the length of the divided segments is infinitesimal, i.e., a point, e.g., line f in Fig. 3–4. The visibility of the point is then determined. The result is to perform a logarithmic search for the intersection point. The maximum number of subdivisions is equal to the precision (number of bits) of the representation of the end points of the line.

To illustrate the technique, consider lines c and f of Fig. 3–4. Although line f is not visible, it crosses the corner and cannot be trivially rejected. Subdivision at the midpoint, P_{m_1}, allows the half, $P_{m_1}P_2$, to be trivially rejected. The half, $P_{m_1}P_1$, again crosses the corner and cannot be trivially rejected. Further, subdivision at P_{m_2} allows rejection of $P_{m_2}P_1$ as invisible. Subdivision of the remaining portion, $P_{m_1}P_{m_2}$, continues until the intersection of the line with the extension of the right-hand window edge is found within some specified accuracy. This point is then examined and found to be invisible. Hence, the entire line is invisible.

From the end point codes, line c of Fig. 3–4 is also neither totally visible, nor can it be trivially rejected as invisible. Subdivision at the midpoint P_{m_1} yields the same result for both halves. Setting aside the segment $P_{m_1}P_1$ for later consideration, the segment $P_{m_1}P_2$ is further subdivided at P_{m_2}. The segment

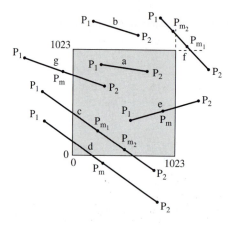

Figure 3–4 Midpoint subdivision.

$P_{m_1}P_{m_2}$ is now totally visible, and the segment $P_{m_2}P_2$ partially visible. The segment $P_{m_1}P_{m_2}$ can now be drawn. However, this would result in the visible portion of the line being inefficiently drawn as a series of short segments. Instead the point P_{m_2} is remembered as the current farthest visible point from P_1.

Subdivision of the segment $P_{m_2}P_2$ continues. Each time a visible midpoint is found it is declared the farthest visible point from P_1, until the intersection with the bottom edge of the window is determined to some specified accuracy. This intersection is then declared the farthest visible point from P_1. The segment $P_{m_1}P_1$ is then examined in the same way. For line c of Fig. 3–4 the farthest visible point from P_2 is the intersection with the left-hand window edge. The visible portion of the line P_1P_2 is then drawn between the two intersections.

For lines like c and d of Fig. 3–4, the midpoint subdivision algorithm performs two logarithmic searches for the two farthest visible points from the ends of the line. These are the intersections with the window edges. Each midpoint subdivision is a crude guess at these points. For lines like e and g, which have one end point visible, one of these searches is trivial. In a software implementation the two searches are performed sequentially; in a hardware implementation they are performed in parallel. The algorithm is formalized in three steps [Newm73, 79].

For each end point:

> If the end point is visible, then it is the farthest visible point. The process is complete. If not, continue.
>
> If the line is trivially invisible, no output is generated. The process is complete. If not, continue.
>
> Guess at the farthest visible point by dividing the line P_1P_2 at its midpoint, P_m. Apply the previous tests to the two segments P_1P_m and P_mP_2. If P_mP_2 is rejected as trivially invisible, the midpoint is an overestimation of the farthest visible point. Continue with P_1P_m.

Otherwise, the midpoint is an underestimation of the farthest visible point. Continue with $P_2 P_m$. If the segment becomes so short that the midpoint corresponds to the accuracy of the machine or, as specified, to the end points, evaluate the visibility of the point and the process is complete.

A specific example better illustrates the algorithm.

Example 3–3   Midpoint Subdivision

Consider the window in the screen coordinates shown in Fig. 3–4 to have left, right, bottom and top edges of 0, 1023, 0, 1023, respectively. The line c has end points $P_1(-307, 631)$ and $P_2(820, -136)$ in screen coordinates. The end point code for P_1 is (0001), and that for P_2 is (0100). Both end point codes are not zero, so the line is not totally visible. The logical intersection of the end point codes is (0000). The line is not trivially invisible. Look for the intersections.

The midpoint is

$$x_m = \frac{x_2 + x_1}{2} = \frac{820 - 307}{2} = 256.5 = 256$$

$$y_m = \frac{y_2 + y_1}{2} = -136 + 6312 = 247.5 = 247$$

using integer arithmetic. The end point code for the midpoint is (0000). Neither segment $P_1 P_m$ nor $P_2 P_m$ is totally visible or trivially invisible. First looking for the farthest visible point from P_1 followed by the farthest visible point from P_2 the subdivision process continues as shown in Table 3–2. The actual equation of the line $P_1 P_2$ yields intersection points at $(0, 422)$ and $(620, 0)$. The differences are due to integer arithmetic truncation.

A pseudocode implementation of the algorithm shown here uses the Endpoint, Sum and Logical subroutines used in Sec. 3–2 for the Cohen–Sutherland algorithm.

Midpoint subdivision clipping algorithm

subroutine $\mathrm{mid}(P_1, P_2, x_L, x_R, y_B, y_T)$

Window *is a* 1×4 *array containing the window edges* x_L, x_R, y_B, y_T
P_1 *and* P_2 *are the line end points with components* $P_1 x$, $P_1 y$, $P_2 x$, $P_2 y$
P1code *and* P2code *are* 1×4 *arrays containing the end point codes*

   set up for visibility checks

   call Endpoint(P1, Window; P1code)
   call Endpoint(P2, Window; P2code)
   call Sum(P1code; Sum1)
   call Sum(P2code; Sum2)
   call Visible(P1code, P2code, Sum1, Sum2; Vflag)

   check for trivially visible line

   if Vflag = yes **then**

Table 3–2   Midpoint Subdivision

P_1		P_2		P_m		Comment
−307,	631	820,	−136	256,	247	Save P_1,
						continue $P_m P_2$
256,	247	820,	−136	538,	55	Continue $P_m P_2$
538,	55	820,	−136	679,	−41	Reject $P_m P_2$, $P_2 \leftarrow P_m$
						continue $P_m P_2$
538,	55	679,	−41	608,	7	Continue $P_m P_2$
608,	7	679,	−41	643,	−17	Reject $P_m P_2$, $P_2 \leftarrow P_m$
						continue $P_m P_2$
608,	7	643,	−17	625,	−5	Reject $P_m P_2$, $P_2 \leftarrow P_m$
						continue $P_m P_2$
608,	7	625,	−5	616,	1	Continue $P_m P_2$
616,	1	625,	−5	620,	−2	Reject $P_m P_2$, $P_2 \leftarrow P_m$
						continue $P_m P_2$
616,	1	620,	−2	618,	−1	Reject $P_m P_2$, $P_2 \leftarrow P_m$
						continue $P_m P_2$
616,	1	618,	−1	617,	0	Success
						Recall saved P_1,
						$P_2 \leftarrow P_1, P_1 \leftarrow P_m$
617,	0	−307,	631	155,	315	Continue $P_m P_2$
155,	315	−307,	631	−76,	473	Reject $P_m P_2$, $P_2 \leftarrow P_m$
						continue $P_m P_2$
155,	315	−76,	473	39,	394	Continue $P_m P_2$
39,	394	−76,	473	−19,	433	Reject $P_m P_2$, $P_2 \leftarrow P_m$
						continue $P_m P_2$
39,	394	−19,	433	10,	413	Continue $P_m P_2$
10,	413	−19,	433	−5,	423	Reject $P_m P_2$, $P_2 \leftarrow P_m$
						continue $P_m P_2$
2,	418	−5,	423	2,	418	Continue $P_m P_2$
2,	418	−5,	423	−2,	420	Reject $P_m P_2$, $P_2 \leftarrow P_m$
						continue $P_m P_2$
2,	418	−2,	420	0,	419	Continue $P_m P_2$
0,	419	−2,	420	−1,	419	Reject $P_m P_2$, $P_2 \leftarrow P_m$
						continue $P_m P_2$
0,	419	−1,	419	−1,	419	Success

        draw visible line

          exit subroutine

      end if

    check for trivially invisible line

    if Vflag = no **then**

        trivially invisible

          exit subroutine

    end if

the line is partially visible or crosses a corner invisibly

Error = 1

for i = 1 to 2

    if P_1 or P_2 is inside the window, only go through the loop once

    if i = 1 **and** Sum1 = 0 **then**   *P_1 inside — switch P_1, P_2*

        SaveP$_2$ = P_1

        Temp = P_2

        P_2 = P_1

        P_1 = Temp

        i = 2

    end if

    if i = 1 **and** Sum2 = 0 **then**   *P_2 inside — switch P_1, P_2*

        Temp = P_2

        P_2 = P_1

        P_1 = Temp

        SaveP$_2$ = P_1

        i = 2

    end if

    SaveP$_1$ = P_1

    TempSum1 = Sum1

    SaveP1code = P1code

    while $\mathbf{Abs}(P_2x - P_1x) >$ Error **or** $\mathbf{Abs}(P_2y - P_1y) >$ Error

        P_m = **Integer**$((P_2 + P_1)/2)$

        Temp = P_1 *temporarily save P_1*

        P_1 = P_m *assume P_m is the far end of the line*

        call Endpoint(P_1, Window; P1code)

        call Sum(P1code; Sum1)

        call Visible(P1code, P2code, Sum1, Sum2; Vflag)

        if Vflag = no **then**   *reject $P_m P_2$*

            P_1 = Temp   *backup to P_1*

            P_2 = P_m *P_m is now the far end of the line*

            P2code = P1code   *switch the end point codes and sums*

            Sum2 = Sum1

            call Endpoint(P1, Window; P1code)

            call Sum(P1code; Sum1)

        end if

    end while

    if i = 1 **then**

        SaveP$_2$ = P_m

        P_1 = P_m

        P_2 = SaveP$_1$

        Sum2 = TempSum1

$\qquad$ P2code = SaveP1code

$\quad$ **else**

$\qquad$ $P_1 = P_m$

$\qquad$ $P_2 = SaveP_2$

$\quad$ **end if**

$\quad$ **call** Endpoint(P_1, Window; P1code)

$\quad$ **call** Endpoint(P_2, Window; P2code)

$\quad$ **call** Sum(P1code; Sum1)

$\quad$ **call** Sum(P2code; Sum2)

$\quad$ **call** Visible(P1code, P2code, Sum1, Sum2; Vflag)

next i

the partially visible line is found — check for invisible point

call Logical(P1code, P2code; Inter)

if Inter $<>$ 0 **then**

$\quad$ *draw* P_1P_2

end if

return

3–4 $\quad$ Two-dimensional Parametric Line Clipping for Convex Boundaries

The algorithms presented previously assume that the clipping window has a regular rectangular polygonal boundary. For many purposes, the clipping window is not a regular rectangular polygon. For example, suppose that the rectangular clipping window is rotated with respect to the coordinate system, as shown in Fig. 3–5. If the clipping window is not a rectangular polygon, then neither of the algorithms discussed previously is applicable. Cyrus and Beck developed an algorithm for clipping to arbitrary convex regions [Cyru78].

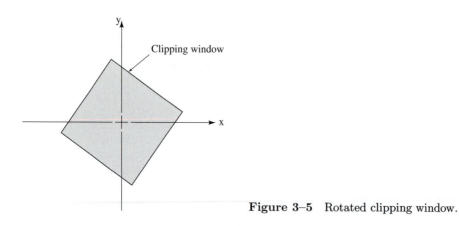

$\qquad\qquad\qquad\qquad\qquad\qquad\qquad\qquad$ **Figure 3–5** $\quad$ Rotated clipping window.

Before specifically developing the Cyrus–Beck algorithm in the next section, consider clipping a parametrically defined line to a window. The parametric equation of a line segment from P_1 to P_2 is

$$P(t) = P_1 + (P_2 - P_1)t \qquad 0 \le t \le 1 \tag{3 – 1}$$

where t is the parameter. Restricting the range of t to $0 \le t \le 1$ makes it a line segment rather than an infinite line. The parametric description of a line is independent of any coordinate system. This attribute makes the parametric form particularly useful for determining the intersection between a line and the edge of an arbitrary convex polygon. The technique is first illustrated with a regular rectangular window.

For a two-dimensional Cartesian coordinate system, Eq. $(3 – 1)$ yields a pair of parametric equations, one for each coordinate, i.e.

$$x(t) = x_1 + (x_2 - x_1)t \qquad 0 \le t \le 1 \tag{3 – 2a}$$

$$y(t) = y_1 + (y_2 - y_1)t \qquad 0 \le t \le 1 \tag{3 – 2b}$$

For a rectangular clipping window, one of the coordinates of the intersection with each edge is known. Only the other intersection needs to be calculated. From Eq. $(3 – 1)$ the value of the parameter t for any point on the line segment is

$$t = \frac{P(t) - P_1}{P_2 - P_1}$$

From Eq. $(3 – 2)$ the specific value of t corresponding to the intersection with the window edge is

For the left edge: $\qquad t = \dfrac{x_L - x_1}{x_2 - x_1} \qquad 0 \le t \le 1$

For the right edge: $\qquad t = \dfrac{x_R - x_1}{x_2 - x_1} \qquad 0 \le t \le 1$

For the top edge: $\qquad t = \dfrac{y_T - y_1}{y_2 - y_1} \qquad 0 \le t \le 1$

For the bottom edge: $\qquad t = \dfrac{y_B - y_1}{y_2 - y_1} \qquad 0 \le t \le 1$

where x_L, x_R, y_B, y_T are the coordinates of the left, right, bottom and top window edges. If solutions of these equations yield values of t outside the range $0 \le t \le 1$, then those solutions are discarded because they represent points beyond the end of the line segment.

Partially Visible Lines

An example for partially visible lines serves to illustrate the basic concept of parametric line clipping.

Example 3–4   Simple Partially Visible Line

Consider the partially visible line from $P_1(-3/2, -3/4)$ to $P_2(3/2, 1/2)$ clipped to the window $(-1, 1, -1, 1)$, i.e., x_L, x_R, y_B, y_T, as shown in Fig. 3–6.

For the left edge:

$$t = \frac{x_L - x_1}{x_2 - x_1} = \frac{-1 - (-3/2)}{3/2 - (-3/2)} = \frac{1/2}{3} = \frac{1}{6}$$

For the right edge:

$$t = \frac{x_R - x_1}{x_2 - x_1} = \frac{1 - (-3/2)}{3/2 - (-3/2)} = \frac{5/2}{3} = \frac{5}{6}$$

For the bottom edge:

$$t = \frac{y_B - y_1}{y_2 - y_1} = \frac{-1 - (-3/4)}{1/2 - (-3/4)} = \frac{-1/4}{5/4} = \frac{-1}{5}$$

which is less than zero and is thus rejected.

For the top edge:

$$t = \frac{y_T - y_1}{y_2 - y_1} = \frac{1 - (-3/4)}{1/2 - (-3/4)} = \frac{7/4}{5/4} = \frac{7}{5}$$

which is greater than one and is also rejected. The visible portion of the line is then from $1/6 \le t \le 5/6$.

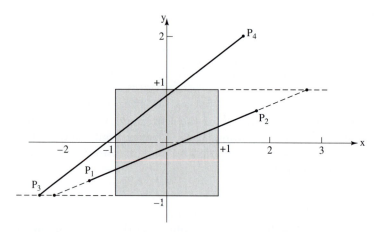

Figure 3–6   Parametric clipping of partially visible lines.

The x and y coordinates of the intersection points are obtained from the parametric equations. In particular, for $t = \frac{1}{6}$ Eq. $(3-2)$ yields

$$x\left(\frac{1}{6}\right) = -\frac{3}{2} + \left[\frac{3}{2} - \left(-\frac{3}{2}\right)\right]\left(\frac{1}{6}\right) = -1$$

which of course is already known, since $x = -1$ represents the intersection with the left edge of the window. The y coordinate is

$$y\left(\frac{1}{6}\right) = -\frac{3}{4} + \left[\frac{1}{2} - \left(-\frac{3}{4}\right)\right]\left(\frac{1}{6}\right) = -\frac{13}{24}$$

Similarly, for $t = \frac{5}{6}$

$$\left[x\left(\frac{5}{6}\right) \quad y\left(\frac{5}{6}\right)\right] = \left[-\frac{3}{2} \quad -\frac{3}{4}\right] + \left[\frac{3}{2} - \left(-\frac{3}{2}\right)\frac{1}{2} \quad -\left(-\frac{3}{4}\right)\right]\left(\frac{5}{6}\right)$$

$$= \left[1 \quad \frac{7}{24}\right]$$

where the separate calculations for the x and y coordinates have been combined. Again, since the line intersects the right-hand edge the x coordinate for the parameter value of $\frac{5}{6}$ is already known.

From Ex. 3–4 the technique appears to be simple and straightforward. However, there are some difficulties which are best illustrated by further examples.

Example 3–5   Partially Visible Line

Consider the line from $P_3(-\frac{5}{2}, -1)$ to $P_4(\frac{3}{2}, 2)$ also shown in Fig. 3–6 and again clipped to the window $(-1, 1, -1, 1)$. Here, the intersection points are given by the parametric values

$$t_L = \frac{3}{8} \qquad t_R = \frac{7}{8} \qquad t_B = 0 \qquad t_T = \frac{2}{3}$$

and all four values of t fall in the range $0 \leq t \leq 1$.

It is well known that if a straight line segment intersects a convex polygon, it does so in at most two points. Hence, only two of the four parameter values found in Ex. 3–5 are required. Rearranging the four parameter values into the numerically increasing sequence t_B, t_L, t_T, t_R and inspecting Fig. 3–6 shows that the required values are $t_L = \frac{3}{8}$ and $t_T = \frac{2}{3}$ which yield intersection points at $(-1, \frac{1}{8})$ and $(\frac{1}{6}, 1)$, respectively. These parameter values are the maximum minimum value and the minimum maximum value of the t parameters. Formally determining these values is a simple classical problem in linear programming. An algorithm for this is given in Sec. 3–5.

As in any clipping algorithm, the ability to quickly identify and separate totally visible and totally invisible lines is important. The next two examples illustrate some further difficulties.

Example 3–6   Totally Visible Lines

Consider the entirely visible line $P_1(-\frac{1}{2}, \frac{1}{2})$ to $P_2(\frac{1}{2}, -\frac{1}{2})$, again clipped to the window $(-1, 1, -1, 1)$ as shown in Fig. 3–7. The parameter values for the window edge intersections are

$$t_L = -\frac{1}{2} \qquad t_R = \frac{3}{2} \qquad t_B = \frac{3}{2} \qquad t_T = -\frac{1}{2}$$

All these values are outside the range $0 \le t \le 1$.

From Ex. 3–6 it appears that a technique for identifying totally visible lines has been found. However, Ex. 3–7 illustrates that this is not the case.

Example 3–7   Totally Invisible Lines

Consider the totally invisible line $P_3(\frac{3}{2}, -\frac{1}{2})$ to $P_4(2, \frac{1}{2})$ also shown in Fig. 3–7. The clipping window is again $(-1, 1, -1, 1)$. Here the parametric values for the window edge intersections are

$$t_L = -5 \qquad t_R = -1 \qquad t_B = -\frac{1}{2} \qquad t_T = \frac{3}{2}$$

Again, all these values are outside the range $0 \le t \le 1$.

The result given in Ex. 3–7 is the same condition previously identified with a totally visible line. But in contrast to the line $P_1 P_2$ of Ex. 3–6, the line $P_3 P_4$ is invisible. From these two examples it is evident that for parametric lines no simple, unique method for distinguishing totally visible or totally invisible lines is available. It is also evident that a more formal approach to the problem is required.

3–5   Cyrus–Beck Algorithm

To develop a reliable clipping algorithm it is necessary to find a reliable technique for determining whether a point on a line is inside, on, or outside a window. The Cyrus–Beck algorithm [Cyru78] uses the normal vector to accomplish this.

Consider a convex clipping region R. Although R is not limited to a two-dimensional region, the examples used for the present discussion assume one. Thus, R can be any convex planar polygon. It *cannot* be a concave polygon. An inner normal vector, n, for any point a on the boundary of R must satisfy the vector dot product

$$n \cdot (b - a) \ge 0$$

where b is any other point on the boundary of R. To see this, recall that the dot product of two vectors V_1 and V_2 is given by

$$V_1 \cdot V_2 = |V_1||V_2| \cos \theta$$

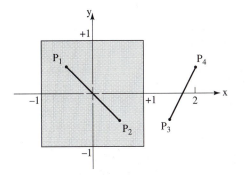

Figure 3–7   Parametric clipping of visible and invisible lines.

where θ is the smaller of the angles formed by $\mathbf{V}_1$ and $\mathbf{V}_2$. Note that if $\theta = \pi/2$ then $\cos \theta = 0$ and $\mathbf{V}_1 \cdot \mathbf{V}_2 = 0$; i.e., when the dot product of two vectors is zero the two vectors are perpendicular. Figure 3–8 shows a convex region R, i.e., a clipping window. At the point a on the boundary, both the inner normal, $\mathbf{n}_i$, and the outer normal, $\mathbf{n}_o$, are shown, along with several vectors to other points on the region boundary. The angle between $\mathbf{n}_i$ and any of the vectors is always in the range $-\pi/2 \le \theta \le \pi/2$. In this range the cosine is always positive, hence the dot product is always positive, as stated previously. However, the angle between the outer normal and any of these vectors is always $\pi - \theta$; and $\cos(\pi - \theta) = -\cos \theta$ is always negative. To further illustrate this, consider the following example.

Example 3–8   Inner and Outer Normals

Consider the rectangular region in Fig. 3–8. Here the inner and outer normals at a are $\mathbf{n}_i = \mathbf{i}$ and $\mathbf{n}_o = -\mathbf{i}$, respectively, where $\mathbf{i}$ is the unit vector in the x direction. Table 3–3 shows the values of the dot product of the inner and

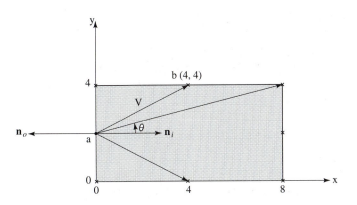

Figure 3–8   Inner and outer normals.

outer normals and vectors from a to various points b on the region boundary. As a specific example, note that the inner normal at a is

$$\mathbf{n}_i = \mathbf{i}$$

The vector from $a(0, 2)$ to $b(4, 4)$ is

$$\mathbf{b} - \mathbf{a} = 4\mathbf{i} + 2\mathbf{j}$$

The dot product is

$$\mathbf{n}_i \cdot (\mathbf{b} - \mathbf{a}) = \mathbf{i} \cdot (4\mathbf{i} + 2\mathbf{j}) = 4$$

Table 3–3

a	b	$\mathbf{n}_i \cdot (\mathbf{b} - \mathbf{a})$	$\mathbf{n}_o \cdot (\mathbf{b} - \mathbf{a})$
$(0, 2)$	$(0, 4)$	0	0
	$(4, 4)$	4	-4
	$(8, 4)$	8	-8
	$(8, 2)$	8	-8
	$(8, 0)$	8	-8
	$(4, 0)$	4	-4
	$(0, 0)$	0	0

The zero values in Table 3–3 indicate that the vector and the inner and outer normals are perpendicular.

Returning to the determination of the intersection of a line and a window edge, again consider the parametric representation of the line from P_1 to P_2

$$P(t) = P_1 + (P_2 - P_1)t \qquad 0 \le t \le 1$$

If f is a boundary point of the convex region R and $\mathbf{n}$ is an inner normal for one of its boundaries, then for any particular value of t, i.e., any particular point on the line $P_1 P_2$

$$\mathbf{n} \cdot [\mathbf{P}(t) - \mathbf{f}] < 0$$

implies that the vector $\mathbf{P}(t) - \mathbf{f}$ is pointed away from the interior of R

$$\mathbf{n} \cdot [\mathbf{P}(t) - \mathbf{f}] = 0$$

implies that $\mathbf{P}(t) - \mathbf{f}$ is pointed parallel to the plane containing f and perpendicular to the normal

$$\mathbf{n} \cdot [\mathbf{P}(t) - \mathbf{f}] > 0$$

implies $\mathbf{P}(t) - \mathbf{f}$ is pointed toward the interior of R as illustrated in Fig. 3–9. Together these conditions show that, if the convex region R is closed, i.e., for the two-dimensional case a closed convex polygon, an infinite line which intersects

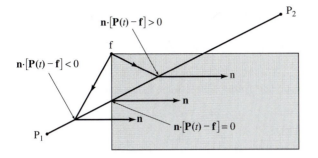

Figure 3–9   Vector directions.

the boundary of the region does so at precisely two points. Further, these two points do not lie on the same boundary plane or edge. Thus,

$$\mathbf{n} \cdot [\, \mathbf{P}(t) - \mathbf{f} \,] = 0$$

has only one solution. If the point f lies in the boundary plane or edge for which $\mathbf{n}$ is the inner normal, then that point t on the line $P(t)$ which satisfies this condition is the intersection of the line and the boundary plane.

Partially Visible Lines

We use an example to illustrate the technique for partially visible lines.

Example 3–9   Cyrus–Beck Clipping — Partially Visible Lines

Consider the line from $P_1(-1, 1)$ to $P_2(9, 3)$ clipped to the rectangular region shown in Fig. 3–10. The equation of the line $P_1 P_2$ is $y = (x + 6)/5$ which

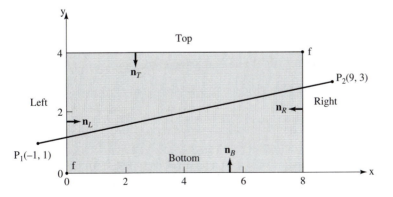

Figure 3–10   Cyrus–Beck clipping — partially visible line.

intersects the window at $(0, {}^6\!/_5)$ and $(8, {}^{14}\!/_5)$. The parametric representation of the line $P_1 P_2$ is

$$P(t) = P_1 + (P_2 - P_1)t = [-1 \quad 1] + [10 \quad 2]t$$

$$= (10t - 1)\mathbf{i} + (2t + 1)\mathbf{j} \qquad 0 \leq t \leq 1$$

where $\mathbf{i}, \mathbf{j}$ are the unit vectors in the x and y directions, respectively. The four inner normals are

Left:	$\mathbf{n}_L$	$=$	$\mathbf{i}$
Right:	$\mathbf{n}_R$	$=$	$-\mathbf{i}$
Bottom:	$\mathbf{n}_B$	$=$	$\mathbf{j}$
Top:	$\mathbf{n}_T$	$=$	$-\mathbf{j}$

Choosing $f = (0, 0)$ for the left edge yields

$$P(t) - \mathbf{f} = (10t - 1)\mathbf{i} + (2t + 1)\mathbf{j}$$

and

$$\mathbf{n}_L \cdot [P(t) - \mathbf{f}] = 10t - 1 = 0$$

or

$$t = \frac{1}{10}$$

is the intersection of the line and the left edge of the clipping window. Hence

$$P\left(\frac{1}{10}\right) = [-1 \quad 1] + [10 \quad 2]\left(\frac{1}{10}\right) = \left[0 \quad \frac{6}{5}\right]$$

which is the same as that explicitly calculated.

Choosing $f = (8, 4)$ for the right edge yields

$$P(t) - \mathbf{f} = (10t - 9)\mathbf{i} + (2t - 3)\mathbf{j}$$

and

$$\mathbf{n}_R \cdot [P(t) - \mathbf{f}] = -(10t - 9) = 0$$

or

$$t = \frac{9}{10}$$

as the intersection point of the line and the right edge. Specifically

$$P\left(\frac{9}{10}\right) = [-1 \quad 1] + [10 \quad 2]\left(\frac{9}{10}\right) = \left[8 \quad \frac{14}{5}\right]$$

which is also the same as the explicit calculation.

Using $f = (0, 0)$ for the bottom edge yields

$$\mathbf{n}_B \cdot [P(t) - \mathbf{f}] = (2t + 1) = 0$$

or

$$t = -\frac{1}{2}$$

which is outside the range $0 \leq t \leq 1$ and is thus rejected.

Using $f = (8, 4)$ for the top edge yields

$$\mathbf{n}_T \cdot [P(t) - \mathbf{f}] = -(2t - 3) = 0$$

or

$$t = \frac{3}{2}$$

which is also outside the range $0 \leq t \leq 1$ and is also rejected. The visible range for the line $P_1 P_2$ clipped to the rectangular region of Fig. 3–10 is ${}^1\!/_{10} \leq t \leq {}^9\!/_{10}$, or from $(0, {}^6\!/_5)$ to $(8, {}^{14}\!/_5)$.

This example shows that the intersection points are easily found.

Totally Visible Lines

Identifying totally visible and totally invisible lines is illustrated by three further examples.

Example 3–10   Cyrus–Beck — Totally Visible Lines

Consider the line $P_1(1,1)$ to $P_2(7,3)$ clipped to the rectangular window shown in Fig. 3–11. The parametric representation of the line P_1P_2 is

$$P(t) = [1 \quad 1] + [6 \quad 2]t$$

Using the inner normals and boundary points of Ex. 3–9, the results are given in Table 3–4.

Table 3–4

Edge	n	f	$P(t) - f$	$n \cdot [P(t) - f]$	t
Left	$-i$	$(0,0)$	$(\ 1+6t)i + (\ 1+2t)j$	$1 + 6t$	$-\frac{1}{6}$
Right	$-i$	$(8,4)$	$(-7+6t)i + (-3+2t)j$	$7 - 6t$	$-\frac{7}{6}$
Bottom	j	$(0,0)$	$(\ 1+6t)i + (\ 1+2t)j$	$1 + 2t$	$-\frac{1}{2}$
Top	$-j$	$(8,4)$	$(-7+6t)i + (-3+2t)j$	$3 - 2t$	$\frac{3}{2}$

All the intersection values for t are outside the range $0 \le t \le 1$. The entire line is visible.

Totally Invisible Lines

The next two examples consider two types of invisible lines. One line is totally to the left of the window and can be declared invisible using the end point codes

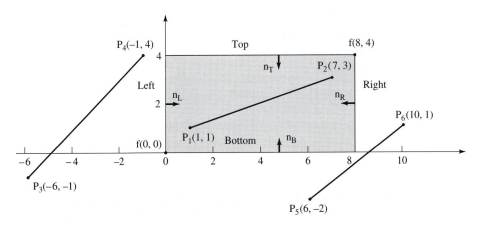

Figure 3–11   Cyrus–Beck clipping — visible and invisible lines.

discussed in Sec. 3–1. The second crosses the window corner outside the window itself. It cannot be declared invisible using the end point codes.

Example 3–11   Cyrus–Beck — Trivially Invisible Line

Consider the line $P_3(-6, -1)$ to $P_4(-1, 4)$ clipped to the rectangular window shown in Fig. 3–11. The line is invisible. The parametric representation is

$$P(t) = [-6 \quad -1] + [5 \quad 5]\,t$$

Using the inner normals and boundary points of the previous examples, the results are given in Table 3–5.

Table 3–5

Edge	n	f	$P(t) - f$	$n \cdot [P(t) - f]$	t
Left	i	(0,0)	$(-6 + 5t)\,i + (-1 + 5t)\,j$	$-6 + 5t$	$6/5$
Right	$-i$	(8,4)	$(-14 + 5t)\,i + (-5 + 5t)\,j$	$-(-14 + 5t)$	$14/5$
Bottom	j	(0,0)	$(-6 + 5t)\,i + (-1 + 5t)\,j$	$-1 + 5t$	$1/5$
Top	$-j$	(8,4)	$(-14 + 5t)\,i + (-5 + 5t)\,j$	$-(-5 + 5t)$	1

Examination of the results in Table 3–5 shows that the intersection values for the left and right edges are both outside the range $0 \le t \le 1$, but those for the top and bottom are both within the range $0 \le t \le 1$. Based on this, the line might initially be assumed visible in the range $1/5 \le t \le 1$. However, further consideration of the intersections for the left and right edges shows that both intersection values of the parameter are greater than one. This shows that the window is completely to the right of the line, hence the line is invisible. Similarly, if both values are less than zero the window is completely to the left of the line, and the line is invisible.

If in Ex. 3–11 P_3 and P_4 are interchanged, then the results show that the window is completely to the left of the line. The direction of the line is important in arriving at the decision about the invisibility of the line. The next example further explores this question.

Example 3–12   Cyrus–Beck — Nontrivially Invisible Line

Here the line from $P_5(6, -2)$ to $P_6(10, 1)$, again clipped to the rectangular window of Fig. 3–11, is considered. The parametric representation is

$$P(t) = [6 \quad -2] + [4 \quad 3]\,t$$

Using the inner normals and boundary points of the previous examples yields the results given in Table 3–6. These results show that the intersections for the left and the top edges fall outside the required range. However, the intersections for the right and bottom edges are within the proper range. But, considering the direction of the line to be from P_5 to P_6, it is not possible for the line to intersect the right edge at $t = 1/2$ before it intersects the bottom edge at $t = 2/3$ and still pierce the region R, i.e., the window. Thus, the line is invisible.

Table 3–6

Edge	n	f	$P(t) - \mathbf{f}$	$\mathbf{n} \cdot [\mathbf{P}(t) - \mathbf{f}]$	t
Left	i	$(0,0)$	$(\ \ 6 + 4t)\mathbf{i} + (-2 + 3t)\mathbf{j}$	$6 + 4t$	$-3/2$
Right	$-$i	$(8,4)$	$(-2 + 4t)\mathbf{i} + (-6 + 3t)\mathbf{j}$	$-(-2 + 4t)$	$1/2$
Bottom	j	$(0,0)$	$(6 + 4t)\mathbf{i} + (-2 + 3t)\mathbf{j}$	$-2 + 3t$	$2/3$
Top	$-$j	$(8,4)$	$(-2 + 4t)\mathbf{i} + (-6 + 3t)\mathbf{j}$	$-(-6 + 3t)$	2

From these examples, it is clear that apparently visible lines are correctly identified by also considering the direction of the line. This observation is exploited in the formal statement of the Cyrus–Beck algorithm given below.

Formal Statement of Cyrus–Beck Algorithm

To formalize the algorithm, again recall that the parametric representation of a line is

$$P(t) = P_1 + (P_2 - P_1)t \qquad 0 \le t \le 1 \tag{3 – 3}$$

and that the dot product of an inner normal and the vector from any point on the parametric line to any other point on the boundary, i.e.

$$\mathbf{n}_i \cdot [\mathbf{P}(t) - \mathbf{f}_i] \qquad i = 1, 2, 3, \ldots \tag{3 – 4}$$

is positive, zero or negative for a point on the parametric line interior to the region, on the region boundary or exterior to the region. This relation is applied for each boundary plane or edge, i, of the region. Combining Eqs. $(3 - 3)$ and $(3–4)$ yields

$$\mathbf{n}_i \cdot [\mathbf{P}_1 + (\mathbf{P}_2 - \mathbf{P}_1)t - \mathbf{f}_i] = 0 \tag{3 – 5}$$

as the condition for a point on the parametric line which lies on the boundary of the region, i.e., the intersection point. Alternatively, Eq. $(3 - 5)$ becomes

$$\mathbf{n}_i \cdot [\mathbf{P}_1 - \mathbf{f}_i] + \mathbf{n}_i \cdot [\mathbf{P}_2 - \mathbf{P}_1]t = 0 \tag{3 – 6}$$

Noting that the vector $\mathbf{P}_2 - \mathbf{P}_1$ defines the direction of the line and that the vector $\mathbf{P}_1 - \mathbf{f}_i$ is proportional to the distance from the end point of the line to the boundary point, let

$$\mathbf{D} = \mathbf{P}_2 - \mathbf{P}_1$$

be the direction of the line and

$$\mathbf{w}_i = \mathbf{P}_1 - \mathbf{f}_i$$

be a weighting factor. Equation (3–6) then becomes

$$t(\mathbf{n}_i{\cdot}\mathbf{D}) + \mathbf{w}_i{\cdot}\mathbf{n}_i = 0 \qquad\qquad (3-7)$$

Solving for t yields

$$t = -\frac{\mathbf{w}_i{\cdot}\mathbf{n}_i}{\mathbf{D}{\cdot}\mathbf{n}_i} \qquad \mathbf{D} \neq 0 \qquad i = 1, 2, 3, \ldots \qquad (3-8)$$

$\mathbf{D}{\cdot}\mathbf{n}_i$ is zero if $\mathbf{D} = 0$, which implies that $P_2 = P_1$, i.e., a point, or $\mathbf{D}$ and $\mathbf{n}_i$ are perpendicular. If $\mathbf{D}$ and $\mathbf{n}_i$ are perpendicular, the line does not intersect the edge. If $P_2 = P_1$ then for

$$\begin{aligned}\mathbf{w}_i{\cdot}\mathbf{n}_i \quad &< 0, \quad \text{the point is outside}\\ &= 0, \quad \text{on the boundary of}\\ &> 0, \quad \text{inside}\end{aligned}$$

the region or window.

Equation (3–8) is used to obtain the value of t for the intersection of the line with each edge of the window. If t is outside the range $0 \le t \le 1$, then it is ignored. Although it is known that the line intersects the convex window in at most two points, i.e., at two values of t, Eq. $(3-8)$ can yield several values of t in the range $0 \le t \le 1$, one for each edge of the convex region not parallel to the line. These values separate into two groups, a lower limit group near the beginning of the line and an upper limit group near the end of the line. What is required is to find the largest lower limit, the maximum of the minimum, and the smallest upper limit, the minimum of the maximum. If $\mathbf{D}{\cdot}\mathbf{n}_i > 0$, then the calculated value of t is near the beginning of the line and the lower limit value of t is sought. If $\mathbf{D}{\cdot}\mathbf{n}_i < 0$, then the value of t is near the end of the line and the upper limit value of t is sought. Figure 3–12 gives a flowchart of an algorithm which uses these conditions to solve the resulting linear programming problem. A pseudocode implementation of the algorithm is:

Cyrus–Beck two-dimensional clipping algorithm
subroutine cb($\mathrm{P}_1, \mathrm{P}_2, \mathbf{n}_i, \mathbf{f}_i, \mathrm{k}$)
P_1 *and* P_2 *are the end points of the line*
the number of edges for the clipping region is k
the $\mathbf{n}_i$ *are the* k *normal vectors*
the $\mathbf{f}_i$ *are the* k *boundary points, one in each edge*
$\mathbf{D}$ *is the direction of the line,* $\mathrm{P}_2 - \mathrm{P}_1$
$\mathbf{w}_i$ *is the weighting function,* $\mathrm{P}_1 - \mathbf{f}_i$
t_{L}, t_{U} *are the lower and upper parameter limits*

 initialize the parameter limits, assuming the entire line is visible
 $t_{\mathrm{L}} = 0$
 $t_{\mathrm{U}} = 1$

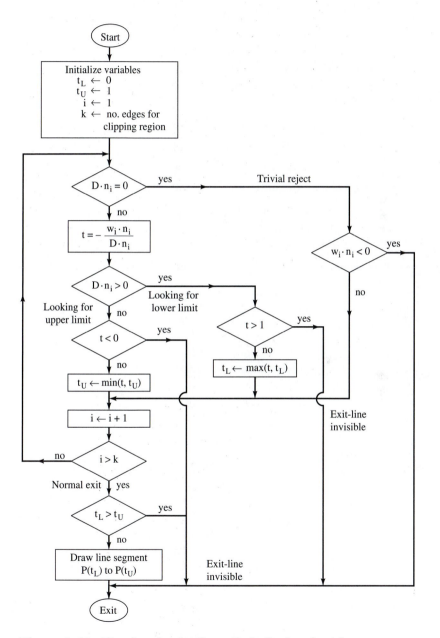

Figure 3–12   Flowchart for the Cyrus–Beck clipping algorithm.

calculate the directrix **D**

$D = P_2 - P_1$

start the main loop

for $i = 1$ **to** k

    calculate $\mathbf{w}_i$, $\mathbf{D} \cdot \mathbf{n}_i$ *and* $\mathbf{w}_i \cdot \mathbf{n}_i$ *for this value of* i

    $\mathbf{w}_i = P_1 - f_i$

    call Dotproduct$(D, n_i;$ Ddotn$)$

    call Dotproduct$(w_i, n_i;$ Wdotn$)$

    is the line a point?

    if Ddotn $<> 0$ **then**

        the line is not a point, calculate t

        $t = -$Wdotn/Ddotn

        looking for the upper or the lower limit?

        if Ddotn > 0 **then**

            looking for the lower limit
            is t *within the range 0 to 1?*

            if t > 1 **then**   *region entirely right of line*
                exit subroutine   *line trivially invisible — exit*

            else

                $t_L = $ **Max**(t, t_L)

            end if

        else   *at this point* Ddotn < 0

            looking for the upper limit
            is t *within the range 0 to 1?*

            if t < 0 **then**   *region entirely left of line*
                exit subroutine   *line trivially invisible — exit*

            else

                $t_U = $ **Min**(t, t_U)

            end if

        end if

    else   *here Ddotn = 0*

        if Wdotn < 0 **then**

            the line is trivially invisible or an invisible point
            abnormal exit from the routine occurs

            exit subroutine

        end if

    end if

next i

a normal exit from the loop has occurred

check if the line is in fact invisible

if $t_L <= t_U$ **then**   *the = catches a visible corner point*

Draw line segment $P(t_L)$ *to* $P(t_U)$

end if

return

subroutine module to calculate the dot product

subroutine Dotproduct(Vector1,Vector2; Dproduct)

Vector1 *is the first vector with components* x *and* y
Vector2 *is the second vector with components* x *and* y
Dproduct *is the dot or inner product*

Dproduct = Vector1x * Vector2x + Vector1y * Vector2y

return

Irregular Windows

To illustrate that the algorithm is not limited to rectangular windows consider the following example.

Example 3–13   Cyrus–Beck — Irregular Window

An eight-sided polygonal clipping window is shown in Fig. 3–13. The line $P_1(-1,1)$ to $P_2(3,3)$ is to be clipped to this window. Table 3–7 illustrates the complete results of the Cyrus–Beck algorithm. As a specific example, consider the edge from V_5 to V_6. The algorithm yields

$$\mathbf{D} = \mathbf{P}_2 - \mathbf{P}_1 = [3 \quad 3] - [-1 \quad 1] = [4 \quad 2]$$

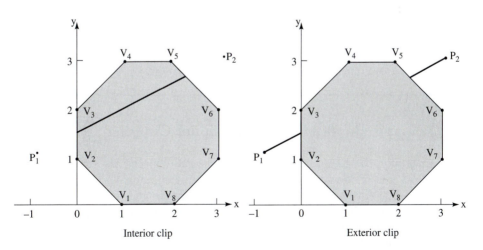

Interior clip   Exterior clip

Figure 3–13 Cyrus–Beck interior and exterior clipping of a many-sided polygon.

For the boundary point $f(2,3)$

$$\mathbf{w} = \mathbf{P}_1 - \mathbf{f} = [-1 \quad 1] - [2 \quad 3] = [-3 \quad -2]$$

For the edge $V_5 V_6$ the inner normal is

$$\mathbf{n} = [-1 \ -1]$$

Hence
$$\mathbf{D} \cdot \mathbf{n} = -6 < 0$$

and the upper limit is sought.

$$\mathbf{w} \cdot \mathbf{n} = 5$$

and
$$t_U = -\frac{5}{-6} = \frac{5}{6}$$

Examining Table 3–7 shows that the maximum lower limit is $t_L = \frac{1}{4}$ and the minimum upper limit is $t_U = \frac{5}{6}$. As shown in Fig. 3–13, the line is visible from $\frac{1}{4} \le t \le \frac{5}{6}$ or from $(0, \frac{3}{2})$ to $(\frac{7}{3}, \frac{8}{3})$.

Table 3–7

Edge	n		f	w		$\mathbf{w}\cdot\mathbf{n}$	$\mathbf{D}\cdot\mathbf{n}^\dagger$	t_L	t_U
$V_1 V_2$	[1	1]	(1,0)	[2	1]	-1	6	$\frac{1}{6}$	
$V_2 V_3$	[1	0]	(0,2)	$[-1 \ -1]$		-1	4	$\frac{1}{4}$	
$V_3 V_4$	[1	-1]	(0,2)	$[-1 \ -1]$		0	2	0	
$V_4 V_5$	[0	-1]	(2,3)	$[-3 \ -2]$		2	-2		1
$V_5 V_6$	$[-1$	-1]	(2,3)	$[-3 \ -2]$		5	-6		$\frac{5}{6}$
$V_6 V_7$	$[-1$	0]	(3,1)	$[-4 \quad$	0]	4	-4		1
$V_7 V_8$	$[-1$	1]	(3,1)	$[-4 \quad$	0]	4	-2		2
$V_8 V_1$	[0	1]	(1,0)	$[-2 \quad$	1]	1	2	$-\frac{1}{2}$	

† $\mathbf{D}\cdot\mathbf{n} < 0$ upper limit (t_U), $\mathbf{D}\cdot\mathbf{n} > 0$ lower limit (t_L).

3–6 Liang–Barsky Two-dimensional Clipping

Fundamentally, the Liang–Barsky two-dimensional clipping algorithm [Lian84] is a special case of the Cyrus–Beck parametric line clipping algorithm [Cyru78] (see Sec. 3–5). Although the Liang–Barsky algorithm generalizes to arbitrary convex two- and three-dimensional clipping regions, it is usually presented for rectangular clipping regions aligned with the coordinate axes (regular or upright clipping regions), as shown in Fig. 3–14, where x_L, x_R, y_B, y_T represent the left, right, bottom and top edges of the clipping region or window.

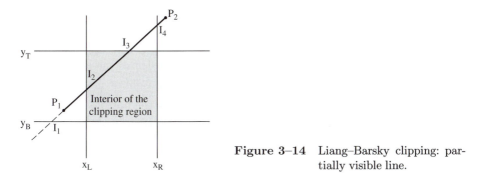

Figure 3–14 Liang–Barsky clipping: partially visible line.

The interior of the clipping region is represented by the inequalities

$$x_L \leq x \leq x_R$$

$$y_B \leq y \leq y_T$$

Substituting the components of the parametric line $P(t) = P_1 + (P_2 - P_1)t$, $0 \leq t \leq 1$, i.e.

$$x(t) = x_1 + (x_2 - x_1)t = x_1 + t\Delta x \qquad 0 \leq t \leq 1$$

$$y(t) = y_1 + (y_2 - y_1)t = y_1 + t\Delta y \qquad 0 \leq t \leq 1$$

into these inequalities yields an alternate representation of the interior of the clipping region given by

$$-t\Delta x \leq x_1 - x_L \qquad -t\Delta y \leq y_1 - y_B$$

$$t\Delta x \leq x_R - x_1 \qquad t\Delta y \leq y_T - y_1$$

Each of these inequalities is of the form

$$td_i \leq q_i \qquad i = 1, 2, 3, 4 \tag{3-9}$$

where

$$d_1 = -\Delta x \qquad d_2 = \Delta x \qquad d_3 = -\Delta y \qquad d_4 = \Delta y$$

$$q_1 = x_1 - x_L \qquad q_2 = x_R - x_1 \qquad q_3 = y_1 - y_B \qquad q_4 = y_T - y_1$$

and $i = 1, 2, 3, 4$ represent the left, right, bottom and top edges of the clipping region, respectively.

Each of the window edges divides the two dimensional clipping plane into two regions: one region is exterior to the clipping region, and one is interior. For example, in Fig. 3–14 the region to the left of the infinite line labelled x_L is exterior to the clipping region, and the region to the right is interior to the clipping region. The inequalities given in Eq. $(3-9)$ are used to establish the geometrical relationship of a point or line segment to the clipping region.

If $q_i < 0$, then P_1 is on the exterior (invisible) side of the ith edge of the clipping region. To see this, consider

$$q_1 = x_1 - x_L < 0 \quad \Rightarrow \quad x_L > x_1 \quad \Rightarrow \quad P_1 \text{ is to the left of the left edge}$$
$$q_2 = x_R - x_1 < 0 \quad \Rightarrow \quad x_1 > x_R \quad \Rightarrow \quad P_1 \text{ is to the right of the right edge}$$
$$q_3 = y_1 - y_B < 0 \quad \Rightarrow \quad y_B > y_1 \quad \Rightarrow \quad P_1 \text{ is below the bottom edge}$$
$$q_4 = y_T - y_1 < 0 \quad \Rightarrow \quad y_1 > y_T \quad \Rightarrow \quad P_1 \text{ is above the top edge}$$

In essence, this is an alternate technique for generating the Cohen–Sutherland outcodes of Sec. 3–1.

Similarly, if $q_i \geq 0$ then P_1 is on the interior (visible) side of that edge of the clipping region. The particular case of $q_i = 0$ implies that P_1 is on the boundary of the clipping region. If $d_i = 0$, then the line is parallel to the edge. Consequently, if $d_i = 0$ and $q_i < 0$, the complete line is exterior to that edge of the clipping region and can be trivially rejected.

Recalling Eq. $(3-9)$, we see that the intersection of the parametric line $P(t)$ and an edge of the clipping region is given by

$$t = \frac{q_i}{d_i}$$

Assuming that $P(t)$ is not parallel to an edge, there is an intersection of the infinite line $P(t)$, $-\infty \leq t \leq \infty$, for each edge of the clipping region. These intersections are labelled I_i in Fig. 3–14. However, for the line segment $P(t)$, $0 \leq t \leq 1$, any intersection with a parameter value outside of the range $0 \leq t \leq 1$, e.g., I_1 in Fig. 3–14, can be eliminated.

As shown in Fig. 3–14, even after the values of t outside the range $0 \leq t \leq 1$ are eliminated, more than two values of t may remain. The 'proper' intersection values are determined by recalling our discussion of the Cyrus–Beck algorithm (see Sec. 3–5). Recall from that discussion that the parameter values cluster into an upper and a lower group. Here we seek the maximum t value for the lower group and the minimum t value for the upper group. A flow chart for the Liang–Barsky two-dimensional clipping algorithm is shown in Fig. 3–15. Pseudocode for the Liang–Barsky algorithm, adapted from [Lian84], is

Liang–Barsky two-dimensional clipping algorithm

P_1 *and* P_2 *are the line end points with components* x_1, y_1, x_2, y_2
t_L *and* t_U *are the lower and upper parametric limits*
x_L, x_R, y_B, y_T *are the left, right, bottom and top window edges*

> **function** clipt(d, q; t_L, t_U)
>
> *clipt performs trivial rejection tests and finds*
> *the maximum of the lower set of parameter values and*
> *the minimum of the upper set of parameter values*
>
> visible = true

if d = 0 and q < 0 then   *line is outside and parallel to edge*
    visible = false
else if d < 0 then   *looking for upper limit*
    t = q/d
    if t > t_U then   *check for trivially invisible*
        visible = false
    else if t > t_L then   *find the minimum of the maximum*
        t_L = t
    end if
else if d > 0 then   *looking for the lower limit*

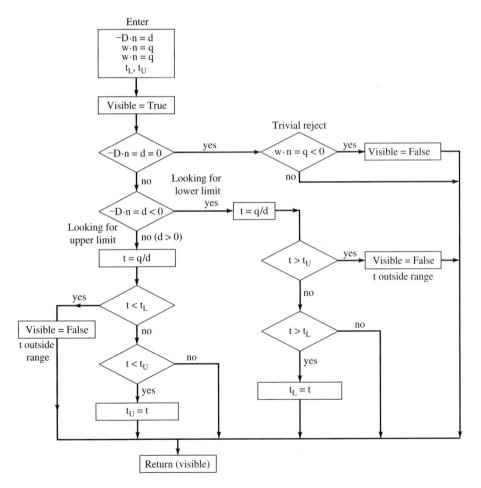

Figure 3–15   Flowchart for the Liang–Barsky clipping algorithm: the Cyrus–Beck parameters, $-\mathbf{D}\cdot\mathbf{n} = d$ and $\mathbf{w}\cdot\mathbf{n} = q$, are shown for comparison with Fig. 3–12.

$t = q/d$

if $t < t_L$ **then**   *check for trivially invisible*

    visible = false

else if $t < t_U$ **then**   *find the maximum of the minimum*

    $t_U = t$

end if

end if

return(visible)

end function

start the main algorithm

$t_L = 0$

$t_U = 1$

deltax = $x_2 - x_1$

if clipt($-$deltax, $x_1 - x_L$, t_L, t_U) = true **then**   *left edge*

    if clipt(deltax, $x_R - x_1$, t_L, t_U) = true **then**   *right edge*

        deltay = $y_2 - y_1$

        if clipt($-$deltay, $y_1 - y_B$, t_L, t_U) = true **then**   *bottom edge*

            if clipt(deltay, $y_T - y_1$, t_L, t_U) = true **then**   *top edge*

                if $t_U < 1$ **then**

                    $x_2 = x_1 + t_U * $deltax

                    $y_2 = y_1 + t_U * $deltay

                end if

                if $t_L > 0$ **then**

                    $x_1 = x_1 + t_L * $deltax

                    $y_1 = y_1 + t_L * $deltay

                end if

                Draw $P_1 P_2$

            end if

        end if

    end if

end if

finish

Comparison with the Cyrus–Beck Algorithm

Recalling the discussion of the Cyrus–Beck algorithm (see Sec. 3–5) and that $D = P_2 - P_1$ and $w_i = P_1 - f_i$, Table 3–8 and the flow charts in Figs. 3–12 and 3–15 show that the two-dimensional Liang–Barsky algorithm is a special case of the Cyrus–Beck algorithm. A series of examples further clarifies the algorithm and compares it to the Cyrus–Beck algorithm of Sec. 3–5.

**Example 3–14 Liang–Barsky Two-dimensional Clipping —
Partially Visible Line**

Use the Liang–Barsky clipping algorithm to clip the line $P_1(-1,1)$ to $P_2(9,3)$
to the rectangular region shown in Fig. 3–10. Compare the results to the
Cyrus–Beck algorithm used in Ex. 3–9.

The parametric representation of the line is

$$P(t) = P_1 + (P_2 - P_1)t = [-1 \quad 1] + [10 \quad 2]t$$

$$x(t) = x_1 + (x_2 - x_1)t = -1 + 10t \qquad\qquad 0 \le t \le 1$$

$$y(t) = y_1 + (y_2 - y_1)t = -1 + 2t$$

$$d_1 = -\Delta x = -(x_2 - x_1) = -10$$

$$d_2 = \Delta x = x_2 - x_1 = 10$$

$$d_3 = -\Delta y = -(y_2 - y_1) = -2$$

$$d_4 = \Delta y = y_2 - y_1 = 2$$

From Fig. 3–10 $x_L = 0$, $x_R = 8$, $y_B = 0$, $y_T = 4$. Thus

$$q_1 = x_1 - x_L = -1 - 0 = -1$$

$$q_2 = x_R - x_1 = 8 - (-1) = 9$$

$$q_3 = y_1 - y_B = 1 - 0 = 1$$

$$q_4 = y_T - y_1 = 4 - 1 = 3$$

Applying the Liang–Barsky algorithm, we have

$$t_L = 0$$
$$t_U = 1$$
$$\text{deltax} = 10$$
$$\text{clipt}(d = -10,\ q = -1,\ t_L = 0,\ t_U = 1)$$

Table 3–8 Correspondence between Liang–Barsky and Cyrus–Beck algorithms

Edge	n_i	f_i	w_i	$-d_i$ $\mathbf{D}_i \cdot \mathbf{n}_i$	q_i $\mathbf{w}_i \cdot \mathbf{n}_i$	$t = -\dfrac{q_i}{d_i}$ $-\dfrac{\mathbf{w}_i \cdot \mathbf{n}_i}{\mathbf{D}_i \cdot \mathbf{n}_i}$
x_L	$[\ 1 \quad 0]$	$[x_L \ y_T]$	$[x_1 - x_L \ \ y_1 - y_T]$	$x_2 - x_1$	$x_1 - x_L$	$-\dfrac{x_1 - x_L}{x_2 - x_1}$
x_R	$[-1 \quad 0]$	$[x_R \ y_B]$	$[x_1 - x_R \ \ y_1 - y_B]$	$-(x_2 - x_1)$	$-(x_1 - x_R)$	$-\dfrac{x_1 - x_R}{x_2 - x_1}$
y_B	$[\ 0 \quad 1]$	$[x_R \ y_B]$	$[x_1 - x_R \ \ y_1 - y_B]$	$y_2 - y_1$	$y_1 - y_B$	$-\dfrac{y_1 - y_B}{y_2 - y_1}$
y_T	$[\ 0 \ -1]$	$[x_L \ y_T]$	$[x_1 - x_L \ \ y_1 - y_T]$	$-(y_2 - y_1)$	$-(y_1 - y_T)$	$-\dfrac{y_1 - y_T}{y_2 - y_1}$

$$q < 0$$
$$\quad t = {}^1\!/_{10}$$
$$\quad t = {}^1\!/_{10} > t_L = 0$$
$$\quad\quad t_L = t = {}^1\!/_{10}$$
$$\text{return (true)}$$
$$\text{clipt}(d = 10,\ q = 9,\ t_L = {}^1\!/_{10},\ t_U = 1)$$
$$\quad d > 0$$
$$\quad\quad t = {}^9\!/_{10}$$
$$\quad\quad t = {}^9\!/_{10} < t_U = 1$$
$$\quad\quad\quad t_L = t = {}^9\!/_{10}$$
$$\quad\text{return (true)}$$

$$\text{deltay} = 2$$
$$\text{clipt}(d = -2,\ q = 1,\ t_L = {}^1\!/_{10},\ t_U = {}^9\!/_{10})$$
$$\quad d < 0$$
$$\quad\quad t = -{}^1\!/_2$$
$$\quad\quad t = -{}^1\!/_2 < t_L = {}^1\!/_{10}$$
$$\quad\text{return (true)}$$

$$\text{clipt}(d = 2,\ q = 3,\ t_L = {}^1\!/_{10},\ t_U = {}^9\!/_{10})$$
$$\quad d > 0$$
$$\quad\quad t = {}^3\!/_2$$
$$\quad\quad t = {}^3\!/_2 > t_U = {}^9\!/_{10}$$
$$\quad\text{return (true)}$$

$$t_U = {}^9\!/_{10} < 1$$
$$\quad x_2 = -1 + {}^9\!/_{10}\,(10) = 8$$
$$\quad y_2 = 1 + {}^9\!/_{10}\,(2) = {}^{14}\!/_5$$
$$t_L = {}^1\!/_{10} > 0$$
$$\quad x_1 = -1 + {}^1\!/_{10}\,(10) = 0$$
$$\quad y_1 = 1 + {}^1\!/_{10}\,(2) = {}^6\!/_5$$
$$\text{Draw } P_1 P_2$$

The visible range of the line $P_1 P_2$ is for ${}^1\!/_{10} \leq t \leq {}^9\!/_{10}$, or from $P_1(0, {}^6\!/_5)$ to $P_2(8, {}^{14}\!/_5)$. This is the same result obtained in Ex. 3–9 using the Cyrus–Beck clipping algorithm.

In the next example we compare the Cyrus–Beck and Liang–Barsky algorithms for a trivially invisible line.

Example 3–15   Liang–Barsky Two-dimensional Clipping — Invisible Line

Use the Liang–Barsky and Cyrus–Beck algorithms to clip the line $P_3(-6, -1)$ to $P_4(-1, 4)$ to the rectanguler clipping region shown in Fig. 3–11.

$$P(t) = P_3 + (P_4 - P_3)t \quad = [-6 \quad -1] + [5 \quad 5]\,t$$
$$x(t) = x_3 + (x_4 - x_3)t \quad = -6 + 5t \qquad\qquad 0 \leq t \leq 1$$
$$y(t) = y_3 + (y_4 - y_3)t \quad = -1 + 5t$$

<table>
<tr><td>

Liang–Barsky

The values for the Liang–Barsky algorithm are:

$$d_1 = -\Delta x = -(x_4 - x_3) = -5$$
$$d_2 = \Delta x = x_4 - x_3 = 5$$
$$d_3 = -\Delta y = -(y_4 - y_3) = -5$$
$$d_4 = \Delta y = y_4 - y_3 = 5$$

$$q_1 = x_3 - x_L = -6 - 0 = -6$$
$$q_2 = x_R - x_3 = 8 - (-6) = 14$$
$$q_3 = y_3 - y_B = -1 - 0 = -1$$
$$q_4 = y_T - y_3 = 4 - (-1) = 3$$

Referring to the algorithm, we have

$t_L = 0$
$t_U = 1$
deltax = 5
clipt$(d = -5, q = -6, t_L = 0, t_U = 1)$
   visible = true
   $d < 0$
      $t = {}^{-6}\!/_{-5} = {}^{6}\!/_{5}$
      $t > t_U$
         visible = false
   return (false)
trivially invisible

</td><td>

Cyrus–Beck

The values for the inner normals n_i, the boundary points f_i and $P(t) - f$ are given in Table 3–5.

Referring to the Cyrus–Beck algorithm in Sec. 3–5, we have

$t_L = 0$
$t_U = 1$
$D = [5 \quad 5]$
$i = 1$
  $n_1 = [1 \quad 0]$
  $w_1 = P_3 - f_1 = [-6 \quad -1]$
Ddotn = 5
Wdotn = -6
Ddotn <> 0
  $t = -(^{-6}\!/_{5}) = {}^{6}\!/_{5}$
  Ddotn > 0 (*lower limit*)
  $t > 1$
      exit subroutine
      trivially invisible

</td></tr>
</table>

Hence, the Liang–Barsky and Cyrus–Beck algorithms reject trivially invisible lines with equal efficiency.

In the next example we compare the Liang–Barsky and Cyrus–Beck algorithms when an invisible line cuts across one of the corners of the clipping region.

Example 3–16 Liang–Barsky Two-dimensional Clipping — Invisible Corner Crossing Line

Extend the line segment P_3P_4 in Ex. 3–15 from $P_5(-6, -1)$ to $P_6(2, 7)$. This line segment now invisibly crosses the upper left corner of the rectangular clipping region shown in Fig. 3–11. Compare the Liang–Barsky and Cyrus–Beck clipping algorithms for this line segment.

$$P(t) = P_5 + (P_6 - P_5)t = [-6 \quad -1] + [8 \quad 8]t \qquad 0 \le t \le 1$$
$$x(t) = x_5 + (x_6 - x_5)t = -6 + 8t \qquad 0 \le t \le 1$$
$$y(t) = y_5 + (y_6 - y_5)t = -1 + 8t \qquad 0 \le t \le 1$$

Liang–Barsky	Cyrus–Beck

Liang–Barsky

The values for the Liang–Barsky algorithm are:

$$d_1 = -\Delta x = -(x_6 - x_5) = -8$$

$$d_2 = \Delta x \quad = x_6 - x_5 = 8$$

$$d_3 = -\Delta y = -(y_6 - y_5) = -8$$

$$d_4 = \Delta y \quad = y_6 - y_5 = 8$$

The values of q_1, q_2, q_3, q_4 are unchanged from Ex. 3–15.

Referring to the algorithm, we have

$t_L = 0$
$t_U = 1$
deltax = 8
clipt$(d = -8, q = -6, t_L = 0, t_U = 1)$
  visible = true
  $d < 0$
  $t = {}^{-6}/_{-8} = {}^3/_4$
  $t > t_L$
  $t_L = {}^3/_4$
  return (true)
clipt$(d = 8, q = 14, t_L = {}^3/_4, t_U = 1)$
  visible = true
  $d > 0$
  $t = {}^{14}/_8 = {}^7/_4$
  $t > t_L$
  $t > t_U$
  return (true)
clipt$(d = -8, q = -1, t_L = {}^3/_4, t_U = 1)$
  visible = true
  $d < 0$
  $t = {}^{-1}/_{-8} = {}^1/_8$
  $t < t_U$
  $t < t_L$
  return (true)
clipt$(d = 8, q = 5, t_L = {}^3/_4, t_U = 1)$
  visible = true
  $d > 0$
  $t = {}^5/_8$
  $t < t_L$
  visible = false
  return (false)

Cyrus–Beck

The values for the inner normals n_i, the boundary points f_i and $P(t) - f$ are given in Table 3–5. Referring to the Cyrus–Beck algorithm in Sec. 3–5, we have

$t_L = 0$
$t_U = 1$
$D = \begin{bmatrix} 8 & 8 \end{bmatrix}$
$i = 1$
  $n_1 = \begin{bmatrix} 1 & 0 \end{bmatrix}$
  $w_1 = P_5 - f_1 = \begin{bmatrix} -6 & -1 \end{bmatrix}$
  Ddotn = 8
  Wdotn = -6
  Ddotn <> 0
  $t = -({}^{-6}/_8) = {}^3/_4$
  Ddotn > 0   *lower limit*
  $t < 1$
  $t_L = \text{Max}({}^3/_4, 0) = {}^3/_4$
$i = 2$
  $n_2 = \begin{bmatrix} -1 & 0 \end{bmatrix}$
  $w_2 = P_5 - f_2 = \begin{bmatrix} -14 & -5 \end{bmatrix}$
  Ddotn = -8
  Wdotn = 14
  Ddotn <> 0
  $t = -({}^{-14}/_{-8}) = {}^7/_4$
  Ddotn < 0   *upper limit*
  $t > 0$
  $t_U = \text{Min}({}^7/_4, 1) = 1$
$i = 3$
  $n_3 = \begin{bmatrix} 0 & 1 \end{bmatrix}$
  $w_3 = P_5 - f_3 = \begin{bmatrix} -6 & -1 \end{bmatrix}$
  Ddotn = 8
  Wdotn = -1
  Ddotn <> 0
  $t = -({}^{-1}/_8) = {}^1/_8$
  Ddotn > 0   *lower limit*
  $t < 1$
  $t_L = \text{Max}({}^1/_8, {}^3/_4) = {}^3/_4$
$i = 4$
  $n_4 = \begin{bmatrix} 0 & -1 \end{bmatrix}$
  $w_4 = P_5 - f_4 = \begin{bmatrix} -14 & -5 \end{bmatrix}$
  Ddotn = -8
  Wdotn = 5
  Ddotn <> 0
  $t = -({}^5/_{-8}) = {}^5/_8$
  Ddotn < 0   *upper limit*
  $t > 0$
  $t_U = \text{Min}({}^5/_8, 1) = {}^5/_8$
$t_L > t_U$
line is invisible

Each algorithm computes four values of t and hence rejects trivially invisible lines with equal efficiency.

These examples and the flow charts in Figs. 3–12 and 3–15 illustrate that the Liang–Barsky and the Cyrus–Beck algorithms are essentially the same.

3–7   Nicholl–Lee–Nicholl Two-dimensional Clipping

The Nicholl–Lee–Nicholl algorithm [Nich87] capitalizes on the principle of avoidance to generate an efficient two-dimensional clipping algorithm. The algorithm, which does not extend to three-dimensional or polygon clipping, carefully examines the position of the line relative to the clipping region, to trivially reject the line as invisible, or to avoid unnecessary expensive intersection calculations. Using the avoidance principle to either develop or enhance the efficiency of an algorithm generally leads to increased complexity. The Nicholl–Lee–Nicholl algorithm is no exception.

The Nicholl–Lee–Nicholl algorithm divides the two-dimensional plane into three types of regions, interior, edge and corner, as shown in Fig. 3–16. The initial point on a line segment, P_1, lies in one of the three regions, i.e., in either an interior, edge or corner region. The other end point of the line segment, P_2, can lie in any of the nine regions shown in Fig. 3–16.

Drawing lines from P_1 through the corners of the clipping region divides the plane into four regions, as shown in Fig. 3–17, for P_1 in an interior, edge or corner region. Each of these lines is labelled to indicate the corner through which it passes, e.g., the line from P_1 through the corner formed by the left and top edges of the clipping region is labelled LT. Similarly, the lines passing through the corners formed by the right and top, right and bottom, and left and bottom edges are labelled RT, RB and LB, respectively. By comparing the slope of the line $P_1 P_2$ to the slopes of the lines labelled LT, RT, RB, LB, the visibility of the line (if any), the number of intersections and the specific edges of the clipping regions which are intersected is determined.

As an example, consider P_1 to lie in the lower left corner region, as shown in Fig. 3–17c. If P_2 lies in any region exterior to the clipping region, then letting

Figure 3–16   Regions for the Nicholl–Lee–Nicholl algorithm.

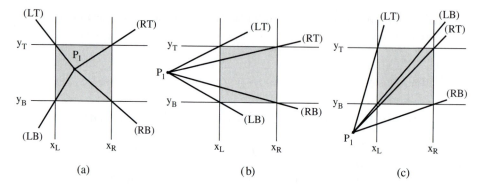

Figure 3–17 Subdivision of the plane. (a) P_1 interior to the clipping region; (b) P_1 in an edge region; (c) P_1 in a corner region.

m be the slope of the line P_1P_2 and m_{LT}, m_{RT}, m_{RB} and m_{LB} be the slopes of the lines through P_1 and the corners of the clipping regions respectively gives

> **if** $m > m_{LT}$ **then** visible = false   *trivially invisible*
> **if** $m < m_{RB}$ **then** visible = false   *trivially invisible*
> **if** $m_{RB} \leq m \leq m_{LT}$ **then** visible = true   *two intersections*
>
> > **if** $m = m_{LT}$ **then**   *special case — one intersection*
> > **if** $m_{LB} < m < m_{LT}$ **then**   *left and top edge intersection*
> > **if** $m_{RT} < m \leq m_{LB}$ **then**   *bottom and top edge intersection*
> > **if** $m_{RB} < m < m_{RT}$ **then**   *bottom and right edge intersection*
> > **if** $m = m_{RB}$ **then**   *special case — one intersection*

Calculating the slopes requires two subtractions and a division. The expense of these calculations is avoided by first checking if P_2 is left of the left edge or below the bottom edge. These tests also eliminate lines for which P_2 lies in the regions between the bottom edge of the clipping region and the line RB, and between the left edge and the line LT. These initial tests are

> **if** $x_2 < x_L$ **then** visible = false   *trivially invisible*
> **if** $y_2 < y_B$ **then** visible = false   *trivially invisible*

Assuming that P_2 is exterior to the clipping region, the complete algorithm for P_1 in the lower left corner region is

> **Nicholl–Lee–Nicholl two-dimensional clipping algorithm**
> **subroutine** nln($P_1, P_2, x_L, x_R, y_B, y_T$)
> P_1 *and* P_2 *are the line end points with components* x_1, y_1, x_2, y_2
> P_1 *is assumed to be in the lower left corner, and not coincident with the lower left corner, of the clipping region*
> x_L, x_R, y_B, y_T *are the left, right, bottom and top window edges*

m, m_{LT}, m_{LB}, m_{RT}, m_{RB} *are the slopes of the line, the line through the left-top, left-bottom, right-top and right-bottom clipping region corners.*

if $x_1 < x_L$ **then** P_1 *in lower left corner*

   if $y_1 < y_B$ **then**

      if $x_2 < x_L$ **then**

         visible = false   *trivially invisible*

         exit subroutine

      else if $y_2 < y_B$ **then**

         visible = false   *trivially invisible*

         exit subroutine

      else   *may be partially visible, 1 or 2 intersections*

         deltax = $x_2 - x_1$

         deltay = $y_2 - y_1$

         deltaxLT = $x_L - x_1$

         deltayLT = $y_T - y_1$

         m = deltay/deltax

         mLT = deltayLT/deltaxLT

         if m > mLT **then**   *passes left of LT corner*

            visible = false

            exit subroutine

         else

            if m = mLT **then**   *LT corner intersection*

               $x_1 = x_2 = x_L$

               $y_1 = y_2 = y_T$

            else

               deltaxLB = deltaxLT   *not really needed*

               deltayLB = $y_B - y_1$

               mLB = deltayLB/deltaxLB

               if mLB < m **and** m < mLT **then**   *left & top*

                  $x_2 = x_1 + \text{deltayLT}/m$

                  $y_2 = y_T$

                  $x_1 = x_L$

                  $y_1 = y_1 + m * \text{deltaxLT}$

               else

                 deltaxRT = $x_R - x_1$

                 deltayRT = deltayLT   *not really needed*

                 mRT = deltayRT/deltaxRT

                 if mRT < m **and** m $\leq$ mLB **then** *bottom & top*

                   $x_2 = x_1 + \text{deltayRT}/m$

                   $y_2 = y_T$

                   $x_1 = x_1 + \text{deltayLB}/m$

                   $y_1 = y_B$

                 else

$$\text{deltaxRB} = \text{deltaxRT} \qquad \textit{not really needed}$$
$$\text{deltayRB} = \text{deltayLB} \qquad \textit{not really needed}$$
$$\text{mRB} = \text{deltayRB}/\text{deltaxRB}$$
if $\text{mRB} < \text{m}$ **and** $\text{m} < \text{mRT}$ **then**   *bottom*
$$y_2 = y_1 + m * \text{deltaxRB} \qquad \textit{\& right}$$
$$x_2 = x_R$$
$$x_1 = x_1 + \text{deltayRB}/m$$
$$y_1 = y_B$$
else if $\text{m} = \text{mRB}$ **then**   RB *corner inter.*
$$x_1 = x_2 = x_R$$
$$y_1 = y_2 = y_B$$
else if $\text{m} < \text{mRB}$ **then**   *passes below* RB
$$\text{visible} = \text{false}$$
exit subroutine
end if   *end bottom & right*
end if   *end bottom & top*
end if   *end left & top*
end if   *end LT corner intersection*
end if   *end passes left of LT corner*
end if   *end* $x_2 < x_L$
end if   *end* $y_1 < y_B$
end if P_1 *in lower left corner*
return

Routines similar to this must be developed for P_1 in each of the corner and edge regions for P_2 exterior and interior to the clipping region. Similarly, routines must be developed for P_1 interior to the clipping region and P_2 exterior and interior to the clipping region. In the latter case, $P_1 P_2$ is trivially visible. These routines are then hierarchically arranged into an efficient algorithm. Obviously, there are a large number of cases and the resulting algorithm is quite complex. Consequently, development, testing and validation are of considerable concern.

Nicholl, Lee and Nicholl point out that the development, testing and validation task is reduced by the symmetry of the problem. Because of the symmetry, once a single routine for a corner or edge region is completed all others can be obtained by rotations by 90°, 180° or 270° about the origin, or reflection through the axes or through the line $y = -x$. Further, it is possible to machine translate the code for the base routine to any of the other routines (e.g., see [Arsa79]).

Duvanenko et al. [Duva93], using a machine operation analysis accounting for data types (integer or floating point), assuming a scalar computing environment and that addition is faster than subtraction, that multiplication and division are slower than addition or subtraction and that multiplication is faster than division, conclude that the Nicholl–Lee–Nicholl (NLN) algorithm is faster than the Cohen–Sutherland algorithm as presented by Newman and Sproull [Newm79]. Further, they show that the NLN algorithm is no faster for the trivial rejection case than the modified Cohen–Sutherland algorithm (see [Duva93] and Sec. 3–2). However, both the NLN and the modified Cohen–Sutherland algorithms are faster than the Liang–Barsky algorithm. Duvanenko et al. also find that the Sutherland–Hodgman polygon clipping algorithm, which is also applicable to two-dimensional line clipping (see Sec. 3–19), is generally as fast as or faster than any of these algorithms, especially when the algorithm is implemented for parallel execution.

3–8   Interior and Exterior Clipping

The emphasis of the discussions in Sec. 3–7 was on clipping a line to the interior of a region or polygon. However, it is also possible to clip a line to the exterior of a region or polygon, i.e., to determine what portion or portions of a line lie outside a region and to draw those exterior portions. For example, the visible portions of the line P_1P_2 of Fig. 3–13 exterior to the window are $0 \leq t < \frac{1}{4}$ and $\frac{5}{6} < t \leq 1$, or from $(-1, 1)$ to $(0, \frac{3}{2})$ and $(\frac{7}{3}, \frac{8}{3})$ to $(3, 3)$. The results of both an interior and an exterior clip of the line are shown in Fig. 3–13.

Exterior clipping is important in a multiwindow display environment, as shown in Fig. 3–18. In Fig. 3–18 windows 1 to 3 have priority over the display window, and windows 1 and 3 have priority over window 2. Consequently, data in the display window is clipped to the interior of the display window itself and to the exterior of windows 1 to 3. Data in window 2 is clipped to the interior of the window itself and to the exterior of windows 1 and 3. Data in windows 1 and 3 is only clipped to the interior of the individual windows.

Exterior clipping can also be used to clip a line to a concave polygonal window. In Fig. 3–19 a concave polygon described by the vertices $V_1V_2V_3V_4V_5V_6V_1$ is shown. A convex polygon is formed from this concave polygon by connecting the vertices V_3 and V_5, as shown by the dashed line in Fig. 3–19. Using the Cyrus–Beck algorithm, the line P_1P_2 is clipped to the interior of the convex polygon formed by $V_1V_2V_3V_5V_6V_1$. An exterior clip to the polygon $V_3V_5V_4V_3$ of the resulting line, $P_1'P_2'$, then yields the required result, i.e., $P_1'P_2''$.

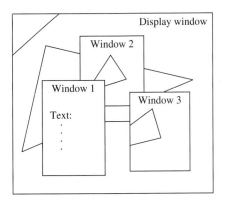

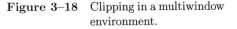

Figure 3–18   Clipping in a multiwindow environment.

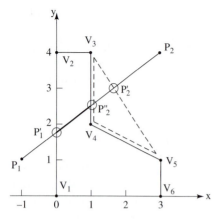

Figure 3–19   Clipping a line to a concave polygon.

3–9   Identifying Convex Polygons and Determining the Inner Normal

The Cyrus–Beck clipping algorithm requires a convex region. Thus, it is necessary to ensure that the clipping region is convex and then to determine the inner normals for each edge. Two-dimensional polygons are convex provided that a line drawn from any point on the polygon boundary to any other point on the boundary is completely contained within the polygon. In practice the convexity of a polygon is determined by calculating the vector cross products of adjacent edges and examining the signs of the results. The conclusions drawn from the signs of the vector cross products are:

All zero	— the polygon is colinear
Some positive and some negative	— concave polygon
All positive or zero	— convex polygon and the inner normal points to the left looking along the direction of the edge
All negative or zero	— convex polygon and the inner normal points to the right looking along the direction of the edge

This is illustrated in Fig. 3–20.

Alternatively, one of the polygon vertices is selected as a base, and the vector cross products are calculated using the vectors from this base to successive pairs of polygon vertices. The interpretation of the results is unchanged.

The vector cross product is normal to the plane of the polygon. For two planar vectors, $\mathbf{V}_1$ and $\mathbf{V}_2$, the cross product is $(V_{x_1} V_{y_2} - V_{y_1} V_{x_2})\mathbf{k}$, where $\mathbf{k}$ is the unit vector perpendicular to the plane of the polygon edge vectors.

The normal vector for a polygon edge is determined by recalling that the dot product of two perpendicular vectors is zero. If n_x and n_y are the unknown

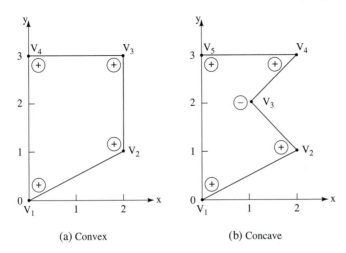

(a) Convex

(b) Concave

Figure 3–20   Signs for vector cross products.

components of the normal and V_{e_x} and V_{e_y} are the components of a known edge vector, then

$$\mathbf{n} \cdot V_e = (n_x \mathbf{i} + n_y \mathbf{j}) \cdot (V_{e_x} \mathbf{i} + V_{e_x} \mathbf{j}) = n_x V_{e_x} + n_y V_{e_y} = 0$$

or

$$n_x V_{e_x} = -n_y V_{e_y}$$

Because only the direction of the normal is required, n_y is assumed equal to 1 without loss of generality. Hence, the normal vector is

$$\mathbf{n} = -\frac{V_{e_y}}{V_{e_x}} \mathbf{i} + \mathbf{j}$$

If the edge vector is formed from two polygon vertices, V_{i-1} and V_i, and if the dot product of the vector from V_{i-1} to V_{i+1} and the normal is positive, $\mathbf{n}$ is the inner normal. Otherwise, $\mathbf{n}$ is the outer normal. In this case, the inner normal is obtained by reversing the signs of the x and y components. A simple example illustrates the technique.

Example 3–17   Vector Cross Products

Figure 3–20a shows a simple convex polygon and Fig. 3–20b a concave polygon. Tables 3–9 and 3–10 give complete results. As a specific example, the vector cross product at V_2 and the inner normal for the edge $V_1 V_2$ for the polygon of Fig. 3–20a are determined.

For the adjacent edges at V_2

$$V_1 V_2 = 2\mathbf{i} + \mathbf{j} \qquad V_2 V_3 = 2\mathbf{j}$$

The vector cross product is

$$\mathbf{V_1 V_2} \otimes \mathbf{V_2 V_3} = 4\mathbf{k}$$

where $\mathbf{k}$ is the unit normal perpendicular to the plane of the vectors. The cross product is positive. Table 3–9 shows that the cross products for all the vertices are positive; thus, the polygon is convex.

Table 3–9

Vertex	Vectors	Cross product
V_1	$\mathbf{V_4 V_1} \otimes \mathbf{V_1 V_2}$	$[\ \ 0\ \ -3\ ] \otimes [\ \ 2\ \ \ \ 1\ ] = +6$
V_2	$\mathbf{V_1 V_2} \otimes \mathbf{V_2 V_3}$	$[\ \ 2\ \ \ \ 1\ ] \otimes [\ \ 0\ \ \ \ 2\ ] = +4$
V_3	$\mathbf{V_2 V_3} \otimes \mathbf{V_3 V_4}$	$[\ \ 0\ \ \ \ 2\ ] \otimes [-2\ \ \ \ 0\ ] = +4$
V_4	$\mathbf{V_3 V_4} \otimes \mathbf{V_4 V_1}$	$[-2\ \ \ \ 0\ ] \otimes [\ \ 0\ \ -3\ ] = +6$

Table 3–10 shows that for the polygon of Fig. 3–20b the cross product at V_3 is negative, whereas all the others are positive. Hence, this polygon is concave.

Table 3–10

Vertex	Vectors	Cross product
V_1	$\mathbf{V_5 V_1} \otimes \mathbf{V_1 V_2}$	$[\ \ 0\ \ -3\ ] \otimes [\ \ 2\ \ \ \ 1\ ] = +6$
V_2	$\mathbf{V_1 V_2} \otimes \mathbf{V_2 V_3}$	$[\ \ 2\ \ \ \ 1\ ] \otimes [-1\ \ \ \ 1\ ] = +3$
V_3	$\mathbf{V_2 V_3} \otimes \mathbf{V_3 V_4}$	$[-1\ \ \ \ 1\ ] \otimes [\ \ 1\ \ \ \ 1\ ] = -2$
V_4	$\mathbf{V_3 V_4} \otimes \mathbf{V_4 V_5}$	$[\ \ 1\ \ \ \ 1\ ] \otimes [-2\ \ \ \ 0\ ] = +2$
V_5	$\mathbf{V_4 V_5} \otimes \mathbf{V_5 V_1}$	$[-2\ \ \ \ 0\ ] \otimes [\ \ 0\ \ -3\ ] = +6$

The normal for the edge vector $\mathbf{V_1 V_2}$ is

$$\mathbf{n} = -\frac{1}{2}\mathbf{i} + \mathbf{j}$$

or alternatively

$$\mathbf{n} = -\mathbf{i} + 2\mathbf{j}$$

The vector $\mathbf{V_1 V_3}$ is

$$\mathbf{V_1 V_3} = 2\mathbf{i} + 3\mathbf{j}$$

Hence

$$\mathbf{n} \cdot \mathbf{V_1 V_3} = (-\mathbf{i} + 2\mathbf{j}) \cdot (2\mathbf{i} + 3\mathbf{j}) = 4 > 0$$

and this is an inner normal.

A procedure involving translation and rotation of the polygonal window may be used to determine both the convexity of the polygon and the inner normal for each edge. The procedure is:

For each vertex of the polygon, translate the polygon such that the ith vertex is at the origin.

Rotate the polygon about the origin such that the $(i + 1)$th vertex is on the positive x-axis.

Examine the sign of the y component of the $(i + 2)$th vertex.

If all the $(i + 2)$th vertices have the same sign for the y component, the polygon is convex; if not, it is concave.

If the $(i + 2)$th vertex has a zero y component, then the ith, $(i + 1)$th, $(i + 2)$th vertices are collinear.

If all the $(i + 2)$th vertices have zero y components, the polygon is degenerate, i.e., a line.

For each edge of a convex polygon, the inner normal has components in the rotated coordinate system of zero and the sign of the $(i+2)$th y component.

In determining the original direction of the inner normal, only the inverse rotations are applied.

Figure 3–21 illustrates the various stages in the procedure for both the convex and concave polygons of Fig. 3–20. The appropriate rotation and translation algorithms are given by Rogers [Roge90a].

3–10   Splitting Concave Polygons

Many algorithms require that polygonal clipping regions be convex. The Cyrus–Beck clipping algorithm presented in Sec. 3–5 is an example. Additional examples are presented in subsequent sections. A simple extension of the translation and rotation technique for determining whether a polygon is convex or concave allows splitting or dividing simple concave polygons into multiple convex polygons. If the polygon vertices are specified counterclockwise, the procedure is:

For each vertex of the polygon, translate such that the ith vertex is at the origin.

Rotate the polygon clockwise about the origin such that the $(i+1)$th vertex is on the positive x-axis.

Examine the sign of the y component of the $(i + 2)$th vertex. If the sign is positive or zero, the polygon is convex with respect to this edge. If the sign is negative, the polygon is concave. Split the polygon.

The polygon is split by examining each successive vertex greater than $i+2$ until a vertex with a y component more than or equal to zero is found. This vertex is on or above the x-axis and is called $i + j$. The split off polygon is formed from $V_{i+1}V_{i+2} \ldots V_{i+j}$ and back to V_i. The remainder polygon is $V_i V_{i+1} V_{i+j} \ldots$ and back to V_i.

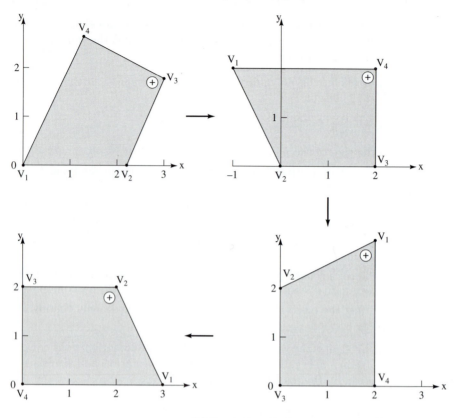

(a) Convex

Figure 3–21   Using rotations and translations to determine convex and concave polygons.

The algorithm is reentered with the split-off polygons until they are all declared convex.

The algorithm does not yield an optimum split in the sense of the minimum number of convex polygons. Also, the algorithm does not properly split polygons whose edges intersect, e.g., nonsimple polygons such as the classic schoolboy star or bowtie. An example further illustrates the procedure.

Example 3–18   Splitting Concave Polygons

Consider the concave polygon shown in Fig. 3–21b. With the vertex V_2 at the origin and V_3 on the positive x-axis, the sign of the y component of V_4 is negative. Hence, the polygon is concave. Examining the y components of successive vertices shows that the y component of V_5 is zero, hence $i + j = 5$. The split off polygon is then $V_3 V_4 V_5$, and the remainder polygon is $V_1 V_2 V_3 V_5$. Reentering the algorithm with $V_3 V_4 V_5$ and $V_1 V_2 V_3 V_5$ shows that they are both convex. Hence, the algorithm is complete.

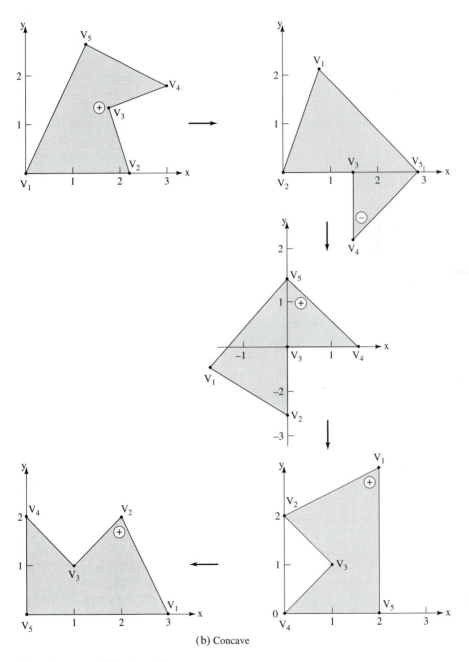

(b) Concave

Figure 3–21 (*Continued.*)

3–11   Three-dimensional Clipping

Before extending the methods discussed above to three dimensions, it is necessary to discuss the shape of the clipping volume. The two common three-dimensional clipping volumes are a rectangular parallelepiped, i.e., a box, used for parallel or axonometric projections, and a truncated pyramidal volume, frequently called a frustum of vision, used for perspective projections. These volumes, shown in Fig. 3–22, are six-sided — left, right, top, bottom, near (hither) and far (yon) planes. There is also a requirement to clip to unusual volumes, e.g., the cargo bay of the space shuttle.

As in two-dimensional clipping, lines that are totally visible or trivially invisible can be identified using an extension of the Cohen–Sutherland end point codes (see Sec. 3–1). For three-dimensional clipping, a 6 bit end point code is used. Again, the first bit is the rightmost bit. The bits are set to 1 using an extension of the two-dimensional scheme. Specifically

First-bit set   —   if the end point is to the left of the window
Second-bit set   —   if the end point is to the right of the window
Third-bit set   —   if the end point is below the window
Fourth-bit set   —   if the end point is above the window
Fifth bit set   —   if the end point is in front of the volume
Sixth bit set   —   if the end point is behind the volume

Otherwise, the bit is set to zero. Again, if both end point codes are *zero* both ends of the line are visible, and the line is visible. Also, if the bit-by-bit logical intersection of the two end point codes is *not zero*, then the line is totally invisible.

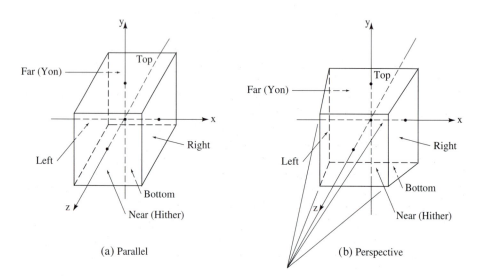

(a) Parallel   (b) Perspective

Figure 3–22   Three-dimensional clipping.

If the logical intersection is zero, the line may be partially visible or totally invisible. In this case it is necessary to determine the intersection of the line and the clipping volume.

Determining the end point codes for a rectangular parallelepiped clipping volume is a straightforward extension of the two-dimensional algorithm. However, the perspective clipping volume shown in Fig. 3–22b requires additional consideration. One technique (see [Newm73 or Newm79]) is to transform the clipping volume into a canonical volume with $x_{\text{right}} = 1$, $x_{\text{left}} = -1$, $y_{\text{top}} = 1$, $y_{\text{bottom}} = -1$, at $z_{\text{far}} = 1$. If $z_{\text{near}} = a$, where $0 < a \leq 1$ and the center of projection is at the origin in a left-hand coordinate system, then the end point code conditions are considerably simplified.

A more straightforward technique, which requires less distortion of the clipping volume, makes the line connecting the center of projection and the center of the perspective clipping volume coincident with the z-axis in a right-hand coordinate system, as shown in Fig. 3–22b.

A top view of the perspective clipping volume is shown in Fig. 3–23. The equation of the line which represents the right-hand plane in this view is

$$x = \frac{z - z_{CP}}{z_Y - z_{CP}} x_R = z\alpha_1 + \alpha_2$$

where $\qquad \alpha_1 = \dfrac{x_R}{z_Y - z_{CP}} \qquad$ and $\qquad \alpha_2 = -\alpha_1 z_{CP}$

The equation of this plane is used to determine whether a point is to the right, on or to the left of the plane, i.e., outside the volume, on the right-hand plane or inside the volume. Substituting the x and z coordinates of a point P into $x - z\alpha_1 - \alpha_2$ yields

$$f_R = x - z\alpha_1 - \alpha_2 > 0 \quad \text{if } P \text{ is to the right of the plane}$$
$$= 0 \quad \text{if } P \text{ is on the plane}$$
$$< 0 \quad \text{if } P \text{ is to the left of the plane}$$

Test functions for the left, top and bottom planes are

$$f_L = x - z\beta_1 - \beta_2 < 0 \quad \text{if } P \text{ is to the left of the plane}$$
$$= 0 \quad \text{if } P \text{ is on the plane}$$
$$> 0 \quad \text{if } P \text{ is to the right of the plane}$$

where $\qquad \beta_1 = \dfrac{x_L}{z_Y - z_{CP}} \qquad$ and $\qquad \beta_2 = -\beta_1 z_{CP}$

and $\qquad f_T = y - z\gamma_1 - \gamma_2 > 0 \quad \text{if } P \text{ is above the plane}$
$$= 0 \quad \text{if } P \text{ is on the plane}$$
$$< 0 \quad \text{if } P \text{ is below the plane}$$

where $\qquad \gamma_1 = \dfrac{y_T}{z_Y - z_{CP}} \qquad$ and $\qquad \gamma_2 = -\gamma_1 z_{CP}$

and
$$f_B = y - z\delta_1 - \delta_2 \; < 0 \quad \text{if } P \text{ is below the plane}$$
$$= 0 \quad \text{if } P \text{ is on the plane}$$
$$> 0 \quad \text{if } P \text{ is above the plane}$$

where $\qquad \delta_1 = z_{CP} \qquad$ and $\qquad \delta_2 = -\delta_1 z_{CP}$

Finally, the test functions for the near and far planes are

$$f_N = z - z_N \; > 0 \quad \text{if } P \text{ is in front of the plane}$$
$$= 0 \quad \text{if } P \text{ is on the plane}$$
$$< 0 \quad \text{if } P \text{ is behind the plane}$$

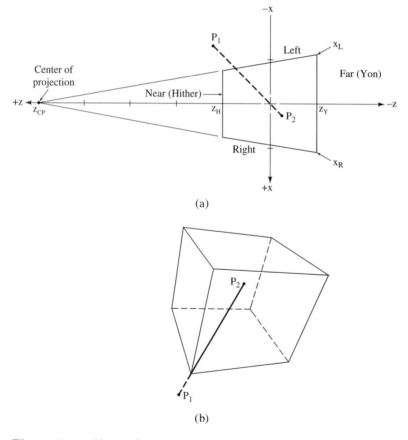

(a)

(b)

Figure 3–23 Views of perspective clipping volume.

and $\qquad$ $f_F = z - z_F\ < 0\quad$ if P is behind the plane

$\qquad\qquad\qquad\qquad = 0\quad$ if P is on the plane

$\qquad\qquad\qquad\qquad > 0\quad$ if P is in front of the plane

As z_{CP} approaches infinity, the clipping volume approaches a rectangular parallelepiped. The test functions also approach those for a rectangular parallelepiped.

As pointed out by Liang and Barsky [Lian84], this approach may not yield the correct codes if the end points lie behind the center of projection. This is because the left and right and the top and bottom planes of the perspective clipping volume intersect at the center of projection. Thus, a point can be right of right and left of left simultaneously. Liang and Barsky suggest that in principle it is only necessary to reverse the left-right, top-bottom code bits if $z < z_{CP}$ to correct this; see also Sec. 3–15.

3–12   Three-dimensional Midpoint Subdivision Algorithm

The midpoint subdivision algorithm given in Sec. 3–3 extends directly to three dimensions. For the pseudocode implementation, the array dimensions for the Pcodes and Window arrays must be changed and the Endpoint and Sum subroutines rewritten for three dimensions. A pseudocode implementation for the three-dimensional Endpoint and Sum subroutines is

> **subroutine module for calculating three-dimensional perspective volume end point codes**
>
> subroutine Endpoint(P, Window; Pcode)
>
> P_x, P_y, P_z *are the* x, y *and* z *components of the point* P
>
> Window *is a* 1×7 *array containing the left, right, bottom, top, near, far edges and the center of projection,* x_L, x_R, y_B, y_T, z_N, z_F, z_{CP}, *respectively*
>
> Pcode *is a* 1×6 *array containing the end point code*
>
> *calculate* α_1, α_2, β_2, γ_1, γ_2, δ_1, δ_2
>
> $\alpha_1 = x_R / (z_Y - z_{CP})$
> $\alpha_2 = -\alpha_1 z_{CP}$
> $\beta_1 = x_L / (z_Y - z_{CP})$
> $\beta_2 = -\beta_1 z_{CP}$
> $\gamma_1 = y_T / (z_Y - z_{CP})$
> $\gamma_2 = -\gamma_1 z_{CP}$
> $\delta_1 = y_B / (z_Y - z_{CP})$
> $\delta_2 = -\delta_1 z_{CP}$
>
> *determine the end point codes*
>
> **if** $P_x - P_z\beta_1 - \beta_2 < 0$ **then** Pcode(6) $= 1$ **else** Pcode(6) $= 0$
> **if** $P_x - P_z\alpha_1 - \alpha_2 > 0$ **then** Pcode(5) $=\ 1$ **else** Pcode(5) $= 0$

> if $P_y - P_z\delta_1 - \delta_2 < 0$ then Pcode(4) $= 1$ else Pcode(4) $= 0$
> if $P_y - P_z\gamma_1 - \gamma_2 > 0$ then Pcode(3) $= 1$ else Pcode(3) $= 0$
> if $P_z - z_N > 0$ then Pcode(2) $= 1$ else Pcode(2) $= 0$
> if $P_z - z_F < 0$ then Pcode(1) $= 1$ else Pcode(1) $= 0$

return

subroutine Sum(Pcode; Sum)

Pcode *is a* 1×6 *array containing the end point code*
Sum *is the element-by-element sum of* Pcode

> *calculate the sum*
>
> Sum $= 0$
> **for** i $= 1$ **to** 6
>   Sum $=$ Sum $+$ Pcode(i)
> **next** i

return

An example for the three-dimensional midpoint clipping algorithm follows.

Example 3–19   Three-dimensional Midpoint Subdivision

Consider a line from $P_1(-600, -600, 600)$ to $P_2(100, 100, -100)$ in screen units clipped to the perspective volume with $x_R = y_T = 500$, $x_L = y_B = -500$ at the far clipping plane. The near and far clipping planes are $z_H = 357.14$, $z_Y = -500$. The center of projection is $z_{CP} = 2500$. A top view is shown in Fig. 3–23a, and a perspective view in 3–23b. The clipping volume test functions are:

Right: $f_R = 6x + z - 2500$
Left: $f_L = 6x - z + 2500$
Top: $f_T = 6y + z - 2500$
Bottom: $f_B = 6y - z + 2500$
Near: $f_H = z - 357.14$
Far: $f_Y = z + 2500$

The end point code for P_1 is (010101), and that for P_2 is (000000). Because both end point codes are not zero, the line is not totally visible. The logical intersection of the end point codes is (00000). The line is not trivially invisible. Because the end point code for P_2 is (000000), P_2 is inside the volume, hence it is the farthest visible point from P_1. Thus, only one intersection with the volume occurs. The midpoint is

$$x_m = \frac{x_2 + x_1}{2} = \frac{100 + (-600)}{2} = -250$$

$$y_m = \frac{y_2 + y_1}{2} = \frac{100 + (-600)}{2} = -250$$

$$z = \frac{z_2 + z_1}{2} = \frac{-100 + 600}{2} = 250$$

using integer arithmetic. The end point code for the midpoint is (000000). The segment $P_m P_2$ is totally visible. The segment $P_1 P_m$ is partially visible. Continue with $P_1 P_m$. The subdivision continues in Table 3–11.

Table 3–11

P_1	P_2	P_m	Comment
−600, −600, 600	−100, −100, −100	−250, −250, 250	Continue $P_1 P_m$
−600, −600, 600	−250, −250, 250	−425, −425, 425	Continue $P_m P_2$
−425, −425, 425	−250, −250, 250	−338, −338, 337	Continue $P_1 P_m$
−425, −425, 425	−338, −338, 337	−382, −382, 381	Continue $P_m P_2$
−382, −382, 381	−338, −338, 337	−360, −360, 359	Continue $P_m P_2$
−360, −360, 359	−338, −338, 337	−349, −349, 348	Continue $P_1 P_m$
−360, −360, 359	−349, −349, 348	−355, −355, 353	Continue $P_1 P_m$
−360, −360, 359	−355, −355, 353	−358, −358, 356	Continue $P_m P_2$
−358, −358, 356	−355, −355, 353	−357, −357, 354	Continue $P_1 P_m$
−358, −358, 356	−357, −357, 354	−358, −358, 355	Continue $P_m P_2$
−358, −358, 355	−357, −357, 354	−358, −358, 354	Success

The actual intersection point is $(-357.14, -357.14, 357.14)$. The difference is due to the use of integer arithmetic in the algorithm.

3–13   Three-dimensional Cyrus–Beck Algorithm

In developing the Cyrus–Beck algorithm [Cyru78] for two-dimensional clipping, no restriction was placed on the shape of the clipping region except that it be convex. The clipping region can therefore be a three-dimensional convex volume. The algorithm developed previously is directly applicable. Instead of k being the number of edges, it is now the number of planes (see Fig. 3–12). All vectors now have three components: x, y, z. The extension of the Dotproduct subroutine module to three-dimensional vectors is straightforward. To more fully illustrate the algorithm, consider the following examples. The first considers clipping to a rectangular parallelepiped, i.e., to a box.

Example 3–20   Three-dimensional Cyrus–Beck Algorithm

A line from $P_1(-2, -1, 1/2)$ to $P_2(3/2, 3/2, -1/2)$ is to be clipped to the volume $(x_L, x_R, y_B, y_T, z_H, z_Y) = (-1, 1, -1, 1, 1, -1)$, as shown in Fig. 3–24. By inspection the six inner normals are

$$
\begin{aligned}
\text{Top:} &\quad \mathbf{n}_T = -\mathbf{j} = [\ 0 \ \ -1 \ \ \ 0\ ] \\
\text{Bottom:} &\quad \mathbf{n}_B = \ \ \mathbf{j} = [\ 0 \ \ \ \ 1 \ \ \ 0\ ] \\
\text{Right:} &\quad \mathbf{n}_R = -\mathbf{i} = [-1 \ \ \ \ 0 \ \ \ 0\ ] \\
\text{Left:} &\quad \mathbf{n}_L = \ \ \mathbf{i} = [\ 1 \ \ \ \ 0 \ \ \ 0\ ] \\
\text{Near:} &\quad \mathbf{n}_H = -\mathbf{k} = [\ 0 \ \ \ \ 0 \ \ -1\ ] \\
\text{Far:} &\quad \mathbf{n}_Y = \ \ \mathbf{k} = [\ 0 \ \ \ \ 0 \ \ \ 1\ ]
\end{aligned}
$$

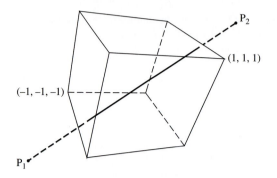

Figure 3–24 Cyrus–Beck clipping—three-dimensional rectangular volume.

The points in each clipping plane are also selected by inspection. By choosing points at the end of a diagonal between opposite corners of the clipping volume, two are sufficient. Thus

$$f_T = f_R = f_H (1, 1, 1)$$

and
$$f_B = f_L = f_Y (-1, -1, -1)$$

Alternatively, the center or a corner point of each clipping plane can be used.

The direction of the line $P_1 P_2$ is

$$\mathbf{D} = \mathbf{P}_2 - \mathbf{P}_1 = \begin{bmatrix} \frac{3}{2} & \frac{3}{2} & -\frac{1}{2} \end{bmatrix} - \begin{bmatrix} -2 & -1 & \frac{1}{2} \end{bmatrix}$$

$$= \begin{bmatrix} \frac{7}{2} & \frac{5}{2} & -1 \end{bmatrix}$$

For the boundary point $f_L(-1, -1, -1)$

$$\mathbf{w} = \mathbf{P}_1 - \mathbf{f} = \begin{bmatrix} -2 & -1 & \frac{1}{2} \end{bmatrix} - \begin{bmatrix} -1 & -1 & -1 \end{bmatrix}$$

$$= \begin{bmatrix} -1 & 0 & \frac{3}{2} \end{bmatrix}$$

and for the left-hand clipping plane the inner normal is

$$\mathbf{n}_L = \begin{bmatrix} 1 & 0 & 0 \end{bmatrix}$$

Hence
$$\mathbf{D} \cdot \mathbf{n}_L = \begin{bmatrix} \frac{7}{2} & \frac{5}{2} & -1 \end{bmatrix} \cdot \begin{bmatrix} 1 & 0 & 0 \end{bmatrix} = \frac{7}{2} > 0$$

and the lower limit is being sought

$$\mathbf{w} \cdot \mathbf{n}_L = \begin{bmatrix} -1 & 0 & \frac{3}{2} \end{bmatrix} \cdot \begin{bmatrix} 1 & 0 & 0 \end{bmatrix} = -1$$

and
$$t_L = -\frac{1}{7/2} = \frac{2}{7}$$

Table 3–12 gives the complete results.

Table 3–12

Plane	n	f	w	w·n	D·n[†]	t_L	t_U
Top	$[\ \ 0\ \ -1\ \ \ \ 0]$	$(\ \ 1,\ \ 1,\ \ 1)$	$[-3\ \ -2\ \ -1/2]$	2	$-5/2$		$4/5$
Bottom	$[\ \ 0\ \ \ \ 1\ \ \ \ 0]$	$(-1,-1,-1)$	$[-1\ \ \ \ 0\ \ \ \ 3/2]$	0	$5/2$	0	
Right	$[-1\ \ \ \ 0\ \ \ \ 0]$	$(\ \ 1,\ \ 1,\ \ 1)$	$[-3\ \ -2\ \ -1/2]$	3	$-7/2$		$6/7$
Left	$[\ \ 1\ \ \ \ 0\ \ \ \ 0]$	$(-1,-1,-1)$	$[-1\ \ \ \ 0\ \ \ \ 3/2]$	-1	$7/2$	$2/7$	
Near	$[\ \ 0\ \ \ \ 0\ \ -1]$	$(\ \ 1,\ \ 1,\ \ 1)$	$[-3\ \ -2\ \ -1/2]$	$1/2$	1	$-1/2$	
Far	$[\ \ 0\ \ \ \ 0\ \ \ \ 1]$	$(-1,-1,-1)$	$[-1\ \ \ \ 0\ \ \ \ 3/2]$	$3/2$	-1		$3/2$

[†] If $\mathbf{D \cdot n} < 0$, test upper limit t_U; if $\mathbf{D \cdot n} > 0$, test lower limit t_L.

Examining Table 3–12 shows that the maximum lower limit is $t_L = 2/7$ and the minimum upper limit is $t_U = 4/5$. The parametric equation of the line P_1P_2 is

$$P(t) = \begin{bmatrix} -2 & -1 & \frac{1}{2} \end{bmatrix} + \begin{bmatrix} \frac{7}{2} & \frac{5}{2} & -1 \end{bmatrix} t$$

Substituting t_L and t_U yields

$$P\left(\frac{2}{7}\right) = \begin{bmatrix} -2 & -1 & \frac{1}{2} \end{bmatrix} + \begin{bmatrix} \frac{7}{2} & \frac{5}{2} & -1 \end{bmatrix} \left(\frac{2}{7}\right)$$

$$= \begin{bmatrix} -1 & -\frac{2}{7} & \frac{3}{14} \end{bmatrix}$$

as the intersection point with the left clipping plane and

$$P\left(\frac{4}{5}\right) = \begin{bmatrix} -2 & -1 & \frac{1}{2} \end{bmatrix} + \begin{bmatrix} \frac{7}{2} & \frac{5}{2} & -1 \end{bmatrix} \left(\frac{4}{5}\right)$$

$$= \begin{bmatrix} \frac{4}{5} & 1 & -\frac{3}{10} \end{bmatrix}$$

as the intersection with the top clipping plane.

Clipping to a standard perspective volume is only slightly more complex. Here, except for the near and far clipping planes, the inner normals must be determined formally rather than by inspection.

Example 3–21   Clipping to a Perspective Volume

Again consider $P_1(-2, -1, 1/2)$ to $P_2(3/2, 3/2, -1/2)$, i.e., the same line as in Ex. 3–20, clipped to the perspective volume with $(x_L, x_R, y_B, y_T, z_H, z_Y) = (-1, 1, -1, 1, 1, -1)$, with a center of projection at $z_{CP} = 5$. See Fig. 3–22b.

The inner normals for the near and far clipping planes are obtained by inspection. Those for the remaining four clipping planes are calculated from the cross products of vectors from the center of projection to the corners at $z = 0$, the plane of projection. These vectors are

$$V1 = \begin{bmatrix} 1 & 1 & -5 \end{bmatrix}$$
$$V2 = \begin{bmatrix} -1 & 1 & -5 \end{bmatrix}$$
$$V3 = \begin{bmatrix} -1 & -1 & -5 \end{bmatrix}$$
$$V4 = \begin{bmatrix} 1 & -1 & -5 \end{bmatrix}$$

The inner normals are then

$$T = V1 \otimes V2 = \begin{bmatrix} 0 & -10 & -2 \end{bmatrix}$$
$$L = V2 \otimes V3 = \begin{bmatrix} 10 & 0 & -2 \end{bmatrix}$$
$$B = V3 \otimes V4 = \begin{bmatrix} 0 & 10 & -2 \end{bmatrix}$$
$$R = V4 \otimes V1 = \begin{bmatrix} -10 & 0 & -2 \end{bmatrix}$$
$$H = \begin{bmatrix} 0 & 0 & -1 \end{bmatrix}$$
$$Y = \begin{bmatrix} 0 & 0 & 1 \end{bmatrix}$$

Since the center of projection is in four of the six planes, it is convenient to take

$$f_T = f_L = f_B = f_R(0, 0, 5)$$

and the center of the near and far planes

$$f_H(0, 0, 1) \quad \text{and} \quad f_Y(0, 0, -1)$$

as the boundary points.

The directrix for $P_1 P_2$ is again

$$D = P_2 - P_1 = \begin{bmatrix} \dfrac{7}{2} & \dfrac{5}{2} & -1 \end{bmatrix}$$

For the boundary point in the left-hand clipping plane

$$w = P_1 - f_L = \begin{bmatrix} -2 & -1 & \dfrac{1}{2} \end{bmatrix} - \begin{bmatrix} 0 & 0 & 5 \end{bmatrix}$$
$$= \begin{bmatrix} -2 & -1 & -\dfrac{9}{2} \end{bmatrix}$$

Noting that

$$D \cdot n_L = \begin{bmatrix} \dfrac{7}{2} & \dfrac{5}{2} & -1 \end{bmatrix} \cdot \begin{bmatrix} 10 & 0 & -2 \end{bmatrix} = 37 > 0$$

and the lower limit is being sought, then

$$w \cdot n_L = \begin{bmatrix} -2 & -1 & -\dfrac{9}{2} \end{bmatrix} \cdot \begin{bmatrix} 10 & 0 & -2 \end{bmatrix} = -11$$

and
$$t_L = -\frac{-11}{37} = \frac{11}{37} = 0.297$$

Table 3–13 gives the complete results.

Table 3–13

Plane	n	f	w	w·n	D·n[†]	t_L	t_U
Top	[0 −10 −2]	(0, 0, 5)	[−2 −1 −9/2]	19	−23		0.826
Bottom	[0 10 −2]	(0, 0, 5)	[−2 −1 −9/2]	−1	27	0.037	
Right	[−10 0 −2]	(0, 0, 5)	[−2 −1 −9/2]	29	−33		0.879
Left	[10 0 −2]	(0, 0, 5)	[−2 −1 −9/2]	−11	37	0.297	
Near	[0 0 −1]	(0, 0, 1)	[−2 −1 −1/2]	1/2	1	−0.5	
Far	[0 0 1]	(0, 0,−1)	[−2 −1 3/2]	3/2	−1		1.5

[†] If D·n < 0, test upper limit t_U; if D·n > 0, test lower limit t_L.

Table 3–13 shows that the maximum lower limit is $t_L = 0.297$ and the minimum upper limit is $t_U = 0.826$. From the parametric equation the intersection values are
$$P(0.297) = [-0.961 \quad -0.258 \quad 0.203]$$
and
$$P(0.826) = [0.891 \quad 1.065 \quad -0.323]$$
for the left and top clipping planes.

As a final example, a nonstandard clipping volume with seven clipping planes is considered.

Example 3–22   Clipping to an Arbitrary Volume

The clipping volume is shown in Fig. 3–25. It is a cube with one corner removed. The polygons describing each face have vertices

Right:	$(1, -1, 1), (1, -1, -1), (1, 1, -1), (1, 1, 1)$
Left:	$(-1, -1, 1), (-1, -1, -1), (-1, 1, -1), (-1, 1, 0), (-1, 0, 1)$
Bottom:	$(1, -1, 1), (1, -1, -1), (-1, -1, -1), (1, -1, -1)$
Top:	$(1, 1, 1), (1, 1, -1), (-1, 1, -1), (-1, 1, 0), (0, 1, 1)$
Near:	$(1, -1, 1), (1, 1, 1), (0, 1, 1), (-1, 0, 1), (-1, -1, 1)$
Far:	$(-1, -1, -1), (1, -1, -1), (1, 1, -1), (-1, 1, -1)$
Skew:	$(-1, 0, 1), (0, 1, 1), (-1, 1, 0)$

Table 3–14 gives the complete results for the line $P_1(-2, 3/2, 1)$ to $P_2(3/2, -1, -1/2)$ clipped to this volume.

Table 3–14

Plane	n	f	w	w·n	D·n†	t_L	t_U
Top	[0 −1 0]	(1, 1, 1)	[−3 ½ 0]	−½	5/2	1/5	
Bottom	[0 1 0]	(−1, −1, −1)	[−1 5/2 2]	5/2	−5/2		1
Right	[−1 0 0]	(1, 1, 1)	[−3 ½ 0]	3	−7/2		6/7
Left	[1 0 0]	(−1, −1, −1)	[−1 5/2 2]	−1	7/2	2/7	
Near	[0 0 −1]	(1, 1, 1)	[−3 ½ 0]	0	3/2	0	
Far	[0 0 1]	(−1, −1, −1)	[−1 5/2 2]	2	−3/2		4/3
Skew	[1 −1 −1]	(−1, 0, 1)	[−1 3/2 0]	−5/2	15/2	1/3	

† If $\mathbf{D \cdot n} < 0$, test upper limit t_U; if $\mathbf{D \cdot n} > 0$, test lower limit t_L.

From the table the maximum lower limit is $t_L = 1/3$, and the minimum upper limit is $t_U = 6/7$. The intersection points are thus

$$P\left(\frac{1}{3}\right) = \left[-\frac{5}{6} \quad \frac{2}{3} \quad \frac{1}{2}\right]$$

in the skew plane and

$$P\left(\frac{6}{7}\right) = \left[1 \quad -\frac{9}{14} \quad -\frac{2}{7}\right]$$

in the right-hand plane.

Note that the computational expense of the Cyrus–Beck algorithm grows linearly with the number of edges or planes clipped.

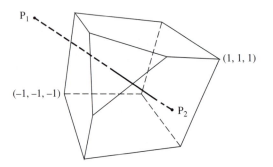

Figure 3–25 Cyrus–Beck clipping — odd three-dimensional volume.

3–14 Liang–Barsky Three-dimensional Clipping

The Liang–Barsky two-dimensional clipping algorithm conveniently extends to three dimensions. Consider the viewing pyramid defined by the two viewing angles, θ_x and θ_y, and the center of projection or eyepoint at the origin, as shown in Fig. 3–26a.[†] The interior of the volume is defined by

$$-z_e \le \cot\left(\frac{\theta_x}{2}\right) x_e \le z_e$$

$$-z_e \le \cot\left(\frac{\theta_y}{2}\right) y_e \le z_e$$

where the e subscript refers to the 'eye' coordinate system. These inequalities also imply that $-z_e \le z_e$ and $z_e \ge 0$, i.e., the scene lies in the positive half plane. Examining these inequalities suggests a convenient transformation. Letting

$$x = \cot\left(\frac{\theta_x}{2}\right) x_e$$

$$y = \cot\left(\frac{\theta_y}{2}\right) y_e$$

$$z = z_e$$

transforms the inequalities defining the viewing pyramid to

$$-z \le x \le z$$

$$-z \le y \le z$$

where $z \ge 0$ is implied. Effectively these transformations yield a clipping pyramid with 90° included angles, as shown in Fig. 3–26b.

Again considering the parametric line segment represented by $P(t) = P_1 + (P_2 - P_1)t$, $0 \le t \le 1$, with components

$$
\begin{aligned}
x(t) &= x_1 + (x_2 - x_1)t &= x_1 + \Delta x t \\
y(t) &= y_1 + (y_2 - y_1)t &= y_1 + \Delta y t \qquad 0 \le t \le 1 \\
z(t) &= z_1 + (z_2 - z_1)t &= z_1 + \Delta z t
\end{aligned}
$$

and substituting into the inequalities yields

$$-(\Delta x + \Delta z)t \le x_1 + z_1 \qquad \text{and} \qquad (\Delta x - \Delta z)t \le z_1 - x_1$$

$$-(\Delta y + \Delta z)t \le y_1 + z_1 \qquad \text{and} \qquad (\Delta y - \Delta z)t \le z_1 - y_1$$

[†]Note that this is a left-hand coordinate system.

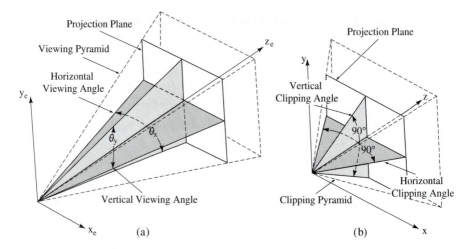

Figure 3–26   Three-dimensional clipping volumes. (a) Viewing pyramid; (b) transformed viewing pyramid with 90° included angles.

Recalling our discussion of the two-dimensional Liang–Barsky clipping algorithm (see Sec. 3–6), we write these inequalities as

$$d_i t \le q_i \qquad i = 1, 2, 3, 4 \tag{3–9}$$

where

$$
\begin{aligned}
d_1 &= -(\Delta x + \Delta z) & q_1 &= x_1 + z_1 \\
d_2 &= \Delta x - \Delta z & q_2 &= z_1 - x_1 \\
d_3 &= -(\Delta y + \Delta z) & q_3 &= y_1 + z_1 \\
d_4 &= \Delta y - \Delta z & q_4 &= z_1 - y_1
\end{aligned}
$$

and the left, right, bottom and top edges are defined by the inequalities for $i = 1, 2, 3, 4$, respectively.

The viewing pyramid is turned into a frustum of vision by adding near (hither) and far (yon) clipping planes (see Fig. 3–22), $z = n$ and $z = f$, respectively. The inside of the frustum of vision along the z-axis is indicated by

$$n \le z \le f$$

Substituting the parametric representation of the line segment yields

$$-\Delta z t \le z_1 - n$$
$$\Delta z t \le f - z_1$$

or in the form of Eq. (3–9)

$$
\begin{aligned}
d_5 &= -\Delta z & q_5 &= z_1 - n \\
d_6 &= \Delta z & q_6 &= f - z_1
\end{aligned}
$$

The intersection of the parametric line and one of the clipping planes is given by $t = q_i/d_i$. The sign of q_i indicates the side of the clipping plane on which P_1 lies.[†] If $q_i \geq 0$, then P_1 lies on the visible side of the plane; if $q_i < 0$, then it lies on the invisible side. Finally, if $d_i = 0$ and $q_i < 0$, the line is on the invisible side of the clipping plane and parallel to the plane, hence it is trivially invisible. These are the same conditions and constraints used for the two-dimensional Liang–Barsky algorithm. Consequently, the clipt routine is identical. The three-dimensional Liang–Barsky algorithm is

Liang–Barsky three-dimensional clipping algorithm

P_1 and P_2 are the line end points with components x_1, y_1, z_1, x_2, y_2, z_2
t_L and t_U are the lower and upper parametric limits
x_L, x_R, y_B, y_T are the left, right, bottom and top window edges

the clipt function is the same as in the two-dimensional Liang–Barsky
   algorithm (see Sec. 3-6)

  $t_L = 0$
  $t_U = 1$
  deltax $= x_2 - x_1$
  deltaz $= z_2 - z_1$
  if clipt$(-$deltax $-$ deltaz, $x_1 + z_1, t_L, t_U) =$ true then
     if clipt$($deltax $-$ deltaz, $z_1 - x_1, t_L, t_U) =$ true then
       deltay $= y_2 - y_1$
       if clipt$(-$deltay $-$ deltaz, $y_1 + z_1, t_L, t_U) =$ true then
         if clipt$($deltay $-$ deltaz, $z_1 - y_1, t_L, t_U) =$ true then
           if $t_U < 1$ then
              $x_2 = x_1 + t_U *$ deltax
              $y_2 = y_1 + t_U *$ deltay
              $z_2 = z_1 + t_U *$ deltaz
           end if
           if $t_L > 0$ then
              $x_1 = x_1 + t_L *$ deltax
              $y_1 = y_1 + t_L *$ deltay
              $z_1 = z_1 + t_L *$ deltaz
           end if
           Draw P_1P_2
        end if

[†]Since each of the sides of the frustum of vision is perpendicular to one of the coordinate planes, the equation of the plane of the side does not involve the perpendicular coordinate. Consequently, the q_i are test functions giving the relationship between a point and the plane, e.g., the left side of the frustum of vision is perpendicular to the xz plane. The plane equation is $x + z = 0$. The test function is $x_1 + z_1$.

> end if
>> end if
>>> end if
> finish

An example further illustrates the algorithm.

Example 3–23   Liang–Barsky Three-dimensional Clipping

Clip the line $P_1(0, 0, -10)$ to $P_2(0, 0, 10)$, using the Liang–Barsky three-dimensional clipping algorithm, with near and far clipping planes at $n = 1$ and $f = 2$.

The values for the Liang–Barsky algorithm are

$$
\begin{aligned}
d_1 &= -(\Delta x + \Delta z) = -20 & q_1 &= x_1 + z_1 = -10 \\
d_2 &= \Delta x - \Delta z = -20 & q_2 &= z_1 - x_1 = -10 \\
d_3 &= -(\Delta y + \Delta z) = -20 & q_3 &= y_1 + z_1 = -10 \\
d_4 &= \Delta y - \Delta z = -20 & q_4 &= z_1 - y_1 = -10 \\
d_5 &= -\Delta z = -20 & q_5 &= z_1 - n = -11 \\
d_6 &= \Delta z = 20 & q_6 &= f - z_1 = 12
\end{aligned}
$$

Referring to the Liang–Barsky three-dimensional clipping algorithm, we have

$\texttt{clipt}(d_1 = -20,\ q_1 = -10,\ t_L = 0,\quad t_U = 1) \Rightarrow t_L = \frac{1}{2}$ visible = true
$\texttt{clipt}(d_2 = -20,\ q_2 = -10,\ t_L = \frac{1}{2},\ t_U = 1) \Rightarrow t_L = \frac{1}{2}$ visible = true
$\texttt{clipt}(d_3 = -20,\ q_3 = -10,\ t_L = \frac{1}{2},\ t_U = 1) \Rightarrow t_L = \frac{1}{2}$ visible = true
$\texttt{clipt}(d_4 = -20,\ q_4 = -10,\ t_L = \frac{1}{2},\ t_U = 1) \Rightarrow t_L = \frac{1}{2}$ visible = true
$\texttt{clipt}(d_5 = -20,\ q_5 = -9,\ t_L = \frac{1}{2},\ t_U = 1) \Rightarrow t_L = \frac{11}{20}$ visible = true
$\texttt{clipt}(d_6 = 20,\ q_6 = -12,\ t_L = \frac{11}{20},\ t_U = 1) \Rightarrow t_L = \frac{12}{20}$ visible = true

The visible range of t is thus $t_L = \frac{11}{20} \le t \le \frac{12}{20} = t_U$. P_1 and P_2 are then

$$
\begin{aligned}
x_1 &= x_1 + t_L \Delta x = x_1 = 0 \\
y_1 &= y_1 + t_L \Delta y = y_1 = 0 \\
z_1 &= z_1 + t_L \Delta z = -10 + \frac{11}{20}(20) = 1 \\[6pt]
x_2 &= x_1 + t_U \Delta x = x_1 = 0 \\
y_2 &= y_1 + t_U \Delta y = y_1 = 0 \\
z_2 &= z_1 + t_U \Delta z = -10 + \frac{12}{20}(20) = 2
\end{aligned}
$$

The visible portion of $P_1 P_2$ is from $1 \le z \le 2$, i.e., between the near and far clipping planes along the z-axis, as expected.

3–15   Clipping in Homogeneous Coordinates

If clipping is to be performed in homogeneous coordinates (see Rogers [Roge90a]) considerable care must be taken if a perspective transformation is also used. The fundamental reason is that a single plane does not necessarily divide a line into two parts, one inside the clipping region and one outside the clipping region. The line may 'wrap around' through infinity such that two segments are visible inside the region. Blinn [Blin78a] shows that clipping all line segments *before* completing the perspective transformation by dividing by the homogeneous coordinate eliminates the segments that 'return from infinity'.

The Cyrus–Beck Algorithm

The Cyrus–Beck and Liang–Barsky algorithms correctly clip a line to the perspective frustum of vision, provided that the line exists entirely in front of the eyepoint or center of projection (see Ex. 3–21). However, if the line passes behind the center of projection, the algorithms reject the line even if partially visible. In practice, the correct result is obtained by first clipping the line to the physical volume described in ordinary coordinate space and then applying the perspective transformation to the results. Note that any affine transformations (e.g., rotations, translations, etc.) are applied to both the clipping volume and the line before the perspective transformation is applied. A further example illustrates these points.

Example 3–24   Cyrus–Beck Algorithm for a Line Passing Behind the Center of Projection

Consider the line $P_1(0, 1, 6)$ to $P_2(0, -1, -6)$ clipped to the physical volume $(x_L, x_R, y_B, y_T, z_N, z_F) = (-1, 1, -1, 1, -1, 1)$ from a center of projection at $z = 5$. The line $P_1 P_2$ passes through the clipping volume but originates behind the center of projection.

After applying the perspective transformation (see Rogers [Roge90a]) the end points of the line in homogeneous coordinates are

$$
\begin{matrix} P_1 \\ P_2 \end{matrix}
\begin{bmatrix} 0 & 1 & 6 & 1 \\ 0 & -1 & -6 & 1 \end{bmatrix}
\begin{bmatrix} 1 & 0 & 0 & 0 \\ 0 & 1 & 0 & 0 \\ 0 & 0 & 1 & -\frac{1}{5} \\ 0 & 0 & 0 & 1 \end{bmatrix}
\begin{bmatrix} 0 & 1 & 6 & -\frac{1}{5} \\ 0 & -1 & -6 & \frac{11}{5} \end{bmatrix}
$$

Note that the homogeneous coordinates of the transformed end points, P_1 and P_2, now have opposite signs indicating that the line has 'wrapped around' through infinity. This means that when projected onto the $h = 1$ (homogeneous) plane the line now extends from P_1 *away* from P_2 through infinity and then back to P_2 – it 'wraps around' through infinity.

Dividing through by the homogeneous coordinate yields the ordinary coordinates

$$P_1(0, -5, -30) \quad \text{and} \quad P_2\left(0, -\frac{5}{11}, -\frac{30}{11}\right)$$

Thus P_1, which was originally in front of the clipping volume but behind the center of projection, is now wrapped around through infinity to a location behind the clipping volume. Since both end points are now outside the clipping volume, the Cyrus–Beck algorithm rejects the line as invisible.

We now clip the line to the cubical physical volume and then perform the perspective transformation. Recalling the inner normals and the points in each clipping plane from Ex. 3–20, the line is first clipped to the physical volume $(-1, 1, -1, 1, -1, 1)$. Here, the direction of $P_1 P_2$ is

$$\mathbf{D} = \mathbf{P}_2 - \mathbf{P}_1 = [0 \quad -1 \quad -6] - [0 \quad 1 \quad 6] = [0 \quad -2 \quad -12]$$

The results are given in Table 3–15.

Table 3–15

Plane	n	f	w	w·n	D·n[†]	t_L	t_U
Top	$[\;0 \; -1 \quad 0]$	$(\;1, \; 1, \; 1)$	$[-1 \; 0 \; 5]$	0	2	0	
Bottom	$[\;0 \quad 1 \quad 0]$	$(-1, -1, -1)$	$[\;1 \; 2 \; 7]$	2	-2		1
Right	$[-1 \quad 0 \quad 0]$	$(\;1, \; 1, \; 1)$	$[-1 \; 0 \; 5]$	1	0		
Left	$[\;1 \quad 0 \quad 0]$	$(-1, -1, -1)$	$[\;1 \; 2 \; 7]$	1	0		
Near	$[\;0 \quad 0 \; -1]$	$(\;1, \; 1, \; 1)$	$[-1 \; 0 \; 5]$	-5	12	$5/12$	
Far	$[\;0 \quad 0 \quad 1]$	$(-1, -1, -1)$	$[\;1 \; 2 \; 7]$	7	-12		$7/12$

[†] If $\mathbf{D} \cdot \mathbf{n} < 0$, test upper limit t_U; if $\mathbf{D} \cdot \mathbf{n} > 0$, test lower limit t_L.

Examining Table 3-15 shows that the line is visible from $5/12 \leq t \leq 7/12$. The end points of the clipped line in physical space are

$$P\left(\frac{5}{12}\right) = [0 \quad 1 \quad 6] + [0 \quad -2 \quad -12]\left(\frac{5}{12}\right) = \left[0 \quad \frac{1}{6} \quad 1\right]$$

$$P\left(\frac{7}{12}\right) = [0 \quad 1 \quad 6] + [0 \quad -2 \quad -12]\left(\frac{7}{12}\right) = \left[0 \quad -\frac{1}{6} \quad -1\right]$$

Transforming these end points to perspective space using homogeneous coordinates (see [Roge90a]) yields

$$\begin{bmatrix} 0 & \frac{1}{6} & 1 & 1 \\ 0 & -\frac{1}{6} & -1 & 1 \end{bmatrix} \begin{bmatrix} 1 & 0 & 0 & 0 \\ 0 & 1 & 0 & 0 \\ 0 & 0 & 1 & -\frac{1}{5} \\ 0 & 0 & 0 & 1 \end{bmatrix} = \begin{bmatrix} 0 & \frac{5}{24} & \frac{5}{4} & 1 \\ 0 & -\frac{5}{36} & -\frac{5}{6} & 1 \end{bmatrix}$$

as the visible portion of the line. This is the correct result.

The Liang–Barsky Algorithm

Liang and Barsky [Lian84] extended their line clipping algorithm to homogeneous coordinates by effectively distorting the clipping volume. Clipping is performed after the perspective transformation in perspective space but *before* projection back into physical space, i.e., before division by the homogeneous coordinate. Recall from the discussion of the three-dimensional Liang–Barsky clipping algorithm in Sec. 3-14 that the perspective center of projection or eyepoint is at the origin and that in the eye coordinate system $z_e \geq 0$, i.e., the scene lies in the positive half plane. Thus, the Liang–Barsky homogeneous clipping algorithm incorrectly clips a line originating behind the center of projection or eyepoint.

After transforming the viewing pyramid into a right pyramid with 90° included angles limited by near and far clipping planes (see Fig. 3-26), i.e., a frustum of vision, the clipping limits are

$$-z \leq x \leq z \qquad -z \leq y \leq z \qquad n \leq z \leq f$$

where n and f specify the near and far clipping planes.

Performing a perspective transformation (see [Roge90a]) shows the transformed z coordinate in the physical plane is of the form

$$z^* = \frac{z}{h}$$

where h is the homogeneous weighting factor or coordinate. z^* is normalized to the range $0 \leq z^* \leq 1$ by the transformation

$$z^* = \frac{f}{f-n}\left(1 - \frac{n}{z}\right)$$

After substituting, the clipping limits become

$$-h \leq x \leq h \qquad -h \leq y \leq h \qquad 0 \leq z \leq h$$

Recall that

$$x = x_1 + \Delta x\, t \qquad y = y_1 + \Delta y\, t \qquad z = z_1 + \Delta z\, t$$

and

$$h = h_1 + \Delta h\, t$$

where $\Delta h = h_2 - h_1$. Substituting into the clipping limits yields

$$\begin{array}{lll}
-(\Delta x + \Delta h)t \leq x_1 + h_1 & \text{and} & (\Delta x - \Delta h)t \leq h_1 - x_1 \\
-(\Delta y + \Delta h)t \leq y_1 + h_1 & \text{and} & (\Delta y - \Delta h)t \leq h_1 - y_1 \\
-\Delta z\, t \leq z_1 & \text{and} & (\Delta z - \Delta h)t \leq h_1 - z_1
\end{array}$$

Thus the d_i and q_i are

$$d_1 = -(\Delta x + \Delta h) \qquad q_1 = x_1 + h_1 \qquad \text{left}$$
$$d_2 = \Delta x - \Delta h \qquad q_2 = h_1 - x_1 \qquad \text{right}$$
$$d_3 = -(\Delta y + \Delta h) \qquad q_3 = y_1 + h_1 \qquad \text{bottom}$$
$$d_4 = \Delta y - \Delta h \qquad q_4 = h_1 - y_1 \qquad \text{top}$$
$$d_5 = -\Delta z \qquad q_5 = z_1 \qquad \text{near}$$
$$d_6 = \Delta z - \Delta h \qquad q_6 = h_1 - z_1 \qquad \text{far}$$

Pseudocode for the Liang–Barsky homogeneous clipping algorithm is given below. Again, the clipt function is the same as in the Liang–Barsky two-dimensional clipping algorithm given in Sec. 3-6.

Liang–Barsky three-dimensional homogeneous clipping algorithm

P_1 and P_2 are the end points with components
  x_1, y_1, z_1, h_1, x_2, y_2, z_2, h_2
t_L and t_U are the lower and upper parametric limits
x_L, x_R, y_B, y_T are the left, right, bottom and top window edges

the clipt function is the same as in the two-dimensional Liang–Barsky algorithm (see Sec. 3–6)

```
t_L = 0
t_U = 1
deltax = x_2 − x_1
deltah = h_2 − h_1
if clipt(−deltax − deltah, x_1 + h_1, t_L, t_U) = true then
    if clipt(deltax − deltah, h_1 − x_1, t_L, t_U) = true then
        deltay = y_2 − y_1
        if clipt(−deltay − deltah, y_1 + h_1, t_L, t_U) = true then
            if clipt(deltay − deltah, h_1 − y_1, t_L, t_U) = true then
                deltaz = z_2 − z_1
                if clipt(−deltaz, z_1, t_L, t_U) = true then
                    if clipt(deltaz−deltah, h_1−z_1, t_L, t_U) = true then
                        if t_U < 1 then
                            x_2 = x_1 + t_U * deltax
                            y_2 = y_1 + t_U * deltay
                            z_2 = z_1 + t_U * deltaz
                            h_2 = h_1 + t_U * deltah
                        end if
                        if t_L > 0 then
                            x_1 = x_1 + t_L * deltax
                            y_1 = y_1 + t_L * deltay
                            z_1 = z_1 + t_L * deltaz
                            h_1 = h_1 + t_L * deltah
```

$$\text{end if}$$
$$\text{Draw } P_1P_2$$
$$\text{end if}$$
$$\text{end if}$$
$$\text{end if}$$
$$\text{end if}$$
$$\text{end if}$$
$$\text{end if}$$
$$\text{finish}$$

In the next example, we consider a line which originates behind the center of projection, to illustrate the problems with the Liang–Barsky homogeneous clipping algorithm. If the line does not originate behind the center of projection, the Liang–Barsky algorithm correctly performs the clip.

Example 3–25   Liang–Barsky Homogeneous Clipping

The Liang–Barsky homogeneous clipping volume is a $90°$ frustum of vision, with the eyepoint at the origin (see Fig. 3–26). Assume near and far clipping planes at $z = n = 1$ and $z = f = 2$, respectively. Consider the line $P_1 [0 \ 0 \ -10 \ -9]$ to $P_2 [0 \ 0 \ 10 \ 11]$ in homogeneous coordinates. This line lies along the z-axis, beginning behind the center of projection, or eyepoint, passing through the clipping volume and ending beyond the clipping volume. (Note that $h_1 = -9 < 0$ and $h_2 = 11 > 0$.)

Referring to the Liang–Barsky homogeneous clipping algorithm we have

$$d_1 = -(\Delta x + \Delta h) = -20 \qquad q_1 = x_1 + h_1 = -9$$
$$d_2 = \Delta x - \Delta h = -20 \qquad q_2 = h_1 - x_1 = -9$$
$$d_3 = -(\Delta y + \Delta h) = -20 \qquad q_3 = y_1 + h_1 = -9$$
$$d_4 = \Delta y - \Delta h = -20 \qquad q_4 = h_1 - y_1 = -9$$
$$d_5 = -\Delta z = -20 \qquad q_5 = z_1 = -10$$
$$d_6 = \Delta z - \Delta h = 0 \qquad q_6 = h_1 - z_1 = 1$$

```
clipt(d1 = -20, q1 = -9,  tL = 0,    tU = 1)  ⇒ tL = 9/20  visible = true
clipt(d2 = -20, q2 = -9,  tL = 9/20, tU = 1)  ⇒ t  = 9/20  visible = true
clipt(d3 = -20, q3 = -9,  tL = 9/20, tU = 1)  ⇒ t  = 9/20  visible = true
clipt(d4 = -20, q4 = -9,  tL = 9/20, tU = 1)  ⇒ t  = 9/20  visible = true
clipt(d5 = -20, q5 = -10, tL = 9/20, tU = 1)  ⇒ tL = 1/2   visible = true
clipt(d6 =   0, q6 =   1, tL = 1/2,  tU = 1)  ⇒            visible = true
```

The visible range of t is thus $t_L = 1/2 \le t \le 1 = t_U$. Since $t_U = 1$, P_2 is unchanged. Calculating P_1, we have

$$x_1 = x_1 + t_L \Delta x = x_1 = 0$$
$$y_1 = y_1 + t_L \Delta y = y_1 = 0$$

$$z_1 = z_1 + t_L \Delta z = -10 + \frac{1}{2}(20) = 0$$

$$h_1 = h_1 + t_L \Delta z = -9 + \frac{1}{2}(20) = 1$$

and in homogeneous coordinates $P_1 = [0\ \ 0\ \ 0\ \ 1]$. Examining these results immediately shows that, as with the Cyrus–Beck algorithm, the Liang–Barsky homogeneous clipping algorithm incorrectly clips lines that originate behind the center of projection or eyepoint and that terminate in front of the center of projection. The correct result is obtained by first clipping to the physical volume as shown in Ex. 3–24. The details are left as an exercise (see Prob. 3–15).

3–16   Determining The Inward Normal and Three-dimensional Convex Sets

The two-dimensional technique using rotations and translations previously used to identify convex polygons and to determine the inward normal can be extended to three-dimensional polygonal volumes. The three-dimensional procedure is

For each polygonal face plane of the volume:

Translate the volume such that one of the vertices of the polygon face is at the origin.

Rotate about the origin such that one of the two adjacent polygon edges is coincident with one of the coordinate axes, e.g., the x-axis.

Rotate about this coordinate axis until the polygonal face lies in a coordinate plane, e.g., the $z = 0$ plane.

Examine the sign of the coordinate component perpendicular to this plane for all other vertices of the volume, e.g., the z component.

If all the vertices have the same sign or are zero, then the volume is convex with respect to this plane. If the volume is convex for all its face planes, then it is convex; if not, it is concave.

If for each face the value of the coordinate component perpendicular to this plane is zero, then the volume is degenerate; i.e., it is a plane.

For each convex plane, the inner normal has components in the rotated coordinate system of zero and the sign of the coordinate component perpendicular to the plane in which the face plane lies.

In determining the original direction of the inner normal, only the inverse rotations need be applied.

Example 3–26   Determining the Convexity of a Volume

As a specific example, again consider the cube with one corner removed previously described in Ex. 3–22. The cube is shown in Fig. 3–27a. Determine the convexity of the clipping volume with respect to the face labeled abc in Fig. 3–27a using the above algorithm.

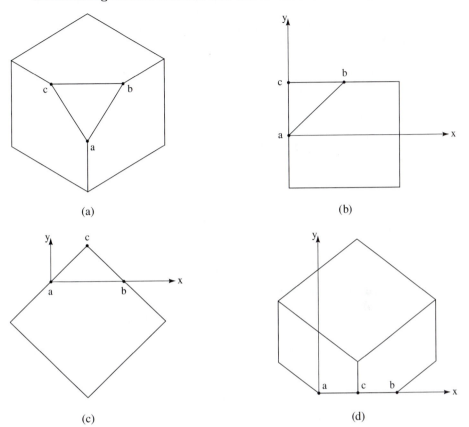

(a)

(b)

(c)

(d)

Figure 3–27 Determining a convex volume and the inner normal.

The volume is first translated such that point a is at the origin. The 4×4 homogeneous coordinate transformation matrix is (see [Roge90a])

$$[T] = \begin{bmatrix} 1 & 0 & 0 & 0 \\ 0 & 1 & 0 & 0 \\ 0 & 0 & 1 & 0 \\ 1 & 0 & -1 & 1 \end{bmatrix}$$

The result is shown, projected onto the $z = 0$ plane, in Fig. 3–27b.

Rotation about the z-axis by $\theta = -45°$ makes the edge ab coincident with the x-axis. The homogeneous coordinate transformation matrix is (see [Roge90a])

$$[R_z] = \begin{bmatrix} \cos\theta & \sin\theta & 0 & 0 \\ -\sin\theta & \cos\theta & 0 & 0 \\ 0 & 0 & 1 & 0 \\ 0 & 0 & 0 & 1 \end{bmatrix}$$

The result is shown in Fig. 3–27c, again projected onto the $z = 0$ plane. It remains to rotate about the x-axis to make the plane abc coincident with the coordinate plane, $y = 0$. The coordinates of the point c in Fig. 3–27c are $(0.565685, 0.565685, -0.8)$. The rotation angle about x is given by

$$\alpha = \tan^{-1}\left(\frac{y}{z}\right) = \tan^{-1}\left(\frac{0.565685}{-0.8}\right) = -35.2644°$$

Rotation by this angle places the volume below the coordinate plane, $y = 0$. Rotation by $(180 - \alpha)°$ places the volume above the plane. The latter result is shown in Fig. 3–27d projected onto the $z = 0$ plane. The rotation matrix is

$$\begin{bmatrix} 1 & 0 & 0 & 0 \\ 0 & \cos\alpha & \sin\alpha & 0 \\ 0 & -\sin\alpha & \cos\alpha & 0 \\ 0 & 0 & 0 & 1 \end{bmatrix}$$

The y coordinates of all the other points in the volume are positive. Hence, the volume is convex with respect to the plane abc.

The inner normal for the plane abc in this orientation is

$$n' = \begin{bmatrix} 0 & \text{Sign}(y) & 0 \end{bmatrix} = \begin{bmatrix} 0 & 1 & 0 \end{bmatrix}$$

Applying the inverse rotations yields

$$n = \begin{bmatrix} 0.5774 & -0.5774 & -0.5774 \end{bmatrix}$$

or

$$n = \begin{bmatrix} 1 & -1 & -1 \end{bmatrix}$$

as expected. To prove the volume convex, this operation must be performed for each face plane.

3–17   Splitting Concave Volumes

Clipping to concave volumes can be accomplished by internal and external clipping to appropriate convex volumes which constitute the concave volume, in a manner similar to the technique previously discussed for clipping to concave polygons (Sec. 3–8). The task of splitting simple concave volumes into constituent convex volumes can be accomplished by an extension of the translation and rotation technique presented in Sec. 3–16. The algorithm assumes that the volume is polyhedral. The procedure is

For each polygonal face plane of the volume:

Translate such that one of the vertices of the polygon face is at the origin.

Rotate about the origin such that one of the adjacent polygon edges is coincident with one of the coordinate axes, e.g., the x-axis.

Rotate about this coordinate axis until the polygon face lies in the coordinate plane, e.g., the $z = 0$ plane.

Examine the sign of the coordinate component perpendicular to this plane for all other vertices of the volume, e.g., the z component.

If all the vertices have the same sign or are zero, then the volume is convex with respect to this plane; if not, it is concave. Split the volume along the coordinate plane in which the face polygon lies.

Reenter the algorithm with each of the split-off volumes. Continue until each is shown to be convex.

An example illustrates the technique.

Example 3–27   Splitting Concave Volumes

Consider the concave volume shown in Fig. 3–28a. The polygons describing each face are

Back:	$P_1(3,0,0), P_2(0,0,0), P_3(0,2,0), P_4(1,2,0)$
	$P_5(1, {}^3\!/_2, 0), P_6({}^3\!/_2, {}^3\!/_2, 0), P_7({}^3\!/_2, 2, 0), P_8(3, 2, 0)$
Front:	$P_9(3,0,2), P_{10}(0,0,2), P_{11}(0,2,2), P_{12}(1,2,2)$
	$P_{13}(1, {}^3\!/_2, 2), P_{14}({}^3\!/_2, {}^3\!/_2, 2), P_{15}({}^3\!/_2, 2, 2), P_{16}(3, 2, 2)$
Left:	$P_2(0,0,0), P_{10}(0,0,2), P_{11}(0,2,2), P_3(0,2,0)$
Right:	$P_1(3,0,0), P_8(3,2,0), P_{16}(3,2,2), P_9(3,0,2)$
Bottom:	$P_1(3,0,0), P_2(0,0,0), P_{10}(0,0,2), P_9(3,0,2)$
Top left:	$P_{10}(0,0,2), P_4(1,2,0), P_3(0,2,0), P_{11}(0,2,2)$
Left notch:	$P_{13}(1, {}^3\!/_2, 2), P_5(1, {}^3\!/_2, 0), P_4(1,2,0), P_{12}(1,2,2)$
Bottom notch:	$P_{13}(1, {}^3\!/_2, 2), P_{14}({}^3\!/_2, {}^3\!/_2, 2), P_6({}^3\!/_2, {}^3\!/_2, 0), P_5(1, {}^3\!/_2, 0)$
Right notch:	$P_6({}^3\!/_2, {}^3\!/_2, 0), P_7({}^3\!/_2, 2, 0), P_{15}({}^3\!/_2, 2, 2), P_{14}({}^3\!/_2, {}^3\!/_2, 2)$
Top right:	$P_{16}(3, 2, 2), P_8(3, 2, 0), P_7({}^3\!/_2, 2, 0), P_{15}({}^3\!/_2, 2, 2)$

Using the above algorithm, the convexity of the volume with respect to the face called the left notch and labeled abc in Fig. 3–28a is examined. The volume is first translated such that the point P_5, labeled a in Fig. 3–28a, is at the origin. This also places P_{13}, labeled b in Fig. 3–28a, on the positive z-axis. The translation factors are $-1, -{}^3\!/_2, 0$ in the x, y, z directions, respectively. The result is shown projected onto the $z = 0$ plane in Fig. 3–28b. Rotation about the z-axis by $-90°$ makes the plane abc coincident with the $y = 0$ coordinate plane. The result is shown in Figs. 3–28c and 3–28d, projected onto the $z = 0$ plane.

Examination of the y coordinates shows that the volume is concave. It is split into two volumes, V_1 and V_2, along the plane $y = 0$. V_1 is above the plane $y = 0$, and V_2 is below it. The face planes in the original orientation are

V_1:

Left:	$P_2(0,0,0), P_{10}(0,0,2), P_{11}(0,2,2), P_3(0,2,0)$
Right lower:	$P_{10}'(1,0,2), P_5'(1,0,0), P_5(1, {}^3\!/_2, 0), P_{13}(1, {}^3\!/_2, 2)$
Right upper:	$P_{13}(1, {}^3\!/_2, 2), P_5(1, {}^3\!/_2, 0), P_4(1,2,0), P_{12}(1,2,2)$

Top: $P_{10}(0,0,2), P_4(1,2,0), P_3(0,2,0), P_{11}(0,2,2)$

Bottom: $P_2(0,0,0), P_5'(1,0,0), P_{10}'(1,0,2), P_{10}(0,0,2)$

Front: $P_{10}(0,0,2), P_{10}'(1,0,2), P_{13}(1,\sfrac{3}{2},2), P_{12}(1,2,2), P_{11}(0,2,2)$

Back: $P_5'(1,0,0), P_2(0,0,0), P_3(0,2,0), P_4(1,2,0), P_5(1,\sfrac{3}{2},0)$

V_2:

Left: $P_5'(1,0,0), P_{10}'(1,0,2), P_{13}(1,\sfrac{3}{2},2), P_5(1,\sfrac{3}{2},0)$

Right: $P_1(3,0,0), P_8(3,2,0), P_{16}(3,2,2), P_9(3,0,2)$

Right notch: $P_6(\sfrac{3}{2},\sfrac{3}{2},0), P_7(\sfrac{3}{2},2,0), P_{15}(\sfrac{3}{2},2,2), P_{14}(\sfrac{3}{2},\sfrac{3}{2},2)$

Bottom notch: $P_{13}(1,\sfrac{3}{2},2), P_{14}(\sfrac{3}{2},\sfrac{3}{2},2), P_6(\sfrac{3}{2},\sfrac{3}{2},0), P_5(1,\sfrac{3}{2},0)$

Top right: $P_{16}(3,2,2), P_8(3,2,0), P_7(\sfrac{3}{2},2,0), P_{15}(\sfrac{3}{2},2,2)$

Bottom: $P_5'(1,0,0), P_1(3,0,0), P_9(3,0,2), P_{10}'(1,0,2)$

When the two volumes are passed through the algorithm a second time, V_1 is declared convex and V_2 is split into two volumes which are subsequently found to be convex. The result is shown in Fig. 3–28e in an exploded view.

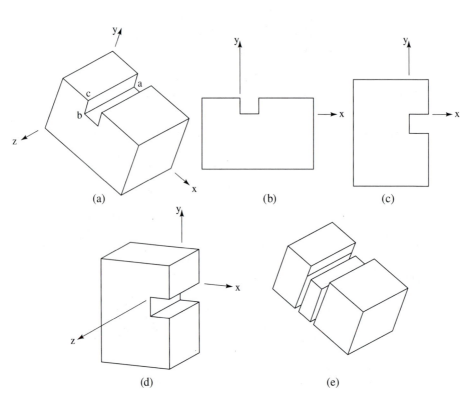

Figure 3–28   Concave volume splitting.

3–18   Polygon Clipping

The previous discussion concentrated on clipping lines. Polygons can, of course, be considered as collections of lines. For line drawing applications, it is not too important if polygons are subdivided into lines before clipping. When a closed polygon is clipped as a collection of lines, the original closed polygon becomes one or more open polygons or discrete lines, as shown in Fig. 3–29.

However, when polygons are considered as solid areas, it is necessary that closed polygons remain closed. In Fig. 3–29 this requires that the lines bc, ef, fg and ha be added to the polygon description. Adding ef and fg is particularly difficult. Considerable difficulty also occurs when clipping a polygon results in several disjoint smaller polygons, as shown in Fig. 3–30. For example, the lines ab and cd shown in Fig. 3–30 are frequently included in the clipped polygon description. If, for example, the original polygon is declared red on a blue background, the lines ab and cd will also appear red on a blue background. This is contrary to expectation.

3–19   Reentrant Polygon Clipping— Sutherland–Hodgman Algorithm

The fundamental idea behind the Sutherland–Hodgman algorithm [Suth74b] is that it is easy to clip a polygon against a single edge or clipping plane. The procedure is to clip the original polygon and each resulting intermediate polygon against a single edge, each edge in succession. Figure 3–31 illustrates the procedure for a rectangular window. The polygon is originally defined by a list of vertices $P_1, \ldots, P_n$ which imply a list of edges $P_1P_2, P_2P_3, \ldots, P_{n-1}P_n, P_nP_1$.

In Fig. 3–31 these edges are first clipped against the left edge of the window to yield the intermediate polygon shown. The clipping algorithm is then reentered, with the intermediate polygon to be clipped against the top edge. This

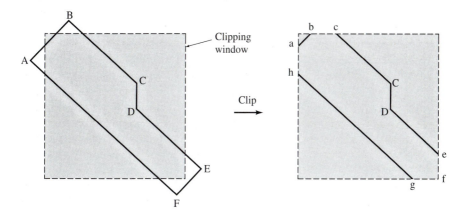

Figure 3–29   Polygon clipping, resulting in open polygons.

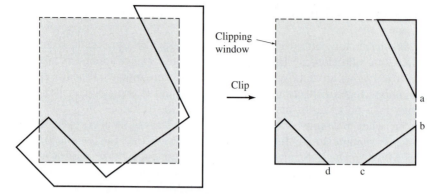

Figure 3–30 Polygon clipping — disjoint polygons.

yields a second intermediate polygon. The process is repeated until the polygon is clipped against all the window edges; the steps are shown in Fig. 3–31. Notice that the addition of the corner point, labeled Q_8 in the final clipped polygon, is now trivial. The algorithm clips any polygon, convex or concave, planar or nonplanar, against any convex polygonal clipping window. The order in which the polygon is clipped against the various window edges is immaterial.

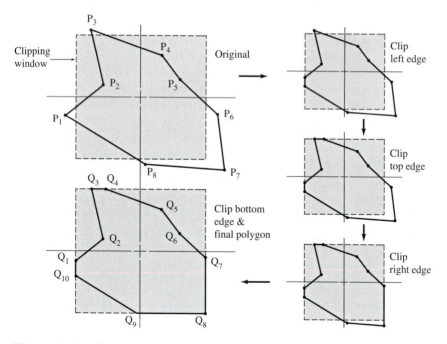

Figure 3–31 Reentrant polygon clipping.

The output of the algorithm is a list of polygon vertices, all of which are on the visible side of a clipping plane. Since each edge of the polygon is individually compared with the clipping plane, only the relationship between a single edge and a single clipping plane need be considered. If each point P in the polygon vertex list, except the first, is considered as the terminal vertex of an edge, and if the starting vertex S of that edge is the vertex just previous to P in the list, then there are only four possible relationships between the edge and the clipping plane. These are shown in Fig. 3–32.

The result of each polygon edge-clipping plane comparison is the output to the clipped polygon list of zero, one or two vertices. If the edge is entirely visible, then P is output. It is not necessary to output S, the starting vertex, since, if each vertex is considered sequentially, S is the terminating vertex of the previous edge and has already been output. If the edge is entirely invisible, no output is required.

If the edge is partially visible, then it is either entering or leaving the visible side of the clipping plane. If the edge is leaving the visible region, the intersections of the polygon edge and the clipping plane must be calculated and output. If the edge is entering the visible region, the intersection with the clipping plane must again be calculated and output. Since P, the terminating vertex, is now visible, it must also be output.

For the first point of the polygon, it is only necessary to determine if it is visible. If it is visible, then it is output and saved as S. If it is not visible no output occurs; but it is still saved as S, the starting point.

The final edge, $P_n P_1$, must be considered separately. This is done by saving the first point of the polygon as F. Thus, the final edge becomes $P_n F$ and is considered exactly as any other edge.

Determining the Visibility of a Point

Before presenting the complete algorithm, there are two additional considerations: determining the visibility of a point, and determining the intersection of

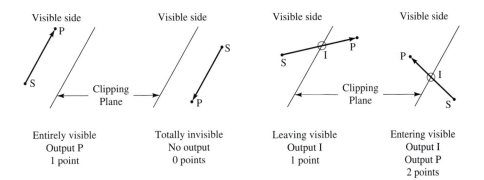

Visible side	Visible side	Visible side	Visible side
Entirely visible	Totally invisible	Leaving visible	Entering visible
Output P	No output	Output I	Output I
1 point	0 points	1 point	Output P
			2 points

Figure 3–32   Edge-clipping plane relationships.

the polygon edge and the clipping plane. Determining the visibility of a point is equivalent to determining on which side of the clipping plane the point lies. If successive edges of the clipping polygon are considered in a clockwise direction, the inside of the polygon is always to the right; if counterclockwise, the inside is to the left. Previously, two methods of determining the location (visibility) of a point with respect to a line or plane were considered: examining the sign of the dot product of the normal vector and a vector from a point in the line or plane to the point under consideration (see Sec. 3–5), and substitution of the point coordinates into the equation of the line or plane (see Sec. 3–9). This latter technique is a variation of that proposed by Sutherland and Hodgman [Suth74b].

Another technique is to examine the sign of the z component of the cross product of two vectors which lie in a plane. If two points in the clipping plane are P_1 and P_2, and the point under consideration is P_3, then these three points define a plane. Two vectors which lie in that plane are $\mathbf{P_1P_2}$ and $\mathbf{P_1P_3}$. If this plane is considered the xy plane, then the vector cross product $\mathbf{P_1P_3} \otimes \mathbf{P_1P_2}$ has only a z component given by $(x_3 - x_1)(y_2 - y_1) - (x_3 - y_1)(x_2 - x_1)$. If the sign of the z component is positive, zero or negative, then P_3 is to the right, on or to the left of the line P_1P_2.

All these techniques are particularly simple for rectangular clipping windows parallel to the coordinate axes.

Example 3–28   Relation of a Point to a Plane

Consider a clipping plane at $x = w = -1$ perpendicular to the x-axis, as shown in Fig. 3–33. The locations of two points, $P_3(-2, 1)$ and $P_3'(2, 1)$, with respect to the clipping plane are required.

Using the cross-product technique with $P_1(-1, 0)$ and $P_2(-1, 2)$ yields for P_3

$$(y_3 - y_1)(x_3 - x_2) = (1 - 0)[-2 - (-1)] = -1 < 0$$

which indicates P_3 is to the left of $\mathbf{P_1P_2}$, and for P_3'

$$(y_3' - y_1)(x_3' - x_2) = (1 - 0)[2 - (-1)] = 3 > 0$$

which indicates P_3' is to the right of $\mathbf{P_1P_2}$

The substitution technique is particularly simple. Here the test function is $x - w$. For P_3

$$x_3 - w = -2 - (-1) = -1 < 0$$

and for P_3'

$$x_3' - w = 2 - (-1) = 3 > 0$$

which indicates that P_3 and P_3' are to the left and right of $\mathbf{P_1P_2}$, respectively.

Choosing the inner normal as $\mathbf{n} = [1 \ \ 0]$ and the point in the clipping plane as $f(-1, 0)$, and taking the dot product of the vectors, yields for P_3

$$\mathbf{n} \cdot [\mathbf{P_3} - \mathbf{f}] = [1 \ \ 0] \cdot [-1 \ \ 1] = -1 < 0$$

and for P_3'

$$\mathbf{n}\cdot[\,\mathbf{P}_3' - \mathbf{f}\,] = [\,1 \quad 0\,]\cdot[\,3 \quad 1\,] = 3 > 0$$

which again indicates P_3 is to the left and P_3' is to the right of the clipping plane.

Using these visibility tests, a polygon edge is totally visible or totally invisible if both end points are totally visible or totally invisible. If one end point is visible and the other invisible, then the polygon edge intersects the clipping plane and its intersection point must be calculated.

Line Intersections

Any of the line intersection (clipping) techniques discussed above can be used, e.g., Cyrus–Beck (see Sec. 3–5), parametric (see Sec. 3–4) or the midpoint subdivision (see Sec. 3–3). Again, as illustrated previously, these techniques are particularly simple for rectangular clipping windows parallel to the coordinate axis. The Cyrus–Beck and midpoint subdivision techniques are completely general. However, the intersection of two general parametric lines in the two-dimensional plane requires further discussion.

Two line segments with end points P_1, P_2 and P_3, P_4, respectively, are parametrically represented by

$$P(s) = P_1 + (P_2 - P_1)s \qquad 0 \le s \le 1$$

and

$$P(t) = P_3 + (P_4 - P_3)t \qquad 0 \le t \le 1$$

At the intersection point $P(s) = P(t)$. Recalling that $P(s)$ and $P(t)$ are vector valued functions, i.e., $P(s) = [\,x(s) \ y(s)\,]$ and $P(t) = [\,x(t) \ y(t)\,]$, yields two equations in the two unknown parameter values, s and t, at the intersection; i.e., $x(s) = x(t)$, $y(s) = y(t)$ at the intersection point. If there is no solution, then the lines are parallel. If either s or t is outside the required range, the segments do not intersect. A matrix formulation is particularly convenient.

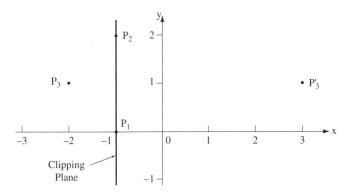

Figure 3–33 Visibility tests.

Example 3–29   Intersection of Parametric Lines

Consider two line segments, $P_1[0\ 0]$ to $P_2[3\ 2]$ and $P_3[3\ 0]$ to $P_4[0\ 2]$, as shown in Fig. 3–34. Then

$$P(s) = [0\ 0] + [3\ 2]\,s$$

$$P(t) = [3\ 0] + [-3\ 2]\,t$$

Equating the x and y components yields

$$3s = 3 - 3t$$

$$2s = 2t$$

Solving yields

$$s = t = \frac{1}{2}$$

The intersection point is then

$$P_i(s) = [0\ 0] + \frac{1}{2}[3\ 2]$$

$$= \left[\frac{3}{2}\ \ 1\right]$$

The Algorithm

Recall that in the Sutherland–Hodgman algorithm developed above each polygon edge is considered successively. Hence, with minor changes the same code is used for each edge. The last vertex is handled specially. Figure 3–35, adapted from the original paper [Suth74b], gives a flowchart of the algorithm. While

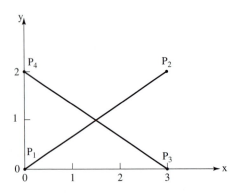

Figure 3–34   Intersection of parametric lines.

Fig. 3–35a is applied to every vertex, Fig. 3–35b is used only for the last vertex. Sutherland and Hodgman [Suth74b] show how the generation and storage of intermediate polygon vertices can be avoided. Specifically, instead of clipping each edge (vertex) of the polygon against a single window plane, each polygon edge (vertex) is clipped successively against all the window planes. As soon as a polygon edge (vertex) is clipped against a window plane the algorithm calls itself recursively to clip the result against the next window plane. This makes the algorithm more suitable for hardware implementation.

A pseudocode implementation which generates and stores intermediate polygons is given here:

Sutherland–Hodgman polygon clipping algorithm

This is a sequential implementation

P *is the input polygon array*
Q *is the output polygon array*

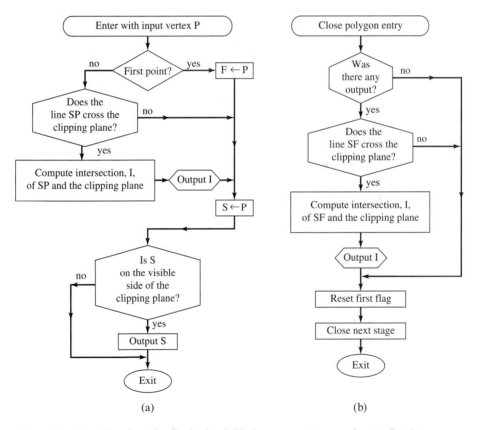

(a)

(b)

Figure 3–35   Flowchart for Sutherland–Hodgman reentrant polygon clipping.

W *is the clipping window array; the first vertex is repeated*
  as the last vertex
Nin *is the number of input polygon vertices*
Nout *is the number of output polygon vertices*
Nw *is the number of clipping polygon vertices plus one*
all polygon vertices are given in counterclockwise order

  for each window edge

  for $i = 1$ **to** Nw $- 1$

    set the output counter and zero the output array

    Nout $= 0$

    $Q = 0$

    clip each polygon edge against this window edge

    for $j = 1$ **to** Nin $- 1$

      treat the first point specially

      if $j = 1$ **then**

        save first point

        $F = P_j$

        set S to the first point

        $S = P_j$

        check the visibility of the first point

        call Visible$(S, W_i, W_{i+1}; \text{Svisible})$

        if Svisible ≥ 0 **then**

          the point is visible; output it

          call Output$(S, \text{Nout}; Q)$

        end if

      end if

      check if this polygon edge crosses the window edge

      call Cross$(S, P_{j+1}, W_i, W_{i+1}; \text{Spcross})$

      if Spcross $=$ no **then**

        replace the first point

        $S = P_{j+1}$

      else

        the polygon edge crosses the window edge
        calculate the intersection point

        call Intersect$(S, P_j, W_i, W_{i+1}; \text{Pintersect})$

        output the intersection point

        call Output $(\text{Pintersect}, \text{Nout}; Q)$

        $S = P_{j+1}$

      end if

check if the second point on the edge (now S) is visible

call Visible(S, W_i, W_{i+1}; Svisible)
if Svisible $\geq$ 0 **then**

    the point is visible; output it

    call Output(S, Nout; Q)
end if

next j

closure—treat the edge P_nP_1
if there was no output, skip to the next window edge

if Nout = 0 **then**

    P = Q
    Nin = Nout

else

    check if the last polygon edge crosses the window edge

    call Cross(S, F, W_i, W_{i+1}; Spcross)
    if Spcross = no **then**

        P = Q
        Nin = Nout

    else

        the polygon edge crosses the window edge
        calculate the intersection

        call Intersect(S, F, W_i, W_{i+1}; Pintersect)

        output the intersection

        call Output(Pintersect,Nout; Q)
        Nin = Nout

    end if
end if

the polygon is now clipped against the edge W_i to W_{i+1}
the algorithm is now reentered with the clipped polygon

next i
finish

subroutine module to determine if the polygon edge and
  the window edge intersect

subroutine Cross(Start,Point,W1,W2; Spcross)

  determine the visibility of the starting point of the polygon edge

  call Visible(Start,W1,W2;Pvisible)
  Pvisible1 = Pvisible

  determine the visibility of the end point of the polygon edge

  call Visible(Point,W1,W2;Pvisible)
  Pvisible2 = Pvisible

a polygon edge which begins or ends on a window edge is considered
not to cross the edge. This point will have previously been output

if Pvisible1 < 0 **and** Pvisible2 > 0 **or**
>   Pvisible1 > 0 **and** Pvisible2 < 0 **then**
>   Spcross = yes

else
>   Spcross = no

end if

return

subroutine module to determine visibility

subroutine Visible(Point,P1,P2;Pvisible)

determine the visibility of Point *with respect to the edge* P_1P_2

Pvisible < 0 Point *is to the left (visible)*
>   = 0 Point *is on the edge* P_1P_2
>   > 0 Point *is to the right (invisible)*

the routine uses the cross-product technique
the Sign *function returns* −1, 0, 1 *as the argument is*
>   *negative, zero or positive*
the direction of the edge is assumed to be from P_1 *to* P_2
the window is assumed specified counterclockwise, so that the inside
>   *(visible side) is always to the left looking from* P_1 *to* P_2

>   Temp1 = (Pointx − P1x) ∗ (P2y − P1y)
>   Temp2 = (Pointy − P1y) ∗ (P2x − P1x)
>   Temp3 = Temp1 − Temp2
>   Pvisible = −**Sign**(Temp3)

return

subroutine module to calculate intersection of two lines

subroutine Intersect(P1,P2,W1,W2;Pintersect)

the routine uses a parametric line formulation
the lines P_1P_2 *and* W_1W_2 *are assumed two-dimensional*
the matrix for the parameter values is obtained by equating the x *and* y
>   *components of the two parametric lines*
Coeff *is a* 2 × 2 *matrix containing the parameter coefficients*
Parameter *is a* 2 × 1 *matrix containing the parameters*
Right *is a* 2 × 1 *matrix for the right-hand sides of the equations*
Invert *is the matrix inversion function*
Parameter(1, 1) *is the polygon edge intersection value*
Multiply *is the matrix multiply function*

>   *fill the coefficient matrix*

>   Coeff(1, 1) = P2x − P1x
>   Coeff(1, 2) = W1x − W2x

$\text{Coeff}(2,1) = \text{P2y} - \text{P1y}$
$\text{Coeff}(2,2) = \text{W1y} - \text{W2y}$

fill the right-hand side matrix

$\text{Right}(1,1) = \text{W1x} - \text{P1x}$
$\text{Right}(2,1) = \text{W1y} - \text{P1y}$

invert the coefficient matrix
it is not necessary to check for a singular matrix because
  intersection is ensured

$\text{Coeff} = \text{Invert}(\text{Coeff})$

solve for the parameter matrix

$\text{Parameter} = (\text{Coeff})\ \text{Multiply}\ (\text{Right})$

calculate the intersection points

$\text{Pintersect} = \text{P1} + (\text{P2} - \text{P1}) * \text{Parameter}(1,1)$

return

subroutine module for polygon output

subroutine Output(Vertex; Nout,Q)

Vertex contains the output point

  increment the number of output vertices and add to Q

$\text{Nout} = \text{Nout} + 1$
$\text{Q(Nout)} = \text{Vertex}$

return

Example 3–30 further illustrates the Sutherland–Hodgman algorithm. It also illustrates a particular characteristic of the algorithm, i.e., degenerate boundaries. An example of a degenerate boundary is one that coincides with a window edge, connects two 'disjoint' pieces of the clipped polygon and is traversed twice, once in each direction, as shown in Fig. 3–16. The existence of these degenerate boundaries is not important in many applications, e.g., solid area scan conversion. However, some applications, e.g., some hidden surface algorithms, necessitate their elimination. This can be accomplished by sorting the vertices as suggested by Sutherland and Hodgman [Suth74b].

Example 3–30   Sutherland–Hodgman Polygon Clipping

Consider the polygon with vertices given in Table 3–16 and shown in Fig. 3–36 clipped to the square window with planes $x_{\text{left}} = -1$, $x_{\text{right}} = 1$, $y_{\text{bottom}} = -1$, $y_{\text{top}} = 1$. As a specific example, consider the edge from P_1 to P_2 clipped to the left-hand window plane. Considering the window planes in clockwise order, the inside or visible side is to the right. With the use of the substitution method (see Ex. 3–28), the test function $x - w$ is

$$x - w = x - (-1) = x + 1$$

Table 3–16

	Original polygon	Clipped against left edge	Clipped against top edge	Clipped against right edge	Final polygon
P_1	$(1/2, -3/2)$	$(1/2, -3/2)$	$(1/2, -3/2)$	$(1/2, -3/2)$	$(-1, -1)$
P_2	$(-2, -3/2)$	$(-1, -3/2)$	$(-1, -3/2)$	$(-1, -3/2)$	$(-1, 1)$
P_3	$(-2, 2)$	$(-1, 2)$	$(-1, 1)$	$(-1, 1)$	$(1, 1)$
P_4	$(3/2, 2)$	$(3/2, 2)$	$(3/2, 1)$	$(1, 1)$	$(1, 0)$
P_5	$(3/2, 0)$	$(3/2, 0)$	$(3/2, 0)$	$(1, 0)$	$(1/2, 0)$
P_6	$(1/2, 0)$	$(1/2, 0)$	$(1/2, 0)$	$(1/2, 0)$	$(1/2, 1)$
P_7	$(1/2, 3/2)$	$(1/2, 3/2)$	$(1/2, 1)$	$(1/2, 1)$	$(-1, 1)$
P_8	$(-3/2, 3/2)$	$(-1, 3/2)$	$(-1, 1)$	$(-1, 1)$	$(-1, 0)$
P_9	$(-3/2, 1/2)$	$(-1, 0)$	$(-1, 0)$	$(-1, 0)$	$(0, -1)$

For $P_1(1/2, -3/2)$

$$x_1 + 1 = \frac{1}{2} + 1 > 0$$

Thus, P_1 is to the right of the clipping plane and visible.

For $P_2(-2, -3/2)$

$$x_2 + 1 = -2 + 1 < 0$$

Thus, P_2 is invisible. The edge $P_1 P_2$ crosses the clipping plane. Hence, the intersection must be calculated. Using the parametric line solution (see Ex. 3–29) yields $x = -1$, $y = -3/2$.

The results are shown in Fig. 3–36. Of particular interest is the last clipping stage, i.e., against the bottom window plane. Up to this stage, P_1 has survived. Hence, the intermediate polygon vertex lists remained in the same order as the original vertex list. However, P_1 is eliminated by the clip against the bottom window plane. The vertex list now starts at the intermediate vertex corresponding to P_2. The last vertex in the final clipped polygon list represents the intersection of the polygon edge, $P_9 P_1$, with the bottom window plane.

Note the four degenerate edges, or boundaries, in the upper left corner of the clipping window, as shown in Fig. 3–36 for the final polygon.

The Sutherland–Hodgman algorithm as presented here concentrates on clipping to a two-dimensional window. In fact, the algorithm is more general. Any planar or nonplanar polygon can be clipped to a convex clipping volume, by calculating the intersection with a three-dimensional clipping plane using the

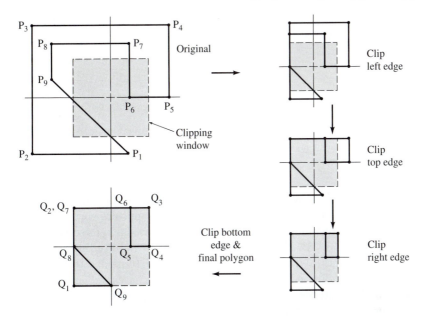

Figure 3–36   Results for Ex. 3–28.

Cyrus–Beck algorithm. The Sutherland–Hodgman clipping algorithm can also be used to split concave polygons (see Sec. 3–10 and [Suth74b]).

3–20   Liang–Barsky Polygon Clipping

Liang and Barsky [Lian83] developed a new algorithm for polygon clipping. As presented, the algorithm is optimized for rectangular clipping windows but is extensible to arbitrary convex windows. The algorithm is based on concepts from their two- and three-dimensional line clipping algorithm [Lian84]. Tests indicate that for rectangular windows the optimized algorithm is twice as fast as the Sutherland–Hodgman algorithm.

The Liang–Barsky algorithm assumes that the clipping region and polygon are coplanar. Each edge of the clipping region or window divides the plane into two half planes. The side of the half plane containing the window is called the inside or visible half plane. The other half plane is the outside or invisible half plane. The four window edges divide the clipping plane into nine regions, as shown in Fig. 3–37. Each of the regions is on the visible side of the number of half planes indicated in Fig. 3-37. Notice that only the window is on the inside of all four window edges.

Entering and Leaving Vertices

Provided that a polygon edge, represented by P_iP_{i+1}, is not horizontal or vertical, then the infinite line, L_i, containing the polygon edge intersects each of the four

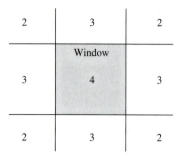

2	3	2
3	Window 4	3
2	3	2

Figure 3–37   Nine regions of the clipping plane.

window edges. In fact, as shown in Fig. 3-38, such an infinite line always starts in a corner region, labeled 2, and ends in the diagonally opposite corner region, whether it intersects the window or not. The four window edge intersections are marked with ×s in Fig. 3–38. The first intersection of the infinite line, L_i, with a window edge represents a transition from an invisible (outside) to a visible (inside) side of the window edge. Such an intersection is called an *entering* intersection. The last intersection of the infinite line, L_i, with a window edge represents a transition from a visible to an invisible side of the window edge and is classed as a *leaving* intersection. The two intermediate intersections can occur in either entering–leaving order, as illustrated by the lines labeled A and C, or in leaving–entering order, as illustrated by the line labeled B in Fig. 3–38.

If the intermediate intersections occur in entering–leaving order, then the infinite line, L_i, intersects the window and the polygon edge, P_iP_{i+1}, may be visible in the window. Whether any part or all of the polygon edge, P_iP_{i+1},

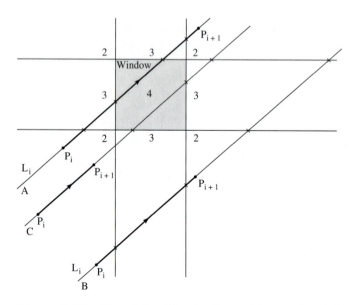

Figure 3–38   The relationship of a diagonal line to the window.

is visible depends on the location of P_iP_{i+1} along L_i, as shown by the polygon edges on lines A and C in Fig. 3–38.

If the intermediate intersections occur in leaving–entering order (line B), then no part of the infinite line, L_i, is visible in the window; hence no part of the polygon edge, P_iP_{i+1}, contained in L_i is visible in the window. This is equivalent to determining the visibility of a nontrivially invisible line in the Cyrus–Beck algorithm (see Sec. 3–5 and Ex. 3–12). In particular, line B in Fig. 3–38 intersects the right window edge before it intersects the bottom edge and thus cannot be visible.

Turning Vertices

Whether a visible, partially visible or invisible polygon edge, P_iP_{i+1}, affects the output polygon also depends on subsequent polygon edges. If a subsequent polygon edge reenters the window through a different window edge, then it is necessary to include one or more of the window corners in the output polygon. This, of course, is the fundamental difference between line and polygon clipping. Liang and Barsky call such a window corner a *turning vertex*. Figure 3–39 shows two examples of turning vertices.

A necessary, but not sufficient, condition that a turning vertex exist is if an entering intersection occurs on $P_{i+1}P_{i+2}$ and outside the window (see lines B and C in Fig. 3–39). When this condition occurs, the Liang–Barsky polygon clipping algorithm adds the turning vertex closest to the entering vertex to the output

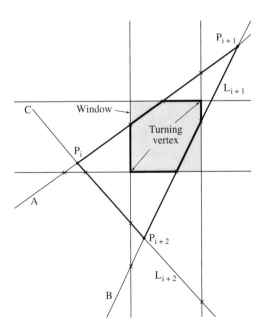

Figure 3–39   Turning vertices.

polygon. This is a necessary but not sufficient condition, because the entire polygon could lie outside the window. Thus, extraneous turning vertices can be added to the output polygon. This is a major weakness of the Liang–Barsky algorithm. For example, the output or clipped polygon for the polygon shown in Fig. 3–40 is the window itself, although the polygon does not intersect the window. In contrast, the Sutherland–Hodgman algorithm (see Sec. 3–19) yields only the degenerate polygon represented by the bottom edge of the window, and the Weiler–Atherton algorithm (see Sec. 3–21) yields the correct result.

However, noting that unless the first entering intersection is a window corner and hence coincident with the second entering intersection, and thus that the first entering intersection cannot be in the window, yields a sufficient condition for including a turning vertex in the output polygon. Specifically, the sufficient condition requires that the polygon edge, $P_i P_{i+1}$, contain the first entering intersection. This condition is not used in the algorithm.

Calculation of the actual intersections of the line L_i and the window edges, as well as the ordering of the intersections, is most conveniently developed using the parametric equation of the polygon edge

$$P(t) = P_i + (P_{i+1} - P_i)t$$

where $0 < t \leq 1$ represents the polygon edge except for the initial point, P_i, and $-\infty < t < \infty$ represents the infinite line containing the polygon edge. Excluding the initial polygon edge vertex prevents considering the vertex twice as each successive polygon edge is considered.

Development of the Algorithm

Because the Liang–Barsky algorithm assumes a regular clipping region, the algorithm is most efficiently developed using the components of the parametric line, i.e.

$$x = x_i + (x_{i+1} - x_i)t = x_i + \Delta x\, t$$
$$y = y_i + (y_{i+1} - y_i)t = y_i + \Delta y\, t$$

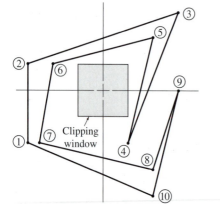

Figure 3–40 A nonintersecting polygon surrounding the window.

For a regular clipping region, the edges are given by

$$x_{\text{left}} \leq x \leq x_{\text{right}}$$

$$y_{\text{bottom}} \leq y \leq y_{\text{top}}$$

Using subscripts e and ℓ to denote entering and leaving intersections, the parametric values for the four intersections with the window edges are

$$t_{x_e} = (x_e - x_i)/\Delta x_i \qquad \Delta x_i \neq 0$$
$$t_{x_\ell} = (x_\ell - x_i)/\Delta x_i \qquad \Delta x_i \neq 0$$
$$t_{y_e} = (y_e - y_i)/\Delta y_i \qquad \Delta y_i \neq 0$$
$$t_{y_\ell} = (y_\ell - y_i)/\Delta y_i \qquad \Delta y_i \neq 0$$

where

$$x_e = \begin{cases} x_{\text{left}} & \Delta x_i > 0 \\ x_{\text{right}} & \Delta x_i \leq 0 \end{cases}$$

$$x_\ell = \begin{cases} x_{\text{right}} & \Delta x_i > 0 \\ x_{\text{left}} & \Delta x_i \leq 0 \end{cases}$$

$$y_e = \begin{cases} y_{\text{bottom}} & \Delta y_i > 0 \\ y_{\text{top}} & \Delta y_i \leq 0 \end{cases}$$

$$y_\ell = \begin{cases} y_{\text{top}} & \Delta y_i > 0 \\ y_{\text{bottom}} & \Delta y_i \leq 0 \end{cases}$$

The first and second entering and leaving intersections are then

$$t_{e_1} = \min(t_{x_e}, t_{y_e})$$
$$t_{e_2} = \max(t_{x_e}, t_{y_e})$$
$$t_{\ell_1} = \min(t_{x_\ell}, t_{y_\ell})$$
$$t_{\ell_2} = \max(t_{x_\ell}, t_{y_\ell})$$

For the polygon edge, $P_i P_{i+1}$, three conditions result in no contribution to the output polygon:

1. The edge terminates *before* the first entering intersection ($1 < t_{e_1}$), e.g., line A in Fig. 3–41.

2. The edge begins *after* the first entering intersection ($0 \geq t_{e_1}$) and ends *before* the second entering intersection ($1 < t_{e_2}$), e.g., line B in Fig. 3–41.

3. The edge begins *after* the second entering intersection ($0 \geq t_{e_2}$) and *after* the first leaving intersection ($0 \geq t_{\ell_1}$), e.g., line C in Fig. 3–41.

Three conditions also yield a contribution to the output polygon. The first of these considers partially or wholly visible polygon edges:

4. The edge is either partially or wholly contained within the window, hence partially or wholly visible, if the second entering intersection occurs *before*

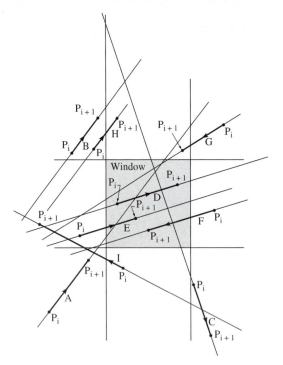

Figure 3–41   Polygon edge conditions.

the first leaving intersection $(t_{e_2} \leq t_{\ell_1})$, and P_i lies on L_i *before* the first leaving intersection $(0 < t_{\ell_1})$, and P_{i+1} lies on L_i *after* the second entering intersection $(1 \geq t_{e_2})$, e.g., lines D, E and F in Fig. 3–41.

If the edge is partially visible, the intersection point is obtained and output by substituting the appropriate parametric value t into the parametric equation for the appropriate coordinate. The other coordinate is given by the value of the window edge.

The next two conditions consider the addition of a turning vertex to the output. These conditions occur when an entering intersection is on the edge, P_iP_{i+1}, and outside the window:

5. If the first entering intersection lies on P_iP_{i+1} $(0 < t_{e_1} \leq 1)$, then the turning vertex is (x_e, y_e), e.g., line G in Fig. 3–41.

6. If the second entering intersection lies on P_iP_{i+1} $(0 < t_{e_2} \leq 1)$ and is outside the window $(t_{\ell_1} < t_{e_2})$, then the turning vertex is either (x_e, y_e) when the second entering intersection lies on a vertical edge of the window $(t_{x_e} > t_{y_e})$, e.g., line H in Fig. 3–41, or (x_ℓ, y_e) when the second entering intersection lies on a horizontal edge of the window $(t_{y_e} > t_{x_e})$, e.g., line I in Fig. 3–41.

These six conditions are summarized in Table 3–17.

Table 3–17 Output Conditions for Polygon Edges

	Condition	Contribution
1	$1 < t_{e_1}$	reject
2	$0 \geq t_{e_1}$ and $1 < t_{e_2}$	reject
3	$0 \geq t_{e_2}$ and $0 \geq t_{\ell_1}$	reject
4	$t_{e_2} \leq t_{\ell_1}$ and $0 \leq t_{\ell_1}$ and $1 \geq t_{e_2}$	visible segment
5	$0 \leq t_{e_1} \leq 1$	turning vertex (x_e, y_e)
6	$0 < t_{e_2} \leq 1$ and $t_{\ell_1} < t_{e_2}$	turning vertex (x_e, y_e) for $t_{x_e} > t_{y_e}$ (x_ℓ, y_e) for $t_{y_e} > t_{x_e}$

With the exception of condition 5, each of the conditions in Table 3–17 is independent of the others. However, after the turning vertex is generated by condition 5, if the polygon edge penetrates the window, a visible segment may be generated by condition 4; or if the polygon edge is completely outside the window, another turning vertex may be generated by condition 6. Obviously, both of these conditions cannot occur simultaneously. Consequently, the algorithm must be carefully constructed to account for these possibilities, i.e., evaluation of condition 5 must occur prior to evaluation of conditions 4 and 6.

Horizontal and Vertical Edges

Up to this point, horizontal and vertical polygon edges have been ignored. These polygon edges are easily detected by looking for Δy or $\Delta x = 0$, respectively. There are two techniques for considering horizontal and vertical polygon edges. The first handles them as special cases. For example, a horizontal polygon edge can only intersect the two vertical window edges, and a vertical polygon edge can only intersect the two horizontal window edges (see Prob. 3–14). Alternatively, horizontal and vertical polygon edges may be completely outside the window but still add a turning vertex to the output. The second technique forces horizontal and vertical polygon edges to conform to the general algorithm. We adopt this technique.

Consider a nearly horizontal line intersecting the window, e.g., line E or F in Fig. 3–41. For such a line

$$t_{y_e} \leq t_{x_e} \leq t_{x_\ell} \leq t_{y_\ell}$$

As the line approaches the horizontal, $\Delta y \to 0$ and $t_{ye} \to -\infty$ and $t_{y\ell} \to +\infty$. Thus, the horizontal line is characterized by

$$-\infty \leq t_{x_e} \leq t_{x_\ell} \leq +\infty$$

Similarly, considering a nearly vertical line intersecting the window, e.g., line C in Fig. 3–41

$$t_{x_e} \leq t_{y_e} \leq t_{y_\ell} \leq t_{x_\ell}$$

As the line approaches the vertical, $\Delta x \to 0$ and $t_{x_e} \to -\infty$ and $t_{x_\ell} \to +\infty$, and the line is characterized by

$$-\infty \leq t_{y_e} \leq t_{y_\ell} \leq +\infty$$

For a nearly vertical or horizontal line entirely outside the window, e.g., line B in Fig. 3–41 either

$$t_{y_e} \leq t_{y_\ell} \leq t_{x_e} \leq t_{x_\ell} \quad \text{or} \quad t_{x_e} \leq t_{x_\ell} \leq t_{y_e} \leq t_{y_\ell}$$

depending on the direction of the line.

If the line is horizontal, t_{y_e} and t_{y_ℓ} are infinite and the inequalities become

$$-\infty \leq -\infty \leq t_{x_e} \leq t_{x_\ell} \quad \text{or} \quad t_{x_e} \leq t_{x_\ell} \leq +\infty \leq +\infty$$

depending on the line direction.

If the line is vertical, t_{x_e} and t_{x_ℓ} are infinite and the inequalities become

$$t_{y_e} \leq t_{y_\ell} \leq +\infty \leq +\infty \quad \text{or} \quad -\infty \leq -\infty \leq t_{y_e} \leq t_{y_\ell}$$

depending on the line direction. Algorithmically, using the $-\infty$ is somewhat more efficient.

The Algorithm

An outline clarifies the structure of the algorithm.

> *Outline of Liang–Barsky polygon clipping algorithm*
> *for regular rectangular windows*
>
> **for** *each polygon edge* P(i)P(i+1)
> > *determine the direction of the edge*
> > *and whether it is diagonal, vertical or horizontal*
> > *determine the order of the edge–window intersections*
> > *determine the t-values of the entering edge–window intersections*
> > *and the t-value for the first leaving intersection*
> > *analyze the edge*
> > **if** $1 \geq$ t_enter_1 **then**   *condition 2 or 3 or 4 or 6 and not 1*
> > > **if** $0 <$ t_enter_1 **then**   *condition 5 — turning vertex*
> > > > **call** output(turning vertex)
> > >
> > > **end if**
> > > **if** $1 \geq$ t_enter_2 **then**   *condition 3 or 4 or 6 and not 1 or 2*
> > > > *determine second leaving t-value*
> > > > *there is output*
> > > > > **if** $(0 <$ t_enter_2$)$ **or** $(0 <$ t_leave_1$)$ **then** *cond. 4 or 6, not 3*
> > > > > > **if** t_enter_2 $\leq$ t_leave_1 **then**   *cond. 4 — visible segment*

call output(appropriate edge intersection)
  else *end condition 4 and begin condition 6 — turning vertex*
  call output(appropriate turning vertex)
 end if *end condition 6*
 end if *end condition 4 or 6*
 end if *end condition 3 or 4 or 6*
end if *end condition 2 or 3 or 4 or 6*
next i *end edge P(i)P(i+1)*

A pseudocode implementation of the complete algorithm is:

Liang–Barsky polygon clipping algorithm
 for regular rectangular windows

subroutine lbpoly(Nin,x,y,W;Nout,Q)

x *is the* x *component of the input polygon array*
y *is the* y *component of the input polygon array*
Q *is the output polygon array*
W *is the clipping window array.*
 W(1) = xleft
 W(2) = xright
 W(3) = ybottom
 W(4) = ytop
Nin *is the number of input polygon vertices*
Nout *is the number of output polygon vertices*
all polygon vertices are given in counterclockwise order
assume that infinity is represented by some real number

set up window edges

xleft = W(1)
xright = W(2)
ybottom = W(3)
ytop = W(4)

close the polygon

x(Nin + 1) = x(1)
y(Nin + 1) = y(1)

begin the main loop

for i = 1 **to** Nin
 deltax = x(i + 1) − x(i)
 deltay = y(i + 1) − y(i)

 determine the direction of the edge
  and whether it is diagonal, vertical or horizontal
 determine the order of the edge–window intersections

 if deltax > 0 **then** *not a vertical line*
  x_enter = xleft *diagonal line running left to right*

```
        x_leave = xright
    else if deltax < 0 then        diagonal line running right to left
        x_enter = xright
        x_leave = xleft
    else     vertical line (insure correct x_enter,x_leave,y_enter,y_leave)
        if y(i + 1) > y(i) then
            y_enter = ybottom
            y_leave = ytop
        else
            y_enter = ytop
            y_leave = ybottom
        endif
    endif
    if deltay > 0 then        not a horizontal line
        y_enter = ybottom        diagonal line running bottom to top
        y_leave = ytop
    else if deltay < 0 then        diagonal line running top to bottom
        y_enter = ytop
        y_leave = ybottom
    else     horizontal line (insure correct x_enter,x_leave,y_enter,y_leave)
        if x(i + 1) > x(i) then
            x_enter = xleft
            x_leave = xright
        else
            x_enter = xright
            x_leave = xleft
        end if
    end if
```

determine the t-values of the entering edge–window intersections and the t-value for the first leaving intersection

```
    if deltax <> 0 then
        t_enter_x = (x_enter − x(i))/deltax        diagonal line
    else
        t_enter_x = −∞        vertical line
    end if
    if deltay <> 0 then
        t_enter_y = (y_enter − y(i))/deltay        diagonal line
    else
        t_enter_y = −∞        horizontal line
    end if
    if t_enter_x < t_enter_y then        first entry at x then y
        t_enter_1 = t_enter_x
        t_enter_2 = t_enter_y
    else     first entry at y then x
        t_enter_1 = t_enter_y
```

```
    t_enter_2 = t_enter_x
end if
```

analyze the edge

if 1 >= t_enter_1 **then**   *condition 2 or 3 or 4 or 6 and* not *1*
    if 0 < t_enter_1 **then**   *condition 5 — turning vertex*
      call output(xin,yin,Nout,Q)
    end if
    if 1 >= t_enter_2 **then**   *condition 3 or 4 or 6 and* not *1 or 2*
      determine second leaving t-value
      if deltax <> 0 **then**   *diagonal line*
        t_leave_x = (x_leave − x(i))/deltax
      else   *vertical line*
        if (xleft <= x(i)) **and** (x(i) <= xright) **then**   P(i) *inside*
          t_leave_x = ∞
        else   P(i) *outside*
          t_leave_x = −∞
        end if
      end if
      if deltay <> 0 **then**   *diagonal line*
        t_leave_y = (y_leave − y(i))/deltay
      else   *horizontal line*
        if (ybottom <= y(i)) **and** (y(i) <= ytop) **then**
          t_leave_y = ∞   P(i) *inside*
        else
          t_leave_y = −∞   P(i) *outside*
        end if
      end if
      if t_leave_x < t_leave_y **then**   *first exit at* x
        t_leave_1 = t_leave_x
      else   *first exit at* y
        t_leave_1 = t_leave_y
      end if
      there is output
      if (0 < t_enter_2) **or** (0 < t_leave_1) **then**   *cond. 4 or 6, not 3*
        if t_enter_2 <= t_leave_1 **then**   *cond. 4 — visible segment*
          if 0 < t_enter_2 **then**   P(i) *outside window*
            if t_enter_x > t_enter_y **then**   *vertical boundary*
              call output(xin,y(i) + tinx*deltay; Nout,Q)
            else   *horizontal boundary*
              call output(x(i) + tiny*deltax,yin; Nout,Q)
            end if
          end if
          if 1 > t_leave_1 **then**   P(i+1) *outside window*

        if t_leave_x < t_leave_y then   *vertical boundary*
          call output(xout,y(i)+toutx∗deltay; Nout,Q)
        else   *horizontal boundary*
          call output(x(i) + touty∗deltax,yout; Nout,Q)
        end if
      else   P(i+1) *inside window*
        call output(x(i+1),y(i+1); Nout,Q)
      end if   *end condition 4*
    else   *condition 6 — turning vertex*
      if t_enter_x > t_enter_y then   *second entry at* x
        call output(xin,yout; Nout,Q)
      else   *second entry at* y
        call output(xout,yin; Nout,Q)
      end if
    end if   *end condition 6*
   end if   *end condition 4 or 6*
  end if   *end condition 3 or 4 or 6*
 end if   *end condition 2 or 3 or 4 or 6*
next i   *end edge* P(i)P(i+1)
return

3–21   Concave Clipping Regions— Weiler–Atherton Algorithm

The clipping algorithms previously discussed require a convex clipping region. In the context of many applications, e.g., hidden surface removal, the ability to clip to concave regions is required. A powerful but somewhat more complex clipping algorithm developed by Weiler and Atherton [Weil77] meets this requirement. The Weiler–Atherton algorithm is capable of clipping a concave polygon with interior holes to the boundaries of another concave polygon, also with interior holes. The polygon to be clipped is the *subject polygon*. The clipping region is the *clip polygon*. The new boundaries created by clipping the subject polygon against the clip polygon are identical to portions of the clip polygon. No new edges are created, hence the number of resulting polygons is minimized.

    The algorithm describes both the subject and the clip polygon by a circular list of vertices. The exterior boundaries of the polygons are described clockwise, and the interior boundaries or holes counterclockwise. When traversing the vertex list, this convention ensures that the inside of the polygon is always to the right. The boundaries of the subject polygon and the clip polygon may or may not intersect. If they intersect, then the intersections occur in pairs. One of the intersections occurs when a subject polygon edge enters the inside of the clip polygon and one when it leaves. Fundamentally, the algorithm starts at an entering intersection and follows the exterior boundary of the subject polygon clockwise until an intersection with the clip polygon is found. At the intersection a right turn is made, and the exterior boundary of the clip polygon is followed clockwise until an intersection with the subject polygon is found. Again, at the intersection, a right turn is made, with the subject polygon now being followed. The process is continued until the starting point is reached. Interior boundaries of the subject polygon are followed counterclockwise; see Fig. 3–42.

A more formal statement of the algorithm is:

Determine the intersections of the subject and clip polygons.

Add each intersection to the subject and clip polygon vertex lists. Tag each intersection vertex, and establish a bidirectional link between the subject and clip polygon lists for each intersection vertex.

Process nonintersecting polygon borders.

Establish two holding lists, one for boundaries which lie inside the clip polygon and one for boundaries which lie outside. Ignore clip polygon boundaries which are outside the subject polygon. Clip polygon boundaries inside the subject polygon form holes in the subject polygon. Consequently, a copy of the clip polygon boundary goes on both

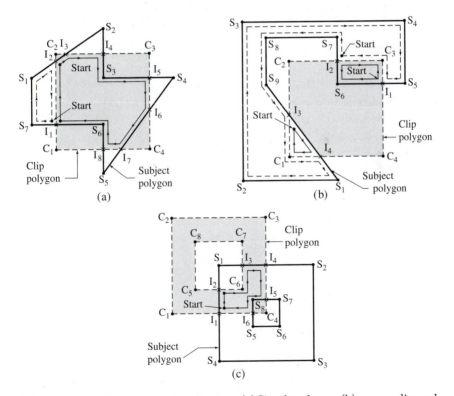

Figure 3–42   Weiler–Atherton clipping. (a) Simple polygon; (b) surrounding polygon; (c) polygon and window with holes.

the inside and the outside holding list. Place the boundaries on the appropriate holding list.

Create two intersection vertex lists.

One, the entering list, contains only the intersections for the subject polygon edge entering the inside of the clip polygon. The other, the leaving list, contains only the intersections for the subject polygon edge leaving the inside of the clip polygon. The intersection type alternates along the boundary. Thus, only one determination is required for each pair of intersections.

Perform the actual clipping.

Polygons inside the clipping polygon are found using the following procedure:

Remove an intersection vertex from the entering list. If the list is empty, the process is complete.

Follow the subject polygon vertex list until an intersection is found. Copy the subject polygon list up to this point to the inside holding list.

Using the link, jump to the clip polygon vertex list.

Follow the clip polygon vertex list until an intersection is found. Copy the clip polygon vertex list up to this point to the inside holding list.

Jump back to the subject polygon vertex list.

Repeat until the starting point is again reached. At this point the new inside polygon is closed.

Polygons outside the clipping polygon are found using the same procedure, except that the initial intersection vertex is obtained from the leaving list, and the clip polygon vertex list is followed in the *reverse* direction. The polygon lists are copied to the outside holding list.

Attach any holes, i.e., interior boundaries, to their associated exterior boundaries. Since exterior boundaries are specified clockwise and interior boundaries counterclockwise, this is most conveniently accomplished by testing the directionality of the boundaries. The process is complete.

Several examples serve to more fully illustrate the algorithm.

Example 3–31 Weiler–Atherton Polygon Clipping — Simple Polygon

Consider the subject polygon shown in Fig. 3–42a, clipped to the square clipping polygon shown in Fig. 3–42a. The intersection points between the two polygons are also shown and labeled I_i. The subject polygon and the clip polygon vertex lists are shown here. The intersection vertices, I_2, I_4, I_6 and I_8, are placed on the entering list and the vertices I_1, I_3, I_5, I_7 on the leaving list.

	Subject polygon list	Clip polygon list	Subject polygon list	Clip polygon list
	S_1	C_1	S_1	C_1
Start	I_2	I_1	I_2	I_1 Finish
	I_3	I_2 Finish	I_3	I_2
	S_2	C_2	S_2	C_2
	I_4	I_3	I_4	I_3
	S_3	I_4	S_3	I_4
	I_5	C_3	I_5	C_3
	S_4	I_5	S_4	I_5
	I_6	I_6	I_6	I_6
	I_7	C_4	I_7	C_4
	S_5	I_7	S_5	I_7
	I_8	I_8	I_8	I_8
	S_6	C_1	S_6	C_1
	I_1		I_1 Start	
	S_7		S_7	
	S_1		S_1	
	Inside polygon		Outside polygon	

To form the inside polygon, the first intersection on the entering list, I_2, is removed. The procedure described earlier yields the results shown by the solid line with the arrows in Fig. 3–42a and in the subject and clip polygon lists. The resulting inside polygon is

$$I_2 I_3 I_4 S_3 I_5 I_6 I_7 I_8 S_6 I_1 I_2$$

The other intersection vertices on the entering list, i.e. I_4, I_6, and I_8, yield the same clipped polygon.

To form the outside polygons, the first intersection on the leaving list, I_1, is removed. The procedure described earlier yields the results shown by the dashed line with the arrows in Fig. 3–42a and in the subject and clip polygon lists. Notice that the clip polygon list is traversed in the reverse direction from I_2 to I_1. The resulting outside polygon is

$$I_1 S_7 S_1 I_2 I_1$$

Removing I_3, I_5 and I_7 from the leaving list yields the outside polygons

$$I_3 S_2 I_4 I_3 \quad \text{and} \quad I_5 S_4 I_6 I_5 \quad \text{and} \quad I_7 S_5 I_8 I_7$$

respectively.

A somewhat more complex subject polygon, which partially surrounds the clip polygon, is considered in Ex. 3–32.

Example 3–32   Weiler–Atherton Polygon Clipping — Surrounding Polygon

The subject and clip polygons and their intersections are shown in Fig. 3–42b. The intersection vertices, I_1 and I_3, are placed on the entering list and I_2 and I_4 on the leaving list. The subject and clip polygon lists are then

Subject polygon list	Clip polygon list	Subject polygon list	Clip polygon list
S_1	C_1	S_1	C_1
S_2 Finish	I_3	S_2	I_3
S_3	C_2	S_3	C_2
S_4	I_2	S_4 Finish	I_2
S_5	C_3	S_5	C_3
Start I_1 Finish	I_1	I_1	I_1
S_6	C_4	S_6	C_4
I_2	I_4	I_2 Start	I_4
S_7	C_1	S_7	C_1
S_8		S_8	
S_9		S_9	
Start I_3		I_3	
I_4		I_4	
S_1		S_1	
Inside polygon		Outside polygon	

To form the inside polygons, remove first I_1 and then I_3 from the entering list. The results are shown by the solid line with arrows in Fig. 3–42b and in the subject and clip polygon lists. The resulting clipped inside polygons are

$$I_1 S_6 I_2 C_3 I_1 \quad \text{and} \quad I_3 I_4 C_1 I_3$$

respectively.

Removing I_2 from the leaving polygon list yields

$$I_2 S_7 S_8 S_9 I_3 C_1 I_4 S_1 S_2 S_3 S_4 S_5 I_1 C_3 I_2$$

for the outside polygon; I_4 yields the same polygon. The results are indicated by the dashed line in Fig. 3–42b and in the polygon lists above. Again, notice that the clip polygon list is traversed in the reverse direction for the outside polygon.

The final example considers a concave polygon, with a hole, clipped to a concave window, also having a hole.

**Example 3–33 Weiler–Atherton Clipping—Boundaries
With Holes**

The subject and clip polygons and their intersections are shown in Fig. 3–42c.
The intersection vertices, I_1, I_3 and I_5, are placed on the entering list and I_2,
I_4 and I_6 on the leaving list. The subject and clip polygon lists are

Subject polygon list	Clip polygon list		Subject polygon list	Clip polygon list
S_1	C_1		S_1	C_1
I_3	C_2		I_3	C_2
I_4	C_3	Outer	I_4	C_3
S_2	I_4	border	S_2	I_4
S_3	I_5		S_3	I_5
S_4	C_4		S_4	C_4
Start I_1	I_6		I_1	I_6
I_2	I_1 Finish		I_2 Start	I_1
S_1	C_1		S_1	C_1
S_5	C_5		S_5	C_5
S_6	I_2		S_6	I_2 Finish
S_7	C_6	Hole	S_7	C_6
I_5	I_3	border	I_5	I_3
S_8	C_7		S_8	C_7
I_6	C_8		I_6	C_8
S_5	C_5		S_5	C_5
Inside polygon			Outside polygon	

Notice that the interior boundaries, i.e., the hole vertices, are listed in counterclockwise order. The interior and exterior boundary lists are individually
circular.

When I_1 is removed from the entering list, the algorithm yields

$$I_1 I_2 C_6 I_3 I_4 I_5 S_8 I_6 I_1$$

for the inside polygon, as shown by the solid lines with arrows in Fig. 3–42c,
and the subject and clip polygon lists. I_3 and I_5 from the entering list yield
the same polygon.

Removing I_2 from the leaving list yields the outside polygon

$$I_2 S_1 I_3 C_6 I_2$$

Note that the subject polygon list contains two separate boundaries, an inner boundary and an outer boundary, each of which is individually circular.

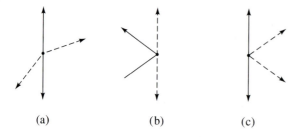

Figure 3–43   Single vertex polygon edge intersections — dashed line represents the clip polygon, solid line the subject polygon. (a) True intersection — one intersection; (b) grazing intersection — no intersection; (c) grazing intersection — no intersection, possible degenerate polygon.

Therefore, the transfer from S_1 at the bottom of the outer boundary list is to S_1 at the top of the outer boundary list rather than to S_5 on the hole boundary list. Transfer from an exterior to an interior boundary always occurs by a jump from the subject to the clip polygon list or vice versa, as shown by the dashed line in the subject and clip polygon lists. Similarly, I_4 and I_6 from the leaving list both yield the outside polygon

$$I_4 S_2 S_3 S_4 I_1 I_6 S_5 S_6 S_7 I_5 I_4$$

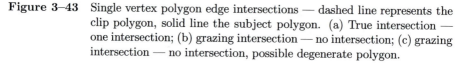

Special Cases

In order for the Weiler–Atherton algorithm to work correctly, care must be taken with the identification and placement of intersections. For example, grazing conditions, i.e., when a subject polygon vertex or edge lies on or is coincident with a clip polygon edge, are not considered intersections.

Polygon edge intersections can occur at a single polygon vertex, as shown in Fig. 3–43, or at two polygon vertices, as shown in Fig. 3–44. In these figures, clip polygon edges are shown dashed and subject polygon edges solid. The arrows indicate the direction of the polygon edge. Arrows in both directions indicate that the edge can be in either direction.

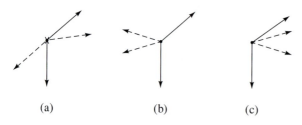

Figure 3–44   Double vertex polygon edge intersections — dashed line represents the clip polygon, solid line the subject polygon. (a) True intersection — one intersection; (b) grazing intersection — no intersection; (c) grazing intersection — no intersection, possible degenerate polygon.

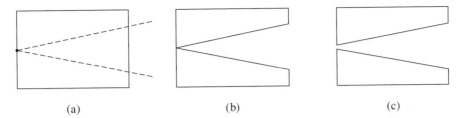

Figure 3–45   Degenerate edges. (a) Original polygons with grazing vertex; (b) degenerate polygon; (c) required nondegenerate polygons.

Figures 3–43a and 3–44a represent true intersections which are added to the subject and clip polygon lists. Figures 3–43b and 3–43c and their reflections about the clip edge are grazing intersections, which are not added to the subject and clip polygon lists. Figures 3–44b and 3–44c also represent grazing intersections which are not added to the subject and clip polygon lists.

Defining a degenerate polygon as one whose edges fold or touch back on themselves at one or more points, then Figs. 3–43c and 3–44c, but not their reflections, possibly yield degenerate edges, as illustrated in Fig. 3–45. The algorithm must identify and prevent the occurrence of these degenerate edges.

Polygon edges may abut or be coincident, as shown in Fig. 3–46:

> If the edges abut, as shown in Fig. 3–46a, no intersections are added to the subject and clip polygon lists.

> If the clip polygon starts on the inside of the subject polygon, becomes coincident with a subject polygon edge and leaves the subject polygon edge toward the inside, as shown in Fig. 3–46b, then two intersections, indicated by the ×s in Fig. 3–46b, are added to the subject and clip polygon lists.

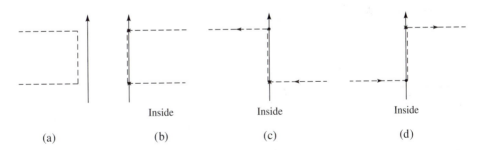

Figure 3–46   Coincident polygon edges — dashed line represents the clip polygon, solid line the subject polygon. (a) A butting edge — one intersection; (b) coincident edge, arrives and leaves from the inside of the subject polygon — two intersections, indicated by the ×s; (c) coincident edge, arrives from the inside and leaves to the outside of the subject polygon — one intersection, indicated by the ×; (d) coincident edge, arrives from the outside and leaves to the inside of the subject polygon — one intersection, indicated by the ×.

If the clip polygon starts inside the subject polygon, becomes coincident with a subject polygon edge and leaves toward the outside of the subject polygon, as shown in Fig. 3–46c, then only the first intersection, indicated by the ×s in Fig. 3–46c, is added to the subject and clip polygon lists.

If the clip polygon starts outside the subject polygon, becomes coincident with a subject polygon edge and leaves toward the inside of the subject polygon, as shown in Fig. 3–46d, then only the second intersection, indicated by the ×s in Fig. 3–46d, is added to the subject and clip polygon lists.

The relationship of one polygon edge to another is determined by carefully applying the tests given in Sec. 3–19 to determine the relation of a point to a plane (see Ex. 3–28). For example, the single vertex edge intersection shown in Fig. 3–43a is identified by determining that the vertices before and after the intersected vertex on the clip polygon lie on opposite sides of the subject polygon edge. Double vertex intersections require the use of techniques similar to that described for the Schumacker cluster priority tests given in Sec. 4–13.

The subject and clip polygons may not intersect; these are called loose polygons. If a loose clip polygon is outside the subject polygon, it can be ignored. Loose clip polygons inside the subject polygon form holes in the subject polygon. Loose subject or clip polygons are placed on either the entering or leaving lists. Specifically,

Loose subject polygon

if inside clip polygon, add to the inside holding list (see Fig. 3–47a);

if outside clip polygon, add to the outside holding list (see Fig. 3–47b).

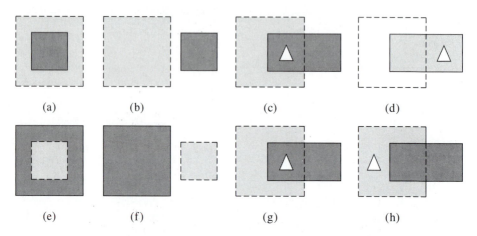

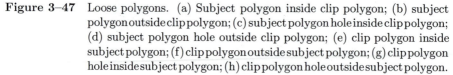

Figure 3–47   Loose polygons. (a) Subject polygon inside clip polygon; (b) subject polygon outside clip polygon; (c) subject polygon hole inside clip polygon; (d) subject polygon hole outside clip polygon; (e) clip polygon inside subject polygon; (f) clip polygon outside subject polygon; (g) clip polygon hole inside subject polygon; (h) clip polygon hole outside subject polygon.

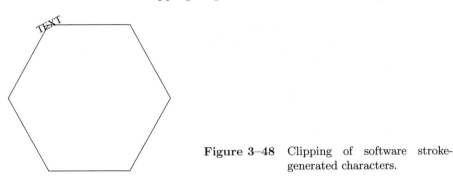

Figure 3–48   Clipping of software stroke-generated characters.

Loose hole subject polygon

    if inside clip polygon, add to the inside hole holding list (see Fig. 3–47c);

    if outside clip polygon, add to outside hole holding list (see Fig. 3–47d).

Loose clip polygon

    add to the inside holding list (see Fig. 3–47e);

    reverse the direction of the polygon, and also add it to the outside holding list (see Fig. 3–47f).

Loose hole clip polygon

    add to outside holding list (see Fig. 3–47g);

    reverse the direction of the polygon, and also add to the inside holding list (see Fig. 3–47h).

The existence of loose polygons is determined using the disjoint and contained polygon tests described in Sec. 4–4 for the Warnock hidden surface algorithm. Additional implementation details are given by Weiler [Weil78].

Weiler [Weil80] restructures the clipping algorithm using graph theoretic concepts, specifically to simplify the handling of grazing conditions and degenerate polygons. The presentation is conceptually somewhat more complex than that given here. Consequently, the original presentation was used here.

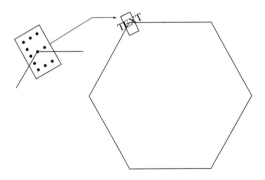

Figure 3–49   Clipping of software dot matrix or bit mapped characters.

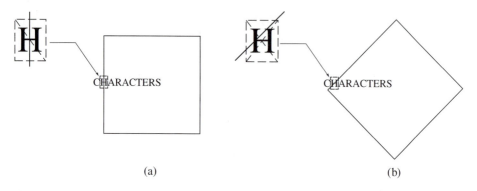

(a)   (b)

Figure 3–50   Clipping of hardware-generated characters.

3–22   Character Clipping

Characters or text are generated in software, firmware, or hardware. Characters can be formed from individual lines or strokes or from dot matrix (bit map) representations. Stroke characters generated in software are treated like any other line; i.e., they can be rotated, translated, scaled and clipped to arbitrary windows in arbitrary orientations using the algorithms discussed in preceding sections. Figure 3–48 shows a typical example.

Dot matrix character representations generated in software are treated in a similar fashion. The process is, however, somewhat more tedious. In particular, if the character box surrounding the character is clipped to an arbitrary window, then each pixel of the character mask is compared with the clip window to determine if it is inside or outside. If inside, it is activated; if outside, no action is taken. Figure 3–49 illustrates this.

Clipping of hardware-generated characters is more limited. Generally, any character which is not totally visible is eliminated. This is accomplished by clipping the character box against the window. If the entire box is inside the window, the character is displayed; otherwise, it is not. When the rectangular character box is aligned with a rectangular window, only one diagonal of the character box is compared with the window (see Fig. 3–50a). For odd-shaped windows, or when the rectangular character box is not aligned with the window, both diagonals are compared with the window, as shown in Fig. 3–50b.

When characters are generated in firmware, character clipping facilities may be very limited or very extensive. The extent depends on the clipping algorithm also implemented in firmware.

VISIBLE SURFACES

The visible surface problem is one of the more difficult in computer graphics. Visible surface algorithms attempt to determine the lines, edges, surfaces or volumes that are visible to an observer located at a specific point in space.

4–1   Introduction

In the early days of computer graphics visible surface algorithms were called hidden line or hidden surface algorithms. The need for eliminating hidden lines, edges, surfaces or volumes, or determining the visible surfaces, is illustrated in Fig. 4–1. Figure 4–1a shows a typical wire frame drawing of a cube. A wire frame drawing represents a three-dimensional object as a line drawing of its edges. Figure 4–1a can be interpreted as a view of the cube either from above and to the left or from below and to the right. The alternate views can be seen by blinking and refocusing the eyes. This ambiguity is eliminated by determining the lines or surfaces that are visible from the two alternate viewpoints and displaying only those lines or surfaces. The results are shown in Figs. 4–1b and 4–1c.

The complexity of the visible surface problem results in a large number of diverse solutions. Many of these are for specialized applications. There is no best solution to the visible surface problem. Fast algorithms that provide solutions at high frame rates are required for real-time simulations, e.g., for flight simulation. Algorithms that provide detailed realistic solutions, including shadows, transparency and texture effects, with reflections and refractions in a multitude of subtle shades of color, are also required, e.g., for computer animation. These algorithms are slower, often requiring several minutes or even hours of computation. There is a tradeoff between speed and detail. No single algorithm provides both. As faster algorithms and computers are developed, more rendering detail is incorporated. However, inevitably more detail is required.

Technically, transparency, texture, reflection, etc., are not part of the visible surface problem. They are more appropriately part of the rendering of the picture. Rendering is the process of interpreting or presenting a picture or scene realistically. These effects are discussed in detail in Chapter 5. However, many of these effects are incorporated into visible surface algorithms and consequently are touched on in the present discussion.

All visible surface algorithms involve sorting [Suth74a]. The order in which sorting of the geometric coordinates occurs is generally immaterial to the efficiency of the algorithms. The principal sort is based on the geometric distance of a volume, surface, edge or point from the viewpoint. The fundamental assumption made is that the farther an object is from the viewpoint, the more likely the object is to be totally or partially obscured by one closer to the viewpoint. After establishing the distance or depth priority, it remains to sort laterally and vertically to determine whether in fact an object is obscured by those closer to the viewpoint. The efficiency of a visible surface algorithm depends significantly on the efficiency of the sorting process. Coherence, i.e., the tendency for the characteristics of a scene to be locally constant, is used to increase the efficiency of the sort. For raster scan visible surface algorithms, the use of coherence to improve sorting results in a number of algorithms that bear a strong resemblance to the scan-conversion algorithms discussed previously in Chapter 2.

Visible surface algorithms are often classified based on the coordinate system or space in which they are implemented [Suth74a]. Object space algorithms are implemented in the physical coordinate system in which the objects are described. Very precise results, generally to the precision of the machine, are available. These results can be satisfactorily enlarged many times. Object space algorithms are particularly useful in precise engineering applications. Image space algorithms are implemented in the screen coordinate system in which the objects are viewed. Calculations are performed only to the precision of the screen representation. This is generally quite crude, typically 1280×1024 integer points. Scenes calculated in image space and significantly enlarged do not give acceptable results. For example, the end points of lines may not match. List priority algorithms are partially implemented in both coordinate systems.

Theoretically, the computational work for an object space algorithm that compares every object in a scene with every other object in the scene grows as

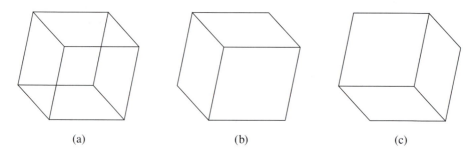

(a) (b) (c)

Figure 4-1 Need for hidden surfaces. (a) Wireframe; (b) viewed from left above; (c) viewed from right below.

the number of objects squared, i.e., as n^2. Similarly, the work for an image space algorithm which compares every object in the scene with every pixel location in screen coordinates theoretically grows as nN. Here, n is the number of objects (volumes, planes or edges) in the scene, and N is the number of pixels. Theoretically, object space algorithms require less work than image space algorithms for $n < N$. Since N is typically of order $1.3 - 2.0 \times 10^6$, most algorithms should theoretically be implemented in object space. In practice, this is not the case; image space algorithms are more efficient because it is easier to take advantage of coherence in a raster scan implementation of an image space algorithm.

The following sections examine several object, image space and list priority algorithms in detail. Each algorithm illustrates one or more fundamental ideas in the implementation of visible surface algorithms.

4–2   Floating Horizon Algorithm

The floating horizon algorithm is most frequently used for three-dimensional representations of surface functions of the form

$$F(x, y, z) = 0$$

Functions of this form arise from diverse applications in mathematics, engineering and science, as well as in other disciplines.

A number of algorithms using this technique have been developed (see, e.g., [Will72; Wrig73; Watk74; Gott78; Butl79]). Since the representation of the function is of principal interest, the algorithm is usually implemented in image space. The fundamental idea behind the technique is to convert the three-dimensional problem to two dimensions by intersecting the surface with a series of parallel cutting planes at constant values of x, y or z. This is shown in Fig. 4–2,

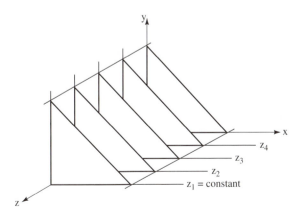

Figure 4–2   Constant-coordinate cutting planes.

where constant values of z define the parallel planes. The function $F(x, y, z) = 0$ is reduced to a planar curve in each of these parallel planes, i.e., to

$$y = f(x, z) \qquad \text{or} \qquad x = g(y, z)$$

where z is constant for each of the parallel planes.

Upper Horizon

The surface is built up of a series of curves in each of these planes, as shown in Fig. 4–3. Here, it is assumed that the resulting curves are single-valued functions of the independent variables. If the result is projected onto the $z = 0$ plane, as shown in Fig. 4–4, an algorithm for removing the hidden portions of the surface is immediately recognized. The algorithm first sorts the $z = $ constant planes by increasing distance from the viewpoint. Beginning with the $z = $ constant plane closest to the viewpoint, the curve in each plane is generated; i.e., for each x coordinate in image space, the appropriate y value is determined. The visible line algorithm is then

> If at any given value of x the y value of the curve in the current plane is larger than the y value for any previous curve at that x value, then the curve is visible; otherwise it is hidden.

This is shown by the dashed lines in Fig. 4–4. Implementation of the algorithm is quite simple. An array of size equal to the resolution of image space in the x direction is used to contain the largest value of y at each x location. The values in this array represent the current 'horizon'. Thus, the horizon 'floats up' as each succeeding curve is drawn. Effectively, this is a one-line visible line algorithm.

Lower Horizon

The algorithm works fine unless some of the succeeding curves dip below the first curve, as shown in Fig. 4–5a. These curves are normally visible as the bottom of

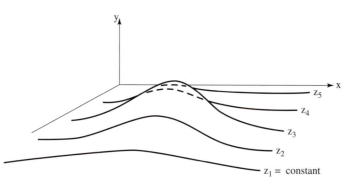

Figure 4–3 Curves in constant-coordinate cutting planes.

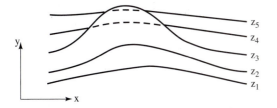

Figure 4–4   Projection of curves onto the $z = 0$ plane.

the surface; however, this algorithm treats them as invisible. The lower side of the surface is made visible by modifying the algorithm to accommodate a lower horizon that floats down as the algorithm progresses. This is implemented by using a second array, of size equal to the resolution of the image space in the x direction, containing the smallest value of y at each x location. The algorithm is now

> If at any given value of x the y value of the curve in the current plane is larger than the maximum y value or smaller than the minimum y value for any previous curve at that x value, then the curve is visible; otherwise it is hidden.

The result is shown in Fig. 4–5b.

Function Interpolation

These algorithms assume that the value of the function, i.e., y, is available at each x location in image space. If, however, y is not available (calculated) at each x location, then the upper and lower floating horizon arrays cannot be maintained. In this case, linear interpolation between the known locations is used to fill the upper and lower floating horizon arrays, as shown in Fig. 4–6. If the visibility of the line changes, this simple interpolation technique does not yield the correct result; the effect is shown in Fig. 4–7a. Assuming that the fill operation occurs after the visibility check, then when the current line goes from visible to invisible

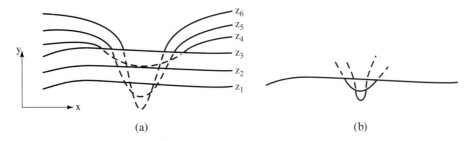

(a)   (b)

Figure 4–5   Handling the lower side of the surface. (a) Incorrect result; (b) correct result.

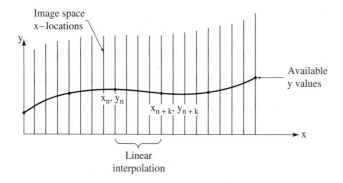

Figure 4–6   Linear interpolation between data points.

(segment AB in Fig. 4–7a), the point at x_{n+k}, y_{n+k} is declared invisible, the line from x_n, y_n to x_{n+k}, y_{n+k} is not drawn, and the fill operation is not performed. A gap is left between the current line and the previous line. When a segment of the current line goes from invisible to visible (segment CD in Fig. 4–7a), the point at x_{m+k}, y_{m+k} is declared visible, the line from x_m, y_m to x_{m+k}, y_{m+k} is drawn, and the fill operation is performed. Thus, an invisible portion of the segment is drawn. Further, the floating horizon arrays now contain incorrect values. This leads to additional adverse effects for subsequent lines. Hence, it is necessary to solve for the intersection of the segments of the current and previous lines.

There are several techniques for obtaining the intersection of the lines. On a raster scan display, x can be incremented by 1 beginning at x_n or x_m (see Fig. 4–7a). The y value at this image space x coordinate is obtained by adding the slope of the line to the y value at the previous x coordinate. The visibility of the new point at $x + 1$ and $y + \Delta y$ is determined. If the point is visible, its associated pixel is activated; if not, the pixel is not activated and x is incremented. The process is repeated until $x_n + k$ or $x_m + k$ is reached. This technique provides a sufficiently accurate intersection for raster scan displays. A similar, but somewhat more elegant, method is to perform a binary search for the intersection [Gott78].

An accurate intersection of the two interpolated straight lines between x_n, y_n and x_{n+k}, y_{n+k} (see Fig. 4–7) on the current and previous lines is given by

$$x = x_n - \frac{\Delta x(y_{n_p} - y_{n_c})}{(\Delta y_p - \Delta y_c)}$$

and

$$y = m(x - x_n) + y_n$$

where

$$\Delta x = x_{n+k} - x_n$$

$$\Delta y_p = (y_{n+k})_p - (y_n)_p$$

$$\Delta y_c = (y_{n+k})_c - (y_n)_c$$

$$m = \frac{[(y_{n+k}) - (y_n)]}{\Delta x}$$

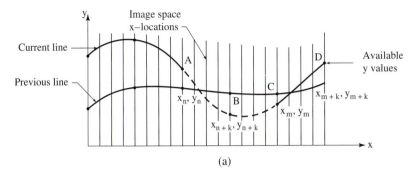

(a)

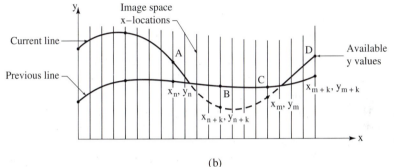

(b)

Figure 4-7 The effect of intersecting lines. (a) Incorrect result leaves gap; (b) solving for intersection and filling the horizon give correct result.

and the subscripts c and p refer to the current and previous lines, respectively. The result is shown in Fig. 4–7b. The algorithm is now

> If, at any given value of x, the y value of the curve in the current plane is larger than the maximum y value or smaller than the minimum y value for any previous curve at that x value, then the curve is visible; otherwise it is hidden.

> If the line from the previous x value (x_n) to the current x value (x_{n+k}) is becoming visible or invisible, calculate the intersection (x_i).

> Draw the line from x_n to x_{n+k} if the segment is totally visible, from x_n to x_i if the segment becomes invisible, or from x_i to x_{n+k} if the segment becomes visible.

> Fill the upper and lower floating horizons.

This algorithm exhibits an anomaly when the curve in one of the planes further from the viewpoint extends beyond the 'edge' of the curves in the planes closer to the viewpoint. The effect is shown in Fig. 4–8, where planes $n-1$ and n are closer to the viewpoint and have already been processed. The result shows the effect when the current plane, $n+1$, is processed. After processing the lines $n-1$ and n, the upper horizon contains the initial value for x locations 0 and 1, the value for the line n for x locations 2 to 17 and the value for the line $n - 1$ for x locations 18 to 20. The lower horizon contains the initial value for x locations 0 and 1, values for the line n at x locations 2 to 4, and values for the line $n - 1$ for x locations 5 to 20. In processing the current line $(n + 1)$, the algorithm declares it to be visible at $x = 4$. This is shown by the solid line in Fig. 4–8. A similar effect occurs at the right-hand edge at $x = 18$. The effect gives the appearance of a ragged edge. The solution to this ragged edge problem is to insert values into the upper and lower horizon arrays corresponding to the dashed lines in Fig. 4–8. Effectively, this creates a false edge. An algorithm for accomplishing this for both edges is:

Left-side fill:

If P_n is the first point on the first line, save P_n as P_{n-1} and continue; otherwise, create the edge from P_{n-1} to P_n.

Fill in the upper and lower horizons from this edge and save P_n as P_{n-1}.

Right-side fill:

If P_n is the last point on the first line, save P_n as P_{n-1} and continue; otherwise, create the edge from P_{n-1} to P_n.

Fill in the upper and lower horizons from this edge, and save P_n as P_{n-1}.

The complete algorithm is now

For each $z =$ constant plane.
Fill in the left edge.
For each point on the curve in a $z =$ constant plane:

If, at any given value of x, the y value of the curve in the current plane is larger than the maximum y value or smaller than the minimum y value for any previous curve at that x value, then the curve is visible; otherwise it is hidden.

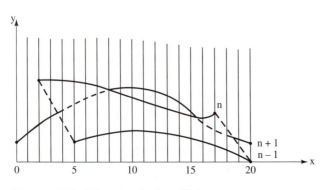

Figure 4–8 The ragged edge effect.

If the line from the previous x value (x_n) to the current x value (x_{n+k}) is becoming visible or invisible, calculate the intersection.

Draw the line from x_n to x_{n+k} if the segment is totally visible, from x_n to x_i if the segment becomes invisible or from x_i to x_{n+k} if the segment becomes visible.

Fill the upper and lower floating horizons.

Fill in the right edge.

Aliasing

If the function contains very narrow regions (spikes), then the algorithm yields incorrect results. Figure 4–9 illustrates the effect. Here, the lowest line $(z = 1)$ contains a spike. At $x = 8$, the next line $(z = 2)$ is declared visible. At $x = 12$, the line $(z = 2)$ is declared invisible, the intersection is determined and the line $(z = 2)$ is drawn visibly from $x = 8$ to the intersection. From $x = 12$ to $x = 16$, the line $(z = 2)$ again becomes visible, the intersection is determined and the line is drawn visibly from the intersection to $x = 16$. On the next line $(z = 3)$ at $x = 8$, the line is visible and is also declared visible at $x = 12$. Hence, the line is drawn visibly from $x = 8$ to $x = 12$, even though it passes behind the spike. This effect is caused by computing the function and evaluating the visibility at less than the image space resolution; i.e., the function is undersampled (see Sec. 2–16) and aliasing results. When narrow regions occur, the function must be computed at more points. In Fig. 4–9, if the function is computed at 0, 2, 4, $\cdots$, 18, 20 rather than at 0, 4, $\cdots$, 16, 20, the algorithm correctly draws the line $z = 3$. Figure 4–10 shows a typical floating horizon result.

The Algorithm

A pseudocode implementation of the algorithm, including cross-hatching, is:

floating horizon algorithm

subroutine fhalg(Xmin,Xmax,Zmin,Zmax,Xsamples,Zsamples)

Hscreen *is the resolution of the screen in the horizontal direction*
Vscreen *is the resolution of the screen in the vertical direction*
Upper *is the array containing the upper horizon values*
Lower *is the array containing the lower horizon values*
y *is the current value of the function* y = f(x, z) *for* z = *constant*
Cflag *is the visibility flag for the current point*
Pflag *is the visibility flag for the previous point*
    0 = *invisible*
    1 = *visible above upper horizon*
    −1 = *visible below lower horizon*
Draw *draws a visible line between the specified coordinates*
Xmin, Xmax *are the minimum and maximum* x *coordinates*

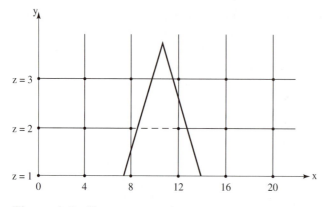

Figure 4–9   Very narrow regions.

Zmin, Zmax *are the minimum and maximum z coordinates*
Zinc *is the increment between* z = *constant planes*

    Dimension Upper(Hscreen), Lower(Hscreen)

    initialize variables

    Zinc = (Zmax − Zmin)/Zsamples

    initialize the horizon arrays

    Upper = 0
    Lower = Vscreen

    evaluate the function for each constant z plane
    start with the closest plane, Zmax

    for z = Zmax **to** Zmin **step** − Zinc

        initialize the previous x and y values, Xprev, Yprev

        Xprev = Xmin
        Yprev = f(Xprev, z)

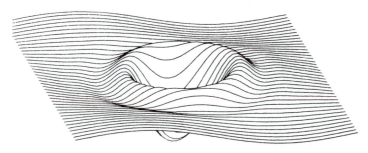

Figure 4–10   The function $y = \frac{1}{5}\sin x \cos z - \frac{3}{2}\cos(7a/4)\exp(-a), a = (x - \pi)^2 + (z - \pi)^2$, displayed for 0 to 2π using a floating horizon algorithm.

perform any viewing transformations

call Transform(Xprev,Yprev,z)

call Visibility(Xprev,Yprev,Upper,Lower; Pflag)

for each point on the curve in the constant z plane

for xr = Xmin **to** Xmax **step** (Xmax − Xmin)/Xsamples

    x = xr

    y = f (x, z)

    perform any viewing transformations

    call Transform(x,y,z)

    check the visibility of the current point
      and fill the horizon as appropriate

    call Visibility(x,y,Upper,Lower; Cflag)

    call Drawline(Xprev,Yprev,Pflag,x,y,Cflag; Upper,Lower)

next xr

if z − Zinc ≥ Zmin **then**

    for xr = Xmin **to** Xmax **step** (Xmax − Xmin)/(Zsamples)

      Xprev = xr

      Yprev = f (xr, z)

      call Transform(Xprev,Yprev,z)

      call Visibility(Xprev,Yprev,Upper,Lower; Pflag)

      for each point on the orthogonal curve,
        do the cross-hatching

      for hz = z **to** z − Zinc **step** (Zmin − Zmax)/Xsamples

        x = xr

        y = f (x, hz)

        call Transform(x,y,hz)

        call Visibility(x,y,Upper,Lower; Cflag)

        call Drawline(Xprev,Yprev,Pflag,x,y,Cflag;

                                 Upper,Lower)

      next hz

    next xr

  end if

next z

end sub

subroutine Drawline(Xprev,Yprev,Pflag,x,y,Cflag; Upper,Lower)

fills the horizons and draws the lines

  make sure the current point is inside the screen

if (0 ≤ x **and** x < Hscreen **and** 0 ≤ y **and** y < Vscreen) **and**

  (0 ≤ Xprev **and** Xprev < Hscreen **and**

  0 ≤ Yprev **and** Yprev < Vscreen) **then**

    if Cflag = Pflag **then**

               the visibility has not changed

```
            the visibility has not changed
            if Cflag = 1 or Cflag = −1 then
                call Draw(Xprev,Yprev,x,y)
                call Horizon(Xprev,Yprev,x,y; Upper,Lower)
            end if
    else
            visibility changed — calculate the intersection
            draw the appropriate piece and fill the horizons
            if Cflag = 0 then
                if Pflag = 1 then
                    call Intersect(Xprev,Yprev,x,y,Upper; Xi,Yi)
                else
                    call Intersect(Xprev,Yprev,x,y,Lower; Xi,Yi)
                end if
                call Draw(Xprev,Yprev,Xi,Yi)
                call Horizon(Xprev,Yprev,Xi,Yi; Upper,Lower)
            else
                if Cflag = 1 then
                    if Pflag = 0 then
                        call Intersect(Xprev,Yprev,x,y,Upper; Xi,Yi)
                        call Draw(Xi,Yi,x,y)
                        call Horizon(Xi,Yi,x,y; Upper,Lower)
                    else
                        call Intersect(Xprev,Yprev,x,y,Lower; Xi,Yi)
                        call Draw(Xprev,Yprev,Xi,Yi)
                        call Horizon(Xprev,Yprev,Xi,Yi; Upper,Lower)
                        call Intersect(Xprev,Yprev,x,y,Upper; Xi,Yi)
                        call Draw(Xi,Yi,x,y)
                        call Horizon(Xi,Yi,x,y; Upper,Lower)
                    end if
                else
                    if Pflag = 0 then
                        call Intersect(Xprev,Yprev,x,y,Lower; Xi,Yi)
                        call Draw(Xi,Yi,x,y)
                        call Horizon(Xi,Yi,x,y; Upper,Lower)
                    else
                        call Intersect(Xprev,Yprev,x,y,Upper; Xi,Yi)
                        call Draw(Xprev,Yprev,Xi,Yi)
                        call Horizon(Xprev,Yprev,Xi,Yi; Upper,Lower)
                        call Intersect(Xprev,Yprev,x,y,Lower; Xi,Yi)
                        call Draw(Xi,Yi,x,y)
                        call Horizon(Xi,Yi,x,y; Upper,Lower)
                    end if
```

```
                    end if
                end if
            end if
        end if
        Pflag = Cflag
        Xprev = x
        Yprev = y
end sub
```

subroutine Visibility (x,y,Upper,Lower; Cflag)

the visibility of the point is to be determined with respect to
the upper and lower floating horizons. If the point is on
the horizon, it is declared visible.

Cflag = 0 *invisible*
       = 1 *visible above the upper horizon*
       = −1 *visible below the lower horizon*

x *is assumed integer*

    check if the current point is within the screen

```
        if 0 ≤ x and x < Hscreen and 0 ≤ y and y < Vscreen then
            if y < Upper(x) and y > Lower(x) then Cflag = 0
            if y ≥ Upper(x) then Cflag = 1
            if y ≤ Lower(x) then Cflag = −1
        else
            Cflag = 0
        end if
end sub
```

subroutine Horizon(x1,y1,x2,y2; Upper,Lower)

the algorithm uses linear interpolation to fill the
horizon arrays between x1 and x2

Max(a,b) *yields the larger of a and b*
Min(a,b) *yields the smaller of a and b*
Sign *returns* −1, 0, 1 *if the sign of its argument is* < 0, = 0, > 0

    check for infinite slope

```
        if (x2 − x1) = 0 then
            Upper(x2) = Max(Upper(x2), y2)
            Lower(x2) = Min(Lower(x2), y2)
        else
            Slope = (y2 − y1)/(x2 − x1)
            for x = x1 to x2 step Sign(x2 − x1)
                y = Slope ∗ (x − x1) + y1
                Upper(x) = Max(Upper(x), y)
                Lower(x) = Min(Lower(x), y)
```

```
        next x
      end if
   end if
end sub
```

subroutine Intersect(x1,y1,x2,y2,Array; Xi,Yi)

the routine calculates the intersection between two straight lines

Array *contains the appropriate horizon*
Inc *is used to determine the direction of the line*

```
   Inc = −1
   if x1 < x2 then Inc = 1
```

check for infinite slope

```
   if (x2 − x1) = 0 then
      Xi = x2
      Yi = Array(x2)
   else
```

calculate the intersection by marching

```
      Slope = (y2 − y1)/(x2 − x1)
      Ysign = Sign(y1 + Slope * Inc − Array(x1 + Inc))
      Csign = Ysign
      Yi = y1 + Slope * Inc
      Xi = x1 + Inc
      while (Csign = Ysign) and (Xi * Inc < x2 * Inc)
         Yi = Yi + Slope * Inc
         Xi = Xi + Inc
         Csign = Sign(Yi − Array(Xi))
      end while
      if Abs(Yi−Slope−Array(Xi−Inc)) ≤ Abs(Yi−Array(Xi)) then
         Yi = Yi − Slope * Inc
         Xi = Xi − Inc
      end if
      if Abs(Slope) > 1 and Array(Xi) <> Array(0) then
         Yi = Array(Xi)
      end if
   end if
end sub
```

An example further illustrates the technique.

Example 4–1   Floating Horizon

Consider the geometric functions described in Table 4–1. The functions are given in the $z = 0$, 30 and 60 planes. Two curves are given in each plane. The first is a straight line, and the second describes a sawtooth wave above and below the plane in which the straight line lies. Two lines at the same constant

z values are easily processed by the floating horizon algorithm. However, the order in which they are processed affects the final appearance. Here, the straight line is considered first.

Table 4–1

Curve number	Point number	x	y	z	Comment
1	1	0	0	0	Sawtooth
	2	2	4	0	wave
	3	6	−4	0	
	4	8	0	0	
2	5	0	0	0	Straight
	6	8	0	0	line
3	7	0	0	3	Sawtooth
	8	2	4	3	wave
	9	6	−4	3	
	10	8	0	3	
4	11	0	0	3	Straight
	12	8	0	3	line
5	13	0	0	6	Sawtooth
	14	2	4	6	wave
	15	6	−4	6	
	16	8	0	6	
6	17	0	0	6	Straight
	18	8	0	6	line

Before displaying the surface described in Table 4-1, it is necessary to apply a viewing transformation. First, the surface is rotated $30°$ about the y-axis, then by $15°$ about the x-axis. The result is projected onto the $z = 0$ plane from a point of projection at infinity on the $+z$-axis (see [Roge90a]). The resulting 4×4 homogeneous coordinate transformation matrix is

$$\begin{bmatrix} 0.866 & 0.129 & 0 & 0 \\ 0 & 0.966 & 0 & 0 \\ 0.5 & -0.224 & 0 & 0 \\ 0 & 0 & 0 & 1 \end{bmatrix}$$

Applying the transformation yields the results given in Table 4–2. These results are transformed (scaled) to an integer grid, with $0 \le x \le 100$ and $-50 \le y \le 50$, i.e., to image space coordinates.

Sorting the curves into z priority order, and recalling that the straight line in each constant z plane is processed first, shows that the curves are processed in the reverse order to that given in Table 4–2, namely, 6, 5, 4, 3, 2, 1.

Table 4–2

Curve number	Point number	x	y
1	1	0	0
	2	17	41
	3	52	−31
	4	69	10
2	5	0	0
	6	69	10
3	7	15	−7
	8	32	35
	9	67	−38
	10	84	36
4	11	15	−7
	12	84	36
5	13	30	−13
	14	47	28
	15	82	−44
	16	99	−3
6	17	30	−13
	18	99	−3

Table 4–3

	x	0	10	20	30	40	50	60	70	80	90	100
Initially	U	−50	−50	−50	−50	−50	−50	−50	−50	−50	−50	−50
	L	50	50	50	50	50	50	50	50	50	50	50
Fig. 4–11a	U	−50	−50	−50	−13	−12	−10	−9	−7	−6	−4	−50
curve 6	L	50	50	50	−13	−12	−10	−9	−7	−6	−4	50
Fig. 4–11b	U	−50	−50	−50	−13	10	22	1	−7	−6	−4	−50
curve 5	L	50	50	50	−13	−12	−10	−9	−19	−40	−25	50
Fig. 4–11c	U	−50	−50	−6	−4	10	22	1	1	3	1	−50
curve 4	L	50	50	−9	−13	−12	−10	−9	−19	−40	−25	50
Fig. 4–11d	U	−50	−50	5	29	19	22	1	1	3	1	−50
curve 3	L	50	50	−9	−13	−12	−10	−23	−30	−40	−25	50
Fig. 4–11e	U	0	1	5	29	19	22	9	10	5	1	−50
curve 2	L	0	−4	−9	−13	−12	−10	−23	−30	−40	−25	50
Fig. 4–11f	U	0	24	36	29	19	22	9	10	5	1	−50
curve 1	L	0	−4	−9	−13	−12	−28	−23	−30	−40	−25	50

The upper and lower horizons are initialized to -50 and 50, respectively, as shown in Table 4–3 for selected horizontal screen locations. Also shown in Table 4–3 and Figs. 4–11a to 4–11f are the values (to the nearest integer) as the algorithm processes each line. The dashed lines are the false edges created by the left- and right-edge fill.

Cross-hatching

The previous algorithm and Ex. 4–1 consider the function $y = F(x, z)$ for constant z only. Frequently, it is convenient to plot curves of both constant z and constant x. When this is done, a cross-hatching effect is obtained. Initially, it might seem that cross-hatching is accomplished by superimposing two results, one with $z = $ constant planes, and one with $x = $ constant planes. Figure 4–12 shows that this is not the case (see [Wrig73]). Notice, in particular, Fig. 4–12c, where the arrows indicate the incorrect result. The correct result, shown in Fig. 4–12d, is obtained by processing the curves in either the z or $x = $ constant planes, whichever is most nearly horizontal, in the usual order. However, after each nearly horizontal curve is processed, the parts of the curves in the orthogonal constant planes between this curve and the next curve must be processed. Of course, the same upper and lower floating horizon arrays must be used for both sets of curves. In particular, if for the function $y = F(x, y)$, $z = $ constant curves are most nearly horizontal, then, after processing the curve for z_1, the curves for $x = $ constant between z_1 and z_2 are processed (in the same direction) before the curve for z_2 is processed. If cross-hatching is used, left- and right-edge fills are not used.

The basic assumption for the floating horizon algorithm is that the function, and specifically the silhouette edge, in each cutting plane is a function of either x or y only. Anderson [Ande82] pointed this out and developed an algorithm to handle situations where this is not the case. An example, rendered with his algorithm, is shown in Fig. 4–13. Skala [Skal87] discusses a modification of Bresenham's line drawing algorithm (see Sec. 2–3) that implements the floating horizon algorithm for raster scan displays.

4–3   Roberts Algorithm

The Roberts algorithm represents the first known solution to the visible surface problem [Robe64; Pett77]. It is a mathematically elegant solution which operates in object space. The algorithm first eliminates the edges or planes from each volume that are hidden by the volume itself. Subsequently, each remaining edge of each volume is compared to each of the remaining volumes to determine what portion or portions, if any, are hidden by these volumes. Thus, computational requirements for the Roberts algorithm theoretically increase as the number of objects squared. Historically, this, in combination with increased interest in raster scan displays that operate in image space, led to a lack of interest in the Roberts algorithm. However, the mathematical techniques used in the

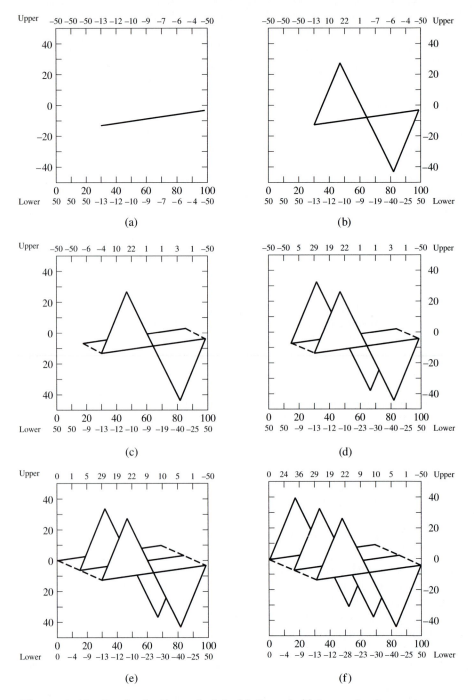

Figure 4–11   Results for Example 4–1. (a) through (f) Image development.

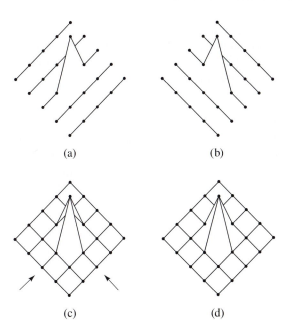

Figure 4–12 Cross-hatching. (a) Lines of constant z; (b) lines of constant x; (c) superposition of (a) and (b); (d) correct result.

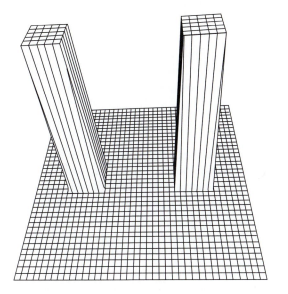

Figure 4–13 A scene for which the silhouette edge is not solely a function of x or y. Rendered correctly by Anderson's algorithm.

algorithm are simple, powerful and accurate. Furthermore, the algorithm is useful in illustrating several important concepts. Finally, implementations using a preliminary z priority sort, and simple boxing or minimax tests, exhibit a near-linear growth with the number of objects.

Volume Matrices

The Roberts algorithm requires that all volumes or objects in a scene be convex; concave volumes must be subdivided into component convex volumes (see Sec. 3–17). The algorithm considers a convex planar polygonal volume to be represented by a collection of intersecting planes. The equation of a plane in three-space is

$$ax + by + cz + d = 0 \qquad (4-1)$$

In matrix notation, the plane equation is represented by

$$\begin{bmatrix} x & y & z & 1 \end{bmatrix} \begin{bmatrix} a \\ b \\ c \\ d \end{bmatrix} = 0$$

or

$$\begin{bmatrix} x & y & z & 1 \end{bmatrix} [P]^T = 0$$

where $[P] = [a\ b\ c\ d]$ represents the plane. Thus, a convex solid is represented by a volume matrix of plane equation coefficients, e.g.

$$\begin{bmatrix} a_1 & a_2 & \cdots & a_n \\ b_1 & b_2 & & b_n \\ c_1 & c_2 & & c_n \\ d_1 & d_2 & & d_n \end{bmatrix}$$

where each column represents the coefficients of a single plane.

Recall that a general point in space is represented in homogeneous coordinates by the position vector (see [Roge90a])

$$[S] = \begin{bmatrix} x & y & z & 1 \end{bmatrix}$$

In addition, recall that, if $[S]$ is on the plane, then $[S] \cdot [P] = 0$ (see Sec. 3–5). If $[S]$ is not on the plane, the sign of the dot product indicates which side it is on. The Roberts algorithm uses the convention that points on the side of a plane corresponding to the inside of a volume yield positive dot products. To illustrate these ideas, consider Ex. 4–2.

Example 4–2   Volume Matrix

The six planes describing an origin-centered unit cube are $x_1 = \frac{1}{2}$, $x_2 = -\frac{1}{2}$, $y_3 = \frac{1}{2}$, $y_4 = -\frac{1}{2}$, $z_5 = \frac{1}{2}$ and $z_6 = -\frac{1}{2}$, as shown in Fig. 4–14. The equation of the right-hand plane is

$$x_1 + 0y_1 + 0z_1 - \frac{1}{2} = 0$$

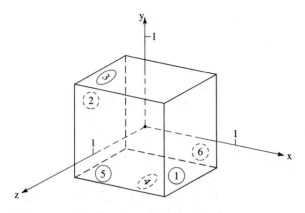

Figure 4–14 Origin-centered unit cube.

or
$$2x_1 - 1 = 0$$

The complete volume matrix is

$$[V] = \begin{array}{c} \begin{array}{cccccc} ① & ② & ③ & ④ & ⑤ & ⑥ \end{array} \\ \begin{bmatrix} 1 & 1 & 0 & 0 & 0 & 0 \\ 0 & 0 & 1 & 1 & 0 & 0 \\ 0 & 0 & 0 & 0 & 1 & 1 \\ -\frac{1}{2} & \frac{1}{2} & -\frac{1}{2} & \frac{1}{2} & -\frac{1}{2} & \frac{1}{2} \end{bmatrix} \end{array} = \begin{array}{c} \begin{array}{cccccc} ① & ② & ③ & ④ & ⑤ & ⑥ \end{array} \\ \begin{bmatrix} 2 & 2 & 0 & 0 & 0 & 0 \\ 0 & 0 & 2 & 2 & 0 & 0 \\ 0 & 0 & 0 & 0 & 2 & 2 \\ -1 & 1 & -1 & 1 & -1 & 1 \end{bmatrix} \end{array}$$

This volume matrix is tested against a point known to be inside the volume to ensure that the signs of each plane equation are correct. If the sign of the dot product for any plane is not greater than zero, then the plane equation must be multiplied by -1. A point inside the cube at $x = \frac{1}{4}, y = \frac{1}{4}, z = \frac{1}{4}$ has the homogeneous coordinate position vector

$$[S] = \begin{bmatrix} \frac{1}{4} & \frac{1}{4} & \frac{1}{4} & 1 \end{bmatrix} = \begin{bmatrix} 1 & 1 & 1 & 4 \end{bmatrix}$$

Taking the dot product with the volume matrix yields

$$[S] \cdot [V] = \begin{bmatrix} 1 & 1 & 1 & 4 \end{bmatrix} \begin{array}{c} \begin{array}{cccccc} ① & ② & ③ & ④ & ⑤ & ⑥ \end{array} \\ \begin{bmatrix} 2 & 2 & 0 & 0 & 0 & 0 \\ 0 & 0 & 2 & 2 & 0 & 0 \\ 0 & 0 & 0 & 0 & 2 & 2 \\ -1 & 1 & -1 & 1 & -1 & 1 \end{bmatrix} \end{array}$$

$$= \begin{array}{c} \begin{array}{cccccc} ① & \quad ② & \quad ③ & \quad ④ & \quad ⑤ & \quad ⑥ \end{array} \\ \begin{bmatrix} -2 & 6 & -2 & 6 & -2 & 6 \end{bmatrix} \end{array}$$

Here, the results for the first, third and fifth plane equations (columns) are negative and hence are constituted incorrectly. Multiplying these equations (columns) by -1 yields the correct volume matrix for the cube

$$[V] = \begin{bmatrix} \overset{①}{-2} & \overset{②}{2} & \overset{③}{0} & \overset{④}{0} & \overset{⑤}{0} & \overset{⑥}{0} \\ 0 & 0 & -2 & 2 & 0 & 0 \\ 0 & 0 & 0 & 0 & -2 & 2 \\ 1 & 1 & 1 & 1 & 1 & 1 \end{bmatrix}$$

Plane Equations

In Ex. 4–2, the plane equations were determined by inspection. Of course, this is not always possible. There are several useful techniques for the more general case. Although the equation of a plane, Eq. $(4-1)$, contains four unknown coefficients, the equation can always be normalized so that $d = 1$. Hence, only three noncollinear points are required to determine the coefficients. Applying the normalized form of Eq. $(4-1)$ to three noncollinear points (x_1, y_1, z_1), (x_2, y_2, z_2), (x_3, y_3, z_3) yields

$$ax_1 + by_1 + cz_1 = -1$$

$$ax_2 + by_2 + cz_2 = -1$$

$$ax_3 + by_3 + cz_3 = -1$$

In matrix form this is

$$\begin{bmatrix} x_1 & y_1 & z_1 \\ x_2 & y_2 & z_2 \\ x_3 & y_3 & z_3 \end{bmatrix} \begin{bmatrix} a \\ b \\ c \end{bmatrix} = \begin{bmatrix} -1 \\ -1 \\ -1 \end{bmatrix}$$

or

$$[X][C] = [D] \qquad (4-2)$$

Solving for the coefficients of the plane yields

$$[C] = [X]^{-1}[D]$$

Alternatively, if the normal vector to the plane is known, e.g.

$$n = a\mathbf{i} + b\mathbf{j} + c\mathbf{k}$$

where $\mathbf{i}$, $\mathbf{j}$ and $\mathbf{k}$ are the unit vectors in the x, y, z directions, respectively, then the plane equation is

$$ax + by + cz + d = 0 \qquad (4-3)$$

The value of d is obtained from any point in the plane. In particular, if the components of a point in the plane are (x_1, y_1, z_1) then

$$d = -(ax_1 + by_1 + cz_1) \qquad (4-4)$$

Because the computational work involved in visible surface algorithms increases with the number of polygons, it is advantageous to use polygons with more than three sides to describe surfaces. These polygons can be both concave and nonplanar. A technique due to Martin Newell [Suth74] gives both an exact solution for the plane equation for planar polygons and a 'best' approximation for almost-planar polygons. The technique is equivalent to determining the normal at each polygon vertex by taking the cross product of the adjacent edges and averaging the results. If a, b, c, d are the coefficients of the plane equation, then Newell's technique gives

$$a = \sum_{i=1}^{n}(y_i - y_j)(z_i + z_j)$$

$$b = \sum_{i=1}^{n}(z_i - z_j)(x_i + x_j)$$

$$c = \sum_{i=1}^{n}(x_i - x_j)(y_i + y_j) \qquad (4-5)$$

where $\qquad$ **if** $i = n$ **then** $j = 1$ **else** $j = i+1$

and d is obtained using any point in the plane. Example 4–3 illustrates these techniques.

Example 4–3 Plane Equations

Consider the quadrilateral planar polygon described by the four vertices $V_1(1,0,0)$, $V_2(0,1,0)$, $V_3(0,0,1)$ and $V_4(1,-1,1)$ (see Fig. 4–15). Using the vertices V_1, V_2, V_4 and Eq. $(4-2)$ yields

$$\begin{bmatrix} 1 & 0 & 0 \\ 0 & 1 & 0 \\ 1 & -1 & 1 \end{bmatrix} \begin{bmatrix} a \\ b \\ c \end{bmatrix} = \begin{bmatrix} -1 \\ -1 \\ -1 \end{bmatrix}$$

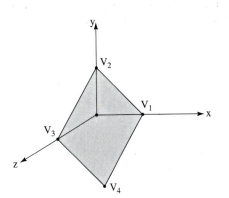

Figure 4–15 Plane in three-space.

Solving for the coefficients of the plane equation gives

$$\begin{bmatrix} a \\ b \\ c \end{bmatrix} = \begin{bmatrix} 1 & 0 & 0 \\ 0 & 1 & 0 \\ -1 & 1 & 1 \end{bmatrix} \begin{bmatrix} -1 \\ -1 \\ -1 \end{bmatrix} = \begin{bmatrix} -1 \\ -1 \\ -1 \end{bmatrix}$$

The plane equation is then

$$-x - y - z + 1 = 0$$

or

$$x + y + z - 1 = 0$$

Alternatively, the normal to the plane is obtained by finding the cross product of two adjacent vectors at one of the vertices, e.g., V_1

$$\mathbf{n} = \mathbf{V_1 V_2} \otimes \mathbf{V_1 V_3} = \begin{vmatrix} \mathbf{i} & \mathbf{j} & \mathbf{k} \\ (x_2 - x_1) & (y_2 - y_1) & (z_2 - z_1) \\ (x_3 - x_1) & (y_3 - y_1) & (z_3 - z_1) \end{vmatrix}$$

$$\mathbf{n} = \begin{vmatrix} \mathbf{i} & \mathbf{j} & \mathbf{k} \\ -1 & 1 & 0 \\ -1 & 0 & 1 \end{vmatrix} = \mathbf{i} + \mathbf{j} + \mathbf{k}$$

where $\mathbf{i}, \mathbf{j}, \mathbf{k}$ are the unit vectors in the x, y, z directions, respectively. Using Eq. $(4-4)$ and V_4, the constant term in the plane equation is

$$d = -1(1 - 1 + 1) = -1$$

Hence, the plane equation is again

$$x + y + z - 1 = 0$$

Turning now to Newell's technique for $n = 4$, Eq. $(4 - 5)$ yields

$$a = (y_1 - y_2)(z_1 + z_2) + (y_2 - y_3)(z_2 + z_3) + (y_3 - y_4)(z_3 + z_4)$$
$$+ (y_4 - y_1)(z_4 + z_1)$$
$$= (-1)(0) + (1)(1) + (1)(2) + (-1)(1) = 2$$

$$b = (z_1 - z_2)(x_1 + x_2) + (z_2 - z_3)(x_2 + x_3) + (z_3 - z_4)(x_3 + x_4)$$
$$+ (z_4 - z_1)(x_4 + x_1)$$
$$= (0)(1) + (-1)(0) + (0)(1) + (1)(2) = 2$$

$$c = (x_1 - x_2)(y_1 + y_2) + (x_2 - x_3)(y_2 + y_3) + (x_3 - x_4)(y_3 + y_4)$$
$$+ (x_4 - x_1)(y_4 + y_1)$$
$$= (1)(1) + (0)(1) + (-1)(-1) + (0)(-1) = 2$$

and using V_4, the constant term is

$$d = -(2 - 2 + 2) = -2$$

After dividing by 2, the plane equation is again

$$x + y + z - 1 = 0$$

A further example illustrates Newell's technique for almost-planar polygons.

Example 4–4   Nonplanar Polygons

Consider the almost-planar polygon described by the four vertices $V_1(1, 0, 0)$, $V_2(0, 1, 0)$, $V_3(0, 0, 1)$ and $V_4(1.1, -1, 1)$. Calculating the normal at each vertex by taking the cross product of the two adjacent edges yields

$$\mathbf{n}_1 = \mathbf{V}_1\mathbf{V}_2 \otimes \mathbf{V}_1\mathbf{V}_4 = \mathbf{i} + \mathbf{j} + 0.9\mathbf{k}$$

$$\mathbf{n}_2 = \mathbf{V}_2\mathbf{V}_3 \otimes \mathbf{V}_2\mathbf{V}_1 = \mathbf{i} + \mathbf{j} + \mathbf{k}$$

$$\mathbf{n}_3 = \mathbf{V}_3\mathbf{V}_4 \otimes \mathbf{V}_3\mathbf{V}_2 = \mathbf{i} + 1.1\mathbf{j} + 1.1\mathbf{k}$$

$$\mathbf{n}_4 = \mathbf{V}_4\mathbf{V}_1 \otimes \mathbf{V}_4\mathbf{V}_3 = \mathbf{i} + 1.1\mathbf{j} + \mathbf{k}$$

Averaging the normals yields

$$\mathbf{n} = \mathbf{i} + 1.05\mathbf{j} + \mathbf{k}$$

Solving for the constant term in the plane equation, using one of the vertices, e.g., V_1, yields $d = -1$. Hence, the approximate plane equation is

$$x + 1.05y + z - 1 = 0$$

Newell's method gives the same result. In particular, from Eq. $(4 - 5)$

$$a = (-1)(0) + (1)(1) + (1)(2) + (-1)(1) = 2$$

$$b = (0)(1) + (-1)(0) + (0)(1.1) + (1)(2.1) = 2.1$$

$$c = (1)(1) + (0)(1) + (-1.1)(-1) + (0.1)(-1) = 2$$

Using V_1 to solve for d, and dividing by 2, yields the same approximate plane equation. The approximate plane passes through the line $x = z$ and contains the vertices V_1 and V_3. However, V_2 and V_4 are slightly displaced on either side of the plane.

Viewing Transformations and Volume Matrices

Before applying a visible surface algorithm, a three-dimensional viewing transformation is frequently used to obtain the desired view of the scene. The volume matrices for the objects in the transformed scene are obtained by either transforming the original volume matrices or calculating new volume matrices from the transformed vertices or points.

If $[B]$ is the homogeneous coordinate volume matrix representing the original vertices of a volume, and $[T]$ is a 4×4 viewing transformation matrix, then the transformed vertices are (see [Roge90a])

$$[BT] = [B][T] \qquad (4-6)$$

where $[BT]$ is the transformed vertex matrix. Referring to Eq. $(4-2)$, we write the original plane equations for the volume as

$$[B][V] = [D] \qquad (4-7)$$

where $[V]$ is the volume matrix and $[D]$ is the right-hand matrix of zeros. Similarly, the transformed plane equations are given by

$$[BT][VT] = [D] \qquad (4-8)$$

where $[VT]$ is the transformed volume matrix. Equating Eqs. $(4-7)$ and $(4-8)$ yields

$$[BT][VT] = [B][V]$$

Substituting Eq. $(4-6)$, eliminating $[B]$ and premultiplying by $[T]^{-1}$ gives

$$[VT] = [T]^{-1}[V]$$

Thus, the transformed volume matrix is obtained by premultiplying the original volume matrix by the inverse of the viewing transformation. An example illustrates this.

Example 4–5   Volume Manipulation

Consider translating the unit cube centered at the origin three units to the right in the positive x direction. The appropriate 4×4 transformation matrix (see [Roge90a]) is

$$[T] = \begin{bmatrix} 1 & 0 & 0 & 0 \\ 0 & 1 & 0 & 0 \\ 0 & 0 & 1 & 0 \\ 3 & 0 & 0 & 1 \end{bmatrix}$$

and its inverse is

$$[T]^{-1} = \begin{bmatrix} 1 & 0 & 0 & 0 \\ 0 & 1 & 0 & 0 \\ 0 & 0 & 1 & 0 \\ -3 & 0 & 0 & 1 \end{bmatrix}$$

Premultiplying the volume matrix for the unit cube obtained in Ex. 4–2 by $[T]^{-1}$ yields the volume matrix for the translated cube

$$[VT] = [T]^{-1}[V] = \begin{bmatrix} 1 & 0 & 0 & 0 \\ 0 & 1 & 0 & 0 \\ 0 & 0 & 1 & 0 \\ -3 & 0 & 0 & 1 \end{bmatrix} \overset{\textstyle\substack{① \quad ② \quad ③ \quad ④ \quad ⑤ \quad ⑥}}{\begin{bmatrix} -2 & 2 & 0 & 0 & 0 & 0 \\ 0 & 0 & -2 & 2 & 0 & 0 \\ 0 & 0 & 0 & 0 & -2 & 2 \\ 1 & 1 & 1 & 1 & 1 & 1 \end{bmatrix}}$$

$$= \overset{\textstyle\substack{① \quad ② \quad ③ \quad ④ \quad ⑤ \quad ⑥}}{\begin{bmatrix} -2 & 2 & 0 & 0 & 0 & 0 \\ 0 & 0 & -2 & 2 & 0 & 0 \\ 0 & 0 & 0 & 0 & -2 & 2 \\ 7 & -5 & 1 & 1 & 1 & 1 \end{bmatrix}}$$

Translating an origin-centered unit cube three units to the right places the left-hand face at $x = 2\frac{1}{2}$ and the right-hand face at $x = 3\frac{1}{2}$. The first column of the transformed volume matrix yields the plane equation for the right-hand face

$$-2x + 7 = 0 \qquad \text{or} \qquad x = 3\frac{1}{2}$$

as required. Similarly, the second column yields

$$2x - 5 = 0 \qquad \text{or} \qquad x = 2\frac{1}{2}$$

for the left-hand face, as expected.

Recall from Ex. 4–2 that the point

$$[S] = \begin{bmatrix} \frac{1}{4} & \frac{1}{4} & \frac{1}{4} & 1 \end{bmatrix} = \begin{bmatrix} 1 & 1 & 1 & 4 \end{bmatrix}$$

was inside the untransformed volume, hence $[S] \cdot [V] \geq 0$. However, the point $[S]$ is outside the translated volume. Examining the dot product of $[S]$ and the transformed volume matrix

$$[S] \cdot [VT] = \begin{bmatrix} 1 & 1 & 1 & 4 \end{bmatrix} \cdot [VT] = \overset{\textstyle\substack{① \qquad ② \qquad ③ \quad ④ \quad ⑤ \quad ⑥}}{\begin{bmatrix} 26 & -18 & 2 & 6 & 2 & 6 \end{bmatrix}}$$

yields a negative element in the second column corresponding to the left-hand face of the cube. This shows that the point is outside the volume. In fact, it is to the left of the left-hand face, i.e., on the wrong side of the left-hand face, as shown by the negative sign.

If the point matrix, $[S]$, is transformed by postmultiplying by the transformation matrix, then

$$[ST] = [S][T] = \begin{bmatrix} 1 & 1 & 1 & 4 \end{bmatrix}[T] = \begin{bmatrix} 13 & 1 & 4 \end{bmatrix} = \begin{bmatrix} 3\frac{1}{4} & \frac{1}{4} & \frac{1}{4} & 1 \end{bmatrix}$$

Testing the transformed point at $x = 3\frac{1}{4}$ against the transformed volume matrix yields

$$[ST] \cdot [VT] = \overset{\textstyle\substack{① \quad ② \quad ③ \quad ④ \quad ⑤ \quad ⑥}}{\begin{bmatrix} 2 & 6 & 2 & 6 & 2 & 6 \end{bmatrix}}$$

which shows that it is inside the transformed volume.

Self-hidden Planes

Recalling that planes are of infinite extent, and that the dot product of a point and the volume matrix is negative when the point is outside the volume, suggests a method for using the volume matrix to identify planes which are hidden by the volume itself. Example 4–5 shows that only the specific plane (column) in the volume matrix for which a point is declared outside yields a negative dot product. In Example 4–5, this is the left-hand plane (second column) for the transformed volume $[VT]$ and the untransformed point $[S]$. The concept is illustrated in Fig. 4–16.

If the view, or eyepoint, is at infinity on the positive z-axis looking toward the origin, then the view direction is toward negative infinity on the z-axis. In homogeneous coordinates, this vector is represented by (see [Roge90a])

$$[E] = [0 \quad 0 \quad -1 \quad 0]$$

$[E]$ also represents the point at infinity on the negative z-axis. In fact $[E]$ represents any point on the plane at $z = -\infty$, i.e., any point $(x, y, -\infty)$. Thus, if the dot product of $[E]$ and the plane in the volume matrix is negative, then $[E]$ is outside these planes. Consequently, these planes are hidden with respect to a viewpoint anywhere on the plane at $z = \infty$, and the test point at $z = -\infty$ is hidden by the volume itself, as illustrated in Fig. 4–17. These planes are called self-hidden planes, or backfaces, hence

$$[E] \cdot [V] < 0$$

identifies self-hidden planes or backfaces. Note that for axonometric projections (eyepoint at infinity) this is equivalent to looking for positive values in the third row of the volume matrix.

This technique is the simplest visible surface algorithm for single convex polygonal volumes. It is also used to eliminate the self-hidden, or backplanes,

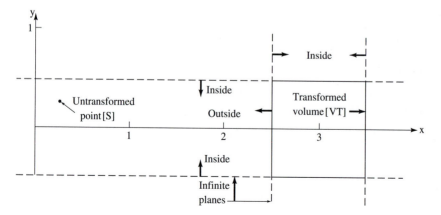

Figure 4–16 A point outside a volume.

from a scene before applying most of the hidden surface algorithms subsequently discussed in this chapter. When used this way, it is frequently called backplane culling. For convex polygonal volumes, the number of polygonal faces is reduced by approximately half. The technique is equivalent to calculating the surface normal for each individual polygon. A negative surface normal indicates that the normal points away from the viewer, and hence the polygon is hidden. The technique can also be used for simple shading (see Chapter 5). The intensity, or shade, of the polygon is made proportional to the magnitude of the surface normal. An example further illustrates the concept.

Example 4–6   Self-hidden Planes

Again consider the origin-centered unit cube, as shown in Fig. 4–17. The eyepoint is on the positive z-axis at $[0\ 0\ 1\ 0]$, looking toward the origin. Thus, the test point, or direction of view, is given by $[E] = [0\ 0\ -1\ 0]$. Taking the dot product with the volume matrix yields

$$[E]\cdot[V] = [0\ 0\ -1\ 0]\begin{array}{cccccc} \text{①} & \text{②} & \text{③} & \text{④} & \text{⑤} & \text{⑥} \\ \left[\begin{array}{cccccc} -2 & 2 & 0 & 0 & 0 & 0 \\ 0 & 0 & -2 & 2 & 0 & 0 \\ 0 & 0 & 0 & 0 & -2 & 2 \\ 1 & 1 & 1 & 1 & 1 & 1 \end{array}\right] \end{array} [0\ 0\ 0\ 0\ 2\ -2]$$

and the negative sign in the sixth column indicates that this face is self-hidden. Inspection of Fig. 4–17 confirms this. The zero results indicate planes that are parallel to the direction of view.

This technique for identifying self-hidden planes in effect performs an axonometric projection onto a plane at infinity from any point in three-space. Viewing transformations, including perspective, are applied prior to identifying the self-hidden planes. When the viewing transformation includes perspective,

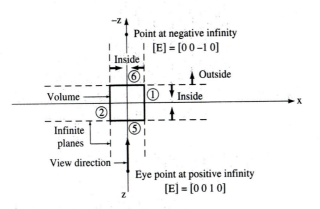

Figure 4–17   Self-hidden planes.

the full perspective transformation from one three-space to another three-space must be used, not a perspective projection onto some two-dimensional plane (see [Roge90a]). The full perspective transformation yields a distorted three-dimensional volume, which, in effect, is then projected onto a plane at infinity when the self-hidden planes are identified. The effect is equivalent to a perspective projection from some point of projection onto a finite plane of projection.

The viewing transformation can be applied to the volume with the eyepoint fixed. Alternatively, the volume is fixed and the eyepoint moves. The equivalent eyepoint and view direction are obtained by postmultiplying by the inverse of the viewing transformation. The next example illustrates these techniques.

Example 4–7   Self-hidden Plane with Viewing Transformation

Consider the origin-centered unit cube rotated about the y-axis by $45°$. The viewing transformation is (see [Roge90a])

$$[R_y] = \begin{bmatrix} \cos\phi & 0 & -\sin\phi & 0 \\ 0 & 1 & 0 & 0 \\ \sin\phi & 0 & \cos\phi & 0 \\ 0 & 0 & 0 & 1 \end{bmatrix}_{\phi=45°} = \begin{bmatrix} \dfrac{1}{\sqrt{2}} & 0 & -\dfrac{1}{\sqrt{2}} & 0 \\ 0 & 1 & 0 & 0 \\ \dfrac{1}{\sqrt{2}} & 0 & \dfrac{1}{\sqrt{2}} & 0 \\ 0 & 0 & 0 & 1 \end{bmatrix}$$

The transformed volume matrix is obtained by premultiplying by the inverse of the viewing transformation. For a pure rotation, the inverse of the viewing transformation is its transpose. Thus

$$[R_y]^{-1} = [R_y]^T = \begin{bmatrix} \cos\phi & 0 & \sin\phi & 0 \\ 0 & 1 & 0 & 0 \\ -\sin\phi & 0 & \cos\phi & 0 \\ 0 & 0 & 0 & 1 \end{bmatrix}_{\phi=45°} = \begin{bmatrix} \dfrac{1}{\sqrt{2}} & 0 & \dfrac{1}{\sqrt{2}} & 0 \\ 0 & 1 & 0 & 0 \\ -\dfrac{1}{\sqrt{2}} & 0 & \dfrac{1}{2} & 0 \\ 0 & 0 & 0 & 1 \end{bmatrix}$$

The transformed volume matrix is

$$[VT] = [R_y]^{-1}[V] = \begin{bmatrix} \overset{①}{-\dfrac{2}{\sqrt{2}}} & \overset{②}{\dfrac{2}{\sqrt{2}}} & \overset{③}{0} & \overset{④}{0} & \overset{⑤}{-\dfrac{2}{\sqrt{2}}} & \overset{⑥}{\dfrac{2}{\sqrt{2}}} \\ 0 & 0 & -2 & 2 & 0 & 0 \\ \dfrac{2}{\sqrt{2}} & -\dfrac{2}{\sqrt{2}} & 0 & 0 & -\dfrac{2}{\sqrt{2}} & \dfrac{2}{\sqrt{2}} \\ 1 & 1 & 1 & 1 & 1 & 1 \end{bmatrix}$$

From an eyepoint on the positive z-axis, $[0 \quad 0 \quad 1 \quad 0]$, looking toward the origin, the view direction or test point is given by

$$[E] = [0 \quad 0 \quad -1 \quad 0]$$

Taking the dot product of $[E]$ and the transformed volume matrix yields

$$[E] \cdot [VT] = \begin{bmatrix} \overset{①}{-\dfrac{2}{\sqrt{2}}} & \overset{②}{\dfrac{2}{\sqrt{2}}} & \overset{③}{0} & \overset{④}{0} & \overset{⑤}{\dfrac{2}{\sqrt{2}}} & \overset{⑥}{-\dfrac{2}{\sqrt{2}}} \end{bmatrix}$$

Hence, the first and sixth planes, which correspond to the left and rear planes in the original orientation, are self-hidden. Figure 4–18a confirms this. Notice also that, when the volume is transformed and the view direction fixed, taking the dot product of the test point and the transformed volume matrix, and looking for negative signs, is equivalent to looking for positive terms in the third row of the transformed volume matrix.

The equivalent eyepoint for the untransformed volume corresponding to the rotation about the y-axis is

$$[0 \ \ 0 \ \ 1 \ \ 0][R_y]^{-1} = \begin{bmatrix} -\dfrac{1}{\sqrt{2}} & 0 & \dfrac{1}{\sqrt{2}} & 0 \end{bmatrix} = [-1 \ \ 0 \ \ 1 \ \ 0]$$

i.e., a point at positive infinity on the line $-x = z$, as shown in Fig. 4–18b. Similarly, the equivalent view direction and test point are

$$[ET] = [E][R_y]^{-1} = [0 \ \ 0 \ \ -1 \ \ 0][R_y]^{-1} = \frac{1}{\sqrt{2}}[1 \ \ 0 \ \ -1 \ \ 0]$$

This is a point at negative infinity on the line $-x = z$. Taking the dot product of the equivalent view direction and the untransformed volume matrix yields

$$[ET] \cdot [V] = \frac{1}{\sqrt{2}} \begin{bmatrix} \overset{①}{-2} & \overset{②}{2} & \overset{③}{0} & \overset{④}{0} & \overset{⑤}{2} & \overset{⑥}{-2} \end{bmatrix}$$

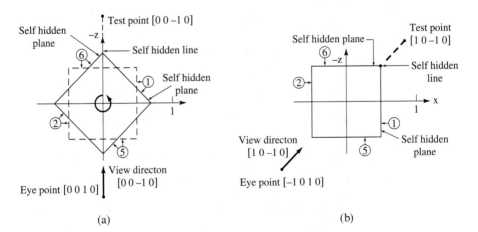

(a) (b)

Figure 4–18 Viewing transformation and self-hidden planes. (a) Transforming object; (b) transforming viewpoint.

where again the negative signs indicate that the first and sixth planes are self-hidden. Figure 4–18b confirms this.

Having identified the self-hidden planes, it remains to identify the self-hidden lines. A self-hidden line is formed by the intersection of two self-hidden planes. Although in Ex. 4–6 plane 6 is self-hidden, no lines are self-hidden because only one plane is self-hidden. However, in Ex. 4–7 the edge formed by the intersection of planes 1 and 6 is self-hidden.

Lines Hidden by Other Volumes

After first eliminating the self-hidden lines, it is necessary to consider whether an individual line is hidden by any other volume in the scene. In order to accomplish this, every remaining line or edge is compared with all the other volumes in the scene. Here, using a priority sort (z sort) and simple minimax or bounding box tests (see Sec. 2–9) allows the elimination of entire groups or clusters of lines and volumes. For example, if all volumes in the scene are sorted into a priority list using the z value of the nearest vertex to represent the distance from the eye, then no volume on the list for which the nearest vertex is farther from the eye than the farthest end point of a line can obscure that line. Furthermore, of the remaining volumes, no volume whose bounding box is completely to the right, to the left, above or below that for the line can obscure the line. Using these techniques significantly reduces the number of volumes with which an individual line or edge must be compared.

To compare a single line, P_1P_2, with a single volume, it is convenient to use a parametric representation of the line

$$P(t) = P_1 + (P_2 - P_1)t \qquad 0 \le t \le 1$$

or
$$\mathbf{v} = \mathbf{s} + \mathbf{d}t$$

where $\mathbf{v}$ is the position vector of the line, $\mathbf{s}$ is the starting point and $\mathbf{d}$ is the direction of the line. The objective is to determine whether the line is hidden. If it is hidden, then the objective is to determine the values of t for which it is hidden. To accomplish this, another parametric line from any point on $P(t)$ to the eyepoint at $\mathbf{g}$ is formed

$$\mathbf{Q}(\alpha, t) = \mathbf{u} = \mathbf{v} + \mathbf{g}\alpha = \mathbf{s} + \mathbf{d}t + \mathbf{g}\alpha \qquad 0 \le t \le 1, \ \alpha \ge 0$$

Here, α and t perform similar functions. A given value of t yields a point on the line $P(t)$, and α yields a point on the line from this point to the eyepoint. In fact, $Q(\alpha, t)$ represents a plane in three-space. Specifying both α and t locates a point on this plane. The value of α is positive, because only the part of the plane between the line $P(t)$ and the eyepoint can contain volumes which obscure the line.

Example 4–8   Parametric Plane

Consider the line from $P_1(-2, 0, -2)$ to $P_2(2, 0, -2)$ viewed from a position at positive infinity in the z direction (see Fig. 4–19). In homogeneous coordinates, P_1 and P_2 are

$$P_1 = [-2 \quad 0 \quad -2 \quad 1]$$

$$P_2 = [\ 2 \quad 0 \quad -2 \quad 1]$$

Hence $P(t) = \mathbf{v} = \mathbf{s} + \mathbf{d}t = [-2 \quad 0 \quad -2 \quad 1] + [4 \quad 0 \quad 0 \quad 0]t$

The eyepoint vector is

$$\mathbf{g} = [0 \quad 0 \quad 1 \quad 0]$$

and $$Q(\alpha, t) = \mathbf{s} + \mathbf{d}t + \mathbf{g}\alpha = [-2 \quad 0 \quad -2 \quad 1]$$
$$+ [4 \quad 0 \quad 0 \quad 0]t + [0 \quad 0 \quad 1 \quad 0]\alpha$$

Figure 4–19 and Table 4–4 show the effect of varying t and α. As a specific example, assume $t = \frac{1}{2}$ and $\alpha = 3$. Then

$$P\left(\frac{1}{2}\right) = \mathbf{v} = [-2 \quad 0 \quad -2 \quad 1] + [4 \quad 0 \quad 0 \quad 0]\left(\frac{1}{2}\right)$$

$$= [0 \quad 0 \quad -2 \quad 1]$$

which is the point on the line $P_1 P_2$ where it crosses the z-axis at $z = -2$. For $\alpha = 3$

$$Q\left(3, \frac{1}{2}\right) = \mathbf{v} + \mathbf{g}\alpha = [0 \quad 0 \quad -2 \quad 1] + [0 \quad 0 \quad 1 \quad 0](3)$$

$$= [0 \quad 0 \quad 1 \quad 1]$$

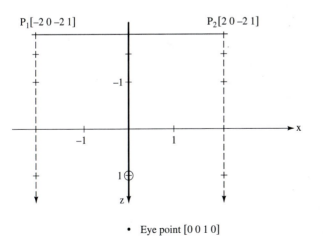

- Eye point $[0\ 0\ 1\ 0]$

Figure 4–19   The parametric plane.

which is the point on the z-axis at $z = 1$. This point is shown by the dot in Fig. 4–19. Each of the points given in Table 4–4 is indicated by crosses in Fig. 4–19. Notice that each of the lines is parallel to the z-axis.

Table 4–4

t	α	$\mathbf{v}(t)$	$Q(\alpha, t)$
0	0	$\begin{bmatrix} -2 & 0 & -2 & 1 \end{bmatrix}$	$\begin{bmatrix} -2 & 0 & -2 & 1 \end{bmatrix}$
	$\frac{1}{2}$		$\begin{bmatrix} -2 & 0 & -\frac{3}{2} & 1 \end{bmatrix}$
	1		$\begin{bmatrix} -2 & 0 & -1 & 1 \end{bmatrix}$
	2		$\begin{bmatrix} -2 & 0 & 0 & 1 \end{bmatrix}$
	3		$\begin{bmatrix} -2 & 0 & 1 & 0 \end{bmatrix}$
$\frac{1}{2}$	0	$\begin{bmatrix} 0 & 0 & -2 & 1 \end{bmatrix}$	$\begin{bmatrix} 0 & 0 & -2 & 1 \end{bmatrix}$
	$\frac{1}{2}$		$\begin{bmatrix} 0 & 0 & -\frac{3}{2} & 1 \end{bmatrix}$
	1		$\begin{bmatrix} 0 & 0 & -1 & 1 \end{bmatrix}$
	2		$\begin{bmatrix} 0 & 0 & 0 & 1 \end{bmatrix}$
	3		$\begin{bmatrix} 0 & 0 & 1 & 0 \end{bmatrix}$
1	0	$\begin{bmatrix} 2 & 0 & -2 & 1 \end{bmatrix}$	$\begin{bmatrix} 2 & 0 & -2 & 1 \end{bmatrix}$
	$\frac{1}{2}$		$\begin{bmatrix} 2 & 0 & -\frac{3}{2} & 1 \end{bmatrix}$
	1		$\begin{bmatrix} 2 & 0 & -1 & 1 \end{bmatrix}$
	2		$\begin{bmatrix} 2 & 0 & 0 & 1 \end{bmatrix}$
	3		$\begin{bmatrix} 2 & 0 & 1 & 0 \end{bmatrix}$

Recall that, for a point inside a volume, the dot product of the point and the volume matrix is positive. If the point is inside the volume it is hidden. Therefore, to determine the part of a line hidden by a volume, it is only necessary to find the values of α and t for which the dot product of $Q(\alpha, t)$ and the volume is positive. Taking the dot product of $Q(\alpha, t) = \mathbf{u}$ and the transformed volume yields

$$h = \mathbf{u} \cdot [VT] = \mathbf{s} \cdot [VT] + t\mathbf{d} \cdot [VT] + \alpha \mathbf{g} \cdot [VT] > 0 \qquad 0 \le t \le 1, \ \alpha \ge 0$$

If each component of h is nonnegative for some t and α, the line is hidden by the volume for those values of t. Defining

$$p = \mathbf{s} \cdot [VT]$$

$$q = \mathbf{d} \cdot [VT]$$

$$w = \mathbf{g} \cdot [VT]$$

the condition

$$h_j = p_j + tq_j + \alpha w_j > 0 \qquad 0 \leq t \leq 1, \ \alpha \geq 0$$

where j counts the columns in the volume matrix, must hold for all values of j, i.e., for all the planes describing a volume. The dividing case for visibility or invisibility is when $h_j = 0$. For $h_j = 0$ the point lies on the plane. Setting $h_j = 0$ for each of the planes yields a series of equations in α, t, all of which must be satisfied. This is accomplished by solving each of the equations with each of the others in pairs, to find all possible values of α and t for which the line is marginally visible, as shown in Fig. 4–20. The number of possible solutions for j equations (planes) is $j(j-1)/2$. Each of the solutions in the range $0 \leq t \leq 1$, $\alpha \geq 0$ is tested against all the other equations to ensure that the condition $h_j \geq 0$ is satisfied. A search of the valid solutions is performed to yield the minimum maximum value (t_{minmax}) and the maximum minimum value (t_{maxmin}) of the parameter t. The line is hidden from $t_{\text{maxmin}} < t < t_{\text{minmax}}$. This latter requirement is a simple classical linear programming problem. An algorithm, similar to that previously given for the Cyrus–Beck clipping algorithm (see Sec. 3–5), for this solution is given later in Fig. 4–27. First, some examples help clarify the discussion.

Example 4–9   Testing Lines Against Volumes

Again consider the origin-centered unit cube. The line from $P_1\,[-2\ 0\ -2\ 1]$ to $P_2\,[2\ 0\ -2\ 1]$ passes behind the cube and is partially hidden by the cube, as shown in Fig. 4–21. Again

$$P(t) = \mathbf{v} = [-2\ \ 0\ \ -2\ \ 1] + [4\ \ 0\ \ 0\ \ 0]\,t$$

and
$$\mathbf{s} = [-2\ \ 0\ \ -2\ \ 1]$$

$$\mathbf{d} = [4\ \ 0\ \ 0\ \ 0]$$

For an eyepoint at infinity on the positive z-axis

$$\mathbf{g} = [0\ \ 0\ \ 1\ \ 0]$$

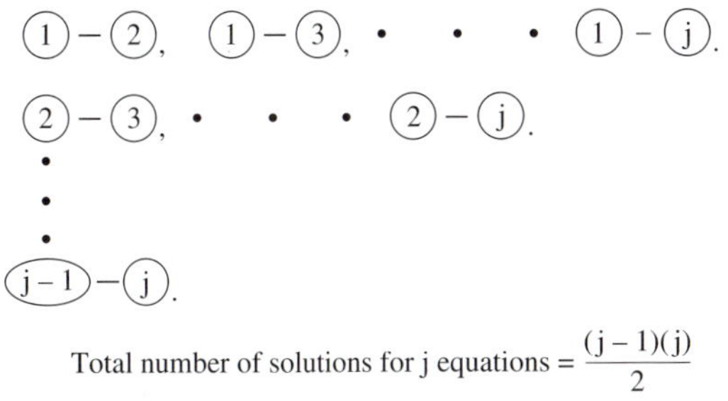

①－②, ①－③, •   •   • ①－ⓙ.

②－③, •   •   • ②－ⓙ.

•

•

•

ⓙ⁻¹－ⓙ.

Total number of solutions for j equations $= \dfrac{(j-1)(j)}{2}$

Figure 4–20   Solution technique for α, t.

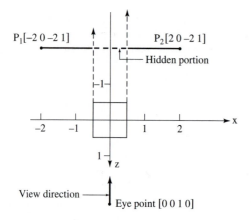

Figure 4–21 Testing a line against a volume.

Here, the untransformed cube is considered. Hence

$$[VT] = [V] = \begin{bmatrix} -2 & 2 & 0 & 0 & 0 & 0 \\ 0 & 0 & -2 & 2 & 0 & 0 \\ 0 & 0 & 0 & 0 & -2 & 2 \\ 1 & 1 & 1 & 1 & 1 & 1 \end{bmatrix}$$

Forming p, q and w by taking the dot product of $\mathbf{s}$, $\mathbf{d}$ and $\mathbf{g}$ with $[VT]$ yields

$$p = \mathbf{s} \cdot [VT] = \begin{bmatrix} 5 & -3 & 1 & 1 & 5 & -3 \end{bmatrix}$$
$$q = \mathbf{d} \cdot [VT] = \begin{bmatrix} -8 & 8 & 0 & 0 & 0 & 0 \end{bmatrix}$$
$$w = \mathbf{g} \cdot [VT] = \begin{bmatrix} 0 & 0 & 0 & 0 & -2 & 2 \end{bmatrix}$$

From these results, six equations corresponding to the condition

$$h_j = p_j + t q_j + \alpha w_j > 0$$

are formed, one for each of the six planes representing the faces of the cube. Specifically

    ① $5 - 8t$ > 0

    ② $-3 + 8t$ > 0

    ③ 1 > 0

    ④ 1 > 0

    ⑤ 5 $- 2\alpha > 0$

    ⑥ -3 $+ 2\alpha > 0$

The third and fourth of these equations simply state that the condition is always satisfied. They correspond to the physical condition that the line is always 'inside' the infinitely extended top and bottom surfaces of the cube. Setting the other four equations to zero yields $t = \frac{5}{8}$, $t = \frac{3}{8}$, $\alpha = \frac{5}{2}$ and $\alpha = \frac{3}{2}$. Of course, this is a particularly simple example. The equations are essentially solved by inspection; however, in general this is not the case.

Each of these equations represents a straight line in α, t space. It is instructive to consider a graphical solution, as shown in Fig. 4–22. The cross-hatching indicates the side of the line on which possible solutions exist. Clearly, all the conditions $h_j > 0$ are satisfied only within the bounded region indicated.

Thus $\qquad\qquad t_{\text{maxmin}} = \dfrac{3}{8} \quad$ and $\quad t_{\text{minmax}} = \dfrac{5}{8}$

The line is hidden for $\frac{3}{8} < t < \frac{5}{8}$ and visible for $0 \le t \le \frac{3}{8}$ and $\frac{5}{8} \le t \le 1$. Using the parametric equation of the line

$$P\!\left(\frac{3}{8}\right) = [\,-2 \;\; 0 \;\; -2 \;\; 1\,] + [\,4 \;\; 0 \;\; 0 \;\; 1\,]\left(\frac{3}{8}\right) = \left[\,-\frac{1}{2} \;\; 0 \;\; -2 \;\; 1\,\right]$$

and

$$P\!\left(\frac{5}{8}\right) = [\,-2 \;\; 0 \;\; -2 \;\; 1\,] + [\,4 \;\; 0 \;\; 0 \;\; 1\,]\left(\frac{5}{8}\right) = \left[\,\frac{1}{2} \;\; 0 \;\; -2 \;\; 1\,\right]$$

as shown in Fig. 4–21.

This example yields two values of t, hence it is possible to assign a t_{maxmin} and a t_{minmax}. What if solution of the equations yields only one value of t? The next examples illustrate this problem and its solution.

Example 4–10   Single Values of t

Continuing to use the origin-centered cube, consider the line $P_1\,[\,1 \;\; 0 \;\; -1 \;\; 1\,]$ to $P_2\,[\,0 \;\; 0 \;\; -1 \;\; 1\,]$, as shown in Fig. 4–23. Here

$$P(t) = \mathbf{v} = [\,1 \;\; 0 \;\; -1 \;\; 1\,] + [\,-1 \;\; 0 \;\; 0 \;\; 0\,]t$$

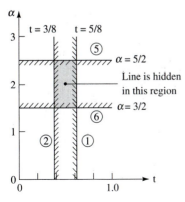

Figure 4–22   Graphical solution for Ex. 4–9.

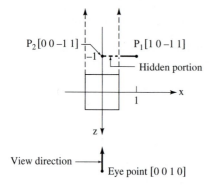

View direction ⎯⎯⎯

Eye point [0 0 1 0]

Figure 4–23   Testing a line with a hidden end point against a volume.

and
$$s = [\ 1\quad 0\quad -1\quad 1\ ]$$

$$d = [-1\quad 0\quad\ \ 0\quad 0\ ]$$

with
$$g = [0\quad 0\quad 1\quad 0\ ]$$

for the untransformed cube, i.e., $[VT] = [V]$, p, q and w become

$$p = s \cdot [VT] = [-1\quad\ \ 3\quad 1\quad 1\quad\ \ 3\quad -1]$$

$$q = d \cdot [VT] = [\ \ 2\quad -2\quad 0\quad 0\quad\ \ 0\quad\ \ 0]$$

$$w = g \cdot [VT] = [\ \ 0\quad\ \ 0\quad 0\quad 0\quad -2\quad\ \ 2]$$

Forming the equations for the $h_j > 0$ condition yields

① $\quad -1 + 2t \qquad\qquad > 0$

② $\qquad 3 - 2t \qquad\qquad > 0$

③ $\qquad\quad 1 \qquad\qquad\quad > 0$

④ $\qquad\quad 1 \qquad\qquad\quad > 0$

⑤ $\qquad\quad 3 \qquad - 2\alpha > 0$

⑥ $\qquad -1 \qquad + 2\alpha > 0$

Solution of these equations for $h_j = 0$ yields $t = \frac{1}{2}$, $t = \frac{3}{2}$, $\alpha = \frac{3}{2}$, $\alpha = \frac{1}{2}$. The solution for $t = \frac{3}{2}$ is rejected, because it is outside the permissible range $0 \le t \le 1$. Hence, only one value of t is found. The graphical solution is shown in Fig. 4–24a. Again, the cross-hatching indicates the side of the line on which possible solutions exist. Clearly, no bounded region is formed. However, the stated solution technique did not consider the boundary conditions represented by the lines $t = 0$ and $t = 1$. As shown in Fig. 4–24b, adding these lines to the solution clearly forms the required bounded region. Thus

$$t_{\text{maxmin}} = \frac{1}{2} \qquad \text{and} \qquad t_{\text{minmax}} = 1$$

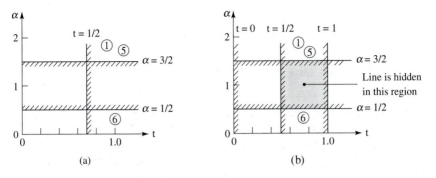

Figure 4–24   Graphical solution for Ex. 4–10. (a) No solution; (b) adding $t = 1$ yields solutions.

Furthermore, the conditions $h_j > 0$ are all satisfied by both these values of t, hence the line is visible for $0 \le t \le \frac{1}{2}$, i.e. for

$$P(0) = [1 \quad 0 \quad -1 \quad 1] + [-1 \quad 0 \quad 0 \quad 0](0) = [1 \quad 0 \quad -1 \quad 1]$$

to

$$P\!\left(\frac{1}{2}\right) = [1 \quad 0 \quad -1 \quad 1] + [-1 \quad 0 \quad 0 \quad 0]\left(\frac{1}{2}\right) = \left[\frac{1}{2} \quad 0 \quad -1 \quad 1\right]$$

Reversing the direction of the line, i.e., interchanging P_1 and P_2, places the solution region between $t = 0$ and $t = \frac{1}{2}$.

A further example illustrates that the $\alpha = 0$ boundary must also be considered.

Example 4–11   Alpha Boundary

Consider the line $P_1\,[1 \; 0 \; 2 \; 1]$ to $P_2\,[-1 \; 0 \; -2 \; 1]$ and the untransformed cube, as shown in Fig. 4–25. The line $P_1 P_2$ penetrates the volume. Here

$$P(t) = \mathbf{v} = [1 \quad 0 \quad 2 \quad 1] + [-2 \quad 0 \quad -4 \quad 0]\,t$$

and

$$\mathbf{s} = [\,1 \quad 0 \quad 2 \quad 1\,]$$

$$\mathbf{d} = [-2 \quad 0 \quad -4 \quad 0\,]$$

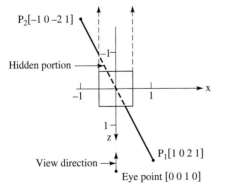

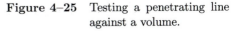

Figure 4–25   Testing a penetrating line against a volume.

Again, the eyepoint is at infinity and

$$\mathbf{g} = [0 \quad 0 \quad 1 \quad 0]$$

For the untransformed cube, i.e., $[VT] = [V]$

$$p = \mathbf{s} \cdot [VT] = [-1 \quad 3 \quad 1 \quad 1 \quad -3 \quad 5]$$

$$q = \mathbf{d} \cdot [VT] = [4 \quad -4 \quad 0 \quad 0 \quad 8 \quad -8]$$

$$w = \mathbf{g} \cdot [VT] = [0 \quad 0 \quad 0 \quad 0 \quad -2 \quad 2]$$

The resulting equations for $h_j > 0$ are

① $-1 + 4t \qquad > 0$

② $3 - 4t \qquad > 0$

③ $1 \qquad > 0$

④ $1 \qquad > 0$

⑤ $-3 + 8t - 2\alpha > 0$

⑥ $5 - 8t + 2\alpha > 0$

Solution of these equations for $h_j = 0$ yields a single valid result, $t = \frac{3}{4}$. The solution is shown graphically in Fig. 4–26a. Again, cross-hatching indicates the side of the line on which possible solutions exist. No valid bounded region exists. Adding the boundaries at $t = 0$ and $t = 1$, as shown in Fig. 4–26b, yields a bounded region between $t = \frac{3}{4}$ and $t = 1$. However, as shown by the cross-hatching, this region is not valid, because, for $t > \frac{3}{4}, h_j > 0$ is not satisfied for $j = 2$. Adding the boundary at $\alpha = 0$ also yields a valid bounded

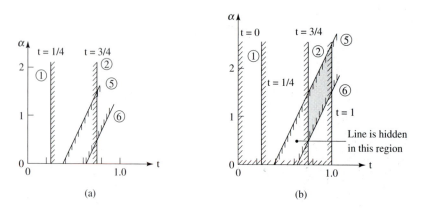

(a) (b)

Figure 4–26 Graphical solution for Ex. 4–11. (a) No solution; (b) adding $t = 1$ yields solution.

region, with solutions at $t = \frac{3}{8}$ and $t = \frac{5}{8}$. It is this region that yields $t_{\text{maxmin}} = \frac{3}{8}$ and $t_{\text{minmax}} = \frac{5}{8}$. Hence, the line is visible for

$$0 \le t \le \frac{3}{8} \quad \text{and} \quad \frac{3}{4} \le t \le 1$$

or for

$$P(0) = \begin{bmatrix} 1 & 0 & 2 & 1 \end{bmatrix} \quad \text{to} \quad P\left(\frac{3}{8}\right) = \begin{bmatrix} \frac{1}{4} & 0 & \frac{1}{2} & 1 \end{bmatrix}$$

and

$$P\left(\frac{5}{8}\right) = \begin{bmatrix} -\frac{1}{4} & 0 & -\frac{1}{2} & 1 \end{bmatrix} \quad \text{to} \quad P(1) = \begin{bmatrix} -1 & 0 & -2 & 1 \end{bmatrix}$$

The $\alpha = 0$ boundary solutions occur for penetrating (objects).

Penetrating Volumes

One technique for adding the lines at these penetrating junctures to the scene is to save all the penetrating points. Lines are formed by connecting each penetrating point in a pair of penetrating volumes to every other penetrating point in that pair of volumes. These lines are then tested against all remaining volumes; the visible lines are the juncture lines.

These examples show that solutions satisfying $h_j > 0$ also exist for the boundaries of the region described by $0 \le t \le 1$ and $\alpha \ge 0$. Thus, the three equations corresponding to these boundaries, i.e., $t = 0$, $t - 1 = 0$ and $\alpha = 0$, must be added to the solution set, $h_j = 0$. The number of solutions is now $(j + 2)(j + 3)/2$, where j is the number of planes describing a convex volume.

As previously mentioned, selecting the maximum minimum and the minimum maximum values of t from the possible valid solutions is a simple linear programming problem. Its solution is equivalent to identifying the valid bounded region for the graphical solutions shown in Figs. 4–22, 4–24 and 4–26. The flowchart in Fig. 4–27 provides a solution algorithm for the minimax problem. The algorithm is used only for lines that are known to be partially or totally hidden. All self-hidden lines and all totally visible lines are identified and eliminated before the algorithm is used. The algorithm is similar to that for the Cyrus–Beck clipping algorithm discussed in Sec. 3–5 (see Fig. 3–12). It is entered with t and α from the solution of the pair of linear equations numbered e_1 and e_2, t_{min} and t_{max} (the current minimum and maximum values of t), and with n (the number of equations in the solution set). The first part of the algorithm ensures that the condition $h_j > 0$ is satisfied. If this condition is satisfied, the second part looks for t_{min} and t_{max}. The result is t_{maxmin} and t_{minmax}.

Totally Visible Lines

The solution technique just discussed is computationally expensive, hence it is efficient to look for ways to quickly identify totally visible lines. The basic idea is to determine if both end points of a line lie between the eyepoint and a visible plane. Recall that

$$\mathbf{u} = \mathbf{s} + t\mathbf{d} + \alpha\mathbf{g}$$

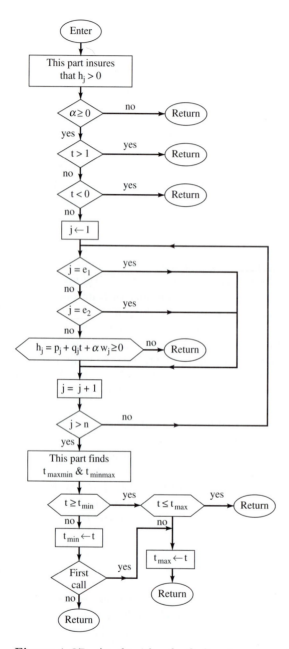

Figure 4–27   An algorithm for finding t_{maxmin} and t_{minmax} for the Roberts hidden line technique.

For $\alpha = 0$, **u** represents the line itself. Furthermore, if $\alpha = 0$, then $t = 0$ and $t = 1$ yield the end points of the line. Also recall that

$$h_j = \mathbf{u} \cdot [VT] = p_j + q_j t + w_j \alpha$$

and note that for $t = 0$, p_j is the dot product of the end point of the line and the jth plane of the volume. Similarly, $p_j + q_j$ is the dot product of the other end point of the line and the jth plane of the volume. Finally, recall that the jth plane of a volume is visible if $w_j \leq 0$. Thus, if $w_j \leq 0$ and $p_j \leq 0$, then one end point of the line is either on the visible plane or between the visible plane and the eyepoint. If $p_j + q_j \leq 0$, then the other end point is also either on the visible plane or between the plane and the eyepoint. Hence, the line is totally visible if for any j

$$w_j \leq 0 \qquad \text{and} \qquad p_j \leq 0 \qquad \text{and} \qquad p_j + q_j \leq 0$$

These conditions ensure that $h_j \leq 0$ cannot be satisfied for any $\alpha \leq 0$ and $0 \leq t \leq 1$. Thus, no part of the line can be hidden, and it is totally visible.

Example 4–12   Totally Visible Lines

For the origin-centered cube, consider the line from $P_1 [-2 \ \ 0 \ \ 2 \ \ 1]$ to $P_2 [2 \ 0 \ 2 \ 1]$ which, as shown in Fig. 4–28, passes in front of the cube. Here

$$\mathbf{v} = \mathbf{s} + \mathbf{d} = [-2 \ \ 0 \ \ 2 \ \ 1] + [4 \ \ 0 \ \ 0 \ \ 0] t$$

and with the eyepoint at infinity in the z direction

$$\mathbf{s} = [-2 \ \ 0 \ \ 2 \ \ 1]$$

$$\mathbf{d} = [4 \ \ 0 \ \ 0 \ \ 0]$$

$$\mathbf{g} = [0 \ \ 0 \ \ 1 \ \ 0]$$

For the untransformed cube, $[VT] = [V]$ and

$$
\begin{array}{rcccccccc}
 & & & ① & ② & ③ & ④ & ⑤ & ⑥ \\
p & = \mathbf{s} \cdot [VT] & = [& 5 & -3 & 1 & 1 & -3 & 5 \ ] \\
q & = \mathbf{d} \cdot [VT] & = [& -8 & 8 & 0 & 0 & 0 & 0 \ ] \\
w & = \mathbf{g} \cdot [VT] & = [& 0 & 0 & 0 & 0 & -2 & 2 \ ]
\end{array}
$$

Note that

$$w_5 < 0 \qquad \text{and} \qquad p_5 < 0 \qquad \text{and} \qquad p_5 + q_5 < 0$$

Thus, the line is totally visible.

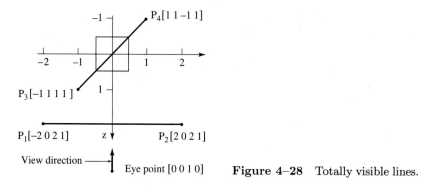

Figure 4–28   Totally visible lines.

As an example, consider the line from $P_3 [-1\ 1\ 1\ 1]$ to $P_4 [1\ 1\ -1\ 1]$, which passes diagonally above the cube and is also shown in Fig. 4–28. Here

$$\mathbf{s} = [-1 \quad 1 \quad 1 \quad 1]$$

$$\mathbf{d} = [\ 2 \quad 0 \quad -2 \quad 0]$$

$$\mathbf{g} = [0 \quad 0 \quad 1 \quad 0]$$

and

$$
\begin{array}{llll}
& & \ ①\ \ ②\ \ ③\ \ ④\ \ ⑤\ \ ⑥ \\
p & = \mathbf{s}\cdot[VT] & = [\ \ 3\ -1\ -1\ \ \ 3\ -1\ \ \ 3\ ] \\
q & = \mathbf{d}\cdot[VT] & = [-4\ \ \ 4\ \ \ 0\ \ \ 0\ \ \ 4\ -4\ ] \\
w & = \mathbf{g}\cdot[VT] & = [\ \ 0\ \ \ 0\ \ \ 0\ \ \ 0\ -2\ \ \ 2\ ]
\end{array}
$$

Note that

$$w_5 < 0 \qquad \text{and} \qquad p_5 < 0 \qquad \text{but} \qquad p_5 + q_5 > 0$$

However

$$w_3 = 0 \qquad \text{and} \qquad p_3 < 0 \qquad \text{and} \qquad p_3 + q_3 < 0$$

Again, the line is totally visible.

Although the top plane (plane 3) is 'edge-on' to an eyepoint at infinity on the z-axis, mathematically the line $P_3 P_4$ in Ex. 4–12 is between the eye and the visible plane. A similar condition occurs for the bottom and the two side planes.

Unfortunately, there is no easy test for totally invisible lines. It is, of course, possible to determine that the end points of a line are both behind a hidden plane. However, because the plane is of infinite extent, it is not possible to determine if the ends of the line extend beyond the volume (see Fig. 4–23). Totally invisible lines must be found using the general solution technique. In this case, the hidden portion is from $t = 0$ to $t = 1$.

We now give an efficient implementation of the Roberts algorithm.

The Algorithm

The algorithm is divided into three parts. The first part analyzes each volume separately, to eliminate the self-hidden planes. The second part compares the remaining edges of each volume against all the others, to find the line segments hidden by the others. The third part constructs the junction lines for penetrating volumes. The algorithm assumes that a volume consists of planar polygonal faces, the faces consist of edges and the edges consist of individual vertices. All vertices, edges and faces are associated with a specific volume.

Roberts hidden line algorithm

Eliminate the self-hidden planes.

For each volume in the scene:

Form face polygons and edges from the volume vertex list.

Calculate the plane equation for each face polygon of the volume.

Check the sign of the plane equation.

Calculate a point inside the volume as the average of the vertices.

Calculate the dot product of the plane equation and the point inside the volume.

If the dot product is < 0, change the sign of the plane equation.

Form the volume matrix.

Premultiply by the inverse of the viewing transformation, including perspective.

Calculate and save the bounding box values, x_{max}, x_{min}, y_{max}, y_{min}, z_{max}, z_{min}, for the transformed volume.

Identify the self-hidden planes.

Take the dot product of the test point, at infinity, and the transformed volume matrix.

If the dot product is < 0, then the plane is hidden.

Eliminate the entire polygon forming the plane; this eliminates the necessity for separately identifying hidden lines as the intersection of two hidden planes.

Eliminate the line segments for each volume hidden by all other volumes in the scene.

If there is only one volume, the algorithm is complete.

Form a priority list of the volumes.

Perform a z sort. Sort on the maximum z coordinate of the vertices of the transformed volumes. The first and highest priority volume on the sorted list is the one with minimum maximum z. In the right-hand coordinate system used, this is the farthest volume from an eyepoint at z infinity.

For each volume on the priority list:

Test the non-self-hidden edges against all other volumes in the scene. The volume whose edges are being tested is the test object; the volume against which it is currently being tested is the test volume. A test object normally need be tested only against lower priority test volumes.

Perform bounding box tests for the test object and the test volume.

if x_{min}(test volume) $> x_{max}$(test object) **or**

x_{max} (test volume) $< x_{min}$(test object) **or**

y_{min} (test volume) $> y_{max}$(test object) **or**

y_{max} (test volume) $< y_{min}$(test object)

then the test volumes cannot hide any edges of the test object; continue to the next test volume. Otherwise

Perform preliminary penetration tests to see if the test object penetrates the test volume and possibly obscures part of it.

Test the maximum z value of the test object against the minimum z value of the test volume.

if z_{max}(test object) $< z_{min}$ (test volume), **then** penetration is not possible; continue with the next volume. Otherwise

Test for visible penetration.

if z_{max}(test object) $> z_{max}$ (test volume), **then** the test object may penetrate the front face of the test volume.

Set the visible penetration flag for later use; place the penetrating volume on the penetration list.

if x_{max}(test object) $> x_{min}$(test volume) **or**

x_{min} (test object) $< x_{max}$(test volume)

then the test object may penetrate the side of the volume.

Set the visible penetration flag for later use; place the penetrating volume on the penetration list.

if y_{max}(test object) $> y_{max}$(test volume) **or**

y_{min}(test object) $< y_{min}$(test volume)

then the test object may penetrate the top or bottom of the test volume.

Set the visible penetration flag for later use; place the penetrating volume on the penetration list.

If the penetration list is empty, set the no penetration flag.

Perform edge tests.

Calculate **s** and **d** for the edge.

Calculate p, q, w for each plane of the test volume.

Test for total visibility; if the edge is totally visible, skip to the next edge.

Form the $h_j = 0$ equations and solve simultaneously in pairs, including the $t = 0$ and $t = 1$ boundaries. If the visible penetration flag is set, then include the $\alpha = 0$ boundary; save the penetrating points. Otherwise, ignore the $\alpha = 0$ boundary.

For each t, α solution check $0 \leq t \leq 1$, $\alpha \geq 0$ and $h_j > 0$ for all other planes; if these conditions are satisfied, find t_{maxmin} and t_{minmax}.

Calculate the visible line segments and save to test against lower priority volumes.

Determine visible junction lines for penetrating volumes.

If the visible penetration flag is not set, skip to the display routine.

If no penetrating points have been recorded, skip to the display routine.

Form possible junction edges by connecting all penetrating points for the two penetrating volumes.

Test all junction edges against both penetrating volumes for visibility.

Test the surviving visible junction edges against all volumes in the scene for visibility; save the visible segments.

Display remaining visible edge segments.

Note that the algorithm can also be implemented with a reverse priority list. This algorithm was used to produce the dimetric view of the three objects shown in Fig. 4–29.

Timing results for scenes similar to that shown in Fig. 4–30, with up to 1152 blocks, indicate a very nearly linear growth in computational expense with the number of blocks [Roge82]. Petty and Mach [Pett77] note a similar result for a Roberts algorithm implemented using Warnock-style area subdivision (see Sec. 4–4). The principal disadvantage of the Roberts algorithm is the requirement for convex volumes. Example 4–13 is a detailed illustrative example of this.

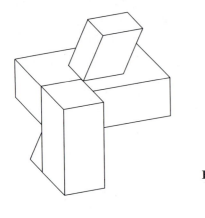

Figure 4–29 Hidden lines removed from a dimetric view of penetrating objects.

Example 4–13 Complete Roberts Algorithm

Consider the two intersecting blocks shown in Fig. 4–31. The blocks are described by these vertex point data bases:

Block 1				Block 2			
Vertex number	x	y	z	Vertex number	x	y	z
1	0	0	1	9	1	2	0
2	2	0	1	10	3	2	0
3	2	0	3	11	3	2	4
4	0	0	3	12	1	2	4
5	0	6	1	13	1	4	0
6	2	6	1	14	3	4	0
7	2	6	3	15	3	4	4
8	0	6	3	16	1	4	4

The vertex numbers are shown in Fig. 4–31a. The edge lists are:

Block 1		Block 2	
Edge	Joins vertices	Edge	Joins vertices
11	1–2	13	19–10
12	2–3	14	10–11
13	3–4	15	11–12
14	4–1	16	12–19
15	5–6	17	13–14
16	6–7	18	14–15
17	7–8	19	15–16
18	8–5	20	16–13
19	1–5	21	19–13
10	2–6	22	10–14
11	3–7	23	11–15
12	4–8	24	12–16

These edges are formed into face polygons for two blocks:

Block 1		Block 2	
Polygon number	Edges	Polygon number	Edges
1	2, 11, 6, 10	7	14, 23, 18, 22
2	4, 12, 8, 9	8	21, 20, 24, 16
3	5, 6, 7, 8	9	17, 18, 19, 20
4	1, 2, 3, 4	10	13, 14, 15, 16
5	3, 12, 7, 11	11	15, 24, 19, 23
6	1, 10, 5, 9	12	13, 22, 17, 21

The volume matrices for the blocks in the given orientation can be developed at this point, checked for correct sign by taking a point inside, and then transformed by premultiplying by the inverse of the viewing transformation. However, in this example we use the alternate approach of first transforming the volume vertex matrices by postmultiplying by the viewing transformation, and then determining the transformed plane equations and hence the transformed volume matrices.

Here, a viewing transformation, comprised of a $-30°$ rotation about the y-axis ($\phi = 30°$), followed by a $+15°$ rotation about the x-axis ($\theta = 15°$), is used. The combined transformation is (see [Roge90a])

$$[T] = [R_x][R_y] = \begin{bmatrix} \cos\phi & \sin\phi\sin\theta & -\sin\phi\cos\theta & 0 \\ 0 & \cos\theta & \sin\theta & 0 \\ \sin\phi & -\cos\phi\sin\theta & \cos\phi\cos\theta & 0 \\ 0 & 0 & 0 & 1 \end{bmatrix}$$

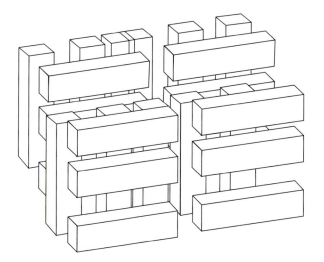

Figure 4–30   Test scene for the Roberts algorithm.

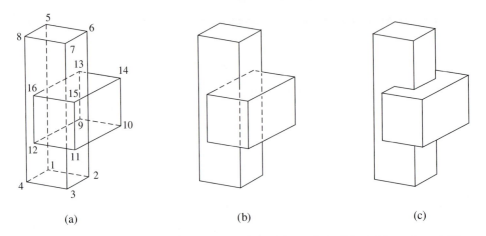

Figure 4–31 Penetrating blocks for Ex. 4–13. (a) Vertices; (b) visible surfaces with no penetration shown; (c) visible surfaces with penetration lines shown.

$$= \begin{bmatrix} 0.866 & -0.129 & 0.483 & 0 \\ 0.0 & 0.966 & 0.259 & 0 \\ -0.5 & -0.224 & 0.837 & 0 \\ 0.0 & 0.0 & 0.0 & 1 \end{bmatrix}$$

Transforming, the point data bases become

$$[PT_1] = [P_1][T] = \begin{bmatrix} -0.5 & -0.224 & 0.837 & 1 \\ 1.232 & -0.483 & 1.802 & 1 \\ 0.232 & -0.933 & 3.475 & 1 \\ -1.5 & -0.672 & 2.510 & 1 \\ -0.5 & 5.571 & 2.389 & 1 \\ 1.232 & 5.313 & 3.355 & 1 \\ 0.232 & 4.864 & 5.028 & 1 \\ -1.5 & 5.123 & 4.062 & 1 \end{bmatrix} \begin{matrix} 1 \\ 2 \\ 3 \\ 4 \\ 5 \\ 6 \\ 7 \\ 8 \end{matrix}$$

and

$$[PT_2] = [P_2][T] = \begin{bmatrix} 0.866 & 1.802 & 1.001 & 1 \\ 2.598 & 1.544 & 1.967 & 1 \\ 0.598 & 0.647 & 5.313 & 1 \\ -1.134 & 0.906 & 4.347 & 1 \\ 0.866 & 3.734 & 1.518 & 1 \\ 2.598 & 3.475 & 2.484 & 1 \\ 0.598 & 2.579 & 5.830 & 1 \\ -1.134 & 2.838 & 4.864 & 1 \end{bmatrix} \begin{matrix} 9 \\ 10 \\ 11 \\ 12 \\ 13 \\ 14 \\ 15 \\ 16 \end{matrix}$$

The plane equations for each of the faces of the two blocks in this orientation can be obtained by Newell's technique, as discussed previously. For example, the face described by polygon 1 uses the four vertices labeled 2, 3, 7, 6 in Fig. 4–31a. Newell's technique (see Ex. 4–3) using the transformed points yields the plane equation

$$-20.791x + 3.106y - 11.593z + 48.001 = 0$$

Rewriting this result to correspond to that obtained by transforming the volume matrix from the original orientation yields

$$-0.866x + 0.129y - 0.483z + 2 = 0$$

The transformed volume matrix in this form is then

$$[VT_1] = \begin{array}{cccccc} \textcircled{1} & \textcircled{2} & \textcircled{3} & \textcircled{4} & \textcircled{5} & \textcircled{6} \\ \begin{bmatrix} -0.866 & 0.866 & 0 & 0 & 0.5 & -0.5 \\ -0.483 & 0.483 & -0.259 & 0.259 & -0.837 & 0.837 \\ 2 & 0 & 6 & 0 & 3 & -1 \end{bmatrix} \end{array}$$

and similarly

$$[VT_2] = \begin{array}{cccccc} \textcircled{1} & \textcircled{2} & \textcircled{3} & \textcircled{4} & \textcircled{5} & \textcircled{6} \\ \begin{bmatrix} -0.866 & 0.866 & 0 & 0 & 0.5 & -0.5 \\ 0.129 & -0.129 & -0.966 & 0.966 & 0.224 & -0.224 \\ -0.483 & 0.483 & -0.259 & 0.259 & -0.837 & 0.837 \\ 3 & -1 & 4 & -2 & 4 & 0 \end{bmatrix} \end{array}$$

With the eyepoint at $[0\ 0\ 1\ 0]$, the test point is

$$[E] = [0 \quad 0 \quad -1 \quad 0]$$

Looking for the self-hidden planes in volume 1 yields

$$[E] \cdot [VT_1] = \begin{array}{cccccc} \textcircled{1} & \textcircled{2} & \textcircled{3} & \textcircled{4} & \textcircled{5} & \textcircled{6} \\ [\ 0.483 & -0.483 & 0.259 & -0.259 & 0.837 & -0.837\ ] \end{array}$$

Similarly, for volume 2

$$[E] \cdot [VT_2] = \begin{array}{cccccc} \textcircled{7} & \textcircled{8} & \textcircled{9} & \textcircled{10} & \textcircled{11} & \textcircled{12} \\ [\ 0.483 & -0.483 & 0.259 & -0.259 & 0.837 & -0.837\ ] \end{array}$$

The negative signs show that planes (polygons) 2, 4 and 6 in volume 1, and 8, 10 and 12 in volume 2, are self-hidden. Intersections of these polygons represent invisible edges. In particular, the edges 1, 4 and 9 in the first volume, and 13, 16 and 21 in the second volume, represent the intersection of two self-hidden planes and are thus hidden. The result is shown in Fig. 4–31b.

The remaining lines in each volume are checked to see if they are hidden by the other volume. First check if the volumes interpenetrate. Testing volume 1 against volume 2, using the transformed point vertices, shows that

$$(z_{max})_{vol.1} = 5.028 > (z_{min})_{vol.2} = 1.001$$

Hence, penetration is possible. Furthermore

$$(x_{max})_{vol.1} = 1.232 > (x_{min})_{vol.2} = -1.134$$

and penetration occurs. Thus, the $\alpha = 0$ boundary is included in the solution set.

The remaining edges of volume 1 are tested against volume 2. As a specific example, consider edge 2 between vertices 2 and 3. Here

$$\mathbf{v} = \mathbf{s} + \mathbf{d}t = [\,1.232 \quad -0.483 \quad 1.802 \quad 1\,] + [\,-1 \quad -0.45 \quad 1.673 \quad 0\,]\,t$$

Taking the dot product of $\mathbf{s}$ and $\mathbf{d}$ with $[\,VT_2\,]$ yields

$$
\begin{array}{ccccccc}
 & \text{①} & \text{②} & \text{③} & \text{④} & \text{⑤} & \text{⑥} \\
p = \mathbf{s} \cdot [\,VT_2\,] = [& 1 & 1 & 4 & -2 & 3 & 1\,]
\end{array}
$$

$$
\begin{array}{ccccccc}
 & \text{①} & \text{②} & \text{③} & \text{④} & \text{⑤} & \text{⑥} \\
q = \mathbf{d} \cdot [\,VT_2\,] = [& 0 & 0 & 0 & 0 & -2 & 3\,]
\end{array}
$$

For an eyepoint at positive infinity in the z direction

$$\mathbf{g} = [\,0 \quad 0 \quad 1 \quad 0\,]$$

and
$$
\begin{array}{ccccccc}
 & \text{①} & \text{②} & \text{③} & \text{④} & \text{⑤} & \text{⑥} \\
w = \mathbf{g} \cdot [\,VT_2\,] = [\,-0.483 & & 0.483 & -0.259 & 0.259 & -0.837 & 0.837\,]
\end{array}
$$

Checking to see if the line is totally visible shows that the conditions

$$w_j \le 0 \quad \text{and} \quad p_j \le 0 \quad \text{and} \quad p_j + q_j \le 0$$

are not satisfied for any plane, because the infinite plane containing the bottom (plane 4) of volume 2 could hide the edge. Forming the hidden edge conditions, h_j yields

$$
\begin{array}{lll}
\text{①} & 1 & -0.483\alpha \ge 0 \\
\text{②} & 1 & +0.483\alpha \ge 0 \\
\text{③} & 4 & -0.259\alpha \ge 0 \\
\text{④} & -2 & +0.259\alpha \ge 0 \\
\text{⑤} & 3 - 2t & -0.837\alpha \ge 0 \\
\text{⑥} & 1 + 2t & +0.837\alpha \ge 0
\end{array}
$$

Solving these equations successively in pairs shows that the condition $h_j \ge 0$ for all j cannot be met. Hence, no portion of the edge is hidden, and it is totally visible. The details of the remaining solutions for the edges of volume 1 hidden by volume 2 are given in Tables 4–5 and 4–6. Note that $\mathbf{g}$ and w are constant.

The solution diagrams for edges 10 and 11 are shown in Figs. 4–32a and 4–32b. Both edges penetrate volume 2. Edge 10 is hidden for $0.244 < t < 0.667$. This corresponds to the line from the point $[\,1.232 \quad 0.815 \quad 2.150\,]$ to the point $[\,1.232 \quad 3.381 \quad 2.837\,]$. Edge 11 is hidden for $0.282 < t < 0.667$, which corresponds to the line from $[\,0.232 \quad 0.703 \quad 3.913\,]$ to $[\,0.232 \quad 2.933 \quad 4.510\,]$.

Table 4-5

Edge	Joins vertices	s				d			
2	2 − 3	[1.232	−0.483	1.802	1]	[−1.0	−0.45	1.673	0]
3	3 − 4	[0.232	−0.931	3.46	1]	[−1.732	0.259	−0.966	0]
5	5 − 6	[−0.5	5.571	2.389	1]	[1.732	−0.259	0.966	0]
6	6 − 7	[1.232	5.313	3.355	1]	[−1.0	−0.448	1.673	0]
7	7 − 8	[0.232	4.864	5.028	1]	[−1.732	0.259	−0.966	0]
8	8 − 5	[−1.5	5.123	4.062	1]	[1.0	0.448	−1.673	0]
10	2 − 6	[1.232	−0.483	1.802	1]	[0.0	5.796	1.553	0]
11	3 − 7	[0.232	−0.931	3.475	1]	[0.0	5.796	1.553	0]
12	4 − 8	[−1.5	−0.672	2.510	1]	[0.0	5.796	1.553	0]

The $\alpha = 0$ boundary yields penetrating points at $t = 0.333$ and 0.667 for both edges. These values of t correspond to the points $[1.232\ 1.449\ 2.320]$ and $[1.232\ 3.381\ 2.837]$ for edge 10, and to the points $[0.232\ 1.001\ 3.993]$ and $[0.232\ 2.933\ 4.510]$ for edge 11. These four points are saved as penetration points.

Comparing the non-self-hidden edges of volume 2 against volume 1 yields the results shown in Tables 4–7 and 4–8. Edge 17 is partially hidden by volume 1.

Table 4–7

Edge	Joins vertices	s				d			
14	10 − 11	[2.598	1.544	1.967	1]	[−2.0	−0.897	3.346	0]
15	11 − 12	[0.598	0.647	5.313	1]	[−1.732	0.259	−0.966	0]
17	13 − 14	[0.866	3.734	1.518	1]	[1.732	−0.259	0.966	0]
18	14 − 15	[2.598	3.475	2.484	1]	[−2.0	−0.897	3.346	0]
19	15 − 16	[0.598	2.579	5.830	1]	[−1.732	0.259	−0.966	0]
20	16 − 13	[−1.134	2.838	4.864	1]	[2.0	0.897	−3.346	0]
22	10 − 14	[2.60	1.544	1.967	1]	[0	1.932	0.518	0]
23	11 − 15	[0.598	0.647	5.313	1]	[0	1.932	0.518	0]
24	12 − 16	[−1.134	0.906	4.347	1]	[0	1.932	0.518	0]

As shown in Fig. 4–32c, edge 17 is hidden from $0 \leq t < 0.211$, which corresponds to the line from $[0.866\ 3.734\ 1.518]$ to $[1.232\ 3.679\ 1.722]$. Edge 20 penetrates the front face (plane 5) of volume 1 at $t = 0.25$. Hence, it is hidden from $0.25 < t \leq 1.0$, which corresponds to the line from $[-0.634\ 3.062\ 4.28]$ to $[0.866\ 3.734\ 1.518]$. The solution region is shown in Fig. 4–32d. The point

Table 4–6

Edge	Joins vertices	p						q						Comment
2	2 – 3	[1	1	4	−2	3	1]	[0	0	0	0	−2	2]	Totally visible; full solution
3	3 – 4	[1	1	4	−2	1	3]	[2	−2	0	0	0	0]	Totally visible; full solution
5	5 – 6	[3	−1	−2	4	3	1]	[−2	2	0	0	0	0]	Totally visible; $w_3 < 0, p_3 < 0, p_3 + q_3 < 0$
6	6 – 7	[1	1	−2	4	3	1]	[0	0	0	0	−2	2]	Totally visible; $w_3 < 0, p_3 < 0, p_3 + q_3 < 0$
7	7 – 8	[1	1	−2	4	1	3]	[2	−2	0	0	0	0]	Totally visible; $w_3 < 0, p_3 < 0, p_3 + q_3 < 0$
8	8 – 5	[3	−1	−2	4	1	3]	[0	0	0	0	2	−2]	Totally visible; $w_3 < 0, p_3 < 0, p_3 + q_3 < 0$
10	2 – 6	[1	1	4	−2	3	1]	[0	0	−6	6	0	0]	Penetrating; hidden$0.244 < t < 0.667$; see Fig. 4–31a
11	3 – 7	[1	1	4	−2	1	3]	[0	0	−6	6	0	0]	Penetrating; hidden$0.282 < t < 0.667$; see Fig. 4–31b
12	4 – 8	[3	−1	4	−2	1	3]	[0	0	−6	6	0	0]	Totally visible; full solution

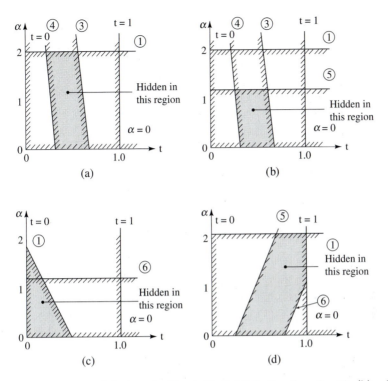

Figure 4–32 Solutions for Ex. 4–13. (a) Solution for edge 10; (b) solution for edge 11; (c) solution for edge 17; (d) solution for edge 20.

$[-0.634 \ 3.062 \ 4.028]$ is saved as a penetrating point. The solution region also shows that the point for $t = 0.75, \alpha = 0$ is a penetrating point. This value of t corresponds to the point $[0.366 \ 3.511 \ 2.355]$.

There are six penetrating points

$$[PP] = \begin{bmatrix} 1.232 & 1.449 & 2.320 & 1 \\ 1.232 & 3.381 & 2.837 & 1 \\ 0.232 & 1.001 & 3.993 & 1 \\ 0.232 & 2.933 & 4.510 & 1 \\ -0.634 & 3.062 & 4.028 & 1 \\ 0.366 & 3.511 & 2.355 & 1 \end{bmatrix} \begin{matrix} ⑰ \\ ⑱ \\ ⑲ \\ ⑳ \\ ㉑ \\ ㉒ \end{matrix}$$

Connecting each of these lines to each of the others in turn yields 30 possible junction lines. Each of these lines must be tested against each of the volumes. The large majority are invisible. By inspection, only the lines connecting points 18 and 20, and 20 and 21 are of interest. These lines are totally visible. In fact, they are the junction lines. The details of the complete solution are left as an exercise. The complete result is shown in Fig. 4–31c.

Table 4-8

Edge	Joins vertices	p	q	Comment
14	10 – 11	[-1 3 4 2 3 -1]	[0 0 0 -4 -4]	Totally visible; $w_1 < 0, p_1 < 0, p_1 + q_1 < 0$
15	11 – 12	[-1 3 4 2 -1 3]	[2 -2 0 0 0]	Totally visible; $w_5 < 0, p_5 < 0, p_5 + q_5 < 0$
17	13 – 14	[1 1 2 4 3 -1]	[-2 2 0 0 0]	Partially hidden; $0 \le t < 0.211$
18	14 – 15	[-1 3 2 4 3 -1]	[0 0 0 -4 -4]	Totally visible; $w_1 < 0, p_1 < 0, p_1 + q_1 < 0$
19	15 – 16	[-1 3 2 4 -1 3]	[2 -2 0 0 0]	Totally visible; $w_5 < 0, p_5 < 0, p_5 + q_5 < 0$
20	16 – 13	[1 1 2 4 -1 3]	[0 0 0 4 -4]	Penetrating, hidden; $0.25 < t \le 1.0$
22	10 – 14	[-1 3 4 2 3 -1]	[0 0 -2 2 0]	Totally visible; $w_1 < 0, p_1 < 0, p_1 + q_1 < 0$
23	11 – 15	[-1 3 4 2 -1 3]	[0 0 0 2 0]	Totally visible; $w_1 < 0, p_1 < 0, p_1 + q_1 < 0$
24	12 – 16	[1 1 4 2 -1 3]	[0 0 -2 2 0]	Totally visible; $w_5 < 0, p_5 < 0, p_5 + q_5 < 0$

4–4   Warnock Algorithm

The basic ideas behind the Warnock algorithm are very general. They are, by analogy, based on an hypothesis of how the human eye–brain combination processes information contained in a scene. The hypothesis is that very little time or effort is expended on areas that contain little information. The majority of the time and effort is spent on areas of high information content. As an example, consider an otherwise empty table top with a bowl of fruit on it. The color, texture, etc., of the entire table top require minimal time to perceive. Attention is focused on the fruit bowl. Where on the table is it located? How large is it? What kind of bowl: wooden, ceramic, plastic, glass, metal? What color bowl: red, blue, silver, dull, glossy, etc.? What kind of fruit does it contain: peaches, grapes, pears, bananas, apples? What color apples: red, yellow, green? Does the apple have a stem? In each case the area of interest narrows, and the level of detail sought increases. Furthermore, if at a particular level a specific question cannot be answered immediately, it is temporarily put aside for later consideration. Fundamentally, this is a divide and conquer strategy.

The Warnock algorithm and its derivatives attempt to take advantage of the fact that large areas of a display are similar, e.g., the table top in the previous paragraph. This characteristic is known as *area coherence*; i.e., adjacent areas (pixels) in both the x and y directions tend to be similar.

The Warnock algorithm considers a window (or area) in image (or object) space, and seeks to determine if the window is empty or if the contents of the window are simple enough to resolve. If not, the window is subdivided until either the contents of a subwindow are simple enough to determine, or the subwindow size is at the limit of desired resolution. In the latter case, the remaining information in the window is evaluated. If an object space implementation is required, the precision information is written to a file for further processing. If only image space precision is required, the result is displayed at a single intensity or color. For an image space implementation, antialiasing is incorporated by carrying the subdivision process to less than display pixel resolution and averaging the subpixel attributes to determine the display pixel attributes (see Sec. 2–16).

Specific implementations of the Warnock algorithm vary, in the method of subdividing the window, and in the details of the criteria used to decide whether the contents are simple enough to display directly. In Warnock's original presentation of the algorithm [Warn68, 69a, 69b], each window is subdivided into four equal subwindows. This implementation of the algorithm, and a common variation allowing for subdivision of the window at polygon boundaries, are discussed in the present section. Another variation that subdivides the window into polygonal windows, developed by Weiler and Atherton [Weil77], is discussed in Sec. 4–7. Catmull [Catm74, 75] has also applied the basic subdivision concept to the display of curved surfaces. This technique is discussed in Sec. 4–8.

Figure 4–33 illustrates the progress of the simplest implementation of the Warnock algorithm in image space. Here, a window that is too complicated to display is subdivided into four equal windows. Also, a window that contains

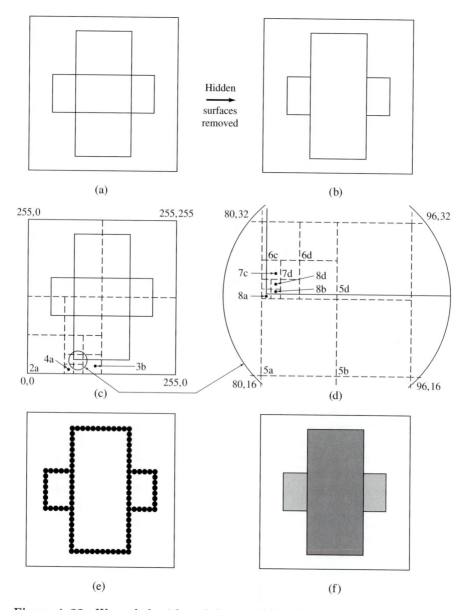

Figure 4–33   Warnock algorithm subdivision. (a) Original surface; (b) hidden surfaces removed; (c) and (d) subdivision process; (e) result for hidden line algorithm; (f) result for hidden/visible surface algorithm.

anything is always subdivided until the resolution of the display is reached. Figure 4–33a shows a scene composed of two simple polygons. Figure 4–33b shows the result with the hidden surfaces removed. Notice that the horizontal rectangle is partially hidden by the vertical rectangle. Figures 4–33c and 4–33d show the process of subdivision for a display resolution of 256×256. Since $2^8 = 256$, a maximum of eight subdivisions are required to reach the resolution of the display. If the subwindows are considered in the order lower left, lower right, upper left, upper right, then the subwindows of level 1a, labeled 2a, 4a, 4b, 4c, 5a, 5b, are declared empty and are displayed at the background intensity during the course of the subdivision. Here, the number indicates the subdivision level, and the letter the quadrant. The first subwindow examined at pixel level that contains a feature of interest is the one labeled 8a. At this point it is necessary to decide whether a visible line or a visible surface algorithm is desired. If a visible line algorithm is desired, then the pixel corresponding to subwindow 8a is activated, because a visible edge passes through it. The result is to display the visible edges of the polygons as a series of pixel-sized dots, as shown in Fig. 4–33e.

Subsequent consideration of the window labeled 8d in Fig. 4–33d best illustrates the difference between implementation as a visible line and as a visible surface algorithm. For a visible line algorithm, the pixel-sized window, 8d, does not contain any polygon edges. Therefore, it is declared empty and displayed at the background intensity or color. For a visible surface algorithm, the pixel-sized window, 8d, is examined to see if it is surrounded by any of the polygons in the scene. If it is, all the polygons surrounding the pixel are tested to see which one is closer to the eyepoint at this pixel location. The test is performed at the pixel center. The pixel is then displayed at the intensity or color of the closest polygon. If no surrounding polygons are found, the pixel-sized window is empty. Thus, it is displayed at the background color or intensity. The pixel-sized window labeled 8d is surrounded by the vertical rectangle; thus, it is displayed at the color or intensity for that rectangle. The result is shown in Fig. 4–33f.

The addition of antialiasing to the visible surface algorithm is illustrated by reconsidering window 8a in Fig. 4–33d. Subdividing this window yields four subpixel-sized windows. Only one of these windows, the upper right-hand one, is surrounded by the polygon; the other three are empty. Averaging the results for the four subpixels (see Sec. 2–16) shows that the pixel-sized window, 8a, should be displayed at one-quarter the intensity of the rectangle. Similarly, the pixel labeled 8b is displayed at half the intensity of the rectangle. The pixel-sized windows can, of course, be subdivided more than once to allow for weighted averaging of the subpixel characteristics, as discussed in Sec. 2–16.

Quadtree Data Structure

The subdivision process yields a tree structure for the subwindows, as shown in Fig. 4–34.[†] The root of the tree is the display window. Each node represented

---

[†]Warnock's algorithm is the first known implementation of a quadtree data structure.

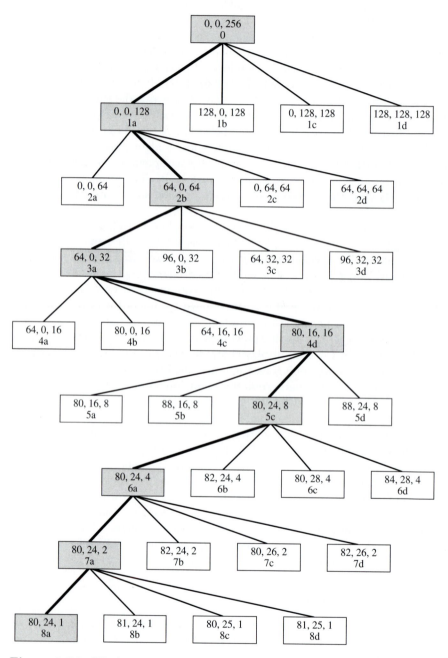

Figure 4–34 Window quadtree structure.

by the box contains the coordinates of the lower left-hand corner and the length of the side of the subwindow. Assuming that subdivided windows are processed in the order *abcd*, i.e., from left to right at a particular subdivision level in the tree, then Fig. 4–34 shows the active path through the tree structure to the pixel-sized window labeled 8a. The active node at each level is indicated by a heavy line. Examination of Figs. 4–33 and 4–34 shows that, at a particular level, all windows to the left of the active node are empty. Thus, they have been previously displayed at the background color or intensity. All windows to the right of the active node at a particular level remain to be processed, i.e., declared empty or subdivided, as the tree is traversed in the reverse direction.

Subdivision Criteria

The preceding algorithm is sufficient to solve either the visible line or visible surface problem. However, both the simplicity of the subdivision criteria and the rigidity of the subdivision algorithm maximize the number of subdivisions. The algorithm is made more efficient by using both more complex subdivision algorithms and more complex subdivision criteria. Figure 4–35a illustrates one common alternate subdivision algorithm and compares it to the previous fixed subdivision algorithm, as shown in Fig. 4–35b.

The subdivisions shown in Fig. 4–35a are obtained by using the bounding box of the polygon. Note that the subwindows are not necessarily square. The algorithm is recursively applied to any polygon wholly contained within the window or subwindow. If only a single polygon exists within the window, and if it is wholly contained within the window, then it is easy to display that polygon without further subdivision. A subdivision algorithm such as the one described here is particularly useful in minimizing the number of subdivisions for simple scenes such as is shown in Fig. 4–35. However, as the scene complexity increases, its advantage decreases.

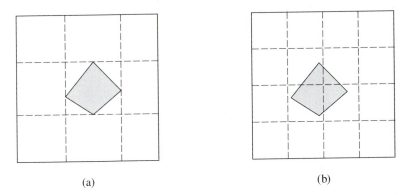

(a)   (b)

Figure 4–35   Comparison of subdivision algorithms. (a) Complex subdivision using polygon boundary box; (b) fixed subdivision.

When considering more complex subdivision criteria, it is convenient to define the relationship of several types of polygons to a window. In particular, a polygon is

disjoint if it is totally outside the window

contained if it is totally inside the window

intersecting if it intersects the window

surrounding if it completely contains the window

An example of each of these polygon types is shown in Fig. 4–36. Using these definitions, decision criteria are applied to a window. Assembled into an algorithm, they yield:

For each window:

If all the polygons in the scene are disjoint from the window, then the window is empty; it is displayed at the background intensity or color without further subdivision.

If only a single polygon is contained within the window, the area of the window outside the polygon is filled with the background intensity or color; and the polygon is filled with the appropriate intensity or color.

If a single polygon intersects the window, the area of the window outside the polygon is filled with the background intensity or color; and the portion of the intersecting polygon within the window is filled with the appropriate intensity or color.

If the window is surrounded by a single polygon, and if there are no other polygons in the window, then the window is filled with the intensity or color appropriate for the surrounding polygon.

If at least one surrounding polygon is found, and if it is the polygon closest to the eye, then the window is filled with the intensity or color appropriate for the surrounding polygon.

Otherwise, subdivide the window.

The first four of these criteria deal with the relationship of single polygons to the window. They are used to reduce the number of subdivisions. The last criterion is the key to the visible surface problem. It attempts to find a single

| Disjoint | Contained | Intersecting | Surrounding |

Figure 4–36   Polygon types.

surrounding polygon that is closer to the eye then any other polygon in the window. Obviously, this surrounding polygon obscures or hides all the other polygons in the window. Thus, it represents the visible feature in the scene for this window.

The Relationship of a Polygon to a Window

Implementing these decision criteria requires techniques for determining whether a polygon is disjoint from, contained within, intersects or surrounds a window. For rectangular windows, bounding box or minimax tests are used to determine whether a polygon is disjoint from a window (see Secs. 2–13 and 3–2). In particular, if x_L, x_R, y_B, y_T define the four edges of a window and $x_{min}, x_{max}, y_{min}, y_{max}$ the bounding box surrounding a polygon, then the polygon is disjoint from the window if any of the conditions

$$x_{min} > x_R$$

$$x_{max} < x_L$$

$$y_{min} > y_T$$

$$y_{max} < y_B$$

is satisfied, as shown in Fig. 4–37a. Furthermore, the polygon is contained within the window if the bounding box is contained within the window, i.e., if

$$x_{min} \geq x_L \quad \text{and} \quad x_{max} \leq x_R \quad \text{and} \quad y_{min} \geq y_B \quad \text{and} \quad y_{max} \leq y_T$$

as shown in Fig. 4–37b.

Example 4–14   Disjoint and Contained Polygons

Consider a square window with edges x_L, x_R, y_B, y_T equal to $0, 32, 0, 32$. Two polygons, the first with vertices $P_1(36, 8)$, $P_2(48, 24)$ and $P_3(56, 4)$, and the second with vertices $P_1(8, 4)$, $P_2(12, 24)$ and $P_3(24, 12)$, as shown in Fig. 4–37a, are to be tested against this window.

The bounding box for the first polygon, $x_{min}, x_{max}, y_{min}, y_{max}$, is $36, 56, 4, 24$. Since

$$(x_{min} = 36) > (x_R = 32)$$

the polygon is disjoint from the window.

Similarly, the bounding box for the second polygon, $x_{min}, x_{max}, y_{min}, y_{max}$, is $8, 24, 4, 24$, as shown in Fig. 4–37b. Here the condition

$$(x_{min} = 8) > (x_L = 0) \quad \text{and} \quad (x_{max} = 24) < (x_R = 32) \quad \text{and}$$

$$(y_{min} = 4) > (y_B = 0) \quad \text{and} \quad (y_{max} = 24) < (y_T = 32)$$

is satisfied, hence the polygon is contained within the window.

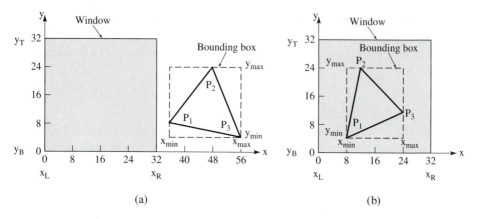

Figure 4–37 Boxing tests for disjoint and contained polygons. (a) Disjoint; (b) contained.

A simple substitution test is used to determine if a polygon intersects a window. The coordinates of the window vertices are substituted into a test function formed from the equation of the line defining a polygon edge (see Sec. 3–19 and Ex. 3–28). If the sign of the test function is the same for each window vertex, then all the vertices lie on the same side of the line and there is no intersection. If the signs are different, then the polygon intersects the window. If none of the polygon edges intersects the window, the polygon is either disjoint or surrounds the window. If the equation of the line through two polygon vertices $P_1(x_1, y_1)$ and $P_2(x_2, y_2)$ is $y = mx + b$, then the test function is

$$T.F. = y - mx - b$$

where
$$m = \frac{y_2 - y_1}{x_2 - x_1} \qquad x_2 - x_1 \neq 0$$

$$b = y_1 - mx_1$$

and
$$T.F. = x - x_1 \qquad x_2 - x_1 = 0$$

An example illustrates the technique.

Example 4–15   Intersecting Polygons

Consider the square window with x_L, x_R, y_B, y_T equal to $8, 32, 8, 32$, and the two polygons with vertices $P_1(8, 4)$, $P_2(12, 24)$ and $P_3(40, 12)$, and $P_1(4, 4)$, $P_2(4, 36)$, $P_3(40, 36)$ and $P_4(32, 4)$, as shown in Fig. 4–38. The test function for the polygon edge $P_1 P_2$ in Fig. 4–38a is obtained from

$$m = \frac{y_2 - y_1}{x_2 - x_1} = \frac{24 - 4}{12 - 8} = \frac{20}{4} = 5$$

$$b = y_1 - mx_1 = 4 - 5(8) = -36$$

$$T.F. = y - mx - b = y - 5x + 36$$

Substituting the coordinates of each window corner into the test function yields

$$T.F.(8,8) = 8 - 5(8) + 36 = 4$$
$$T.F.(8,32) = 32 - 5(8) + 36 = 28$$
$$T.F.(32,32) = 32 - 5(32) + 36 = -92$$
$$T.F.(32,8) = 8 - 5(32) + 36 = -116$$

Since the test function changes sign, the polygon edge intersects the window edge, as shown in Fig. 4–38a. Hence, the polygon is an intersector; there is no need to check the other polygon edges.

Table 4-9

Polygon edge	Test function	Window coordinates	Test function result	Comment
P_1P_2	$x - 4$	$(8,8)$	4	Nonintersecting
		$(8,32)$	4	
		$(32,32)$	28	
		$(32,8)$	28	
P_2P_3	$y - 36$	$(8,8)$	-28	Nonintersecting
		$(8,32)$	-4	
		$(32,32)$	-4	
		$(32,8)$	-28	
P_3P_4	$y - 4x + 124$	$(8,8)$	100	Nonintersecting
		$(8,32)$	124	
		$(32,32)$	28	
		$(32,8)$	4	
P_4P_1	$y - 4$	$(8,8)$	4	Nonintersecting
		$(8,32)$	28	
		$(32,32)$	28	
		$(32,8)$	4	

The results for the polygon shown in Fig. 4–38b are given in Table 4–9. None of the polygon edges intersects the window, hence the polygon is either disjoint or a surrounder. Figure 4–38b shows that it is a surrounder.

The simple bounding box test discussed above does not identify all disjoint polygons, e.g., a polygon that encloses a corner of the window, as shown in Fig. 4–39a. More complex tests are required. Two are of particular interest,

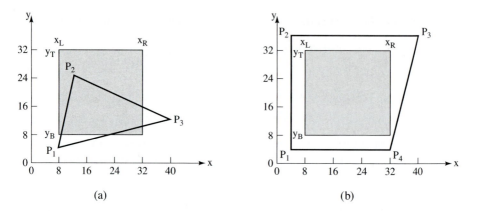

(a) (b)

Figure 4–38 Intersection tests. (a) Intersector; (b) surrounder.

the infinite line test and the angle counting test. Both assume that intersecting and contained polygons were previously identified. Both can be used to identify disjoint and surrounding polygons.

For the infinite line test, a line is drawn from any part of the window, e.g., a corner, to infinity. The number of intersections of the line and the polygon of interest are counted. If the number is even (or zero), the polygon is disjoint; if odd, the polygon surrounds the window, as shown in Fig. 4–39a. If the line passes through a vertex of the polygon, as shown in Fig. 4–39b, uncertainty results. This uncertainty is resolved by counting two intersections at a concave vertex (P_2 in Fig. 4–39b) and only one at a convex vertex (P_4 in Fig. 4–39b) (see also Sec. 2–10). Changing the slope or direction of the line also eliminates the uncertainty. For example, first choose a horizontal line extending to the right for

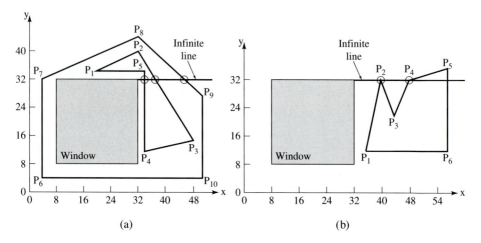

(a) (b)

Figure 4–39 Surrounding polygon test. (a) Unambiguous test; (b) ambiguous test when the line passes through a vertex.

the selected vertex. If this line intersects another polygon vertex, choose a horizontal line to the left, or a vertically upward or downward line, or a line at 45°, etc. Haines [Hain89] and Forrest [Forr85] give further implementation details.

The angle counting or winding number test is illustrated in Fig. 4–40. Proceeding either clockwise or counterclockwise around the polygon, the angles formed between lines from any point in the window to the initial and final vertices of a polygon edge are summed. As shown in Fig. 4–40, the center of the window is a convenient point. The sum of these angles is interpreted as:

$$\text{Sum} = 0 \qquad \text{the polygon is disjoint from the window.}$$
$$\text{Sum} = \pm 360n \quad \text{the polygon surrounds the window } n \text{ times.}$$

The actual determination of the sum is considerably simplified by realizing that the precision of the individual angle calculations need not be high. In fact, sufficient precision is obtained by counting only the whole octants (45° increments) subtended by the individual angles, as shown in Fig. 4–41. The implementation is similar to that for the line end point codes used for clipping (see Sec. 3–1). Here, the octant regions are numbered 0 to 7, counterclockwise. The number of whole octants subtended is obtained by taking the difference between the region numbers of the polygon edge end points and applying the algorithm

$$\Delta\alpha = \text{second end point region number } - \text{ first end point region number:}$$

$$\text{if } \Delta\alpha > 4 \quad \text{then } \Delta\alpha = \Delta\alpha - 8$$
$$\text{if } \Delta\alpha < -4 \text{ then } \Delta\alpha = \Delta\alpha + 8$$
$$\text{if } \Delta\alpha = 0 \quad \text{then the polygon edge is split at a window edge, and}$$
$$\text{the process is repeated with the two segments.}$$

Summing the individual polygon edge contributions yields

$$\sum\Delta\alpha \ = 0 \qquad \text{the polygon is disjoint from the window.}$$
$$= \pm 8n \ \text{the polygon surrounds the window.}$$

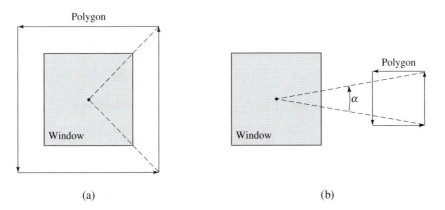

(a)   (b)

Figure 4–40 Angle counting test. (a) Surrounding polygon; (b) intersecting polygon.

Example 4–16   Angle Test for Surrounding and Disjoint Polygons

Consider the window and the polygons shown in Fig. 4–41. For the polygon shown in Fig. 4–41a, the number of octants subtended by the edge $P_1 P_2$ is

$$\Delta\alpha_{12} = 2 - 7 = -5 < -4$$

$$= -5 + 8 = 3$$

Similarly, for the remaining polygon edges

$$\Delta\alpha_{23} = 3 - 2 = 1$$

$$\Delta\alpha_{34} = 5 - 3 = 2$$

$$\Delta\alpha_{41} = 7 - 5 = 2$$

The sum of the angles subtended by all the polygon edges is

$$\sum\Delta\alpha = 3 + 1 + 2 + 2 = 8$$

Thus, the polygon surrounds the window.

For the polygon shown in Fig. 4–41b

$$\Delta\alpha_{12} = 1 - 7 = -6 < -4$$

$$= -6 + 8 = 2$$

$$\Delta\alpha_{23} = 2 - 1 = 1$$

$$\Delta\alpha_{34} = 0 - 2 = -2$$

$$\Delta\alpha_{45} = 6 - 0 = 6 > 4$$

$$= 6 - 8 = -2$$

$$\Delta\alpha_{51} = 7 - 6 = 1$$

and $$\sum\Delta\alpha = 2 + 1 - 2 - 2 + 1 = 0$$

Thus, the polygon is disjoint from the window.

Hierarchical Application of Polygon–Window Relations

A hierarchical application of these techniques based on the computational work involved is advantageous. If only the simplest image space Warnock algorithm is implemented, then it is not necessary to identify either contained or intersecting polygons. Subdivision eventually makes contained or intersecting polygons either disjoint or surrounding polygons. Any remaining conflicts are resolved at the pixel level. For this simple algorithm, only the bounding box test need be used to identify empty windows. If this simple test fails, the algorithm subdivides the

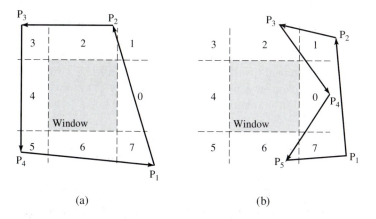

Figure 4-41   Angle test for disjoint and surrounding polygons.   (a) Surrounding polygon; (b) disjoint polygon.

window until the pixel level is reached. Because even at the pixel level a disjoint polygon of the form shown in Fig. 4–41b can exist, it is necessary to apply a more rigorous algorithm to determine if the window is empty or surrounded by one or more polygons.

The more complex algorithm discussed here attempts to identify contained, intersector, more complex disjoint polygons, and surrounding polygons for larger windows in order to avoid subdivision. These tests require more work. Hence, there is a tradeoff between the work associated with subdivision and the work associated with early identification of displayable windows. A more complex algorithm might implement the tests at each window in this order:

> The simple bounding box test for identifying most empty windows and windows with a single contained polygon: these windows are immediately displayed.
>
> The simple intersector test for identifying windows with a single intersecting polygon. The polygon is clipped and displayed; for example, the polygon in Fig. 4–35b is displayed after one subdivision.
>
> The more complex disjoint and surrounder tests for identifying additional empty windows, and windows with a single surrounding polygon: these windows are immediately displayed.

At this point, either subdivision occurs, or an attempt is made to find a single surrounding polygon that is closer to the eyepoint than any other polygon. If subdivision occurs, this question is delayed until the pixel level. In either case, a depth calculation is required.

Finding Surrounder Polygons

The depth calculation is performed by comparing the depth (z coordinate) of the planes of the polygons at the window corners. If the depth of a surrounding polygon is greater than the depth of all other polygons at the corners of the window, then the surrounding polygon hides all the other polygons in the window. Hence, the window is displayed at the intensity or color of the surrounding polygon. Note that this is a sufficient, but not a necessary, condition for a surrounding polygon to hide all other polygons in the window. Figure 4–42 illustrates that extending the plane of a polygon to intersect the window corners may result in failure to identify a surrounding polygon that hides all others in the window.

In particular, if an extended polygon is hidden by a surrounding polygon at the window corners, then the polygon itself is hidden by the surrounding polygon (as seen in Fig. 4–42). If an extended polygon is not hidden by the surrounding polygon, it is not obvious whether the polygon itself is hidden or not (see b in Fig. 4–42). The conflict is resolved by subdividing the window.

The depth of an extended polygon at the window corners is obtained from the plane equations for the polygons (see Sec. 4–3 and Ex. 4–3). For example, if the plane equation is

$$ax + by + cz + d = 0$$

and the window corner coordinates are x_w, y_w, then

$$z = \frac{-(d + ax_w + by_w)}{c} \qquad c \neq 0$$

yields the depth of the extended polygon at the window corner.

This discussion assumes that every polygon is compared to every window. For complex scenes, this is very inefficient. The efficiency of the algorithm is improved by performing a depth priority sort (z sort). The sort order of the polygons is based on the z coordinate of the polygon vertex nearest the eyepoint. In a right-hand coordinate system, the polygon with the maximum z coordinate value for its nearest vertex is closest to the eyepoint. This polygon appears first on the sorted polygon list.

When processing each window, the algorithm looks for surrounding polygons. When a surrounding polygon is found, its vertex farthest from the eye

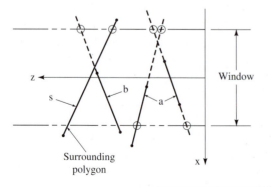

Figure 4–42 Depth comparisons for surrounding polygons.

is remembered as z_{smin}. As each successive polygon on the list is considered, the z coordinate value of its nearest vertex, z_{pmax}, is compared to z_{smin}. If $z_{pmax} < z_{smin}$, then clearly this polygon is hidden by the surrounding polygon and is not considered further. Figure 4–42 illustrates that this is a sufficient, but not a necessary, condition; e.g., the polygon labeled a in Fig. 4–42 is not considered further, but the polygon labeled b is.

The size of the list of polygons processed for each window is reduced by taking advantage of information about the polygon obtained earlier in the algorithm. In particular, if a polygon surrounds a window, then clearly it surrounds all subwindows of that window and need not be processed further. In addition, if a polygon is disjoint from a window, then it is disjoint from all subwindows of that window and need not be considered when processing those subwindows. Only intersector and contained polygons from the previous window need be processed further.

To take advantage of this information, three lists are used: one for surrounding polygons, one for disjoint polygons and one for intersecting and contained polygons (see [Warn69a, 69b]). As the subdivision progresses, polygons are added or removed from the appropriate list. The level at which a polygon is first added to a particular list is retained. This information is used when the tree in Fig. 4–34 is traversed in the reverse direction. At each subdivision level, the surrounding polygon list is processed first to find the closest surrounding polygon. The intersector/contained polygon list is then processed to see if the surrounding polygon hides all the intersector and contained polygons. The disjoint polygon list is ignored.

The Basic Algorithm

The underlying concept and a number of possible enhancements of the Warnock algorithm have been discussed. It should be clear that no single Warnock algorithm exists. The implementation details vary from algorithm to algorithm. A pseudocode implementation of the most basic algorithm in image space is given here. In the algorithm given here, if the window size is greater than the display resolution and contains any feature of interest, the algorithm always subdivides the window. For windows greater than pixel size, a simple bounding box test is used to identify disjoint polygons. For pixel-sized windows, a more sophisticated test is used that determines the visible polygon by examining the z coordinate of each polygon at the center of the pixel. No depth priority sort is used, nor is advantage taken of prior information about window-polygon relationships. The algorithm is implemented using a pushdown stack. The maximum stack length is

$$3 \text{ (screen resolution in bits} - 1) + 5$$

This simple algorithm is sufficient to demonstrate the principle without becoming submerged in data structures. For convex polygonal volumes, a backplane cull (see Sec. 4–2) is performed before passing polygons to the algorithm. A flowchart is shown in Fig. 4–43.

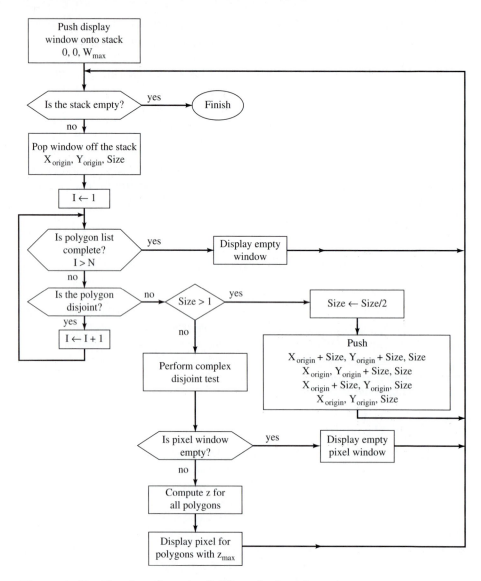

Figure 4–43   Flowchart for a simple Warnock algorithm.

a simple implementation of the Warnock algorithm

a square display window is assumed
if there is anything in a window, the algorithm always subdivides
the window is subdivided into four equal-sized square windows
every polygon is compared with every window
all data are assumed transformed to display window
  (image space) coordinates

an initial backplane cull is assumed prior to entering the algorithm

Vertex *is an* $m \times 3$ *array containing the* x,y,z *coordinates of each polygon vertex.*

m *is the total number of polygon vertices in the scene; the vertices are assumed specified in clockwise order*

N *is the number of polygons in the scene*

Polygon *is an* $N \times 11$ *array containing information about individual polygons*

Polygon(,1) *is a pointer to the location of the first polygon vertex in the* Vertex *array*

Polygon(,2) *is the number of vertices for the polygon*

Polygon(,3) *is the intensity or color associated with the polygon*

Polygon(,4–7) *contain the coefficients of the plane equation, a,b,c,d, for the polygon*

Polygon(,8–11) *contain the bounding box values,* $x_{min}, x_{max}, y_{min}, y_{max}$, *for the polygon*

Push *is a function that places windows on a pushdown stack*

Pop *is a function that removes windows from a pushdown stack*

Wmax *is the maximum* x *and* y *extent of the window; the origin of the display window is assumed at* $(0, 0)$.

Window *is a* 1×3 *array containing the current window origin and size as* Window(Xorigin, Yorigin, Size)

Disjoint *is a flag,*

> $= 0$ *for empty windows*
> ≥ 1 *for nonempty windows*

> *initialize the background color to black*

> Background $= 0$

> *push the display window onto the stack*

> **Push** Window$(0, 0, \text{Wmax})$
> **while** (stack not empty)

>> *get a window from the stack*

>> **Pop**Window(Xorigin, Yorigin, Size)

>> *initialize polygon counter*

>> i $= 1$
>> Disjoint $= 0$

>> *for each polygon, perform a bounding box test to find disjoint polygons*

>> **while** (i $\leq$ N **and** Disjoint $= 0$)
>>> **call** Box(i, Polygon, Window; Disjoint)
>>> i $= i + 1$
>> **end while**

       if at least one polygon is not disjoint, subdivide or display pixel
      if Disjoint > 0 **then**

          if window is not pixel size, subdivide
          if Size > 1 **then**
              Size $=$ Size$/2$
              Push Window(Xorigin $+$ Size, Yorigin $+$ Size, Size)
              Push Window(Xorigin, Yorigin $+$ Size, Size)
              Push Window(Xorigin $+$ Size, Yorigin, Size)
              Push Window(Xorigin, Yorigin, Size)
          else

              if window is pixel-sized, calculate attributes
              call Cover(Vertex, N, Polygon, Window; Pnumber)
              if Pnumber > 0 **then**
                  call Display(Window, Polygon(Pnumber, 3))
              else

                  display the empty window
                  call Display(Window, Background)
              end if
          end if
      else
          call Display(Window, Background)
      end if
    end while
finish

subroutine to perform a simple bounding box test
subroutine Box(i, Polygon, Window; Disjoint)

    calculate Xleft, Xright, Ybottom, Ytop

    Xleft $=$ Window$(1, 1)$
    Xright $=$ Window$(1, 1) +$ Window$(1, 3) - 1$
    Ybottom $=$ Window$(1, 2)$
    Ytop $=$ Window$(1, 2) +$ Window$(1, 3) - 1$

    perform bounding box tests

    Disjoint $= 1$
    if Polygon$(i, 8) >$ Xright **then** Disjoint $= 0$
    if Polygon$(i, 9) <$ Xleft **then** Disjoint $= 0$
    if Polygon$(i, 10) >$ Ytop **then** Disjoint $= 0$
    if Polygon$(i, 11) <$ Ybottom **then** Disjoint $= 0$
return

subroutine to display a window

subroutine Display(Window, Intensity)

Setpixel(x, y, I)*sets a pixel at coordinates* x,y *to the intensity* I

    for j = Window(1, 2) **to** Window(1, 2) + Window(1, 3) − 1

        for i = Window(1, 1) **to** Window(1, 1) + Window(1, 3) − 1

            Setpixel(i, j, Intensity)

        next i

    next j

return

subroutine to check if a polygon covers the center of a window

subroutine Cover(Vertex, N, Polygon, Window; Pnumber)

*a polygon covers a pixel-sized window if the center of the window is
inside the polygon*

*if the polygon vertices are specified in clockwise order, then the inside is
always to the right*

the algorithm uses the Visibility *subroutine presented in Sec. 3–19*

if no covering polygon is found, Pnumber = 0

if at least one covering polygon is found, then Pnumber *is set to the visible
polygon*

    initialize Zmax *to zero; this assumes that all polygons are in
the positive half space,* z ≥ 0

    Zmax = 0

    initially assume there are no covering polygons

    Pnumber = 0

    set up window center

    Pointx = Window(1, 1) + Window(1, 3)/2

    Pointy = Window(1, 2) + Window(1, 3)/2

    for each polygon

    for i = 1 **to** N

        Index = Polygon(i, 1)

        for each polygon edge

        j = 1

        while (j ≤ Polygon(i, 2) − 1 **and** Pvisible ≥ 0)

            P1x = Vertex(Index, 1)

            P1y = Vertex(Index, 2)

            P2x = Vertex(Index + 1, 1)

            P2y = Vertex(Index + 1, 2)

        note that Point, P1, P2 *are shorthand for* Pointx, Pointy *etc.*

```
            call Visible(Point, P1, P2; Pvisible)
            Index = Index + 1
            j = j + 1
        end while
```

take care of last edge

```
        if Pvisible ≥ 0 then
            P1x = Vertex(Index, 1)
            P1y = Vertex(Index, 2)
            P2x = Vertex(Polygon(i, 1), 1)
            P2y = Vertex(Polygon(i, 1), 2)
            call Visible(Point, P1, P2; Pvisible)
            if Pvisible ≥ 0 then
                call Compute(Vertex, i, Polygon, Window; z)
                if z > Zmax then
                    Zmax = z
                    Pnumber = i
                end if
            end if
        end if
    next i
return
```

subroutine to calculate the pixel intensity

subroutine Compute(Vertex, N, Polygon, Window; z)

the equation of the polygon plane is used to calculate the polygon nearest the eyepoint for this pixel

Max *is the maximum function*

   calculate the x *and* y *coordinates of the pixel center*

```
    Xcenter = Window(1, 1) + Window(1, 3)/2
    Ycenter = Window(1, 2) + Window(1, 3)/2
```

   determine z *at the pixel center*
   check for an edge on the polygon through the pixel center
   note that a polygon of this nature may be totally missed or appear as a disconnected series of dots — an example of aliasing

```
    if Polygon(i, 6) = 0 then
        for j = 2 to Polygon(i, 2)
            z = Max(Vertex(j, 3), Vertex(j − 1, 3))
        next j
    else
        calculate z from the plane equation
```

$$A = \text{Polygon}(i, 4)$$
$$B = \text{Polygon}(i, 5)$$
$$C = \text{Polygon}(i, 6)$$
$$D = \text{Polygon}(i, 7)$$
$$z = -(A * \text{Xcenter} + B * \text{Ycenter} + D)/C$$

    end if

  return

An example serves to illustrate the algorithm.

Example 4–17   Warnock Algorithm

Consider the three polygons

   1 : $(10, 3, 20), (20, 28, 20), (22, 28, 20), (22, 3, 20)$

   2 : $(5, 12, 10), (5, 20, 10), (27, 20, 10), (27, 12, 20)$

   3 : $(15, 15, 25), (25, 25, 5), (30, 10, 5)$

to be displayed at a resolution of 32×32 pixels using the simple Warnock algorithm just described. The first two polygons are rectangles perpendicular to the z axis at $z = 20$ and $z = 10$, respectively. The third polygon is a triangle that penetrates both rectangles, as shown in Fig. 4–44a. Figure 4–44b shows a visible surface view from a point at infinity on the positive z-axis. Figure 4–44c shows the contents of the frame buffer upon completion of the algorithm. The numbers in the boxes correspond to the polygon descriptions given. The algorithm proceeds from the lower left corner to the right and upward. The box outlines indicate the size of the window subdivisions processed at each step in the algorithm. For example, notice the large (8×8) empty window in the lower left corner. This window is displayed without further subdivision. The figures show that the triangle is partially obscured by the second rectangle, penetrates the rectangle, is partially visible, is then obscured by the first rectangle, and then penetrates the first rectangle with the apex visible.

4–5   Appel's Algorithm

An early visible line algorithm due to Arthur Appel [Appe67] introduces the notion of the quantitative invisibility of a line. Appel defines quantitative invisibility as the number of potentially visible surfaces that lie between the line segment and the eyepoint. A surface is potentially visible if the angle between the outward normal to the surface and the line to the eyepoint is less than $90°$, and is invisible if the angle is greater than $90°$. If the quantitative invisibility is zero, the line segment is visible.

    The quantitative invisibility changes by ±1 only at contour edges or lines. For polyhedra, a contour line is shared by both a potentially visible and an invisible surface, while for single potentially visible polygons all edges are contour lines. The quantitative invisibility increases by $+1$ when a line segment enters the

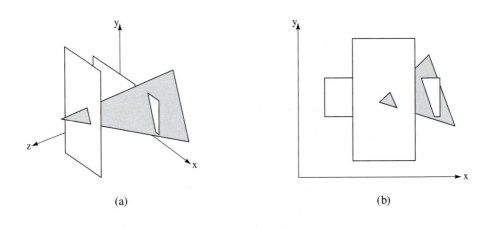

(a)   (b)

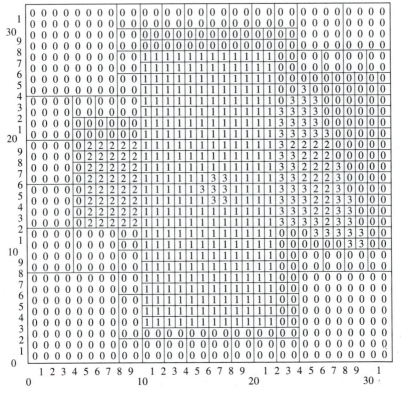

(c)

Figure 4–44   Polygon example for the simple Warnock algorithm. (a) A three-dimensional view; (b) a two-dimensional visible surface view; (c) pseudo-frame-buffer results.

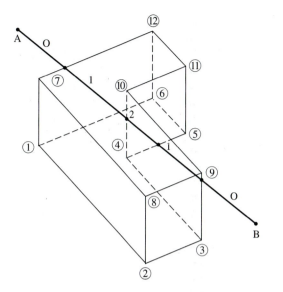

Figure 4–45   An illustration of quantitative invisibility, as the line AB passes completely behind the object.

region bounded by a contour line, and decreases by -1 when it exits the region. In Fig. 4–45 lines 2–3, 3–9, 9–10, 5–11, 11–12, 12–7, 7–1, 4–10 are contour lines. The line AB begins with a quantitative invisibility of zero, passes behind contour line 7–12, where the quantitative invisibility increases to $+1$, then behind contour line 4–10, where it increases to $+2$. Passing behind contour line 4–5 reduces the quantitative invisibility by -1 to $+1$. The line then emerges from behind contour line 9–3, after which the quantitative invisibility is again zero. The portions of the line AB with a quantitative invisibility of zero are visible, i.e., those portions from A to the contour line 7–12, and from the contour line 3–9 to B.

If a line is parametrically described, deciding whether it is entering or exiting a region bounded by a contour line can be accomplished using the technique described in the Cyrus–Beck clipping algorithm (see Sec. 3–5). Alternatively, if the vertices of the polyhedral face or polygon containing the contour edge are described counterclockwise, e.g., 1, 6, 12, 7, about the outer normal to the face, then upon substituting a vertex of the line into the test function formed from the plane equation of the face, i.e.

$$\text{T.F.} = ax + by + cz + d$$

the test function is negative, the line is entering the region. If the test function is zero, the vertex lies on the plane. If the test function is positive, then the line is exiting the region (see also Sec. 4–12).

To determine if a line passes in front of or behind a contour edge, consider the triangle formed with the end points of the contour edge as its base and the eyepoint as its apex. If the line pierces the plane of the triangle *and* the piercing point is contained within the triangle, the line passes in *front* of the contour edge; otherwise it passes behind the contour edge. Appel recommends using the infinite line containment test (see Sec. 4-4) to determine if the piercing point lies within the triangle. He ascribes the containment test to J. Rutledge.[†]

It remains to determine the initial quantitative invisibility of at least one point (vertex) in the scene; basically, ray tracing is used (see Sec. 4–20). A surface (polygon) hides a point when the piercing point of a line from the point to the eyepoint for the surface is closer to the eye than the point, and the piercing point is contained within the surface (polygon). If a surface hides a point, the quantitative invisibility of the point increases by one. Spatial subdivision techniques are used to reduce the number of surfaces (polygons) examined.

Assuming scenes are composed of polyhedra and polygons, lines or edges have common vertices, e.g., lines 7–1 and 1–2 in Fig. 4–45 have a common vertex at 1. Lines or edges that meet at a common vertex have the same quantitative invisibility at the common vertex. Thus, the quantitative invisibility at the end of one edge becomes the quantitative invisibility at the beginning of edges originating at the common vertex. However, there are some exceptions. These exceptions are handled by noting that

> if an edge originating at a common vertex at an *external* corner terminates at an *internal* corner, quantitative invisibility *increases* only if contour lines are present at both corners;

> if an edge originating at a common vertex at an *internal* corner terminates at an *external* corner, quantitative invisibility *decreases* only if a contour line exists at both the common vertex and the internal corner;

> quantitative invisibility does not change at a common vertex if no contour line exists at the vertex.

Fundamentally, these rules detect an invisible internal corner.

4–6   The Haloed Line Algorithm

In some applications, it is both convenient and informative to see the underlying structure of the hidden portions of an object. This effect is obtained with the haloed line algorithm of Appel, Rohlf and Stein [Appe79]. The algorithm is particularly useful for line drawings, because it does not require that a line be part of an underlying geometric entity such as a polygon, volume or surface. Arbitrary lines simply stand by themselves.

The algorithm surrounds the projection of each line with a 'halo', consisting of a symmetrically placed rectangle of width $2H$ with semicircular ends of radius H, as shown in Fig. 4–46. The depth of the line is retained. If line A in Fig. 4–46a is closer to the viewpoint than line B, then the segment within the

---

[†]To the best of the author's knowledge, Appel's paper [Appe67] is the first to describe the infinite line containment test. He gives no reference source for J. Rutledge's original description.

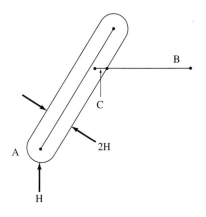

Figure 4-46 Haloed line segments.

halo, labelled C, is not drawn. The effect, in comparison to typical wire frame and visible surface drawings, is shown in Fig. 4–47. A particularly useful effect when annotating illustrations is shown in Fig. 4–48. If the halo is wider than the typical line spacing in the scene, then the algorithm gives a visible surface effect.

The algorithm presented here follows Franklin [Fran80a, 87] and is similar to those reported by him [Fran80b, 81]. The algorithm, based on area subdivision concepts (see Sec. 4–4), is divided into two parts. The first part uses an adaptive grid to find all the line intersections in the scene. The grid size is a function of the average length of a line in the scene. Information about the line segments in each cell of the grid, and their intersections, if any, are saved. Given a halo width, H, the second part of the algorithm subtracts and adds the halo width to each intersection found in the first part to determine the points at which a

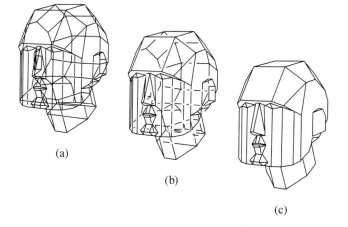

(a)

(b)

(c)

Figure 4-47 Effect of the haloed line algorithm.(a) Wire frame drawing showing all lines; (b) haloed line drawing; (c) visible surface drawing with all hidden lines eliminated. (Courtesy of Arthur Appel, IBM T.J. Watson Research Center.).

line becomes visible or invisible. After sorting the visible/invisible points along the line, the visible portions are drawn using Appel's concept of quantitative invisibility [Appe67] (see Sec. 4–5). Specifically, the algorithm is

Prepare the data:

Scale the data to the range $0, 1$.

Determine the average line length, L.

Generate an overlay grid with cells of approximate size $1/L$.

Determine and store the equation of each line in three-space, i.e., $z = ax + by + d$.

for each line, L_i, in the scene:

Determine the cells that the projection of L_i passes through. Using the bounding box of L_i saves computational effort, at the expense of adding some additional cells to the list.

Generate a list of these cells $(C_{i,j}, L_i)$.

Sort $(C_{i,j}, L_i)$ into a lineal list, using the cells as the key.

Group all the segments in one cell together.

for each nonempty cell:

Compare each line segment, L_i, with the other line segments in the cell, $L_j (i \neq j)$, to determine if an intersection exists (see Sec. 4–3).

if L_i and L_j intersect, calculate the intersection point I.

if I is not within the cell, ignore it.

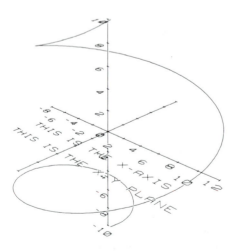

Figure 4–48 Haloed line effect used for graphical annotations. (Courtesy of Arthur Appel, IBM T.J. Watson Research Center.).

if I is within the cell, determine if L_i or L_j is closest to the eye at the intersection point. Use the precalculated equation of the line; note that for lines perpendicular to the projection plane, the equation is singular.

Assuming, with no loss of generality, that L_i is behind L_j at I, calculate the angle, θ, between L_i and L_j.

Save the result in an array (L_i, I, θ).

Sort the array (L_i, I, θ) by L_i.

If a line, L_i, does not appear in the array (L_i, I, θ), the line is trivially visible; add a dummy element to the array for the line.

Pass this array to the display routine.

Display routine:

for each line in (L_i, I, θ):

for each intersection in the array (L_i, I, θ) subtract and add an *effective* halo length, using H and θ to compute I_1 and I_2, where the halo on L_i starts and stops.

Add elements $(I_1, -1)$ and $(I_2, +1)$ to an array, S.

With E_1 and E_2 the first and second end points of L_i, add elements $(E_1, +1)$ and $(E_2, -1)$ to the array, S.

Sort the array S in order along L_i.

Process S in order along L_i

Add the -1's and $+1$'s along L_i.

Start drawing when the sum is $= 1$.

Stop drawing when the sum is ≤ 0.

The sum should never be more than one. When the sum is less than or equal to zero, a region of overlapping halos exists; at the last point, the sum equals zero.

One advantage to splitting the algorithm into two parts is that the scene can be redrawn with various halo widths without recalculating the first part. Furthermore, the algorithm is conveniently parallelized.

Beatty, Booth and Matthies [Beat81] developed an implementation of the haloed line effect based on the scan line algorithm of Watkins [Watk70]. Elber [Elbe95] extended the basic haloed line algorithm using the facilities of the PostScript language [Post85] to include additional illustration techniques (see, for example, [Magn70; Thom68]). Examples include: decreasing the line thickness as a function of distance from the eye, as shown in Fig. 4–49; changing the color or gray level (depth cueing) as a function of distance from the eye; and decreasing or increasing the line width slightly at a hidden edge. Fundamentally, the algorithm breaks each line into small segments, sorts the segments by depth, makes the appropriate attribute proportional to the depth, invokes the appropriate PostScript command and writes the result to the display.

4–7 Weiler–Atherton Algorithm

Weiler and Atherton [Weil77] attempt to minimize the number of subdivisions in a Warnock-style algorithm by subdividing along polygon boundaries. The basis of the algorithm is the Weiler–Atherton polygon clipper previously discussed in Sec. 3–21. The output of the algorithm, which operates in object space to an arbitrary accuracy, is polygons. Since the output consists of complete polygons, the algorithm is easily used for visible line, as well as visible surface, elimination. The visible surface algorithm involves four steps:

A preliminary depth sort.

A clip or polygon area sort based on the polygon nearest the eyepoint.

Removal of the polygons behind that nearest the eyepoint.

Recursive subdivision, if required, and a final depth sort to remove any ambiguities.

A preliminary depth sort is used to establish an approximate depth priority list. Assuming that the eyepoint is located at infinity on the positive z-axis, the polygon closest to the eyepoint and the first polygon on the list is the one with the vertex having the largest z coordinate.

A copy of the first polygon on the preliminary depth-sorted list is used as the clip polygon. The remaining polygons on the list, including the first polygon, are subject polygons. Two lists are established, an inside list and an outside list. Using the Weiler–Atherton clipping algorithm, each of the subject polygons is

Figure 4–49   Haloed line effect with decreased line thickness proportional to distance from the eye. (Courtesy of Gershon Elber.).

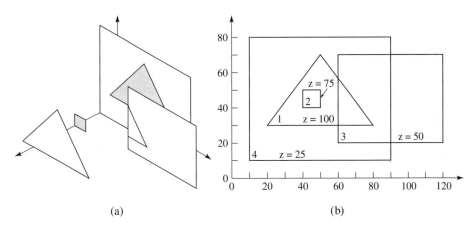

(a)   (b)

Figure 4–50   Priority polygon clipping for the Weiler–Atherton visible surface algorithm. (a) Three-dimensional view; (b) two-dimensional projection.

clipped against the clip polygon. This is a two-dimensional clip of the projection
of the clip and the subject polygons. The portion of each subject polygon inside
the clip polygon, if any, is placed on the inside list. The portion outside the clip
polygon, if any, is placed on the outside list. This part of the algorithm is an
x, y, or area, sort. An example is shown in Fig. 4–50. Figure 4–51 illustrates the
inside and outside polygon lists for the scene in Fig. 4–50. The depth of each
polygon on the inside list is now compared to that of the clip polygon. Using
the x, y coordinates of the vertices of the subject polygons on the inside list, and
their plane equations, the depth (z coordinate) of each vertex is calculated and
compared with the minimum z coordinate value (z_{cmin}) for the clip polygon. If
none of the z coordinate values of the subject polygons on the inside list is larger
than z_{cmin}, then all the subject polygons on the inside list are hidden by the clip
polygon (see Fig. 4–50). These polygons are eliminated, and the inside polygon
list is displayed. Note that here the only remaining polygon on the inside list is
the clip polygon. The algorithm continues with the outside list.

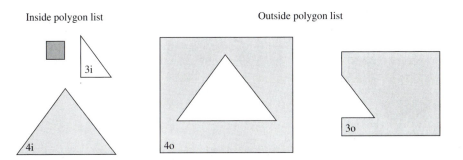

Figure 4–51   Inside and outside polygon lists.

If the z coordinate for any polygon on the inside list is greater than z_{cmin}, then the subject polygon on the inside list lies at least partially in front of the clip polygon. Figure 4–52 illustrates how this occurs. In this case, the original preliminary depth sort is in error. The algorithm recursively subdivides the area, using the offending polygon as the new clip polygon. The inside list is used as the subject polygon list. The original clip polygon is now clipped against the new clip polygon. Note that the new clip polygon is a copy of the complete original polygon, not the remainder after the original clip. Using a copy of the complete polygon for the new clip polygon minimizes the number of subdivisions.

A simple example more fully illustrates the algorithm.

Example 4–18   Weiler–Atherton Hidden Surface Algorithm

Consider the two rectangular polygons shown in Fig. 4–52. Polygon A has vertices $(5, 0, 25)$, $(40, 0, 5)$, $(40, 40, 5)$ and $(5, 40, 25)$. Polygon B has vertices $(25, 0, 20)$, $(55, 0, 20)$, $(55, 30, 20)$ and $(25, 30, 20)$. Figure 4–53a shows the unclipped scene from an eyepoint at infinity on the positive z-axis. Although polygon B obscures part of polygon A, the preliminary depth sort places A before B on the sorted list. A copy of polygon A is used as the initial clip polygon. The initial subject polygon list contains both A and B, as shown in Table 4–10. Table 4–10 and Fig. 4–53b show the result of clipping the subject polygon list against polygon A. The inside list now contains polygons A and C, and the outside list polygon B'. Comparing the depths of polygons A and C to the clip polygon shows that C is in front of the clip polygon. The algorithm recursively subdivides the area by using polygon B, of which C is a part, as the clip polygon and the inside list as the subject polygon list. The portion labeled A' is clipped away and placed on the outside list; the portion labeled D is placed on the inside list. Comparing polygons C and D on the inside list with the clip polygon B shows that D is obscured, hence it is eliminated. C is coincident with B, the clip polygon; it remains on the inside list. Recursion is not necessary. Polygon C is displayed. The algorithm continues to completion by extracting polygons B' and A' from the outside list. The details are given in Table 4–10.

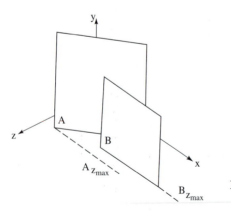

Figure 4–52   Condition for an error in the initial z sort.

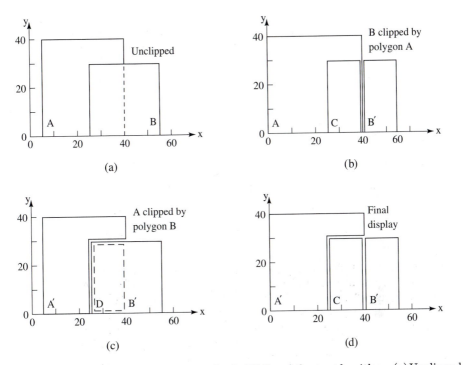

Figure 4–53 Recursive subdivision for the Weiler–Atherton algorithm. (a) Unclipped; (b) polygon B clipped by polygon A; (c) polygon A clipped by polygon B; (d) the result.

Table 4–10

Clip polygon	Subject polygons	Inside list	Beginning outside list	Final outside list	Display	Comment
A	A B	A C		B′		Recursion
B	A C	C D	B′	A′	C	Continue with outside list
				B′		
A′	A′	A′ — B′	B′	B′	A′	
B′	B′	B′	B′		B′	

One additional detail of the algorithm is of interest. When a single polygon cyclically overlaps the clip polygon, i.e., lies both in front of and behind the clip polygon (see Fig. 4–54a), no recursive subdivision is required. Here, all material behind the cyclical polygon has already been removed by the previous clip. It is only necessary to clip the original polygon against the cyclical polygon and display the result. The unnecessary recursive subdivision is prevented by

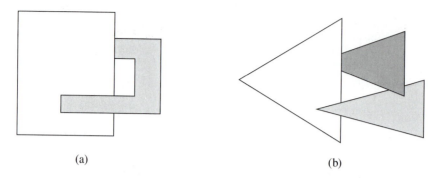

(a)

(b)

Figure 4–54 Cyclically overlapping polygons. (a) Two polygons; (b) multiple polygons.

maintaining a list of polygons previously used as clipping polygons. If during recursive subdivision the current clipping polygon appears on this list, then a cyclical overlapping polygon has been found. No additional recursion is necessary. Note that the algorithm directly handles cases of cyclical overlap among several polygons, as shown in Fig. 4–54b.

4–8   A Subdivision Algorithm For Curved Surfaces

Both the basic Warnock and the Weiler–Atherton subdivision algorithms assume that the scene is represented by a collection of planar polygons. However, many objects are represented by curved surfaces, e.g., aircraft, ships, automobiles, chinaware, etc. Polygonal approximations to these curved surfaces do not always yield adequate representations; e.g., silhouette edges appear as short, connected, straight line segments rather than as continuous curves. Catmull [Catm74, 75] developed the first visible surface algorithm for curved surfaces, a Warnock-style subdivision algorithm. Although Catmull applied the algorithm to bicubic surface patches, it is general enough to be applied to any curved surface. In contrast to the Warnock algorithm that recursively divides image or object space, the Catmull algorithm recursively subdivides the surface. Simply stated, the algorithm is

> Recursively subdivide the surface until a subpatch, transformed into image space, covers at most one pixel center.
> Determine the depth of the subpatch at the pixel center.
> Using a z-buffer algorithm (see Sec. 4–9), determine if the patch is visible.
> **if** the patch is visible **then**
> > compute the attributes of the surface at this pixel and display the pixel.

Figure 4–55a shows a surface patch and its subdivision into pixel-sized subpatches. Unless the surface is highly curved, it is usually sufficient to use a polygonal approximation to the curved subpatch to decide whether it covers just

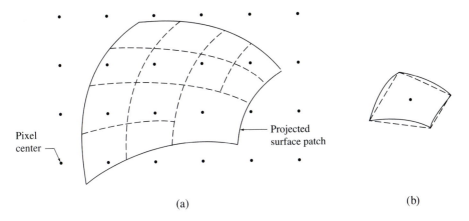

Figure 4–55   Curved surface subdivision. (a) Subdivided curved surface; (b) polygonal approximation to a subpatch.

one pixel center (see Fig. 4–55b). The subdivision process results in subpatches that do not cover any pixel center; the attributes of these patches are assigned to the nearest pixel center. Subpatches that are outside the viewing window are, of course, discarded. Subpatches that intersect the viewing window edge are further subdivided, until a clear inside or outside decision is possible.

The efficiency of the algorithm depends on the efficiency of the curved surface subdivision technique. Catmull [Catm74] has suggested one technique for bicubic surface patches. Cohen, Lyche and Riesenfeld [Cohe80] suggest a more general technique for B-spline surfaces.

4–9   *Z*-Buffer Algorithm

The *z*-buffer, or depth buffer, is one of the simplest of the visible surface algorithms. The technique was originally proposed by Catmull [Catm75] and is an image space algorithm. The *z*-buffer is a simple extension of the frame buffer idea. A frame buffer is used to store the attributes (intensity or shade) of each pixel in image space. The *z*-buffer is a separate depth buffer used to store the z coordinate, or depth, of every visible pixel in image space. In use, the depth or z value of a new pixel to be written to the frame buffer is compared to the depth of that pixel stored in the *z*-buffer. If the comparison indicates that the new pixel is in front of the pixel stored in the frame buffer, then the new pixel is written to the frame buffer and the *z*-buffer updated with the new z value. If not, no action is taken. Conceptually, the algorithm is a search over x, y for the largest value of $z(x, y)$.

The simplicity of the algorithm is its greatest advantage. In addition, it handles the visible surface problem and the display of complex surface intersections trivially. Although frequently implemented for polygonally represented scenes, the *z*-buffer algorithm is applicable for any object for which depth and shading characteristics can be calculated. Furthermore, a scene can contain mixed object types. Scenes are of any complexity. Since image space is of fixed size, the increase in computational work with the complexity of the scene is, at most, linear. Since elements of a scene or picture are written to the frame or z-buffer in arbitrary order, they need not be sorted into depth priority order. Hence, the computation time associated with a depth sort is eliminated.

The storage required is the principal disadvantage of the algorithm. If the scene is transformed and clipped to a fixed range of z coordinates, then a z-buffer of fixed precision can be used. Because large complex scenes may contain elements with dimensions that vary by more than six orders of magnitude, i.e., by a factor of more than a million, depth information must be maintained to a higher precision than lateral x, y information. An additional precision problem occurs because of compression of the z coordinate values when a perspective transformation is used. Furthermore, a perspective transformation changes the object-to-object intersections. Thus, only the perspective projection of a polygon or object is passed to a z-buffer algorithm. Generally, a 24 bit deep z-buffer is sufficient. A $1280 \times 1024 \times 24$-bit-plane frame buffer, in combination with a $1280 \times 1024 \times 24$ bit z-buffer, requires nearly *eight megabytes* of storage. However, comparatively low memory costs make dedicated z-buffer memory and associated hardware practical.

An alternative to dedicated z-buffer memory is to use main memory for the z-buffer. Smaller storage requirements also result from subdividing the image space into 4, 16 or more subsquares, or bands. The limit is a single-scan-line z-buffer (see Sec. 4–15). Because each scene element is processed multiple times, segmenting the z-buffer generally increases the time required to process a scene. However, area sorting, in the sense of an active polygon list (see Sec. 2–12), so that only active polygons are processed for each subsquare or band, significantly reduces the increase.

A further disadvantage of the z-buffer is the difficulty and expense of implementing antialiasing, transparency and translucency effects. Because the algorithm writes pixels to the frame buffer in arbitrary order, the necessary information for prefiltering antialiasing techniques (see Sec. 2–16) is not easily available. For transparency and translucency effects (see Sec. 5–10), pixels can be written to the frame buffer in incorrect order, leading to local errors.

Although prefiltering antialiasing techniques are possible (see [Catm74]), they are difficult to apply. However, postfiltering (subpixel averaging) techniques (see Sec. 2–16) are relatively easy to apply. Recalling that postfiltering antialiasing techniques compute the scene at image space resolutions greater than the display resolution, two approaches to postfiltering antialiasing are possible. The first uses a larger than display space resolution image space frame buffer, and a display space resolution z-buffer. The depth of the image is computed only at the center of the group of subpixels to be averaged. If intensity scaling is used to indicate distance from the observer, this technique is not adequate.

The second technique maintains both increased image space resolution frame and z-buffers. Upon displaying the image, both the pixel and the depth information are averaged. This technique requires very large amounts of storage. For example, a $1280 \times 1024 \times 24$-bit-plane image, with 24 bits of z-buffer computed at a factor of 2 increase in both x and y resolution and antialiased using uniform averaging (see Fig. 2–62a), requires approximately 32 *megabytes* of storage.

More formally stated, the *z*-buffer algorithm is

Set the frame buffer to the background intensity or color.

Set the *z*-buffer to the minimum z value.

Scan-convert each polygon in arbitrary order.

For each Pixel(x,y) in the polygon, calculate the depth z(x,y) at that pixel.

Compare the depth z(x,y) with the value stored in the *z*-buffer at that location, Zbuffer(x,y).

If z(x,y) > Zbuffer(x,y), then write the polygon attributes (intensity, color, etc.) to the frame buffer and replace Zbuffer(x,y) with z(x,y).

Otherwise, no action is taken.

The *z*-buffer algorithm is also used for surface sectioning. Here the comparison is modified to

$$z(x, y) > \text{Zbuffer}(x, y) \quad \textbf{and} \quad z(x, y) \leq \text{Zsection}$$

where Zsection is the desired section location. The effect is to retain only those elements at or behind Zsection. Atherton [Athe81] applied the *z*-buffer algorithm to a three-dimensional voxel representation, to render constructive solid geometry (CSG) models with sectioning, including curved section surfaces, cut away views, transparency and translucency effects (see also Sec. 5–10). The efficiency of Atherton's implementation is enhanced by saving a list of all the points along a particular *z* vector, ordered in *z*, in an object buffer. The existence of the object buffer considerably speeds rendering sectioning, cut away views, transparency and translucency views. Rossignac and Requicha [Ross86] also used a modified *z*-buffer algorithm to render constructive solid geometry models. They cover each face of the CSG primitives used to construct the model with a dense array of points. Only those points that are both on the model surface and closest to the eye are rendered.

A pseudocode outline of the algorithm, which only considers scan lines and pixels within the bounding box of a polygon or object and calculates the shade of a pixel only if it is written to the frame buffer, is

> *initialize the frame buffer to the background color*
> *initialize the z-buffer to the minimum z value*
> **for** *the projection of each polygon or object*
>> **for** *each scan line within the polygon projection's bounding box*
>>> **for** *each pixel within the polygon projection's bounding box*
>>>> *calculate the depth of the pixel* z(x, y)
>>>> **if** z(x, y) > Zbuffer(x, y) **then**
>>>>> *calculate the shade of the pixel at* z(x, y)
>>>>> *write the pixel to the frame buffer*
>>>>> *write* z(x, y) *to the z-buffer*
>>>> **end if**
>>> **next** *pixel*

> **next** *scan line*
> **next** *polygon or object*
> *Display the frame buffer*

Where appropriate, a preliminary backface cull (see Sec. 4–3) is used.

Incrementally Calculating the Depth

If the plane equation for each polygon is available, calculation of the depth at each pixel on a scan line is done incrementally with a single subtraction. Recall the plane equation

$$ax + by + cz + d = 0$$

and

$$z = -\frac{(ax + by + d)}{c} \qquad c \neq 0$$

On a scan line, $y = $ constant. Thus, the depth of the pixel at $x_1 = x + \Delta x$ along the scan line is

$$z_1 - z = -\frac{(ax_1 + d)}{c} + \frac{(ax + d)}{c} = \frac{a(x - x_1)}{c}$$

or

$$z_1 = z - \left(\frac{a}{c}\right)\Delta x$$

But $\Delta x = 1$, so

$$z_1 = z - \frac{a}{c}$$

The increment from scan line to scan line is also accomplished with a single subtract. The depth of the pixel on the next scan line at the same value of x is

$$z_1 = z - \frac{(by_1 + d)}{c} + \frac{(by + d)}{c} = \frac{b(y - y_1)}{c} = -\left(\frac{b}{c}\right)\Delta y$$

Because $\Delta y = 1$

$$z_1 = z - \frac{b}{c}$$

where again b/c is a precomputed constant.

For nonplanar polygons the depth, z, of each pixel is obtained using bilinear interpolation (see also Sec. 5–6). Referring to Fig. 4–56, the depth of the polygon where the scan line, y_s, and the polygon edge, P_1P_4, intersect is

$$z_a = z_1 + (z_4 - z_1)\frac{y_1 - y_s}{y_1 - y_4}$$

while that for the intersection of y_s and the polygon edge P_1P_2 is

$$z_b = z_1 + (z_2 - z_1)\frac{y_1 - y_s}{y_1 - y_2}$$

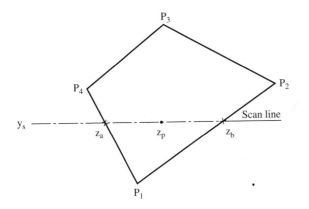

Figure 4–56 Bilinear interpolation of pixel depth values.

Finally, the depth of the pixel z_p on scan line y_s is

$$z_p = z_a + (z_b - z_a)\,\frac{x_a - x_p}{x_a - x_b}$$

If shading calculations are computationally expensive, the efficiency of the algorithm is increased by performing an initial depth priority sort. Starting with the polygon or object closest to the eyepoint, the shading calculation is performed only if a pixel is visible and is written to the frame buffer.

Efficiently adding temporary information to a z-buffered display is accomplished by saving the original z-buffer and frame buffer values when the temporary information is written to the frame buffer. Removal is accomplished by restoring the original values. Alternatively, the temporary information is written to separate overlay planes in the frame buffer. Clearing the overlay planes removes the temporary information from the display. These techniques are used to display a three-dimensional cursor or a grid, or to show the motion of objects within a mostly static scene.

An example serves to further illustrate the algorithm.

Example 4–19   Z-Buffer Algorithm

Consider the rectangle with corner coordinates $P_1(10, 5, 10)$, $P_2(10, 25, 10)$, $P_3(25, 25, 10)$, $P_4(25, 5, 10)$ and the triangle with vertices $P_5(15, 15, 15)$, $P_6(25, 25, 5)$, $P_7(30, 10, 5)$. The triangle penetrates the rectangle from behind, as shown in Fig. 4–57. The polygons are to be displayed at an image resolution of 32×32, using a simple 2-bit-plane frame buffer. In the frame buffer, the background is represented by 0, the rectangle by 1 and the triangle by 2. The z-buffer is $32 \times 32 \times 4$ bit planes, thus the z-buffer range is from 0 to 16. The viewpoint is at infinity on the positive z-axis, as shown in Fig. 4–57b.

Initially, both the frame buffer and the z-buffer are set to zero. After scan-converting the rectangle, the frame buffer contents are:

```
0 0 0 0 0 0 0 0 0 0 0 0 0 0 0 0 0 0 0 0 0 0 0 0 0 0 0 0 0 0 0 0 0 0
0 0 0 0 0 0 0 0 0 0 0 0 0 0 0 0 0 0 0 0 0 0 0 0 0 0 0 0 0 0 0 0 0 0
0 0 0 0 0 0 0 0 0 0 0 0 0 0 0 0 0 0 0 0 0 0 0 0 0 0 0 0 0 0 0 0 0 0
0 0 0 0 0 0 0 0 0 0 0 0 0 0 0 0 0 0 0 0 0 0 0 0 0 0 0 0 0 0 0 0 0 0
0 0 0 0 0 0 0 0 0 0 0 0 0 0 0 0 0 0 0 0 0 0 0 0 0 0 0 0 0 0 0 0 0 0
0 0 0 0 0 0 0 0 0 0 0 0 0 0 0 0 0 0 0 0 0 0 0 0 0 0 0 0 0 0 0 0 0 0
0 0 0 0 0 0 0 0 0 0 0 0 0 0 0 0 0 0 0 0 0 0 0 0 0 0 0 0 0 0 0 0 0 0
0 0 0 0 0 0 0 0 0 0 1 1 1 1 1 1 1 1 1 1 1 1 1 0 0 0 0 0 0 0 0
0 0 0 0 0 0 0 0 0 0 1 1 1 1 1 1 1 1 1 1 1 1 1 0 0 0 0 0 0 0 0
0 0 0 0 0 0 0 0 0 0 1 1 1 1 1 1 1 1 1 1 1 1 1 0 0 0 0 0 0 0 0
0 0 0 0 0 0 0 0 0 0 1 1 1 1 1 1 1 1 1 1 1 1 1 0 0 0 0 0 0 0 0
0 0 0 0 0 0 0 0 0 0 1 1 1 1 1 1 1 1 1 1 1 1 1 0 0 0 0 0 0 0 0
0 0 0 0 0 0 0 0 0 0 1 1 1 1 1 1 1 1 1 1 1 1 1 0 0 0 0 0 0 0 0
0 0 0 0 0 0 0 0 0 0 1 1 1 1 1 1 1 1 1 1 1 1 1 0 0 0 0 0 0 0 0
0 0 0 0 0 0 0 0 0 0 1 1 1 1 1 1 1 1 1 1 1 1 1 0 0 0 0 0 0 0 0
0 0 0 0 0 0 0 0 0 0 1 1 1 1 1 1 1 1 1 1 1 1 1 0 0 0 0 0 0 0 0
0 0 0 0 0 0 0 0 0 0 1 1 1 1 1 1 1 1 1 1 1 1 1 0 0 0 0 0 0 0 0
0 0 0 0 0 0 0 0 0 0 1 1 1 1 1 1 1 1 1 1 1 1 1 0 0 0 0 0 0 0 0
0 0 0 0 0 0 0 0 0 0 1 1 1 1 1 1 1 1 1 1 1 1 1 0 0 0 0 0 0 0 0
0 0 0 0 0 0 0 0 0 0 1 1 1 1 1 1 1 1 1 1 1 1 1 0 0 0 0 0 0 0 0
0 0 0 0 0 0 0 0 0 0 1 1 1 1 1 1 1 1 1 1 1 1 1 0 0 0 0 0 0 0 0
0 0 0 0 0 0 0 0 0 0 1 1 1 1 1 1 1 1 1 1 1 1 1 0 0 0 0 0 0 0 0
0 0 0 0 0 0 0 0 0 0 1 1 1 1 1 1 1 1 1 1 1 1 1 0 0 0 0 0 0 0 0
0 0 0 0 0 0 0 0 0 0 1 1 1 1 1 1 1 1 1 1 1 1 1 0 0 0 0 0 0 0 0
0 0 0 0 0 0 0 0 0 0 1 1 1 1 1 1 1 1 1 1 1 1 1 0 0 0 0 0 0 0 0
0 0 0 0 0 0 0 0 0 0 0 0 0 0 0 0 0 0 0 0 0 0 0 0 0 0 0 0 0 0 0 0 0 0
0 0 0 0 0 0 0 0 0 0 0 0 0 0 0 0 0 0 0 0 0 0 0 0 0 0 0 0 0 0 0 0 0 0
0 0 0 0 0 0 0 0 0 0 0 0 0 0 0 0 0 0 0 0 0 0 0 0 0 0 0 0 0 0 0 0 0 0
0 0 0 0 0 0 0 0 0 0 0 0 0 0 0 0 0 0 0 0 0 0 0 0 0 0 0 0 0 0 0 0 0 0
0 0 0 0 0 0 0 0 0 0 0 0 0 0 0 0 0 0 0 0 0 0 0 0 0 0 0 0 0 0 0 0 0 0
```

Frame buffer after scan converting rectangle.

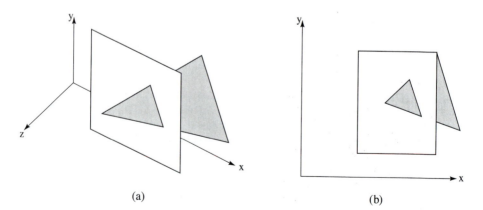

(a)   (b)

Figure 4–57   Penetrating triangle. (a) Three-dimensional view; (b) two-dimensional projection.

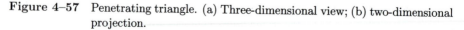

The *z*-buffer contents are as shown:

```
0 0 0 0 0 0 0 0 0 0 0 0 0 0 0 0 0 0 0 0 0 0 0 0 0 0 0 0 0 0 0 0 0 0 0 0
0 0 0 0 0 0 0 0 0 0 0 0 0 0 0 0 0 0 0 0 0 0 0 0 0 0 0 0 0 0 0 0 0 0 0 0
0 0 0 0 0 0 0 0 0 0 0 0 0 0 0 0 0 0 0 0 0 0 0 0 0 0 0 0 0 0 0 0 0 0 0 0
0 0 0 0 0 0 0 0 0 0 0 0 0 0 0 0 0 0 0 0 0 0 0 0 0 0 0 0 0 0 0 0 0 0 0 0
0 0 0 0 0 0 0 0 0 0 0 0 0 0 0 0 0 0 0 0 0 0 0 0 0 0 0 0 0 0 0 0 0 0 0 0
0 0 0 0 0 0 0 0 0 0 0 0 0 0 0 0 0 0 0 0 0 0 0 0 0 0 0 0 0 0 0 0 0 0 0 0
0 0 0 0 0 0 0 0 0 0 0 0 0 0 0 0 0 0 0 0 0 0 0 0 0 0 0 0 0 0 0 0 0 0 0 0
0 0 0 0 0 0 0 0 0 10 10 10 10 10 10 10 10 10 10 10 10 10 10 10 10 10 0 0 0 0 0 0 0
0 0 0 0 0 0 0 0 0 10 10 10 10 10 10 10 10 10 10 10 10 10 10 10 10 10 0 0 0 0 0 0 0
0 0 0 0 0 0 0 0 0 10 10 10 10 10 10 10 10 10 10 10 10 10 10 10 10 10 0 0 0 0 0 0 0
0 0 0 0 0 0 0 0 0 10 10 10 10 10 10 10 10 10 10 10 10 10 10 10 10 10 0 0 0 0 0 0 0
0 0 0 0 0 0 0 0 0 10 10 10 10 10 10 10 10 10 10 10 10 10 10 10 10 10 0 0 0 0 0 0 0
0 0 0 0 0 0 0 0 0 10 10 10 10 10 10 10 10 10 10 10 10 10 10 10 10 10 0 0 0 0 0 0 0
0 0 0 0 0 0 0 0 0 10 10 10 10 10 10 10 10 10 10 10 10 10 10 10 10 10 0 0 0 0 0 0 0
0 0 0 0 0 0 0 0 0 10 10 10 10 10 10 10 10 10 10 10 10 10 10 10 10 10 0 0 0 0 0 0 0
0 0 0 0 0 0 0 0 0 10 10 10 10 10 10 10 10 10 10 10 10 10 10 10 10 10 0 0 0 0 0 0 0
0 0 0 0 0 0 0 0 0 10 10 10 10 10 10 10 10 10 10 10 10 10 10 10 10 10 0 0 0 0 0 0 0
0 0 0 0 0 0 0 0 0 10 10 10 10 10 10 10 10 10 10 10 10 10 10 10 10 10 0 0 0 0 0 0 0
0 0 0 0 0 0 0 0 0 10 10 10 10 10 10 10 10 10 10 10 10 10 10 10 10 10 0 0 0 0 0 0 0
0 0 0 0 0 0 0 0 0 10 10 10 10 10 10 10 10 10 10 10 10 10 10 10 10 10 0 0 0 0 0 0 0
0 0 0 0 0 0 0 0 0 10 10 10 10 10 10 10 10 10 10 10 10 10 10 10 10 10 0 0 0 0 0 0 0
0 0 0 0 0 0 0 0 0 10 10 10 10 10 10 10 10 10 10 10 10 10 10 10 10 10 0 0 0 0 0 0 0
0 0 0 0 0 0 0 0 0 10 10 10 10 10 10 10 10 10 10 10 10 10 10 10 10 10 0 0 0 0 0 0 0
0 0 0 0 0 0 0 0 0 10 10 10 10 10 10 10 10 10 10 10 10 10 10 10 10 10 0 0 0 0 0 0 0
0 0 0 0 0 0 0 0 0 10 10 10 10 10 10 10 10 10 10 10 10 10 10 10 10 10 0 0 0 0 0 0 0
0 0 0 0 0 0 0 0 0 10 10 10 10 10 10 10 10 10 10 10 10 10 10 10 10 10 0 0 0 0 0 0 0
0 0 0 0 0 0 0 0 0 10 10 10 10 10 10 10 10 10 10 10 10 10 10 10 10 10 0 0 0 0 0 0 0
0 0 0 0 0 0 0 0 0 10 10 10 10 10 10 10 10 10 10 10 10 10 10 10 10 10 0 0 0 0 0 0 0
0 0 0 0 0 0 0 0 0 10 10 10 10 10 10 10 10 10 10 10 10 10 10 10 10 10 0 0 0 0 0 0 0
0 0 0 0 0 0 0 0 0 0 0 0 0 0 0 0 0 0 0 0 0 0 0 0 0 0 0 0 0 0 0 0 0 0 0 0
0 0 0 0 0 0 0 0 0 0 0 0 0 0 0 0 0 0 0 0 0 0 0 0 0 0 0 0 0 0 0 0 0 0 0 0
0 0 0 0 0 0 0 0 0 0 0 0 0 0 0 0 0 0 0 0 0 0 0 0 0 0 0 0 0 0 0 0 0 0 0 0
0 0 0 0 0 0 0 0 0 0 0 0 0 0 0 0 0 0 0 0 0 0 0 0 0 0 0 0 0 0 0 0 0 0 0 0
0 0 0 0 0 0 0 0 0 0 0 0 0 0 0 0 0 0 0 0 0 0 0 0 0 0 0 0 0 0 0 0 0 0 0 0
```

z-buffer after scan converting rectangle.

Recall that the lower left corner pixel is $(0, 0)$.

Using Newell's method (see Sec. 4–3, Ex. 4–3), the plane equation for the triangle is

$$3x + y + 4z - 120 = 0$$

hence the depth of the triangle at any location is

$$z = -\frac{(3x + y - 120)}{4}$$

For succeeding pixels on a scan line

$$z_1 = \frac{z - 3}{4}$$

Calculating the intersections of the triangle edges with the scan lines, using the half scan line convention, yields the intersection pairs $(24.5, 25.2)$, $(23.5, 25.5)$,

(22.5, 25.8), (21.5, 26.2), (20.5, 26.5), (19.5, 26.8), (18.5, 27.2), (17.5, 27.5), (16.5, 27.8), (15.5, 28.2), (16.5, 28.5), (19.5, 28.8), (22.5, 29.2), (25.5, 29.5), (28.5, 29.8) for scan lines 24 to 10. Recall that a pixel whose center is inside or on the triangle edge, i.e., for $x_1 \le x \le x_2$, is activated. Scan-converting and comparing the depth of each pixel with the z-buffer value yields the new frame buffer contents:

```
0 0 0 0 0 0 0 0 0 0 0 0 0 0 0 0 0 0 0 0 0 0 0 0 0 0 0 0 0 0 0 0 0 0
0 0 0 0 0 0 0 0 0 0 0 0 0 0 0 0 0 0 0 0 0 0 0 0 0 0 0 0 0 0 0 0 0 0
0 0 0 0 0 0 0 0 0 0 0 0 0 0 0 0 0 0 0 0 0 0 0 0 0 0 0 0 0 0 0 0 0 0
0 0 0 0 0 0 0 0 0 0 0 0 0 0 0 0 0 0 0 0 0 0 0 0 0 0 0 0 0 0 0 0 0 0
0 0 0 0 0 0 0 0 0 0 0 0 0 0 0 0 0 0 0 0 0 0 0 0 0 0 0 0 0 0 0 0 0 0
0 0 0 0 0 0 0 0 0 0 0 0 0 0 0 0 0 0 0 0 0 0 0 0 0 0 0 0 0 0 0 0 0 0
0 0 0 0 0 0 0 0 0 0 0 0 0 0 0 0 0 0 0 0 0 0 0 0 0 0 0 0 0 0 0 0 0 0
0 0 0 0 0 0 0 0 0 0 1 1 1 1 1 1 1 1 1 1 1 1 1 1 0 0 0 0 0 0 0
0 0 0 0 0 0 0 0 0 0 1 1 1 1 1 1 1 1 1 1 1 1 1 1 2 0 0 0 0 0 0
0 0 0 0 0 0 0 0 0 0 1 1 1 1 1 1 1 1 1 1 1 1 1 1 2 0 0 0 0 0 0
0 0 0 0 0 0 0 0 0 0 1 1 1 1 1 1 1 1 1 1 1 1 1 1 2 0 0 0 0 0 0
0 0 0 0 0 0 0 0 0 0 1 1 1 1 1 1 1 1 1 1 1 1 1 1 2 2 0 0 0 0 0
0 0 0 0 0 0 0 0 0 0 1 1 1 1 1 1 1 1 2 1 1 1 1 1 2 2 0 0 0 0 0
0 0 0 0 0 0 0 0 0 0 1 1 1 1 1 1 1 2 2 1 1 1 1 1 2 2 0 0 0 0 0
0 0 0 0 0 0 0 0 0 0 1 1 1 1 1 1 2 2 2 2 1 1 1 1 2 2 2 0 0 0 0
0 0 0 0 0 0 0 0 0 0 1 1 1 1 1 2 2 2 2 2 1 1 1 1 2 2 2 0 0 0 0
0 0 0 0 0 0 0 0 0 0 1 1 1 1 2 2 2 2 2 2 1 1 1 1 2 2 2 0 0 0 0
0 0 0 0 0 0 0 0 0 0 1 1 1 1 1 2 2 2 2 2 2 1 1 1 2 2 2 2 0 0 0
0 0 0 0 0 0 0 0 0 0 1 1 1 1 1 1 1 1 2 2 2 1 1 1 2 2 2 2 0 0 0
0 0 0 0 0 0 0 0 0 0 1 1 1 1 1 1 1 1 1 1 1 1 1 1 2 2 2 2 0 0 0
0 0 0 0 0 0 0 0 0 0 1 1 1 1 1 1 1 1 1 1 1 1 1 1 2 2 2 2 0 0
0 0 0 0 0 0 0 0 0 0 1 1 1 1 1 1 1 1 1 1 1 1 1 1 0 0 0 2 2 0 0
0 0 0 0 0 0 0 0 0 0 1 1 1 1 1 1 1 1 1 1 1 1 1 1 0 0 0 0 0 0 0
0 0 0 0 0 0 0 0 0 0 1 1 1 1 1 1 1 1 1 1 1 1 1 1 0 0 0 0 0 0 0
0 0 0 0 0 0 0 0 0 0 1 1 1 1 1 1 1 1 1 1 1 1 1 1 0 0 0 0 0 0 0
0 0 0 0 0 0 0 0 0 0 1 1 1 1 1 1 1 1 1 1 1 1 1 1 0 0 0 0 0 0 0
0 0 0 0 0 0 0 0 0 0 1 1 1 1 1 1 1 1 1 1 1 1 1 1 0 0 0 0 0 0 0
0 0 0 0 0 0 0 0 0 0 0 0 0 0 0 0 0 0 0 0 0 0 0 0 0 0 0 0 0 0 0 0 0 0
0 0 0 0 0 0 0 0 0 0 0 0 0 0 0 0 0 0 0 0 0 0 0 0 0 0 0 0 0 0 0 0 0 0
0 0 0 0 0 0 0 0 0 0 0 0 0 0 0 0 0 0 0 0 0 0 0 0 0 0 0 0 0 0 0 0 0 0
0 0 0 0 0 0 0 0 0 0 0 0 0 0 0 0 0 0 0 0 0 0 0 0 0 0 0 0 0 0 0 0 0 0
0 0 0 0 0 0 0 0 0 0 0 0 0 0 0 0 0 0 0 0 0 0 0 0 0 0 0 0 0 0 0 0 0 0
```

Frame buffer after scan converting rectangle and triangle.

After processing the triangle, the z-buffer contents are:

As a specific example, consider the pixel at $(20, 15)$. Evaluating z at the center of the pixel yields

$$z = \frac{-[(3)(20.5) + 15.5 - 120]}{4} = \frac{43}{4} = 10.75$$

Comparing it to the z-buffer value at $(20, 15)$ after processing the rectangle shows that the triangle is in front of the rectangle. Thus, the frame buffer value at $(20, 15)$ is changed to 2. Since, for the purposes of this example, the z-buffer is only 4 bits deep and thus has a range of only 0 to 15, the z value is rounded to the nearest whole number. Consequently, the value 11 is placed in the z-buffer at location $(20, 15)$.

```
0 0 0 0 0 0 0 0 0 0 0 0 0 0 0 0 0 0 0 0 0 0 0 0 0 0 0 0 0 0 0 0
0 0 0 0 0 0 0 0 0 0 0 0 0 0 0 0 0 0 0 0 0 0 0 0 0 0 0 0 0 0 0 0
0 0 0 0 0 0 0 0 0 0 0 0 0 0 0 0 0 0 0 0 0 0 0 0 0 0 0 0 0 0 0 0
0 0 0 0 0 0 0 0 0 0 0 0 0 0 0 0 0 0 0 0 0 0 0 0 0 0 0 0 0 0 0 0
0 0 0 0 0 0 0 0 0 0 0 0 0 0 0 0 0 0 0 0 0 0 0 0 0 0 0 0 0 0 0 0
0 0 0 0 0 0 0 0 0 0 0 0 0 0 0 0 0 0 0 0 0 0 0 0 0 0 0 0 0 0 0 0
0 0 0 0 0 0 0 0 0 0 0 0 0 0 0 0 0 0 0 0 0 0 0 0 0 0 0 0 0 0 0 0
0 0 0 0 0 0 0 0 0 10 10 10 10 10 10 10 10 10 10 10 10 10 10 0 0 0 0 0 0 0
0 0 0 0 0 0 0 0 0 10 10 10 10 10 10 10 10 10 10 10 10 10 10 5 0 0 0 0 0 0
0 0 0 0 0 0 0 0 0 10 10 10 10 10 10 10 10 10 10 10 10 10 10 5 0 0 0 0 0 0
0 0 0 0 0 0 0 0 0 10 10 10 10 10 10 10 10 10 10 10 10 10 10 6 0 0 0 0 0 0
0 0 0 0 0 0 0 0 0 10 10 10 10 10 10 10 10 10 10 10 10 10 10 6 5 0 0 0 0 0
0 0 0 0 0 0 0 0 0 10 10 10 10 10 10 10 10 10 10 11 10 10 10 10 6 5 0 0 0 0
0 0 0 0 0 0 0 0 0 10 10 10 10 10 10 10 10 10 12 11 10 10 10 10 6 6 0 0 0 0
0 0 0 0 0 0 0 0 0 10 10 10 10 10 10 10 13 12 11 10 10 10 10 7 6 5 0 0 0 0
0 0 0 0 0 0 0 0 0 10 10 10 10 10 10 14 13 12 11 11 10 10 10 10 7 6 5 0 0 0
0 0 0 0 0 0 0 0 0 10 10 10 10 10 15 14 13 12 12 11 10 10 10 10 7 6 6 0 0 0
0 0 0 0 0 0 0 0 0 10 10 10 10 10 14 13 13 12 11 10 10 10 10 7 7 6 5 0 0 0
0 0 0 0 0 0 0 0 0 10 10 10 10 10 10 10 10 12 11 11 10 10 10 8 7 6 5 0 0 0
0 0 0 0 0 0 0 0 0 10 10 10 10 10 10 10 10 10 10 10 10 10 10 8 7 6 6 0 0 0
0 0 0 0 0 0 0 0 0 10 10 10 10 10 10 10 10 10 10 10 10 10 10 8 7 7 6 5 0 0
0 0 0 0 0 0 0 0 0 10 10 10 10 10 10 10 10 10 10 10 10 10 10 0 0 6 5 0 0 0
0 0 0 0 0 0 0 0 0 10 10 10 10 10 10 10 10 10 10 10 10 10 10 0 0 0 0 0 0 0
0 0 0 0 0 0 0 0 0 10 10 10 10 10 10 10 10 10 10 10 10 10 10 0 0 0 0 0 0 0
0 0 0 0 0 0 0 0 0 10 10 10 10 10 10 10 10 10 10 10 10 10 10 0 0 0 0 0 0 0
0 0 0 0 0 0 0 0 0 10 10 10 10 10 10 10 10 10 10 10 10 10 10 0 0 0 0 0 0 0
0 0 0 0 0 0 0 0 0 10 10 10 10 10 10 10 10 10 10 10 10 10 10 0 0 0 0 0 0 0
0 0 0 0 0 0 0 0 0 0 0 0 0 0 0 0 0 0 0 0 0 0 0 0 0 0 0 0 0 0 0 0
0 0 0 0 0 0 0 0 0 0 0 0 0 0 0 0 0 0 0 0 0 0 0 0 0 0 0 0 0 0 0 0
0 0 0 0 0 0 0 0 0 0 0 0 0 0 0 0 0 0 0 0 0 0 0 0 0 0 0 0 0 0 0 0
0 0 0 0 0 0 0 0 0 0 0 0 0 0 0 0 0 0 0 0 0 0 0 0 0 0 0 0 0 0 0 0
0 0 0 0 0 0 0 0 0 0 0 0 0 0 0 0 0 0 0 0 0 0 0 0 0 0 0 0 0 0 0 0
0 0 0 0 0 0 0 0 0 0 0 0 0 0 0 0 0 0 0 0 0 0 0 0 0 0 0 0 0 0 0 0
```

z-buffer after scan converting rectangle and triangle.

The line of intersection of the triangle and the rectangle is obtained by substituting $z = 10$ into the plane equation for the triangle. The result is

$$3x + y - 80 = 0$$

Intersection of this line with the triangle edges is at $(20, 20)$ and $(22.5, 12.5)$. This line of intersection where the triangle becomes visible is clearly shown by the frame buffer contents.

Hierarchical Z-Buffer

Greene, Kass and Miller discuss modifications of the classical z-buffer algorithm for complex scenes containing tens or hundreds of millions of polygons [Gree93]. Their hierarchical z-buffer algorithm takes advantage of object space coherence, i.e., the ability to resolve the visibility of a collection of *objects* with a single computation; image space coherence, i.e., the ability to resolve the visibility of a collection of *pixels* with a single computation; and temporal coherence, i.e., the use of information from the previous frame to resolve the visibility of objects/pixels in the current frame.

An octree spatial subdivision (see Sec. 4–18) is used to reduce the number of polygons scan converted. Fundamentally, if an octree cube is hidden by the current z-buffer, then all the polygons within the octree cube are hidden by the z-buffer and can be ignored. To determine if the octree cube is hidden, each potentially visible face of the cube is scan converted. If every pixel on each of the potentially visible faces is hidden with respect to the z-buffer, then the octree cube is hidden. If the octree cube is not hidden, then the cube is subdivided and the algorithm applied recursively.

To reduce the cost of scan converting the octree cube faces, an image space z pyramid is used. The z pyramid uses the original z-buffer as the finest, or bottom, level of the pyramid. Subsequent levels are developed by recursively tiling a square four pixel area (or mask) across the current pyramid level, determining the farthest z value of the four pixels and using that value as the z value of the next higher level in the z pyramid. At the apex of the pyramid is a single z value representing the farthest z value in the scene.

When determining the visibility of a polygon, the depth of the pyramid level corresponding to the area of the image space bounding box of the polygon, i.e., its window, is compared to the nearest z value of the polygon. If the nearest z value of the polygon is farther from the eyepoint than the z value at this level in the z pyramid, then no part of the polygon is visible, and it is discarded without being scan converted; if not, then the polygon's window is subdivided into four parts (see the discussion of the Warnock algorithm, Sec. 4–4), and the algorithm is applied recursively to each of the parts of the window using the nearest z value of the original polygon. If each part of the polygon is invisible, the entire polygon is invisible. Eventually, either the entire polygon is declared invisible or a visible pixel is found and rendered, i.e., scan conversion is done hierarchically.

If multiple frames are to be rendered, then a temporal coherence list, comprised of all the visible cubes from the previous frame, is constructed and initially rendered at the beginning of the current frame. The rendered cubes are marked to avoid rerendering them. The resulting z-buffer is then used to construct the z pyramid for the current frame prior to invoking the hierarchical z-buffer algorithm. Consequently, with sufficient frame-to-frame coherence, most of the visible segments of the scene are already rendered. Thus, the z pyramid test is more efficient. Color Plate 2 shows an office scene containing 538 million polygons, rendered in 6.45 seconds on an SGI Crimson Elan with a software implementation of the algorithm. Figure 4–58 shows a grey level rendering of Color Plate 2.

4–10   The A-Buffer Algorithm

The A-buffer has its genesis in an early scan line visible surface algorithm incorporating antialiasing developed by Catmull [Catm78]. After sorting the polygons

Figure 4–58   Gray level rendering of Color Plate 2, showing an office scene containing 538 million polygons.

in the scene by y, those on an active polygon list for a particular scan line are sorted by x and then by z. The pixels within a given polygon on the scan line are divided into two groups: pixels that are completely covered by the polygon, and pixels intersected by an edge of the polygon.

If a given pixel is completely covered by at least one polygon and that polygon is the closest to the eye, i.e, it is a surrounder polygon (see the Warnock algorithm, Sec. 4–4), then the pixel is displayed with that polygon's color. If a polygon edge intersects the pixel, then the polygon is clipped against the pixel window using a modification of the Sutherland–Hodgman clipping algorithm (see Sec. 3–19). Multiple polygons or clipped pieces of polygon may be contained within the pixel window. Using the previously z-sorted polygon list and starting with the closest polygon, each successive polygon is clipped against all previous polygon pieces until a surrounding polygon (or the background) is found.

The intensity, or shade, of the pixel is determined using a weighted average of the visible areas of the clipped polygons (see Fig. 4–59). This is equivalent to convolving a box filter over the pixel window, i.e., area antialiasing (see Secs. 2–28 and 2–29).

Transparency is added to the algorithm by starting with the closest polygon and clipping each successive polygon against all previous polygon pieces until an opaque surrounding polygon (or the background) is found. When a visible polygon piece is transparent, its intensity or shade is recursively combined with the next polygon piece on the z-sorted list, until an opaque polygon piece is found (see Sec. 5-10). The resulting shade is used in determining the weighted average of the visible areas of the clipped polygons.

Unfortunately, the precise clipping operations used to obtain the precise area weighted averages in the Catmull algorithm are computationally expensive. Carpenter's A-buffer algorithm [Carp84] approximates these precise areas using a subpixel bit mask. Although for computation convenience Carpenter used a 4×8 subpixel bit mask (one 32 bit word), any convenient size mask can be used.

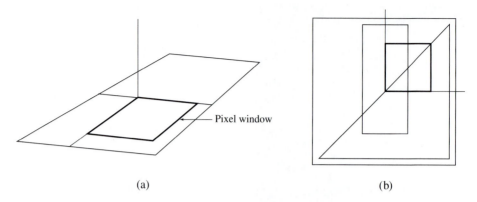

(a)   (b)

Figure 4–59   Precise area averaging for a single pixel.

All elements of the subpixel bit mask for a given polygon piece are initially set
to zero. The area of each polygon piece inside the pixel window is approximated
by complimenting (**xor**ing) all subpixel elements of the bit mask to the right
of each edge of the polygon piece, as shown in Fig. 4–60. Horizontal edges are
ignored. Essentially, this operation is an edge fill scan conversion algorithm
(see Sec. 2–13).

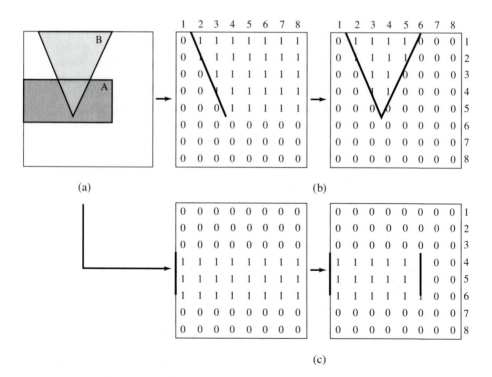

Figure 4–60   Area approximation using 8×8 subpixel masks. (a) Pixel contents;
(b) triangle area equals $^{12}/_{64}$ ths; (c) rectangle area equals $^{18}/_{64}$ ths.

The visibility of each polygon piece, the surrounder polygon or the background is determined using the z sort list and the pixel masks. For example, by recursively **and**ing the bit masks of successive polygon pieces, the visible portion of each polygon piece is determined, and hence the approximate visible area of each polygon piece. It is this approximate area that is used in the area average to determine the pixel shade. Specifically consider the bit masks for polygon pieces A and B of Fig. 4–60. Taking the logical (Boolean) **and** of the bit masks shows that only the two subpixels at locations $(4, 3)$ and $(4, 4)$ overlap. Assuming that polygon A occurs before polygon B on the z sort list, the approximate area of polygon B is reduced by $^{2}/_{64}$ths to $^{10}/_{64}$ths, to obtain the approximate visible area for polygon piece B.

Since the A-buffer keeps only the location of each polygon piece on the z sort list and not the actual z values, if the z priority sort is not definitive errors result (see the discussion of the Newell–Newell–Sancha algorithm in Sec. 4–12). For example, if the point of polygon B just penetrates polygon A from below, then a z sort, using the nearest polygon vertex as the key, places polygon B before polygon A on the z sort list. Thus, the area of the tip of polygon piece B is incorrectly subtracted from the area of polygon piece A when determining the visible areas of the polygon pieces.

As discussed here, the A-buffer uses simple single pixel area averaging for antialiasing. Multiple pixel support is achieved by expanding the pixel bit masks to encompass several pixels, e.g., the eight surrounding pixels, and using weighted area averaging (see Sec. 2–16). Abram, Westover and Whitted [Abra85] extended the A-buffer using convolution kernels centered on the eight surrounding pixels and the subject pixel. They considered nine simple polygon pieces comprised of 45° half pixel triangles in each of the four pixel corners, half pixel rectangles adjacent to each of the four pixel edges and a completely covered pixel. The convolutions of each of these fragments is precomputed for each of the pixels in the support base, multiplied by the fragment area and stored in a small look-up table. More complex polygon pieces are approximated by sums and differences of these simple fragments or, if necessary, by bit masks. The technique both improves and speeds up A-buffer antialiasing.

4–11 List Priority Algorithms

All visible surface algorithms attempt to establish the priority, i.e., the depth or distance from the viewpoint, of objects in a scene. The list priority algorithms attempt to capitalize on this by performing the depth or priority sort first. The objective of the sort is to obtain a definitive list of scene elements in depth priority order, based on distance from the viewpoint. If the list is definitive, then no two elements overlap in depth. Starting with the scene element farthest from the viewpoint, each element in turn is written to a frame buffer. Closer elements on the list overwrite the contents of the frame buffer. Thus, the visible surface problem is trivially solved. Transparency effects are incorporated into the algorithm by only partially overwriting the contents of the frame buffer with the attributes of the transparent element (see [Newe72] and Sec. 5–10).

For simple scene elements, e.g., polygons, for which a definitive priority sort is available, the technique is sometimes called the painter's algorithm, because it is analogous to that used by an artist in creating a painting. The artist first paints the background, then the elements in the intermediate distance, and finally the elements in the foreground. The artist solves the visibility problem by constructing the painting in reverse priority order.

In computer graphics, several important applications are inherently layered, for example window management systems, VLSI chip layout and cartographic applications. For these and similar applications, a definitive depth priority sort and the simple painter's algorithm is appropriate.

For more general but simple scenes, such as that shown in Fig. 4–61a, obtaining a definitive depth priority list is also straightforward; for example, the polygons can be sorted by either their maximum or minimum z coordinate value. However, for the scene shown in Fig. 4–61b, a definitive depth priority list cannot be obtained by simply sorting in z. If P and Q in Fig. 4–61b are sorted by the minimum z coordinate value (z_{min}), then P appears on the depth priority list before Q. If P and Q are written to the frame buffer in this order, then Q will partially hide P; however, P in fact partially hides Q. The correct order in the priority list is obtained by interchanging P and Q.

A further difficulty is illustrated by Fig. 4–62. Here, the polygons cyclically overlap each other. In Fig. 4–62a, P is in front of Q, which is in front of R, which in turn is in front of P. For Fig. 4–62b, P is in front of Q which is in front of P. A similar cyclical overlap occurs for penetrating polygons, e.g., the triangle that penetrates the rectangle in Fig. 4–57. There, the rectangle is in front of the triangle, which is in front of the rectangle. In both examples, a definitive depth priority list cannot be immediately established. The solution is to cyclically split the polygons along their plane of intersection until a definitive priority list is obtained. This is shown by the dashed lines in Figs. 4–62a and 4–62b.

In outline, a typical list priority algorithm consists of three steps:

Initially sort all objects in depth priority order, using some metric.

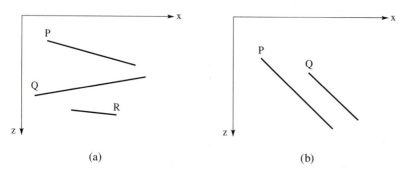

(a)   (b)

Figure 4–61 Polygonal priority. (a) Correct depth priority; (b) incorrect depth priority.

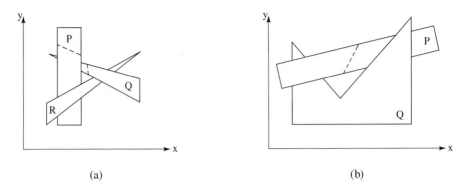

Figure 4–62   Cyclical overlapping polygons. (a) Convex polygons; concave polygons.

Identify and resolve any ambiguities, to obtain a definitive depth priority. Scan convert the resulting depth priority list back to front.

4–12   Newell–Newell–Sancha Algorithm

Newell, Newell and Sancha [Newe72] developed a special sorting technique for resolving priority conflicts on the depth priority list. This special sorting technique is incorporated into the Newell–Newell–Sancha algorithm. The algorithm dynamically computes a new depth priority list before processing each frame of a scene. No restrictions are placed on the complexity of the scene environment, nor on the type of polygon used to describe elements of the scene. The Newell–Newell–Sancha algorithm is designed to process polygons. Newell [Newe74] extended the concept to three-dimensional volumes. Newell's extension is not restricted to polyhedral volumes; it also allows the processing of volumes of mixed types within the same scene.

The Newell–Newell–Sancha algorithm for polygons is:

Establish a preliminary depth priority list, using $z_{\min}$ for each polygon as the sort key. The first polygon on the list is the one with the smallest value of $z_{\min}$. This polygon, labeled P, is the farthest from a viewpoint at infinity on the positive z axis. The next polygon on the list is labeled Q.

For each polygon on the list examine the relationship of P to Q.

If the nearest vertex of P, $P_{z_{\max}}$, is farther from the viewpoint then the farthest vertex of Q, $Q_{z_{\min}}$, i.e. $Q_{z_{\min}} \geq P_{z_{\max}}$, then no part of P can hide Q. Write P to the frame buffer (see Fig. 4–61a).

If $Q_{z_{\min}} < P_{z_{\max}}$, then P potentially obscures not only Q but also any polygon on the list for which $Q_{z_{\min}} < P_{z_{\max}}$. This is the set $\{Q\}$. However, P may not hide any part of any polygon in the set $\{Q\}$. If this can be determined, then P can be written to the frame buffer. A series of tests of increasing computational difficulty is used to answer this question. The tests are posed as questions. If the answer to any question is yes, then P cannot obscure $\{Q\}$. P is then immediately written to the frame buffer. The tests are:

Are the bounding boxes of P and Q disjoint in x?

Are the bounding boxes of P and Q disjoint in y?

Is P wholly on the side of the plane of Q farther from the viewpoint? (See Fig. 4–63a.)

Is Q wholly on the side of the plane of P nearer the viewpoint? (See Fig. 4–63b.)

Are the projections of P and Q disjoint?

Each test is applied to each element of $\{Q\}$. If none of these tests successfully writes P to the frame buffer, then P can obscure Q.

Interchange P and Q, marking the position of Q on the list. Repeat the tests with the rearranged list. This is successful for Fig. 4–61b.

If an attempt is made to swap Q again, a cyclical overlap exists (see Fig. 4–62). In this case P is split along the plane of Q, the original polygon is removed from the list, and the two parts of P are inserted into the list. The tests are then repeated with the new list. This step prevents infinite looping.

Implementing the Tests

Combined, the first two steps for determining whether P obscures Q are a normal bounding box test (see Secs. 2–13 and 3–1). Since many scenes are not square, it is more likely that the polygon bounding boxes overlap in one direction rather than in the other. When polygons are primarily horizontal or vertical, using individual tests is more efficient. As written, the algorithm assumes the scene is wider than it is high; and thus polygons are primarily horizontal. The order of the tests is interchanged if the scene is higher than it is wide. If the scene is square, or if its composition is isomorphic, then the order of the tests is immaterial.

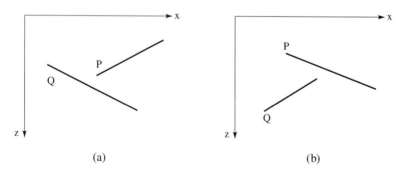

(a)   (b)

Figure 4–63   Tests for overlapping polygons. (a) P wholly on the side of Q farther from the viewpoint; (b) Q wholly on the side of P nearer the viewpoint.

The third and fourth tests are implemented using any of the visibility tests previously discussed (see Sec. 3–19 and Ex. 3–28). Since the plane equation or the normal for each polygon is frequently available, a simple substitution test is convenient. If the relationship of the polygon Q to the polygon P is desired, then the coordinates of the vertices of Q are substituted into the plane equation of P. If the signs of the results are all the same, then Q lies wholly on one side of P. As with the hidden surface algorithms discussed previously, a preliminary backface cull is used if appropriate. Example 4–20 more fully illustrates this for polygons skewed in space.

Example 4–20   Relationship Test for Skewed Polygons

Consider the three polygons P, Q_1, Q_2 shown in Fig. 4–64. The polygon vertices are

$$P: \ (1,1,1), (4,5,2), (5,2,5)$$
$$Q_1: \ (2,2,0.5), (3,3,1.75), (6,1,0.5)$$
$$Q_2: \ (0.5,2,5.5), (2,5,3), (4,4,5)$$

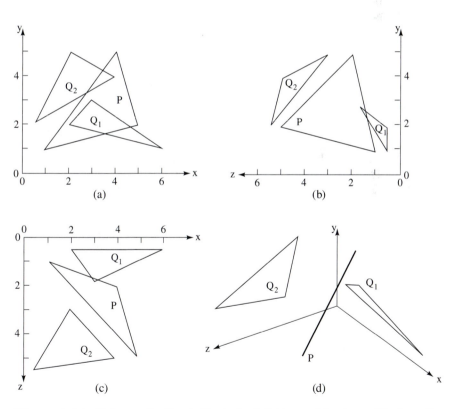

Figure 4–64   Polygons for Ex. 4–20. (a, b, c) Orthographic views; (d) three-dimensional view.

It is desired to determine if Q_1 and Q_2 are wholly on one side of P; this is not clear from the three orthographic views in Fig. 4–64. The plane equation of P is

$$15x - 8y - 13z + 6 = 0$$

The test function is then

$$T.F. = 15x - 8y - 13z + 6$$

Substituting the vertices of Q_1 into the test function yields

$$T.F._1 = 15(2) - 8(2) - 13(0.5) + 6 = 13.5 > 0$$
$$T.F._2 = 15(3) - 8(3) - 13(1.75) + 6 = 4.25 > 0$$
$$T.F._3 = 15(6) - 8(1) - 13(0.5) + 6 = 81.5 > 0$$

Since the sign of all the test functions is positive, the polygon Q_1 lies wholly on one side of the plane of P.

Substituting the vertices of Q_2 into the test function yields

$$T.F._4 = 15(0.5) - 8(2) - 13(5.5) + 6 = -74 < 0$$
$$T.F._5 = 15(2) - 8(5) - 13(3) + 6 = -43 < 0$$
$$T.F._6 = 15(4) - 8(4) - 13(5) + 6 = -31 < 0$$

Again, all the signs of the test functions are the same, and the polygon Q_2 lies wholly on one side of the plane of P.

Figure 4–64d clearly shows that Q_1 is on the side of the plane of P away from a viewpoint at infinity on the positive z-axis. Hence, it is partially obscured by P. Similarly, Fig. 4–64d clearly shows that Q_2 is on the side of the plane of P nearer a viewpoint at infinity on the positive z-axis. Thus, it partially obscures P.

From this example it is clear that:

If the signs of the test function for every vertex of a polygon are the same and positive or zero, then the polygon is on the far (hidden) side of the plane of P.

If the signs of the test function for every vertex of a polygon are the same and negative or zero, then the polygon is on the near (visible) side of the plane of P.

If the test functions for every vertex of a polygon are zero, then the polygon lies in the plane of P.

The last of the series of tests is particularly expensive, because it requires a full determination of whether the projections of P and Q are disjoint. These techniques were previously discussed in the context of the Warnock algorithm (see Sec. 4–4).

If a cyclical overlap exists, a polygon clipping algorithm, e.g., the Sutherland-Hodgman algorithm (see Sec. 3–19), is used to split the polygons along the line of the intersections of their planes. Here the plane of Q is used as the clipping plane. Each edge of P is clipped against Q to form the two new polygons. A line clipping algorithm, e.g., the three-dimensional Cyrus–Beck algorithm (see Sec. 3–13), is used to find the intersection of each edge of P with the plane of Q.

Occasionally a pair of polygons is unnecessarily split by the sort algorithm. Consider polygons P and Q shown in Fig. 4–65. z_{min} for polygon P is smaller than z_{min} for polygon Q. Thus, P is placed on the preliminary depth priority list before polygon Q. When comparing P to Q notice that all the tests in the Newell–Newell–Sancha special sort fail. Hence, P is unnecessarily split along the plane of Q. This is a small price to pay to obtain a definitive depth priority sort.

4–13   Binary Space Partitioning Algorithms

The Newell–Newell–Sancha algorithm attempts to solve the hidden surface problem dynamically by processing all the polygons in the scene as each frame is presented. If the scene is complex and the frame rate high, as in real-time simulation systems, sufficient processing capability may not be available (see [Scha83]). However, for many real-time simulations, e.g., aircraft flight simulators, the scene is static and only the viewpoint changes. Schumacker et al. [Schu69] take advantage of several more general priority characteristics to precompute, off-line, the priority list for simulations of such static environments.

The Schumacker Algorithm

The Schumacker algorithm allows only convex polygons in the scene. These polygons are grouped into clusters of polygons that are linearly separable. Clusters are linearly separable if a nonintersecting, dividing plane can be passed between them. Several two-dimensional clusters are shown in Fig. 4–66a. The separating planes are labeled α and β. They divide the scene into four regions, A, B,

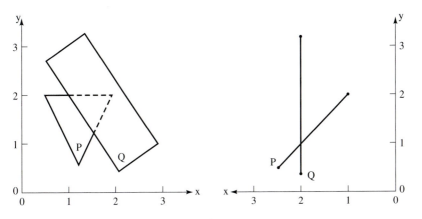

Figure 4–65   Unnecessarily split polygons.

C, D. A viewpoint can be located in any of the four regions. The binary tree structure shown in Fig. 4–66b establishes the cluster priority for the scene. For any viewpoint in the two-dimensional plane the cluster priority is precomputed. Substituting the coordinates of the viewpoint into the equations for the separating planes locates the appropriate node in the cluster priority tree. The hidden surface problem is then solved for each of the clusters in reverse priority order.

Example 4–21   Cluster Priority

Assume that the separating planes α and β, shown in Fig. 4–66a, intersect at the origin of the coordinate system. Further assume that α is the $y = 0$ plane and β the plane through the line $y = x$, both perpendicular to the paper. The plane equations and appropriate test functions are then

$$\alpha : y = 0 \qquad (T.F.)_1 = y$$
$$\beta : y - x = 0 \quad (T.F.)_2 = y - x$$

A viewpoint on the line $2y - x = 0$, e.g., at $(20, 10)$, yields

$$(T.F.)_1 = 10 > 0$$
$$(T.F.)_2 = 10 - 20 = -10 < 0$$

Thus, the viewpoint is in region D. From Fig. 4–66b, the cluster priority is $3, 1, 2$.

Clusters are used to subdivide a scene. The simplest cluster is a single polygon. Clusters can be complex polygonal or nonpolygonal surfaces or volumes. As described by Newell [Newe74], an appropriate visible surface technique can be applied within each cluster.

Within certain types of clusters, the priority of individual polygons is independent of the viewpoint [Schu69; Fuch83]. This observation is one of the major

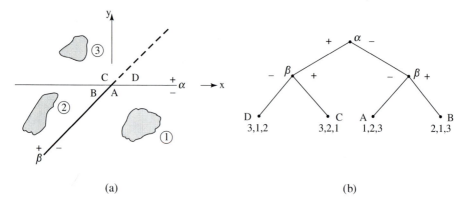

(a)   (b)

Figure 4–66   Cluster priority. (a) Scene; (b) binary tree showing cluster priority.

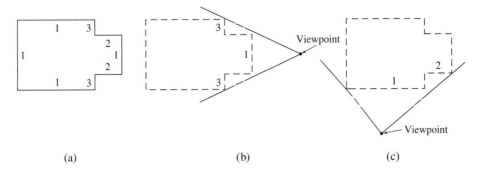

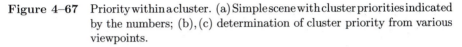

(a)   (b)   (c)

Figure 4–67   Priority within a cluster. (a) Simple scene with cluster priorities indicated by the numbers; (b), (c) determination of cluster priority from various viewpoints.

contributions of the Schumacker algorithm. It allows precomputation of the entire priority list. Figure 4–67a shows a two-dimensional cluster for which the individual polygonal priorities can be precalculated. The priority of each polygon is established by considering whether a given polygon hides any other polygon from any viewpoint. The more polygons a given polygon hides, the higher its priority. To establish the polygonal priority within a cluster for a given viewpoint, the self-hidden polygons are first removed. The remaining polygons are then in priority order, as shown in Figs. 4–67b and 4–67c. The cluster priorities for the Schumacker algorithm were generally determined *by hand*. This limited the utility of the algorithm.

Binary Space Partition Trees

In contrast to the Schumacker algorithm the Binary Space Partitioning (BSP) tree visible surface algorithm [Fuch80] assumes that for a given viewpoint a polygon is correctly rendered if all the polygons on its side away from the viewpoint are rendered first; then the polygon itself is rendered; and finally, all the polygons on the side nearer the viewpoint are rendered. Like the Schumacker algorithm, the BSP tree algorithm is a two-part algorithm. First the BSP tree is constructed, and then it is displayed.

Constructing the BSP Tree

Like the Schumacker algorithm, the BSP tree algorithm recursively subdivides space into two half spaces. However, the BSP tree algorithm uses one of the polygons in the scene as the separating or dividing plane. Other polygons in the scene that are entirely on one side of the separating plane are placed in the appropriate half space. Polygons that intersect the separating plane are split along the separating plane, and each portion is placed in the appropriate half space. Each half space is then recursively subdivided, using one of the polygons in the half space as the separating plane; subdivision continues until there is only a single polygon in each half space. The subdivided space is conveniently represented by a binary tree, with the original separating polygon as the root. Construction of the BSP tree is accomplished in object space

Figure 4–68 shows a simple scene and the resulting BSP tree as it is constructed. Here, for simplicity, each of the polygons and the separating plane are assumed perpendicular to the paper. Figure 4–68 uses polygon 1 as the separating plane. The separating plane intersects polygon 2. After dividing polygon 2, polygons 2a and 3 are in front of the separating plane, while polygons 2b, 4 and 5 are behind the separating plane, as shown in the accompanying incomplete BSP tree.

Selecting polygon 3 from the 'front' branch of the tree as the separating polygon places polygon 2a on the front branch and nothing on the back branch of the tree. This branch of the tree in now complete. Returning to the root and selecting polygon 5 as the separating plane shows that only polygon 4 is in front and polygon 2b is in back of the separating plane. This branch of the tree is now complete. Actually, polygon 4 is coplanar with the separating plane and can be placed on either branch of the tree.

The determination of the side of the separating plane on which a polygon lies is accomplished with any of the tests discussed previously, e.g., a simple substitution test (see Sec. 3–19 Ex. 3–28, Sec. 4–4 Ex. 4–15 or Sec. 3–19 Ex. 3–28.

Since the selection of the polygon used as the initial separating plane and in each subsequent half space is arbitrary, there is no unique BSP tree representation for a given scene. An example of an alternative BSP tree for the scene in Fig. 4–68a is shown in Fig. 4–69.

To reduce the number of polygons ultimately rendered, it is advantageous if separating planes create the minimum number of polygon splits. To accomplish this, every polygon in the initial scene and in all subsequent subspaces must be tested as the separating plane. However, Fuchs, Abram and Grant [Fuch83] show that testing only 5 or 6 polygons as potential separating planes gave a near optimal result while significantly decreasing the effort required to build the BSP tree. Pseudocode for constructing a BSP tree is:

```
if polylist is empty then
    BSPtree = null
else
    call SelectPolygon(polylist; root)
    backlist = null
    frontlist = null
    for each remaining polygon on polylist
        if polygon in front of root then
            call AddtoBSPlist(polygon; frontlist)
        else if polygon behind root then
            call AddtoBSPlist(polygon; backlist)
        else
            call SplitPolygon(polygon, root; frontpart, backpart)
```

1 Motion capture. A three-dimensional wireless motion capture system (see Sec. 1–9). *(Courtesy of Ascension Technology Corp.)*

2 Office scene. Rendered with a hierarchical z-buffer algorithm (see Sec. 4–9). *(Courtesy of N. Greene, NYIT Computer Graphics Lab.)*

3   1983 Chevrolet Camaro. Rendered by D. Warn with a Watkins algorithm and the special effects illumination model of Sec. 5–8. *(Courtesy General Motors Research Laboratory.)*

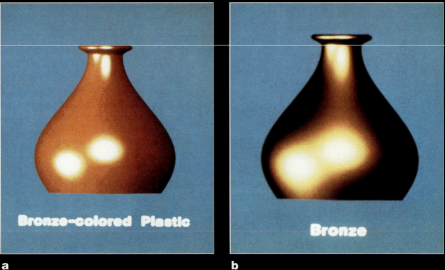

Bronze-colored Plastic

Bronze

a   **b**

4   Bronze vases. (a) The vase is bronze-colored plastic; (b) the vase is metallic bronze. Each vase is illuminated with two light sources and rendered using the Cook–Torrance illumination model of Sec. 5–9. *(Courtesy R. Cook and the Program of Computer Graphics, Cornell University.)*

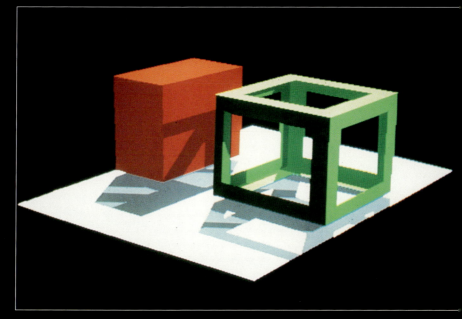

5 Shadows. The Weiler–Atherton algorithm of Sec. 5–11 is used to determine the shadows from the two light sources. *(Courtesy of P. Atherton and the Program of Computer Graphics, Cornell University.)*

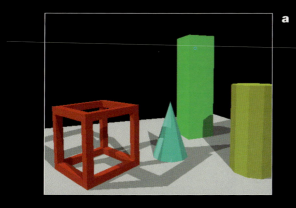

a

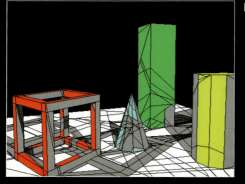

b

6 Shadows (SVBSP). (a) The scene is illuminated by three light sources. (b) The shaded scene shows the fragmented polygons generated by the scene BSP tree and the shadow volume SVBSP tree. Shadow colors indicate the number of illuminating light sources (see Sec. 5–11). *(Courtesy of N. Chin, Silicon Graphics, Inc.)*

7 Shadow volumes. Penumbra and umbra shadows from linear light sources (see Sec. 5–11). (Courtesy of Professors Nishita and Nakamae.)

a

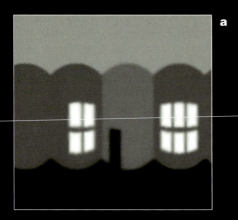

b

8 Teapot. A teapot with a window. (a) Environment map; (b) reflection in the teapot (see Sec. 5–12). *(Courtesy of Jim Blinn.)*

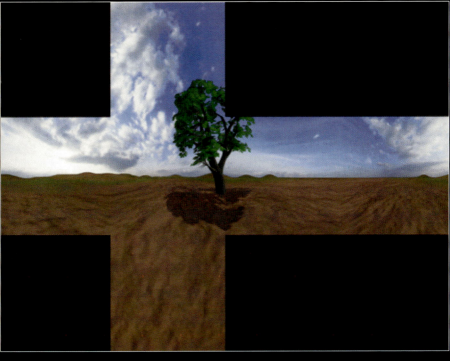

9 Environment map. Unfolded cube projection of a three-dimensional environment map (see Sec. 5–12). *(Courtesy of N. Greene, NYIT Computer Graphics Lab.)*

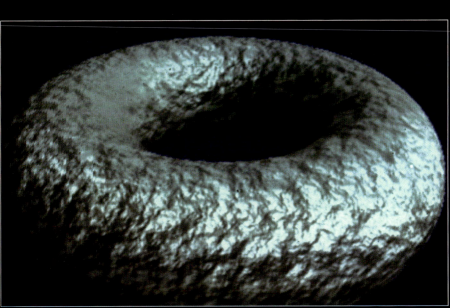

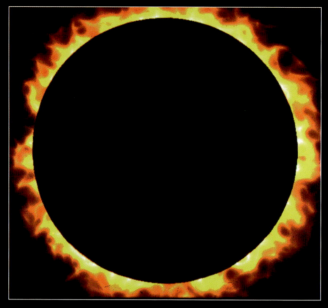

11   Corona. The corona of the sun simulated using procedural texture (see Sec. 5–12). *(Courtesy of K. Perlin.)*

a

b

12   Fractal mountains. The image in Color Plate 12a contains 16,384 fractal triangles. The image in Color Plate 12b contains 262,144 fractal triangles. Notice the self-shadowing from the light source at the right (see Sec. 5–13). *(Courtesy of J. Kajiya, Cal Tech.)*

13 Balls over a red-yellow checkerboard. Rendered with a ray tracing algorithm and a global illumination model incorporating reflections, shadows and transparency with refraction effects (see Sec. 5–14). *(Courtesy T. Whitted, Bell Laboratories, reprinted with permission from Communications of the ACM, Vol. 23, June 1980, Copyright 1980, Association for Computing Machinery.)*

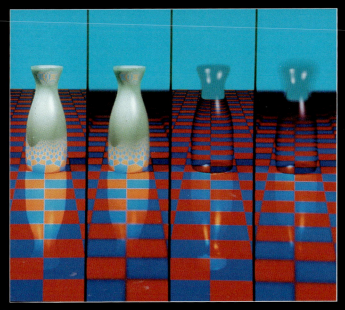

14 Vases. Opaque and transparent vases rendered with a ray tracing algorithm. In each case the right-hand image illustrates the effects of limited depth of field (see Sec. 5–14). *(Courtesy M. Potmesil and the Image Processing Laboratory, Rensselaer Polytechnic Institute.)*

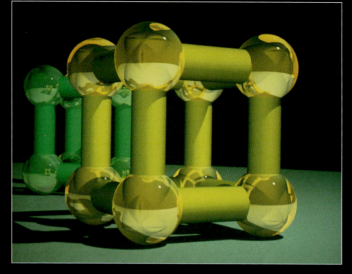

15 Spheres and cylinders with reflection and refraction. Computed using the Whitted ray tracing algorithm and illumination model (see Sec. 5–14). *(Courtesy A. Barr, Raster Technologies, Inc.)*

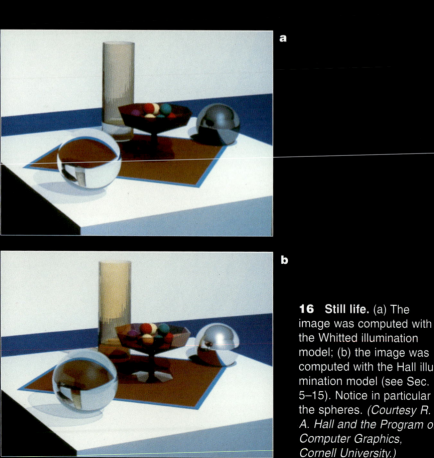

a

b

16 Still life. (a) The image was computed with the Whitted illumination model; (b) the image was computed with the Hall illumination model (see Sec. 5–15). Notice in particular the spheres. *(Courtesy R. A. Hall and the Program of Computer Graphics, Cornell University.)*

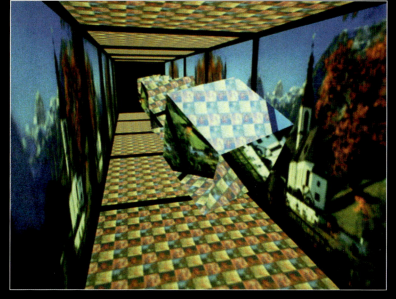

17 Beam tracing. A recursive texture mapped reflective cube (see Sec. 5–16). *(Courtesy of P. Heckbert.)*

18 1984. Stochastic sampling showing motion blur and penumbra shadows. Notice that reflections and shadows are also motion blurred (see Sec. 5–16). *(©1984 PIXAR. Courtesy of T. Porter.)*

 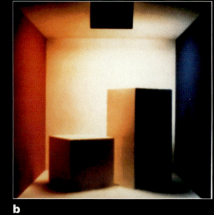

a   b

19 Radiosity. Experimental comparison of a real image with a computer-generated image. The real image is on the left (see Sec. 5–17). *(Courtesy of G. Meyer, H. Rushmeier, M. T. Cohen, D. Greenberg, K. Torrance and the Program of Computer Graphics, Cornell University.)*

20 Chartres Cathedral. A radiosity solution for the Chartres Cathedral nave (see Sec. 5–17). *(Courtesy of J. Wallace, K. Elmquist and E. Haines, 3DEye, Inc.)*

21 A radiosity solution with diffuse and nondiffuse reflections (see Sec. 5–17). *(Courtesy of D. Immel, M. Cohen, D. Greenberg and the Program of Computer Graphics, Cornell University.)*

a

b

c

22 Two pass lighting solution. (a) Direct illumination only; (b) direct illumination plus diffuse to diffuse transfer; (c) full solution (see Sec. 5–18). *(Courtesy of J. Wallace, M. Cohen, D. Greenberg and the Program of Computer Graphics, Cornell University.)*

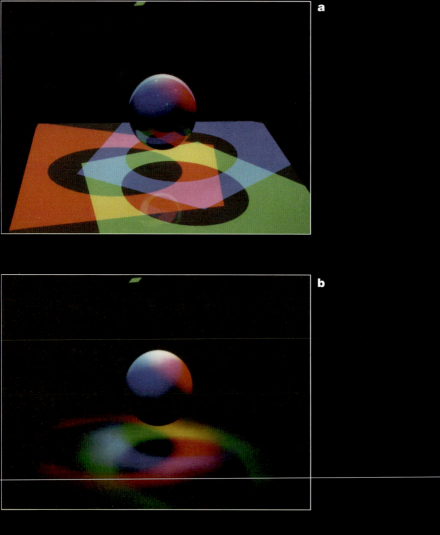

a

b

c **23 Refraction effects.** A two-pass combined radiosity and ray-tracing algorithm. (a) Conventional ray tracing image; (b) conventional radiosity image; (c) combined radiosity and ray tracing, index of refraction 1.1 (see Sec. 5–18).
(Courtesy F. Sillion iMAGIS-GRAVIR, CNRS.)

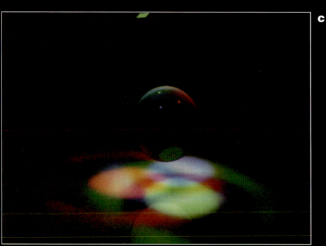

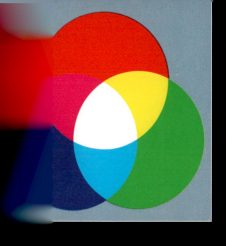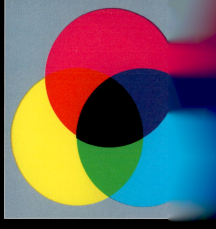

b

r systems. (a) The additive RGB color system; (b) the subtractive
m (see Sec. 5–19).

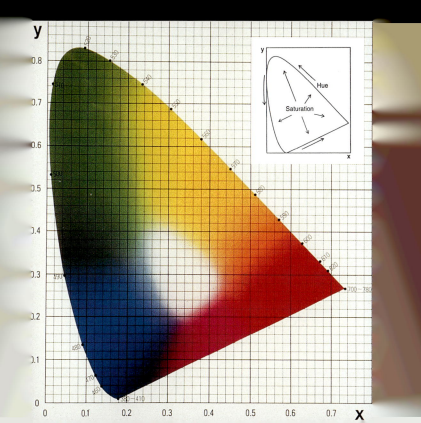

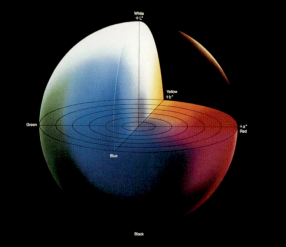

White
+L*

Yellow
+b*

Green

Blue

+a*
Red

Black

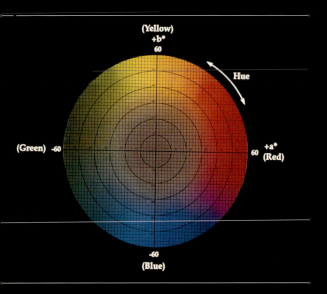

(Yellow)
+b*
60

Hue

(Green) -60

60 +a*
(Red)

-60
(Blue)

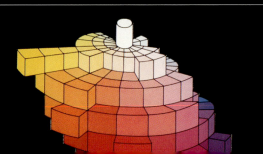

a

b

c

d

29 White sands. The flowering plants were grown from a single cell using an algorithm developed by the artist Alvy Ray Smith, based on the mathematics of Paulien Hogeweg. The grasses were rendered by Bill Reeves using a particle system. The hidden surface software is by Loren Carpenter and the compositioning software by Thomas Porter (see Sec. 5–22). *(Courtesy of Alvy Ray Smith, ©Lucasfilm Ltd. All rights reserved.)*

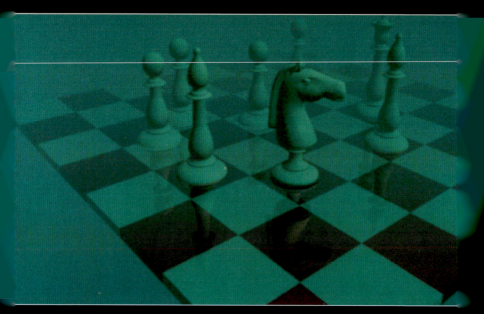

30 Foggy chessmen. Created using a scan line algorithm and combining separate

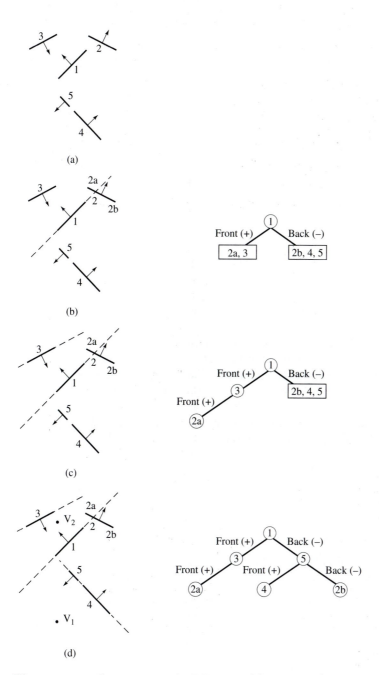

Figure 4–68 Construction of a BSP tree. (a) Original scene; (b) scene partitioned using polygon 1; (c) scene split further using polygon 3; (d) final partition using polygon 5.

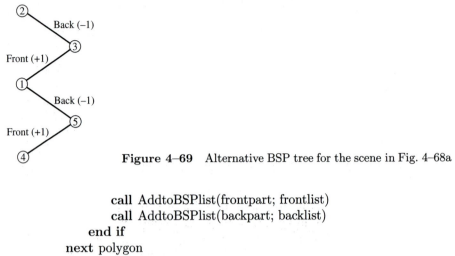

Figure 4–69   Alternative BSP tree for the scene in Fig. 4–68a

```
            call AddtoBSPlist(frontpart; frontlist)
            call AddtoBSPlist(backpart; backlist)
        end if
      next polygon
    end if
    call Combine(frontlist, root, backlist; BSPtree)
    finish
```

BSP Tree Traversal

One of the significant advantages of the BSP tree algorithm is that the BSP tree itself is independent of the location of the eye or viewpoint. In addition, the display algorithm operates in image space. In order to generate the visible surfaces from the BSP tree, it is only necessary to know the spatial relationship of the viewpoint to the root polygon of the tree. A variant of an in order tree traversal, i.e., traverse one subtree, visit the root, traverse the other subtree, is then used to generate the visible surfaces. The tree traversal is a linear time algorithm.

In the context of a list priority algorithm, the basic idea is to write those polygons farthest from the viewpoint to the frame buffer or to display them first, i.e., a back-to-front ordering of the polygons. There are two possibilities. If the viewpoint is in front of the root polygon, then the BSP tree is traversed in the order

Back branch (all polygons in the root's rear half space)

Root (node) polygon

Front branch (all polygons in the root's front half space)

while if the viewpoint is in back of the root polygon, then the BSP tree is traversed in the order

Front branch (all polygons in the root's front half space)

Root (node) polygon

Rear branch (all polygons in the root's rear half space.

If we consider the half space of the root polygon which does not contain the viewpoint as the far half space, and the half space containing the viewpoint as the near half space, then the two traversal algorithms collapse to a single traversal algorithm.

Far branch

Root (node) polygon

Near branch

A pseudocode algorithm for back-to-front traversal of the BSPtree is:

> **if** BSPtree not empty **then**
>> **if** viewpoint in front of root polygon **then**
>>> **call** DisplayBSPtree(back_branch)
>>> **call** DisplayBSPtree(root_polygon) *only without backface culling*
>>> **call** DisplayBSPtree(front_branch)
>> **else**   *viewpoint in back of root polygon*
>>> **call** DisplayBSPtree(front_branch)
>>> **call** DisplayBSPtree(root_polygon) *only without backface culling*
>>> **call** DisplayBSPtree(back_branch)
>> **end if**
> **end if**
> **finish**

The algorithm is applied recursively as the BSP tree is traversed. An example illustrates the algorithm.

Example 4–22   Display BSP Tree

Consider the BSP tree in Fig. 4–68d, with the viewpoint located as shown by v_1. The root polygon is 1, and v_1 is on the back, or negative, side of the root polygon. Thus, the BSP tree traversal order is front-root-back.

Applying the algorithm recursively at polygon 3 shows that the viewpoint, v_1, is on the front, or positive, side. Thus, the traversal order is back-root-front. Here there is no back branch. The root polygon, polygon 3, is now displayed. Traversing the front branch yields polygon 2a, which is a leaf polygon; it is now displayed. Moving back up the tree, the root polygon, polygon 1, is displayed.

Traversing the back (negative) branch of the BSP tree originating at the root, i.e., polygon 1, we encounter polygon 5 as the root of the subtree. The viewpoint is on the front, or positive, side of polygon 5, thus the traversal order for the subtree is back-root-front. Polygon 2b is a leaf polygon and is displayed. The root of the subtree, polygon 5, is now displayed, and then the front branch of the subtree is traversed. Polygon 4 is a leaf polygon and is displayed. The scene is complete. The final display order is 3, 2a, 1, 2b, 5, 4.

If the viewpoint is at v_2, as shown in Fig. 4–68d, then the polygon display order is 4, 5, 2b, 1, 3, 2a.

Notice that the back-to-front ordering is independent of distance to the viewpoint. Furthermore, it is also independent of direction [Chin95], because those polygons *behind* the viewer are subsequently clipped away before final display.

A back-to-front display order assumes that obscured pixels are overwritten by visible pixels as the scene is generated. Consequently, shading calculations are unnecessarily performed for pixels that are ultimately overwritten. A front-to-back display order is also possible by simply reversing the order of the traversal of the BSP tree, i.e., near branch, root (node) polygon, far branch. In this case, shading calculations are performed for a pixel only if that pixel has not already been written to the display (see, e.g., [Gord91]).

Culling

If the viewpoint is in the negative, or back, half space of a polygon, then that polygon can be culled. For example, for viewpoint v_1 in Fig. 4–68d, polygons 1, 2a, 2b and 4 are marked as backface polygons. Similarly, polygons 2a, 2b and 5 are marked as backface polygons for viewpoint v_2.

If all of the view space (vertices) lies completely on one side of the root polygon, the opposite side of the BSP tree is eliminated from the traversal. This concept is applied recursively as the BSP tree is traversed.

Summary

In addition to their use as the basis for a visible surface algorithm, BSP trees are used for constructive solid geometry (see, e.g., [Thib87]), point and line classification (see, e.g., [Tilo80; Thib87; Chin95]), ray tracing (see, e.g., [Nayl86]) and shadow generation (see, e.g., [Chin92]). Fuchs, Abram and Grant [Fuch83] also suggest a technique for incorporating antialiasing into a back-to-front BSP visible surface algorithm.

The list priority algorithms operate in both object and image space. In particular, the priority list calculations are carried out in object space, and the result is written to an image space frame buffer. The use of a frame buffer is critical to the algorithm.

Like the Warnock (see Sec. 4–4) and z-buffer (see Sec. 4–9) algorithms, the list priority algorithms process polygons in arbitrary order; therefore, applying antialiasing techniques to the resulting images is difficult. However, as with the Warnock and z-buffer algorithms, the postfiltering antialiasing technique is applicable (see Secs. 2–27 and 2–28).

The list priority, Warnock and z-buffer algorithms may also be implemented as visible line algorithms. When implemented as visible line algorithms, the edge of each polygon is written to the frame buffer with a unique attribute. However, the interior of each polygon is written to the frame buffer with the background attribute. In this way polygons nearer the viewpoint 'obscure' polygon edges further from the viewpoint.

4–14   Scan Line Algorithms

The Warnock, z-buffer and list priority algorithms process scene elements or polygons in arbitrary order with respect to the display. The scan line algorithms, as originally developed by Wylie et al. [Wyli67], Bouknight [Bouk69, 70b], Bouknight and Kelly [Bouk70a], Romney et al. [Romn68, 69a] and Watkins [Watk70], and subsequently by Myers [Myer75], Hamlin and Gear [Haml77] and Jackson [Jack80b], process the scene in scan line order. Scan line algorithms operate in image space.

Scan conversion of single polygons is discussed in Chapter 2. Scan line visible surface and visible line algorithms are extensions of those techniques. Scan line algorithms reduce the visible line/visible surface problem from three dimensions to two. A scan plane is defined by the viewpoint at infinity on the positive z-axis and a scan line, as shown in Fig. 4–70. The intersection of the scan plane and the three-dimensional scene defines a one-scan-line-high window. The visible surface problem is solved in this scan plane window. Figure 4–70b shows the intersection of the scan plane with the polygons. The figure illustrates that the visible surface problem is reduced to deciding which line segment is visible for each point on the scan line.

At first glance it might appear that the ordered edge list algorithm discussed in Sec. 2–12 is directly applicable. However, Fig. 4–70b clearly shows that this yields incorrect results. For example, for the scan line shown in Fig. 4–70 there

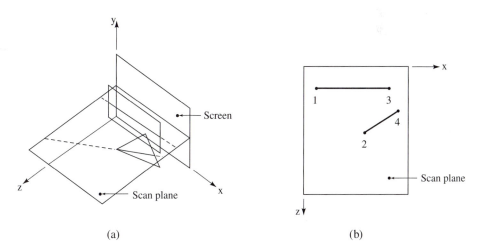

(a)   (b)

Figure 4–70   Scan plane.

are four active edges on the active edge list. The intersections of these edges with the scan line are shown by the small dots in Fig. 4–70b. The ordered edge list is shown by the numbers in Fig. 4–70b. Extracting the intersections in pairs causes the pixels between 1 and 2 and between 3 and 4 to be activated. The pixels between 2 and 3 are not activated. The result is incorrect. A 'hole' is left on the scan line, where in fact the scan line intersects two polygons. Correct scan line algorithms are discussed in the next two sections.

4–15   Scan Line z-Buffer Algorithm

One of the simplest scan line algorithms that solves the hidden surface problem is a special case of the z-buffer algorithm discussed in the previous section. It is called a scan line z-buffer algorithm [Myer75]. In this algorithm, the display window is one scan line high by the horizontal resolution of the display wide. Both the frame buffer and the z-buffer are only one bit high by the horizontal resolution of the display wide by the requisite precision deep. The required depth precision depends on the range of z. For example, the frame buffer might be $1 \times 1280 \times 24$ bits and the z-buffer $1 \times 1280 \times 20$ bits. Alternatively, the z-buffer is implemented in floating point for additional precision.

Conceptually, the algorithm is quite simple. For each scan line, the frame buffer is initialized to the background and the z-buffer to the minimum z. The intersection of the scan line with the two-dimensional projection of each polygon in the scene, if any, is found. These intersections occur in pairs, as discussed in Sec. 2–12. As each pixel on the scan line between the intersection pairs is considered, its depth is compared to the depth recorded in the z-buffer at that location. If the pixel depth is greater than that in the z-buffer, then this line segment is the currently visible segment. Hence, the polygon attributes for this line segment are written to the frame buffer at that pixel location, and the z-buffer for that location is updated. When all the polygons in the scene have been processed, the scan line frame buffer contains the visible surface solution for that scan line. It is copied in scan line order, i.e., left to right, to the display. Both pre- and postfiltering antialiasing techniques can be used with the scan line z-buffer algorithm.

In practice, examining each polygon for each scan line is inefficient. A variation of the ordered edge list discussed in Sec. 2–12 is adopted. In particular, a y bucket sort, an active polygon list and an active edge list are used to increase the efficiency of the algorithm.

Using these techniques, a scan line z-buffer algorithm is:

> To prepare the data:
>
>> For each polygon determine the highest scan line intersected.
>>
>> Place the polygon in the y bucket corresponding to this scan line.
>>
>> Store, e.g., on a linked list, at least Δy, the number of scan lines crossed by the polygon, a list of the polygon edges, the coefficients

of the plane equation (a, b, c, d), and the rendering attributes for each polygon in a linked list.

To solve the hidden surface problem:

Initialize the display frame buffer.

For each scan line:

Initialize the scan line frame buffer to the background.

Initialize the scan line z-buffer to $z_{\min}$.

Examine the scan line y bucket for any new polygons; add any new polygons to the active polygon list.

Examine the active polygon list for any new polygons; add any new polygon edge pairs to the active edge list.

If either element of a polygon edge pair has dropped off the active edge list, determine if that polygon is still on the active polygon list. If it is, complete the edge pair for this polygon on the active edge list; if not, remove the other element of the edge pair from the active edge list.

The active edge list contains the following information for each polygon edge intersection pair:

x_l the intersection of the left element of the polygon edge pair with the current scan line.

Δx_l the increment in x_l from scan line to scan line.

Δy_l the number of scan lines crossed by the left side.

x_r the intersection of the right element of the polygon edge pair with the current scan line.

Δx_r the increment in x_r from scan line to scan line.

Δy_r the number of scan lines crossed by the right side.

z_l the depth of the polygon at the center of the pixel corresponding to the left element of a polygon edge pair.

Δz_x the increment in z along the scan line; equal to a/c for $c \neq 0$.

Δz_y the increment in z from scan line to scan line; equal to b/c for $c \neq 0$.

The polygon edge pairs are placed on the active edge list in arbitrary order; within an edge pair, the intersections are sorted into left–right order. More than one edge pair may occur for a polygon.

For each polygon edge pair on the active edge list:

Extract polygon edge pairs from the active edge list.

Initialize z to z_l.

For each pixel such that $x_l \le x + \frac{1}{2} \le x_r$, calculate the depth $z(x + \frac{1}{2}, y + \frac{1}{2})$ at the center of the pixel using the plane equation for the polygon. On a scan line, this reduces to the incremental calculation.

$$z_x + \Delta x = z_x - \Delta z_x$$

Compare the depth $z(x + \frac{1}{2}, y + \frac{1}{2})$ with the z value stored in the scan line z-buffer at Zbuffer(x). If $z(x + \frac{1}{2}, y + \frac{1}{2}) >$ Zbuffer(x), then write the polygon attributes to the scan line frame buffer and replace Zbuffer(x) with $z(x + \frac{1}{2}, y + \frac{1}{2})$.

Otherwise, no action is taken.

Write the scan line frame buffer to the display.

Update the active edge list:

For each polygon edge pair decrement Δy_l and Δy_r. If either Δy_l or $\Delta y_r < 0$, remove that edge from the list. Flag both its location on the list and the polygon that generated it.

Calculate the new x intercepts:

$$x_{lnew} = x_{lold} + \Delta x_l$$
$$x_{rnew} = x_{rold} + \Delta x_r$$

Calculate the polygon depth at the left edge using the plane equation for the polygon; between scan lines this reduces to the incremental calculation

$$z_{lnew} = z_{lold} - \Delta z_x \Delta x - \Delta z_y$$

Decrement the active polygon list; if Δy for any polygon is less than zero, remove that polygon from the list.

Again, a preliminary backplane cull is used if appropriate. An example serves to illustrate the algorithm more fully.

Example 4–23   Scan Line Z-Buffer Algorithm

Reconsider the rectangle and triangle previously discussed in Ex. 4–19. Recall that the rectangle had corner coordinates $P_1(10, 5, 10)$, $P_2(10, 25, 10)$, $P_3(25, 25, 10)$, $P_4(25, 5, 10)$ and triangle vertices $P_5(15, 15, 15)$, $P_6(25, 25, 5)$, $P_7(30, 10, 5)$, as shown in Fig. 4–57. The display resolution is again $32 \times 32 \times 2$ bit planes. Again, the background is represented by 0, the rectangle by 1 and the triangle by 2. The viewpoint is at infinity on the positive z-axis. Using the half scan line convention for both polygons, the maximum scan line that intersects the polygons is at $y = 24$. Thus, only the $y = 24$ bucket contains any information; all others are empty. The active polygon list at $y = 24$ for the rectangle (polygon 1) and the triangle (polygon 2) contains

rectangle: $19, 2, P_1 P_2, P_3 P_4, 0, 0, 1, -10, 1$
triangle: $14, 3, P_5 P_6, P_6 P_7, P_7 P_5, 3, 1, 4, -120, 2$

The entries in this list correspond to Δy, the number of edges, the edge list, the coefficients of the plane equation (a, b, c, d), and the polygon number, respectively. Note that for the rectangle the list contains only two edges. Horizontal edges are ignored.

At scan line 15 (see Fig. 4–71) the active polygon list contains both polygons. For the rectangle, $\Delta y = 11$; for the triangle, $\Delta y = 5$. Initially the active edge list contains two pairs of intersections, the first for the rectangle and the second for the triangle:

rectangle: $10, 0, 19, 25, 0, 19, 10, 0, 0$
triangle: $24\,^1/_2, -1, 9, 25\,^1/_6, \,^1/_3, 14, 5\,^1/_2, \,^3/_4, \,^1/_4$

where the elements correspond to x_l, Δx_l, Δy_l, x_r, Δx_r, Δy_r, z_l, Δz_x, Δz_y. Just prior to processing scan line 15, the active edge list contains

rectangle: $10, 0, 10, 25, 0, 10, 10, 0, 0$
triangle: $15\,^1/_2, -1, 0, 28\,^1/_6, \,^1/_3, 5, 14\,^1/_2, \,^3/_4, \,^1/_4$

After first resetting the scan line frame and z-buffers to 0, and then scan-converting the rectangle, the buffers contain

Scan line frame buffer

---

0 0 0 0 0 0 0 0 0 0 1 1 1 1 1 1 1 1 1 1 1 1 1 1 1 0 0 0 0 0 0 0

Scan line z-buffer

---

0 0 0 0 0 0 0 0 0 0 10 10 10 10 10 10 10 10 10 10 10 10 10 10 10 0 0 0 0 0 0 0

Now the triangle is considered. At the left edge, $z = 14\,^1/_2$, which is greater than Zbuffer(15) = 10. Thus, the triangle attributes are written to the frame buffer, and the scan line z-buffer is updated. The results, after scan-conversion is complete, are

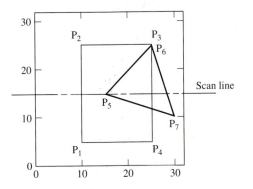

Figure 4–71   Polygons for Ex. 4–23.

Scan line frame buffer

---

0 0 0 0 0 0 0 0 0 0 1 1 1 1 2 2 2 2 2 2 2 2 1 1 1 1 2 2 0 0 0 0 0 0

Scan line z-buffer

---

0 0 0 0 0 0 0 0 0 0 10 10 10 10 15 14 13 12 12 11 10 10 10 10 10 6 6 0 0 0 0 0

---

where the z-buffer values are rounded to integers to save space. The result is the same as the corresponding scan line in Ex. 4–19. The frame buffer is copied, in left to right order, to the display.

At this point, the active edge list is updated. Decrementing yields $\Delta y_l = -1 < 0$. Consequently, the edge $P_6 P_5$ is deleted from the active edge list, and the polygon is flagged. Updating the right edge of the triangle yields

$$x_{rnew} = x_{rold} + \Delta x_r = 28\frac{1}{6} + \frac{1}{3} = 28\frac{1}{2}$$

$$\Delta y_{rnew} = \Delta y_{rold} - 1 = 5 - 1 = 4$$

After updating the active edge list, the active polygon list is decremented. Since the rectangle remains on the list, the next pass through the algorithm will insert the edge $P_5 P_7$ into the active edge list at the flagged location. At scan line 14 ($y = 14\frac{1}{2}$) the intersection with the edge $P_5 P_7$ yields a new $x_l = 16\frac{1}{2}$. The triangle depth is

$$z_l = -\frac{[ax + by + d]}{c} = -\frac{[(3)(16.5) + (1)(14.5) - 120]}{4} = 14$$

The resulting active edge list at scan line 14 is then

rectangle: $10, 0, 9, 25, 0, 9, 10, 0, 0$

triangle: $16\frac{1}{2}, 3, 4, 28\frac{1}{2}, 4, 14, \frac{3}{4}, \frac{1}{4}$

The complete results are shown in Ex. 4–19.

4–16   A Spanning Scan Line Algorithm

The scan line z-buffer algorithm calculates the polygon depth at every pixel on the scan line. The number of depth calculations is reduced by introducing the concept of spans, as in the original Watkins algorithm [Watk70]. Figure 4–72a shows the intersection of two polygons with a scan plane. By dividing the scan line at each edge crossing into segments called spans (see Fig. 4–72a), the solution of the visible surface problem is reduced to selection of the visible segment in each span. Figure 4–72a shows that only three types of spans are possible:

The span is empty, e.g., span 1 in Fig. 4–72a; display the background.

The span contains only one segment, e.g., spans 2 and 4 in Fig. 4–72a; the polygon attributes for that segment are displayed for the span.

The span contains multiple segments, e.g., span 3 in Fig. 4–72a. The depth of each segment in the span is calculated; the segment with the largest z value is the visible segment. The polygon attributes for that segment are displayed for the span.

If penetrating polygons are not allowed, it is sufficient to calculate the depth of each segment in a span at one end of the span. If two segments touch but do not penetrate at the end of a span, the depth calculation is performed at the opposite end of the span or at the midpoint of the span, as shown in Fig. 4–72b. For span 3, a depth calculation performed at the left end of the span yields inconclusive results. Performing the depth calculation at the midpoint of the span, as shown by the +s in Fig. 4–72b, yields the correct results.

If penetrating polygons are allowed, then the scan line is divided not only at each edge crossing but also at each intersection, as shown in Fig. 4–72c. Depth calculations at each span end point yield indeterminate results. Here it is sufficient to perform the depth calculation at the midpoint of each span, as shown by the +s in Fig. 4–72c.

More sophisticated span generation techniques reduce the number of spans and hence the computational requirements. Frequently, simple methods also yield surprising results. For example, Watkins [Watk70] suggested a simple midpoint subdivision technique. In Fig. 4–73a, a simple comparison of the end point depths of the lines ab and cd shows that cd is always visible; but Fig. 4–73b shows that this is not always the case. However, by dividing at the midpoint of cd it is easy to show that both segments of cd are visible.

It is frequently possible to avoid depth calculations altogether. Romney et al. [Romn68] showed that if penetration is *not* allowed, and if exactly the same polygons are present, and if the order of the edge crossings is exactly the same on a given scan line as on the previous scan line, then the depth priority of the segments in each span remains unchanged. Hence, depth priority calculations for the new scan line are not required. Hamlin and Gear [Haml77] show how,

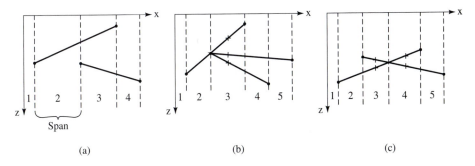

Figure 4–72   Scan line spans. (a) Nonintersecting, nontouching spans; (b) touching spans; (c) intersecting spans.

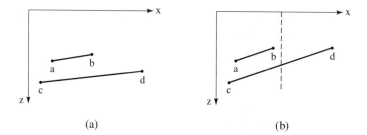

(a)   (b)

Figure 4–73   Alternate spanning technique. (a) Line cd clearly visible; (b) line cd may be partially visible — resolved by midpoint subdivision.

in some circumstances, the depth priority is maintained, even if the order of the edge crossings changes.

The basic structure developed for the scan line z-buffer algorithm is also applicable to a Watkins-style spanning scan line algorithm. Only the inner loop, i.e., how an individual scan line is processed, and the contents of the active edge list are changed. Here it is not necessary to maintain the polygon edge–scan line intersections in pairs. Individual edges are placed on the active edge list. The active edge list is sorted into increasing x order. A polygon identifier and a polygon active flag are used to identify left and right elements of the edge pair. In a manner similar to that discussed for the simple parity polygon scan conversion algorithm given in Sec. 2–11, the polygon active flag is initially set to *false* at the beginning of a scan line and complemented each time an edge for that polygon is processed. Encountering a left edge for a polygon causes that polygon's flag to be set to *true*, while encountering a right edge for that polygon returns it to *false*. Example 4–24 more fully illustrates the use of the flag.

The spans for each polygon are determined as a scan line is processed. If penetration is not allowed, each edge intersection on the active edge list represents a span boundary. Recall that the number of polygons active within a span determines how a span is processed. Depth calculations are performed only if more than one polygon is active in a span. If penetration is allowed, and more than one polygon is active within a span determined by the edge intersections, then it is necessary to check for possible intersecting segments within the span (see Fig. 4–72c). A convenient method for doing this is to compare the signs of the differences in the depths of pairs of segments at the span end points. Each pair of segments in the span must be examined. For example, if two segments have depths $z_{1_l}, z_{1_r}, z_{2_l}, z_{2_r}$ at the left and right end points, then

$$\textbf{if Sign}(z_{1_l} - z_{2_l}) \neq \textbf{Sign}(z_{1_r} - z_{2_r}) \tag{4-9}$$

the segments intersect. If the segments intersect, the intersection is calculated and the span is subdivided at the intersection. The process is repeated with the left-hand span until the span is clear of intersections. For these spans, the depth calculation is performed at the midpoint of the span.

If either sign in this test is zero, the segments intersect at the end of the span, i.e., the spans touch. Here, it is sufficient to determine the depth at the opposite end of the span rather than subdividing the span.

The structure of the spanning scan line algorithm is then

To prepare the data:

Determine the highest scan line intersected by each polygon.

Place the polygon in the y bucket corresponding to this scan line.

Store at least Δy, the number of scan lines crossed by the polygon, a list of the polygon edges, the coefficients of the plane equation (a, b, c, d), and the rendering attributes for each polygon on a linked list.

To solve the visible surface problem:

For each scan line:

Examine the scan line y bucket for any new polygons; add any new polygons to the active polygon list.

Examine the active polygon list for any new polygons; add any new polygon edges to the active edge list. The active edge list contains the following information for each polygon edge intersection:

x the intersection of the polygon edge with the current scan line

Δx the increment in x from scan line to scan line

Δy number of scan lines crossed by the edge

P a polygon identifier

$Flag$ a flag indicating whether the polygon is active on a given scan line.

Sort the active edge list into increasing x order.

Process the active edge list; the details are shown in the flowchart in Fig. 4–74 and the modifications in Figs. 4–75 and 4–76.

Update the active edge list:

For each edge intersection, decrement Δy; if $\Delta y < 0$, remove the edge from the active edge list.

Calculate the new x intercepts:

$$x_{\text{new}} = x_{\text{old}} + \Delta x$$

Decrement the active polygon list:

For each polygon, decrement Δy_p; if Δy_p for any polygon < 0, remove the polygon from the list.

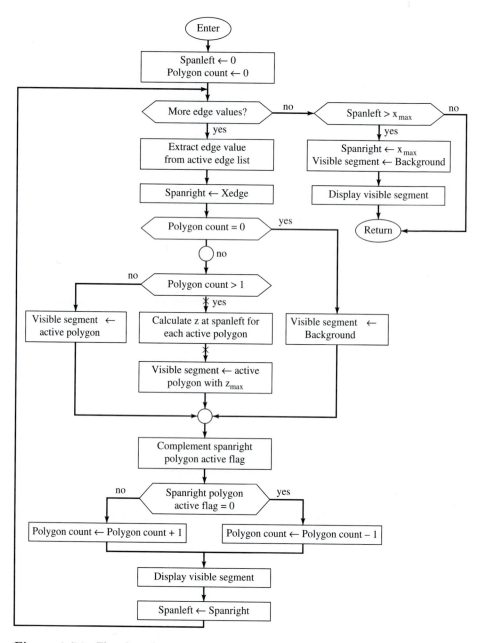

Figure 4–74 Flowchart for spanner for nonpenetrating polygons.

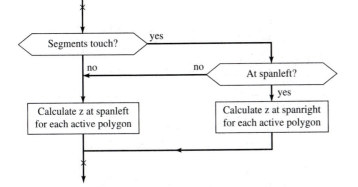

Figure 4–75   Flowchart for modified depth calculation for Fig. 4–74.

This algorithm does not take advantage of depth priority coherence, as suggested by Romney [Romn68]. If penetration is not allowed, modification of the algorithm to take advantage of depth priority coherence results in significant savings.

The simple spanning algorithm given in Fig. 4–74 assumes that polygon segments in a span do not intersect. If the segments intersect at a span end, i.e., touch, then, as just discussed, the depth calculation is performed at the opposite end of the span for these segments. A simple modification of the calculation block for the flowchart shown in Fig. 4–74 is given in Fig. 4–75.

If the segments intersect within a span, i.e., the polygons penetrate, then either a more complex spanner is used or the intersections must be inserted into the ordered edge list. The spanning algorithm shown in Fig. 4–74 is applicable when penetrating polygons are allowed, provided the active edge list includes the intersections, each intersection is flagged, the polygon flag complementation is modified and the depth priority calculations are carried out at the center of the span.

Figure 4–76 illustrates a modification of the algorithm given in Fig. 4–74. The modified algorithm assumes that the active edge list does not contain the intersection points. The intersection segments are discovered and processed on the fly. Here, each span is examined for intersecting segments. If any are found, the intersection point is calculated and the span subdivided at the intersection point. The right-hand subspan is pushed onto a stack. The algorithm is recursively applied to the left-hand subspan, until a subspan with no intersections is found. This subspan is displayed, and a new subspan is popped from the stack. The process is repeated until the stack is empty. The technique is similar to that suggested by Jackson [Jack80b]. As a matter of interest, the front and back cover photos for the first edition of this book [Roge85] were generated with a spanning scan line algorithm.

For simplicity, the modified algorithm shown in Fig. 4–76 assumes that segments intersect only if they cross. Because segments may touch at the ends of the spans, the depth calculation is carried out at the center of the span. The modified

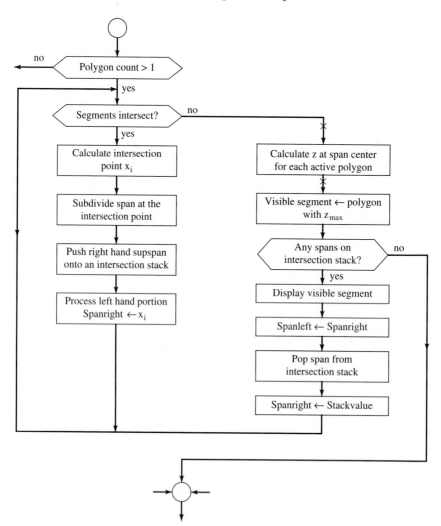

Figure 4–76 Modification of the flowchart in Fig. 4–74 for penetrating polygons.

calculation block shown in Fig. 4–75 can be substituted to avoid this additional computational expense. A further modification of the algorithm performs a z priority sort for spans with intersections, to determine if the intersecting segments are visible before subdividing the span. This modification reduces the number of subspans and increases the algorithm's efficiency. If appropriate, a preliminary backplane cull is also used to increase efficiency.

***

Example 4–24   Spanning Scan Line Algorithm

Again consider the rectangle and penetrating triangle previously discussed in Exs. 4–19 and 4–23. Scan line 15 is considered. The half scan line convention

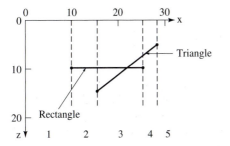

Figure 4–77   Scan plane for Ex. 4–24.

is used. The intersection of the scan plane at $y = 15\,^1/_2$ with the polygons is shown in Fig. 4–77. Figure 4–71 shows a projection of the polygons onto the xy plane. Just prior to processing scan line 15, the active edge list, sorted into x increasing order, contains

$$10, 0, 10, 1, 0, 15\,^1/_2, -1, 0, 2, 0, 25, 0, 10, 1, 0, 28\,^1/_6, \,^1/_3, 5, 2, 0$$

where the numbers are considered in groups of five, representing x, Δx, Δy, P, *Flag*, as defined in the previous algorithm. Figure 4–77 shows the five spans that result from the four intersections given on the active edge list. Figure 4–77 also shows that the polygon segments intersect within the third span.

The scan line is processed from left to right in scan line order. The first span contains no polygons. It is displayed (pixels 0 to 9) with the background attributes. In the second span the rectangle becomes active. Its flag is complemented to 1

$$Flag = -Flag + 1$$

The span contains only one polygon. Consequently, it is displayed (pixels 10 to 14) with the rectangle's attributes.

The third span starts at $x = 15\,^1/_2$. The triangle becomes active, and its flag is complemented to 1, the polygon count is increased to 2, *Spanleft* becomes $15\,^1/_2$ and the next edge at $x = 25$ is extracted from the active edge list. *Spanright* is set equal to 25. The polygon count is greater than one. The segments are examined for possible intersection (see Fig. 4–76).

From Ex. 4–19, the plane equation for the triangle is

$$3x + y + 4z - 120 = 0$$

For scan line 15, $y = 15\,^1/_2$; and the triangle depth at any pixel becomes

$$z = \frac{(120 - y - 3x)}{4} = \frac{(120 - 15.5 - 3x)}{4} = \frac{(104.5 - 3x)}{4}$$

Thus, using the center of the pixel, i.e., $x + \,^1/_2$

$$z_{2_l} = \frac{[104.5 - (3)(15.5)]}{4} = 14.5$$

$$z_{2_r} = \frac{[104.5 - (3)(25.5)]}{4} = 7.0$$

Since the rectangle is of constant depth

$$z_{1_l} = 10$$

$$z_{1_r} = 10$$

Recalling Eq. $(4-9)$

$$\mathbf{Sign}\,(z_{1_l} - z_{2_l}) = \mathbf{Sign}\,(10 - 14.5) < 0$$

$$\mathbf{Sign}\,(z_{1_r} - z_{2_r}) = \mathbf{Sign}\,(10 - 7) > 0$$

Since $\mathbf{Sign}\,(z_{1_l} - z_{2_l}) \neq \mathbf{Sign}\,(z_{1_r} - z_{2_r})$, the segments intersect. The intersection of the two segments is

$$z = \frac{(120 - 15.5 - 3x)}{4} = 10$$

$$x_i = 21.5$$

The span is subdivided at $x_i = 21\,^1/_2$. The value for *Spanright* is pushed onto the stack. *Spanright* is set to x_i, i.e., $21\,^1/_2$.

The subspan from $x = 15\,^1/_2$ to $x = 21\,^1/_2$ contains no intersections. The depth at the center of the subspan, i.e., at $x = 18\,^1/_2$, for the triangle is

$$z_2 = \frac{(104.5 - 3x)}{4} = \frac{[104.5 - (3)(18.5)]}{4} = 12.25$$

which is greater than $z_1 = 10$ for the rectangle. Thus, the triangle is displayed for this subspan (pixels 15 to 20).

Spanleft is set to *Spanright*, and the right-hand subspan is popped from the stack. *Spanright* is set to the stack value, i.e., $x = 25$. The subspan from $x = 21\,^1/_2$ to $x = 25$ contains no intersections. The depth at the center of the subspan, i.e., at $x = 23\,^1/_4$, for the triangle is

$$z_2 = \frac{(104.5 - 3x)}{4} = \frac{[104.5 - (3)(23.25)]}{4} = 8.69$$

which is less than $z_1 = 10$ for the rectangle. Thus, the rectangle is visible for this subspan (pixels 21 to 24).

The intersection stack is now empty. The routine given in Fig. 4–76 exits to that in Fig. 4–74. The span right polygon is the rectangle; the rectangle becomes inactive. Its flag is complemented to 0, which also causes the polygon count to be reduced to 1. The segment is now displayed using the rectangle's attributes. *Spanleft* is reset to *Spanright*.

The next edge extracted from the active edge list is for the triangle at $x = 28\,^1/_6$. The span is from $x = 25$ to $x = 28\,^1/_6$. The polygon count is 1. The active polygon in the span is the triangle. Consequently, the segment is displayed with the triangle's attributes (pixels 25 to 27). The span right polygon is the triangle. Its flag is complemented to 0, and the triangle becomes inactive. The polygon count is now 0. *Spanleft* is set to *Spanright*, i.e., $28\,^1/_6$.

There are no more edges on the active edge list. Here, $x_{max} = 32$, so *Spanleft* $< x_{max}$. Thus, *Spanright* is set to x_{max} and the display segment to the background. The span (pixels 28 to 31) is displayed with the background attributes, and *Spanleft* is reset to *Spanright*. Again, there are no more edges; but *Spanleft* $= x_{max}$, and the processing of the scan line is complete.

The final results are identical to those shown in Example 4–19.

Beatty, Booth and Matthies [Beat81] revisited Watkins' spanning scan line algorithm [Watk70] and suggested several techniques for increasing the efficiency of the basic algorithm. The suggested improvements centered around utilizing multiple scan line coherence. They noted that except at critical events, defined to be the visible entry, exit or crossing of scene edges, the visibility along scan lines does not change. Thus, the active edge list does not require resorting. Furthermore, they noted that the scan line on which a critical event might occur is predictable from the stored data in the same manner as the position of the intersection of an edge with a succeeding scan line is predictable. They also subjected the algorithm to a formal complexity analysis. In the worst case, they found that the basic algorithm exhibited quadratic behavior.

Scan line algorithms are also implemented as visible line algorithms; e.g., Archuleta [Arch72] implemented a visible line version of the Watkins algorithm.

Invisible Coherence

An interesting modification applicable to scan line visible surface algorithms due to Crocker [Croc84] uses the concept of invisibility coherence to increase the efficiency of the algorithms. Invisible coherence compares the depth of the polygons to be added to the active polygon list with the depth of visible polygons on the previous scan line. If the depth of the new polygon is farther from the eyepoint than the depth of the previous scan line, then it is likely, but not necessarily, invisible. If it is likely to be invisible, it is added to an invisibility list instead of to the active polygon list.

The depth of the previous scan line is maintained in a scan line z-buffer (see Sec. 4–15). To determine the likely invisibility of the new polygon, its depth at its intersections, x_{min} and x_{max}, with the current scan line are compared with the depths stored at the corresponding locations in the scan line z-buffer. The active polygon list is then processed normally.

Because the polygons on the invisible list are not necessarily invisible, the maximum depth of the polygons on the invisible list is compared to the depth of the visible surface as the active polygon list is processed. If the maximum depth of the polygon on the invisible list is less than the visible polygon, then the polygon on the invisible list is added to the active polygon list and the active polygon list reprocessed. Examples of invisible polygons correctly and incorrectly placed on the invisible list are shown in Fig. 4–78. The most common case is a polygon behind another polygon with a hole in it, as shown in Fig. 4–78d.

The efficiency of the scan line algorithms is increased by eliminating the necessity of processing large numbers of invisible polygons in complex scenes.

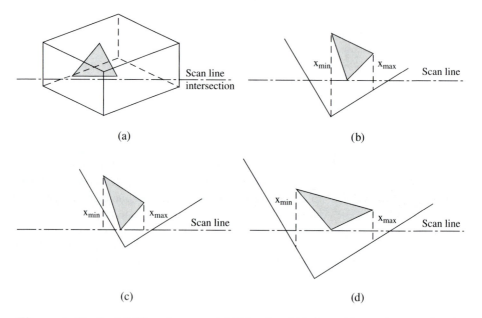

Figure 4–78   Invisibility coherence. (a) Triangle within box; (b) top view — triangle eliminated and placed on invisible list; (c) top view — triangle not eliminated; (d) top view — triangle incorrectly eliminated and placed on invisible list.

Crocker tested the algorithm using Atherton's [Athe83] visible surface algorithm for constructive solid geometry. The invisible coherence modification is also applicable to the polygonal visible surface algorithms of Watkins [Watk70], Romney [Romn70] and Bouknight [Bouk70b], as well as others. It is also applicable to the curved surface scan line algorithms of Lane and Carpenter [Lane79], Whitted [Whit78] and Blinn [Blin78b] (see also [Lane80]).

An Object Space Scan Line Algorithm

In contrast to most of the classical scan line algorithms which operate in image space, Sechrest and Greenberg [Sech82] present a scan-line-like algorithm for nonintersecting polygons, that operates in object space. By recognizing that visibility changes only at edge crossings and vertices in polygonal scenes, the algorithm incorporates some aspects of Appel's idea of quantitative visibility by dividing the scene vertically into horizontal bands in which the visibility does not change (see Fig. 4–79). Initially the scene is divided at only vertices that are local minima of each object. A y sort is used, along with an elaborate data structure, to develop an active edge list. The initial scene banding is refined on-the-fly to include all vertices and edge crossings as the active edge list is processed. The algorithm outputs object space precision visible edge segments, plus sufficient information to reconstruct visible polygons. A backface cull is used to eliminate self-hidden planes.

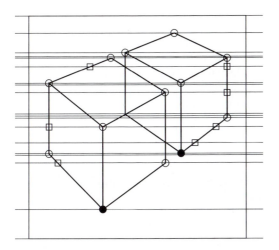

Figure 4–79 Horizontal constant visibility bands for a simple scene. • Local minima vertices; ○ nonminimal vertices; □ typical edge intersections (not all are shown).

4–17   Scan Line Algorithms For Curved Surfaces

The Catmull subdivision algorithm for curved surfaces (see Sec. 4–8), although simple and elegant, does not present the result in scan line order. This is inconvenient for raster scan output devices. A curved surface can, of course, be polygonally approximated and scan-converted using any of the scan line algorithms discussed previously. However, to obtain a high degree of accuracy, the number of polygons in a reasonably complex scene becomes excessive. Furthermore, unless shading interpolation techniques are used (see Chapter 5), the result has a faceted appearance. In any case, the silhouette edges are piecewise linear, i.e., represented as connected, short, straight line segments.

Algorithms that display parametric bipolynomial, typically bicubic, surfaces directly from the surface description in scan line order were developed by Blinn [Blin78b], Whitted [Whit78], Lane and Carpenter [Lane79, 80] and Clark [Clar79]. First the Blinn and Whitted algorithms, which are similar, are discussed; then the similar Lane–Carpenter and Clark algorithms are considered.

Recalling that a scan line algorithm intersects the scene with a scan plane through the eyepoint and a scan line immediately shows the difference between polygonal and curved (sculptured) parametric surfaces. For a polygonal surface, all the intersections are straight lines. These straight lines are easily represented by their end points. For a curved parametric surface, the intersection of the scan plane and the surface is given by the relation

$$y(u, w) = yscan = \text{constant}$$

where u and w are the parametric values for the surface. The result is a curve, called either a contour or a level curve. The curve is not necessarily single-valued.

Furthermore, there may be multiple curves at any contour level. Finally, having found the curve(s) of intersection with the scan line, it is also necessary to find each location along the scan line, i.e., each $x = x(u, w)$, and to calculate the depth at that location, $z = z(u, w)$, to determine its visibility.

Mathematically, the requirement is stated as: Given a scan line value y and a location of a point on that scan line x, obtain the inverse solution for the parameters u, w, i.e., find

$$u = u(x, y)$$

$$w = w(x, y)$$

Once the parameters u, w are known, the depth is obtained from

$$z = z(u, w)$$

Hence, the visibility of that point on the scan line can now be determined. Unfortunately, there is no known closed form solution for these equations. Both Blinn and Whitted use numerical procedures to obtain a solution. Specifically, a Newton–Raphson iteration technique is used (see [Kunz57]). The Newton–Raphson technique requires an initial estimate. Both algorithms take advantage of scan line coherence to provide this initial estimate and reduce the number of iterations per pixel. Unfortunately, Newton–Raphson iteration can become unstable. Kajiya [Kaji82] presents a more robust but more complex procedure based on concepts from algebraic geometry.

Briefly, in the context of the structure of a scan line algorithm, the inner loop for the Blinn and Whitted algorithms is

Given a parametric surface from the active patch list with

$$x = x(u, w)$$

$$y = y(u, w)$$

$$z = z(u, w)$$

For each scan line y:

For each pixel x on a scan line:

For each surface intersecting that scan line at x :

Solve for $u = u(x, y), w = w(x, y)$.

Calculate the depth of the surface $z = z(u, w)$.

Determine the visible surface at x, y and display it.

The algorithm illustrates another fundamental difference between a polygonal surface and a curved parametric surface. The algorithm says "For each surface intersecting that scan line." Surfaces become active at the highest intersecting scan line, and inactive at the lowest intersecting scan line. These intersections occur at local maxima and minima of the surface. For polygonal surfaces, local maxima and minima always occur at a vertex. Scan line algorithms use these vertices and the surface edges that connect them to decide when a polygon is added to or deleted from the active polygon and active edge lists.

For curved surfaces, local maxima and minima do not necessarily occur at vertices; they frequently occur interior to the surface along silhouette edges. A silhouette edge interior to a surface is identified by the vanishing of the z component of the surface normal; several examples are shown in Fig. 4–80. For a curved surface, surfaces may be added to or deleted from the active surface list at silhouette edges, and scan line spans may start and stop at silhouette edges. Both the Blinn and Whitted algorithms solve this problem by effectively dividing the surface along the silhouette edges.

The Lane–Carpenter and the Clark parametric curved surface algorithms are basically subdivision techniques. However, in contrast to the original Catmull subdivision algorithm, which proceeds in arbitrary order, these algorithms proceed in scan line order. The algorithms perform a y bucket sort of the surface patches, based on the maximum y value for each patch. At each scan line, patches from an active patch list that intersect that scan line are subdivided, until each subpatch either meets a flatness criterion or no longer intersects the scan line. Subpatches that no longer intersect the scan line are placed on an inactive patch list for subsequent consideration. Subpatches that meet the flatness criterion are treated as planar polygons and are scan converted, using a polygonal scan conversion algorithm. However, each of these approximately planar polygons is a parametric subpatch. All the information available for the parametric subpatch is available for determining individual pixel attributes during polygonal scan-conversion. Using this information allows subpatches to be blended together smoothly. In fact, if the flatness criterion is less than one pixel, then a smooth silhouette results. Back facing or self-hidden polygons are eliminated by simply determining the normal to the surface (see Sec. 4–3). If the normal points away from the viewpoint, the subpatch is eliminated. This saves considerable processing.

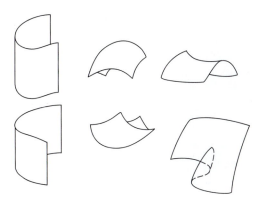

Figure 4–80   Silhouette edges.

Although both the Lane–Carpenter and the Clark algorithms use the idea expressed above, the Clark algorithm preprocesses the patches before scan-converting, while the Lane–Carpenter algorithm subdivides the patches dynamically as the frame is processed. The Lane–Carpenter algorithm requires considerably less memory but performs more subdivisions than the Clark algorithm. Figure 4–81 was generated with the Lane–Carpenter algorithm.

Briefly, in the context of a scan line algorithm, the inner loop for the Lane–Carpenter algorithm is

> For each scan line y:
>> For each patch on the active patch list:
>>> if the patch is flat **then**
>>>> add the patch to the polygon list
>>> else
>>>> split the patch into subpatches
>>>> if a subpatch still intersects the scan line **then**
>>>>> add it to the active patch list
>>>> else
>>>>> add it to the inactive patch list
>>>> end if
>>> end if
>> Scan-convert the polygon list

Both the Lane–Carpenter and the Clark algorithms take advantage of the characteristics of particular basis functions used to generate parametric patches to efficiently subdivide the patch. However, the algorithms are applicable for any parametric surface patch for which an efficient subdivision algorithm is available.

Figure 4–81   Teapot defined by 28 bicubic patches rendered with the Lane–Carpenter algorithm. (Courtesy of Loren Carpenter).

One disadvantage of these adaptive subdivision algorithms is that tears or holes in the surface can result from mismatches between the approximate polygonal subpatches and the exact parametric surface subpatches.

Quadric surfaces are generally somewhat simpler than parametric surface patches. Quadric surfaces are defined by the general quadratic equation

$$a_1 x^2 + a_2 y^2 + a_3 z^2 + a_4 xy + a_5 yz + a_6 zx + a_7 x + a_8 y + a_9 z + a_{10} = 0$$

Common examples of quadric surfaces are spheres, cones, cylinders, and ellipsoids and hyperboloids of revolution. If a_1 through a_6 are zero, then the equation reduces to that of a planar polygon.

Spheres as a subset of quadric surfaces are of particular interest in molecular modeling. Several scan line algorithms specifically for spheres have been developed. In particular, the algorithms by Porter [Port78, 79] and Staudhammer [Stau78] implement scan line z-buffer algorithms for spheres. By restricting the algorithm to orthographic views, Porter effectively uses Bresenham's circle algorithm (see Sec. 2–4) to generate the silhouette of the sphere. Further, since the intersection of the scan plane with a sphere is also a circle, Bresenham's circle algorithm can be used to incrementally calculate the depth of each sphere on the scan line. Finally, by maintaining a priority list of the spheres based on the depth of the sphere center, Bresenham's algorithm is used to antialias the silhouette edges (see Sec. 2–16). The priority sort also allows transparency effects to be added.

4–18   Octrees

Octrees are three-dimensional analogs of quadtrees discussed previously in the section on the Warnock algorithm (see Sec. 4–4). Consider a three-dimensional cubical scene space, as shown in Fig. 4–82a. In order to simplify processing objects in the scene, subdivide the space by recursively passing cutting planes through the center of each face of the cube perpendicular to the faces. Thus, the cube is subdivided into eight equal cubes or octants, or voxels. The octants, or voxels, are usually numbered from 0–7, as shown in Fig. 4–82a. Alternate numbering schemes are frequently used (for example, see Sec. 4–20), as are directional alphabetic schemes, for example Left/Right, Up/Down, Front/Back. In the directional alphabetic scheme the octant labeled 01 in Fig. 4–82a is the Right-Down-Front, or RDF, octant. Figure 4–82b shows three levels of subdivision of the cube, while Fig. 4–82c illustrates the corresponding octree data structure. Notice that here the root node is labeled 0, and each succeeding child node appends 0–7, recursively.

Figure 4–83a shows a single object within the scene, and Fig. 4–83b shows the resulting octree. Notice that each node is labeled full (F), empty (E) or partially full (P). As the octree is built, each voxel is examined to determine whether it is empty, full or partially full. If the voxel is either full or empty, the tree terminates at that level; if the voxel is partially full, i.e., contains any

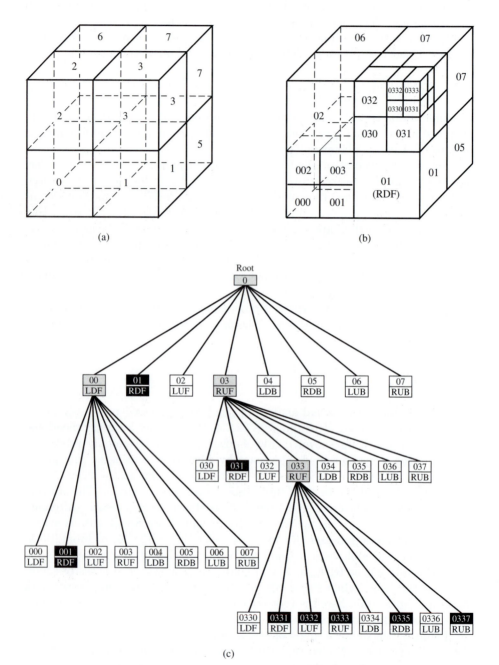

Figure 4–82 Octree subdivision and numbering scheme. (a) First subdivision; (b) three levels of subdivision; (c) octree data structure.

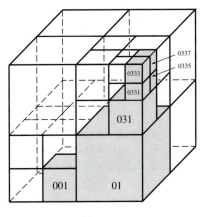

(a)

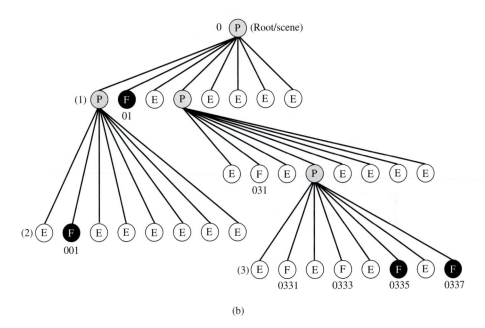

(b)

Figure 4–83   Octree representation of an object. (a) Scene octree and object; (b) octree with nodes 'numbered' left to right.

object or parts of objects, the voxel is subdivided, provided that it is either larger than the minimum size (maximum resolution) or above a minimum complexity level. For example, the minimum complexity level might be a single object that did not 'fill' the voxel. Thus, an object is represented to the resolution of the smallest voxel.

Octree Display

Assuming that at maximum resolution a partially full voxel is declared and stored as full, and that the view direction is from an eyepoint at infinity on and along the positive z-axis, then the visible surface display algorithm for a scene encoded as an octree is relatively simple. Notice from Figs. 4–82 and 4–83 that the octree data structure is generated from the top down, left-to-right, bottom-to-top and front-to-back. If each voxel is written to the frame buffer or display in back-to-front order, then hidden voxels are successively overwritten. The result is a visible surface display.

Examining Figs. 4–82 and 4–83 again shows that processing the octree from the top down, right-to-left, top-to-bottom and back-to-front, while following any partial nodes downward through the octree, yields the desired result. Assuming that the routine processlevel can call itself, a pseudocode fragment for the algorithm is

level = 0

subroutine processlevel(octree, level, maxlevel)

    if level $\leq$ maxlevel **then**

        for node 7 to 0 **step** -1

            if node <> empty **then**

                if node = full **then**

                    call Display

                else if node = partial **then**

                    call processlevel(octree, level + 1, maxlevel)

                end if

            end if

        next node

    end if

    return

An example illustrates the process.

Example 4–25   Octree Display

Display the octree encoded scene given in Fig. 4–83 using the pseudocode algorithm fragment given above. Stepping through the algorithm yields

    level = 0 $\leftarrow$ P (0)

        level = 1

            node = 7 $\leftarrow$ E (07)

                6 $\leftarrow$ E (06)

                5 $\leftarrow$ E (05)

                4 $\leftarrow$ E (04)

$$3 \leftarrow \text{P (03)}$$

level = 2

 node = 7 ← E (037)

  6 ← E (036)

  5 ← E (035)

  4 ← E (034)

  3 ← E (033)

  level = 3

   node = 7 ← F (0337) **Display**

    6 ← E (0336)

    5 ← F (0335) **Display**

    4 ← E (0334)

    3 ← F (0333) **Display**

    2 ← E (0332)

    1 ← F (0331) **Display**

    0 ← E (0330)

 level = 2

  node = 2 ← E (032)

   1 ← F (031) **Display**

   0 ← E (030)

level = 1

 node = 2 ← E (02)

  1 ← F (01) **Display**

  0 ← P (00)

 level = 2

  node = 7 ← E (007)

   6 ← E (006)

   5 ← E (005)

   4 ← E (004)

   3 ← E (003)

   2 ← E (002)

   1 ← F (001) **Display**

   0 ← E (000)

The result is the front face of the cube shown in Fig. 4–83a, comprised of visible elements (01), (001), (031), (0331) and (0333).

A number of alternate display algorithms have been developed by Doctor and Torborg [Doct81], Meagher [Meag82a, 82b], Oliver [Oliv84], Frieder, Gordon and Reynolds [Frie85], Gargantini, Walsh and Wu [Garg86], and Gargantini, Schrack and Atkinson [Garg89] and Zhao and Davis [Zhao91], to cite only a few. In addition, a number of ray tracing algorithms use an octree data structure (see Sec. 4–20). Generally, the algorithms use a back-to-front paradigm, as discussed here, or attempt to prevent overwriting of obscured voxels using a front-to-back paradigm, or divide the scene into slices using a back-to-front or front-to-back paradigm for each slice, to improve efficiency. The octree can also be converted into a quadtree and the quadtree displayed [Doct81; Meag82b]. Voxels can also be sorted into depth priority order, using a classical 'bucket' or radix sort [Garg89] prior to display using a list priority-style algorithm. Veenstra and Ahuja [Veen88] describe a technique for generating line drawings (wire frames) from octrees.

Linear Octrees

A $2^n \times 2^n \times 2^n$ octree with reasonable values of n requires huge amounts of storage. For example, if $n = 10$, i.e., a $1024 \times 1024 \times 1024$ scene cube, approximately 1×10^9 voxels must potentially be stored in the octree; most of these voxels are empty. Linear octrees concentrate on reducing the storage requirements by storing and accessing only full voxels and encoding the voxel location in the octree [Garg82a, 86, 89]. Gargantini [82a, 82b] describes an efficient encoding technique using octal numbers. Glassner [Glas84] utilized a similar scheme for ray tracing (see Sec. 4–20 for a description).

Manipulation of Octrees

Orthographic views along the z-axis of the scene cube in its original orientation are rather uninteresting. Consequently, the scene is normally manipulated, i.e., scaled, rotated, translated, etc., prior to rendering. Manipulating the scene itself, and then regenerating the octree before rendering, is computationally expensive. Thus, manipulating the scene by directly manipulating the octree is of interest.

Scaling by a factor of 2 is the easiest manipulation [Jack80a]. To double the size of an object represented by an octree, select a child of the root, remove its children and make the child the new root. To halve the size of an object, form a new parent of the root and make it the new root while declaring all the children of the original root empty.

Rotation by 90° about a coordinate axis is done by recursively rotating each of the children of the root node by 90° about the axis. General rotations are more complex (see [Meag82]), as are translations. Jackins and Tanimoto [Jack80a] give an algorithm for general translation. Implementing the perspective transformation is discussed by Meagher [Meag82] and Sandor [Sand85].

Boolean Operations

The Boolean operations of union, intersection and difference are frequently used in constructive solid geometry (CSG). These operations are straightforward for objects represented as either quadtrees or octrees. Hunter and Steiglitz [Hunt79] present algorithms for quadtrees. Extension to octrees is straightforward.

Consider the intersection of two objects represented by octrees. First, an intersection must contain some volume. If two objects intersect and do not contain any volume, then they touch, e.g., along a surface, and do not actually intersect. To determine the intersection:

Starting at the root, examine corresponding pairs of nodes.

If either node is empty, add an empty node to the octree representing the intersection.

If either node is full, create a node in the intersection octree with the value of the other node.

If both nodes are partially full, create a partially full node in the intersection octree and recursively apply the algorithm to the children of the nodes.

Examine the children of this node in the intersection octree.

If all the children are either empty or full, delete them and change the partially full parent appropriately.

Determining the union of two objects is identical, except that the roles of empty and full are interchanged.

Finding Neighboring Voxels

Operations on quadtrees and octrees frequently require finding adjacent nodes. These nodes are called neighbors; the process is referred to as neighbor finding. An example use is when 'walking' a ray through a scene described by an octree (see Sec. 4–20). In two dimensions, nodes can be adjacent to any of four edges or four vertices, i.e., there are eight possible neighbors. In three dimensions, nodes can be adjacent along any of six faces (face nodes), twelve edges (edge nodes) or eight vertices (vertex nodes), i.e., there are 26 possible neighbors. Neighbors are not necessarily of the same size. Assuming that the adjacent node of a specific type in a specific direction is desired, and that the node exists, i.e., is not a boundary node, the fundamental algorithm ascends the tree until a common ancestor to the nodes is found. The tree is then descended while searching for the neighbor. The algorithms are most efficient if the root is not reached when ascending the tree, i.e., the nearest common ancestor is desired. The details for locating the nearest common ancestor depend upon the specific data structure used to represent the quadtree or octree. Samet [89a, 90a, 90b] extensively discusses these details, which are beyond the scope of this text. An alternate technique is briefly discussed in Sec. 4–20.

4–19   Marching Cubes

The marching cubes [Lore87; Clin87] and algorithms by Wyvill, McPheeters and Wyvill [Wyvi86] and Bloomenthal [Bloo88] consider data on a regular three-dimensional lattice, as shown in Fig. 4–84. Examples of such data are computer tomography (CT), magnetic resonance (MR), single-photon emission computer tomography (SPECT), seismography, electron microscope, barometric pressure, etc. The data are generally presented as discrete values on two-dimensional slices through the surface. The problem is to reconstruct a three-dimensional polygonal (triangular) surface representation from the data. Goldsmith and Jacobson [Gold96] consider data in cylindrical and spherical coordinates.

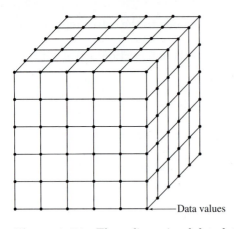

—Data values

Figure 4–84   Three-dimensional data lattice.

Lorensen and Cline [Lore87] consider a data cube such as that shown in Fig. 4–85. The cube is created from eight data values on two adjacent data slices, as shown by the dots at each corner vertex. Frequently it is desirable to construct surfaces at constant values of the sampled variables; such surfaces are called level surfaces, or isosurfaces. Examples are isobaric or constant pressure lines on a weather map, or locations where the gradient of the variable is large. For example, in CT data the density of soft tissue and bone is significantly different; thus the boundary, represented by the large gradient in density, outlines the bones. The desired level surface seldom passes through the data values. Consequently, interpolation between the data slices is required. If the level surface intersects the cube, then it also intersects the edges of the cube. Lorensen and Cline reconstruct an approximation to the level surface within a cube and piece the surface together as the cube moves (marches) through the data set, hence 'marching cube' algorithm.

For a given value of the level surface, the value of the data at each vertex of the cube (see Fig. 4–85) is either greater than, less than or equal to that of the level surface. If the value of the data is greater than or equal to that of the level surface, the vertex is above the level surface; the vertex is assigned a value of one. If the data value at the vertex is less than the level surface value, then the vertex is below the level surface; the vertex is assigned a zero value. The surface intersects those edges where the vertices have different values, e.g., if vertex V_4 in Fig. 4–85 is assigned a value of one and vertex V_1 a value of zero, then the surface intersects edge e_4. Because there are eight vertices, each with two possible values, the surface can intersect the cube in at most 256 (2^8) ways. Encoding the assigned values at each vertex into a single byte yields an index into a lookup table containing the 256 possible intersections. For example, referring to Fig. 4–85, the index might be

V_8	V_7	V_6	V_5	V_4	V_3	V_2	V_1

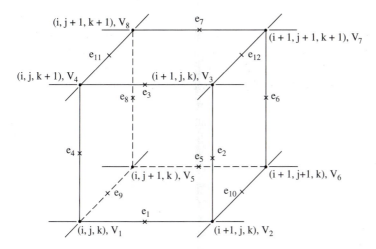

Figure 4–85   Marching cube.

Thus, 00001000 binary (or 8 decimal) indicates a level surface that intersects the cube along edges e_3, e_4 and e_{11}; i.e., vertex V_4 is above the level surface, and all the other vertices are below the level surface.

Lorensen and Cline use two symmetries to reduce the 256 cases to 15 when triangulating the level surface. First, note that complementing the vertices, i.e., interchanging the relationship of vertices above the level surface with those below the level surface (complementing the binary index) yields equivalent triangulations. Hence, the number of cases is halved, because only cases with zero to four vertices above the level surface need be considered. Second, Lorensen and Cline claim that rotational symmetry further reduces the number of cases to 15. These 15 cases, including case 0 with no intersections and hence no triangles, are shown in Fig. 4–86. Using the index into the edge intersection table yields the edges intersected by the level surface, along with the appropriate triangulation of the cube. Linear interpolation between the vertices forming an edge and the level surface value yields the exact intersection value of the level surface and the edge. Note from Fig. 4–86 that as few as one (case 1) and as many as four (cases 9–14) triangles may result from the level surface intersection with the cube. Lorensen and Cline claim that higher degree interpolating surfaces yield little improvement compared to linear interpolation.

Ambiguous faces

Durst [Durs88] originally pointed out that using only Lorensen and Cline's original 15 cases, as given in Fig. 4–86, with the marching cubes algorithm yields ambiguous faces, as shown in Fig. 4–87. The left-hand cube is Lorensen and Cline's case 6, while the right-hand cube is the complement of their case 3, i.e., $\bar{3}$. Connecting the edge intersections of the abutting faces, as shown by the dotted lines, results in a hole in the level surface. Although the appearance of holes

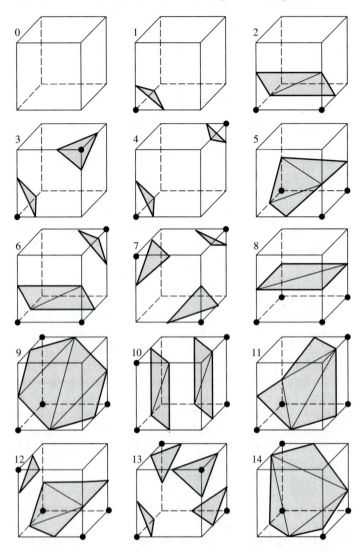

Figure 4–86   Lorensen and Cline's 15 cube triangulation cases.

is infrequent and is often eliminated by reducing the cube size, holes do occur in practice.

Nielson and Hamann [Niel91] proposed a solution to the hole problem using bilinear interpolation, called the asymptotic decider, that required 18 triangulations in addition to Lorensen and Cline's original 15 triangulations. Zhou et al. [Zhou94] show that only three additional triangulations, as illustrated in Fig. 4–88, are required to eliminate holes in the level surface. They point out that complementary symmetry as used by Lorensen and Cline [Lore87] does not apply when at least one cube face has an intersection point on each of its four edges, i.e., cases 3, 6, 7, 10, 12 and 13 of Fig. 4–86. However, the complementary

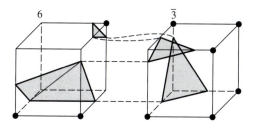

Figure 4–87   An ambiguous surface (hole) in the marching cubes algorithm.

operation is never performed on cases 10, 12, and 13, because each of these faces has four vertices on one side of the level surface; the complementary operation is only performed when three or fewer vertices are on a single side of the level surface. Thus, holes only result from cases 3, 6 and 7. Zhou and his colleagues eliminate complementary symmetry for these three cases and propose the three additional triangulations shown as 3b, 6b and 7b in Fig. 4–88. Consequently, their scheme uses a total of 18 triangulations. Figure 4–89 illustrates how the alternate triangulation, 3b, eliminates the hole in the level surface when abutting case 6a.

Shu et al. [Shu95] developed an adaptive marching cube algorithm to increase the computational efficiency of the basic marching cube algorithm. Their algorithm varies the size of the cubes based on the curvature of the surface. One

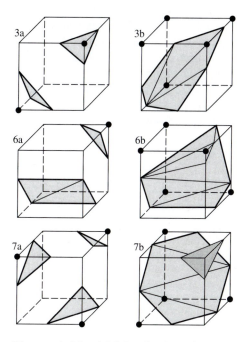

Figure 4–88   Additional triangularizations required to eliminate ambiguous faces (holes).

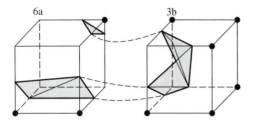

Figure 4–89   Corrected ambiguous face with no hole.

significant problem found in many adaptive subdivision algorithms is the existence of cracks in the resulting surface. Figure 4–90 illustrates how a crack is formed. Shu et al. solve the crack problem by identifying 22 basic arbitrary-sized crack configurations. The cracks are then patched with polygons the same shape as the crack.

4–20   A Visible Surface Ray Tracing Algorithm

All the hidden surface algorithms discussed in the previous sections depend upon some coherence characteristic of the scene to efficiently find the visible portions of the scene. In contrast, ray tracing is a brute force technique. The basic idea underlying the technique is that an observer views an object by means of light from a source that strikes the object and then somehow reaches the observer. The light may reach the observer by reflection from the surface, or by refraction or transmission through the surface. If light rays from the source are traced, very few reach the viewer. Consequently, the process is computationally inefficient. Appel [Appe68] originally suggested that rays should be traced in the opposite direction, i.e., from the observer to the object, as shown in Fig. 4–91. Appel's original algorithm included the generation of shadows. Ray tracing was born. Mathematical Applications Group Inc. (MAGI) [MAGI68; Gold71] successfully implemented ray tracing, including application to Boolean set operations in a

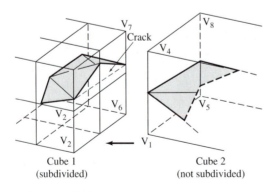

Figure 4–90   Origin of a surface crack.

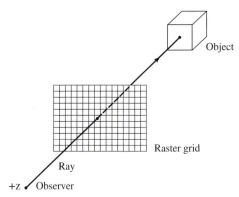

Figure 4–91   Simple ray tracing.

constructive solid geometry (CSG) modeling display system. In the original MAGI implementation, rays terminated when they intersected the surface of a visible opaque object; i.e., it was used only as a visible surface processor. The system included the ability to declare some objects fully transparent in order to peel away an object's outer shell [Gold71]. They also applied ray tracing to computer animation, including an early director's language.

Subsequent to the work of Appel and MAGI, Kay [Kay79a, 79b] and Whitted [Whit79] implemented ray tracing algorithms in conjunction with global illumination models. These algorithms account for reflection of one object in the surface of another, refraction, transparency and shadow effects. The images are also antialiased. An algorithm incorporating these effects is discussed in Sec. 5–14. The present discussion is limited to ray tracing as an opaque visible surface technique.

Figure 4–91 illustrates the simplest ray tracing algorithm. The algorithm assumes that the scene is transformed to image space. A perspective transformation is not applied. The viewpoint or observer is assumed to be at infinity, on the positive z-axis; hence all the light rays are parallel to the z-axis. Each ray passes from the observer, through the center of a pixel in the raster, into the scene. The path of each ray is traced to determine which objects in the scene, if any, are intersected by the ray. Every object in the scene must be examined for every ray. If a ray intersects an object, all possible intersections of the ray and the object are determined. This process potentially yields multiple intersections for multiple objects. The intersections are sorted in depth. The intersection of the object closest to the observer, i.e., the one with the maximum z value, represents the visible surface for that pixel. The attributes for this object are used to determine the pixel's characteristics.

When the viewpoint is not located at infinity, the algorithm is only slightly more complex. Here, the observer is assumed located on the positive z-axis. The image plane, i.e., the raster, is perpendicular to the z-axis, as shown in Fig. 4–92. The effect is to perform a single-point perspective projection onto the image plane (see [Roge76, 90]). Pseudocode for this simple algorithm is

```
for each scan line of the raster
    for each pixel on the scan line
        calculate the ray from the eye point to the pixel
        for each object in the scene
            determine and store ray–object intersections, if any, on an
            intersection list
        end if
        if the intersection list is not empty then
            determine the closest intersection
            set the pixel to the attributes of the object with the closest
            intersection
        else
            set the pixel to the background attributes
        end if
    next pixel
next pixel
```

The most important element of a visible surface ray tracing algorithm is the intersection routine. Any object for which an intersection routine can be written may be included in a scene. Objects in the scene may be composed of a mixture of planar polygons, polyhedral volumes or volumes defined or bounded by quadric, algebraic or bipolynomial parametric surfaces. Since a simple ray tracing algorithm spends $75 - 95\%$ of its effort in determining intersections [Whit80], the efficiency of the intersection routine significantly affects the efficiency of the algorithm. Determining the intersections of an arbitrary line in space (a ray) with a particular object can be computationally expensive (see, for example, [Kaji82]). To eliminate unnecessary intersections, the intersection of a ray with the bounding volume of an object is examined. If a ray fails to intersect the bounding volume of an object, then that object need not be considered further for that ray. Spheres [Whit80], rectangular parallelepipeds (RPPs) or boxes [Rubi80, Toth85], triangular pyramids [Kaji83], ellipses [Bouv85], convex polyhedra or slabs [Kay86] or three-dimensional convex hull constructs are used as bounding volumes.

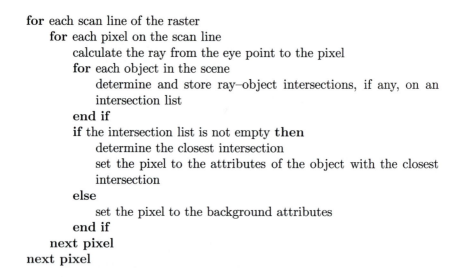
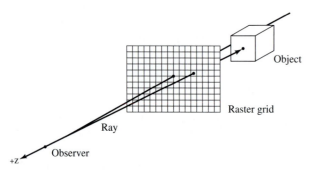

Figure 4–92   Ray tracing with perspective.

Bounding Volumes

Although, as shown in Fig. 4–93, a bounding sphere can be inefficient, determining whether a three-dimensional ray intersects a sphere is simple. In particular, if the distance from the center of the bounding sphere to the ray is more than the radius of the sphere, then the ray does not intersect the bounding sphere. Hence, it cannot intersect the object.

The bounding sphere test thus reduces to determining the distance from a point, i.e., the center of the sphere, to a three-dimensional line, i.e., the ray. A parametric representation of the line segment, i.e., the ray, between the points $P_1(x_1, y_1, z_1)$ and $P_2(x_2, y_2, z_2)$ is

$$P(t) = P_1 + (P_2 - P_1)t \qquad t \geq 0$$

with components

$$x = x_1 + (x_2 - x_1)t \ = x_1 + at$$

$$y = y_1 + (y_2 - y_1)t \ = y_1 + bt$$

$$z = z_1 + (z_2 - z_1)t \ = z_1 + ct$$

Here $(P_2 - P_1)$ and (a, b, c) represent the direction of the ray. The minimum distance, d, from the line to the point $P_c(x_c, y_c, z_c)$, i.e., the center of the sphere, is

$$d^2 = (x - x_c)^2 + (y - y_c)^2 + (z - z_c)^2$$

where the parameter, t, specifying the point on $P(t)$ for minimum distance is

$$t = -\frac{a(x_1 - x_c) + b(y_1 - y_c) + c(z_1 - z_c)}{a^2 + b^2 + c^2}$$

If $d^2 > R^2$, where R is the radius of the bounding sphere, then the ray cannot intersect the object. Although this solution is relatively simple and efficient, Haines [Hain89] discusses techniques for further improving the efficiency of an implementation.

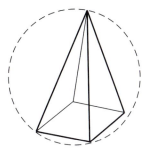 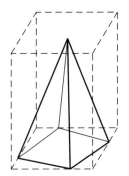

Figure 4–93 Bounding volumes.

Welzl [Welz91] presents a technique for determining the smallest (optimum) bounding sphere. A less than optimum technique that yields an acceptable result is to find the maximum and minimum x, y, z coordinates of the objects to be enclosed, i.e., x_{max}, x_{min}, y_{max}, y_{min}, z_{max}, z_{min}. The center of the sphere is then

$$x_c = \frac{x_{max} + x_{min}}{2} \qquad y_c = \frac{y_{max} + y_{min}}{2} \qquad z_c = \frac{z_{max} + z_{min}}{2}$$

The radius is

$$R = \sqrt{(x_\ell - x_c)^2 + (y_\ell - y_c)^2 + (z_\ell - z_c)^2}$$

and $x_\ell = \max(|x_{max}|, |x_{min}|)$, $y_\ell = \max(|y_{max}|, |y_{min}|)$, $z_\ell = \max(|z_{max}|, |z_{min}|)$.

As shown in Fig. 4–93, a bounding box test may be spatially more efficient than a bounding sphere test. However, performing a bounding box test in three dimensions is computationally more expensive then the bounding sphere test. In general, intersection of the ray with at least three of the infinite planes forming the bounding box must be tested. Since intersections of the ray with the planes forming the bounding box may occur outside a face of the bounding box, a containment or inside test (see Secs. 3–5 and 4–5) must be performed for each intersection. Consequently, when performed in three dimensions, the bounding box test is slower than the bounding sphere test.

A simple procedure reduces the bounding box test to sign comparison, simplifies the intersection calculation for the object and simplifies the depth comparisons among the intersections. The procedure uses translations and rotations about the coordinate axes (see [Roge76, 90]) to make the ray coincident with the z-axis. Note that if a perspective transformation is not used, only a simple translation of the original ray and bounding box are required.

The same transformations are applied to the bounding box of the object. The ray intersects the projection of the bounding box if, in the translated and rotated coordinate system, the signs of x_{min} and x_{max} *and* of y_{min} and y_{max}

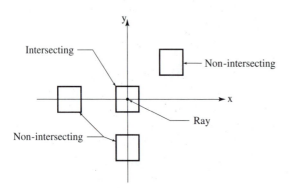

Figure 4–94   Bounding box intersections in the transformed coordinate system.

are opposite, as shown in Fig. 4–94. Effectively, the test is performed on the projected rectangle containing the transformed bounding box.

If the bounding volumes are confined to convex polyhedra, then the intersection of the ray and the bounding volume is conveniently and inexpensively performed using a modification of the Cyrus–Beck three-dimensional line clipping algorithm (see Sec. 3–13). When using the Cyrus–Beck algorithm, there is no need to include a separate containment test.

Kay and Kajiya [Kay86] present a simple and elegant technique for defining convex bounding polyhedra, called slabbing. A slab consists of a pair of parallel infinite planes which may be oriented in any direction in three space, as shown in Fig. 4–95, and a distance between the slabs. Figure 4–95 shows the two-dimensional analog of three-dimensional slabbing. Figure 4–95a shows slabs parallel to the coordinate planes, while Fig. 4–95b shows that increasing the number of slabs and reorienting them tightens the bounding volume around the object at the expense of increased computation when determining the intersections, if any (see Sec. 3–13). A minimum of three slabs is required, in three dimensions, to form a closed polyhedral volume for the bounding box.

Assuming a polyhedral object and a known slab orientation (normal direction), the distance between the planes forming the slab is found by taking the dot product of the normal to the slab and each of the vertices of the object. The distance between the slabs is then the difference between the minimum and maximum of these values.

If the orientation of the slabs is predetermined, the computational expense is significantly reduced. For example, assuming that all slabs are parallel to the coordinate planes means that the normals to the slabs are simple. Consequently, the computations are considerably simplified. Determining the intersection of the ray and the slab, if any, is conveniently determined using the Cyrus–Beck algorithm (see Sec. 3–13). In fact, the technique used by Kay and Kajiya [Kay86] is essentially equivalent to the Cyrus–Beck algorithm. An example illustrates the fundamentals of slabbing.

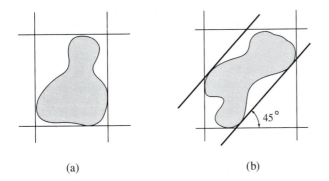

(a)   (b)

Figure 4–95 Two-dimensional analog of slabbing. (a) Slabs parallel to the coordinate planes; (b) slabs parallel and skew to the coordinate planes.

Example 4–26   Slabbing

Consider the origin-centered cube with diagonal corners given by $(-1, -1, -1)$ and $(1, 1, 1)$. Rotating the cube about first the y-axis by $45°$ and then the z-axis by $30°$, followed by translation in x and y by 2 units, yields (see [Roge90])

$$
\begin{array}{ccc}
y \text{ rotation} & z \text{ rotation} & \text{translation}
\end{array}
$$

$$
[T] =
\begin{bmatrix}
\cos 45 & 0 & -\sin 45 & 0 \\
0 & 1 & 0 & 0 \\
\sin 45 & 0 & \cos 45 & 0 \\
0 & 0 & 0 & 1
\end{bmatrix}
\begin{bmatrix}
\cos 30 & 0 & \sin 30 & 0 \\
0 & 1 & 0 & 0 \\
-\sin 30 & 0 & \cos 30 & 0 \\
0 & 0 & 0 & 1
\end{bmatrix}
\begin{bmatrix}
1 & 0 & 0 & 0 \\
0 & 1 & 0 & 0 \\
0 & 0 & 1 & 0 \\
\tfrac{1}{2} & 2 & 0 & 1
\end{bmatrix}
$$

and

$$
\begin{array}{cc}
\text{Cube vertices} & \text{Rotated cube vertices}
\end{array}
$$

$$
\begin{bmatrix}
-1 & -1 & 1 & 1 \\
1 & -1 & 1 & 1 \\
1 & 1 & 1 & 1 \\
-1 & 1 & 1 & 1 \\
-1 & -1 & -1 & 1 \\
1 & -1 & -1 & 1 \\
1 & 1 & -1 & 1 \\
-1 & 1 & -1 & 1
\end{bmatrix}
[T] =
\begin{bmatrix}
2.5 & 1.134 & 1.414 & 1 \\
3.725 & 1.841 & 0 & 1 \\
2.725 & 3.573 & 0 & 1 \\
1.5 & 2.866 & 1.414 & 1 \\
1.275 & 0.4269 & 0 & 1 \\
2.5 & 1.134 & -1.414 & 1 \\
1.5 & 2.866 & -1.414 & 1 \\
0.275 & 2.159 & 0 & 1
\end{bmatrix}
$$

where $[T]$ is the combined transformation matrix. Let us now form a bounding box around this rotated and translated cube, using slabbing.

Assuming three slabs, each perpendicular to one of the coordinate axes, then inspection of the transformed cube vertex matrix shows that $x_{min} = 0.275$, $x_{max} = 3.725$ and $d_x = 3.45$; $y_{min} = 0.427$, $y_{max} = 3.573$ and $d_y = 3.146$; $z_{min} = -1.414$, $z_{max} = 1.414$, and $d_z = 2.828$.

The normal vectors for the slab perpendicular to the x-axis are given by $n^+ = i + 0j + 0k = i$ and $n^- = -i + 0j + 0k = i$. Taking the dot product of the positive normal vector with the position vector for the first vertex in the transformed vertex matrix yields

$$
n^+ \cdot V_i = i \cdot (2.5i + 1.134j + 1.414k) = 2.5
$$

Notice that here the effect of the dot product calculation is simply to pick out the x component of the position vector of each vertex. Similarly, the normals to slabs perpendicular to the y- and z-axes pick out the y and z components of the position vectors. Consequently, the results are identical to those obtained by visual inspection. Using slabs perpendicular to the coordinate axes eliminates the requirement to actually perform the dot product calculation. However, notice that in this particular example the resulting bounding volume is not very efficient.

Clusters

Clustering groups of spatially related objects together [Hall83] increases the efficiency of bounding volume intersection calculations. For example, suppose that a scene consists of a room containing a table, with a bowl of fruit and a candy dish on it. The bowl of fruit contains an apple, a banana, a pear and a bunch of grapes. The candy dish contains several pieces of candy of different shapes and colors. Bounding volumes are defined for groups or clusters of related objects, e.g., the fruit bowl and all the fruit in it, the candy dish and all the candy in it and the table, including the fruit dish and fruit and the candy dish and candy. Bounding volumes that enclose more than one object are called cluster volumes. Typically, the highest level bounding volumes are spheres. If appropriate, cluster bounding polyhedra are also defined. The largest cluster volume, called the scene cluster, contains all the objects in the scene. The bounding volumes are processed hierarchically. The hierarchy is commonly represented as a tree, as shown in Fig. 4–96 [Hall83]; the hierarchy is processed from the top down.

If a ray does not intersect the scene cluster, then it cannot intersect any object in the scene. Hence, the associated pixel is displayed at the background intensity; no further processing is required. If the ray intersects the scene cluster, then the cluster volumes, or objects, on the next lower level of the tree are examined. If a ray intersects a cluster at any level, the process is repeated

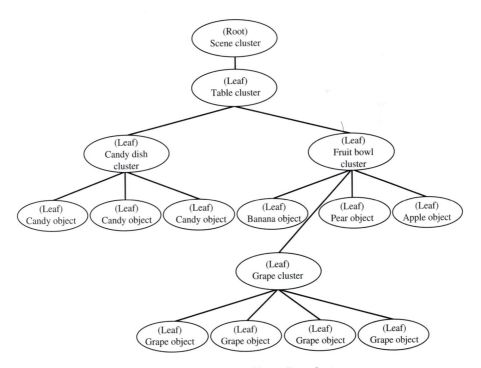

Figure 4–96   Hierarchical representation of bounding clusters.

recursively until all clusters and objects are considered. If at any point a ray intersects an individual object bounding volume, the object is placed on the active object list. This procedure significantly reduces the number of ray bounding volume intersections that must be calculated, and hence increases the efficiency of the algorithm.

Constructing the Cluster Tree

Constructing the cluster tree is a nontrivial task. Both the type of bounding volume and cluster construction significantly affect the efficiency of the tree. Many simple cluster trees are constructed by inspection. Rubin and Whitted [Rubi80] developed an interactive editor to simplify cluster selection. Weghorst et al. [Wegh84] suggested using the modeling tree as the cluster tree. However, Goldsmith and Salmon [Gold87] present a method based on incrementally adding primitive objects as the tree grows, while minimizing the surface area of the bounding volumes. Addition starts at the root; as subbranches are encountered, the subbranch that results in the minimum bounding volume surface area is selected. The process continues until a leaf of the tree is reached. Ties are broken by examining all subbranches at that level and selecting the one with the minimum bounding volume surface area. They found that the best trees were obtained by random shuffling of the order of adding bounding volumes to the tree.

A simpler but somewhat less efficient technique, in terms of ray–object intersections, is used by Kay and Kajiya [Kay86]. They sort the centers of the bounding volumes for individual objects by their x coordinate. The resulting list is split into two halves, and a cluster bounding volume is formed for each half. The algorithm is then applied recursively to each half.

Priority Sort

Hall suggests increasing the efficiency of the algorithm by using a priority sort to reduce the number of ray–object intersection calculations [Hall83, Kay86]. Instead of immediately performing a ray–object intersection calculation, as called for in the simple algorithm given above, the object is placed on an intersection object list. When all objects in the scene have been considered, the intersection object list is sorted by depth priority (see Sec. 4–12). The maximum or minimum z value for the bounding volumes is used to establish the priority sort. Intersections of the ray and objects on the intersection object list are determined in priority order. Unfortunately, as previously discussed in Secs. 4–11 and 4–12, the intersection of the ray and the first object on the prioritized intersection object list is not necessarily the visible point. Intersections with all possibly visible objects, the set $\{Q\}$ (see Sec. 4–12 for details), must be determined and placed on the intersection list. The algorithm then proceeds by sorting the intersection list, as described in the simple algorithm. Fortunately, the set of possible visible objects is generally small compared to the number of objects on the intersection object list; hence the algorithm's efficiency is increased.

In practice, the priority sort can be done 'on the fly' by using a parametric representation of the ray and saving the parameter value, t, of the first intersection of this ray with an object. The t values of intersections with subsequent objects are compared to the saved t value and the t value of the closest intersection saved.

Spatial Subdivision

Building a hierarchical bounding volume tree might be considered a divide and conquer algorithm based on subdividing space centered on objects or clusters of objects, i.e., volumes are selected based on objects, a bottom up approach. In contrast, spatial subdivision algorithms subdivide space in a more rigid fashion, typically based on three-dimensional nonintersecting axis aligned cubical volumes, called voxels (see also Sec. 4–18). Only if an object is partially or wholly within a voxel is a ray–object intersection considered, i.e., objects are selected based on volumes, a top down approach. A typical spatial subdivision is shown in Fig. 4–97.

The object list for a voxel is generated by intersecting each of the six planes forming the voxel with the object. If the object does not intersect the voxel, then it is either disjoint from the voxel or wholly contained within the voxel. Once all intersecting objects are found, wholly contained objects are identified by determining if a single point on the object is within the voxel. If it is, then the object is within the voxel; if not, then it is disjoint.

The passage of a ray through the subdivided space orders the voxels. Consequently, the voxels are processed in the order that the ray intersects them; voxels that do not intersect the ray are ignored. In general, once an intersection is found between the ray and an object partially or wholly within a voxel, then voxels and the objects within them further along the ray are also ignored.

Two exceptions, caused by an object partially occupying multiple voxels, are shown in Fig. 4–98 as a two-dimensional analog to three-dimensional voxel space. Object A in Fig. 4–98 is partially within voxels 1 and 2. When performing ray–object intersections, the results of each intersection between a given object and

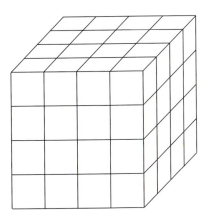

Figure 4–97 Uniform spatial subdivision.

the ray are stored in an intersection list [Arna87]. If the object also is partially within a subsequent voxel along the ray, then the list is consulted; and the results of the ray–object intersection are available without further computation. The actual sorting of the list is avoided by assigning each ray a unique identification. If a ray intersects an object, the object is assigned that ray's identification. Prior to performing an intersection on an object the object's ray identification is checked. If the ray and object identifications match, then the intersection calculation is not performed.

The second exception is illustrated by objects B and C. Notice that object B is partially within voxel 2. Thus, the intersection with the ray which occurs in voxel 4 is determined when the ray passes through voxel 2 and is placed on the intersection list. When the ray passes into voxel 3, the intersection list is examined, the intersection with object B is found and the process is terminated. Thus, the intersection of the ray and object C in voxel 3, which occurs in front of that with object B, is missed. This exception is eliminated by requiring that the voxel–ray intersection occur in the *current* voxel before the process is terminated.

Uniform Spatial Subdivision

Fujimoto et al. [Fuji86] divided space into voxels of uniform size, arranged into a uniform three-dimensional grid called SEADS (Spatially Enumerated Auxiliary Data Structure), as shown in Fig. 4–97. This structure is completely independent of the composition of the environment. Each object in the environment is associated with each voxel in which it is partially or wholly contained. Most voxels in the scene contain few, if any, objects. Hence, the number of ray–object intersections is significantly decreased.

As a ray passes through the divided space, the voxels are processed in the order penetrated. For each voxel penetrated, the list of objects in the voxel is retrieved and examined for intersections, as discussed previously. An efficient technique for 'walking' the ray from one voxel to the next is critical to the success of the algorithm. Fujimoto developed an extension to the classical digital

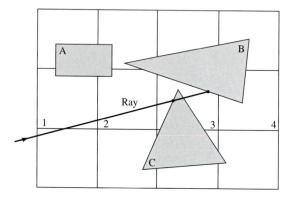

Figure 4–98   Two-dimensional analog of three-dimensional voxel space showing ray–object intersections.

differential analyzer (see Sec. 2–2) to three dimensions, called the 3DDDA (3 Dimensional Digital Differential Analyzer), for 'walking' the ray from one voxel to the next. The 3DDDA is an integer arithmetic incremental algorithm.

On a two-dimensional raster, a line drawing algorithm selects a single pixel in each column (or row) that best represents the line as it passes through the raster, as shown by the squares in Fig. 4–99. In contrast, a ray walking algorithm must select every pixel/voxel through which the ray passes. The additional pixels are indicated by circles in Fig. 4–99. Notice that multiple pixels are selected in some columns. Simple modifications of the digital differential analyzer algorithm of Sec. 2–2 allow walking a ray/line through the raster.

Fujimoto et al. [Fuji86] point out that a three-dimensional walking algorithm is realizable from two synchronized orthogonal two-dimensional algorithms. Each algorithm works sequentially with the projection of the three-dimensional line onto the appropriate plane. When simultaneous movement in both planes is required, the movements must be executed in the correct order or errors result. Although Fujimoto's algorithm is of historical interest, several more efficient algorithms, e.g., Joy [Joy86], Amanatides and Woo [Aman87], Snyder and Barr [Snyd87], Cleary and Wyvill [Clea88] and Klimaszewski [Klim94], exist.

Cleary and Wyvill's algorithm is simple and elegant. Referring to Fig. 4–100, which shows a two-dimensional analog of the three-dimensional problem, a ray enters a cell (voxel) either through a vertical or horizontal plane. Notice that as the ray traverses the grid the distance *along the ray* between intersections with vertical planes is a constant labelled Δx in Fig. 4–100a. Similarly, the distance *along the ray* between intersections with horizontal planes is a constant, labeled Δy in Fig. 4–100a. A third constant, Δz, exists in the three-dimensional case.

As a ray travels through the scene, it enters a voxel through one of three planes. Cleary and Wyvill determine which plane by keeping track of the total distance along the ray traveled in each coordinate direction, measured from some arbitrary origin. In the two-dimensional case shown in Fig. 4–100b, the total distances in the x and y directions traveled along the ray are labeled dx and dy, respectively. In three dimensions there is also a distance dz.

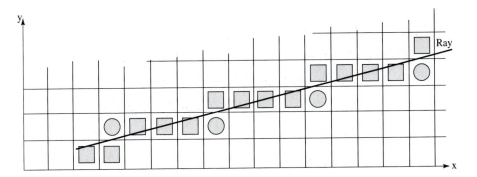

Figure 4–99   Ray walking algorithm. Squares indicate pixels activated by standard line rasterization algorithm; circles indicate extra pixels activated by ray walking algorithm.

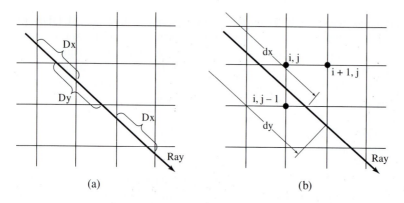

Figure 4-100 Two-dimensional next cell calculation. (a) x and y incremental distances between voxels along the ray; (b) total x and y distances along the ray.

In two dimensions, if $dx < dy$ then the next voxel is entered through the plane perpendicular to the x-axis; and the voxel is located along that axis, with $dx = dx + \Delta x$. Similarly, if $dy < dx$ then the next voxel is entered through the plane perpendicular to the y-axis; and the voxel is located along that axis, with $dy = dy + \Delta y$. Assuming that a voxel (cell) is referenced by one corner with indices i, j, k (i, j), then the index of the next cell is given by $i = i + ix$, $j = j + jy$ and $k = k + kz$, where ix, jy and kz are ± 1 depending on the direction of the ray. For example, for a ray from the lower left rear corner to the upper right front corner of the scene, voxel $ix = iy = iz = +1$. If $dx = dy$, then entry is through a vertex, the next voxel is diagonal to the current voxel and both i and j require updating. In two dimensions, a simple version of the algorithm is

simple 2D Cleary and Wyvill ray walking algorithm
initialize ix, iy, Δx, Δy, dx, dy
while *no object intersections have been found*
    if dx $\leq$ dy **then**
        i = i + ix
        dx = dx + Δx
    end if
    if dx $\geq$ dy **then**
        j = j + jy
        dy = dy + Δy
    end if
end while

Assuming that a three-dimensional voxel is identified by indices i, j, k and stored in a lineal array, then accessing a given voxel requires calculating $p = in^2 + jn + k$, where n^3 is the number of voxels in the original cubical scene voxel. This is an expensive calculation. However, Cleary and Wyvill show that the calculation can be decomposed and inexpensively folded into the algorithm. Because most of the voxels are empty, Cleary and Wyvill suggest maintaining two arrays: a full array of one bit entries showing whether a given voxel is empty, and a small hash table. The hash table, constructed using p mod M as the index with M as the table length as recommended by Glassner [Glas84], is consulted only if a voxel is not empty. Termination of the algorithm is accomplished by first calculating the distances along the ray sx, sy and sz, where the ray exits the scene voxel. The three-dimensional algorithm for walking the ray is then

3D Cleary and Wyvill ray walking algorithm

initialize ix, iy, Δx, Δy, dx, dy, sx, sy, sz, p
while *no object intersections have been found*
    if dx $\leq$ dy **and** dx $\leq$ dz **then**
        if dx $\geq$ sx **then exit**
        p $=$ p $+$ ix
        dx $=$ dx $+$ Δx
    else if dy $\leq$ dx **and** dy $\leq$ dz **then**
        if dy $\geq$ sy **then exit**
        p $=$ p $+$ jy
        dy $=$ dy $+$ Δy
    else if dz $\leq$ dy **and** dz $\leq$ dx **then**
        if dz $\geq$ sz **then exit**
        p $=$ p $+$ kz
        dz $=$ dz $+$ Δz
    end if
    if p $>$ M **then** p $=$ p $-$ M
end while

The significant advantage of uniform spatial subdivision algorithms is that the voxels are easily accessed incrementally. However, there is a memory/speed (space/time) trade-off. In order to more accurately represent the ray, the fineness of the grid is increased, which requires more storage. With a finer grid, individual voxels contain fewer objects; and the number of empty voxels increases. Thus, fewer intersection calculations are necessary; but a larger number of empty voxels are accessed. At some point, the increase in empty voxel access time exceeds the decrease in time required to calculate intersections. One partial solution, used by Glassner for octrees [Glas84], is to store only those voxels that contain objects. These considerations give rise to nonuniform spatial subdivision algorithms.

Nonuniform Spatial Subdivision

Nonuniform spatial subdivision is the three-dimensional analog of two-dimensional subdivision embodied by the Warnock algorithm (see Sec. 4–4). As with the Warnock algorithm, the subdivision is adaptive, i.e., empty, minimal size or simple subdivisions are not further subdivided. Thus, three-dimensional space is subdivided into various sized cubical volumes or voxels which correspond to the complexity of the scene. A typical nonuniform subdivision is shown in Fig. 4–101. Two subdivision techniques are commonly used, octree [Glas84] and binary space partitioning [Jans86; Kapl87]. Octrees (see Sec. 4–18) recursively subdivide a cube, typically axis aligned, into eight subcubes. Binary space partitioning (see Sec. 4–13) divides space into two pieces, using a separating plane (see [Fuch80]). Kaplan [Kapl87] restricts the separating planes to axis aligned, thus his technique yields voxels similar to those for an octree subdivision.

Adaptive nonuniform subdivision provides high resolution spatial subdivision in complex regions, without the large storage requirements associated with uniform spatial subdivision. As the subdivision progresses, a list of each object intersecting a given voxel is generated. Critical to the success of the technique is the method of storing and accessing the voxels as a ray progresses through the scene. Glassner [Glas84] developed an efficient naming technique for voxels. The scene voxel is 'named' 1. As the octree is generated, the eight children of the scene voxel are named by multiplying by ten and adding 1–8 to the parent voxel name. For example, the children of the scene voxel are 11...18. Thus, the eighth child of the seventh child of the sixth child ... etc. is named 12345678. Notice that the parent of any child voxel is obtained by dividing by 10 and taking the integer. Glassner stored only nonempty voxels, using a linked list and a hash table. He found that a convenient hashing function results from calculating the name modulo the size of the hash table.

An alternate technique transforms the ray such that the octree is in the range $(0, 0, 0)$ to $(1, 1, 1)$. The voxel containing any single point is found by converting each coordinate to a 24 bit integer. Thus, the range of each coordinate is 0 to 2^{23}. The most significant bits of each coordinate yield a three bit number (0–7 decimal) identifying the first level of the octree, the next three bits identify the position of the point in the octree at the second level, etc. [Hain97].

If a ray does not intersect an object in a particular voxel, then the ray must be 'walked' into the next voxel. If the minimum voxel edge distance (*minedge*) is kept when the octree is generated, then a simple 'walking' algorithm is:

If the ray exits the voxel interior to a face, then a point, guaranteed to

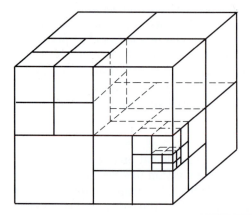

Figure 4–101   Nonuniform spatial subdivision.

exist inside the next voxel, is obtained by moving perpendicular to the exit face a distance $minedge/2$.

If the ray exits through an edge of the voxel, then a point inside the next voxel is obtained by moving a distance $minedge/2$ perpendicular to both faces forming the edge.

If the ray exits through a vertex of the voxel, then a point inside the next voxel is obtained by moving a distance $minedge/2$ perpendicular to all three faces forming the vertex.

Once a point within the next voxel is known, the object list for that voxel is obtained by starting at the scene voxel and recursively determining which octant the point occupies, until a leaf node is reached. The name of the leaf (child) node is then constructed, as discussed above, and the hash table is used to retrieve the object list and status of the child. A nonexistent node indicates an empty voxel. When this occurs, the ray is walked to the next voxel. The algorithm terminates when an intersection is found or the ray exits the scene.

Ray–Object Intersections

The intersection of a ray and an object is important, complex and computationally expensive. Optimizing the ray–object intersection calculation is critical to the success of a ray tracing algorithm. Numerous algorithms specific to a particular object are available. Here, only a few of the simpler or more general techniques are discussed.

The intersection of a sphere and a ray (line) can be calculated based on either parametric or geometric concepts. Recalling our previous discussion for bounding spheres, the ray is represented parametrically as

$$P(t) = P_1 + (P_2 - P_1)t \qquad t \geq 0$$

with components

$$x = x_1 + (x_2 - x_1)t \; = x_1 + at$$

$$y = y_1 + (y_2 - y_1)t \; = y_1 + bt$$

$$z = z_1 + (z_2 - z_1)t \; = z_1 + ct$$

The equation for a sphere with center at (x_c, y_c, z_c) is

$$(x - x_c)^2 + (y - y_c)^2 + (z - z_c)^2 = R^2$$

Substituting and solving for t for the two intersection points yields

$$t_{1,2} = \frac{-B \pm \sqrt{B^2 - 4AC}}{2A}$$

where

$$A = a^2 + b^2 + c^2$$

$$B = 2\Big(a(x_1 - x_c) + b(y_1 - y_c) + c(z_1 - z_c)\Big)$$
$$C = (x_1 - x_c)^2 + (y_1 - y_c)^2 + (z_1 - z_c)^2 - R^2$$

When $\sqrt{B^2 - 4AC} < 0$, there is no intersection. The actual intersection points are obtained by substituting the values of t into the parametric component equations. The smaller value of t gives the 'visible' point. The unit normal vector at the intersection points is given by

$$\hat{\mathbf{n}} = \left[\; \frac{x_i - x_c}{R^2} \quad \frac{y_i - y_c}{R^2} \quad \frac{z_i - z_c}{R^2} \;\right]$$

The outer normal is positive. Haines [Hain89] gives implementation details for an efficient algorithm. He also gives a geometric based solution which yields a somewhat more efficient algorithm.

Recalling that the equation of an infinite plane is

$$Ax + By + Cz + D = 0$$

and substituting the parametric components of the ray yields

$$t = -\frac{Ax_1 + By_1 + Cz_1 + D}{aA + bB + cC} \qquad t \geq 0$$

the parameter value for the intersection point of a ray and an infinite plane. Again, the actual intersection point is obtained by substituting the value of t into the component equations.

The normal to the plane is

$$\mathbf{n} = [\,A \quad B \quad C\,]$$

Notice the normal is formed directly from the coefficients of the plane equation.

If the object is a polygon, it is necessary to also perform a containment test (see Sec. 4–4), which can be expensive. However, provided the polygon is convex, a clever use of the Cyrus–Beck clipping algorithm (see Sec. 3–5) allows determining the intersection point and whether it is contained within the polygon. Specifically, the polygon is considered to be a convex polyhedron with two planes coincident, as shown in Fig. 4–102. The plane equation gives the normals, which are in opposite directions, to these coincident planes. The normals to the polygon sides are determined in the usual way (see Sec. 3–9). If the Cyrus–Beck clipping algorithm yields an intersection, that intersection is contained within the polygon.

General convex volumes are also intersected using the Cyrus–Beck algorithm. For the special case of axis-aligned rectangular parallelepipeds (boxes), Haines [Hain89] gives an efficient algorithm, or the ray is made coincident with the z-axis and the algorithm detailed above is used.

If the polyhedral volume is concave, then each of the planes for each of the polygons forming the volume is intersected by the ray, and a containment

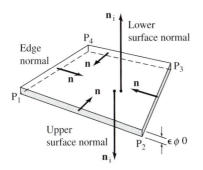

Figure 4–102   Three-dimensional convex polygon intersection and containment using the Cyrus–Beck clipping algorithm.

test is performed to determine if the intersection is inside the polygon. Those intersections inside the face polygons are saved and sorted to determine the visible intersection. Alternatively, the concave polyhedral volume is decomposed into convex polyhedral volumes, using techniques similar to that described in Sec. 3–17.

Spheres, ellipsoids, paraboloids, the hyperbolic paraboloid, the hyperboloid of one and two sheets, the cone and the cylinder are quadric surfaces. In any Cartesian coordinate system, the general quadric surface is the locus of points given by

$$Q(x, y, z) = A_1 x^2 + A_2 y^2 + A_3 z^2 + B_1 yz + B_2 xz + B_3 xy + C_1 x + C_2 y + C_3 z + D = 0$$

Substituting the components of the ray into this equation and solving for t yields

$$t_{1,2} = \frac{-\bar{B} \pm \sqrt{\bar{B}^2 - 4\bar{A}\bar{C}}}{2\bar{A}}$$

where
$$\bar{A} = a^2 A_1 + b^2 A_2 + c^2 A_3 + bcB_1 + acB_2 + abB_3$$
$$\bar{B} = 2(ax_1 A_1 + by_1 A_2 + cz_1 A_3)$$
$$\quad + (cy_1 + bz_1)B_1 + (cx_1 + az_1)B_2 + (bx_1 + ay_1)B_3$$
$$\quad + aC_1 + bC_2 + cC_3$$
$$\bar{C} = x_1^2 A_1 + y_1^2 A_2 + z_1^2 A_3 + y_1 z_1 B_1 + x_1 z_1 B_2 + x_1 y_1 B_3$$
$$\quad + x_1 C_1 + y_1 C_2 + z_1 C_3 + D$$

If $\bar{A} \neq 0$ and $\sqrt{\bar{B}^2 - 4\bar{A}\bar{C}} < 0$, there is no intersection; if $\bar{A} = 0$, then

$$t = -\frac{\bar{C}}{\bar{B}}$$

Again, the actual intersection point is obtained by substituting the values of $t_{1,2}$ into the parametric equation of the ray. The smallest positive value of t yields the intersection point.

The normal to the surface at the intersection point is obtained by taking the partial derivatives of the surface with respect to each of the coordinate directions, that is

$$n_x = 2A_1x_i + B_3y_i + B_2z_i + C_1$$
$$n_y = B_3x_i + 2A_2y_i + B_1z_i + C_2$$
$$n_z = B_2x_i + B_1y_i + 2A_3z_i + C_3$$

where x_i, y_i, z_i are the coordinates of the intersection point, and n_x, n_y and n_z are the components of the normal vector.

The intersection calculation is simplified by transforming the ray to coincide with the z-axis, at the expense of transforming the ray. After applying the combined translation and rotation transformation used to make the ray coincident with the z-axis, the intersection of the ray and the surface, if any, occurs at $x = y = 0$. Thus, in general, the intersection points are given by the solution of

$$A_3'z^2 + C_3'z + D' = 0$$

that is

$$z = \frac{-C_3' \pm \sqrt{C_3'^2 - 4A_3'D'}}{2A_3'}$$

where the prime indicates the coefficients of the general quadric surface in the transformed orientation. If $C_3'^2 - 4A_3'D' < 0$, the solutions are complex and the ray does not intersect the surface. If an infinite quadric surface (e.g., cones and cylinders) is constrained by limit planes, then the limit planes must also be transformed and examined for intersections. If an intersection with an infinite limit plane is found, a containment test must be performed. However, in the transformed coordinate system, this test can be performed on the two-dimensional projection of the intersection of the limit plane and the quadric surface. To obtain the intersections in the original orientation, the inverse transformation is applied.

Intersection calculations for bipolynomial parametric surface patches are less straightforward. Whitted [Whit79] implemented a simple subdivision technique for bicubic surface patches. The calculations are carried out with the surface patch in its original location. If a ray initially intersects the bounding sphere for a patch, the patch is subdivided using Catmull's subdivision algorithm (see Sec. 4–8). The ray is tested against the bounding spheres of the subpatches. If there is no intersection, the ray does not intersect the patch. If the ray intersects a bounding sphere for a subpatch, the patch is further subdivided. The process is continued until no bounding spheres are intersected, or the bounding spheres reach a predetermined minimum size. These minimum-sized bounding spheres represent the intersections of the ray and the patch.

The subdivision technique can be utilized with bounding boxes rather than bounding spheres. This reduces the number of subdivisions and increases the efficiency of the algorithm. For parametric surfaces that exhibit a convex hull property, e.g., Bézier and B-spline surfaces (see [Roge90]), the number of subdivisions can be further reduced, at the expense of further complexity, by using the convex hull (see, e.g., [Barb93]) rather than the bounding box for the subpatches.

Kajiya [Kaji82] implemented a technique for bipolynomial parametric surfaces that does not involve subdivision. The method is based on concepts from algebraic geometry. Solutions of the resulting high-degree algebraic equations are obtained numerically. A similar technique can be implemented in the transformed coordinate system. Recall that a bipolynomial parametric surface is defined by

$$Q(u, w) = 0$$

with components

$$x = f(u, w)$$

$$y = g(u, w)$$

$$z = h(u, w)$$

In the transformed coordinate system $x = y = 0$, hence

$$f(u, w) = 0$$

$$g(u, w) = 0$$

Simultaneous solution of this pair of equations yields the values of u and w for the intersections. Substitution into $z = h(u, w)$ yields the z component of the intersection points. Failure to find a real solution means that the ray does not intersect the surface. The degree of the system of equations for u, w is twice the product of the bipolynomial surface degrees, e.g., eighteenth degree for a bicubic surface. Consequently, numerical solution techniques are generally required. Where applicable, intersections of the ray and the convex hull can be used to obtain an initial estimate of u and w. Again, to obtain the intersections in the original orientation, the inverse transformation is applied.

Hanrahan [Hanr89] provides a useful summary of intersection techniques including blend and join surfaces, bilinear and bicubic patches, simplicial splines and Steiner patches, superquadrics, blobs, sweep surfaces, surfaces of revolution, generalized cylinders, fractals, height fields, deformed surfaces and constructive solid geometry, as well as those discussed here.

Opaque Visible Surface Algorithm

The procedure for a simple opaque visible surface ray tracing algorithm using hierarchical bounding sphere clustering is

Prepare the scene data:

Create an object list containing at least the following information

Complete description of the object: type, surface, characteristics, etc.

Bounding sphere description: center and radius.

Object bounding volume flag. If the flag is true, a bounding volume test is performed; if false, it is skipped.

Bounding volume description and parameters: for example, for a bounding box $x_{min}, x_{max}, y_{min}, y_{max}, z_{min}, z_{max}$.

For each ray to be traced:

For each cluster sphere on the hierarchical tree

Perform a three-dimensional bounding sphere test

If the ray intersects the bounding cluster sphere

If the sphere is an object sphere, place the object on the active object list.

If the active object list is empty, display the pixel at the background intensity and continue.

For each object on the active object list:

If the bounding volume flag is true, perform the bounding volume test

If the ray intersects the bounding volume

Determine the ray's intersections, if any, with the object; place any intersections on an intersection list.

If the intersection list is empty, display the pixel at the background intensity.

Otherwise, determine z_{max} for the intersection list.

Display the pixel using the intersected object's attributes and an appropriate illumination model.

An example serves to more fully illustrate the discussion.

Example 4–27   Ray Tracing Algorithm

Again consider the rectangle and penetrating triangle previously discussed in Exs. 4–19, 4–22, and 4–23. For simplicity, the observer is assumed to be located at infinity on the positive z-axis. Hence, all the rays are parallel to the z-axis. The z-axis passes through the $0, 0$ point on the raster. Recall that the rectangle has corner points $P_1(10, 5, 10)$, $P_2(10, 25, 10)$, $P_3(25, 25, 10)$, $P_4(25, 5, 10)$. The center of its bounding sphere is located at $(17^1/2, 15, 10)$ with radius $12^1/2$. The bounding volume for the rectangle is a bounding box, with $x_{min}, x_{max}, y_{min}, y_{max}, z_{min}, z_{max}$ equal $10, 25, 5, 25, 10, 10$, respectively. Note that both an object bounding sphere *and* an object bounding box for the object increases efficiency.

The triangle has vertices at $P_5(15, 15, 15)$, $P_6(25, 25, 5)$, $P_7(30, 10, 5)$. The center of the bounding sphere is at $(22.885, 15.962, 8.846)$, with radius 10.048. The bounding volume for the triangle is also a bounding box, with x_{min}, $x_{max}, y_{min}, y_{max}, z_{min}, z_{max}$ of $15, 30, 10, 25, 5, 15$.

The ray through the center of the pixel at $(20, 15)$ is considered. Since the observer is at infinity, the ray is parallel to the z-axis.

First, a hierarchical bounding volume tree of spheres is formed. The tree, which is quite simple, consists of a root sphere containing the bounding spheres for the rectangle and the triangle. Thus, the tree has two leaves, one for the rectangle and one for the triangle.

To form the cluster sphere, we use the approximate technique. By inspection, $x_{max} = 30$, $x_{min} = 10$, $y_{max} = 25$, $y_{min} = 5$, $z_{max} = 15$ and $z_{min} = 5$ for the combined rectangle and triangle. The center of the cluster sphere is thus at

$$x_c = \frac{x_{max} - x_{min}}{2} = \frac{30 + 10}{2} = 20$$

$$y_c = \frac{y_{max} - y_{min}}{2} = \frac{25 + 5}{2} = 15$$

$$z_c = \frac{z_{max} - z_{min}}{2} = \frac{15 + 5}{2} = 10$$

with radius

$$R = \sqrt{(x_{max} - x_c)^2 + (y_{max} - y_c)^2 + (z_{max} - z_c)^2}$$

$$= \sqrt{(30 - 20)^2 + (25 - 15)^2 + (15 - 10)^2} = 15$$

Tracing the ray, first consider the intersection of the ray with the cluster sphere. Since the ray is parallel to the z-axis, the distance from the center of the bounding sphere to the ray is a two-dimensional calculation. Specifically, using the center of the pixel, i.e., $(20\,^1\!/_2, 15\,^1\!/_2)$, yields

$$d^2 = (20.5 - 20.0)^2 + (15.5 - 15)^2 = 0.5$$

Since $(d^2 = ^1\!/_2) < (R^2 = 225)$, the ray intersects the cluster sphere. Following the hierarchical tree, the bounding spheres within the cluster sphere are considered.

First consider the rectangle. Again, since the ray is parallel to the z-axis, the distance from the center of the rectangle's bounding sphere to the ray is a two-dimensional calculation. Specifically, using the center of the pixel, i.e., $(20\,^1\!/_2, 15\,^1\!/_2)$, yields

$$d^2 = (20.5 - 17.5)^2 + (15.5 - 15)^2 = 9.25$$

Since $(d^2 = 9\,^1\!/_4) < (R^2 = 156\,^1\!/_4)$, the ray intersects the bounding sphere for the rectangle. This is an object sphere. Thus, the rectangle is placed on the active object list.

Similarly, for the triangle's bounding sphere

$$d^2 = (20.5 - 22.885)^2 + (15.5 - 15.962)^2 = 5.90$$

which is also less than the square of the radius of the bounding sphere; i.e., $(d^2 = 5.90) < (R^2 = 100.96)$. Thus, the ray intersects the bounding sphere for the triangle. Again, this is an object sphere, so the triangle is also placed on the active object list.

The active object list is not empty. For simplicity, the ray is transformed to be coincident with the z-axis. Specifically, the ray is translated by $-20\,{}^1\!/_2$, $-15\,{}^1\!/_2$, 0 in the x, y, z directions, respectively.

Translating the rectangle's bounding box similarly yields $-10\,{}^1\!/_2, 4\,{}^1\!/_2, -10\,{}^1\!/_2$, $9\,{}^1\!/_2, 10, 10$ for $x_{\min}$, $x_{\max}$, $y_{\min}$, $y_{\max}$, $z_{\min}$, $z_{\max}$, respectively. Since the signs of both $x_{\min}$ and $x_{\max}$ *and* $y_{\min}$ and $y_{\max}$ are opposite, the ray intersects the rectangle's bounding box. The intersection of the ray and the rectangle is obtained using the plane equation. In both the transformed and untransformed coordinate systems, the rectangle's plane equation is

$$z - 10 = 0$$

The intersection of the ray thus occurs at $z = 10$. The intersection is inside the rectangle. This value is placed on the intersection list.

Translating the bounding box for the triangle yields $-5\,{}^1\!/_2, 9\,{}^1\!/_2, -5\,{}^1\!/_2, 9\,{}^1\!/_2, 5$, 15 for $x_{\min}$, $x_{\max}$, $y_{\min}$, $y_{\max}$, $z_{\min}$, $z_{\max}$, respectively. Again, the signs of both $x_{\min}$ and $x_{\max}$ *and* $y_{\min}$ and $y_{\max}$ are opposite, so the ray also intersects the triangle's bounding box. In the untransformed coordinate system, the plane equation for the triangle is

$$3x + y + 4z - 120 = 0$$

In the transformed coordinate system it is

$$3x + y + 4z - 43 = 0$$

and the intersection is at

$$z = \frac{(43 - 3x - y)}{4} = \frac{43}{4} = 10\,{}^3\!/_4$$

This value is inside the triangle and is placed on the intersection list.

The intersection list is not empty. The maximum z value is $z_{\max} = 10\,{}^3\!/_4$, and the triangle is visible. Translating back to the original coordinate system yields the intersection point at $(20\,{}^1\!/_2, 15\,{}^1\!/_2, 10\,{}^3\!/_4)$. The pixel at $(20, 15)$ is displayed with the triangle's attributes.

For multiple intersections of the ray being traced and objects in the scene, it is necessary to determine the visible intersection. For the simple opaque visible surface algorithm discussed in this section, the intersection with the maximum z coordinate is the visible surface. For more complex algorithms with reflections and refractions, the intersections must be ordered with respect to the distance from the point of origin of the ray.

The simple algorithm given here does not take advantage of eliminating self-hidden faces for polygonal volumes (see Sec. 4–3), nor does it take advantage of the coherence of the scene. For example, the order in which pixels are considered is arbitrary. Considering the pixels in scan line order would allow the algorithm to take advantage of scan line coherence. Although incorporating these techniques yields a more efficient opaque visible surface algorithm, they are not applicable for a general ray tracing algorithm incorporating reflection, refraction and transparency. For example, when reflection is incorporated into the algorithm an object totally obscured by another object may be visible as a reflection in a third object. Since a ray tracing algorithm is a brute force technique, the opaque visible surface algorithms discussed in previous sections are more efficient and should be used.[†]

Roth [Roth82] points out that a ray tracing algorithm can also be used to generate wire frame line drawings for solid objects. The procedure assumes a scan-line-oriented generation of the rays, i.e., top to bottom and left to right. The procedure is

> If the visible surface at Pixel(x,y) is the background, or is different from the visible surface at $Pixel(x-1, y)$, **or** at $Pixel(x, y-1)$, display the pixel. Otherwise, do not display the pixel.

In addition to the hidden surface problem, ray tracing is useful in a variety of applications, e.g., vision research, medical treatment planning, vulnerability analysis of vehicles (impact and penetration studies), seismic research (density calculation along a ray), interference checking (numerical control and pipe line and chemical plant design and construction).

A ray tracing algorithm can also be used to determine the physical properties of a solid. A complete analysis is beyond the scope of this text. However, a simple example illustrates the concept. In particular, the volume of an arbitrary solid can be determined by approximating it by the sum of a set of small rectangular parallelepipeds. This is accomplished by generating a set of parallel rays at known intervals. The intersections of each ray and the volume are obtained and ordered along the ray. If the ray is translated to be coincident with the z-axis, as described earlier, the volume of each rectangular parallelepiped is then

$$V = l_x l_y [(z_1 - z_2) + (z_3 - z_4) + \cdots + (z_{n-1} - z_n)]$$

where l_x and l_y are the spacing between rays in the horizontal and vertical directions, respectively. Each $(z_{n-1} - z_n)$ represents a portion of the ray inside the volume. The volume of the solid is then the sum of the volumes of all the rectangular parallelepipeds. The accuracy of the result depends on the number of rays used. The accuracy can be increased, at reduced computational expense, by recursively subdividing the 'pixel' size if the volumes of adjacent rectangular parallelepipeds differ by more than a specified amount. This technique more accurately determines the volumes in regions of rapid change, e.g., near the edges of volumes enclosed by curved surfaces.

[†]Implementation of the algorithms as described in the previous sections in the same language, on the same computer system, for the scene described in Exs. 4–19 and 4–22 to 4–24 yields performance ratios of Ray tracing:Warnock:Watkins:Scan line z-buffer:z-buffer as 9.2:6.2:2.1:1.9:1.

Because of the inherently parallel nature of ray tracing (the process for each ray is the same and independent of the results for any other ray), the algorithm can be implemented using parallel processing techniques.

4–21 Summary

The previous sections have discussed, in some detail, a number of fundamental algorithms used to obtain solutions to the visible line or surface problem. These algorithms are by no means all that are available. However, having mastered the concepts presented, the reader should be equipped to understand new algorithms as they are developed, or to invent algorithms specific to a particular application.

RENDERING

5–1 Introduction

Simply defined, rendering is the process of producing realistic images or pictures. Producing realistic images involves both physics and psychology. Light, i.e., electromagnetic energy, reaches the eye after interacting with the physical environment. In the eye, physical and chemical changes take place that generate electrical pulses that are interpreted, i.e. perceived, by the brain. Perception is a learned characteristic. The psychology of visual perception has been extensively studied and written about. An extensive discussion of visual perception is well beyond the scope of this book. The standard reference work on visual perception is Cornsweet [Corn70].

The human eye is a very complex system. The eye is nearly spherical and about 20 mm in diameter. The eye's flexible lens is used to focus received light onto an area of the rear hemisphere of the eye, called the retina. The retina contains two different kinds of receptors: cones and rods. The 6–7 million cones are concentrated in the center of the rear hemisphere of the eye; each one has an individual nerve connected to it. The cones, which are sensitive only to relatively high light levels, are used to resolve fine detail.

The other type of receptor is called a rod. There are between 75 and 150 million rods distributed over the retina. Several rods are connected to a single nerve; thus the rods cannot resolve fine detail. The rods are sensitive to very low levels of illumination. Interestingly enough, only the cones are used in perceiving color. Because the cones are sensitive only to relatively high levels of light, objects viewed with low illumination are seen only with the rods; hence they are not seen in color. In the garden at night a red rose looks black or dark gray.

There is good experimental evidence that the eye's sensitivity to brightness is logarithmic. The total range of brightness sensitivity is very large, on the order of 10^{10}. However, the eye cannot simultaneously respond to this large a brightness range. The eye responds to a much smaller, *relative* brightness range centered around a brightness adaptation level. The relative brightness range is on the order of 100–150 (2.2 log units). The rapidity with which the eye adjusts its brightness adaptation level is different for different parts of the retina. Still, it is remarkable. The eye perceives brightness at the extremes of the relative brightness range as either white or black.

Because the eye adapts to the 'average' brightness in a scene, an area of constant brightness or intensity surrounded by a dark area is perceived to be brighter or lighter than the same area surrounded by a light area. This phenomenon, illustrated in Fig. 5–1, is called simultaneous contrast. On a scale of 0–1, with 1 darkest, the brightness of the center area of Fig. 5–1a is 0.5, and that of the surrounding area is 0.2. In Fig. 5–1b, the brightness of the center area is again 0.5, but that of the surrounding area is 0.8. A common example is the apparent difference in brightness of a single street light viewed against the sky during the day and at night. For either Fig. 5–1a or a street light seen in daylight, the average intensity or brightness of the scene is greater than for the scene in Fig. 5–1b or the street light at night. Consequently, the contrast is lower; the intensity or brightness of the street light or the center of Fig. 5–1a is perceived as lower. A phenomenon similar to simultaneous contrast occurs for color.

Another characteristic of the eye which has implications for computer graphics is that the brightness perceived by the eye tends to overshoot at the boundaries of regions of constant intensity. This characteristic results in areas of constant intensity being perceived as of varying intensity. The phenomenon is called the Mach band effect, after the Austrian physicist Ernst Mach, who first observed it. The Mach band effect occurs whenever the slope of the light intensity curve changes abruptly. At that location, the surface appears brighter or darker: if the inflection in the intensity curve is concave, the surface appears brighter; if convex, it appears darker (see [Ratl72] for a detailed description). Figure 5–2 illustrates both the concept and the results.

(a)

(b)

Figure 5–1   Simultaneous contrast. (a) Lighter square surrounding a darker square; (b) darker square surrounding a lighter square. Both interior squares are the same.

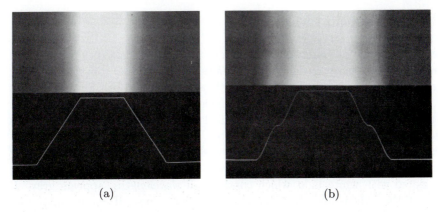

(a)   (b)

Figure 5–2 Mach band effects. (a) Piecewise linear; (b)continuous first-derivative intensity function. (Courtesy of theUniversity of Utah, [Buit75]).

The Mach band effect is particularly important for shaded polygonally represented surfaces. If the direction of the normal vector for each individual polygon composing the surface is used to determine the displayed intensity, then the intensity changes abruptly at the polygon edges. The Mach band effect decreases the ability of the eye to smoothly integrate the scene. Figure 5–3a illustrates this effect. Figure 5–3b shows that increasing the number of facets (polygons) decreases the effect but does not eliminate it. Interestingly enough, because the Mach band effect depends on changes in the spatial derivative of the intensity, the effect tends to disappear as the image is brought closer to the eye because the apparent spatial frequencies decrease [Duff79].

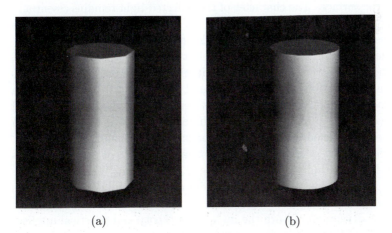

(a)   (b)

Figure 5–3 Mach band effect for plane polygonal surface representations. (a) Eight-sided model; (b) 32-sided model. (Courtesy of the University of Utah [Buit75]).

5–2 Illumination Models

When light energy falls on a surface, it can be absorbed, reflected or transmitted. Some of the light energy incident on a surface is absorbed and converted to heat; the rest is either reflected or transmitted. It is the reflected or transmitted light that makes an object visible. If all the incident light energy is absorbed, the object is invisible. The object is then called a black body. Reflected or transmitted light energy makes an object visible. The amount of energy absorbed, reflected or transmitted depends on the wavelength of the light. If the intensity of incident light is reduced nearly equally for all wavelengths, then an object, illuminated with white light which contains all wavelengths, appears gray. If nearly all the light is absorbed, the object appears black. If only a small fraction is absorbed, the object appears white. If some wavelengths are selectively absorbed, the reflected and/or transmitted light leaving the object has a different energy distribution. The object appears colored. The color of the object is determined by the wavelengths selectively absorbed and reflected.

The character of the light reflected from or transmitted through the surface of an object depends on the composition, direction and geometry of the light source; the surface orientation; and the surface properties of the object. The light reflected from an object is also characterized by being either diffusely or specularly reflected or transmitted. Diffusely reflected or transmitted light can be considered as light that has penetrated below the surface of an object, been absorbed and then reemitted. Diffusely reflected light is scattered equally in all directions. As a result, the position of the observer is unimportant.

Specularly reflected light is reflected from the outer surface of the object. Since it does not penetrate below the surface, it is not scattered. Consequently, if a narrow beam of light is incident on a surface, a narrow beam of light is reflected from the surface. The character of the reflected light remains essentially unchanged, i.e., if the incident light is white (or say red) the reflected light is white (red), essentially independent of the color of the surface.

Surface materials are generally either dielectric (insulating) or conducting. Dielectric materials are transparent, and conducting materials are opaque. This frequently causes confusion. For example, sand is a dielectric material, yet a pile of sand *looks* opaque. However, sand is nearly pure silicon (quartz) and glass, a transparent material, is pure silicon. In fact, if you look at a single grain of sand it is nearly transparent; any slight opaqueness is a result of impurities. A shattered piece of safety glass is another example. A pile of glass fragments looks opaque, but each individual small piece is transparent. Transparent (dielectric) materials have low reflectance, whereas opaque (conducting) materials have high reflectance.

An excellent discussion of both the underlying theory and practical application of the details of the illumination models used in computer graphics is given in the excellent monograph by Hall [Hall89]. In the next few sections, only the basics of illumination models are discussed.

5–3   A Simple Illumination Model

Lambert's cosine law governs the reflection of light from a point source by a perfect diffuser. Lambert's law states that the intensity of light reflected from a perfect diffuser is proportional to the cosine of the angle between the light direction and the normal to the surface. Specifically

$$I(\lambda) = I_\ell(\lambda)k_d(\lambda)\cos\theta \qquad 0 \le \theta \le \frac{\pi}{2}$$

Where $I(\lambda)$ is the reflected intensity, $I_\ell(\lambda)$ is the incident intensity from a point light source, $k(\lambda)_d$ is the diffuse reflection function $(0 \le k_d(\lambda) \le 1)$, λ is the wavelength and θ is the angle between the light direction and the surface normal, as shown in Fig. 5–4. For angles greater than $\pi/2$, the light source is behind the object and thus no reflected light directly reaches an observer. The diffuse reflection coefficient, $k(\lambda)_d$, varies with the wavelength of the light and with the material. The simple illumination models generally assume k_d and I_ℓ to be constant.

Objects rendered with a simple Lambertian diffuse reflection illumination model or shader appear to have a dull matte surface. Because a point light source located at the eye or viewpoint is assumed, objects that receive no light directly from the source appear black. However, in a real scene, objects also receive light scattered back to them from the surroundings, e.g., the walls of a room. This ambient light represents a distributed light source. Because the computational requirements for a distributed light source are very large, simple computer graphics illumination models treat it as a constant diffuse term and linearly combine it with the Lambertian contribution. The simple illumination model is then

$$I(\lambda) = I_a(\lambda)k(\lambda)_a + I_\ell(\lambda)k_d\cos\theta \qquad 0 \le \theta \le \frac{\pi}{2}, \quad k_a + k_d < 1 \qquad (5-1a)$$

where $I_a(\lambda)$ is the incident ambient light intensity and $k(\lambda)_a$ is the ambient diffuse reflection function $(0 \le k_a(\lambda) \le 1)$. Generally k_d and I_a are also assumed

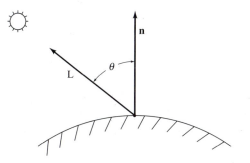

Figure 5–4   Diffuse reflection.

constant in simple illumination models. Thus, the simple illumination model, originally suggested by Bouknight [Bouk70], is then

$$I = I_a k_a + I_\ell k_d \cos\theta \qquad 0 \le \theta \le \frac{\pi}{2}, \quad k_a + k_d < 1 \qquad (5-1b)$$

If this illumination model is used to determine the intensity of light reflected from two objects with the same orientation to the light source but at different distances, the same intensity for both objects results. If the objects overlap, then it is not possible to distinguish between them. However, it is well known that the intensity of light decreases inversely as the square of the distance from the source; i.e., objects farther away appear dimmer. Unfortunately, if the light source is located at infinity, the distance to the object is infinite. Consequently, if the diffuse term in this illumination model is made inversely proportional to the square of the distance from the light source, it yields no contribution. If a perspective transformation is applied to the scene, the distance from the perspective viewpoint to the object, d, is used as the constant of proportionality for the diffuse term. However, when the perspective viewpoint is close to the object, $1/d^2$ varies rapidly. This results in objects at nearly the same distance having large unrealistic variations in intensity. Warnock [Warn69b] suggested that more realistic results are obtained by using a linear, $1/d$ attenuation law, while Romney [Romn69b] suggested using a $1/d^p$ attenuation law. The simple illumination model is then

$$I = I_a k_a + \frac{I_\ell k_d \cos\theta}{d^p + K} \qquad (5-2)$$

where K is an arbitrary constant and $0 \le p \le 2$. When the viewpoint is at infinity, the distance d is frequently determined relative to the location of the object closest to the viewpoint. This has the effect of illuminating the object closest to the viewpoint with the full intensity of the point light source, and all objects farther from the viewpoint at lower intensities. If the surface is colored, the illumination model is applied individually to each of the three primary colors. If additional fidelity is required, the illumination model is applied to several sample wavelengths or bands (see [Hall83; Meyer88].

Specular Reflection

The intensity of specularly reflected light depends on the angle of incidence, the wavelength of the incident light and the material properties. The governing equation is the Fresnel equation, given in any geometric optics book (see, e.g., [Jenk76]). Specular reflection of light is directional. For a perfect reflecting surface (a mirror), the angle of reflection is equal to the angle of incidence. Thus, only an observer located at exactly that angle sees any specularly reflected light. This implies that the sight vector, **S** in Fig. 5–5, is coincident with the reflection vector **R**; i.e., the angle α is zero. For imperfect reflecting surfaces, the amount of light reaching an observer depends on the spatial distribution of the specularly

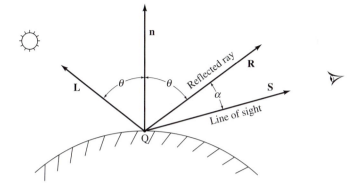

Figure 5–5   Specular reflection.

reflected light. For smooth surfaces, the spatial distribution is narrow or focused, while for rough surfaces it is spread out.

The highlights on a shiny object are due to specular reflection. Because specularly reflected light is focused along the reflection vector, highlights move with the observer. In addition, because the light is reflected from the outer surface, except for some metals and solid dyes, the reflected light exhibits the characteristics of the incident light. For example, the highlights on a shiny blue painted surface illuminated with white light appear white rather than blue.

Because of the complex physical characteristics of specularly reflected light, an empirical model based on a cosine raised to a power originally suggested by Romney [Romn69b], and combined with the ambient and diffuse reflection by Bui-Tuong Phong [Phon75], is usually used for simple illumination models. Specifically

$$I(\lambda)_s = I_\ell(\lambda)w(i, \lambda) \cos^n \alpha \qquad (5-3)$$

where $w(i, \lambda)$, the reflectance curve, gives the ratio of the specularly reflected light to the incident light as a function of the incidence angle, i, and the wavelength λ. Here, n is a power that approximates the spatial distribution of the specularly reflected light. Figure 5–6 shows $\cos^n \alpha$ for $-\pi/2 \leq \alpha \leq \pi/2$ for various values of n. Large values of n yield focused spatial distributions characteristic of metals and other shiny surfaces, while small values of n yield more distributed results characteristic of nonmetallic surfaces, e.g., paper.

Specular reflectance is directional, i.e., it depends on the angle of the incident light. Light that strikes a surface perpendicularly reflects only a percentage of the light specularly; the rest is either absorbed or reflected diffusely. The amount depends on the material properties and the wavelength. For some nonmetallic materials the reflectance is as little as 4%, while for metallic materials it can exceed 80%. Figure 5–7a gives examples of reflectance curves for typical materials at normal incidence as a function of wavelength, and Fig. 5–7b gives results as a function of incidence angle. Notice that at the grazing angle ($\theta = 90°$) all the incident light is reflected (reflectance = 100%).

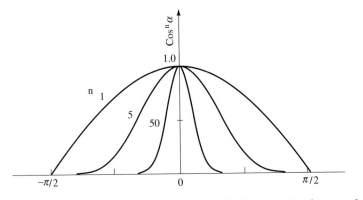

Figure 5–6   Approximate spatial distribution function for specularly reflected light.

Combining the current results with those for ambient and incident diffuse reflection yields the so called Phong [Phon75] illumination model

$$I(\lambda) = I_a(\lambda)k(\lambda)_a + \frac{I_\ell(\lambda)}{d^p + K}(k_d(\lambda)\cos\theta + w(i,\lambda)\cos^n\alpha) \qquad (5-4)$$

Because $w(i,\lambda)$ is such a complex function, it is frequently replaced by an aesthetically or experimentally determined constant, k_s. For a simple illumination model which neglects wavelength variation, we have

$$I = I_a k_a + \frac{I_\ell}{d^p + K}(k_d\cos\theta + k_s\cos^n\alpha) \qquad (5-5)$$

as the illumination model. In computer graphics this model is frequently called a shading function. It is used to determine the intensity or shade of each point

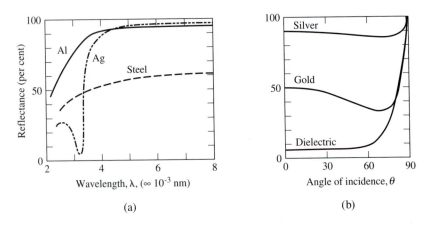

(a)

(b)

Figure 5–7   Reflection curves.

on an object, or of each displayed pixel. Again, individual shading functions are used for each of the three primary colors to yield a colored image. However, since the color of specularly reflected light depends on the color of the incident light, k_s is usually constant for all three primaries.

If multiple light sources are present, the effects are linearly added. The simple illumination model then becomes

$$I = I_a k_a + \sum_{j=1}^{m} \frac{I_{l_j}}{d^p + K} (k_d \cos \theta_j + k_s \cos_j^n \alpha_j) \qquad (5-6)$$

where m is the number of light sources.

Recalling the formula for the dot product of two vectors allows writing

$$\cos \theta = \frac{\mathbf{n} \cdot \mathbf{L}}{|\mathbf{n}|\ |\mathbf{L}|} = \widehat{\mathbf{n}} \cdot \widehat{\mathbf{L}}$$

where $\widehat{\mathbf{n}}$ and $\widehat{\mathbf{L}}$ are the unit vectors in the surface normal and light source directions, respectively.

Similarly

$$\cos \alpha = \frac{\mathbf{R} \cdot \mathbf{S}}{|\mathbf{R}|\ |\mathbf{S}|} = \widehat{\mathbf{R}} \cdot \widehat{\mathbf{S}}$$

where $\widehat{\mathbf{R}}$ and $\widehat{\mathbf{S}}$ are the unit vectors for the reflected ray and line-of-sight directions, respectively. Thus the simple illumination model for a single light source is

$$I = I_a k_a + \frac{I_\ell}{d^p + K} \left[k_d (\widehat{\mathbf{n}} \cdot \widehat{\mathbf{L}}) + k_s (\widehat{\mathbf{R}} \cdot \widehat{\mathbf{S}})^n \right] \qquad (5-7)$$

and for multiple light sources

$$I = I_a k_a + \sum_{j=1}^{m} \frac{I_{\ell_j}}{d^p + K} \left[k_d (\widehat{\mathbf{n}} \cdot \widehat{\mathbf{L}}_j) + k_s (\widehat{\mathbf{R}}_j \cdot \widehat{\mathbf{S}})^n \right]$$

The Halfway Vector

An alternate formulation of the Phong specular reflection model due to Blinn [Blin77] uses the halfway vector, $\mathbf{H}$, defined as the vector halfway between the direction of the light, $\widehat{\mathbf{L}}$, and the line of sight, $\mathbf{S}$, as shown in Fig. 5–8. The unit halfway vector, defined as $\widehat{\mathbf{H}} = (\mathbf{L} + \mathbf{S})/|\mathbf{L} + \mathbf{S}|$, represents the direction of maximum specular reflection. The angle δ, which is not the same as α, is calculated from $\widehat{\mathbf{H}} \cdot \widehat{\mathbf{S}}$; the modified Phong specular reflection function is then $k_s (\widehat{\mathbf{H}} \cdot \widehat{\mathbf{S}})^n$. The modified illumination model for a single light source is

$$I = I_a k_a + \frac{I_l}{d + K} \left[k_d (\widehat{\mathbf{n}} \cdot \widehat{\mathbf{L}}) + k_s (\widehat{\mathbf{H}} \cdot \widehat{\mathbf{S}})^n \right] \qquad (5-8)$$

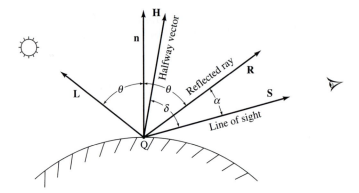

Figure 5–8 The halfway vector **H**.

Because the angles α and δ are different, the same value of the exponent n does not yield the same result. With respect to reflected direction, the shape of the original Phong model is independent of the incidence angle, while the Blinn modification is narrower as the incident angle approaches the grazing angle [Hall89]. As noted by Whitted [Whit82], when the light source and the eye (sight direction) are both at infinity the $\hat{\mathbf{H}}$ vector is constant.

An example more fully illustrates this simple model.

Example 5–1 Simple Illumination Model

Recalling Fig. 5–5, assume that at point P on the surface the normal, light and sight vectors are

$$\mathbf{n} = \quad \mathbf{j}$$
$$\mathbf{L} = -\mathbf{i} + \quad 2\mathbf{j} - \quad \mathbf{k}$$
$$\mathbf{S} = \quad \mathbf{i} + 1.5\mathbf{j} + 0.5\mathbf{k}$$

By inspection the reflection vector, $\mathbf{R}$, is then

$$\mathbf{R} = \mathbf{i} + 2\mathbf{j} + \mathbf{k}$$

Assuming that there is only one object in the scene, $d = 0$ and $K = 1$. The light source is assumed to be 10 times more intense than the ambient light; i.e., $I_a = 1$ and $I_\ell = 10$. The surface is to have a shiny metallic appearance, hence most of the light is specularly reflected. Thus, assume $k_s = 0.8$, $k_d = k_a = 0.15$ and $n = 5$. Note that $k_s + k_d = 0.95$, which implies that 5% of the energy from the light source is absorbed. Determining the various elements of the illumination model yields

$$\hat{\mathbf{n}} \cdot \hat{\mathbf{L}} = \frac{\mathbf{n} \cdot \mathbf{L}}{|\mathbf{n}|\,|\mathbf{L}|} = \frac{\mathbf{j} \cdot (-\mathbf{i} + 2\mathbf{j} - \mathbf{k})}{\sqrt{(-1)^2 + (2)^2 + (-1)^2}} = \frac{2}{\sqrt{6}}$$

or $$\theta = \cos^{-1}\left(\frac{2}{\sqrt{6}}\right) = 35.26°$$

and $$\widehat{\mathbf{R}}\cdot\widehat{\mathbf{S}} = \frac{\mathbf{R}\cdot\mathbf{S}}{|\mathbf{R}|\,|\mathbf{S}|} = \frac{(\mathbf{i}+2\mathbf{j}+\mathbf{k})\cdot(\mathbf{i}+1.5\mathbf{j}+0.5\mathbf{k})}{\sqrt{(1)^2+(2)^2+(1)^2}\sqrt{(1)^2+(1.5)^2+(0.5)^2}}$$

$$= \frac{4.5}{\sqrt{6}\sqrt{3.5}} = \frac{4.5}{\sqrt{21}}$$

or $$\alpha = \cos^{-1}\left(\frac{4.5}{\sqrt{21}}\right) = 10.89°$$

Finally $$I = (1)(0.15) + \left(\frac{10}{1}\right)\left[(0.15)\left(\frac{2}{\sqrt{6}}\right) + (0.8)\left(\frac{4.5}{\sqrt{21}}\right)^5\right]$$

$$= 0.15 + 10(0.12 + 0.73) = 8.65$$

Because the sight vector is almost coincident with the reflection vector, an observer sees a bright highlight at the point P. However, if the position of the observer is changed such that the sight vector is

$$\mathbf{S} = \mathbf{i} + 1.5\mathbf{j} - 0.5\mathbf{k}$$

then $$\widehat{\mathbf{R}}\cdot\widehat{\mathbf{S}} = \frac{\mathbf{R}\cdot\mathbf{S}}{|\mathbf{R}|\,|\mathbf{S}|} = \frac{3.5}{\sqrt{21}}$$

and $$\alpha = 40.2°$$

Here $$I = 0.15 + 10(0.12 + 0.21)$$

$$= 3.45$$

and the observed highlight at P is significantly reduced.

Using the halfway vector to determine the specular highlights yields

$$\widehat{\mathbf{H}} = \frac{\mathbf{L}+\mathbf{S}}{|\mathbf{L}+\mathbf{S}|} = \frac{7/2\,\mathbf{j} - 2\mathbf{k}}{\sqrt{(7/2)^2+(-2)^2}} = \frac{7}{\sqrt{65}}\mathbf{j} - \frac{4}{\sqrt{65}}\mathbf{k}$$

Using the original sight direction

$$\cos\delta = \widehat{\mathbf{H}}\cdot\widehat{\mathbf{S}} = \frac{(7\mathbf{j}-4\mathbf{k})\cdot(\mathbf{i}+1.5\mathbf{j}+0.5\mathbf{k})}{\sqrt{65}\sqrt{(1)^2+(1.5)^2+(0.5)^2}} = 0.563$$

or $$\delta = \cos^{-1}(0.563) = 55.7°$$

Finally $$I = 0.15 + 10(0.12 + 0.563) = 6.98$$

Notice that this value is significantly different from $I = 8.65$ obtained with the original Phong simple illumination model.

5–4   Determining the Surface Normal

The discussion in the previous section shows that the direction of the surface normal is representative of the local curvature of the surface and hence of the direction of specular reflection. If an analytical description of the surface is known, calculation of the surface normal is straightforward. However, for many surfaces only a polygonal approximation is available. If the plane equation for each polygonal facet is known, then the normal for each facet is determined from the coefficients of the plane equation (see Sec. 4–3). Here the outward normal is desired.

Many visible surface algorithms use only vertices or edges. In applying an illumination model in conjunction with these algorithms, an approximation to the surface normal at a vertex and along an edge is required. If the plane equations of the polygonal facets are available, then the normal at a vertex can be approximated by averaging the normals of the polygons surrounding the vertex. For example, the direction of the approximate normal at V_1 in Fig. 5–9 is given by

$$\mathbf{n}_{V_1} = (a_0 + a_1 + a_4)\mathbf{i} + (b_0 + b_1 + b_4)\mathbf{j} + (c_0 + c_1 + c_4)\mathbf{k}$$

where $a_0, a_1, a_4, b_0, b_1, b_4, c_0, c_1, c_4$ are the coefficients of the plane equations of the three polygons, P_0, P_1, P_4, surrounding V_1. Note that if only the direction of the normal is required then it is not necessary to formally divide by the number of surrounding polygons.

Alternately, if the plane equations are not available, the normal at the vertex can be approximated by averaging the cross products of all the edges that terminate at the vertex. Again using the vertex V_1 of Fig. 5–9, the direction of the approximate normal is

$$\mathbf{n}_{V_1} = \mathbf{V}_1\mathbf{V}_2 \otimes \mathbf{V}_1\mathbf{V}_4 + \mathbf{V}_1\mathbf{V}_5 \otimes \mathbf{V}_1\mathbf{V}_2 + \mathbf{V}_1\mathbf{V}_4 \otimes \mathbf{V}_1\mathbf{V}_5$$

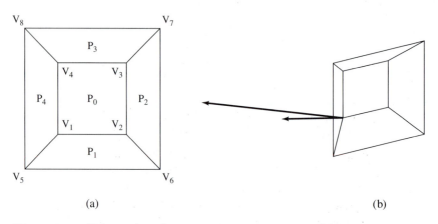

(a)   (b)

Figure 5–9 Polygonal surface normal approximations. (a) Polygonal surface; (b) alternative normals at V_1.

Care must be taken to average only outward normals. Unless a unit normal is calculated, the magnitude of the approximate normal is influenced by the number and area of individual polygons, or the number and length of individual edges. Larger polygons and longer edges have more influence. An example serves to more fully illustrate these techniques.

Example 5–2   Approximating Surface Normals

Consider the polygonal surface shown in Fig. 5–9a. The vertex points are $V_1(-1, -1, 1)$, $V_2(1, -1, 1)$, $V_3(1, 1, 1)$, $V_4(-1, 1, 1)$, $V_5(-2, -2, 0)$, $V_6(2, -2, 0)$, $V_7(2, 2, 0)$, $V_8(-2, 2, 0)$. The surface is a truncated pyramid. The plane equations for the faces labeled P_0, P_1, P_4 surrounding V_1 are

$$\begin{aligned} P_0: & \quad z - 1 = 0 \\ P_1: & \quad -y + z - 2 = 0 \\ P_4: -x & \quad +z - 2 = 0 \end{aligned}$$

Approximating the normal at V_1 by averaging the normals of the surrounding polygons yields

$$\begin{aligned} \mathbf{n}_1 &= (a_0 + a_1 + a_4)\mathbf{i} + (b_0 + b_1 + b_4)\mathbf{j} + (c_0 + c_1 + c_4)\mathbf{k} \\ &= (0 + 0 - 1)\mathbf{i} + (0 - 1 + 0)\mathbf{j} + (1 + 1 + 1)\mathbf{k} \\ &= -\mathbf{i} - \mathbf{j} + 3\mathbf{k} \end{aligned}$$

The magnitude of $\mathbf{n}_1$ is

$$|\mathbf{n}_1| = \sqrt{(-1)^2 + (-1)^2 + (3)^2} = \sqrt{11}$$

and the unit normal is

$$\frac{\mathbf{n}_1}{|\mathbf{n}_1|} = -0.3\mathbf{i} - 0.3\mathbf{j} + 0.9\mathbf{k}$$

Incidentally, note that dividing by 3 does not yield the unit normal. The cross-products of the edges meeting at V_1 are

$$\begin{aligned} \mathbf{V}_1\mathbf{V}_2 \otimes \mathbf{V}_1\mathbf{V}_4 &= 4\mathbf{k} \\ \mathbf{V}_1\mathbf{V}_5 \otimes \mathbf{V}_1\mathbf{V}_2 &= -2\mathbf{j} + 2\mathbf{k} \\ \mathbf{V}_1\mathbf{V}_4 \otimes \mathbf{V}_1\mathbf{V}_5 &= -2\mathbf{i} + 2\mathbf{k} \end{aligned}$$

Approximating the normal at V_1 by averaging the cross-products, i.e., in this case we simply divide by 3 yields

$$\mathbf{n}_1 = -\frac{2}{3}\mathbf{i} - \frac{2}{3}\mathbf{j} + \frac{8}{3}\mathbf{k}$$

The magnitude of $\mathbf{n}_1$ is now

$$|\mathbf{n}_1| = \frac{1}{3}\sqrt{(-2)^2 + (-2)^2 + (8)^2} = \frac{1}{3}\sqrt{72}$$

and the unit normal is

$$\frac{\mathbf{n}_1}{|\mathbf{n}_1|} = -0.24\mathbf{i} - 0.24\mathbf{j} + 0.94\mathbf{k}$$

Notice that both the direction and the magnitude of the normalized and unnormalized surface normals are different for different approximation techniques. This is shown in Fig. 5–9b. Consequently, an illumination model yields subtly different results depending on the technique used to approximate the surface normal.

If the surface normal is used to determine the intensity, and if a perspective transformation is used to display the object or scene, the normal must be determined before the perspective transformation is applied, i.e., before perspective division takes place (see [Roge76, 90a]). Otherwise, the direction of the normal is distorted; consequently the intensity determined by the illumination model is incorrect.

5–5   Determining the Reflection Vector

Determining the direction of the reflection vector is critical in implementing an illumination model. In Ex. 5–1 the direction of the reflection vector was determined by inspection. Several more general techniques are described in this section. Recall the law of reflection, which states that the light vector, the surface normal and reflected light vector lie in the same plane, and that in this plane the angle of incidence is equal to the angle of reflectance (see Fig. 5–10a). Phong [Phon75] used these conditions to obtain a simple solution when the light direction is along the z-axis. For an illumination model consisting of a single point light source, this is often an excellent assumption. If the origin of the coordinate system is taken as the point on the surface, then the projection of

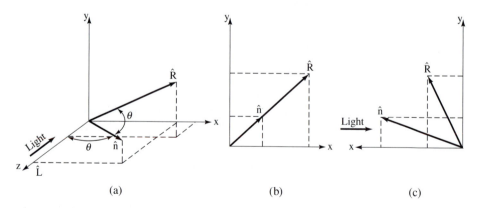

(a)   (b)   (c)

Figure 5–10   Determining the reflection direction.

the normal and reflected vectors onto the xy plane lie on a straight line (see Fig. 5–10b). Thus

$$\frac{R_x}{R_y} = n_x n_y \qquad\qquad (5-8)$$

where R_x, R_y, n_x, n_y are the x and y components of the unit vectors in the reflected and normal directions, respectively.

The angle between the unit normal vector and the z-axis is θ. Thus, the component in the z direction is

$$n_z = \cos\theta \qquad 0 \le \theta \le \frac{\pi}{2}$$

Similarly, the angle between the unit reflection vector and the z-axis is 2θ; hence

$$R_z = \cos 2\theta = 2\cos^2\theta - 1 = 2n_z^2 - 1 \qquad\qquad (5-9)$$

Recalling that

$$R_x^2 + R_y^2 + R_z^2 = 1$$

then

$$R_x^2 + R_y^2 = 1 - R_z^2 = 1 - \cos^2 2\theta$$

or

$$R_y^2\left(\frac{R_x^2}{R_y^2} + 1\right) = 1 - \cos^2 2\theta$$

Using the ratio of the x and y components of the reflected and normal vectors in Eq. $(5-8)$, and recalling that

$$n_x^2 + n_y^2 + n_z^2 = 1$$

yields

$$\frac{R_y^2}{n_y^2}(n_x^2 + n_y^2) = \frac{R_y^2}{n_y^2}(1 - n_z^2) = 1 - \cos^2 2\theta$$

Rewriting the right-hand side gives

$$\frac{R_y^2}{n_y^2}(1 - n_z^2) = 1 - (2\cos^2\theta - 1)^2 = 1 - (2n_z^2 - 1)^2 = 4n_z^2(1 - n_z^2)$$

or

$$R_y = 2n_z n_y \qquad\qquad (5-10)$$

From Eq. $(5-8)$

$$R_x = 2n_z n_x \qquad\qquad (5-11)$$

If the light direction is not along the z-axis, e.g., when multiple light sources are used, this technique is not applicable. Each light source could, of course, be translated and rotated until the light direction is along the z-axis. However, it is simpler to translate and rotate the normal vector until it is along the z-axis, with point P on the object at the origin. Here, the xy plane is now the tangent plane to the surface at P; and the x and y components of the unit light and reflection vectors are the negatives of each other. The z components of the unit light and reflection vectors are, of course, equal. The results in the original orientation are then obtained by applying the inverse transformations. Specifically, in the rotated–translated coordinate system

$$R_x = -L_x \qquad R_y = -L_y \qquad R_z = L_z$$

The third technique uses the cross-products of the unit normal and the unit light and reflection vectors to ensure that the three vectors lie in the same plane. The dot products of the unit normal and the unit light and reflection vectors are used to ensure that the incident and reflection angles are equal; these conditions yield

$$\widehat{\mathbf{n}} \otimes \widehat{\mathbf{L}} = \widehat{\mathbf{R}} \otimes \widehat{\mathbf{n}}$$

or

$$(n_y L_z - n_z L_y)\mathbf{i} + (n_z L_x - L_z n_x)\mathbf{j} + (n_x L_y - L_x n_y)\mathbf{k}$$
$$= (n_z R_y - n_y R_z)\mathbf{i} + (n_x R_z - n_z R_x)\mathbf{j} + (n_y R_x - n_x R_y)\mathbf{k}$$

The directions of the cross-product vectors are the same if their xyz components are the same, thus

$$-n_z R_y + n_y R_z = n_z L_y - n_y L_z$$
$$n_z R_x \qquad -n_x R_z = n_x L_z - n_z L_x$$
$$-n_y R_x + n_x R_y \qquad = n_y L_x - n_x L_y \qquad (5\text{-}12)$$

At first glance, the reflected vector appears to be determined. Unfortunately, for each specific case one of the three equations yields no useful information; i.e., the equations are not independent. Furthermore, the specific equation is not known a priori.

Recalling that the incident and reflected angles are equal yields

$$\widehat{\mathbf{n}} \cdot \widehat{\mathbf{L}} = \widehat{\mathbf{n}} \cdot \widehat{\mathbf{R}}$$

or $\qquad n_x R_x + n_y R_y + n_z R_z = n_x L_x + n_y L_y + n_z L_z \qquad (5-13)$

which yields the required additional condition. A matrix formulation including all four conditions for the three unknowns, R_x, R_y, R_z, is

$$\begin{bmatrix} 0 & -n_z & n_y \\ n_z & 0 & -n_x \\ -n_y & n_x & 0 \\ n_x & n_y & n_z \end{bmatrix} \begin{bmatrix} R_x \\ R_y \\ R_z \end{bmatrix} = \begin{bmatrix} n_z L_y - n_y L_z \\ n_x L_z - n_z L_x \\ n_y L_x - n_x L_y \\ n_x L_x + n_y L_y + n_z L_z \end{bmatrix}$$

or
$$[N][R] = [B]$$

Because $[N]$ is not square, a trick is used to obtain a solution; in particular

$$[R] = \left[[N]^T[N]\right]^{-1}[N]^T[B]$$

and the reflection vector is obtained. However, examine $[N]^T[N]$ more closely, specifically

$$[N]^T[N] = \begin{bmatrix} 0 & n_z & -n_y & n_x \\ -n_z & 0 & n_x & n_y \\ n_y & -n_x & 0 & n_z \end{bmatrix} \begin{bmatrix} 0 & -n_z & n_y \\ n_z & 0 & -n_x \\ -n_y & n_x & 0 \\ n_x & n_y & n_z \end{bmatrix}$$

$$= \begin{bmatrix} n_x^2 + n_y^2 + n_z^2 & 0 & 0 \\ 0 & n_x^2 + n_y^2 + n_z^2 & 0 \\ 0 & 0 & n_x^2 + n_y^2 + n_z^2 \end{bmatrix} = \begin{bmatrix} 1 & 0 & 0 \\ 0 & 1 & 0 \\ 0 & 0 & 1 \end{bmatrix}$$

and
$$[R] = [N]^T[B]$$

and the reflection vector is obtained with a simple matrix multiple.[†]

Referring to Fig. 5–10a, where the $\widehat{\mathbf{L}}$ and $\widehat{\mathbf{n}}$ are assumed in any orientation, a general vector solution[‡] is obtained by again imposing the constraint that $\widehat{\mathbf{R}}$ is in the plane of $\widehat{\mathbf{L}}$ and $\widehat{\mathbf{n}}$. Hence

$$\widehat{\mathbf{R}} = c_1\widehat{\mathbf{n}} + c_2\widehat{\mathbf{L}}$$

where c_1 and c_2 are constants. Recalling that the angle of reflection is equal to the incidence angle, then $\cos\theta = \widehat{\mathbf{n}}\cdot\widehat{\mathbf{R}} = \widehat{\mathbf{n}}\cdot\widehat{\mathbf{L}}$. Thus

$$c_1 + c_2(\widehat{\mathbf{n}}\cdot\widehat{\mathbf{L}}) = \widehat{\mathbf{n}}\cdot\widehat{\mathbf{R}} = \widehat{\mathbf{n}}\cdot\widehat{\mathbf{L}}$$

The angle between $\widehat{\mathbf{R}}$ and $\widehat{\mathbf{L}}$ is 2θ, consequently

$$\widehat{\mathbf{R}}\cdot\widehat{\mathbf{L}} = \cos 2\theta = 2\cos^2\theta - 1 = 2(\widehat{\mathbf{n}}\cdot\widehat{\mathbf{L}})^2 - 1$$

and
$$c_1\widehat{\mathbf{n}}\cdot\widehat{\mathbf{L}} + c_2 = 2(\widehat{\mathbf{n}}\cdot\widehat{\mathbf{L}})^2 - 1$$

Hence
$$\widehat{\mathbf{R}} = 2(\widehat{\mathbf{n}}\cdot\widehat{\mathbf{L}})\widehat{\mathbf{n}} - \widehat{\mathbf{L}}$$

[†] Thanks to both Mike Johnson and Frank Schindler for pointing this out to me. How could I have missed it in the first edition!

[‡] Thanks to Greg Nielson for pointing out this vector solution.

5–6   Gouraud Shading

If an illumination model is applied to a polygonal surface using a single constant normal for each polygon face, a faceted appearance results as illustrated by the face in Fig. 5–11a. A smoother appearance is obtained using a technique developed by Gouraud [Gour71]. If a scan line algorithm is used to render the object, a value for the intensity of each pixel along the scan line must be determined from the illumination model. The normals to the surface are approximated at the polygonal vertices of the surface, as described in the previous section. However, as shown in Fig. 5–12, a scan line does not necessarily pass through the polygon vertices. Gouraud shading first determines the intensity at each polygonal vertex. A bilinear interpolation is then used to determine the intensity of each pixel on the scan line.

In particular, consider the segment of a polygonal surface shown in Fig. 5–12. The intensity at P is determined by linearly interpolating the intensities of the polygon vertices A and B to obtain the intensity of Q, the intersection of the polygon edge with the scan line, i.e.

$$I_Q = uI_A + (1 - u)I_B \qquad 0 \le u \le 1$$

where uAQ/AB. Similarly, the intensities at the polygon vertices B and C are

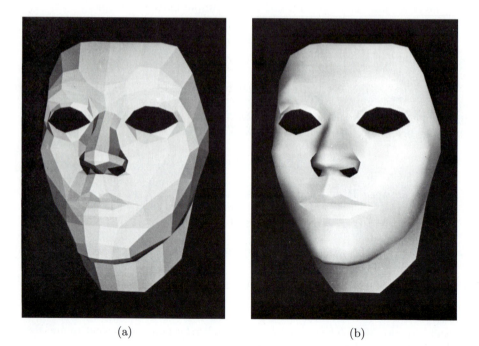

(a)   (b)

Figure 5–11   Gouraud shading. (a) Polygonal model; (b) Gouraud shaded. (Courtesy of the University of Utah).

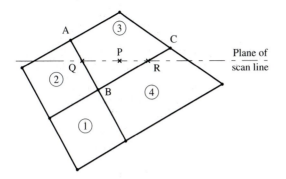

Figure 5–12 Shading interpolation.

linearly interpolated to obtain the intensity at R on the scan line, i.e.

$$I_R = wI_B + (1 - w)I_C \qquad 0 \le w \le 1$$

where $w = BR/BC$. Finally, the intensity at P on the scan line is obtained by linearly interpolating *along* the scan line between Q and R, i.e.

$$I_P = tI_Q + (1 - t)I_R \qquad 0 \le t \le 1$$

where $t = QP/QR$.

The intensity calculation along the scan line can be performed incrementally. For two pixels at t_1 and t_2 on the scan line

$$I_{P_2} = t_2 I_Q + (1 - t_2)I_R$$

and

$$I_{P_1} = t_1 I_Q + (1 - t_1)I_R$$

Subtracting yields

$$I_{P_2} = I_{P_1} + (I_Q - I_R)(t_2 - t_1) = I_{P_1} + \Delta I_{QR}\Delta t$$

along the scan line. The result of applying Gouraud shading to the polygonal approximation for the face in Fig. 5–11a is shown in Fig. 5–11b. The improvement is startling. However, close examination of Fig. 5–11b shows faint evidence of Mach banding, e.g., on the cheek bones, around the eyes and on the chin. This is because the shading interpolation rule yields only continuity of intensity value across polygon boundaries, but not continuity of change in intensity. In addition, silhouette edges, e.g., the eyes and nose, are still polygonal, since the underlying data structure is polygonal.

An additional difficulty with Gouraud shading is illustrated in Fig. 5–13a. If the normals at the vertices B, C, D are computed using polygon averaging, then they all have the same direction and hence the same intensity. Linear interpolation then yields a constant-intensity value from B to D, which makes the surface appear flat in that area. To achieve a smooth appearance at B, C and D it is necessary to introduce additional polygons, as shown in Fig. 5–13b. If an actual crease is required, then the smooth shading must be locally defeated by 'selectively' averaging the surface normals. An example is shown in Fig. 5–13c. Here $\mathbf{n}_{B_1}$ is computed only from the single face to the right of B. $\mathbf{n}_{B_2}$, $\mathbf{n}_{D_1}$ and $\mathbf{n}_{D_2}$ are obtained similarly, while $\mathbf{n}_C$ is computed from the average of the faces to the left and right of C. Gouraud shading then yields a sharp edge at B and D, and an apparent smooth graduation at C. The effect is shown by the lips in Fig. 5–11b.

Because of the simplicity of the shading, the shape of individual highlights from specular reflection is strongly influenced by the polygons used to represent the object or surface. Consequently, a simple diffuse illumination model (see Eq. $(5-1)$ or $(5-2)$) yields the best results with Gouraud shading.

5–7   Phong Shading

Although computationally more expensive, Phong shading [Phon75][†] solves many of the problems of Gouraud shading. Whereas Gouraud shading interpolates intensity values along a scan line, Phong shading interpolates the normal vector along the scan line. The illumination model is then applied at each pixel, using the interpolated normal to determine the intensity. This technique gives a better local approximation to the surface curvature, and hence a better rendering of the surface; in particular, specular highlights appear more realistic.

Phong shading first approximates the surface curvature at polygonal vertices by approximating the normal at the vertex (see Sec. 5–3). A bilinear interpolation is then used to determine the normal at each pixel. In particular, again using Fig. 5–12, the normal at P is determined by linearly interpolating between A and B to obtain Q, between B and C to obtain R and finally between Q and R to obtain P. Specifically

$$\mathbf{n}_Q = u\mathbf{n}_A + (1-u)\mathbf{n}_B \qquad 0 \le u \le 1$$
$$\mathbf{n}_R = w\mathbf{n}_B + (1-w)\mathbf{n}_C \qquad 0 \le w \le 1$$
$$\mathbf{n}_P = t\mathbf{n}_Q + (1-t)\mathbf{n}_R \qquad 0 \le t \le 1$$

where again $u = AQ/AB$, $w = BR/BC$ and $t = QP/QR$. Again, the normal along a scan line can be determined incrementally, i.e.

$$\mathbf{n}_{P_2} = \mathbf{n}_{P_1} + (\mathbf{n}_Q - \mathbf{n}_R)(t_2 - t_1) = \mathbf{n}_{P_1} + \Delta\mathbf{n}_{QR}\,\Delta t$$

where subscripts 1 and 2 indicate successive pixels along the scan line.

[†]Although Phong is Bui-Tong Phong's given (first) name, the use of Phong as the reference is more useful to most readers.

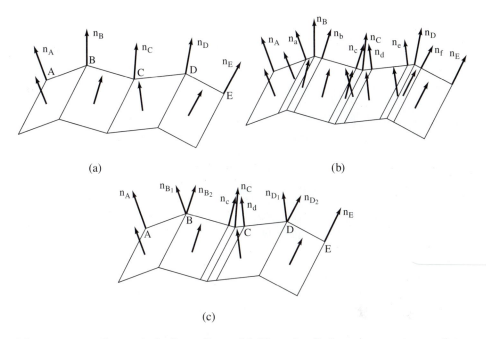

(a)

(b)

(c)

Figure 5–13   Gouraud shading effects. (a) Normals all the same — appears flat; (b) additional normals yield rounded tops; (c) crease obtained by locally defeating Gouraud shading.

Figure 5–14 compares constant, Gouraud and Phong shading. The left-hand torus is rendered with constant normal shading, the middle torus with Gouraud shading and the right-hand torus with Phong shading. The illumination model for the left-hand and middle tori is ambient plus diffuse reflection $\left(\text{Eq. }(5-1)\right)$, while that for the Phong-shaded right-hand torus also includes specular reflection, as shown by the highlights $\left(\text{Eq. }(5-5)\text{, with }d=0, K=1\right)$. Figure 5–15 compares the highlight obtained with specular reflection for Gouraud shading and the more realistic Phong shading. If specular reflection is included in the illumination model and the highlight is not at a polygon vertex, Gouraud shading misplaces the highlight [Duff79]. In general, for Lambertian diffuse reflection, Phong shading produces somewhat brighter images than does Gouraud shading [Duff79].

Even though Phong shading reduces most of the problems associated with Gouraud shading, it is still a linear interpolation scheme. Consequently, discontinuities in the first derivative of the intensity still give rise to Mach band effects. In general, these effects are smaller than for Gouraud shading. However, Duff [Duff79] showed that in some cases, notably for spheres, Phong shading yields worse Mach band effects than Gouraud shading. Mach banding depends on the spatial derivative of the intensity, and for spheres and similar surfaces the spatial derivative of the interpolated intensity derivative is larger for Phong shading then for Gouraud shading. Also, both techniques potentially render concave polygons

Figure 5–14 Comparison of rendering techniques. (Left) constant normal, (middle) Gouraud, (right) Phong. (Courtesy of Turner Whitted).

incorrectly. For example, consider the polygon shown in Fig. 5–16. The scan line labeled 1 uses data from the vertices QRS, while that labeled 2 just below it also uses data from vertex P; this can give rise to a shading discontinuity.

Additional difficulties are exhibited by both Gouraud and Phong shading when used in animation sequences. In particular, the shading varies significantly from frame to frame. This effect is a result of working in image space, and the fact that the shading rule is not invariant with respect to rotation. Consequently,

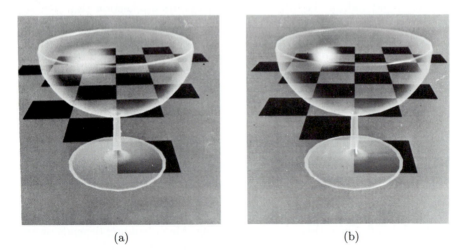

(a)   (b)

Figure 5–15 Comparison of specular reflection highlights. (a) Gouraud shading; (b) Phong shading. (Courtesy of the University of Utah).

as the orientation of an object changes from frame to frame, its shade (color) also changes; this is quite noticeable. Duff [Duff79] presents a technique for rotation independent of the Gouraud and Phong shading rules.

An example that computes constant, Gouraud and Phong shading serves to illustrate the difference between the three techniques.

Example 5–3 Shading

Consider the segment of a surface shown in Fig. 5–12. The equations of the four planes are

$$
\begin{aligned}
1: & & 2z & & -4 = 0 \\
2: & & -x + 1.732y + 7.5z & & -17 = 0 \\
3: & & -2.25x + 3.897y + 10z & -24.5 = 0 \\
4: & & 5.5z & & -11 = 0
\end{aligned}
$$

where z is perpendicular to the plane of the paper, x is positive to the right and y is positive upward. The point B has coordinates of $(0.366, 1.366, 2)$.

The vector to the eye is $S\begin{bmatrix} 1 & 1 & 1 \end{bmatrix}$, and a single point light source is located at positive infinity on the z-axis. The light vector is thus $L\begin{bmatrix} 0 & 0 & 1 \end{bmatrix}$. The illumination model is given by Eq. $(5-7)$, with $d = 0$, $K = 1$, $I_a = 1$, $I_\ell = 10$, $n = 2$, $k_s = 0.8$, $k_d = k_a = 0.15$. Since the light direction is along the z-axis, the Phong technique is used to determine the direction of the reflected light vector (see Sec. 5–4).

For constant shading, the point P is in polygon 3. From the plane equation for polygon 3, the unit normal is

$$
\widehat{n}_3 = \frac{n_3}{|n_3|} = -0.21i + 0.36j + 0.91k
$$

The angle between the normal and light vector is

$$
\widehat{n} \cdot \widehat{L} = (-0.21i + 0.36j + 0.91k) \cdot k = 0.91
$$

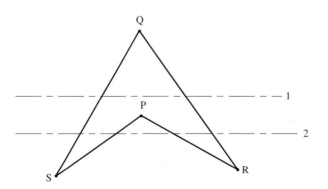

Figure 5–16 Shading anomalies for concave polygons.

which yields an incidence angle of about $24.2°$.

From Eqs. $(5-9)$ to $(5-11)$

$$R_z = 2n_z^2 - 1 = (2)(0.91)^2 - 1 = 0.66$$
$$R_x = 2n_z n_x = (2)(0.91)(-0.21) = -0.38$$
$$R_y = 2n_z n_y = (2)(0.91)(0.36) = 0.66$$

and
$$\widehat{R} = -0.38i + 0.66j + 0.66k$$

The unit vector in the eye direction is

$$\widehat{S} = \frac{S}{|S|} = \frac{S}{\sqrt{3}} = 0.58i + 0.58j + 0.58k$$

Using this value, the angle between the reflected light vector and the line of sight or eye is

$$\widehat{R}\cdot\widehat{S} = (-0.38i + 0.66j + 0.66k)\cdot(0.58i + 0.58j + 0.58k)$$
$$= 0.55$$

which yields an angle of about $57°$.

Recalling the illumination model $(Eq.\ (5-7))$ yields

$$I_P = I_a k_a + \frac{I_\ell}{d+K}\left[k_d\left(\widehat{n}\cdot\widehat{L}\right) + k_s\left(\widehat{R}\cdot\widehat{S}\right)^n\right]$$
$$= (1)(0.15) + \left(\frac{10}{1}\right)\left[(0.15)(0.91) + (0.8)(0.55)y^2\right]$$
$$= 0.15 + 10(0.14 + 0.24) = 0.15 + 3.8$$
$$= 3.95$$

for point P.

For Gouraud shading, the normal vectors for A, B, C in Fig. 5–12 are required. Approximating the normals by the average of the normals of the surrounding planes yields

$$n_A = n_2 + n_3 = -3.25i + 5.63j + 17.5k$$
$$n_B = n_1 + n_2 + n_3 + n_4 = -3.25i + 5.63j + 25k$$
$$n_C = n_3 + n_4 = -2.25i + 3.897j + 15.5k$$

where n_1, n_2, n_3, n_4 are obtained from the plane equations given above. The unit normals are

$$n_A = \frac{n_A}{|n_A|} = -0.17i + 0.3j + 0.94k$$
$$n_B = \frac{n_B}{|n_B|} = -0.12i + 0.22j + 0.97k$$
$$n_C = \frac{n_C}{|n_C|} = -0.14i + 0.24j + 0.96k$$

The unit reflected vectors are

$$\widehat{\mathbf{R}}_A = -0.33\mathbf{i} + 0.57\mathbf{j} + 0.76\mathbf{k}$$

$$\widehat{\mathbf{R}}_B = -0.24\mathbf{i} + 0.42\mathbf{j} + 0.87\mathbf{k}$$

$$\widehat{\mathbf{R}}_C = -0.27\mathbf{i} + 0.46\mathbf{j} + 0.84\mathbf{k}$$

The intensities at A, B, C are

$$I_A = 0.15 + 10(0.14 + 0.27) = 4.25$$

$$I_B = 0.15 + 10(0.15 + 0.30) = 4.65$$

$$I_C = 0.15 + 10(0.14 + 0.29) = 4.45$$

On a particular scan line, $u = AQ/AB = 0.4$ and $w = BR/BC = 0.7$. Interpolating to find the intensities at Q and R yields

$$I_Q = uI_A + (1 - u)I_B = (0.4)(4.25) + (1 - 0.4)(4.65) = 4.49$$

$$I_R = wI_B + (1 - w)I_C = (0.7)(4.65) + (1 - 0.7)(4.45) = 4.59$$

The point P on the scan line is located at $t = QP/QR = 0.5$. Interpolating to find the intensity at P yields

$$I_P = tI_Q + (1 - t)I_R = (0.5)(4.49) + (1 - 0.5)(4.59) = 4.54$$

Phong shading interpolates the normals at A, B, C to first obtain the normal at P. The normal at P is then used to obtain the intensity at P. First, interpolating to obtain the unit normals at Q and R yields

$$\widehat{\mathbf{n}}_Q = u\widehat{\mathbf{n}}_A + (1 - u)\widehat{\mathbf{n}}_B = (0.4)\begin{bmatrix} -0.17 & 0.3 & 0.94 \end{bmatrix} + (0.6)\begin{bmatrix} -0.12 & 0.22 & 0.97 \end{bmatrix}$$

$$= \begin{bmatrix} -0.14 & 0.25 & 0.96 \end{bmatrix} = -0.14\mathbf{i} + 0.25\mathbf{j} + 0.96\mathbf{k}$$

$$\widehat{\mathbf{n}}_R = w\widehat{\mathbf{n}}_B + (1 - w)\widehat{\mathbf{n}}_C = (0.7)\begin{bmatrix} -0.12 & 0.22 & 0.97 \end{bmatrix} + (0.3)\begin{bmatrix} -0.14 & 0.24 & 0.96 \end{bmatrix}$$

$$= \begin{bmatrix} -0.13 & 0.23 & 0.97 \end{bmatrix} = -0.13\mathbf{i} + 0.23\mathbf{j} + 0.97\mathbf{k}$$

Interpolating the normal along the scan line yields

$$\widehat{\mathbf{n}}_P = t\widehat{\mathbf{n}}_Q + (1 - t)\widehat{\mathbf{n}}_R = (0.5)\begin{bmatrix} -0.14 & 0.25 & 0.96 \end{bmatrix} + (0.5)\begin{bmatrix} -0.04 & 0.23 & 0.97 \end{bmatrix}$$

$$= \begin{bmatrix} -0.14 & 0.24 & 0.97 \end{bmatrix}$$

$$= -0.14\mathbf{i} + 0.24\mathbf{j} + 0.97\mathbf{k}$$

The unit reflection vector at P is then

$$\widehat{\mathbf{R}}_P = -0.27\mathbf{i} + 0.46\mathbf{j} + 0.87\mathbf{k}$$

The intensity at P is

$$I_P = 0.15 + (10)(0.15 + 0.30) = 4.65$$

Comparing the different shading models yields

$$
\begin{array}{ll}
\text{Constant:} & I_P = 3.93 \\
\text{Gouraud:} & I_P = 4.54 \\
\text{Phong:} & I_P = 4.65
\end{array}
$$

Fast Phong Shading

The Phong illumination model is expensive to calculate. Implemented without incremental calculation requires performing seven additions, six multiplications, one division and a square root for each pixel. By combining the interpolation and reflection equations and using incremental techniques Duff [Duff79] reduced the number of calculations to three additions, one division and a square root. However, the division and the square root are still expensive. Bishop and Weiner [Bish86], using a two variable Taylor series expansion combined with a table lookup to evaluate the exponential function, reduced the computational requirements to five additions and a memory access per pixel.[†] However, using a coarse lookup table and linear interpolation may increase the appearance of Mach bands.

Occasionally one sees the suggestion that the Phong illumination model can be sped up by *not* renormalizing the normal at each interpolated position. Duff [Duff79] shows that failure to renormalize at each interpolated position results in a *slow* method for doing Gouraud interpolation.

Since the Phong specular reflection model is an approximation, a number of investigators have suggested replacing the expensive exponential calculation using alternate functions. Specifically, Poulin and Fournier [Poul90] suggest using a Chebyshev polynomial approximation. They note that a Chebyshev polynomial of maximum degree six gives an excellent approximation to the Phong $\cos^n \alpha$ model for nearly all values of n. Schlick [Schl94] suggests using the function

$$
\frac{t}{n - nt + t} \quad 0 \le t \le 1
$$

to replace the Phong $\cos^n \alpha$ model. Schlick's function requires one addition, one subtraction, one multiplication and a division to evaluate. Schlick's function decreases more slowly than the Phong function, hence specular highlights are broader than for the Phong function. However, since the function is continuous, Mach banding is decreased significantly. In addition, it requires no memory and thus may be more suitable to hardware implementations.

[†]There are several typographical errors in the original paper. Specifically, p. 104, first column, first equation: remove the $\overrightarrow{L}$ term from the denominator of the second term; first column, second equation, remove the $\overrightarrow{L}$ before $\overrightarrow{Ax}$, $\overrightarrow{By}$, $\overrightarrow{Cz}$ in the denominator; in the second column the first term in T_5's numerator should read $3cg^2$; and on p. 105, first column, second equation, the $\overrightarrow{E}$ is *not* the eye vector.

5–8   A Simple Illumination Model with Special Effects

Warn [Warn83] extended the simple point source illumination model discussed previously in Sec. 5–2 to include special effects. The model was inspired by the lighting controls found in a professional photographer's studio. The special effects included controls for light direction and for light concentration. Further, the area illuminated by a light source can be limited.

The Warn model allows the direction of a light source to be controlled independently of its location. Conceptually, the directed light is modeled as a single point perfect specularly reflecting pseudosurface, illuminated by a point light source, as shown in Fig. 5–17. If the point light source is located along the direction $\mathbf{L}$ normal to the reflecting pseudosurface, then the reflection of that source illuminates the object along the direction $\mathbf{L'}$. Hence, the direction of the light is controlled by rotating the pseudosurface.

With this conceptual model for the directed light source, the same illumination model is used for both directed and point source lights in a scene. The amount of light received at point P from the directed light source, ℓ, as shown in Fig. 5–17, depends on the angle β between $\mathbf{L}$, the light direction vector, and the line from the location of the light to P. Using the Phong approximation for specular reflection from a perfect mirror surface, the intensity of the directed light source along the line from the source to the point P is

$$I_{l_j} \cos^c \beta = I_{\ell_j}(-\widehat{\mathbf{L}} \cdot \widehat{\mathbf{L}'})^c$$

where c is a power that determines the spatial concentration of the directed light source (see Fig. 5–6). If c is large, the beam is narrow, simulating a spotlight. If c is small, the beam is spread out to simulate a flood light. If $c = 0$, a uniformly radiating light source results. The contribution of the directed light source to the overall illumination model $\big($see Eq. $(5 - 6)\big)$ is then

$$I_j = I_{l_j} \cos^c \beta(k_{d_j} \cos \theta_j + k_{s_j} \cos^{n_j} \alpha_j) \tag{5 - 14}$$

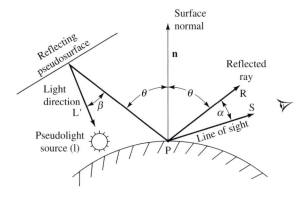

Figure 5–17   Directed lighting model.

where j designates the specific light source.

A studio photographer obtains special effects by limiting the area of concentration of lights using flaps (called barn doors by professional photographers) mounted on the lights and with special reflectors. The Warn model simulates these effects with flaps and cones. Flaps oriented to the coordinate planes are implemented by limiting the maximum and minimum extent in x, y or z of the light, as shown in Fig. 5–18a. If a point on the object is within the range of the flap, e.g., $y_{min} \leq y_{object} \leq y_{max}$, the contribution from that light is evaluated; otherwise it is ignored. Implementation of arbitrarily oriented flaps is straightforward. Flaps can also be used to simulate effects that have no physical counterpart. For example, a flap can be used to drop a curtain across a scene to limit penetration of a particular light source.

A cone, as shown in Fig. 5–18b, is used to produce a sharply delineated spotlight. This is in contrast to the gradual decrease at the edge achieved by varying c in the directed light source model. Again, this simulates an effect available to the commercial photographer. Implementation of the cone effect is straightforward. If the apex of the cone is located at the light source and γ is the cone angle, then if $\beta > \gamma$, the effect of that light source on the point P can be ignored. Otherwise, it is included in the illumination model. In practice, this is accomplished by comparing $\cos \beta$ with $\cos \gamma$, i.e., $\cos \beta > \cos \gamma$.

The effects that can be achieved with this illumination model are shown by the 1983 Chevrolet Camaro in Color Plate 3. Five lights were used. Two lights were used on the left side of the car for back lighting; two lights were also used on the right side of the car. Notice, in particular, the use of light concentration to emphasize the detail line on the right door and along the right rear fender. The fifth light, high and behind the car, was used to emphasize the taillights and the detail on the bumper. The results are exceptional.

5–9   A Physically Based Illumination Model

The illumination models discussed in the previous sections are relatively simple. They are based on aesthetic, heuristic and experimental approximations. This is particularly true of the specular component of the reflected light. More physically based illumination models are anchored in principles developed for

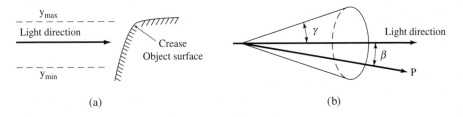

Figure 5–18   Lighting controls. (a) Flaps; (b) cones.

thermal radiation (see, e.g., [Spar78; Sieg81]). To understand these models, it is necessary to understand the terms used in the thermal engineering models, particularly energy and intensity, and how they relate to the common terms used in computer graphics. The nomenclature for thermal and illumination engineering is formally defined in [Nico77] and [IES87].

Energy and Intensity

Frequently, light energy and intensity are used interchangeably; however, they are not the same. To see this, we follow Hall [Hall89] and consider the illuminating hemisphere, with radius $r = 1$ for computational convenience, as shown in Fig. 5–19. Illuminating events, e.g., light sources, either direct or reflected, are described by projecting them onto the illuminating hemisphere.

The amount of illumination associated with a light source depends on the solid angle, ω, subtended by the light source. The solid angle is obtained by projecting the light source onto the illuminating hemisphere. To determine the solid angle, consider a circular source as shown in Fig. 5–19. Projecting the source onto the illuminating hemisphere and integrating over the projected area yields the solid angle, ω. The differential area of the source projected onto the illuminating hemisphere is $dA = \sin\theta d\theta d\phi$ for $r = 1$. Integrating yields

$$\omega = \int^{2\pi}\int^{\tan^{-1}(r_s/r_0)} \sin\theta d\theta d\phi = 2\pi\left(1 - \cos\left(\tan^{-1}\frac{r_s}{r_0}\right)\right)$$

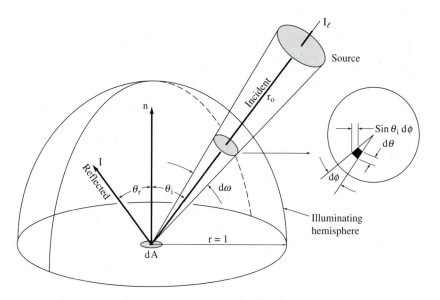

Figure 5–19 The illuminating hemisphere.

Solid angles are measured in steradians (sr). If the intersected area is equal to the square of the hemispheres radius, r, then the angle subtends one steradian (sr). There are 2π sr $(4\pi r^2/2r^2)$ in a hemisphere.

Because accurate calculation of the solid angle is expensive, consider the case for small solid angles, i.e., $r_s/r_0 \ll 1$. Here, $\tan^{-1} r_s/r_0 \approx r_s/r_0$ and $\sin\theta \approx \theta$ Therefore

$$\omega = \int^{2\pi} \int^{(r_s/r_0)} \theta d\theta d\phi = \pi\frac{r_s}{r_0}$$

Noting that πr_s^2 is the projected area of the source toward the illuminating surface, we have [†]

$$d\omega \approx \frac{dA_p}{r_0^2}$$

For $r_s/r_0 < 0.15$, the relative error is less than 2%.

Integrating over the illuminating hemisphere implies that the effect of an illumination source is weighted by the solid angle it subtends. Thus, the energy received from a source depends on both the intensity of the source and the solid angle the source occupies from the viewer's position.

The rate-of-energy received per unit time is the energy flux, Φ, while the energy per unit time per unit area is the energy density $|E^2|$. Intensity is defined as the energy flux per unit projected area, A_{ps}, of its source, per solid angle, ω, occupied by the radiating source, i.e.

$$I = \frac{\Phi}{A_{ps}\omega}$$

Thus, for a spherical source of radius r_s, $A_{ps} = \pi r_s^2$ and $\omega = 4\pi$ so that

$$I = \frac{\Phi}{4\pi r_s^2}$$

which says that intensity is independent of the location of the viewer.

To relate the intensity to the energy of the source, first consider the energy density. For a sphere with radius r_0, with an energy source located along the normal to a point on the sphere, the energy density is the energy flux divided by the area through which the source radiates, i.e.

$$|E^2| = \frac{\Phi}{4\pi r_0^2}$$

For a source not on the normal, the projected area is used. Using the cosine of the angle between the normal and the direction of the source (light), $\hat{n}\cdot\hat{L}$, yields the projected area, i.e.

$$|E^2| = \frac{\Phi}{4\pi r_0^2}\hat{n}\cdot\hat{L}$$

[†] Projected areas are taken perpendicular to the direction of projection.

Substituting for the energy flux yields

$$|E^2| = \frac{4\pi^2 r_s^2 \omega I}{4\pi r_0^2}\, \mathbf{n}\cdot\mathbf{L} = I(\widehat{\mathbf{n}}\cdot\widehat{\mathbf{L}})\,\pi\frac{r_s^2}{r_0^2} = I(\widehat{\mathbf{n}}\cdot\widehat{\mathbf{L}})\omega$$

since $\omega \approx \pi(r_s/r_0)^2$.

Hence, energy and intensity are directly related. Although some illumination models are described in terms of energy and some in terms of intensity, they are easily converted from one form to the other. For additional details see Hall [Hall89].

Physically Based Illumination Models

Torrance and Sparrow [Torr67] and Trowbridge and Reitz [Trow75] present physically based theoretical models for reflected light. Correlation between the theoretical models and experiment is excellent. Blinn [Blin77] used the Trowbridge–Reitz model in his development of a physically based illumination model. In developing the model, he assumes that specular highlights are the same color as the incident light. Cook and Torrance [Cook82a, 82b] used the Torrance–Sparrow model to generate synthetic images. Cook integrates the dependence of the specular reflectance coefficient on wavelength into the model. The results show that the color, i.e., the wavelength, of the specular highlights depends on the material properties. The color of the specular highlights approaches the color of the light source as the incidence angle approaches $\pi/2$.

To develop the physically based illumination model, first consider the solid angle subtended by a light source (Fig. 5–19). The incident energy per unit time per unit area of the reflecting surface is then related to the intensity of the incident light per unit projected area per unit solid angle, ω, subtended by the light source by

$$E_\ell = I_\ell(\widehat{\mathbf{n}}\cdot\widehat{\mathbf{L}})d\omega$$

where I_ℓ is the intensity of a point light source and E_ℓ is the energy density $|E^2|$, as shown previously.

For rough surfaces, the incident light is reflected over a wide range of angles. The reflected light intensity is related to the incident energy by

$$I = \rho E_\ell$$

Here, ρ is the ratio of the reflected intensity for a given direction to the incident energy from another direction. It is called the bidirectional reflectance. Combining the two equations yields

$$I = \rho I_\ell(\widehat{\mathbf{n}}\cdot\widehat{\mathbf{L}})d\omega$$

The bidirectional reflectance is composed of two parts, specular and diffuse, i.e.

$$\rho = k_d\rho_d + k_s\rho_s \quad \text{where} \quad k_d + k_s = 1$$

Here k_d and k_s are properties of the materials (see [Toul70, 72a, 72b]) but are frequently unavailable. Hence, they are usually treated as arbitrary parameters.

Reflection from ambient illumination is needed to complete the model. If a surrounding hemisphere is considered the source of ambient illumination, part of that hemisphere may be blocked by other objects. With this in mind, the reflected intensity due to ambient illumination is

$$I = fk_a\rho_aI_a$$

where f is the unblocked fraction of the hemisphere. The ambient reflectance, ρ_a, results from integrating the bidirectional reflectance ρ over the hemisphere. Consequently, ρ_a is a linear combination of ρ_d and ρ_s. The constant k_a again depends on the material properties; but specific data frequently is not available, and it is taken as an arbitrary parameter.

Combining the results yields the Cook–Torrance illumination model for m multiple light sources, i.e.

$$I = fk_a\rho_aI_a + \sum_{j=1}^{m} I_{l_j}(\hat{\mathbf{n}}\cdot\hat{\mathbf{L}}_j)d\omega_j(k_d\rho_d + k_s\rho_s) \qquad (5-15)$$

Notice that, in contrast to the previous illumination models, the Cook–Torrance model accounts for multiple light sources of both different intensities, I_ℓ, and different projected areas, $\hat{\mathbf{n}}\cdot\hat{\mathbf{L}}d\omega$. This ability is of importance. For example, a light source with the same intensity and illumination angle as another light source, but with twice the solid angle, yields twice the reflected intensity; i.e., the surface appears twice as bright. Quite small solid angles occur for large distant light sources; e.g., the solid angle for the sun is 0.000068 steradian.

The components of the model depend on the wavelength of the incident light, the material properties of the illuminated object, the roughness of the surface and the reflection geometry. Because of their considerable influence on the realism of the resulting synthetic images, the highlights due to specular reflection are of particular interest. The Torrance–Sparrow surface model addresses this problem.

The Torrance–Sparrow Surface Model

The Torrance–Sparrow model [Torr66, Torr67] for reflection from a rough surface is based on the principles of geometric optics. It is applicable to surfaces with an average roughness, large compared to the wavelength of the incident light. The model assumes that the surface is composed of randomly oriented mirror-like microfacets. The specular reflectance component of the reflected light, ρ_s, results from single reflections from the mirror-like microfacets. Diffuse reflection, ρ_d, is a result of multiple reflections among the microfacets, and from internal scattering. Figure 5–20 shows the geometry for reflection from a rough surface. Here, $\hat{\mathbf{n}}$ is the unit normal to the surface, $\hat{\mathbf{L}}$ is the unit vector in the direction of the light source, $\widehat{\mathbf{R}}$ is the unit reflection vector for the surface, $\widehat{\mathbf{H}}$ is the unit normal for a single microfacet in the surface and $\widehat{\mathbf{S}}$ is the unit reflection vector for the microfacet and also the direction of the observer. By the laws of reflection, $\widehat{\mathbf{L}}$, $\widehat{\mathbf{H}}$ and $\widehat{\mathbf{S}}$ all lie in the same plane; and the incident and reflection angles, ϕ, are equal. The angle between the normal to the surface, $\hat{\mathbf{n}}$, and the normal to the microfacet, $\widehat{\mathbf{H}}$, is δ. Since $\widehat{\mathbf{H}}$ is the bisector of the angle between $\widehat{\mathbf{L}}$ and $\widehat{\mathbf{S}}$, i.e., the halfway vector (see Sec. 5–3)

$$\widehat{\mathbf{H}} = \frac{\widehat{\mathbf{S}} + \widehat{\mathbf{L}}}{|\widehat{\mathbf{S}}| + |\widehat{\mathbf{L}}|} = \frac{\widehat{\mathbf{S}} + \widehat{\mathbf{L}}}{2}$$

and

$$\cos \phi = \widehat{\mathbf{L}} \cdot \widehat{\mathbf{H}} = \widehat{\mathbf{S}} \cdot \widehat{\mathbf{H}}$$

Only microfacets with normals in the direction $\widehat{\mathbf{H}}$ contribute to the specular reflection seen by an observer in the direction $\widehat{\mathbf{S}}$.

Using the Torrance–Sparrow model, Cook and Torrance give the specular reflectance ρ_s as

$$\rho_s = \frac{F}{\pi} \frac{DG}{(\hat{\mathbf{n}} \cdot \widehat{\mathbf{L}})(\hat{\mathbf{n}} \cdot \widehat{\mathbf{S}})}$$

where F is the Fresnel term, D is the distribution function for the microfacets on the surface, and G is a geometric attenuation factor due to shadowing and masking of one microfacet by another.

If each microfacet is considered as one side of a symmetric V-groove cavity (see Fig. 5–21), then part of a microfacet may be shadowed from incoming light (see Fig. 5–21b). Alternatively, part of the light reflected from a facet may not leave the cavity because it is masked by the opposite cavity wall. This is shown in Fig. 5–21c. The masking-and-shadowing effect is given by the ratio $\overline{m}/\iota$. Thus, the geometric attenuation is

$$G = 1 - \frac{\overline{m}}{l}$$

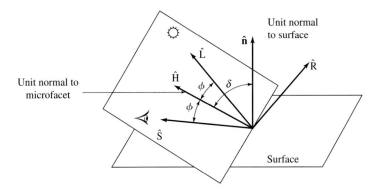

Figure 5–20   Geometry for the Torrance–Sparrow reflection model.

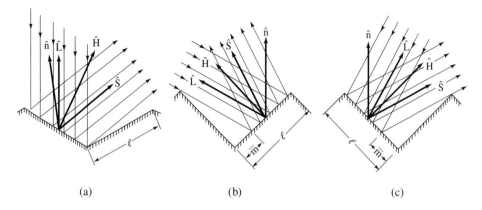

Figure 5–21   Geometric attenuation by the masking-and-shadowing effect. (a) No interference; (b) shadowing; (c) masking.

From the geometry shown in Fig. 5–21 it is obvious that the geometric attenuation is a function of the angle of the incident light, the included angle between the sides of the V groove and the length of the side of the V groove, l. When there is no interference, $\overline{m} = 0$ and $G = 1$. Both Torrance and Sparrow [Torr67] and Blinn [Blin77] determine G for masking and shadowing effects. For masking (Fig. 5–21c)

$$G_{\overline{m}} = \frac{2(\hat{n}\cdot\hat{H})(\hat{n}\cdot\hat{L})}{\hat{H}\cdot\hat{L}}$$

For shadowing (Fig. 5–21b), the result is the same, with $\hat{S}$ and $\hat{L}$ exchanged, that is

$$G_s = \frac{2(\hat{n}\cdot\hat{H})(\hat{n}\cdot\hat{S})}{\hat{H}\cdot\hat{S}} = \frac{2(\hat{n}\cdot\hat{H})(\hat{n}\cdot\hat{S})}{\hat{H}\cdot\hat{L}}$$

since $\hat{H}$ is the bisector of $\hat{L}$ and $\hat{S}$. For any given situation, the geometric attenuation is the minimum of these values; i.e.

$$G = \mathrm{Min}(1, G_m, G_s)$$

Torrance and Sparrow assume that the microfacet distribution on the surface is Gaussian. Thus

$$D = c_1 e^{-(\delta/m)^2}$$

where c_1 is an arbitrary constant and m is the root mean square slope of the microfacets. Cook and Torrance use a more theoretically founded distribution model proposed by Beckmann [Beck63]. The Beckmann distribution is

$$D = \frac{1}{4m^2 \cos^4 \delta}\, e^{-(\tan \delta/m)^2}$$

which provides the absolute magnitude of the distribution function without arbitrary constants. Figure 5–22 compares the Beckmann distributions for $m = 0.2$

and 0.6, corresponding to shiny and matte surfaces, respectively. Each point on the surface shown represents the magnitude of the reflected intensity in the direction $\widehat{S}$ from the point P as the direction of $\widehat{S}$ varies over a hemisphere. For small values of m, the reflected intensity is concentrated along the mirror direction $\widehat{R}$, while for larger values of m it is more evenly distributed. Small values of m yield shiny surfaces, and large values yield dull matte-like surfaces. For small values of m, corresponding to specular reflection, there is little difference between the Gaussian, Beckmann or Phong distribution functions.

For surfaces with more than one roughness scale, a weighted linear combination of the distribution functions for different values of m is used, e.g.

$$D = \sum_i w_i D(m_i)$$

where the sum of the weighting factors, w_i, is unity, i.e., $\sigma w_i = 1$.

Wavelength Dependence — the Fresnel Term

Ambient, diffuse and specular reflection all depend on wavelength λ. The wavelength dependence of ρ_a, ρ_d and F is a result of the material properties of the object. The Fresnel term in the specular reflectance, ρ_s, can be theoretically calculated from the Fresnel equation for unpolarized incident light reflected from a smooth mirror like surface, i.e.

$$F = \frac{1}{2}\left[\frac{\sin^2(\phi - \theta)}{\sin^2(\phi + \theta)} + \frac{\tan^2(\phi - \theta)}{\tan^2(\phi + \theta)}\right]$$

where
$$\sin\theta = \frac{\sin\phi}{\eta}$$

$$\eta = \text{index of refraction of the material}$$

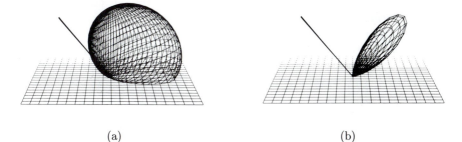

(a)   (b)

Figure 5–22 Beckmann distribution functions for (a) $m = 0.2$; (b) $m = 0.6$. (Courtesy of Rob Cook and the Program of Computer Graphics, Cornell University).

Here $\theta = \cos^{-1}(\widehat{\mathbf{L}} \cdot \widehat{\mathbf{H}}) = \cos^{-1}(\widehat{\mathbf{S}} \cdot \widehat{\mathbf{H}})$, the angle of incidence. Since the index of refraction is a function of wavelength, F is also a function of wavelength. If η is not known as a function of wavelength, F may be obtained from experimental values (see, for example, [Purd70]).[†] Figure 5–23a shows $F(\lambda)$ for bronze at normal incidence. Cook and Torrance suggest the following procedure for obtaining the angular dependence of $F(\lambda)$ when only the normal dependence on wavelength is known. Rewriting F as

$$F = \frac{1}{2} \frac{(g-c)^2}{(g+c)^2} \left\{ 1 + \frac{[c(g+c) - 1]^2}{[c(g-c) + 1]^2} \right\}$$

where
$$c = \cos\phi = \widehat{\mathbf{S}} \cdot \widehat{\mathbf{H}} = \widehat{\mathbf{L}} \cdot \widehat{\mathbf{H}}$$
$$g^2 = \eta^2 + c^2 - 1$$

and noting that at $\phi = 0$, $c = 1$, $g = \eta$ yields

$$F_0 = \left(\frac{\eta - 1}{\eta + 1} \right)^2$$

Solving for η, the index of refraction, yields

$$\eta(\lambda) = \frac{1 + \sqrt{F_0(\lambda)}}{1 - \sqrt{F_0(\lambda)}}$$

This value of η is used to determine $F(\lambda)$ from the Fresnel equation. A typical result is shown in Fig. 5–23b.

Color Shift

The dependence of the specular reflectance on wavelength and angle of incidence implies that there is a color shift in the specular highlights as the angle of incidence approaches $\pi/2$ (see Fig. 5–23b). At near normal incidence, $\phi = 0$; the specular highlights are the color of the material. Near the grazing angle of $\phi = \pi/2$, the specular highlights are the color of the incidence light source ($F = 1$). Because calculation of the color shift is expensive, Cook and Torrance suggest a linear interpolation between the color at normal reflectance ($\phi = 0$) and the color of the light ($\phi = \pi/2$). For example, the red component is

$$\text{Red}_\theta = \text{Red}_0 + (\text{Red}_{\pi/2} - \text{Red}_0) \frac{\text{Max}(0, F_\theta - F_0)}{F_{\pi/2} - F_0}$$

The blue and green components in an RGB color space (see Sec. 5–19) are determined similarly.

[†] Note that the reflectance spectra given in [Toul70, 72a, 72b] are for polished surfaces. They must be multiplied by $1/\pi$ for rough surfaces.

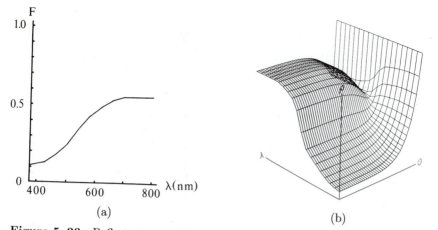

Figure 5–23 Reflectance, ρ, of bronze: (a) at normal incidence; (b) as a function of incidence angle calculated from (a) and the Fresnel equation. (Courtesy of Rob Cook and the Program of Computer Graphics, Cornell University).

Cook and Torrance use the normal reflectance, $\phi = 0$, from the surface for the diffuse reflectance ρ_d. Although the diffuse reflectance varies with angle, the effect is negligible for incidence angles less than about 70°. Hence, this is a reasonable assumption.

The two vases shown in Color Plate 4 illustrate results for the physically based illumination model. The left-hand vase is bronze-colored plastic. The plastic is simulated using a colored diffuse component and white specular highlights ($F = 1$). The right-hand vase is metallic bronze. For metals, reflection occurs from the surface. There is little penetration of the incident light below the surface and hence little if any diffuse reflection. Notice that here the specular reflected highlights have a bronze color. The specific details used by Cook to generate these images are given in Table 5–1.

Blinn [Blin77] also uses the more complex Torrance–Sparrow model with $F = 1$, i.e., without accounting for the color shift. Figure 5–24 by Blinn compares the shape of the specular highlights obtained using the Phong illumination model when the object is edge-lit. Edge-lighting occurs when the observer, $\widehat{\mathbf{S}}$ and the light source, $\widehat{\mathbf{L}}$, are approximately 90° apart. When the light and the observer are at the same location, i.e., $\widehat{\mathbf{L}} = \widehat{\mathbf{S}}$, the results for the two models are indistinguishable.

These results are explained by Fig. 5–25, which shows a comparison of the Phong and Torrance–Sparrow distribution functions for near normal (25°) and near-grazing (65°) angles for incident light. The bump represents the specular reflectance. Figures 5–25a and 5–25b show little difference between the models for near normal incidence. However, for near-grazing angles the Torrance–Sparrow model exhibits a laterally narrower, vertically oriented specular reflectance bump which is not quite in the same direction as that for the Phong model. Incorporating the geometric attenuation factor, G, into the Phong illumination model

Table 5–1 Illumination model data for Color Plate 4

	Plastic vase	Metallic vase
Two lights[†]	I_l = CIE standard illuminant D_{6500} $d\omega_i$ = 0.0001 and 0.0002	I_l = CIE standard illuminant D_{6500} $d\omega_i$ = 0.0001 and 0.0002
Specular	k_s = 0.1 F = reflectance of a vinyl mirror D = Beckmann function with $m = 0.15$	k_s = 1.0 F = S reflectance of a bronze mirror D = Beckmann functions with $m_1 = 0.4$ $w_1 = 0.4$ $m_2 = 0.2$ $w_2 = 0.6$
Diffuse	k_d = 0.9 ρ_d = bidirectional reflectance of bronze at normal incidence	k_d = 0 ρ_d = bidirectional reflectance of bronze at normal incidence
Ambient	I_a = $0.01I_l$ ρ_a = $\pi\rho_d$	I_a = $0.01I_l$ ρ_a = $\pi\rho_d$

[†]See Sec. 5–15.

yields results similar to those produced by the Torrance–Sparrow model for edge-lit objects.

Physical Characteristics of Light Sources

The physical characteristics of light sources are also important in determining both illumination and shadow effects on surfaces. Three characteristics of lights are important: geometry, spectral distribution and luminous intensity distribution. The physical geometry of the light is readily represented by standard modeling techniques. Typical emissive physical geometries are point, line, area and volume light sources.

As we have seen, the spectral characteristics of a light source are wavelength dependent. Restricting the spectral characteristics to the red, green and blue tristimulous values amounts to point sampling in color space. The result is frequently aliasing in color space.

The luminous intensity distribution is one of the most important characteristics of a light source. Frequently, computer graphics considers that the intensity of a light source is equal in all directions. This is seldom true in practice, e.g., shades or reflectors either restrict or redirect the light. Intensity distributions for light sources are given using goniometric diagrams. Goniometric diagrams represent a two-dimensional slice through the three-dimensional vector field representing the spatial luminous intensity distribution. Typical goniometric diagrams used in computer graphics are shown in Fig. 5–26. Verbeck and Greenberg

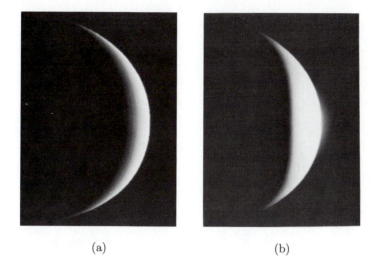

(a)   (b)

Figure 5–24 Comparison of edge-lit specular highlights. (a) Phong; (b) Torrance–Sparrow, magnesium oxide surface. (Courtesy of the University of Utah).

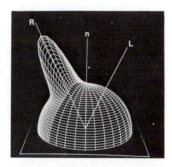

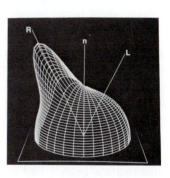

(a)   (b)

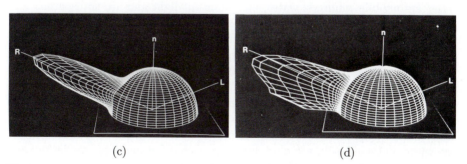

(c)   (d)

Figure 5–25 Comparison of light distribution functions at a near-normal incidence angle (25°): (a) Phong; (b) Torrance–Sparrow; and at a near-grazing incidence angle (65°): (c) Phong; (d) Torrance–Sparrow.

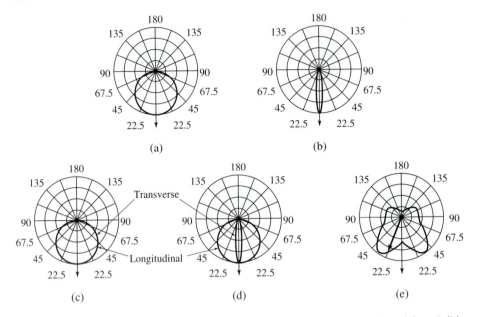

Figure 5-26 Typical goniometric diagrams used in computer graphics. (a) and (b) Point light sources [Verb84]; (c) and (d) line light sources [Verb84]; (e) street lamp [Nish85].

[Verb84] consider the effects of luminous intensity distributions for point, line and area light sources. Nishita, Okamura and Nakamae [Nish85] consider both point and linear sources. They approximate the luminous intensity distributions by multiple partial spheres and use linear interpolation for intervening intensities.

5–10 Transparency

Prior illumination models and visible surface algorithms consider only opaque surfaces or objects. Not all objects are opaque; some transmit light, e.g., glasses, vases, automobile windows, water, etc. transmit light and are transparent. As pointed out by Metelli [Mete74] and others prior to him, transparency is both physical and perceptual. Metelli states that "One perceives transparency when one sees not only surfaces behind a transparent medium but also the transparent medium or object itself". Physical transparency is neither a necessary nor a sufficient condition for the perception of transparency. Some examples illustrate this: A piece of transparent material carefully and evenly glued to a larger opaque object, for example, a piece of black cardboard, disappears. The phenomenon is independent of the color of the opaque object. Conversely, if two opaque squares, one white and one black, are placed next to each other and two smaller opaque squares, one light gray (placed over the white square) and one dark gray (placed over the black square), the gray squares appear to be transparent. Computer graphics typically addresses only the physical manifestations of transparency.

Refraction Effects in Transparent Materials

When light passes from one medium to another, e.g., from air to water, the light ray is bent by refraction. The common childhood observation that a straight stick partially inserted into a pond appears bent is an example of refraction. The amount that the light ray is bent is governed by Snell's law, which states that the refracted ray lies in the same plane as the incident ray and that the relationship between the incident and refracted angles is

$$\eta_1 \sin \theta = \eta_2 \sin \theta'$$

where η_1 and η_2 are the indices of refraction in the first and second mediums. Here, θ is the angle of incidence and θ' the angle of refraction, as shown in Fig. 5–27. No material transmits all the incident light. Some of it is reflected, as is also shown in Fig. 5–27.

By analogy with specular and diffuse reflection, light may be transmitted specularly or diffusely. Transparent materials, e.g., glass, exhibit specular transmission. Except at the silhouette edges of curved surfaces, objects viewed through transparent materials appear undistorted. If the transmitted light is scattered, then diffuse transmission occurs. Materials that diffusely transmit light appear frosted or translucent. Objects viewed through translucent materials appear dim or are distorted.

Some of the practical implications of refraction are shown in Fig. 5–28. Here the objects labeled 1 and 2 have equal indices of refraction greater than that in the surrounding medium. The objects labeled 3 and 4 are opaque. If the effects of refraction are ignored, the light ray labeled a intersects object 3, as shown by the dashed line. However, because the light ray is bent by refraction, it intersects object 4. Consequently, an object that might not otherwise be seen is visible. In contrast, if refraction effects are ignored for the light ray labeled b, then the ray misses object 3 and intersects object 4. However, the refracted ray intersects object 3. Thus, an object that is visible might not be seen. To generate realistic images, these effects must be considered.

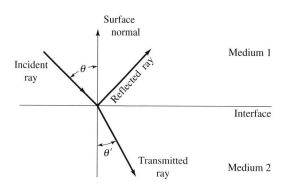

Figure 5–27   Geometry of refraction.

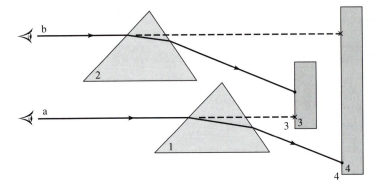

Figure 5–28 Refraction effects.

Similar effects occur when a perspective transformation is incorporated into the viewing transformation. Typically, a perspective transformation is used to obtain a distorted object, which is then displayed using an axonometric projection with the eyepoint at infinity, as shown in Fig. 5–29. Figure 5–29a shows a light ray through P that intersects the undistorted object at i. The refracted ray arrives at the background at point b. Figure 5–29b shows the object after distortion by a perspective transformation. The light ray now intersects the object at the transformed point, i', and the refracted ray now intersects the background at b', on the *opposite* side of the centerline from b. This effect is a result of incorrect angular relationships between the distorted object and the distorted light ray. At first glance, keeping sufficient information to generate the correct angular relations at the light ray–object boundaries might yield a correct result. But the correct result is not obtained, because the length of the light ray path in the distorted object is also different. This difference in path length has two effects. First, the exit point of the refracted ray from the distorted object is not the same as for the undistorted object. Thus, the ray still does not intersect the background at the correct point. Second, the amount of light absorbed within the object is also different. Hence, the intensity of the light ray as it exits the distorted object is changed.

These refraction effects are eliminated either by using an object space algorithm or by appropriately transforming between object and image space. However, they are more easily incorporated into ray tracing visible surface algorithms that utilize a global illumination model (see Sec. 5–14).

Simple Transparency Models

The earliest implementation of transparency is attributed to Newell, Newell and Sancha [Newe72] (see Sec. 4–12). The simplest implementations of transparency effects ignore refraction. When refraction is ignored, the effects illustrated in Figs. 5–28 and 5–29 do not occur. These simple implementations also ignore the effect that the distance a light ray travels in a medium has on the intensity.

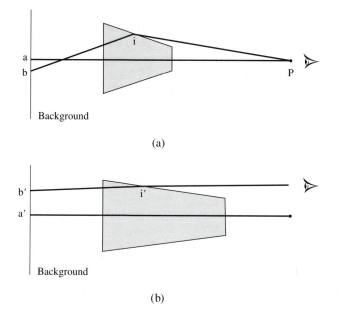

(a)

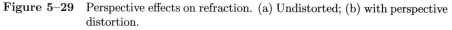

(b)

Figure 5–29   Perspective effects on refraction. (a) Undistorted; (b) with perspective distortion.

Simple transparency models can be directly incorporated into any of the hidden surface algorithms except the z-buffer algorithm. Transparent polygons or surfaces are tagged. When the visible surface is transparent, a linear combination of the two nearest surfaces is written to the frame buffer. The intensity is then

$$I = tI_1 + (1 - t)I_2 \qquad 0 \le t \le 1$$

where I_1 is the visible surface, I_2 is the surface immediately behind the visible surface, and t is the transparency factor for I_1. If $t = 0$, the surface is invisible. If $t = 1$, the surface is opaque. If I_2 is also transparent, the algorithm is applied recursively until an opaque surface or the background is found. When polygons are written to a frame buffer in depth priority order, as in the Newell–Newell–Sancha algorithm, I_2 corresponds to the value stored in the frame buffer and I_1 to the current surface.

The linear approximation does not provide an adequate model for curved surfaces. This is because at the silhouette edge of a curved surface, e.g., a vase or bottle; the thickness of the material reduces its transparency. To more adequately represent these effects, Kay [Kay79a, 79b] suggests a simple nonlinear approximation based on the z component of the surface normal. In particular, the transparency factor is

$$t = t_{\min} + (t_{\max} - t_{\min})[1 - (1 - |n_z|)^p]$$

where $t_{\min}$ and $t_{\max}$ are the maximum and minimum transparencies for the object, n_z is the z component of the unit normal to the surface and p is a transparency power factor, typically 2–3. Here, t is the transparency for any pixel or point on the object. Figure 5–30 compares results for the two models. Figure 5–30a was rendered using the linear model and Fig. 5–30b using the nonlinear model.

Transparent filters that pass selected wavelengths use a transparency model given by

$$I = I_1 + tC_t(\lambda)I_2$$

where $C_t(\lambda)$ is the transparency filter wavelength function. If multiple filters are present, the model is applied recursively to successive polygons.

z-Buffer Transparency

Transparency effects are difficult to add directly to a z-buffer algorithm (see Sec. 4–9). However, transparency effects may be included by using separate transparency, intensity and weighting factor buffers [Myer75] with the transparent polygons tagged in the data structure. For a z-buffer algorithm, the procedure is:

For each polygon:

> If the polygon is transparent, save it on a list.

> If the polygon is opaque, and if $z > z_{\text{buffer}}$, write it to the opaque frame buffer and update the opaque z-buffer.

For each polygon on the transparent list:

> If $z \geq z_{\text{buffer}}$, add its transparency factor to that in the transparency weighting buffer.

$$t_{bn} = t_{bo} + t_c$$

> Combine its intensity with that in the transparency intensity buffer, using

$$I_{bn} = I_{bo}t_{bo} + I_c t_c$$

> where I_{bn} is the new intensity value to be placed in the transparency intensity buffer, I_{bo} is the old value in the transparency intensity buffer, I_c is the intensity of the current polygon, t_{bo} is the old transparency factor in the transparency weighting buffer and t_c is the transparency factor for the current polygon. This gives a weighted sum of the intensities of all the transparent polygons in front of the nearest opaque polygon.

Combine the opaque and transparency intensity frame buffers; a linear combination rule is

$$I_{fb} = t_{bo}I_{bo} + (1 - t_{bo})I_{bfo}$$

where I_{fb} is the final intensity in the opaque frame buffer, and I_{bfo} is the old intensity value in the opaque frame buffer.

(a)   (b)

Figure 5–30   Comparison of simple transparency models.   (a) Linear $t = 0.5$; (b) nonlinear $p = 1$. (Courtesy of D.S. Kay and the Program of Computer Graphics, Cornell University).

Mammen [Mamm89] presents a similar algorithm that uses multiple passes to render depth sorted transparent polygons in back to front order into the opaque frame buffer once the opaque polygons are written to the frame buffer. The results are similar to those of Myer's algorithm [Myer75]. Using Crow's shadow volumes [Crow77b], Brotman and Badler [Brot84] incorporate transparency and penumbra shadows into a z-buffer algorithm (see Sec. 5–10). Transparency is also incorporated into the A-buffer algorithm [Carp84], using the linear transparency model when processing the pixel maps (see Sec. 4–10). Because of the memory requirements for a full z-buffer, the procedure is more appropriate for use with a scan line z-buffer algorithm (see Sec. 4–15).

Pseudotransparency

Pseudotransparency, often called screen door transparency, offers an inexpensive technique for achieving a transparency effect with the z-buffer algorithm. It is frequently implemented in hardware. The technique depends on the ability of the eye to act as an integrator. Specifically, the lower order bits of the pixel address (x, y) are used as an index into a transparency bit mask. If the value in the bit mask is 1, the transparent polygon pixel is written to the frame buffer; otherwise it is ignored. The fewer bits set to one in the transparency mask, the more transparent the polygon. A polygon is made completely transparent by setting all the bits in the transparency mask to zero. However, a number of undesirable side effects occur, e.g., any object drawn with a given transparency bit mask completely obscures any other object previously drawn with the same transparency bit mask.

   One interesting application of transparency is in visualization of the interior of complex objects or spaces. For this technique, each polygon or surface is tagged with a transparency factor. Initially, all transparency factors are 1, i.e. opaque. Rendering produces an opaque hidden surface view of the outside of the object or space. By selectively changing the transparency factor for groups of surfaces to zero, i.e. invisible, the interior of the object or space is revealed when the scene is again rendered.

Adding refraction effects to the illumination model requires that the visible surface problem be solved for both the reflected and transmitted light rays (see Fig. 5–27), as well as for the incident light ray. This is most effectively accomplished with a global illumination model, in conjunction with a ray tracing visible surface algorithm (see Sec. 5–20). Because of the large number of diffusely scattered transmitted rays generated by a translucent surface, only specularly reflected transmitted rays are usually considered. Thus, only transparent materials are simulated. The illumination model used is then a simple extension of those discussed previously (see Secs. 5–3, 5–8 and 5–9). In general the illumination model is

$$I = k_a I_a + k_d I_d + k_s I_s + k_t I_t$$

where the subscripts a, d, s, t specify ambient, diffuse, specular and transmitted effects. Most models assume that k_t is a constant and that I_t, the intensity of the transmitted light, is determined from Snell's law.

5–11   Shadows

When the observer's position is coincident with the light source, no shadows are seen. As the positions of the observer and the light source separate, shadows appear. Shadows contribute considerably to the realism of the scene by increasing depth perception. Shadows are also important in simulation, for example, a specific area of interest may be invisible because it is in shadow. Shadows significantly influence heating, air conditioning and solar power calculations for building and spacecraft design applications, as well as in other application areas.

Observation shows that a shadow consists of two parts, an umbra and a penumbra. The central dense, black, sharply defined shadow area is the umbra; the lighter area surrounding the umbra is the penumbra. The point light sources frequently used in computer graphics generate only umbra shadows. For distributed light sources of finite dimension, both umbra and penumbra shadows result (see [Cook82a]). While light is totally excluded from the umbra shadow, the penumbra receives light from part of the distributed light source.

Because of the computational expense, in many applications only the shadow umbra generated by a point light source is considered. The computational difficulty (and hence expense) of the shadow calculation also depends on the location of the light source. A light source at infinity is easiest to calculate, because an orthographic projection can be used to determine the shadows. A light source at a finite distance, but outside the field of view, is somewhat more difficult, because a perspective projection is required. The most difficult case is a light source located within the field of view. Here, the space must be divided into sectors and the shadows found in each sector separately.

Fundamentally, to add shadows to a scene the visible surface problem must be solved twice: once for the position of each light source, and once for the observer's position, or eyepoint; thus it is a two-step process. This is illustrated in Fig. 5–31 for a single light source at infinity, located above, in front and to the left of the block. The scene is viewed from in front, above and to the right of the block. There are two types of shadows, self-shadows and projected shadows. Self-shadows result when the object itself prevents light from reaching some of its planes, e.g., the right-hand plane of the block in Fig. 5–31. Self-shadowed planes are analogous to self-hidden planes and are found in the same way. They are self-hidden planes when the scene is viewed from the position of the light source.

A projected shadow results when an intervening object prevents light from reaching another object in the scene. The shadow on the base plane in Fig. 5–31b is an example. Projected shadows are found by projecting all non-self-hidden planes into the scene from the position of the light source. The intersections of the projected plane and all other planes in the scene are found; these polygons are tagged as shadow polygons and added to the data structure. The number of polygons added to the data structure is reduced by finding the silhouette of each object and projecting it instead of each individual plane.

After the shadows are added to the data structure, the scene is processed normally from the observer's position to obtain the desired view. Note that multiple views can be obtained without recalculating the shadows. The shadows depend upon the position of the light source and not on that of the observer. An example illustrates these techniques.

Example 5–4   Shadows

As an explicit example, consider the block shown in Fig. 5–31a. The block is described by the points $P_1(1, 0, 3.5)$, $P_2(2, 0, 3.5)$, $P_3(2, 0, 5)$, $P_4(1, 0, 5)$, $P_5(1, 3, 3.5)$, $P_6(2, 3, 3.5)$, $P_7(2, 3, 5)$, $P_8(1, 3, 5)$. The block rests on a base plane given by $B_1(0, 0, 0)$, $B_2(6, 0, 0)$, $B_3(6, 0, 6)$ and $B_4(0, 0, 6)$. The light source is located at infinity along the line connecting P_2 and P_8. The block and the base plane are to be observed from infinity on the positive z-axis,

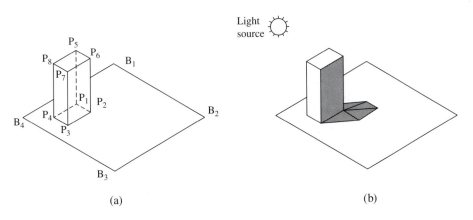

(a)   (b)

Figure 5–31 Shadows.

after first being rotated $-45°$ about the y-axis followed by a $35°$ rotation about the x-axis.

The self-shadowed planes are found by determining the self-hidden planes from the position of the light source. Using the formal techniques discussed in Sec. 4–3 and Exs. 4–2, 4–6 and 4–7, the volume matrix for the block is

$$V = \begin{bmatrix} \overset{\text{\textcircled{R}}}{-1} & \overset{\text{\textcircled{L}}}{1} & \overset{\text{\textcircled{B}}}{0} & \overset{\text{\textcircled{T}}}{0} & \overset{\text{\textcircled{H}}}{0} & \overset{\text{\textcircled{Y}}}{0.5} \\ 0 & 0 & 1 & -1 & 0 & 0.5 \\ 0 & 0 & 0 & 0 & -1 & 1.5 \\ 2 & -1 & 0 & 3 & 5 & 3.5 \end{bmatrix}$$

where R, L, B, T, H, Y refer to the right, left, bottom, top, near (hither), far (yon) planes, based on viewing the untransformed block from a point at infinity on the positive z-axis. The vector from the light source to the block expressed in homogeneous coordinates is

$$[E] = P_2 - P_8 = \begin{bmatrix} 1 & -3 & -1.5 & 0 \end{bmatrix}$$

The dot product of the light source vector and the self-hidden planes yields

$$[E] \cdot [V] = \begin{bmatrix} \overset{\text{\textcircled{R}}}{-1} & \overset{\text{\textcircled{L}}}{1} & \overset{\text{\textcircled{B}}}{-3} & \overset{\text{\textcircled{T}}}{3} & \overset{\text{\textcircled{H}}}{1.5} & \overset{\text{\textcircled{Y}}}{-1.5} \end{bmatrix}$$

The negative signs indicate that, viewed from the light source, the right, bottom and far planes are self-hidden and hence produce self-shadows.

There are several techniques for finding the projected shadows. One is to translate and rotate the block and its base plane until the vector from the light source is coincident with the z-axis. Because the light source is at infinity, an orthographic projection of the visible planes of the block onto the transformed base plane yields the projected shadows. This is accomplished by substituting the x and y coordinates of the transformed vertices of the block into the plane equation for the transformed base plane to obtain z. The coordinates of the projected shadows are then transformed back to the original orientation.

The light vector from infinity through P_8P_2 is made coincident with the x-axis by:

> Translating P_2 to the origin
>
> Rotating about the y-axis by $33.69°$ so that P_4 is on the z-axis
>
> Rotating about the x-axis by $59.04°$ so that P_8 is on the z-axis.

The combined transformation is

$$[T] = \begin{bmatrix} 0.83 & 0.48 & -0.29 & 0 \\ 0 & 0.51 & 0.86 & 0 \\ 0.55 & -0.71 & 0.43 & 0 \\ -3.59 & 1.53 & -0.93 & 1 \end{bmatrix}$$

Transforming the base plane and the block yields

$$
\begin{array}{c}
B_1 \\ B_2 \\ B_3 \\ B_4 \\ \\ P_1 \\ P_2 \\ P_3 \\ P_4 \\ P_5 \\ P_6 \\ P_7 \\ P_8
\end{array}
\begin{bmatrix}
0 & 0 & 0 & 1 \\
6 & 0 & 0 & 1 \\
6 & 0 & 6 & 1 \\
0 & 0 & 6 & 1 \\
1 & 0 & 3.5 & 1 \\
2 & 0 & 3.5 & 1 \\
2 & 0 & 5 & 1 \\
1 & 0 & 5 & 1 \\
1 & 3 & 3.5 & 1 \\
2 & 3 & 3.5 & 1 \\
2 & 3 & 5 & 1 \\
1 & 3 & 5 & 1
\end{bmatrix}
[T] =
\begin{bmatrix}
-3.59 & 1.53 & -0.93 & 1 \\
1.39 & 4.41 & -2.67 & 1 \\
4.69 & 0.15 & -0.09 & 1 \\
-0.29 & -2.73 & 1.65 & 1 \\
-0.84 & -0.48 & 0.29 & 1 \\
0 & 0 & 0 & 1 \\
0.82 & -1.06 & 0.64 & 1 \\
0 & -1.54 & 0.93 & 1 \\
-0.84 & 1.06 & 2.87 & 1 \\
0 & 1.54 & 2.58 & 1 \\
0.82 & 0.47 & 3.22 & 1 \\
0 & 0 & 3.51 & 1
\end{bmatrix}
\begin{array}{c}
\\ \\ \text{Base plane} \\ \\ \\ \\ \\ \\ \text{Block} \\ \\ \\
\end{array}
$$

Using Newell's method (see Sec. 4–3, Ex. 4–3) the equation for the transformed base plane is

$$z = -0.6y$$

Substituting the x and y coordinates of the vertices of the transformed block into the plane equation to obtain z yields the projection of the shadow onto the base plane. Specifically

$$
[P'] =
\begin{bmatrix}
-0.84 & -0.48 & 0.29 \\
0 & 0 & 0 \\
0.82 & -1.06 & 0.64 \\
0 & -1.54 & 0.93 \\
-0.84 & 1.06 & -0.64 \\
0 & 1.54 & -0.93 \\
0.82 & 0.48 & -0.29 \\
0 & 0 & 0
\end{bmatrix}
\begin{bmatrix}
P'_1 \\ P'_2 \\ P'_3 \\ P'_4 \\ P'_5 \\ P'_6 \\ P'_7 \\ P'_8
\end{bmatrix}
$$

where the prime denotes a projected shadow vertex.

Because only the front, left and top planes are visible from the light source, only these planes yield projected shadows. Specifically

$$\text{Front:} \quad P_3P_4P_8P_7 \quad \rightarrow \quad P'_3P'_4P'_8P'_7$$

$$\text{Left:} \quad P_1P_4P_8P_5 \quad \rightarrow \quad P'_1P'_4P'_8P'_5$$

$$\text{Top:} \quad P_7P_8P_5P_6 \quad \rightarrow \quad P'_7P'_8P'_5P'_6$$

Notice that P_2 is not contained in any visible plane, hence its projection, P'_2, is not contained in any visible projected shadow. The projected shadows are obtained in the original orientation by applying the inverse transformation, i.e $[T]^{-1}$ Specifically

$$
[S] = [P'][T]^{-1} =
\begin{bmatrix}
1 & 0 & 3.5 & 1 \\
2 & 0 & 3.5 & 1 \\
2 & 0 & 5 & 1 \\
1 & 0 & 5 & 1 \\
2 & 0 & 2 & 1 \\
3 & 0 & 2 & 1 \\
3 & 0 & 3.5 & 1 \\
2 & 0 & 3.5 & 1
\end{bmatrix}
\begin{bmatrix}
S_1 \\ S_2 \\ S_3 \\ S_4 \\ S_5 \\ S_6 \\ S_7 \\ S_8
\end{bmatrix}
$$

The projected shadow planes projected into the base plane are then $S_3S_4S_8S_7$, $S_1S_4S_8S_5$ and $S_7S_8S_5S_6$. The silhouette polygon is $S_1S_5S_6S_7S_3S_4$.

The result, rotated $-45°$ about the y-axis, followed by a $35°$ rotation about the x-axis and viewed from a point at infinity on the positive z-axis, is shown in Fig. 5–31b. Here the right-hand plane is visible but is self-shadowed, hence its intensity is shown nearly black; the projected shadow is also shown nearly black. Notice that from this viewpoint part of the projected shadow is hidden.

Following Crow [Crow77b], shadow algorithms are divided into five classes:

Algorithms that determine and render the shadows during scan conversion

Algorithms that perform two (or multiple) passes through a visible surface algorithm

Shadow volume algorithms [Crow77b]

Ray tracing algorithms

Radiosity algorithms.

The first four classes are discussed here, and incorporating shadows into radiosity algorithms is discussed in the context of the algorithm itself (see Sec. 5–17).

The Scan Conversion Shadow Algorithms

Incorporating shadows into a hidden surface algorithm was first suggested by Appel [Appe68]. He suggested both a ray tracing and a scan line approach. Bouknight and Kelley [Bouk70a, 70b; Kell70] improved on Appel's scan line approach. Adding shadows to a spanning scan line algorithm, e.g., the Watkins algorithm, requires two steps.

The first step is to determine the self-shadows and the projected shadows for every polygon in the scene for every light source, as discussed in Ex. 5–4. Conceptually, this is a binary matrix. The rows represent polygons that can cast shadows, and the columns represent polygons that are shadowed. In the binary matrix, a 1 indicates that a polygon can possibly cast a shadow on another, and a 0 that it cannot. Along the diagonal, a 1 indicates that a polygon is self-shadowed.

Since, for a scene containing n polygons, the number of possible projected shadows is $n(n-1)$, efficiently determining this matrix is important. Bouknight and Kelley project the scene onto a sphere centered at the light source and use bounding box tests on the projected polygons to eliminate most cases. Similarly, the technique, described in Ex. 5–4, of making the direction of the light source coincident with the z-axis may be used. Simple three-dimensional bounding box tests are then used to eliminate most cases. Additional possibilities are eliminated using more sophisticated sorting techniques, e.g., the Newell–Newell–Sancha priority sort (see Sec. 4–12). A simple example illustrates this.

Example 5–5   Shadow Matrix

For the simple scene shown in Fig. 5–31, the shadow matrix can be constructed by inspection. The result is shown in Table 5–2.

Table 5–2

		Right	Left	Bottom	Top	Hither	Yon	Base plane
Polygon	Right	1	0	0	0	0	0	1
casting	Left	0	0	1	0	0	1	1
the	Bottom	0	0	1	0	0	0	1
shadow	Top	1	0	0	0	0	0	1
	Hither	1	0	1	0	0	0	1
	Yon	0	0	0	0	0	1	1
	Base plane	0	0	0	0	0	0	0

In practice, the matrix is incorporated into a linked list that associates the shadows and the polygons.

The second step processes the scene from the observer's viewpoint. Two scanning processes are involved. In a spanning scan line algorithm, e.g., the Watkins algorithm, the first scanning process determines the visible segment in a span, as described in Sec. 4–16. The second scanning process uses the shadow linked list to determine if any shadows fall on the polygon that generated the visible segment for that span. The second scan for that span then proceeds as follows:

If no shadow polygons are found, the visible segment is displayed.

If shadow polygons are found for the visible segment polygon but none intersect or cover the span, the visible segment is displayed.

If one or more shadow polygons completely cover the span, the intensity of the visible segment is modulated with that of the shadow polygons and the segment displayed.

If one or more shadow polygons partially cover the span, it is subdivided at the intersection of the edges of the shadow polygons; the algorithm is then applied recursively to each subspan until the entire span is displayed.

This algorithm states that the intensity of the visible segment is modulated with that of the shadow polygon. The simplest modulation rule assumes that the shadow is absolutely black. A few minutes experimenting with light sources and two objects shows that shadows are not always absolutely black. The intensity, i.e., the blackness, of the shadow varies with the intensity of the light source and also with the distance between the plane casting the shadow and the plane in shadow. This is because the shadow area receives light from the ambient environment, and because the light source is of finite size.

A simple modulation rule that partially simulates this effect is to make the shadow intensity proportional to the intensity of the light source. For multiple shadows, the shadow intensities are additive. A computationally more expensive rule is to make the shadow intensity proportional to both the intensity of the light source and the distance between the plane casting the shadow and the plane in shadow.

Multiple-pass Visible Surface Shadow Algorithms

The z-buffer algorithm (see Sec. 4–9) can be modified to include shadow effects [Will78a]. Again, a two-step process is used; the modified algorithm is:

> The scene is constructed from the light source direction. The z values for this view are stored in a separate shadow z-buffer; intensity values are ignored.

> The scene is then constructed from the observer's point of view. As each surface or polygon is considered, its depth at each pixel is compared with that in the observer's z-buffer. If it is the visible surface, a linear transformation is used to map the x, y, z values in the observer's view into x', y', z' values in the light source view. The z' value is checked for visibility with respect to the light source by comparing its value with that in the shadow z-buffer at x', y'. If it is visible to the light source, it is rendered normally in the frame buffer at x, y. If not, it is in shadow and is rendered using the appropriate shadow modulation rule. The value in the observer's z-buffer is updated with z'.

This algorithm is directly applicable to the scan line z-buffer algorithm (see Sec. 4–15); here the buffers are only one scan line high. Williams [Will78a] used a modified procedure to render curved shadows on curved surfaces. The complete scene is first computed from the observer's point of view. The point-by-point linear transformation to the light source direction, and consequent shadowing, are then applied as a postprocess. As pointed out by Williams, the modified procedure incorrectly renders highlights, because they are merely darkened if they lie in shadow. Highlights should, of course, not appear in shadowed areas. Williams also discusses the quantization effects that result from performing the transformation from one viewpoint to another in image space.

Atherton [Athe78a, 78b] extended the visible surface algorithm based on the Weiler–Atherton clipping algorithm (see Secs. 3–21 and 4–7), to include shadow generation. The algorithm is important because it operates in object space. Hence, the results can be used for accurate calculations as well as to produce pictures. Again, a two-step process is used.

The first step uses the visible surface algorithm to determine the visible or illuminated polygons from the light source direction. The illuminated polygons are saved, rather than the shadow polygons, in order to increase the efficiency of the algorithm. If shadow polygons, i.e. invisible polygons, are saved, then it is also necessary to save all the self-hidden polygons that are normally culled before application of the visible surface algorithm. For convex polyhedra, this doubles the number of polygons processed by the algorithm.

The illuminated polygons are tagged and transformed back to the original data orientation, where they are attached to the original polygons as surface detail. This operation is accomplished by assigning a unique number to every polygon in the scene. When a polygon is passed through the visible surface algorithm, it may be split into numerous pieces; however, each piece retains the original unique number. Thus, it is possible to associate each of the fragmented illuminated polygons with its original source polygon, or any fragment of the source polygon.

In order to avoid false shadows, it is necessary that the entire scene be contained within the view or clipping volume defined from the location of the light source. If not, then regions outside the clipping volume are incorrectly assumed to be in shadow. The result, viewed from the observer's location, then contains false shadows. This restriction also requires that the light source not be located within the extremes of the scene environment. This restriction occurs because no single perspective or axonometric transformation exists, from the location of the light source, that can contain the entire scene.

The second step processes the combined polygon data from the observer's point of view. If an area is not illuminated, the appropriate shadow modulation rule is applied. The general procedure is shown in Fig. 5–32.

For multiple light sources, multiple sets of illuminated polygons are added to the data base. The color image shown in Color Plate 5 illustrates a result with two light sources.

The Shadow Volume Algorithms

Frank Crow developed a method for determining if a point on an object is in shadow called shadow volumes [Crow77b]. Assuming polyhedral objects, a shadow volume is a semi-infinite region of space defined by lines from the light source passing through each vertex of the polygonal faces forming the polyhedral object. Figure 5–33a shows the shadow volume for a single polygon. Each plane of the shadow volume has an outward facing normal associated with it. Most implementations limit the extent of the semi-infinite shadow volume. Crow [Crow77b] clipped the shadow volume to the frustum of vision, as shown in Fig. 5–33b. When clipped in this way, each plane of the shadow volume forms a quadrilateral polygon. Bergeron [Berg86] limited the shadow volume by a *sphere of influence*, beyond which the effect of a uniformly radiating light source is negligible. Hence, any object beyond the sphere of influence for a given light source is already in shadow with respect to that light source. For nonuniformly radiating light sources, e.g., the flaps and cones of the Warn lighting model [Warn83], the sphere of influence is extended to a *region of influence*.

In determining the visible surface, shadow surfaces are themselves invisible. However, the depth order of shadow and visible surfaces determines whether a visible surface is in shadow with respect to the eyepoint. Crow's method of determining whether a visible surface is in shadow is based on Appel's concept of quantitative invisibility [Appel68].

A shadow surface is *frontfacing* with respect to an eyepoint if the direction of its outward normal is toward the eyepoint and *backfacing* if away from the eyepoint. A frontfacing shadow surface, with respect to an eyepoint, adds +1 to the *shadow depth count* [Berg86], whereas a backfacing shadow surface cancels the effect of a frontfacing shadow surface and adds −1 to the shadow depth count. If the extent of the shadow volume is limited, then the direction of the normal for the limiting shadow surface is reversed.

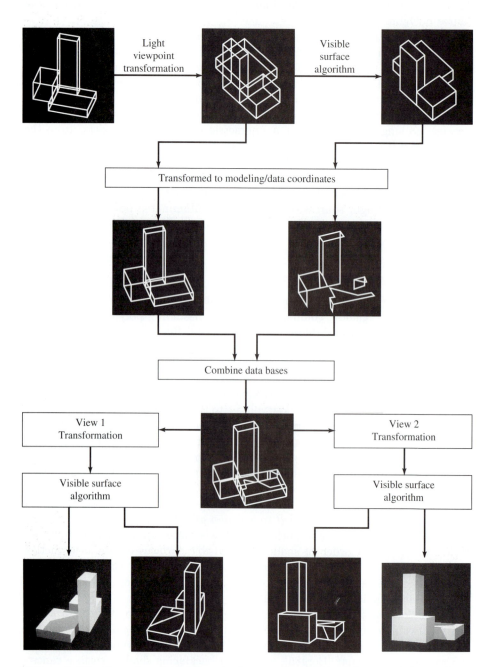

Figure 5–32 Procedure for adding shadows to the Weiler–Atherton visible surface algorithm. (Courtesy of P. Atherton and the Program of Computer Graphics, Cornell University).

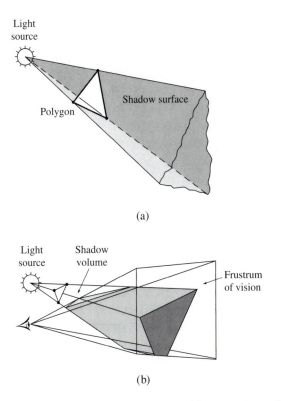

(a)

(b)

Figure 5–33 Shadow volumes. (a) Semi-infinite; (b) limited by clipping to the frustum of vision [Crow77b].

If the eyepoint is not itself in shadow, then, if a line from the eyepoint to a point in the scene intersects more front facing shadow surfaces then backfacing shadow surfaces, i.e., the shadow depth count is positive, it is in shadow. Figure 5–34a illustrates this concept using a two-dimensional analog. The shadow surfaces labelled +1 are frontfacing and those labelled −1 are backfacing with respect to eyepoint E_1. The line from the eyepoint to P_2 intersects three shadow surfaces, as shown by the small ×s. Consequently, P_2 has a shadow depth count of +1 (+1 + 1 − 1) and is in shadow. Similarly, the shadow depth counts for P_1, P_3, P_4 and P_5 are 0, +2, +1 and 0, respectively. Thus, points P_3 and P_4 are also in shadow, while points P_1 and P_5 are not. Notice that if the eyepoint is moved to E_2 the signs of all the shadow depth counts reverse and P_2 is also in shadow from eyepoint E_2, as is required.

If the eyepoint is itself in shadow, as illustrated by E_1 in Fig. 5–34b, the shadow depth counter is initialized to the number of shadow volumes containing the eyepoint. For example, in Fig. 5—34b for eyepoint E_1 the shadow depth counter is initialized to +1. Consequently, P_2 has a shadow depth of +1 (+1 + 1 − 1) and is in shadow, while P_1 has a shadow depth of 0 and is not in shadow.

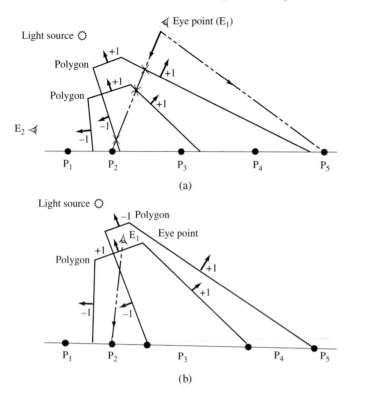

Figure 5–34 Two-dimensional analog of shadow volumes. (a) Eyepoint not in shadow; (b) eyepoint in shadow.

Note in Fig. 5–34a that from eyepoint E_1 both P_1 and P_2 are, in fact, obscured by the polygon itself. Thus, an obvious efficiency in implementing the algorithm is to compute shadow depths only for those points that are visible from the eyepoint. Further efficiencies are possible by creating shadow volumes using only the silhouette edges of a polyhedron. For polyhedral objects, silhouette edges are those edges for which a frontfacing polygon is adjacent to a backfacing polygon with respect to a light source. Silhouette edges are linked together by starting from a known silhouette edge vertex and searching for silhouette edges emanating from the silhouette vertex. For scenes with multiple light sources, shadow volumes are created for each light source.

Bergeron [Berg86] extended Crow's original shadow volume algorithm to include nonplanar polygons and nonpolyhedral objects. He also gives a detailed method for determining if the eyepoint is in shadow, and reasonable approximations for limiting spheres of influence. He implements the shadow volume algorithm in the context of a scan line visible surface algorithm. Fournier and Fussell [Four88] discuss the shadow volume algorithm in the context of a frame buffer.

Chin and Feiner [Chin89] present an object space, BSP-tree-based, shadow algorithm using shadow volumes. Their algorithm considers only point light sources and polyhedral volumes, but it does not require that the shadow volumes be closed; nor does it require that the scene be wholly within a light source's 'view volume'. In developing the algorithm, they capitalize on Thibault and Naylor's [Thib87] use of a BSP tree to represent polyhedral solids. Specifically, they adopt the idea of an 'in' or 'out' value for each empty region at the BSP tree leaves. Assuming outward normals, an 'in' region corresponds to a polygon's backfacing halfspace and an 'out' region to its frontfacing halfspace. Each 'in' and 'out' region forms a convex polyhedral tessellation of the space. The resulting shadow volume BSP (SVBSP) tree represents a union of the convex 'in' regions, possibly concave with holes. The leaves of the BSP tree are the 'in' and 'out' regions, indicating whether the regions are within or without the shadow volume.

Using a normal BSP tree built from the scene polygons to determine the front-to-back order with respect to the eyepoint, the SVBSP tree for each polygon is constructed. The front-to-back ordering means that successive polygons need only be compared with the union of shadow volumes of previously processed polygons, all of which are closer to the light source than the current polygon. The result is a single SVBSP tree constituted as a set of pyramids radiating outward from the light source. Figure 5–35a shows a two-dimensional analog of the result, and Fig. 5–35b illustrates how the combined SVBSP tree is built as each polygon is processed. Polygons are split along shadow surfaces, e.g., *ef* in Fig. 5–35. Polygon fragments split along shadow surfaces that are in shadow reach the 'in' leaves, e.g., *eg* in Fig. 5–35; those that are lit by the light source reach the 'out' leaves, e.g., *gf* in Fig. 5–35. Each fragment that reaches an 'out' cell is lit and thus may shadow later fragments. Consequently, a SVBSP tree is computed for each of the lit fragments and added to the combined SVBSP tree.

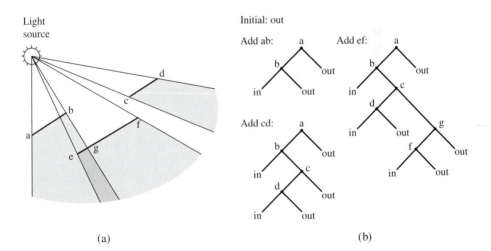

(a) (b)

Figure 5–35 Two-dimensional analog of three-dimensional combined shadow volumes. (a) Shadow volumes; (b) construction of the combined SVBSP tree.

Multiple light sources are handled by building a SVBSP tree for each light source and sequentially combining them as they are built into a single SVBSP tree. Thus, only a single SVBSP tree is kept in memory. The resulting SVBSP tree is then used when rendering the scene either with a software or hardware renderer. Color Plate 6a shows a simple scene with three light sources, while Color Plate 6b shows the shadow volumes for the same scene. Chin [Chin90] gives an optimized and parallelized version.

Penumbra Shadows

Although, as mentioned previously, shadow penumbras are expensive to calculate, Cook [Cook82a] suggests a relatively simple technique for including them. Because the Cook–Torrance illumination model assumes a finite area light source subtending a solid angle $d\omega$ (see Sec. 5–9), blocking a fraction of the area of the light source reduces the effective solid angle and hence the incident intensity from the source. The reflected intensity is then also reduced proportionally.

Figure 5–36 illustrates the effect for a simple straight edge and a spherical light source. The midshadow line is calculated by considering a point light source at the center of the spherical source. From Fig. 5–36, using similar triangles, the projection of the penumbra half-width r in the direction $\mathbf{L}$ is

$$\frac{r(\mathbf{n}\cdot\mathbf{L})}{d} = \frac{R}{D}$$

where d is the distance from the shadow casting point to the corresponding point on the midshadow line, D is the distance from the shadow casting point to the center of the spherical light source and R is the radius of the spherical light source.

Viewed from the polygon casting the shadow, the solid angle of the light source $d\omega$ is

$$d\omega = \pi \left(\frac{R}{D}\right)^2$$

Thus, the penumbra half-width is

$$r = \frac{d}{\widehat{\mathbf{n}}\cdot\widehat{\mathbf{L}}}\frac{R}{D} = \frac{d}{\widehat{\mathbf{n}}\cdot\widehat{\mathbf{L}}}\sqrt{\frac{d\omega}{\pi}}$$

The result shows that the shadow is sharper (i.e., r is smaller) for light resources that subtend smaller solid angles $d\omega$. For a point light source, $d\omega = 0$, which yields $r = 0$. Hence, no penumbra is generated. Further, as the polygon casting the shadow approaches the surface, d and r both decrease. This also makes the shadow sharper.

Within the penumbra, the intensity of each point is determined by the fraction of the light source that is visible. For a spherical light source only partially visible from $-R$ to a, this fraction is

$$A_{\text{frac}} = \frac{1}{\pi R^2}\int_{-R}^{a} 2\sqrt{R^2 - x^2}\, dx = \frac{1}{2} + \frac{1}{\pi}\left[\frac{a}{R}\sqrt{1 - \left(\frac{a}{R}\right)^2} + \sin^{-1}\left(\frac{a}{R}\right)\right]$$

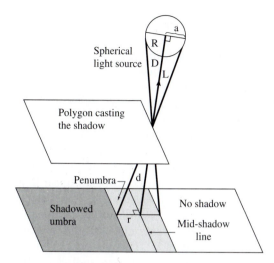

Figure 5–36   Penumbra shadows.

The results show that a shadow penumbra is sharper at one edge. Cook recommends storing the results of this calculation in a lookup table. However, the linear approximation

$$A_{frac} = \frac{1}{2}\left(1 + \frac{a}{R}\right)$$

yields a less than seven percent error and is computationally less expensive.

Brotman and Badler [Brot84] use shadow volumes with a z-buffer algorithm to generate penumbra shadows for area light sources modeled as collections of point light sources on polyhedral surfaces. Objects are assumed to be the union of convex closed polyhedral objects. Transparency is incorporated into the algorithm. They found that a uniform random distribution of point light sources produced more acceptable results than a lattice of evenly spaced points.

To model the penumbra shadows, a shadow volume is generated for each point light source used to model the area light source. At each pixel, the number of shadow volumes, nsv, generated from a given area light source that surround the pixel, is determined. The intensity at the pixel is then attenuated using

$$I_{att} = \frac{I}{n}\left(n - nsv\right)$$

where I is the total intensity of the area light source and n is the number of point light sources used to model the area light source.

Visible objects are rendered into the z-buffer, followed by shadow volumes which are used only to attenuate the intensity. z sorted transparent objects are rendered into a temporary transparency buffer, and the resulting intensity values are used to attenuate those in the frame buffer (see Sec. 5–10). In order to reduce memory requirements, they subdivide the screen into smaller buffer areas and repeat the algorithm for each smaller screen area. Brotman and Badler point out that by using this process transparent objects can cast shadows but cannot have shadows cast on them. Further, if the illumination model includes specular highlights, then highlights appear within shadowed areas.

Nishita and Nakamae [Nish83, 85a, 85b] use Crow's shadow volume technique [Crow77b] to generate both umbra and penumbra shadows from linear, area and volume light sources. The object space (precision) algorithm assumes that objects and light sources are convex polygons and polyhedral volumes. The light sources have Lambertian distributions with uniform brightness. Light sources are *not* modeled as collections of point light sources. Figure 5–37 shows the basic geometry for an area light source which is also applicable to linear light sources. Following the notation used by Nishita and Nakamae, the vertices of the light source are labeled $Q_\ell(\ell = 1, 2, \ldots m)$, and V represents an intervening convex polyhedron. From each vertex of the light source Q_ℓ, a shadow volume $U_\ell(\ell = 1, 2, \ldots m)$ is cast using the silhouette edge of V. The penumbra shadow volume is defined as the *minimum* convex volume (hull) surrounding *all* the $U_\ell(\ell = 1, 2, \ldots m)$ shadow volumes. The umbra shadow is the intersection of the shadow volumes $U_\ell(\ell = 1, 2, \ldots m)$. The intersection of the penumbra and umbra shadow volumes with an object (face) yield the penumbra and umbra shadows.

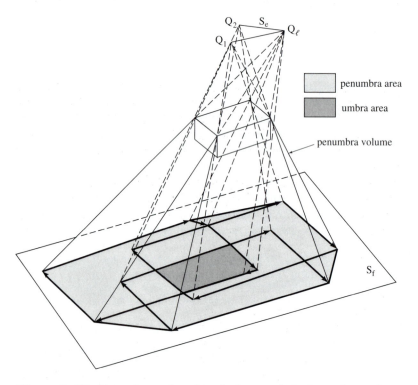

penumbra area

umbra area

penumbra volume

Figure 5–37 Penumbra and umbra shadows and shadow volumes for an area light source [Nish85].

A point, P, that lies within the umbra shadow receives no light from the light source. The illumination of a point, P, lying within the penumbra shadow is proportional to the area of the light source seen from P. Nishita and Nakamae use contour integration to obtain the penumbra illumination for both polygonal and polyhedral light sources. Color Plate 7 shows the direct illumination from a single linear light source. Nishita and Nakamae incorporate the shadow volume technique into an algorithm that also accounts for indirect illumination from interobject reflections [Nish85b].

Ray Tracing Shadow Algorithms

The visible surface ray tracing algorithm previously discussed in Sec. 4–20 can also be extended to include shadows [Appe68]. Again, a two-step process is used. The first step traces the ray from the observer or eyepoint through the plane of projection to determine the visible point, if any, in the scene, as in the previously discussed algorithm.

The second step traces the vector (ray) from the visible point to the light source. If any object in the scene lies between the visible point and the light source, then light from that source cannot reach that point. Hence, the point is in shadow. The technique is illustrated in Fig. 5–38. The techniques previously discussed in Sec. 4–20 makes the search along the local light direction vector more efficient.

5–12   Texture

In computer graphics, the fine surface detail on an object is generated using textures. One example of the motivation for using textures is the contrast between modeling a brick wall from hundreds of polygons and using a single textured

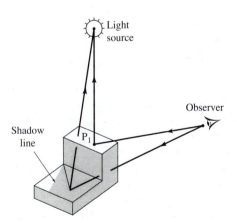

Figure 5–38   Ray tracing with shadows.

polygon. Three aspects of texture are generally considered. The first aspect is the addition of a separately specified pattern to a smooth surface; after the pattern is added, the surface still appears smooth. Adding a pattern to a smooth surface is basically a mapping function. The second is adding the appearance of roughness to the surface; adding the appearance of roughness to a surface is basically a perturbation function. The third is simulating the environment, e.g., shadows and lighting using textures.

Adding a texture pattern to a smooth surface was first suggested by Catmull [Catm74] as a consequence of his subdivision algorithm for curved surfaces (see Sec. 4–8). This basic idea was extended by Blinn and Newell [Blin76] to include reflection and highlights on curved surfaces.

Since the basis of adding texture patterns to smooth surfaces is mapping, the texture problem reduces to transformation from one coordinate system to another. Actually, there are at least two mappings required, as shown in Fig. 5–39. One is from texture space to object space, sometimes called surface parameterization; the second is from object space to image (screen) space, i.e., the viewing transformation. Frequently, the two mappings or transformations are concatenated (composed) into one.

If the texture pattern is defined in an orthogonal coordinate system (u, v) in texture space, and the surface in a second orthogonal coordinate system (x, y, z), represented in parametric space (θ, ϕ) where $x(\theta, \phi)$, $y(\theta, \phi)$, $z(\theta, \phi)$, then adding the texture pattern to the surface involves determining or specifying a mapping function between the two spaces, e.g., the mapping from texture space to parametric space is

$$\theta = f(u, v) \qquad \phi = g(u, v)$$

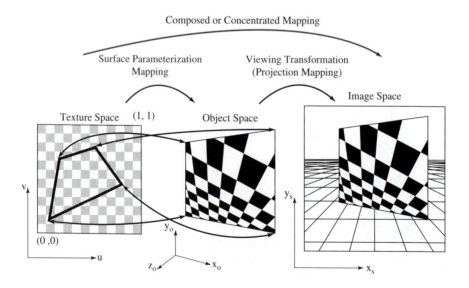

Figure 5–39 Mapping (transformation) from texture space to image space.

and the inverse mapping from parametric space to texture space is

$$u = r(\theta, \phi) \qquad v = s(\theta, \phi)$$

The mapping function is frequently assumed to be linear, i.e.

$$\theta = Au + B \qquad \phi = Cv + D$$

where the constants A, B, C, D are obtained from the relationship between known points in the two coordinate systems. A simple example serves to illustrate the technique.

Example 5–6   Mapping

The pattern shown in Fig. 5–40a in texture space is to be mapped onto the surface patch defined by the octant of the hemisphere in object space, shown in Fig. 5–40b. The pattern is a simple two-dimensional grid of intersecting lines. The parametric representation of the octant of the sphere is given by

$$x = \sin\theta \sin\phi$$
$$0 \le \theta \le \frac{\pi}{2}$$
$$y = \cos\phi$$
$$\frac{\pi}{4} \le \phi \le \frac{\pi}{2}$$
$$z = \cos\theta \sin\phi$$

Assuming a linear mapping function between parametric space and texture space yields

$$\theta = Au + B \qquad \phi = Cv + D$$

and assuming that the corners of the quadrilateral pattern map into the corners of the quadrilateral surface patch, i.e.

$$u = 0, v = 0 \quad \text{at } \theta = 0, \qquad \phi = \frac{\pi}{2}$$

$$u = 1, v = 0 \quad \text{at } \theta = \frac{\pi}{2}, \quad \phi = \frac{\pi}{2}$$

$$u = 0, v = 1 \quad \text{at } \theta = 0, \qquad \phi = \frac{\pi}{4}$$

$$u = 1, v = 1 \quad \text{at } \theta = \frac{\pi}{2}, \quad \phi = \frac{\pi}{4}$$

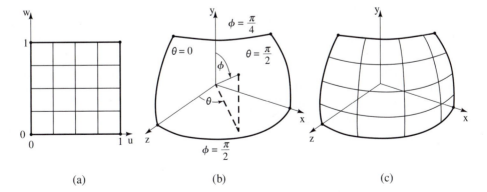

(a)   (b)   (c)

Figure 5–40   Mapping. (a) Texture; (b) surface; (c) textured surface.

yields $\qquad A = \dfrac{\pi}{2} \qquad B = 0 \qquad C = -\dfrac{\pi}{4} \qquad D = \dfrac{\pi}{2}$

Thus, the linear mapping function from uv space to $\theta\phi$ space is

$$\theta = \frac{\pi}{2}u \qquad \phi = \frac{\pi}{2} - \frac{\pi}{4}v$$

The inverse mapping from $\theta\phi$ space to uv space is

$$u = \frac{\theta}{\pi/2} \qquad v = \frac{\pi/2 - \phi}{\pi/4}$$

The results of mapping a single line in uv space into $\theta\phi$ space and thence into xyz Cartesian coordinates is shown in Table 5–3. The complete results are shown in Fig. 5–40c.

Table 5–3

u	w	θ	ϕ	x	y	z
$1/4$	0	$\pi/2$	$\pi/2$	0.38	0	0.92
	$1/4$		$7\pi/16$	0.38	0.20	0.91
	$1/2$		$3\pi/8$	0.35	0.38	0.85
	$3/4$		$5\pi/16$	0.32	0.56	0.77
	1		$\pi/4$	0.27	0.71	0.65

Although the linear mapping in Ex. 5–6 gives a correct and anticipated result, notice the distortion that occurs. The squares in Fig. 5–40a map to curvilinear quadrilaterals in Fig. 5–40c. If the octant of the hemisphere is specified as $0 \le \phi \le \pi/4$, $0 \le \theta \le \pi/2$, which includes one of the 'poles', the distortion is extreme. The topmost row of squares in the texture pattern of Fig. 5–40a map to curvilinear triangles (degenerate curvilinear quadrilaterals), with two coincident vertices at the 'pole' of the hemisphere. If the texture pattern is alternating solid colored squares, e.g., a black and white checkerboard, and we expect to see a pattern of alternating colored solid squares on the sphere, the result is particularly unsatisfying. The fundamental reason is that a nonlinear mapping between texture space and parametric space is required to achieve the desired result.[†] Note that the octants of the hemisphere, which include the 'poles', are particularly pathological cases. In fact, it is well known, particularly among cartographers, that neither a distortion free linear mapping of the polar regions of a sphere onto a flat sheet, nor the inverse mapping of a two-dimensional 'flat' image onto a sphere is possible.

The texture pattern shown in Fig. 5–40a is a simple mathematical definition. Other sources of texture are hand-drawn artwork, or scanned-in (digitized) photographs or procedurally generated patterns. Displaying a texture pattern on a

---

[†]Note that the overall mapping between object space (x, y, z) and texture space (u, v) is nonlinear, because the mapping between parametric space and object space is nonlinear.

surface involves a mapping from object space to image space, as well as the previously discussed mapping (transformation) from texture space to object space. Any viewing transformation must also be applied. Assuming that image space implies a raster device, two slightly different techniques are frequently used.

The first technique is based on Catmull's curved surface subdivision algorithm (see Sec. 4–8). Catmull's algorithm subdivides a surface patch until a subpatch covers a single pixel center. The parametric values of the center of the subpatch or the pixel center are then mapped into texture space, and the texture pattern at that point is used to determine the intensity of the pixel. However, as Catmull points out, this point sampling technique leads to severe aliasing effects. For example, large portions, or perhaps all of the simple mathematically defined texture pattern shown in Fig. 5–40a, is missed if all the sample points occur in the *white* areas of the texture. To alleviate this effect, Catmull subdivides the texture pattern, along with the surface patch. When a subpatch is found that covers only a single pixel center, the average intensity in the associated texture subpatch is used to determine the pixel intensity.

In general, the texture subpatch is not rectangular. If the texture pattern is rasterized, then the intensity of the texture subpatch is taken as the weighted average of the intensities of the texture pixels in the subpatch. The weighting function is the ratio of the area of the texture pixels inside the subpatch to its total area. Blinn and Newell [Blin76] used this technique with a better 2×2 pyramidal (Bartlett) antialiasing filter suggested by Crow (see Sec. 2–16). Results, obtained by Barsky, by texture mapping a simple checkerboard pattern onto a β-spline patch used to construct a bottle, are shown in Fig. 5–41.

Conceptually, the Catmull subdivision algorithm starts with the surface patch in object space and transforms in two directions, one into image space and one into texture space. An example serves to further illustrate the technique.

Example 5–7   Texture Subdivision Algorithm

Again, consider the surface patch formed from the octant of the unit sphere, as shown in Fig. 5–40b, and the simple grid texture pattern shown in Fig. 5–40a. The surface patch is to be rotated about the y-axis by $-45°$ and then about the x-axis by $35°$ and displayed on a 32×32 raster, using an orthographic projection (see Fig. 5–42a). The simple grid texture pattern is rasterized at a resolution of 64×64, with each line assumed to be one pixel wide, as shown in Fig. 5–42b.

First the patch is subdivided, then transformed into image space, with the object space origin corresponding to the center of the 32×32 raster. Figure 5–42a shows that four subdivisions are required before a subpatch covers only a single pixel center. This subpatch is rectangular in image space and is defined by parameters $0 \leq \theta \leq \pi/32$, $59\pi/64 \leq \phi \leq \pi/2$ in object space.

Recalling the inverse mapping functions from $\theta\phi$ object space to uv texture space from Ex. 5–6, i.e.

$$u = \frac{\theta}{\pi/2} \qquad v = \frac{\pi/2 - \phi}{\pi/4}$$

Figure 5–41   Texture pattern mapped to a smooth β-spline defined bottle. (Courtesy of Brian Barsky).

yields the corners of the subpatch in texture space. Specifically, in texture space the vertices of the subpatch are

$$\theta = 0, \quad \phi = \frac{\pi}{2} \quad \rightarrow \quad u = 0, \quad v = 0$$

$$\theta = 0, \quad \phi = \frac{59\pi}{64} \quad \rightarrow \quad u = 0, \quad v = \frac{1}{16}$$

$$\theta = \frac{\pi}{32}, \quad \phi = \frac{59\pi}{64} \quad \rightarrow \quad u = \frac{1}{16}, \quad v = \frac{1}{16}$$

$$\theta = \frac{\pi}{32}, \quad \phi = \frac{\pi}{2} \quad \rightarrow \quad u = \frac{1}{16}, \quad v = 0$$

As shown in Fig. 5–42b, this is a square in texture space. On a 0 to 64 raster, $1/16$ corresponds to 4 raster units, as shown in Fig. 5–42b. The other subdivisions are also shown in Fig. 5–42b.

The intensity of the pixel in image space is obtained by averaging the intensities of the pixels in the subdivided texture space. The diffuse reflection component is scaled by this factor. From Fig. 5–42b there are seven black pixels in the 4×4 subdivision. Thus, the intensity of the displayed pixel in image space (Fig. 5–42a) is $7/16$ on a scale of 0 to 1.

One of the advantages of the Catmull subdivision algorithm is that it does not require knowledge of the inverse transformation from image space to object space, or the depth (z value) of the subpatch in image space. However, one of the disadvantages is that the subpatch may not precisely cover a single pixel in image space (see Fig. 5–42a). Frequently, the depth (z value) is available from the visible surface algorithm. The inverse transformation is determined by saving the three-dimensional viewing and object-to-image space transformations prior to projection onto the image plane. Consequently, the precise area covered by a pixel in image space is transformed to texture space. The procedure is to transform the pixel area from image space to the surface in object space, and

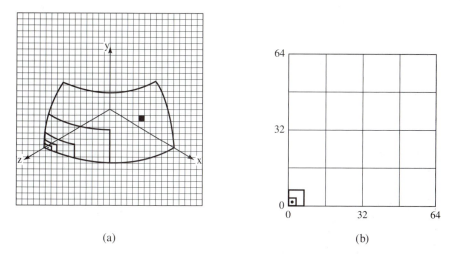

(a)   (b)

Figure 5–42 Texture mapping by patch subdivision. (a) Surface; (b) texture.

then to texture space. The intensity of the pixel in image space is determined by averaging the intensity of the pixels covered by that area in texture space. The diffuse component in the illumination model is then scaled by this factor. Other more sophisticated antialiasing rules may, of course, be used. A simple example serves to illustrate the technique.

Example 5–8 Texture by Inverse Pixel Mapping

Again consider the surface patch formed from the octant of a unit sphere, as shown in Fig. 5–40b, and the simple grid texture problem rasterized at a 64×64 pixel resolution (see Fig. 5–42b). Again, the surface patch is to be rotated about the y-axis by $-45°$ and about the x-axis by $35°,$ and displayed on a 32×32 raster using an orthographic projection (see Fig. 5–42a).

Consider the intensity of the pixel at $P_x = 21$, $P_y = 15$ shown in Fig. 5–42a. Pixels are specified by their lower left hand corners. The pixel area is then specified by $21 \leq P_x \leq 22$ and $15 \leq P_y \leq 16$.

Assuming that the object space window that corresponds to the 32×32 raster in image space is $-1 \leq x' \leq 1$, $-1 \leq y' \leq 1$, yields

$$x' = \frac{P_x}{16} - 1 \qquad y' = \frac{P_y}{16} - 1$$

Recalling the equation for a unit sphere gives

$$z' = \sqrt{1 - (x'^2 + y'^2)}$$

where x', y', z' represent object space coordinates after application of the viewing transformation. The object space coordinates of the corners of the pixel on the surface of the patch are then

P_x	P_y	x'	y'	z'
21	15	0.3125	−0.0625	0.948
22	15	0.3750	−0.0625	0.925
22	16	0.3750	0	0.927
21	16	0.3125	0	0.950

The viewing transformation before projection onto the image plane and its inverse are

$$[T] = \begin{bmatrix} 0.707 & -0.406 & 0.579 & 0 \\ 0 & 0.819 & 0.574 & 0 \\ -0.707 & -0.406 & 0.579 & 0 \\ 0 & 0 & 0 & 1 \end{bmatrix} \quad [T]^{-1} = \begin{bmatrix} 0.707 & 0 & -0.707 & 0 \\ -0.406 & 0.819 & -0.406 & 0 \\ 0.579 & 0.574 & 0.579 & 0 \\ 0 & 0 & 0 & 1 \end{bmatrix}$$

Using the inverse of the viewing transformation yields the corners of the pixel on the surface patch in the original orientation. Specifically

$$[\,x \quad y \quad z \quad 1\,] = [\,x' \quad y' \quad z' \quad 1\,][T]^{-1}$$

and

P_x	P_y	x	y	z
21	15	0.795	0.493	0.341
22	15	0.826	0.479	0.296
22	16	0.802	0.532	0.272
21	16	0.771	0.545	0.329

Recalling that the parametric representation of the unit sphere is

$$x = \sin\theta \sin\phi$$
$$y = \cos\phi$$
$$z = \cos\theta \sin\phi$$

yields

$$\phi = \cos^{-1} y \qquad \phi = sin^{-1}\left(\frac{x}{\sin\phi}\right)$$

in parametric space. Recalling the mapping transformation from parametric space to texture space given in Ex. 5–6, i.e.

$$u = \frac{\theta}{\pi/2} \qquad v = \frac{\pi/2 - \phi}{\pi/4}$$

yields for the corners of the pixel area in texture space

P_x	P_y	ϕ	θ	u	v
21	15	60.50°	66.04°	0.734	0.656
22	15	61.34°	70.30°	0.781	0.636
22	16	57.88°	71.28°	0.792	0.714
21	16	56.99°	66.88°	0.743	0.734

The results are shown in Fig. 5–43, where the curved area is approximated by a quadrilateral.

The rasterized grid pattern passes through the left-hand edge of the pixel area. Again, several techniques can be used to determine the intensity of the display pixel (see Sec. 2–16). One simple technique is to use a weighted average of the intensities of the texture pixels whose centers are inside the display pixel boundaries. Here, the ratio of the 'black' texture pixels representing the grid to the total texture pixels with centers inside the display pixel is $5/18$. The intensity of the diffuse component of the illumination model is scaled by this factor.

Mapping Functions

The previous discussion illustrates the importance of mapping, thus the characteristics of the mapping or transformation are important. Heckbert [Heck86, 89] characterizes the affine, of which the linear transformation is a special case; the bilinear and the two-dimensional projection transformations generally used in texture mapping.

Affine mapping transformations include or are combinations of scales, rotations, translations and shears (see [Roge90a]). They preserve parallel lines and equispaced points along lines. With affine transformations, a triangle transforms into a triangle and a rectangle into a parallelogram. Examples of affine transformations are shown in Figs. 5–44b and 5–44c.

Bilinear mapping transformations are used in Gouraud and Phong shading (see Secs. 5–6 and 5–7). Bilinear mapping transformations map a square into a quadrilateral. The general form is

$$q(u, v) = (1 - u)(1 - v)P_{00} + u(1 - v)P_{10} + (1 - u)vP_{01} + P_{11}$$

where P_{ij} ($i = 0, 1; j = 0, 1$) are the corners of the quadrilateral in the transformed space, while $0 \leq u \leq 1$, $0 \leq v \leq 1$ define the unit square in parameter space, as shown in Fig. 5–44e. A bilinear mapping preserves vertical and

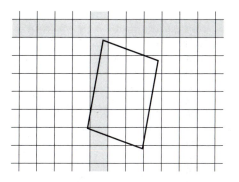

Figure 5–43 Display pixel in texture space.

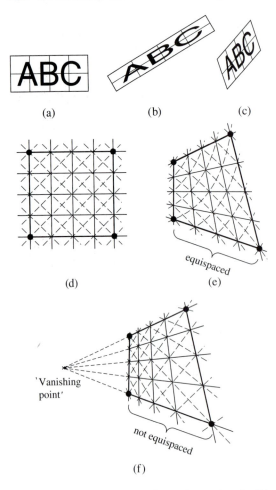

(a) (b) (c)

(d)

equispaced

(e)

'Vanishing point'

not equispaced

(f)

Figure 5–44 Mappings (transformations). (b), (c) Affine mappings of image in (a); (e) bilinear mapping of square in (d); note the curvature of the diagonals; (f) projective map of the square in (d); note the vanishing point, and that the diagonals are straight but diverge.

horizontal lines and equispaced points, but it does not preserve diagonal lines. Concatenated or combined bilinear transformations are biquadratic and not bilinear, as one might expect. The inverse of a bilinear mapping is unfortunately not single-valued.

Two-dimensional projective mapping, sometimes called perspective mapping, generally maps the line at infinity onto the real plane, where it becomes the line of all 'vanishing points' (see [Roge90a]). The projective mapping from (u, v) texture space to (x_s, y_s) image space is given by

$$x_s = \frac{au + bv + c}{gu + hv + i} \qquad y_s = \frac{du + ev + f}{gu + hv + i}$$

Its inverse, the mapping from image space (x_s, y_s) to texture space (u, v) has a similar form with different coefficients. Correct projective texture mapping requires deriving the coefficients a to i explicitly for each textured polygon [Heck89]. Heckbert and Moreton [Heck91] give a more efficient method that avoids computation of the coefficients. If the coefficients g and h are zero, the textured polygon is parallel to the plane of projection of the image. In this case the mapping is affine, and the division at each pixel is unnecessary.

Projective mappings preserve lines of all orientations, but in general they do not preserve equispaced points. Provided the mapping is not degenerate, both forward and inverse projective mappings are single valued except at 'vanishing points'. The inverse projective mapping is also a projective mapping. A projective mapping is shown in Fig. 5–44f.

Although bilinear mapping transformations are occasionally used in texture mapping [Catm80; Hour83], affine and projective mappings are preferred because they are easily inverted. Invertibility is particularly important for planar textures *viewed* with a perspective projection. If the mapping from texture space to object space is affine, then the compound mapping from texture space to image space is projective. When image space scanning is used (see below), projective mappings facilitate rendering of the texture.

Heckbert [Heck86, 89] classifies more recent two-dimensional texture mapping as scan in image space, scan in texture space and two-pass methods. Algorithmically, these are

image space scan

for each y
    for each x
        compute $u(x, y), v(x, y)$
        copy texture(u,v) to image(x,y)
    next x
next y

texture space scan

for each v
    for each u
        compute $x(u, v), y(u, v)$
        copy texture(u,v) to image(x,y)
    next u
next v

two-pass scan

pass one

for each v
    for each u
        compute $x(u, v)$
        copy texture(u,v) to temp(x,v)
    next u

```
      next v
      pass two
      for each x
          for each v
              compute y(x, v)
              copy temp(x,v) to image(x,y)
          next v
      next x
```

In an image space scan or inverse mapping algorithm, each pixel in image space, (x, y), is inverse mapped to texture space, (u, v); the character of the texture at that location determined; any antialiasing applied and the result written to the display.

In texture space scan or forward mapping algorithms, the texture is scanned in texture space (u, v) and the results mapped to image space using the concatenated texture to object and object to image space transformation. Complications arise because uniform sampling in texture space does not result, except for affine transformations, in uniform sampling in image space. This can cause 'holes' in the resulting image. Thus, adaptive sampling is required when nonaffine transformations are used.

Two-pass algorithms, which are particularly effective for affine and projective mappings, seek to simplify the two-dimensional mapping by decomposing it into two sequential one-dimensional mappings typically applied to first the rows and then the columns of an image [Catm80].

Two-part Texture Mapping

Bier and Sloan [Bier86] present a two-step texture mapping procedure for three-dimensional surfaces that predistorts the two-dimensional texture image by mapping it onto a simple three-dimensional surface, e.g., a plane, a cylinder, a sphere or a box, and then mapping the result onto the final three-dimensional surface. The procedure is also useful for environment mapping. Bier and Sloan call the initial mapping from texture space to the intermediate surface the S mapping. The mapping from the intermediate surface to the final three-dimensional surface is called the object, or O, mapping. Thus, the complete mapping is characterized by

$$(u, v) \quad \xrightarrow{\;S\;} \quad (x_i, y_i) \quad \xrightarrow{\;O\;} \quad (x_o, y_o, z_o)$$

$$\text{Texture space} \quad \longrightarrow \quad \text{Intermediate space} \quad \longrightarrow \quad \text{Object space}$$

The simplest of the intermediate surfaces is the plane. Reorienting (making coincident) the texture pattern to align it with and place it appropriately on an arbitrary skew plane in space, in general, requires three rotations and three translations (see [Roge90a]). In addition, the pattern must be scaled to cover the appropriate area of the plane. Ignoring the rotations and translations the transformation is

$$(u, v) \xrightarrow{\ S\ } (ax_i, dy_i)$$

where a and d are scale factors.

When the object is a surface of revolution, a cylinder as an intermediate surface is particularly useful. Representing the cylinder parametrically using (θ, h) yields the mapping from intermediate space to texture space

$$(\theta, h) \xleftarrow{\ S\ } (u, v) = [ar(\theta - \theta_0), d(h - h_0)] \quad -\pi < \theta < \pi$$

where a and d are scale factors and θ_0 and h_0 position the texture on the surface of the cylinder of radius r. A single line of discontinuity parallel to the cylinder axis is inherent in the mapping.

Bier and Sloan suggest using a stereographic projection from a plane to a hemisphere to map a texture onto a sphere as an intermediate surface. Because two hemisphere mappings are required, a discontinuity occurs along the equator. Circular or isotropic texture patterns are recommended. The stereographic projection is

$$(\theta, \phi) \xleftarrow{\ S\ } (u, v) = \left(\frac{2p}{C}, \frac{2q}{C} \right)$$

where
$$C = 1 + \sqrt{1 + p^2 + q^2}$$
$$p = \tan \phi \cos \theta$$
$$q = \tan \phi \sin \theta$$

and (θ, ϕ) are the equatorial and polar parametric variables for the sphere. p and q are the gnomonic projections that map circles in the plane to circles of latitude on the sphere.

Because a box is topologically equivalent to a sphere, using a box as an intermediate surface is particularly advantageous. As shown in Fig. 5–45, the box is first unwrapped and carefully positioned over the texture. Only areas of the texture *inside* the outline of the unwrapped box are mapped to the box and ultimately to the sculptured surface. An additional difficulty is that nonadjacent pieces of the texture are now adjacent both on the box surface and the final three-dimensional surface, potentially leading to a discontinuity. This problem is minimized if the texture fits entirely within the center rectangle, or within the four horizontally or three vertically adjacent rectangles of the unwrapped box. However, if this is possible, a cylinder might be a better choice for an intermediate surface. Alternatively, if the pattern is homogeneous and invariant with respect to 90° rotations, frequently it is possible to hide the seams by careful positioning of the box folds. Finally, if the texture pattern background is a solid color with only a few foreground patterns, then it may be possible to place the texture in the box so as to hide the edges. For environment mapping, the texture pattern *must* fit exactly in the unwrapped box.

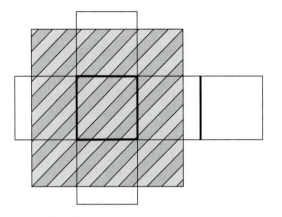

Figure 5–45 Shrink wrapping using a box as an intermediate surface.

Bier and Sloan consider four techniques for mapping the texture from the intermediate surface to the object, as shown in Fig. 5–46.

> *Reflected ray*: Trace a ray from the viewpoint to the object, and then trace the resulting reflected ray from the object to the intermediate surface; the result is the inverse object mapping.
>
> *Object normal*: Find the intersection of the normal to the object surface with the intermediate surface; again, this is the inverse object mapping.

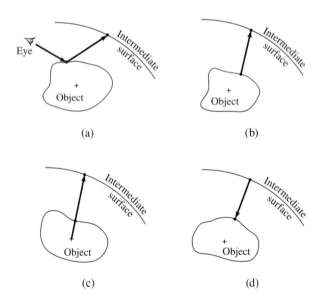

Figure 5–46 Intermediate to object mapping. (a) Reflected ray; (b) object normal; (c) object centroid; (d) intermediate surface normal.

Object centroid: Intersect the line defined by the centroid of the object and a point on the object surface with the intermediate surface; the inverse mapping results.

Intermediate surface normal: Trace a ray in the direction of the normal at a point on the intermediate surface to find its intersection with the object; this is a direct mapping — Peachey [Peac85] uses this mapping.

To be useful, a mapping between the intermediate surface and the object should be single valued, invertible and continuous. Ignoring the reflected ray method, because it is viewpoint dependent and thus not useful for mapping 'artwork' onto surfaces, Bier and Sloan use these criteria to characterize the other three methods, as shown in Fig. 5–47. From Fig. 5–47 five mappings are useful; shrinkwrap, centroid/box, intermediate surface normal (ISN)/box, centroid sphere and slide projector for roughly solids of revolution, approximately spherical objects and approximately planar shapes, respectively.

Bier and Sloan also analyze the five complete mappings from texture space through the intermediate surface to object space for distortion in the final image. In all cases, the results depend on the final object; for example, if the final object is a box of the same size and orientation as the intermediate box, then both box mappings produce no distortion. However, all the mappings can result in infinite distortion; for example, if the object is a cylinder, shrinkwrap produces infinite distortion at the ends. Using a sphere as representative of both a body of revolution and an arbitrary surface, Bier and Sloan conclude that ISN/Box transformations produce the least distortion.

Environment Mapping

Environment or reflection mapping was first introduced by Blinn and Newell [Blin76]. They assume that the scene environment is composed of objects and

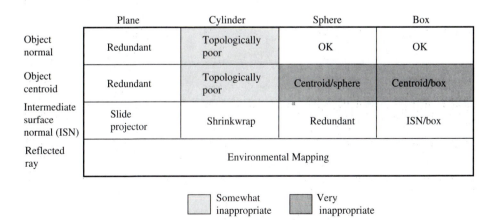

	Plane	Cylinder	Sphere	Box
Object normal	Redundant	Topologically poor	OK	OK
Object centroid	Redundant	Topologically poor	Centroid/sphere	Centroid/box
Intermediate surface normal (ISN)	Slide projector	Shrinkwrap	Redundant	ISN/box
Reflected ray	Environmental Mapping			

☐ Somewhat inappropriate   ■ Very inappropriate

Figure 5–47   Appropriateness of mapping combinations.

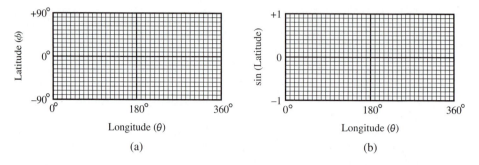

Figure 5–48   Bivariate environment coordinates. (a) Latitude–longitude; (b) Hall's variation, sin(latitude)–longitude.

lights that are far distant from the object being rendered. Effects caused by the object hiding parts of the environment are ignored. In effect, the environment is mapped onto the inside of a large sphere, with the rendered object at its center. The parametric equation of the surface of a sphere is a bivariate function, i.e., it is a two-dimensional function indexed by the coordinates (ϕ, θ), or latitude and longitude, as shown in Fig. 5–48a. Hall [Hall86] suggests using the sine of the latitude for the ordinate, along with the longitude for the indices (see Fig. 5–48b), to insure that equal areas on the sphere map to equal areas on the two-dimensional environment (texture) map, as shown in Fig. 5–48b.

The location in the environment is obtained by tracing a ray from the eye-point (center-of-projection) to the surface of the rendered object, reflecting the ray about the normal to the surface and tracing the reflected ray outward to the sphere, as shown in Fig. 5–49. An image from Blinn and Newell's original paper is given in Fig. 5–50 and Color Plate 8. If the normal direction is used rather than the direction of the reflected ray, the sphere is of infinite radius.

The farther an object is from the eyepoint (center-of-projection) and the larger the object, the greater the distortion relative to full ray tracing. However,

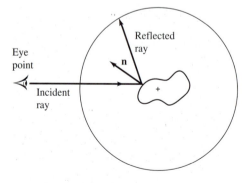

Figure 5–49   Environment mapping.

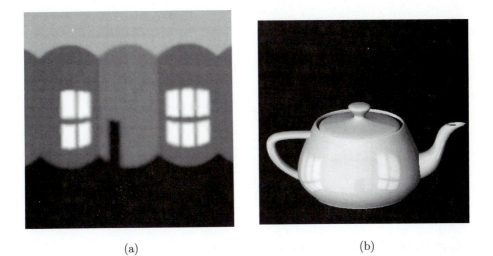

(a)   (b)

Figure 5–50   A teapot with windows. (a) The environment map; (b) reflection in the teapot (see also Color Plate 8). (Courtesy of Jim Blinn)..

by using an individual environment map for each object or group of neighboring objects in the scene distortion is significantly reduced. A spherical map frequently requires that an image be predistorted to obtain the desired image on an object or in a scene. Greene [Gree86] proposes mapping the environment to the inside of a large cube. In contrast to Bier and Sloan's cube, which is conceptual, Greene's cube is represented by six raster images. Here, one method for obtaining the environment map is to take six separate, appropriately oriented photographs of the scene, using a 90° flat field lens. These photographs are then projected onto the six inside faces of the cube. Perspective projections of computer-modeled scenes may also be used. Both Miller and Hoffman [Mill84] and Greene combine Lambertian diffuse and specular reflection in the environment map. Color Plate 9 shows the unwrapped cube projection of an environment map.

Planar objects present special difficulties because of the very slow change in direction of the reflected ray. A mirror image technique, as shown in Fig. 5–51, is used to overcome this problem. Specifically, the eyepoint, or center-of-projection, is reflected through the planer object and the direction of the ray through the mirror eyepoint, and the point on the surface of the planar object is used as the reflected ray direction. The environment map must contain an inverted image of the actual environment.

One-dimensional environment maps are also useful. For example, the colors of a sunset sky from red near the horizon to blue overhead can be used as the index into a table of intensities. Although environment mapping has limited capabilities compared to ray tracing, it is computationally much less expensive; thus, it is a useful technique.

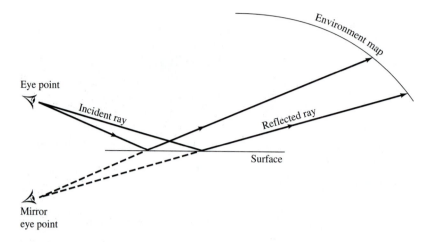

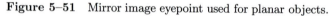

Figure 5–51 Mirror image eyepoint used for planar objects.

Bump Mapping

The preceding techniques add texture patterns to smooth surfaces. The resulting surfaces also appear smooth. To add the appearance of roughness to a surface, a photograph of a rough-textured pattern can be digitized and mapped to the surface. Unfortunately, the results are unsatisfactory because they look like rough-textured patterns painted on a smooth surface. The reason is that true rough-textured surfaces have a small random component in the surface normal and hence in the light reflection direction. Blinn [Blin78c] recognized this and developed a method for perturbing the surface normal. The results give a visual impression of rough-textured surfaces.

At any point on a surface $Q(u, v)$, the partial derivatives in the parameter directions u, v, i.e., Q_u and Q_v, lie in the plane tangent to the surface at that point. The cross-product of Q_u and Q_v defines the surface normal, n, at that point, i.e.

$$\mathbf{n} = \mathbf{Q}_u \otimes \mathbf{Q}_v$$

Blinn defined a new surface giving the visual appearance of having a rough texture by adding a perturbation function, $P(u, v)$, to the surface in the direction of the normal to the original surface. Thus, for any point on the new surface $Q(u, v)$ the position vector is

$$\mathbf{Q}'(u, v) = \mathbf{Q}(u, v) + P(u, v)\frac{\mathbf{n}}{|\mathbf{n}|}$$

The normal vector to the perturbed surface is then

$$\mathbf{n}' = \mathbf{Q}'_u \otimes \mathbf{Q}'_w$$

The partial derivatives Q'_u and Q'_v are

$$\mathbf{Q}'_u = \mathbf{Q}_u + P_u \frac{\mathbf{n}}{|\mathbf{n}|} + P \frac{\mathbf{n}_u}{|\mathbf{n}|}$$

$$\mathbf{Q}'_w = \mathbf{Q}_w + P_v \frac{\mathbf{n}}{|\mathbf{n}|} + P \frac{\mathbf{n}_w}{|\mathbf{n}|}$$

Because P is very small, i.e., a perturbation function, the last term may be neglected. Hence

$$\mathbf{Q}'_u \doteq \mathbf{Q}_u + P_u \frac{\mathbf{n}}{|\mathbf{n}|}$$

$$\mathbf{Q}'_w \doteq \mathbf{Q}_v + P_v \frac{\mathbf{n}}{|\mathbf{n}|}$$

The perturbed normal is then

$$\mathbf{n}' = \mathbf{Q}_u \otimes \mathbf{Q}_v + \frac{P_u(\mathbf{n} \otimes \mathbf{Q}_v)}{|\mathbf{n}|} + \frac{P_v(\mathbf{Q}_u \otimes \mathbf{n})}{|\mathbf{n}|} + \frac{P_u P_v(\mathbf{n} \otimes \mathbf{n})}{|\mathbf{n}|^2}$$

The first term is the normal to the unperturbed surface $\mathbf{n}$, and the last term is zero; therefore

$$\mathbf{n}' = \mathbf{n} + \frac{P_u(\mathbf{n} \otimes \mathbf{Q}_v)}{|\mathbf{n}|} + \frac{P_v(\mathbf{Q}_u \otimes \mathbf{n})}{|\mathbf{n}|}$$

where the last two terms represent the effect of the perturbation on the surface normal, and hence on the illumination model after scaling to unit length. Figure 5–52 illustrates the concept, using a one-dimensional analog. Notice that both the direction and magnitude of the normal vector are perturbed. Notice also that the normal vector, $\mathbf{n}'$, typically should be normalized before use in an illumination model.

Almost any function for which the derivatives are defined may be used as the texture perturbation function P. Blinn used a simple mathematically defined grid pattern, character bit maps, z-buffer patterns, and random hand-drawn patterns. An example, rendered by T. Van Hook, is shown in Fig. 5–53, where a texture pattern is added to bicubic surface patches. For nonmathematically defined patterns, the perturbation function is represented in a two-dimensional lookup table indexed by the parameters u, v. Intermediate values are obtained using bilinear interpolation of the values in the lookup table, and the derivatives P_u and P_v are determined using finite differences.

The rough texture effect is not invariant with scale changes of the object. In particular, if the object size is scaled by a factor of 2, then the magnitude of the normal vector is scaled by a factor of 4, while the perturbation to the normal vector is scaled by only a factor of 2. This results in smoothing the texture effect as the object size increases. However, scale changes due to object movement toward or away from the viewer in perspective space do not affect the texture scale.

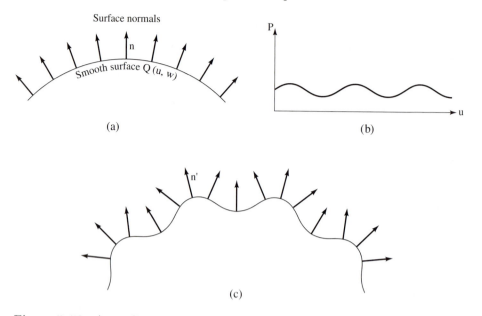

Figure 5–52   A one-dimensional analog of bump mapping. (a) Smooth surface; (b) bump mapping function; (c) perturbed surface normal.

The results of perturbation texture mapping also exhibit aliasing effects. However, if texture area averaging, as described above, or prefiltering antialiasing techniques are used, the result is to smooth out or reduce the texture effect. As pointed out by Blinn [Blin78c], the proper antialiasing technique is to compute the image at a higher-than-display resolution and postfilter, or average the results to obtain the lower resolution display images (see Sec. 2–16).

Procedural Textures

Peachey [Peac85] and Perlin [Perl85] independently developed solid or procedural textures. Solid or procedural textures define a texture function throughout a three-dimensional volume [Eber94]. The object to be textured is embedded in the three-dimensional texture volume. The textured surface of the object is the intersection of the object and the three-dimensional texture volume. Solid textures are coherent, i.e., there are no texture discontinuities because there are no texture joints on the object surface. Solid textures are also independent of the surface geometry or coordinate system.

Peachey gives an example of a wood grain texture built of coaxial alternating light and dark cylinders. The result is shown in Fig. 5–54. The axis of the block in Fig. 5–54 runs from left to right, with its left end rotated slightly upward and away from the viewer. The axis of the sphere in Fig. 5–54 is coincident with the axes of the coaxial cylinders defining the texture volume. Notice the lack of distortion at the poles of the sphere. Also, notice that in solid textures

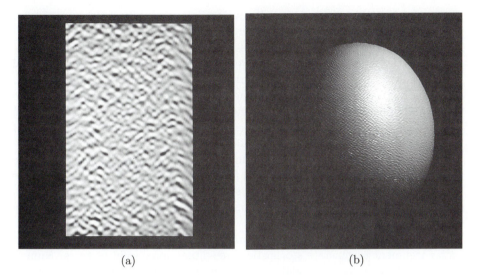

(a) (b)

Figure 5–53   Texture pattern mapped onto bicubic surface patches.   (a) Texture
pattern; (b) result. (Courtesy of T. Van Hook, Adage, Inc.).

aliasing is significantly reduced. However, texture aliasing can be a problem if
the object is distorted by perspective, is very distant or nearly parallel to the
viewing direction or contains high frequencies.

Assuming that the solid texture is defined throughout the texture volume,
the texture shade is obtained at any given point on the object surface by evaluating the texture function using the scene coordinates of the object surface point.

Three-dimensional solid texture functions can be obtained from two-dimensional texture images or functions by sweeping the two-dimensional texture function along a path in three space. Peachey [Peac85] uses an orthogonal projection
as the sweep function. He gives an example using a two-dimensional digitized

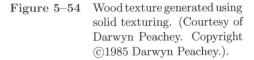

Figure 5–54   Wood texture generated using
solid texturing. (Courtesy of
Darwyn Peachey. Copyright
©1985 Darwyn Peachey.).

image. Interestingly, there are no discontinuities as a result of the 'mapping' of the two-dimensional image onto the three-dimensional surface.

Three-dimensional texture functions are also generated using Fourier synthesis ([Blin76; Scha80, 83; Gard84, 85; Peac85; Perl85]), i.e., a sum of sinusoidal functions of (x, y, z). Peachey uses Fourier synthesis to develop a marble texture. Specifically, the texture consists of numerous 'veins', e.g., thin 'cylinders', whose local direction is determined by two functions comprised of the sum of three sinusoids and whose radius is determined by a third sinusoid while the phases of the sinusoids are randomly specified. Gardner [Gard84, 85] used Fourier synthesized textures and quadric surfaces to model natural terrain and clouds. He also developed a 'translucency' modulation function incorporating a threshold value that 'blacked out' the texture below a certain value and varied it, e.g., linearly, above that value. Use of the modulation function allows the generation of wispy clouds and cloud edges.

Perlin [Perl85] used a *noise*() function which takes a three-dimensional vector as its argument to generate stochastic three-dimensional solid textures. Numerous *noise*() functions are possible. Desirable properties include rotational and translational invariance and a narrow frequency bandpass limit. Perlin's *noise*() function generates a pseudorandom value on an integer lattice. If a point in space is not coincident with a lattice point, cubic polynomial interpolation in three dimensions is used to obtain the value. Perlin uses the *noise*() function to create a number of simple 'random' solid textures. By adding a perturbation capability, *Dnoise*() , he achieves a result similar to bump mapping, as shown in Fig. 5–55 and Color Plate 10. Perlin also uses the *noise*() function to develop a pseudoturbulence function that is then used to generate solid texture fields that simulate marble, fire, clouds and bubbles. The corona of the sun, simulated with

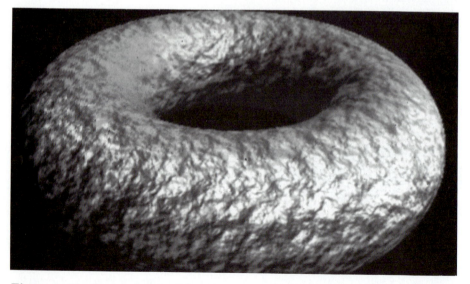

Figure 5–55   Bumpy donut solid texture, mapped using a perturbed *noise*() function (see also Color Plate 10). (Courtesy of Ken Perlin.).

a solid texture, is shown in Fig. 5–56 and Color Plate 11. The details of the turbulence function are given by Perlin [Perl85].

Texture Antialiasing

Aliasing in texture mapping is a serious problem, because silhouette edges and perspective can cause high frequency patterns in image space. Aliasing is a constant aspect of texture mapping. Figure 5–59a shows the results of point sampling a texture pattern, i.e., map the center of an image pixel to texture space and use the value of the nearest texture pixel to render the image space pixel. Catmull [Catm74] (see Sec. 4–8) recognized the problem in his curved surface patch subdivision algorithm. He used an unweighted average quadrilateral box filter. Blinn and Newell [Blin76] used a version of a Bartlett filter (see Sec. 2–16) formed by two-pixel-wide overlapping distorted pyramids. Feibush et al. [Feib80] used a more elaborate (and expensive) filter. For each pixel in image space they

> Find the bounding box of the filter after centering it on the pixel; the filter function may be a box, cone, cylinder, Gaussian, etc.
>
> Transform the bounding box to texture space, approximate the sides of the resulting curvilinear quadrilateral by straight lines and find the bounding box for the quadrilateral.
>
> Map all the pixels inside the bounding box to image space.
>
> Form a weighted average of the mapped texture pixels using a lookup table; the lookup table, which can contain any filter function, is indexed by the location within the pixel.

Gangnet et al. [Gang82] subdivide uniformly in image space rather than in

Figure 5–56 Corona of the sun, using a pseudoturbulence function (see also Color Plate 11). (Courtesy of Ken Perlin.).

texture space, but otherwise their algorithm is similar to the Feibush, Levoy and Cook algorithm.

Greene and Heckbert [Gree86] propose an antialiasing texture filter based on an elliptical weighted average (EWA), and Heckbert [Heck86, 89] suggests using a pyramid data structure for increased efficiency. Because of its efficiency and quality the EWA filter is presented here in some detail.

The EWA filter is an example of a space variant filter, because the shape of the filter varies as it moves across the image. Space variant filters are required when good antialiasing is required and when nonaffine mappings are used. Most texture filters consider square pixels. Nonlinear mappings, e.g., perspective projections, seriously distort square pixels, and significantly increase the area covered by some pixels when mapped to texture space. However, circular regions in image space transform approximately into ellipses in texture space (except near vanishing points, where they transform into parabolas or hyperbolas). Hence, if pixels in image space are approximated by circles, only a single known shape need be considered in texture space even though the size, orientation and eccentricity of the ellipse may change. The EWA filter algorithm is then

> Letting (u, v) denote displacements from the center of the transformed pixel in texture space, inverse map the corners of the square pixel in image space to texture space.

> Use the corner points in texture space to estimate $\partial u/\partial x$, $\partial u/\partial y$, $\partial v/\partial x$, $\partial v/\partial y$, the partial derivatives of u, v in texture space with respect to changes in x, y in image space (see Fig. 5–57).

> Calculate the origin-centered ellipse, that is, the size, orientation and

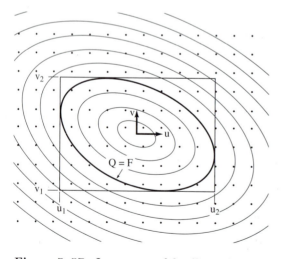

Figure 5–57 Isocontours of the elliptical paraboloid and bounding box around $Q = F$. The dots indicate texture space pixel centers.

eccentricity, in texture space corresponding to the circular pixel in image space (see Fig. 5–57)

$$Q(u, v) = Au^2 + Buv + Cv^2 = F$$

where
$$A = \left(\frac{\partial v}{\partial x}\right)^2 + \left(\frac{\partial v}{\partial y}\right)^2$$

$$B = -2\left(\frac{\partial u}{\partial x}\frac{\partial v}{\partial x} + \frac{\partial u}{\partial y}\frac{\partial v}{\partial y}\right)$$

$$C = \left(\frac{\partial u}{\partial x}\right)^2 + \left(\frac{\partial u}{\partial y}\right)^2$$

and $Q(u, v)$ is an isocontour of a concave upward elliptical paraboloid.

Form the bounding box of $Q = F$ where

$$F = \left(\frac{\partial u}{\partial x}\frac{\partial v}{\partial x} + \frac{\partial u}{\partial y}\frac{\partial v}{\partial y}\right)^2$$

Use the value of Q for the texture pixel centers, satisfying $Q < F$ as the index into a lookup table generated from the filter function.

Heckbert and Greene [Gree86] use a Gaussian filter function, $f(Q) = e^{-\alpha Q}$. They efficiently calculate Q using finite differences. Heckbert [Heck89] notes that an EWA filter with Gaussian filter function is an elliptical Gaussian resampling filter. However, in the original formulation there is no reconstruction term, hence it is a decimation filter which is good if the mapping scales the texture down but poor if it scales it up. He points out that with a simple change the EWA filter becomes a unified resampling filter. Specifically

$$Q(u, v) = A'u^2 + Buv + C'v^2 = F'$$

where
$$A' = A + 1$$
$$C' = C + 1$$
$$F' = A'C' - \frac{B^2}{4}$$

The shape of the filter function is critical. The ideal one-dimensional low-pass filter function is $\text{sinc}(x) = \sin(\pi x)/\pi x$. However, it has infinite width and is thus impractical. Consequently, finite impulse filters are normally used. Examples are a box, a triangle, cubic B-splines and truncated Gaussians, as shown in Fig. 5–58.

An example of a checkerboard in perspective texture mapped using an EWA filter with a Gaussian filter function and a pyramid data structure is shown in Fig. 5–59d. For comparison, the same checkerboard is point sampled and shown

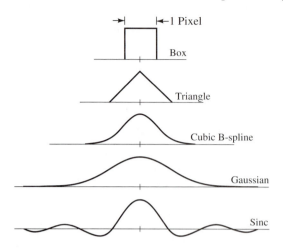

Figure 5–58 Two-dimensional cross sections of finite width impulse filter functions compared to the ideal sinc function.

in Fig. 5–59a. This is an excellent test of texture antialiasing. Notice how point sampling breaks up as the horizon is approached.

In the checkerboard pattern shown in Fig. 5–59b, image space pixels near the horizon map to ellipses with very high eccentricities that cover large areas, e.g., ellipses that are only a few pixels wide and several thousand pixels long in texture space. The result is excessive computational expense. Using a texture image pyramid data structure reduces the computational expense. An image pyramid consists of a sequence of texture images of decreasing resolution, as shown in Fig. 5–60. The decreased resolution images are created by successively reducing the original image resolution, $m \times n$, by a factor of two using 2×2 pixel averaging. The resolution of a given image in the pyramid is thus $m/2^k \times n/2^k$, where k is the resolution level with $k = 0$ representing the original texture image. There are $\log_2 \left(\min(m, n) \right) + 1$ pyramid levels.

Heckbert [Heck89] suggests selecting a pyramid level where the minor axis of the ellipse in texture space covers at least three and less than six pixels. Defining the eccentricity of the ellipse as $e = a/b$, where a is the semimajor axis and b the semiminor axis, Heckbert suggests that if $e > 20$ to 30, then the ellipse is redefined (fattened) so that the minor axis covers at least 3 to 6 pixels. The effect of fattening the ellipse is to blur the image and reduce the filtering time.

Mipmapping (Image Pyramids)

Williams [Will83] developed a texture mapping technique he called mipmapping (from the Latin *multum in parvo*, many things in a small place). Mipmapping generates many images of decreasing resolution from the original image by averaging multiple pixels from the higher resolution image, to obtain a lower resolution image. The original resolution image and the averaged lower resolution

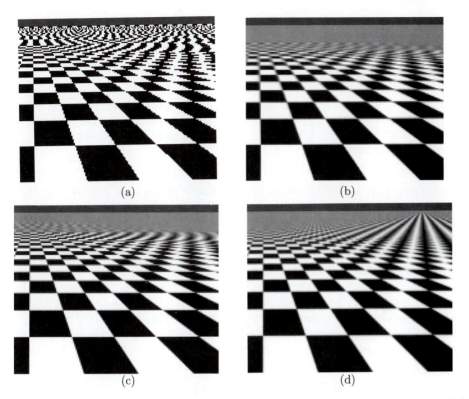

Figure 5–59   Checkerboard in perspective texture mapped. (a) Point sampled; (b) mipmapped (trilinear interpolation); (c) summed area table; (d) EWA filter on a pyramid. (Courtesy of Paul Heckbert).

images are stored in multiple tables. For example, if the resolution is reduced by a factor of two in each direction, then four pixels are averaged to obtain a single pixel in the next lower resolution image. The effect is the same as convolution with a square box filter. The process is represented schematically in Fig. 5–61. Stacking the mipmaps in three space forms a pyramid.

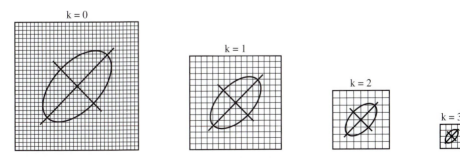

Figure 5–60   A four level image pyramid in texture space.

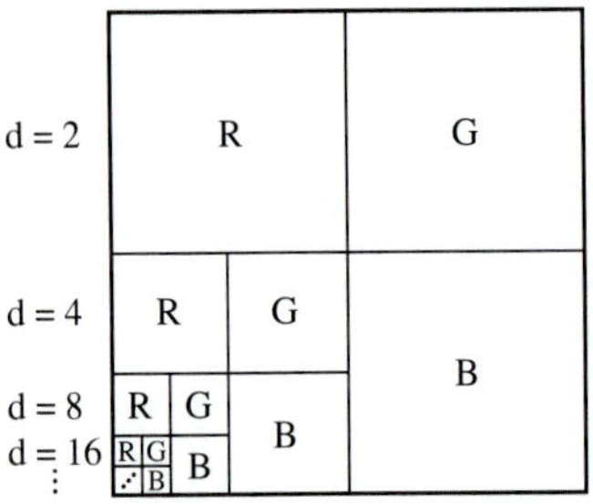

d = 2   R   G

d = 4   R   G

d = 8   R | G   B

d = 16 R|G   B

Figure 5–61   Representation of mipmapping resolution reduction. R,G,B are the red, green and blue components of the image.

Assuming that a pixel covers an approximately planar area in screen space, then a square pixel transforms into a quadrilateral in texture space. Except near singularities, e.g., vanishing points, the quadrilateral is approximately a parallelogram. The size of the approximate parallelogram is given by the partial derivatives $\partial u/\partial x$, $\partial u/\partial y$, $\partial v/\partial x$ and $\partial v/\partial y$. The partial derivatives are approximated by finite differences between the u, v values of adjacent pixels.

Standard mipmaps only properly filter square areas. Thus, the quadrilateral in texture space must be approximated by a square. Choosing the square too small leads to aliasing, too large leads to blurring. Erring on the side of blurring, Heckbert [Heck83] chooses d, the side of the approximating square area in the original texture space, to be

$$d = \max\left(\sqrt{u_x^2 + v_x^2}, \sqrt{u_y^2 + v_y^2}\right)$$

which is the maximum side length of the approximate quadrilateral. d is used to select which of the mipmaps is referenced, and (u, v) selects which pixel within the mipmap is used. Because neither u, v nor d are normally integers, four pixels from each of the two mipmaps at the ends of the intervals in which u, v and d lie are read. Trilinear interpolation is then used to obtain the texture value. Consequently, mipmapping is sometimes called trilinear interpolation.[†] When $d \leq 1$, bilinear interpolation in the largest mipmap is used. The memory requirements of mipmaps is $1 + 1/4 + 1/16 + 1/64 + \cdots = 4/3$ that of the original texture image. Mipmapping is probably the most widely used texture filtering method because it yields acceptable results, is fast and requires little additional memory. An example is shown in Fig. 5–59b.

Summed Area Tables

Pointing out that mipmapping assumes a symmetric square texture region, Crow [Crow84] extended Williams' technique to rectangular regions and reduced the number of tables to one using a summed area table. The basic idea for a summed area table is shown in Fig. 5–62. To calculate the upper right white area for the

---

[†]Mipmapping is currently supported in the Open GL graphics library [Neid93] and available in some three-dimensional graphics hardware.

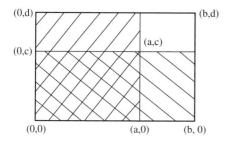

Figure 5–62   The principle behind the summed area table.

rectangle in Fig. 5–62 first calculate the area of the complete rectangle, bd, then subtract the two single cross-hatched areas, bc and ad, and add back in the double cross-hatched area, ac, after noticing that it has been subtracted twice, i.e., Area $= bd - bc - ad + ac$.

Each entry in a summed area table represents the sum of the intensities of all texture pixels in a rectangle defined by the lower left corner of the image $(0,0)$ and the pixel of interest. Dividing by the number of pixels in the rectangle gives the average intensity. Crow prefilters the texture image, using a box filter function prior to summing and storing the intensities. The most efficient technique for creating the summed area table is to invert the method for extracting the areas from the table, i.e., to get the sum for a pixel add the sums for the pixel below and the pixel to the left, and then subtract the sum for the pixel below and to the left. Summed area tables typically require four times the memory needed for the original texture image. If the inverse mapped image pixel is not a rectangle approximately aligned with the texture pattern edges, the simple summed area table results in blurring of the image. Glassner [Glas86] developed techniques for correcting this effect. Ranking the texture filters discussed here from fastest and lowest image quality to slowest with highest image quality yields point sampling, mipmapping, summed area tables and the EWA.

5–13   Stochastic Models

Stochastic, frequently called fractal, modeling systems as used in computer graphics are only approximations to the fractal modeling systems originally discovered by Mandelbrot[†] [Mand77]. Mandelbrot's definition requires statistical self-similarity at any resolution. Typical computer graphics fractal models exhibit approximate statistical self-similarity. Self-similarity is best explained using an example such as the Koch snow flake. Referring to Fig. 5–63, each side of the original image is replaced with an appropriately scaled replica of a side of the original image. A fractal, or more precisely a fractal set, has a fractal dimension (Hausdorff–Besicovitch dimension, [Bese37]) that is more than its topological

---

[†]See [Mand82] for a discussion of Mandelbrot's objections.

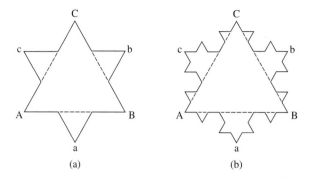

Figure 5–63   Koch snowflake: each side is replaced by a properly scaled replica of a side of the original image, e.g., AaB.[†]

dimension. For example, a fractal Brownian motion path on a plane has a fractal dimension of two, while its topological dimension is one because it is a curve. Fractal dimensions can be noninteger; most fractal sets that occur in nature have noninteger fractal dimensions. For example, if the outline of an island or a continent is measured with an incrementally decreasing length measuring stick (1000, 100, 10, 1, -0.1, 0.01, 0.001 mile long), the length of the measured coast line increases without bound, indicating that its fractal dimension is greater than one (actually, it is about 1.3). Similar results are obtained for rivers, sky lines, blood vessels, tree branches, etc.

A fractal curve is generated by recursively dividing a line, as shown in Fig. 5–64. Starting with a line segment between zero and one on the abscissa, x, the midpoint is perturbed in the y direction by an amount determined by a random real function. The midpoint of each successive line segment is recursively perturbed in a similar fashion, until the length of the line segment falls below some specified value. It is critical that R is a random function, and not a random variable or random number generator. A random function gives repeatable results, consequently it generates a result that is self-similar, or approximately self-similar. A convenient way to generate a random function is to store it in a lookup table, e.g., a *pseudo*random number generator (which is repeatable given the same seed) or a Gaussian distribution can be stored in the lookup table. Smooth 'fractal' curves are obtained by passing a cubic spline (see [Roge90a]) through the perturbed points, or by using the perturbed points as the vertices of the polygon defining a B-spline curve (see [Roge90a]).

Fractal surfaces are typically generated from stochastically defined polygonal or bipolynomial defined surfaces. The technique was originally applied to rough surface definition in computer graphics by Carpenter [Carp80] and

---

[†]To construct the image in Fig. 5–63, start with an equilateral triangle: divide each side into thirds; from each $1/3$ point swing arcs of radius $1/3$ the length of the original side; connect the intersection of the arcs with the $1/3$ points on the side. Recursively repeat for each of the new sides. Do a center opening in the same manner.

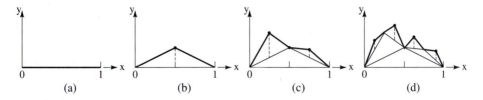

Figure 5–64   Generation of a fractal line.

Fournier and Fussell [Four80] and subsequently in a combined paper [Four82]. Fractal surfaces have been used to render a number of natural surfaces, e.g., terrain [Mill86; Musg89; Szel89; Prus93], trees [Oppe86; Prus86; Vien89], stones [Miya90], marine organisms [Kaan91, 93] and clouds [Stam91; Saka93], to name a few. The fractal technique is based on original work done by Mandelbrot [Mand77].

A polygonal fractal surface is obtained by recursively subdividing an original polygon, as shown in Fig. 5–65. One technique is to define the midpoints of each of the sides of the polygon, and then to perturb the location of these points perpendicular to the plane (or approximate plane) of the original polygon using a random function for each individual point. The center of the polygon is similarly perturbed. Figure 5–65 illustrates the result; notice that neither the original polygon nor any derivative polygon need be planar.

One advantage of fractal surfaces is that they are *infinitely* subdividable. Consequently, any arbitrary level of detail is obtainable. Further, the level of detail can be made dependent on the location of the observer; the closer the observer, the greater the detail. When the observer is far away, the level of detail is reduced and considerable processing is saved. Any appropriate visible surface algorithm and illumination model is used to render the fractal surface. However, the number of subsurfaces increases at a greater than linear rate. Hence, the number of subdivisions and the level of detail is a compromise, or excessive computational requirements result.

A typical result, rendered by Kajiya [Kaji83] using an opaque visible surface ray tracing algorithm, is shown in Color Plate 12. The scene in Color Plate 12a contains 16,384 fractal triangles, and that in Color Plate 12b contains 262,144 fractal triangles. Notice the self-shadowing in the images.

Original polygon

Subdivided fractal surface

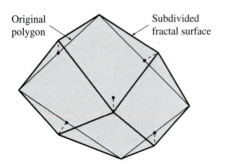

Figure 5–65   Fractal surface subdivision.

5–14   A Global Illumination Model
Using Ray Tracing

An illumination model is designed to determine the intensity of light reflected to an observer's eye at each point (pixel) in an image. The illumination model can be invoked either locally or globally. Invoked locally, only light incident from a light source(s) and the surface orientation is considered by the illumination model in determining the intensity of the light reflected to the observer's eye. Invoked globally, the light that reaches a point by reflection from, or transmission through, other objects in the scene, as well as light incident from any light sources, is also considered in determining the intensity of the light reflected from a point to the observer. Using a global illumination model has significant implications; Fig. 5–66 illustrates some of the effects.

The sphere and the triangular and rectangular blocks shown in Fig. 5–66 are assumed to be opaque and to have surfaces capable of a high degree of specular reflection. An observer located at O looking at the point labeled 1 on the sphere sees not only the sphere but also the triangular block at point 2. The triangular block, which is otherwise obscured by the rectangular block, is thus visible because it is reflected in the sphere. Point 5 on the triangular block is even more indirectly visible at point 3 on the sphere. Here, the image of the triangle at point 5 is reflected from the *back* of the rectangular block at point 4, onto the surface of the sphere at point 3 and then to the observer. Point 5 on the triangle is also visible to the observer at point 1′, with only one reflection from the surface of the sphere. Hence, multiple images of the triangular block are observed reflected in the sphere. Since only one reflection is involved, the image centered around point 1 is reversed. In contrast, the image centered around point 3 is not reversed, since two reflections occur. This second image is also less intense. Finally, the back of the rectangular block is visible as a reflected image in the sphere, even though it does not receive any light directly from the source. It is illuminated by ambient light, and by light reflected from the other objects in the scene.

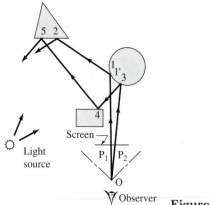

Figure 5–66   Global illumination.

From this discussion it should be clear that the normal backface culling operation commonly used by visible surface algorithms cannot be used with a global illumination model. An initial priority sort to determine visible faces also cannot be used. These two considerations eliminate all the visible surface algorithms discussed in Chapter 4, *except* ray tracing. Consequently, global illumination models are implemented as part of ray tracing visible surface algorithms, or in the context of radiosity models (see Sec. 5–17).

Whitted [Whit80] and Kay [Kay79a, 79b] originally implemented ray tracing algorithms that utilized global illumination models. Whitted's algorithm, which is more general, has been extensively used and extended. Synthetic images generated by Whitted [Whit80], Potmesil [Potm81, 82] and Barr [Barr84] with the Whitted algorithm or extensions of the algorithm are shown in Color Plates 13, 14 and 15. These images illustrate reflection, transparency, refraction, shadows and texture effects.

The Potmesil extension replaces the traditional pinhole camera used in computer graphics with a more realistic model that approximates the lens and aperture characteristics of a real camera. The model considers the effects of depth of field, focus, lens distortion and filtering. In animation sequences it provides a fade-in, fade-out capability. The technique is a two-step process.

The first step uses a traditional pinhole camera ray tracing algorithm to produce a point sampled image. In addition to the usual RGB intensities at each pixel, z depth and visible surface information are also retained. The second step, acting as a postprocessor, invokes the finite aperture camera model. Each sample point is converted to a circle of confusion using the laws of geometric optics. The size and intensity distribution for the circle of confusion are determined by the z value at the sample point, the characteristics of the lens and the lens aperture. The intensity at a given pixel is determined by summing the intensities of all the circles of confusion overlapping that pixel. Results are shown in Color Plate 14.

The illumination model used by Whitted retains the ambient, Lambertian diffuse and Phong specular reflection terms of the local illumination model given in Eq. (5 – 7). The global specular reflection and the transmission terms are based on the model shown in Fig. 5–67. Here, the incoming ray being traced, $\mathbf{v}$, reaches the surface at the point Q. At Q the ray is both reflected in the direction r and, if the surface is transparent, refracted in the direction p. I_t is the intensity incoming to the surface at Q along the p direction that is refracted through the surface and reaches an observer located in the direction $-\mathbf{v}$.

Similarly, I_s is the intensity of the specularly reflected light incoming along the direction $-r$ that is reflected at Q, and that also reaches the observer located in the direction $-\mathbf{v}$. $\mathbf{n}$ is the surface normal at Q, $\mathbf{L}_j$ is the direction of the jth light source, S and R are the local sight and reflection vectors and η is the index of refraction of the media. Here, n is the Phong spatial distribution value for specularly reflected light (see Sec. 5–3). The intensity reaching the observer I is then

$$I = k_a I_a + k_d \sum_j I_{l_j} (\widehat{\mathbf{n}} \cdot \widehat{\mathbf{L}}_j) + k_s \sum_j I_{l_j} (\widehat{\mathbf{S}} \cdot \widehat{\mathbf{R}}_j)^n + k_s I_s + k_t I_t \qquad (5-16)$$

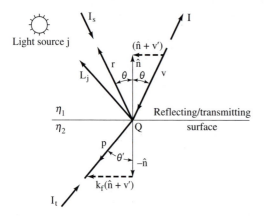

Figure 5–67 Specular reflection and transmission effects for the Whitted global illumination model.

where k_a, k_d, k_s and k_t are the ambient, diffuse and specular reflection coefficients, and k_t is the transmission coefficient. Whitted holds these reflection coefficients constant. However, any of the previously discussed illumination models may be used to determine their variation with incidence angle and wavelength. The first and second summation terms in Eq. $(5-16)$ represent the local diffuse and specular reflection from the light sources.

In contrast to the previous opaque visible surface ray tracing algorithm discussed in Sec. 4–20, the visibility calculations for the global illumination model do not end at the first intersection. Here, the incoming ray, v, is assumed to be reflected from the surface in the direction r and transmitted through the surface in the direction p, as shown at point Q in Fig. 5–67; thus two additional rays are generated at point Q. These two rays are traced to determine their intersections with objects in the scene. The process is repeated until none of the rays intersects any object in the scene. The process, illustrated in Fig. 5–68a for single surface ray intersections, is easily represented using the tree structure shown in Fig. 5–68b. Each node of the tree represents a ray surface intersection. At each node of the tree two subbranches are generated. The right-hand branch is due to refraction, and the left is due to reflection of the ray at the surface. Notice that a branch terminates when the ray leaves the scene.

At each surface ray intersection, the directions of the reflected and transmitted rays are obtained using the laws of geometric optics. In particular, the reflected ray, r, and the incident ray, v, lie in the same plane and make equal angles with the surface normal, n, (see Sec. 5–4). The transmitted ray obeys Snell's law of refraction (see Sec. 5–10). In the context of the present model and notation, the directions of r and p are given by

$$r = \mathbf{v}' + 2\hat{\mathbf{n}}$$

$$\mathbf{p} = k_f\left(\hat{\mathbf{n}} + \mathbf{v}'\right) - \hat{\mathbf{n}}$$

where v', k_f and k_η are

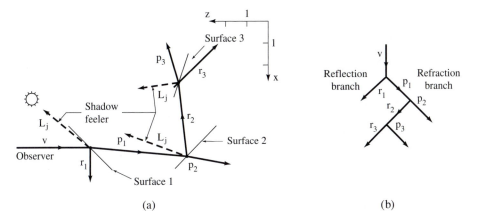

Figure 5–68   Ray tracing surface reflections and refractions. (a) Ray surface intersections; (b) ray tree.

$$v' = \frac{v}{|v \cdot \hat{n}|}$$

$$k_f = \left(k_\eta^2 |v'|^2 - |v' + \hat{n}|^2 \right)^{-1/2}$$

$$k_\eta = \frac{\eta_2}{\eta_1}$$

with k_η the ratio of refractive indices and $\hat{n}$ the unit normal vector in the direction
of the incoming ray. If the denominator of k_f is imaginary, then total internal
reflection occurs and I_t is assumed zero.

Determining the intensity at each ray–surface intersection requires traversing
the ray tracing tree in the reverse direction. The illumination model is applied
recursively at each node of the tree. The intensity at each node of the tree is
attenuated by the distance between the surface intersection points before being used as input for the next node up the tree. When the tree is completely
traversed, the resulting intensity is displayed for that pixel.

Theoretically, the ray tracing tree is infinitely deep. In addition to being
terminated when all rays leave the scene, the tree may be terminated when the
intensity at a node falls below a specified value, or when the allocated storage
is exceeded.

Figure 5–69 shows the effect of internal reflection for a closed transparent
object. The rays specularly reflected from the inside surfaces of the object are
trapped within the object and are eventually absorbed. Hence, they cannot
contribute to the light intensity perceived by the observer. However, at each
ray–surface intersection a transmitted ray, p, is generated. These rays escape
the object and may directly or indirectly reach the observer. Thus, they must
be traced.

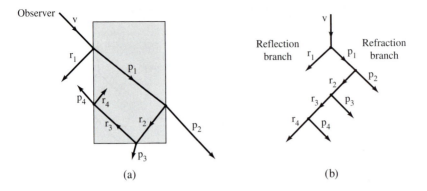

Figure 5–69   Internal reflection for transparent objects. (a) Ray surface intersections; (b) ray tree.

If shadows are also included in the algorithm, then at each ray–surface intersection shadow feelers in the direction of each light source, L_j, are generated. If a shadow feeler intersects an object before reaching the light source, then that ray–surface intersection lies in shadow with respect to that light source. The contribution of that light source to the local diffuse and specular reflection at the point is then attenuated (see Sec. 5–11). If the intervening surface is opaque, no light reaches the surface. If the intervening surface is transparent, the illumination characteristics of the surface are used to attenuate the light. Shadow feelers are shown in Fig. 5–68.

Example 5–9   Global Illumination and Ray Tracing

Consider the simple two-dimensional single plane scene in Fig. 5–68a. The planes are normal to the plane of the paper, which is assumed to be the xz plane. The observer is located at infinity on the positive z-axis at $x = 5$. A single point light source is located at $x = 3$, $z = 10$. The surfaces are defined using the plane equations, i.e.

$$\text{Surface 1:}\quad x + z - 12.5 = 0 \quad 4 \le x \le 6$$

$$\text{Surface 2:}\quad x - z - 2 = 0 \quad 4 \le x \le 6$$

$$\text{Surface 3:}\quad x - 3z + 9 = 0 \quad 1 \le x \le 3$$

The illumination characteristics for each surface are

Surface 1: $k_{a_1} = 0.15, k_{d_1} = 0.15, k_{s_1} = 0.8, k_{t_1} = 0.5, k_{\eta_1} = \dfrac{1}{1.1}$

Surface 2: $k_{a_2} = 0.15, k_{d_2} = 0.15, k_{s_2} = 0.8, k_{t_2} = 0.5, k_{\eta_2} = 1.1$

Surface 3: $k_{a_3} = 0.15, k_{d_3} = 0.15, k_{s_3} = 0.8, k_{t_3} = 0, k_{\eta_3} = 1.1$

The intensity of the ambient light is $I_a = 1.0$, and the intensity of the light source is $I_l = 10$. The Phong spatial distribution value for specularly reflected light is $n = 50$ for each surface.

A ray is fired from the observer toward the scene. The resulting ray tree is shown in Fig. 5–68b. The ray first intersects surface 1. Noting that the equation of the ray before it intersects the surface is $x = 5$ and substituting into the surface equation yields

$$x + z - 12.5 = 5 + z - 12.5 = 0 \quad \rightarrow \quad z = 7.5$$

Thus, the intersection of the ray and the surface, which represents the first node on the ray tree, occurs at $x_1 = 5, z_1 = 7.5$. At that point, the unit normal to the surface is

$$\widehat{\mathbf{n}}_1 = \frac{\mathbf{i}}{\sqrt{2}} + \frac{\mathbf{k}}{\sqrt{2}}$$

Determining the refracted and reflected rays yields

$$\mathbf{v}_1 = -\mathbf{k}$$

and
$$\mathbf{v}_1' = \frac{\mathbf{v}_1}{|\mathbf{v}_1 \cdot \widehat{\mathbf{n}}_1|} = \frac{-\mathbf{k}}{\left| (-\mathbf{k}) \cdot \left(\dfrac{\mathbf{i}}{\sqrt{2}} + \dfrac{\mathbf{k}}{\sqrt{2}} \right) \right|} = -\sqrt{2}\,\mathbf{k}$$

The direction of the reflected ray is

$$\mathbf{r}_1 = \mathbf{v}_1' + 2\widehat{\mathbf{n}}_1 = -\sqrt{2}\,\mathbf{k} + 2\left(\frac{\mathbf{i}}{\sqrt{2}} + \frac{\mathbf{k}}{\sqrt{2}} \right) = \sqrt{2}\,\mathbf{i}$$

Noting that
$$\mathbf{v}_1' + \widehat{\mathbf{n}}_1 = -\sqrt{2}\,\mathbf{k} + \frac{\mathbf{i}}{\sqrt{2}} + \frac{\mathbf{k}}{\sqrt{2}} = \frac{\mathbf{i}}{\sqrt{2}} - \frac{\mathbf{k}}{\sqrt{2}}$$

then
$$k_{f_1} = [\,k_{\eta_1}^2 |\mathbf{v}_1'|^2 - |\mathbf{v}_1' + \widehat{\mathbf{n}}_1|^2\,]^{-1/2} = \left[\left(\frac{1}{1.1} \right)^2 (2) - 1 \right]^{-1/2} = 1.238$$

which yields the refracted ray

$$\mathbf{p}_1 = k_{f_1}(\widehat{\mathbf{n}}_1 + \mathbf{v}_1') - \widehat{\mathbf{n}}_1 = 1.238 \left(\frac{\mathbf{i}}{\sqrt{2}} - \frac{\mathbf{k}}{\sqrt{2}} \right) - \left(\frac{\mathbf{i}}{\sqrt{2}} + \frac{\mathbf{k}}{\sqrt{2}} \right)$$

$$= 0.168\mathbf{i} - 1.582\mathbf{k}$$

At this point the reflected ray leaves the scene and is not considered further. The intersection of the transmitted refracted ray with the second surface yields the second node in the ray tree. Writing the refracted ray, $\mathbf{p}_1$, in parametric form yields

$$x = 5 + 0.168t$$

$$z = 7.5 - 1.582t$$

Substituting into the surface equation yields

$$x - z - 2 = 5 + 0.168t - 7.5 + 1.582t - 2 = 1.75t - 4.5 = 0$$

Consequently, $t = 2.571$, and the intersection point is

$$x_2 = 5 + (0.168)(2.571) = 5.432$$

$$z_2 = 7.5 - (1.582)(2.571) = 3.433$$

The distance between the two intersection points is

$$d_{12} = \sqrt{(x_2 - x_1)^2 + (z_2 - z_1)^2} = \sqrt{(5.432 - 5)^2 + (3.433 - 7.5)^2} = 4.09$$

The reflected and refracted rays at this intersection point are obtained by using $\mathbf{p}_1$ as the incoming ray, i.e.

$$\mathbf{v}_2 = \mathbf{p}_1 = 0.168\mathbf{i} - 1.582\mathbf{k}$$

The unit surface normal is

$$\hat{\mathbf{n}}_2 = \frac{-\mathbf{i}}{\sqrt{2}} + \frac{\mathbf{k}}{\sqrt{2}}$$

The results are

$$\mathbf{p}_2 = 0.215\mathbf{i} - 1.199\mathbf{k}$$

$$\mathbf{r}_2 = -1.278\mathbf{i} + 0.136\mathbf{k}$$

Here, the transmitted refracted ray leaves the scene without intersecting additional objects. Thus, this ray tree branch terminates. The intersection of the reflected ray and the third surface yields the third node in the ray tree. Here, the intersection of $\mathbf{r}_2$ and the third surface is required. Using the parametric form of $\mathbf{r}_2$ and the plane equation for the surface yields

$$x = 5.432 - 1.278t$$

$$z = 3.433 + 0.136t$$

for the ray. Substituting into the plane equation yields

$$x - 3z + 9 = 5.432 - 1.278t - 3(3.433 + 0.136t) + 9 = -1.686t + 4.133 = 0$$

Consequently, $t = 2.451$, and the intersection point is

$$x_3 = 5.432 - (1.278)(2.451) = 2.299$$

$$z_3 = 3.433 + (0.136)(2.451) = 3.766$$

The distance between the two intersection points is

$$d_{23} = \sqrt{(x_3 - x_2)^2 + (z_3 - z_2)^2}$$

$$= \sqrt{(2.299 - 5.432)^2 + (3.766 - 3.433)^2} = 3.151$$

The reflected and refracted rays at this intersection point are obtained using $\mathbf{r}_2$ as the incoming ray, i.e.

$$\mathbf{v}_3 = \mathbf{r}_2 = -1.278\mathbf{i} + 0.136\mathbf{k}$$

The unit surface normal on the incoming ray side of the surface is

$$\hat{\mathbf{n}}_3 = \frac{\mathbf{i}}{\sqrt{10}} - \frac{3\mathbf{k}}{\sqrt{10}}$$

The results are

$$\mathbf{p}_3 = -1.713\mathbf{i} + 0.483\mathbf{k}$$

$$\mathbf{r}_3 = -1.765\mathbf{i} - 1.643\mathbf{k}$$

Here, both the reflected and refracted rays leave the scene. The ray tree terminates at this point. In fact, examination of the illumination characteristics for the surfaces shows that $k_{t_3} = 0$. Hence, the surface is opaque and no transmitted ray is generated.

The intensity calculations begin at the bottom of the ray tree at the third node. Since surface 3 is opaque, there is no light transmitted through the surface. A shadow feeler shows that the surface itself is between the incident ray and the light source. Consequently, the point of intersection of the ray and the surface is in shadow. Thus, the point receives only ambient light. The intensity is

$$I_3 = k_{a_3} I_a = (0.15)(1) = 0.15$$

This intensity is transmitted along the reflection vector, $\mathbf{r}_2$, to the second surface. When it reaches the second surface, it is attenuated by the distance between the intersection points d_{23}. Thus

$$I_{s_2} = \frac{I_3}{d_{23}} = \frac{0.15}{3.151} = 0.0476$$

At the second node in the tree representing the intersection of the ray and the second surface, the shadow feeler does not intersect any object. Hence, the point receives light from the source. The vector from the point to the light source is

$$\mathbf{L}_2 = (x_l - x_2)\mathbf{i} + (z_l - z_2)\mathbf{k} = (3 - 5.432)\mathbf{i} + (10 - 3.433)\mathbf{k}$$

$$= -2.432\mathbf{i} + 6.567\mathbf{k}$$

and

$$\hat{\mathbf{L}}_2 = -0.347\mathbf{i} + 0.938\mathbf{k}$$

Consequently

$$\hat{\mathbf{n}}_2 \cdot \hat{\mathbf{L}}_2 = \left(\frac{-\mathbf{i}}{\sqrt{2}} + \frac{\mathbf{k}}{\sqrt{2}}\right) \cdot (-0.347\mathbf{i} + 0.938\mathbf{k}) = 0.909$$

The reflected direction for the ray from the light source is

$$\hat{\mathbf{R}}_2 = -0.938\mathbf{i} + 0.347\mathbf{k}$$

Here the unit sight vector is $-\hat{\mathbf{p}}_1$ and

$$-\hat{\mathbf{p}}_1 \cdot \hat{\mathbf{R}}_2 = (-0.168\mathbf{i} + 1.582\mathbf{k}) \cdot (-0.938\mathbf{i} + 0.347\mathbf{k}) = 0.707$$

Thus

$$I_2 = k_{a_2} I_a + I_l k_{d_2} (\widehat{\mathbf{n}}_2 \cdot \widehat{\mathbf{L}}_2) + I_l k_{s_2} (-\widehat{\mathbf{p}}_1 \cdot \widehat{\mathbf{R}}_2)^n + k_{s_2} I_{s_2} + k_{t_2} I_{t_2}$$

$$= (0.15)(1) + (10)(0.15)(0.909) + (10)(0.8)(0) + (0.8)(.0476) + (0.5)(0)$$

$$= 1.552$$

This intensity is transmitted along the refraction vector, $\mathbf{p}_1$, to the first surface where, attenuated by the distance between the surfaces d_{12}, it becomes

$$I_{t_1} = \frac{I_2}{d_{12}} = \frac{1.552}{4.09} = 0.379$$

Here, the shadow feeler also does not intersect any object. Hence, the point on the first surface receives light from the source. The vector from the point to the light source is

$$\mathbf{L}_1 = (x_l - x_1)\mathbf{i} + (z_l - z_l)\mathbf{k} = (3 - 5)\mathbf{i} + (10 - 7.5)\mathbf{k}$$

$$= -2\mathbf{i} + 2.5\mathbf{k}$$

and

$$\widehat{\mathbf{L}}_1 = -0.625\mathbf{i} + 0.781\mathbf{k}$$

Consequently

$$\widehat{\mathbf{n}}_1 \cdot \widehat{\mathbf{L}}_1 = \left(\frac{\mathbf{i}}{\sqrt{2}} + \frac{\mathbf{k}}{\sqrt{2}} \right) \cdot (-0.625\mathbf{i} + 0.781\mathbf{k}) = 0.110$$

The reflected direction for the ray from the light source is

$$\widehat{\mathbf{R}}_1 = 0.781\mathbf{i} - 0.625\mathbf{k}$$

Here, the unit sight vector is $-\widehat{\mathbf{v}}_1$ and

$$-\widehat{\mathbf{v}}_1 \cdot \widehat{\mathbf{R}}_1 = (\mathbf{k}) \cdot (0.781\mathbf{i} - 0.625\mathbf{k}) = -0.625$$

Thus

$$I_1 = k_{a_1} I_a + I_l k_{d_1} (\widehat{\mathbf{n}}_1 \cdot \widehat{\mathbf{L}}) + I_l k_{s_1} (-\widehat{\mathbf{v}}_1 \cdot \widehat{\mathbf{R}}_1)^n + k_{s_1} I_{s_1} + k_{t_1} I_{t_1}$$

$$= (0.15)(1) + (10)(0.15)(0.11) + (10)(0.8)(0) + (0.8)(0) + (0.5)(0.379)$$

$$= 0.505$$

This is the intensity transmitted to the observer. Because the resulting intensity is low, the point is only dimly seen. The low intensity results because the surface is almost edge-on to the light source. Furthermore, the results show that more than a third of the intensity is transmitted through the first surface from surface 2. Finally, because of the large value of n local specular highlights are not seen.

If color is used, then the above calculation is performed three times, once for each of the red, green and blue components. In addition, separate illumination characteristics for each component are required.

Figure 5–70 shows a flowchart for a ray tracing algorithm with global illumination. The algorithm is implemented using a pushdown ray stack. The stack serves to communicate reflected and transmitted illumination information among the elements of the ray tree. Since the stack holds only part of the ray tree at any one time, it need only be long enough to contain the longest anticipated branch. A particular branch of the ray tree is terminated when both the reflected and refracted rays at an object intersection leave the scene, or when the available stack length is exceeded. When both rays leave the scene, their contribution to the illumination at the source ray is zero. When the available stack length is exceeded, the algorithm calculates the illumination at the source ray using only the ambient, diffuse and specular reflection components at the source ray intersection. The algorithm can be extended one additional depth in the tree without exceeding the maximum stack depth. The flowchart for this modification is shown in Fig. 5–71.

The efficiency of the algorithm is increased by reducing the average size of the ray tree or stack, and hence the number of required intersection calculations. The average size of the ray stack is reduced by placing on it only rays that significantly contribute to the intensity at the observer's eye. The maximum relative contribution of a particular node of the ray tree to the intensity at the observer's eye is approximated using the following technique. The approximate intensity at the first ray–surface intersection, including any shadow effects, is determined using only a local illumination model, e.g., the ambient, Lambertian diffuse and Phong specular reflection terms from Eq. $(5 - 16)$. This value is saved. At each succeeding ray–surface intersection, the maximum intensity contribution is approximated by the same local illumination model but without considering shadow effects. The resulting intensity is attenuated by the cumulative effects of refraction and reflection, and by the cumulative distance traveled by the ray from the first ray–surface intersection to that under consideration. For example, using this technique, the approximate intensity at surface 3 in Fig. 5–68 is attenuated by $k_{s_2}k_{t_1}/d_{23}d_{12}$ (see Ex. 5–9). If the resulting intensity exceeds a fixed percentage of the approximate intensity at the first ray–surface intersection, then refracted and reflected rays, as appropriate, are placed on the ray stack. If not, then the ray branch is terminated at that point. Hall [Hall83a, 83b], using a similar technique, found that the average tree size and the computational expense is reduced by a factor of more than eight. Unfortunately, the technique is not completely correct. Specifically, if a major contribution to the intensity at the observer's eye due to global illumination effects occurs after the ray tree is terminated, the resulting image is incomplete. However, the probability of this occurring for most general scenes is small. Thus, the significant savings that result justify use of the technique.

The algorithm which is presented here assumes an object description list similar to that discussed in Sec. 4–20 for the opaque visible surface ray tracing algorithm. As a minimum, the ray stack contains the following information for each ray:

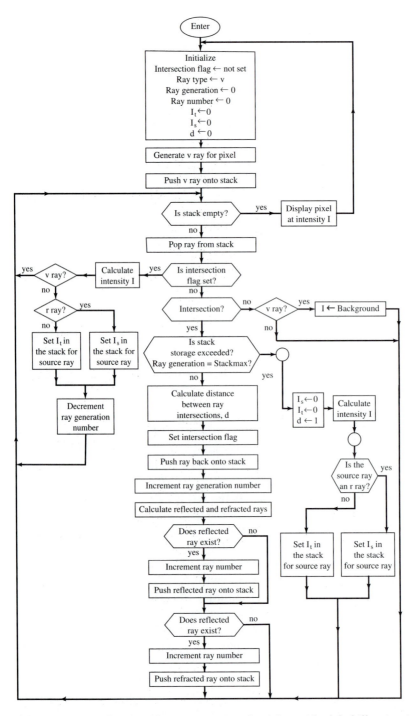

Figure 5–70 Flowchart for a ray tracing algorithm with global illumination.

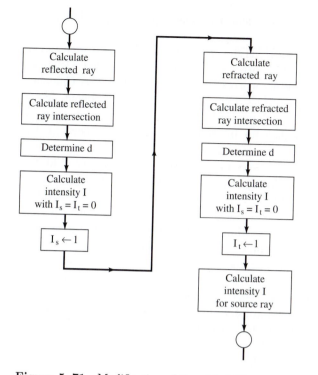

Figure 5–71   Modification of the global illumination ray tracing algorithm.

Ray number	uniquely assigned for each ray
Ray type	**v**, a pixel ray from the eye; **r**, a reflected ray; or **p**, a refracted ray
Ray source number	the number of the ray that generated this ray
Ray source type	**v**, **r** or **p**, as above
Intersection flag	1 if an intersection for this ray was found, otherwise 0
Object pointer	gives the location of the intersected object in the object description list
Intersection values	x, y, z coordinates of the intersection generating this ray
Direction cosines	specify the direction of the ray
d	distance between this ray intersection and the intersection of the source ray
I_t	intensity of transmitted light along this ray
I_s	intensity of specularly reflected light along this ray

When a ray is initially pushed onto the stack, the values of I_s, I_t, d and the intersection flag are set to zero. Subsequent passes through the algorithm update these values as required.

The Whitted illumination model, as shown in Fig. 5–67, is used with the algorithm. The flowchart in Fig. 5–72 corresponds to the block labeled 'Calculate intensity' I, in Fig. 5–70. If color is incorporated into the model, the 'Calculate intensity' block is executed three times, once for each color component. Here, the path of the vectors (shadow feelers) from the surface intersection point to the various light sources is checked for intersection with other objects in the scene. If an intersection occurs with an opaque object, that light source does not contribute to the local diffuse or specular reflection at that point. If all the intersections along the path are transparent, the intensity of the light source, I_{l_j}, is attenuated appropriately. In particular, the attenuation factor is based on the transmission coefficients of the occluding surfaces. Thus, opaque occluding objects produce sharp black shadows, while transparent occluding objects yield faint shadows. Refraction of incident light from the source through transparent objects to the surface is not accounted for. The transmitted and specularly reflected light incident at a point is attenuated by the distance between ray intersections. The algorithm assumes that the surface normal is available from the object description. Other more complex illumination models are incorporated into the model by modifying this routine (see Secs. 5–9 and 5–15).

The intersection processor is described in Sec. 4–20 in the context of an opaque visible surface ray tracing algorithm. The only modification required here is to specifically translate the ray–surface intersection point for each ray to the origin of the coordinate system before rotating to make the ray coincident with the z-axis. The ray points in the direction of $-z$. The same procedure is used to determine the intersections of the shadow feelers with objects.

In operation, the algorithm described in Fig. 5–70 first generates the ray tree along the right hand *refraction* branch from the root node until the branch terminates, as shown in Fig. 5–73 by the dashed line with arrows. The branch is then traversed upward, calculating the intensities at each node until the root node is reached. The left-hand *reflection* branch from the root node is then generated and traversed in the reverse direction. At any intermediate node the process may be repeated. The downward pointing arrows in Fig. 5–73 indicate ray generation (pushed onto the stack), and the upward pointing arrows indicate intensity generation (popped from the stack). After the intensity contribution for a ray at a particular node is determined, the ray is discarded. When only the root node remains, the pixel intensity is determined and sent to the display.

Whitted [Whit80] incorporates antialiasing into the ray tracing algorithm. Aliasing effects are most apparent for regions with high-intensity gradients, e.g., at object edges, at silhouette edges, within texture patterns and for objects smaller than the interval between sample points. To reduce computational requirements, the antialiasing technique used is a dynamically invoked Warnock-style recursive subdivision. Instead of tracing rays through each pixel center, Whitted traces rays through sample points at each corner of the pixel square, as

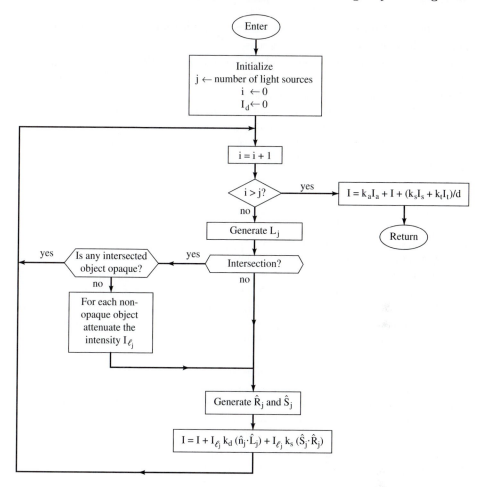

Figure 5–72 Flowchart for the illumination model for the global illumination ray tracing algorithm.

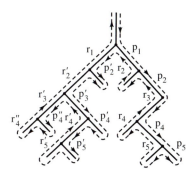

Figure 5–73 Ray tracing tree.

shown in Fig. 5–74a. For an $n \times m$ raster this requires $(n+1) \times (m+1)$ sample points, which is only a modest increase. If the intensities at the four corner sample points are nearly equal, and if no small object lies between them, then the intensity values are averaged and displayed for that pixel. If the four intensity values are not nearly equal (see Fig. 5–74b), the pixel square is subdivided into four subsquares and the process is repeated. Recursive subdivision continues until the corner values are nearly equal, the allotted storage is exceeded or the resolution of the computer is exceeded. The intensity contribution of each subpixel is weighted by its area, and the results are summed to obtain the pixel intensity. Although still a point sampling technique, in the limit the technique is equivalent to area antialiasing (see Sec. 2–16).

Implementation of this scheme requires that either a row or column of sample point intensity values, whichever is smaller, be saved on a rolling basis as the image is generated. Saving the sample point intensity values makes it unnecessary to backtrack or regenerate previously determined intensity values. When a pixel square is subdivided, a stack is used to save intermediate intensity values as the subdivision progresses. (See the Warnock algorithm in Sec. 4–4.)

Whitted prevents small objects from being lost by using a minimum-sized bounding sphere that is larger than the spacing between sample points. When the algorithm encounters a minimum radius bounding sphere and no ray–object intersection is found, the four pixel squares that share the ray through that sample point are recursively subdivided until the object is found. This technique is adequate for directly viewed objects, or for objects viewed indirectly via planar surfaces. However, objects viewed indirectly via curved surfaces can be lost. These objects are lost because closely spaced rays reflected or refracted from highly curved surfaces may diverge sufficiently to miss the object. This effect is shown in Fig. 5–75 for reflection from a sphere. Continued subdivision may

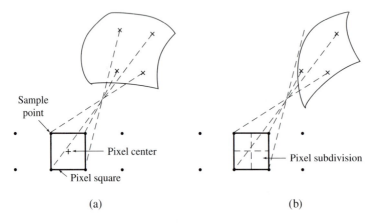

(a)   (b)

Figure 5–74   Antialiasing in ray tracing. (a) Subdivision is not required; (b) subdivision is required.

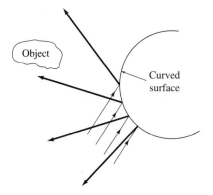

Figure 5–75   Reflection from a curved surface.

exceed machine resolution before an intersecting ray is found. Color Plate 13 was generated using these techniques.

5–15   A More Complete Global Illumination Model Using Ray Tracing

Hall [Hall83a] and Hall and Greenberg [Hall83b] use a more complete global illumination model than that described in the previous section. The Hall global illumination model includes the scattering of light directly from light sources along the refracted or transmitted ray, in addition to along the reflected ray. The scattering model is an adaptation of the Phong model. The model also uses the Fresnel relationships for the wavelength and angle of incidence dependence of refracted and reflected light, and uses the filter properties of specific materials to attenuate light passing through transparent media. Specifically, the Hall global illumination model for j light sources is

$$I = k_d \sum_j I_{l_j} R_d(\hat{\mathbf{n}} \cdot \hat{\mathbf{L}}_j) + k_s \sum_j I_{l_j} R_f(\hat{\mathbf{n}} \cdot \hat{\mathbf{H}})^n$$

$$+ k_t \sum_j I_{l_j} F_t(\hat{\mathbf{n}} \cdot \hat{\mathbf{H}}')^{n'} + k_a R_d I_a + k_s R_f I_s T_r^{d_r}$$

$$+ k_t F_t I_t T_t^{d_t} \tag{5-17}$$

Here, the ambient globally diffuse term $(k_a R_d I_a)$, and the Lambertian diffuse reflection for light scattered directly from light sources, include $R_d(\lambda)$, the material- and wavelength-dependent diffuse reflection curve. Similarly, the specular reflection term for light scattered directly from light sources and the global specular reflection term contain $R_f(\lambda)$, the material- and wavelength-dependent Fresnel reflectance curve (see Sec. 5–9). The third term in Eq. $(5-17)$, which represents the specular transmission of light directly from light sources along the refracted ray, and the global transmission term include F_t, the material- and wavelength-dependent Fresnel transmissivity curve. From conservation-of-energy considerations $F_t = 1 - R_f$. The approximate technique suggested by Cook and described in Sec. 5–9 is used to determine $R_f(\lambda)$ and $F_t(\lambda)$. The global specular reflection and specular refraction terms also include T_r and T_t the transmissivity per unit length for the reflected and transmitted (refracted) rays. The distances traveled by the reflected and transmitted (refracted) rays from the last intersection are given by d_r and d_t, respectively. Following Kay (see Sec. 5–10), T_r and T_t are raised to a power to represent the effects of passage through a material. Here, the distances, d_r and d_t, are used as the powers.

The specular reflection term for light received directly from light sources is adapted from the Torrance–Sparrow model discussed in Sec. 5–9. Here, the angle between the surface normal, $\hat{\mathbf{n}}$, and the bisector of the angle between the light source direction and the observer's direction, $\hat{\mathbf{H}}$, i.e., $\hat{\mathbf{n}}\cdot\hat{\mathbf{H}}$, raised to a power n, is used to represent scattering of specularly reflected light. Similarly, the angle between the surface normal and a vector $\mathbf{H}'$, raised to a power n', is used to represent scattering of specularly transmitted light. The vector $\mathbf{H}'$ represents the normal direction for Torrance–Sparrow surface microfacets (see Sec. 5–9) that refract light received directly from a light source in the direction p (see Fig. 5–67).

The direction of the $\mathbf{H}'$ vector is calculated using Snell's laws (see Sec. 5–10). Referring to Fig. 5–76, using the similar triangles afd and bed, and Snell's law yields

$$\mathbf{ad} = \frac{\eta_2}{\eta_1}\mathbf{bd}$$

Now
$$\mathbf{ab} = \mathbf{v} - \mathbf{p}$$

and
$$\mathbf{ad} = \mathbf{ab} + \mathbf{bd}$$

Thus
$$\mathbf{bd} = \frac{\mathbf{v} - \mathbf{p}}{\eta_2/\eta_1 - 1}$$

Since
$$\mathbf{H}' = \mathbf{bd} - \mathbf{p}$$

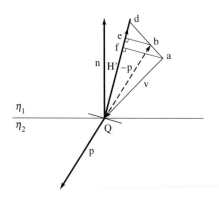

Figure 5–76 Determining the $\mathbf{H}'$ vector.

combining these results yields

$$\mathbf{H}' = \frac{\mathbf{v} - (\eta_2/\eta_1)\mathbf{p}}{\eta_2/\eta_1 - 1}$$

Color Plate 16 compares results for the Whitted and Hall global illumination models. Both images are of the same scene and were created using a ray tracing algorithm. Color Plate 16a was rendered using the Whitted global illumination model described in Eq. $(5-16)$. Color Plate 16b was rendered with the Hall global illumination model described in Eq. $(5-17)$. Compare the appearance of the metallic spheres in both scenes. Notice the color of the blue placemat edge reflected in the metallic sphere. Compare the color of the transparent spheres. Notice the slight bluish-green color of the sphere and its shadow in Color Plate 16b. This color results from including the material filter properties in the Hall model. As shown by Color Plate 16, the Hall global illumination model is empirically derived and hence, as pointed out by Hall [Hall83a], fundamentally incorrect; but the images are still impressive.

5–16   Advances in Ray Tracing

Ray tracing is straightforward but expensive. Most advances lie in the areas of increased efficiency or better image quality. Increased efficiency is strongly associated with the techniques for avoiding intersection calculations, as described in Sec. 4–20. Those techniques are applicable to either original rays or spawned, i.e., reflected and refracted, rays. Increased image quality attempts to reduce aliasing in the image, or to add realism to the image, e.g., soft shadows, motion blur, caustics or physically-based illumination models, as discussed in Secs. 5–9 and 5–11.

Cone Tracing

Fundamentally, ray tracing is a point sampling technique and thus subject to severe aliasing. Whitted [Whit80] introduced adaptive supersampling for antialiasing (see Sec. 5–14). Adaptive supersampling becomes computationally expensive when large repeated variations in intensity occur within small regions. Furthermore, as discussed in Sec. 5–14, small objects, especially when viewed via reflections or refractions, may be missed.

Amanatides [Aman84] expanded the concept of a ray from that of an infinitely thin line to a slender conical ray with a cone half angle, α. The half angle is chosen such that the diameter of the cone equals the width of a pixel at the image plane. The direction of reflected and refracted conical rays is determined by the direction of the reflected or refracted centerline of the cone. Assuming that the reflecting or refracting surface is locally perfectly spherical, the *spread* of the conical ray is determined by the general equations of physical optics for spherical mirrors and lenses [Hect74]. The cone half angle for reflected and refracted rays is obtained by projecting backwards to determine the cone apex.

Calculating the intersection of a cone and an object is more complex than of a ray and an object. Amanatides [Aman84] and Kirk [Kirk87] both discuss the cone sphere intersection as an example. With r the radius of the sphere, α the cone half angle, t the distance from the apex of the cone to a point P on the axis of the cone, the hit/no hit test reduces to

$$S = t + \tan\alpha + \frac{R}{\cos\alpha} < D$$

where D is the distance between P and the center of the sphere. If $S < D$, then there is no intersection of the cone and the sphere, i.e., no hit. The first term in the equation is the radius of the cone at point P; the second term allows for intersections of the cone and sphere at other than the nearest point. There are a number of exceptional cases discussed by Kirk.

Because a cone covers a finite area, if the fractional area of the cone cross section occluded by objects can be calculated, then area antialiasing is possible. Amanatides suggests intersection techniques for spheres and polygons, while Kirk suggests using piecewise or strip integration to estimate the areas. Kirk also precalculates the fractional areas for spheres and planar primitives and stores them in a lookup table. The values stored in the lookup table can be prefiltered. Kirk [Kirk87] significantly reduces the size of the lookup table by storing the values in terms of R_c/R and $D/(R_c + R)$, where R_c is the radius of the cone at the intersection.

By modeling light sources as spheres and broadening the conical shadow feeler to the size of the light source, and modulating the amount of light supplied by that light source based on the fractional area of the light occluded by intervening objects, Amanatides [Aman84] generates penumbra, i.e., fuzzy shadows. Similarly, by broadening reflected rays, dull specular reflections are obtained. By perturbing the size and cone half angles in areas of 'high curvature', Kirk achieves an effect similar to bump mapping (see Sec. 5–12). By modulating the amount of light that a surface diffuses, Kirk creates simulated clouds.

Beam Tracing

Conceptually, beam tracing [Heck86] is similar to cone tracing, i.e., it uses a thick ray to increase the quality of a ray traced image; the implementation is, however, quite different. Beam tracing is a recursive object space algorithm for planar polygonal scenes. The algorithm takes advantage of coherence in the sense that adjacent rays in a scene typically follow similar paths through the scene.

A beam is a polygonal shaped pyramid swept out through space. Beginning with the view pyramid as the initial beam, the algorithm builds a beam tree analogous to the classic ray tracing tree. However, in contrast to classic ray tracing, a beam is finite in size; consequently, it may completely or partially intersect multiple polygons. Beam polygon intersections are accomplished by always transforming the scene into the current beam coordinate system. Polygons are sorted into back-to-front priority order relative to the beam coordinate system, using, for example, the Newell–Newell–Sancha special sort algorithm [Newe72] (see Sec. 4–12). Starting with the first polygon on the sorted list, if a polygon completely or partially intersects the beam, it is visible. The portion of the visible polygon within the beam is subtracted from the beam. The reduced beam is then used to recursively process the next polygon on the depth priority sorted list.

Reflection and refraction are simulated by generating new beams with the cross section of intersected polygons. Reflection from a plane is a linear transformation. However, refraction through a plane is a nonlinear transformation, except for orthographic projections or when the beam is nearly perpendicular to the plane (paraxial rays). Heckbert and Hanrahan [Heck86] approximate refraction by a linear transformation. Consequently, as pointed out by Heckbert and Hanrahan, if a perspective projection is used, refracted optical effects are incorrect.

The resulting object precision beam tree is rendered using any standard visible surface or visible (hidden) line algorithm, e.g., a spanning scan line algorithm (see Sec. 4–16). The depth of the beam tree is controlled in a manner similar to that for classic ray tracing. Gouraud shading (see Sec. 5–6) is implemented using a modified painters algorithm. In rendering the beam tree, the partial polygons are transformed back into the object coordinate system. The first object, i.e., the parent on the beam tree, is rendered, followed by its children, using an appropriate modulation algorithm if the child polygons are transparent. Shadows are added to the scene as lit polygon 'textures', using a technique similar to that of the Atherton–Weiler–Greenberg shadow algorithm [Athe78b] (see Sec. 5–11). Color Plate 17 shows a beam traced scene.

Pencil Tracing

Shinya et al. [Shin87] present the underlying formalism for pencil tracing, of which cone tracing and beam tracing are special cases. A pencil is made up of a centered axial ray and a bundle of *paraxial* rays closely aligned with it. The departure of the paraxial rays from the central axial ray is given by a four-dimensional vector described in a coordinate system referenced to the axial ray. For the typical computer graphics pinhole perspective model (single center-of-projection) a pencil is represented by the pencil spread angle (cone half angle). If the pencil spread angle is small, then the nonlinear refraction transformation can be approximated by a linear 4×4 transformation matrix. Shinya and colleagues developed an error metric for determining the maximum pencil spread angle, along with the appropriate approximate linear matrices for both reflection and refraction. They incorporate their results into three different algorithms, including an extended beam tracing algorithm. One of the algorithms is nearly an order of magnitude faster than conventional ray tracing.

Stochastic Sampling

Stochastic sampling is a Monte Carlo integration technique, of which jitter [Dipp85; Lee85; Cook86; Kaji86; Mitc87, 91] and distributed ray tracing [Cook84, 86, 87, 89] are two examples. Cook et al. [Cook84] originally proposed distributed ray tracing as a means of approximating the integration of the intensity of reflected (transmitted) light at a point on (through) a surface over the surface hemisphere. By integrating around the reflected ray, a blurred reflection or gloss is achieved. By integrating around the transmitted ray, blurred transparency or translucency is achieved. By extending the concept to integration over the solid angle subtended by a light source, shadow penumbras result (see Sec. 5–11). Extending the typical computer graphics pinhole camera model by integrating over the finite lens area achieves a depth of field effect. Finally, by integrating over time (time slicing), motion blur results. Color Plate 18 shows an image generated by Tom Porter, illustrating a number of these effects.

In stochastic sampling, an image is sampled at appropriate nonuniformly spaced intervals. The effect is to replace the aliasing caused by frequencies in the image that exceed the Nyquist limit[†] by noise. The fundamental question is: What is the optimum nonuniform distribution? The characteristics of the eye suggest an answer. There is good experimental evidence [Yell83] that the spacing of the receptors in the retina of the eye conform to a minimum distance Poisson (Poisson disk) distribution. A minimum distance Poisson distribution randomly places points such that no two points are closer than some minimum distance. A minimum distance Poisson distribution is generated by the point diffusion algorithm:

Generate a random point.

Check the distance from all previously generated points.

If the distance is less than the minimum specified distance, keep the point; otherwise discard it.

A minimum distance Poisson distribution is shown in Fig. 5–77a. Alternate, and perhaps more efficient, techniques are given by Mitchell [Mitc87, 91].

The eye is least sensitive to noise in the high frequency range. Thus, if low and medium frequency noise is reduced and high frequency noise increased, a better image is obtained. Low frequency noise is reduced and high frequency noise increased by increasing the minimum distance in the minimum distance Poisson distribution. The eye is approximately twice as sensitive to noise at frequencies corresponding to the color green than to those corresponding to the color red, and approximately four times as sensitive to green frequencies than to those corresponding to the color blue. Hence, the distributions that result from increasing the minimum Poisson distribution distance are referred to as 'blue noise'.

Stochastic sampling, using a minimum distance Poisson distribution, is global in nature and computationally expensive. Jittered stochastic sampling is, however, both local and computationally inexpensive. The basic concept of jittering is shown in Fig. 5–78. A pixel is divided into subpixels. The sample

---

[†]Recall that the Nyquist limit requires that a signal (image) be sampled at twice the highest frequency occurring in the signal (image).

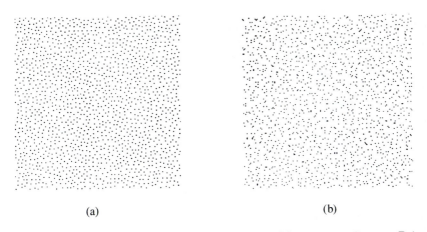

(a)   (b)

Figure 5–77 Stochastic sampling distributions. (a) Minimum distance Poisson distribution; (b) jittering on a rectangular grid.

point within each subpixel is randomly displaced a small distance from the center of the subpixel, as shown in Fig. 5–78 by the small crosses. An example of the stochastic distribution resulting from jittering on a rectangular grid is shown in Fig. 5–77b. An antialiasing filter, e.g., a box, triangular (Bartlett) or Gaussian filter is applied when combining the subpixel samples. Although typically applied on a rectangular grid, jittering is more efficient if a regular hexagonal pattern is used [Dipp85]. For nonspatial dimensions, e.g., time, the frame is divided into slices, with sample points randomly assigned to each time slice. The sample points are then jittered within each time slice.

Adaptive sampling is effective in reducing the number of samples (rays) without reducing image quality [Dipp85]. Initially, a set of stochastically spaced samples at reasonable densities is taken over a region. If the resulting sample values are similar, a lower final sampling rate is used for a given image quality.

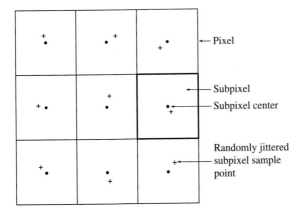

Figure 5–78 Jittered sampling.

If the sample values are sufficiently dissimilar, then a higher final sampling rate is required to achieve a given image quality.

Adaptive rectangular jitter [Dipp85] recursively subdivides the original rectangular cells (pixels or subpixels) in one dimension only, using a randomly chosen subdivision plane with constant x, y or t. The original sample value is assigned to the appropriate subcell, and a new value is determined for the other subcell. Here, the local nature of jittering allows reuse of previously calculated sample values; thus, the total number of sample values (rays) is significantly reduced.

Importance sampling [Lee85; Lane94] is another stochastic sampling refinement. Again, the objective is to reduce the number of rays traced without reducing the image quality. Fundamentally, importance sampling divides the area of the filter or lighting function being sampled, e.g., the reflection function, into equal areas (or volumes) and assigns a fixed number of rays to each area (or volume). The rays are stochastically placed within the area or volume. As an example, if the function falls off quickly from its central core value, few rays are traced at the edges (extremes) of the function, while significant numbers are traced at the core of the function.

Lange [Lang94] uses importance sampling in an implementation of the rendering equation [Kaji86]. She uses a fixed number of rays, $N = 40$, at each pixel. The appropriate reflection model, Lambertian for diffuse reflection and Phong (see Sec. 5–3) for specular reflection, is used to distribute the rays over the surface hemisphere for a given pixel. For specular reflection it is not strictly necessary to sample the entire hemisphere; it is sufficient to consider a smaller solid angle centered around the mirror reflection direction. Varying the size of the solid angle cone determines the glossiness, or softness, of the specular reflection. Diffuse and specular reflection are combined by distributing the number of rays in proportion to k_d and k_s, i.e., $k_s N$ and $k_d N$. Light sources are assumed as circular disks and are sampled with either a uniform distribution over the area or uniformly along the edge in order to generate penumbra shadows. The center of the light sources is sampled by a single ray to determine the directed contribution to the illumination. This contribution is weighted by $w_{\ell s} = \cos^n \theta$, where θ is the angle between the light source direction and the surface normal. The direct light source intensity is then combined with the random intensity samples using $1 - w_{\ell s}$ as the weighting factor. Mitchell provides an interesting discussion of the improvement expected from stochastic (stratified) sampling [Mitc96].

Ray Tracing from the Light Source

Arvo [Arvo86] introduced the idea of illumination maps as a way of including diffuse reflection that results from the intersection of specularly reflected or refracted rays with diffusely reflecting objects in ray traced images. The concept extends nicely to combined ray tracing and radiosity algorithms (see Sec. 5–18). Arvo called the technique backward ray tracing and defined it as tracing rays from the light source into the scene. But to avoid confusion, the technique is more appropriately called *ray tracing from the light source*, or *bidirectional ray tracing.* Ray tracing from the light source is used *only* to determine the diffuse component of the reflected light. Normal ray tracing *from the eyepoint* is still used for visible surface determination, specular reflection and refraction, etc.

Ray tracing from the light source is a two-pass algorithm. In the first, or preprocessing, pass a dense shower of rays emanating *from each of the light sources* is cast into the scene. The rays are traced through the scene, including reflections and refractions. For each of the diffusely reflecting objects in the scene illuminated by specularly reflected/refracted light, an illumination map is constructed. The illumination map is a rectangular array on a 1×1 square, for which a one-to-one correspondence with the object exists, i.e., a parameterization function $T(u, v) \to S(x, y, z)$ and its inverse exists.

When a reflected/refracted ray hits a diffusely reflecting surface with an associated illumination map, the inverse parameterization function is used to deposit the ray's energy at the appropriate grid point using a bilinear interpolation to apportion the energy among the closest four grid points. Once the illumination maps for each surface are completed, the energy at each grid point in the map is converted to intensity by dividing by the corresponding surface area in object space. The surface area is approximated by the partial derivatives of the parameterization function, i.e.,

$$\text{Intensity at the grid point}(u, v) = \frac{\text{Energy}(u, v)}{\left| \dfrac{\partial T(u, v)}{\partial u} \times \dfrac{\partial T(u, v)}{\partial v} \right|}$$

The second pass uses conventional *from the eyepoint* ray tracing. When rendering a point on a surface with an associated illumination map, the parameterization function is used to access the illumination map. The intensity of the specularly reflected/refracted diffuse reflection contribution is obtained using bilinear interpolation among the closest four grid points in the illumination map, and is combined with the direct diffuse and specular reflection/refraction contributions.

5–17   Radiosity

The radiosity method describes an equilibrium *energy* balance within an enclosure. Fundamentally, radiosity accounts for only diffuse reflection. It is based on concepts originally developed for radiative heat transfer in thermal engineering. It was first adapted to computer graphics by Goral et al. [Gora84], and in a somewhat different form by Nishita and Nakamae [Nish85]. Goral's solution was limited to diffuse reflection within convex environments in which no object obscured another. Goral's work is unique in that the computational results were compared to an actual physical environment. Subsequently, Meyer et al. [Meye86b] conducted an extensive comparison of physically real and radiosity generated scenes. Test observers showed no more than a 50% chance of picking the actual physical environment over the computational results, i.e., no better than random guessing. Both the physically real and the computer generated

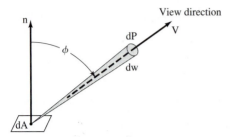

Figure 5–79 Radiant energy falling on a differential area; $d\omega$ is the differential solid angle in steradians.

scenes are shown in Color Plate 19. Cohen and Greenberg [Cohe85] extended the radiosity method to complex environments.

Consider a differential element of area dA. Radiant energy, dP, is assumed to emanate in all directions from dA. The energy, in the current context, is in the form of visible light. The radiant intensity, i, is given by

$$i = \frac{dP}{\cos\phi \, d\omega}$$

where i is the radiant energy per unit time, per unit projected area (in the viewing direction) per unit solid angle, $d\omega$ (see Fig. 5–79).

As shown in Fig. 5–80, for Lambertian diffuse reflection, the distribution of reflected light energy is

$$\frac{dP}{d\omega} = k\cos\phi \qquad k = \text{constant}$$

or

$$dP = k\cos\phi \, d\omega$$

Consequently, the intensity i of the diffusely reflected light is

$$i = \frac{k\cos\phi \, d\omega}{\cos\phi \, d\omega} = k \qquad \text{a constant}$$

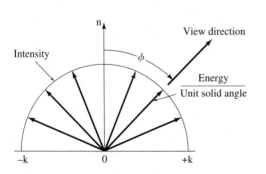

Figure 5–80 Lambertian diffuse reflection.

The total energy is found by integrating over the surface

$$P = \int_{2\pi} dP = \int_{2\pi} i \cos \phi \, d\omega = i \int_{2\pi} \cos \phi \, d\omega = i\pi$$

Thus, the energy and the intensity for ideal Lambertian diffuse reflection differ by a factor of π.

Enclosures

In order to determine the light energy at a surface, *all* the radiant energy from *all* directions in space must be accounted for. Consider a hypothetical enclosure consisting of a set of N surfaces, as shown in Fig. 5–81. The surfaces can be light sources, e.g., emitting surfaces; reflective; or fictitious, e.g., a window. Thus, the surfaces are considered as ideal diffuse reflectors, ideal diffuse emitters, a combination of diffuse reflector and emitter or of uniform composition with uniform illumination, reflection and emission intensities. Light sources are emulated by treating them as surfaces with specified illumination intensities. Directed light sources are handled by first independently computing their direct contribution to surfaces and then treating those surfaces as illuminated (emitting) surfaces in the radiosity solution.

The radiosity $B(i)$ is the hemispherical integral of the energy leaving the surface i. To an observer the surface i appears to be emitting a flux, B_i, from the imaginary surface. The flux consists of two parts: E_i, the rate at which the surface emits energy as a *source*, and $\rho_i H_i$, the rate at which incident energy is reflected back into the environment. Here ρ_i is the reflectivity of the surface, i.e., the fraction of incident energy reflected from the surface; and H_i is the radiant energy incident on the surface. Thus

$$B_i = E_i + \rho_i H_i$$

where the units are energy/unit time/unit area.

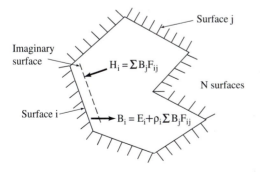

Figure 5–81 A hypothetical enclosure.

The incident flux on surface i, H_i, is the sum of the flux from all the surfaces in the enclosure that 'see' i (see Fig. 5–81). The fraction of the flux leaving surface j, B_j that reaches surface i is given by the form factor F_{ji}. Thus, the incident flux on surface i is

$$H_i = \sum_{j=1}^{N} B_j \frac{A_j F_{ji}}{A_i}$$

where the term within the summation represents the energy leaving patch j, $(B_j A_j)$, that reaches patch i, (F_{ji}), per unit area of patch i, $(1/A_i)$. Intuitively (but see below for more detail), the energy per unit time leaving patch j that reaches patch i is proportional to the area A_j of patch j. Similarly the energy per unit time leaving patch i that reaches patch j is proportional to the area of patch i. Although the energies of the two patches are not necessarily equal, for uniform energy distributions on each patch, the geometry intuitively suggests that $A_i F_{ij} = A_j F_{ji}$ where F_{ij} is the form factor from patch i to patch j. This is the classical radiosity reciprocity relation.

Substituting for H_i and using the reciprocity relation yields

$$B_i = E_i + \rho_i \sum_{j=1}^{N} B_j F_{ij} \qquad 1 \le i \le N$$

Multiplying by the area of patch i gives the energy per unit time leaving patch i, i.e.

$$B_i A_i = E_i A_i + \rho_i \sum_{j=1}^{N} B_j F_{ij} A_i \qquad 1 \le i \le N$$

Dividing each surface into patches and applying this equation to each patch yields a set of linear equations represented in matrix form as

$$\begin{bmatrix} 1 - \rho_1 F_{11} & -\rho_1 F_{12} & \cdots & -\rho_1 F_{1N} \\ -\rho_2 F_{21} & -\rho_2 F_{22} & \cdots & -\rho_2 F_{2N} \\ -\rho_N F_{N1} & -\rho_N F_{N2} & \cdots & -\rho_N F_{NN} \end{bmatrix} \begin{bmatrix} B_1 \\ B_2 \\ . \\ . \\ . \\ B_N \end{bmatrix} = \begin{bmatrix} E_1 \\ E_2 \\ . \\ . \\ . \\ E_N \end{bmatrix}$$

The E_is represent the sources of illumination. If all the E_is equal zero, there is no illumination and all the B_is are zero. This system of equations is applied monochromatically for each bandwidth, for each 'color' (RGB). To get the radiant *intensity*, the B_is and E_is are divided by π. The system of equations can be solved using any standard equation solver. However, a Gauss-Seidel iterative technique is advantageous because the matrix is strictly diagonally dominant, hence rapid convergence to a solution is guaranteed.

Form Factors

To determine the form factors shown in Fig. 5–81, we consider the solid angle subtended by differential surface dA_j (see Fig. 5–82), as seen from differential surface dA_i. This is

$$d\omega = \frac{\cos \phi_j}{r^2} \, dA_j$$

Recalling that

$$i = \frac{dP}{\cos \phi \, d\omega}$$

and

$$P = i \int_{2\pi} \cos \phi \, d\omega = i\pi$$

yields

$$dP_i \, dA_i = i_i \cos \phi_i \, d\omega \, dA_i = \frac{P_i \cos \phi_i \cos \phi_j}{\pi r^2} \, dA_i \, dA_j$$

Recalling that the form factor is the *fraction* of the total energy emanating from dA_j, directly incident on dA_i, yields

$$F_{dA_i - dA_j} = \frac{P_i \cos \phi_i \cos \phi_j \, dA_i \, dA_j / \pi r^2}{P_i \, dA_i} = \frac{\cos \phi_i \cos \phi_j}{\pi r^2} \, dA_j$$

Integrating over A_j yields

$$F_{dA_i - A_j} = \int_{A_j} \frac{\cos \phi_i \cos \phi_j}{\pi r^2} \, dA_j$$

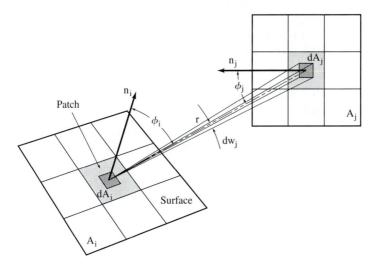

Figure 5–82 The solid angle subtended by dA_j.

which is the fraction of energy leaving dA_j and reaching A_i. The form factor between the finite areas is defined as the area average, i.e.

$$F_{A_i-A_j} = F_{ij} = \frac{1}{A_i} \int\limits_{A_i} \int\limits_{A_j} \frac{\cos\phi_i \cos\phi_j}{\pi r^2} \, dA_i \, dA_j$$

where in arriving at this result the radiosity across each area (patch) is assumed constant. In addition, this result assumes that every part of each area is visible to the other area and that the distance between the patches is large compared to their size. If the distance between the patches is not large compared to their size, then the patches are further subdivided.

Cohen and Greenberg [Cohe85] introduce the factor H_{ij}, where $H_{ij} = 1$ if a straight line between the centers of the differential areas dA_i and dA_j does not intersect any other element in the scene, and $H_{ij} = 0$ if it does. H_{ij} accounts for occluding objects between the areas. Effectively, it produces the projection of area j visible from differential area i. Thus

$$F_{A_i-A_j} = F_{ij} = \frac{1}{A_i} \int\limits_{A_i} \int\limits_{A_j} \frac{\cos\phi_i \cos\phi_j}{\pi r^2} \, H_{ij} \, dA_i \, dA_j$$

From the geometry and the definition of H_{ij}, $H_{ij} = H_{ji}$; and it is obvious that the integrals in this relation are identical. Thus, for uniform diffuse distributions

$$A_i \, F_{ij} = A_j \, F_{ji}$$

which is the reciprocity relation for form factors. Consequently, when calculating form factors only those for $i < j$ need be determined directly. Also, for a plane or convex surface that does not see itself, $F_{ii} = 0$; hence, only $N(N-1)/2$ form factors need actually be calculated.

Because F_{ij} is the fraction of energy that leaves a surface j, which reaches a surface i, and because the environment is enclosed, conservation of energy requires that

$$\sum_{j=1}^{N} F_{ij} = 1 \qquad \text{for } i = 1, N$$

Using this relation further reduces the number of form factors that actually require explicit calculation. Alternatively, it can be used to check the accuracy of numerical calculation of the form factors.

For a limited number of simple geometries analytic formulas give exact form factors. However, in general, numerical methods must be used. For example, Goral [Gora84] used Stoke's theorem to analytically convert the area integrals into contour integrals, that is

$$F_{ij} = \frac{1}{2\pi A_i} \oint\limits_{C_1} \oint\limits_{C_2} [\ln(r)\,dx_i\,dx_j + \ln(r)\,dy_i\,dy_j + \ln(r)\,dz_i\,dz_j]$$

However, it was necessary to solve the resulting integrals numerically by discretizing the boundaries. Thus, because the complexity of the resulting integrals requires a numerical solution, the analytical/numerical approach based on Stokes theorem is also limited to relatively simple environments.

The Hemicube

A geometric analog for the form factor equation is given by the Nusselt Analog (see Fig. 5–83). For a finite area, the form factor is equivalent to the fraction of the circle forming the base of a hemisphere covered by projecting the area onto the surface of the hemisphere and thence orthogonally downward onto the circle. If during projection the hidden (nonvisible) portions of patches are removed, then the procedure includes the effects of hidden surfaces.

Projection onto a sphere is difficult. However, note in Fig. 5–84 that any two patches which have the same area when projected onto the hemisphere have the same form factor. This is also true for any other *surrounding* surface. Cohen and Greenberg [Cohe85] introduced the idea of a hemicube, i.e., half of a cube, to determine a numerical approximation to the integral over the hemisphere, as shown in Fig. 5-85.

An imaginary hemicube is constructed around the center of the patch i in question. For convenience, the environment is transformed such that the center of the patch is at the origin and the normal is along the positive z-axis. The hemicube is divided into subareas, or hemicube 'pixels' (see Fig. 5-86).

All other patches j in the environment are projected onto the hemicube (see Fig. 5–86). If more than one patch projects onto a hemicube subarea, a visible

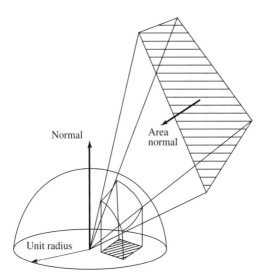

Figure 5–83 The Nusselt Analog. The form factor is equal to the fraction of the base covered by the projection.

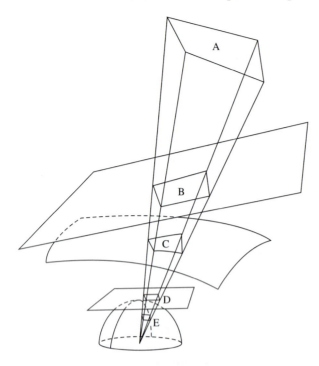

Figure 5–84 The equivalence of projected areas: areas A, B, C, D and E all have the same form factor.

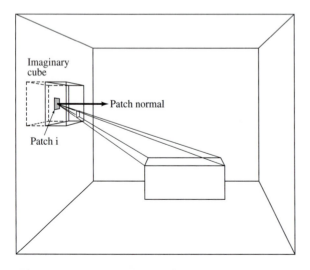

Figure 5-85 Projection of the environment onto the hemicube covering a patch.

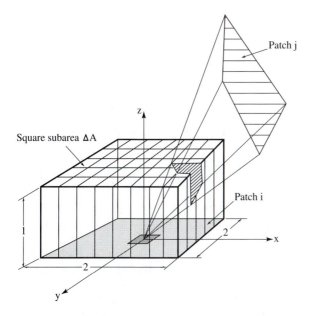

Figure 5–86 A patch projected onto a subdivided hemicube.

surface algorithm, e.g., a modified z-buffer algorithm in the form of an item buffer (see Sec. 4–9 and [Wegh84; Cohe85; Hall89]), determines which patch is seen by that subarea. Thus, occluding objects are handled directly.

A numerical approximation for the form factor between a patch j and the patch i is obtained by determining which subareas of the hemicube are 'covered' by the projection of patch j onto the hemicube. The contribution of this subarea to the total form factor depends on its location, as shown in Fig. 5–87. Effectively, the approximation says that for large distances between patches that are not occluded the form factor is

$$F_{ij} \approx \left(\int_{A_j} \frac{\cos \phi_i \cos \phi_j}{\pi r^2} H_{ij} dA_j \right) \frac{1}{A_i} \int_{A_i} dA_i = \int_{A_j} \frac{\cos \phi_i \cos \phi_j}{\pi r^2} H_{ij} dA_j$$

and then discretizes the resulting integral.

If the patch projects onto the top of the hemicube, then

$$r = \sqrt{x^2 + y^2 + 1}$$

$$\cos \phi_i = \cos \phi_j = \frac{1}{r}$$

and the incremental addition to the form factor is

$$\Delta F_i = \frac{\cos \phi_i \cos \phi_j}{\pi r^2} \Delta A = \frac{1}{\pi(x^2 + y^2 + 1)^2} \Delta A$$

If the patch projects through the side of the hemicube where $x = 1$, then

$$r = \sqrt{1 + y^2 + z^2} \qquad \cos \phi_i = \frac{z}{r} \qquad \cos \phi_j = \frac{1}{r}$$

and the addition to the form factor is

$$\Delta F_i = \frac{\cos \phi_i \cos \phi_j}{\pi r^2} \Delta A = \frac{z}{\pi (1 + y^2 + z^2)^2} \Delta A$$

The form factor for the complete surface is then

$$F_{ij} = \sum_{k=1}^{R} \Delta F_i$$

where R is the number of subareas. The delta form factors for each of the subareas are precalculated and stored in a table. Because of the symmetry of the hemicube, only $1/8$ of the top surface delta form factors and only $1/4$ of those on a single side face are calculated and stored. An example more fully illustrates the computation.

Example 5–10   Form Factors

Consider the example scene shown in Fig. 5–88. Find the form factor between the patch i and the patch j, with $(0, 0, 0)$ at the center of patch i. The vertex list for patch i is $(-1, -1, 0)$, $(1, -1, 0)$, $(1, 1, 0)$, $(-1, 1, 0)$, and for patch j it is $(-0.5, 2, 3)$, $(0.5, 2, 3)$, $(0.5, 3, 2)$, $(-0.5, 3, 2)$.

Erect a hemicube over patch i with vertices $(-1, -1, 0)$, $(1, -1, 0)$, $(1, 1, 0)$, $(-1, 1, 0)$, $(-1, -1, 1)$, $(1, -1, 1)$, $(1, 1, 1)$, $(-1, 1, 1)$, as shown in Fig. 5–88. Grid the hemicube, using 20×20 subareas on the top face $(z = 1)$ of the

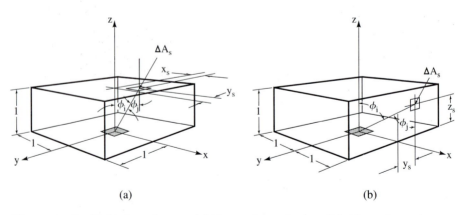

(a)   (b)

Figure 5–87 Delta form factors. (a) Top surface subareas; (b) side surface subareas.

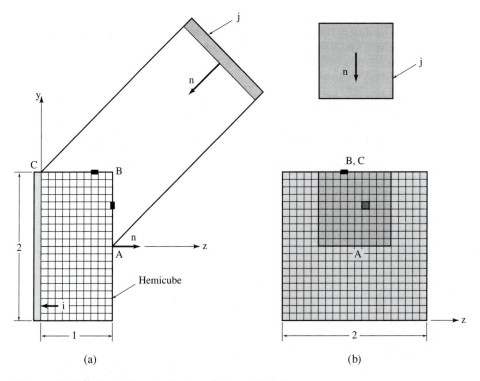

Figure 5–88 Scene for simple form factor calculation.

hemicube, as shown in Fig. 5–88b, and 10×20 subareas on each side face $(y = \pm1, x = \pm1)$, as shown in Fig. 5–88a.

Recalling that the incremental form factors on the top surface of the hemicube where $(z = 1)$ are given by

$$\Delta F_i = \frac{\Delta A_s}{(x_s^2 + y_s^2 + 1)^2}$$

we have for the subarea, with center at $(0.15, 0.55, 1)$ on the top face of the hemicube

$$\Delta F_k = \frac{(0.1)(0.1)}{[(0.15)^2 + (0.55)^2]^2 + 1} = \frac{0.01}{[1.325]^2} = \frac{0.01}{1.7556} = 0.005696$$

Notice that the values in the tables for ΔF_k, given below, are multiplied by 1000. The sum of the ΔF_ks for all the subareas on the top face is $\Delta F_{ij} = 0.567337$, as indicated.

For the subarea on the side face of the hemicube where $y = 1$

$$\Delta F_k = \frac{z_s \Delta A_s}{(x_s^2 + 1 + z_s^2)^2}$$

and for the subarea with center at $(-0.15, 1, 0.75)$ we have

$$\Delta F_k = \frac{(0.75)(0.1)(0.1)}{[(-0.15)^2 + 1 + (0.75)^2]^2} = \frac{0.0075}{[1.585]^2} = \frac{0.0075}{2.5122} = 0.002985$$

The complete results for the top face are

$$1000 \times \Delta F_{ij}$$

y_s/x_s	−0.450	−0.350	−0.250	−0.150	−0.050	0.050	0.150	0.250	0.350	0.450
0.050	6.887	7.901	8.817	9.518	9.901	9.901	9.518	8.817	7.901	6.887
0.150	6.664	7.628	8.495	9.157	9.518	9.518	9.157	8.495	7.628	6.664
0.250	6.249	7.121	7.901	8.495	8.817	8.817	8.495	7.901	7.121	6.249
0.350	5.696	6.452	7.121	7.628	7.901	7.901	7.628	7.121	6.452	5.696
0.450	5.066	5.696	6.249	6.664	6.887	6.887	6.664	6.249	5.696	5.066
0.550	4.415	4.925	5.367	5.696	5.872	5.872	5.696	5.367	4.925	4.415
0.650	3.787	4.189	4.535	4.789	4.925	4.925	4.789	4.535	4.189	3.787
0.750	3.210	3.522	3.787	3.981	4.083	4.083	3.981	3.787	3.522	3.210
0.850	2.699	2.938	3.139	3.284	3.361	3.361	3.284	3.139	2.938	2.699
0.950	2.257	2.439	2.590	2.699	2.756	2.756	2.699	2.590	2.439	2.257

$$\sum \Delta F_{ij} = 0.567337$$

and for the side faces are

$$1000 \times \Delta F_{ij}$$

z_s/x_s	−0.450	−0.350	−0.250	−0.150	−0.050	0.050	0.150	0.250	0.350	0.450
0.050	0.344	0.395	0.441	0.476	0.495	0.495	0.476	0.441	0.395	0.344
0.150	1.000	1.144	1.274	1.374	1.428	1.428	1.374	1.274	1.144	1.000
0.250	1.562	1.780	1.975	2.124	2.204	2.204	2.124	1.975	1.780	1.562
0.350	1.994	2.258	2.492	2.670	2.765	2.765	2.670	2.492	2.258	1.994
0.450	2.280	2.563	2.812	2.999	3.099	3.099	2.999	2.812	2.563	2.280
0.550	2.428	2.709	2.952	3.133	3.230	3.230	3.133	2.952	2.709	2.428
0.650	2.462	2.723	2.948	3.113	3.201	3.201	3.113	2.948	2.723	2.462
0.750	2.408	2.642	2.840	2.985	3.062	3.062	2.985	2.840	2.642	2.408
0.850	2.294	2.497	2.668	2.791	2.857	2.857	2.791	2.668	2.497	2.294
0.950	2.144	2.317	2.460	2.564	2.618	2.618	2.564	2.460	2.317	2.144

$$\sum \Delta F_{ij} = 0.223982$$

The sum of the ΔF_ks for all the subareas on the side face is $\Delta F_{ij} = 0.223982$. Summing the ΔF_{ij}s for the top and side faces yields the form factor

$$F_{ij} = 0.567337 + 0.223982 = 0.791319$$

Rendering

Once the form factors are determined and the matrix equation solved, the radiosities, B_i, are used to render each of the patches in the scene. Notice that the form factors are independent of the location of the viewpoint, i.e., radiosity solutions are *view independent*. Aside from their other attributes, this characteristic makes radiosity solutions particularly useful for scenes in which the viewpoint changes continuously, e.g., so-called walk-throughs.

If the patches are rendered directly, a flat shaded image results. Consequently, the patch radiosity values are extrapolated to the surrounding patch vertices [Cohe85]. The image is then rendered using bilinear interpolation in object space, i.e., a variation on Gouraud shading (see Sec. 5–6). The radiosities at vertices interior to polygon boundaries are determined by averaging the radiosities of the surrounding patches, as shown in Fig. 5–89.

Referring to Fig. 5–89a, the radiosity at vertex o is the average of the radiosities of B_1, B_2, B_3 and B_4

$$B_o = B_1 + B_2 + B_3 + B_4$$

For an edge vertex such as f, observe that the radiosity for the point halfway between vertices o and f, marked by the small square, is given by the average of B_o and B_f, or by the average of B_1 and B_2. Thus

$$\frac{B_o + B_f}{2} = \frac{B_1 + B_2}{2}$$

and $$B_f = B_1 + B_2 - B_o$$

For a corner vertex such as g, note that B_1 is the average of B_g and B_o, i.e.

$$B_1 = \frac{B_g + B_o}{2}$$

and $$B_g = 2B_1 - B_o$$

The case where there are no interior points, as illustrated in Fig. 5–89b [Gate91], is handled by subdividing both patches into four subpatches and applying the

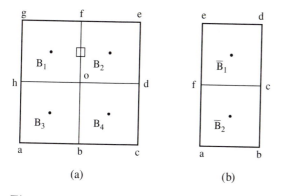

(a)   (b)

Figure 5–89 Extrapolating patch radiosities to the vertices. (a) Interior and boundary vertices; (b) minimal boundary vertices.

equation for the corner vertex, f, of Fig. 5–89a. If each of the subpatches is assumed to have radiosity equal to the parent patch, then the corner vertices a, b are assigned a radiosity equal to $\bar{B}_1$, and corner vertices e, f are assigned a radiosity equal to $\bar{B}_2$. The edge points c, f are assigned a radiosity equal to the average of $\bar{B}_1$ and $\bar{B}_2$, e.g., $\bar{B}_f = (\bar{B}_1 + \bar{B}_2)/2$.

Substructuring

The preceding discussion assumes that the radiosity across a patch is constant. However, there may be areas in the scene where the radiosity varies rapidly, e.g., across a shadow. Increasing the number of patches in the scene corrects this problem, but at considerable computational expense. What is required is a better representation of the radiosity of a patch into smaller elements, locally calculating the radiosity of each of the elements and then using an area-weighted average of the radiosities of the elements to obtain a better radiosity for the patch [Cohe86]. An element is assumed to be the smallest unit for which a radiosity value is determined.

The radiosity for an element, q, due to a patch j is

$$B_q = E_q + \rho_q \sum_{j=1}^{N} B_j F_{qj}$$

Suppose a patch i is subdivided into t elements. Then the radiosity of the patch i is the area-weighted average of the t element radiosities

$$B_i = \frac{1}{A_j} \sum_{q=1}^{t} B_q A_q$$

Combining the equations yields

$$B_i = \frac{1}{A_i} \sum_{q=1}^{t} (E_q + \rho_q \sum_{j=1}^{N} B_j F_{qj}) A_q = \frac{1}{A_i} \sum_{q=1}^{t} E_q A_q + \frac{1}{A_i} \sum_{j=1}^{N} \sum_{q=1}^{t} \rho_q B_j F_{qj} A_q$$

Assuming that neither ρ_q nor E_q vary across the patch yields

$$B_i = E_i + \rho_i \sum_{j=1}^{N} B_j \left(\frac{1}{A_i} \sum_{q=1}^{t} F_{qj} A_q \right)$$

Comparing to the original equation for the form factor F_{ij} shows that

$$F_{ij} = \frac{1}{A_i} \sum_{q=1}^{t} F_{qj} A_q$$

Provided the element form factors, F_{qj}, are known, a more accurate value for the coarse form factor, F_{ij}, is obtained. These element radiosities may also be extrapolated to the element vertices and interpolated across the elements when rendering the patch.

Progressive Refinement

As presented above, the radiosity solution requires both enormous computational effort and enormous storage. Cohen et al. [Cohe88] made a crucial but subtle change to the algorithm that eliminated these requirements by calculating the form factors on-the-fly; they thus reordered the operations in the Gauss-Seidel iteration cycle.

In the restructured algorithm, the radiosity of each patch is updated simultaneously; and patches are processed in sorted order, with the sort order determined by their energy contribution. Fundamentally, an initial approximate solution to the radiosity equation based on known geometric and reflective characteristics of the environment is obtained, and an image is rendered immediately based on the approximate solution. This solution is then *progressively refined*, i.e., iterated, until it converges to the final solution. An image is rendered at each step in the progressive refinement. The image *gracefully* progresses toward realism.

Recalling the fundamental radiosity equation

$$B_i = E_i + \rho_i \sum_{j=1}^{N} B_j F_{ij} \qquad 1 \le i \le N$$

and noting that the iterative solution converges to a solution by solving the matrix one row at a time, then a given row in the matrix, i, represents an estimate of the radiosity of patch i due to the current estimate of the radiosities of all other patches. Consequently, a single element of the summation gives the radiosity of patch i resulting from patch j, i.e, the radiosity leaving patch i is determined by *gathering* light from the environment. Thus

$$B_i \text{ (due to } B_j) = \rho_i B_j F_{ij}$$

Reversing the process, i.e., determining the effect of a single patch on all other patches in the environment using the reciprocity relation, yields

$$B_j \text{ (due to } B_i) = \rho_j B_i F_{ij} \frac{A_i}{A_j}$$

which is the radiosity contribution to the entire environment of patch i. For each iteration, a patch i is selected and a hemicube placed over it to determine its contribution to the illumination of all other patches. Note that the form factors F_{ij} do not change. In effect, light is *shot* from the patch into the environment, as shown in Fig. 5–90.

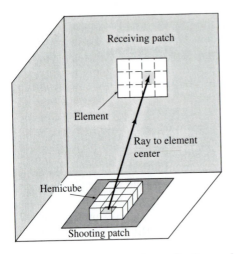

Figure 5–90   Progressive radiosity — shooting a ray from a patch to an element in the scene.

As the system iterates to a solution, this calculation is performed numerous times. Because the radiosity from all previous calculations is already present in the solution, only the *increment* in the radiosity, ΔB_i, need be added to the solution. ΔB_i represents the *unshot* radiosity in the scene. The solution continues until it converges to within some user-supplied tolerance.

Sorting

If patches are sorted based on their contribution to the illumination in the scene, the convergence of the solution is improved. Cohen [Cohe88] uses the product of $B_i A_i$ to estimate the illumination effect. In effect, the solution is started with the emitting patch that makes the largest contribution to the scene. The solution is continued with the patch that has the largest difference, $\Delta B_i A_i$, between the current and previous solution.

The Ambient Contribution

Early images are dark unless an ambient term is added during rendering. The ambient term is used *only* during rendering, it is *not* used to obtain the radiosity solution. As the radiosity solution progresses, the ambient contribution must approach zero.

In order to start the solution, Cohen approximates the initial form factors as the fraction of the total area of the environment covered by patch j, i.e.

$$F_{ij}^{\text{est}} = \frac{A_j}{\sum_{j=1}^{N} A_j}$$

The $\sum F_{ij}^{\text{est}} = 1$, as with the correct form factors.

The average reflectivity for the scene is computed using a weighted average of the individual patch reflectivities

$$\rho_{\text{avg}} = \frac{\sum_{i=1}^{N} \rho_i A_i}{\sum_{i=1}^{N} A_i}$$

For a given energy emitted into the scene, a fraction ρ_{avg} is recursively reflected from each patch. Thus, the overall interreflection coefficient is

$$1 + \rho_{\text{avg}} + \rho_{\text{avg}}^2 + \rho_{\text{avg}}^3 + \cdots = \frac{1}{1 - \rho_{\text{avg}}}$$

by the binomial theorem.

The ambient radiosity term is then the product of the overall interreflection coefficient and the unshot radiosity, i.e.

$$B_{\text{ambient}} = \frac{1}{1 - \rho_{\text{avg}}} \sum_{j=1}^{N} \Delta B_j F_{ij}$$

The radiosity of patch B_i resulting from all the other patches used to *display* the scene is then

$$B_i' = B_i + \rho_i B_{\text{ambient}}$$

Notice that the values of B_i' and B_i converge as the solution progresses, hence the contribution of $B_{\text{ambient}} \to 0$.

Adaptive Subdivision

The overall number of patches and the associated computational effort is reduced using adaptive subdivision. Initially, a relatively coarse patch structure is used. Patches are adaptively subdivided into elements. The elements act as receivers of light from other patches but not from other elements. A hemicube is placed over each patch in the environment, and elements are projected onto the hemicube. The patch to element form factors, F_{iq}, are determined in the same manner as for the full solution, e.g., the radiosity of a patch is determined using the weighted average of the element radiosities. Patches are subdivided only if large gradients in the radiosity occur, or if the area ratio causes the form factor term, $F_{ij} A_i / A_j$, to become more than one. Figure 5–91 shows a patch with a shadow line falling across it. Initially, the patch is divided into four elements (subpatches) and the radiosity of each of the elements is determined. Three of the four elements in Fig. 5–91 contain large radiosity values compared to the fourth. Each of the three patches is recursively subdivided, and the radiosity gradient across the subdivided elements is examined until it falls below some predetermined value. Note that if a particular element is subdivided, only the row of the matrix corresponding to that element need be deleted and replaced. Cohen and Wallace [Cohe93] present a more formal and extensive discussion of adaptive

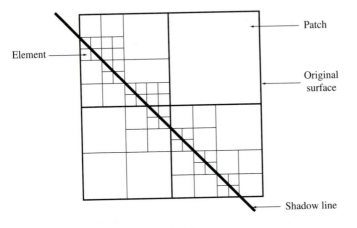

Figure 5-91 Adaptive subdivision.

subdivision. Finally, the images are rendered directly from the elements, using an object space adaptation of Gouraud shading after interpolating the element radiosities to their vertices.

Pseudocode for the progressive refinement algorithm [Cohe88] is:

initialization

  determine overall interreflection factor, ρ

  determine initial ambient contribution

  $B_{\text{ambient}} = (1/(1 - \rho_{\text{avg}})) \sum_{i=1}^{N}(E_i A_i)/\sum_{i=1}^{N} A_i$

  initialize unshot radiosity to emission

  for each patch $\Delta B_i = E_i$

    element e is a subunit of patch i

    for each element $B_e = E_i + \rho_i B_{\text{ambient}}$

      initialize change in ambient radiosity

      $\Delta B_{\text{ambient}} = 0$

    next element

  next patch

radiosity solution

while not converged

    pop patch with largest unshot energy, $\Delta B_i A_i$

    compute patch i to element form factors F_{ie}

    for each element

      determine increase in radiosity of element e due to ΔB_i

      $\Delta Rad = \rho_e \Delta B_i F_{ie} A_i / A_e$

      add area weighted portion of increased radiosity for element e to *the radiosity of the patch j, which contains e*

$$B_e = B_e + \Delta Rad + \rho_e \Delta B_{\text{ambient}}$$
$$\Delta B_j = \Delta B_j + \Delta Rad A_e / A_j$$

next element
interpolate vertex radiosities from neighboring elements
if gradient from neighboring elements too large **then**
    subdivide elements and reshoot patch i
end if
$\Delta B_i = 0$
determine $\Delta B_{\text{ambient}}$ from new unshot radiosities, ΔB_j
display environment as Gouraud-shaded elements
end while
finish

Hemicube Inaccuracies

The hemicube is a numerical approximation to the radiosity integral; as such, several inaccuracies result. Baum et al. [Baum89] point out that these inaccuracies are a result of violating one or more of three critical geometry assumptions in the hemicube approximation:

The proximity assumption

The visibility assumption

The aliasing assumption

As a result of these inaccuracies, the progressive refinement technique does not necessarily converge to the same result as the full matrix solution.

In deriving the hemicube approximation, the assumption is made that the distance between surfaces A_i and A_j is large compared to the effective diameter of A_i. This is the proximity assumption. However, the proximity assumption is violated whenever surfaces are adjacent to each other. An example, taken from [Baum89], is shown in Fig. 5–92. Here, the analytically derived form factors (see [Howe82] or [Walt87]) are given by

$$F_{ij} = \frac{1}{\pi W} \left(W \tan^{-1} \frac{1}{W} + H \tan^{-1} \frac{1}{H} - H^2 + W^2 \tan^{-1} \frac{1}{\sqrt{H^2 + W^2}} \right.$$

$$+ \frac{1}{4} \left\{ \frac{(1+W^2)(1+H^2)}{1+W^2+H^2} \left[\frac{W^2(1+W^2+H^2)}{(1+W^2)(W^2+H^2)} \right]^{W^2} \times \right.$$

$$\left. \left. \left[\frac{H^2(1+W^2+H^2)}{(1+H^2)(W^2+H^2)} \right]^{H^2} \right\} \right)$$

where $H = a/c$ and $W = b/c$, with c the common edge. For the configuration given in Fig. 5–92, $F_{21} = 0.247$ and $F_{12} = 0.0494$, while the limiting values calculated with an infinite resolution hemicube are [Baum89] $F_{hc21} = 0.238$ and $F_{hc12} = 0.0087$. Here we see that the approximation F_{hc21} is reasonable, because the distance from any point on S_2 to any point on S_1 is approximately the same. However, the approximation F_{hc12} is very poor, because the distance from the center of S_1 to points on S_2 is considerably different from the distance from points on the boundary of S_1 to points on S_2. Hemicube proximity errors are not limited to surfaces at right angles. Baum et al. [Baum89] give test results for several different configurations and suggest that for the worst cases patches must be separated by at least five patch 'diameters', assuming square patches.

The visibility assumption requires that an entire patch A_j be visible from a patch A_i. However, the hemicube approximation tests only whether the center of patch A_j is visible from patch A_i, as shown in Fig. 5–93. From the geometry in Fig. 5–93, the hemicube algorithm overestimates the form factor, F_{ij}.

Since the hemicube algorithm is a point sampling algorithm, it is subject to aliasing. The hemicube algorithm determines whether a patch covers a hemicube subarea or hemipixel by sampling the *center* of the hemipixel. Hence, both over- and underestimation of form factors occurs, as shown in Fig. 5–94. This effect is particularly noticeable when sampling lighting sources. Violation of these geometric assumptions results in 'plaiding' effects, and in dark areas where adjacent patches abut.

Baum and colleagues [Baum89] show that progressive radiosity is more susceptible to errors than the full matrix solution. Fundamentally, this is because progressive radiosity finds form factors from the patch to smaller elements which are more likely to be closer; hence, the proximity assumption is more likely to be violated. Baum et al. present a hybrid progressive radiosity solution that analytically determines the form factors using Stoke's theorem when the geometry assumptions are violated. They show that the hybrid solution converges to the correct solution within a very small error.

An alternate technique for determining the form factors for progressive radiosity by Wallace et al. [Wall89] uses ray tracing. They note that although a surface may occupy a significant part of the scene, it may be small enough to

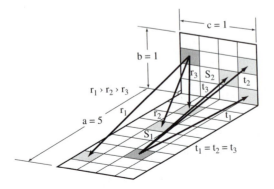

Figure 5–92   Different sized adjacent perpendicular surfaces.

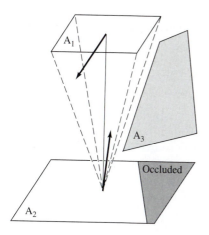

Figure 5–93 Partially occluded surface.

fall between rays from the center of a source patch and the center of hemicube pixels when extended into the scene. They further note that when rendering the scene it is the radiosity of the vertices that is required. Interpolating from the patch radiosity to the vertices also introduces aliasing.

The technique developed by Wallace et al. calculates the form factors by shooting rays from the source patch to the element *vertices* of the receiving patch. The number of sample points on the source may vary from one element vertex to the next. Thus, the form factor for area sources can be computed to any desired accuracy. In addition, the actual surface normal at the vertex can be used when rendering the scene. Thus, polygon meshes approximating curved surfaces are possible. Although radiosity is generally associated with area light sources, the technique allows representation of nonphysical point light sources.

In calculating the delta form factors, they use a simple analytical solution based on a disk to approximate the solution. They also assume that the effect of different orientations between the disk and the differential area is approximated

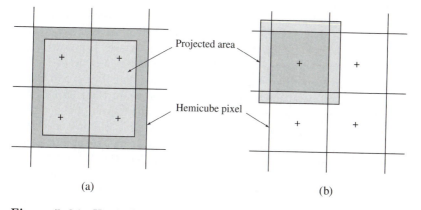

(a)   (b)

Figure 5–94 Hemicube aliasing caused by point sampling. (a) Overestimation; (b) underestimation.

by the cosines of the angles between the normal to each surface, ϕ_1 and ϕ_2, and the direction between source and receiver, i.e.

$$dF_{A_2 - dA_1} = \frac{dA_1 \cos \phi_1 \cos \phi_2}{\pi r^2 + A_2}$$

The effect of occlusion is approximated by shooting a single ray from the receiving vertex to the center of the source delta area. Unless large numbers of sample points are required, a uniform distribution on the source is used. However, for large numbers of sample points adaptive subdivision is implemented. Color Plate 20 was generated using ray traced form factors and progressive radiosity. Only two bays of the nave were actually solved using radiosity. The remaining six were scaled and translated to complete the scene. The two bays contain 9916 polygons, 74,806 element vertices with the stained glass windows represented by 30 light sources.

Alternatives to the Hemicube

Seeking either increased accuracy or speed, a number of investigators in addition to Baum et al. [Baum89] and Wallace et al. [Wall89] developed alternatives to the hemicube algorithm. Malley [Mall88] used a uniform distribution of jittered points on the base circle of a hemisphere centered over patch i. Each point is projected *upward* to the surface of the hemisphere. A ray is then cast radially outward from the center of patch i, through the point on the surface of the hemisphere to patch j, as shown in Fig. 5–95. The result is a *nonuniform* distribution of rays inversely proportional to the cosine of the angle between the normal to the patch and the ray direction, ϕ_i, i.e., concentrated around the normal direction. Provided that patch j is sufficiently far from patch i, $\cos \phi_i$ varies little over patch j. Typically those patches j for which $\cos \phi_i = 1$ make the largest contribution to the radiosity of patch i. Consequently, a nonuniform distribution of rays concentrated around the normal direction yields the most accurate results.

   Sillion and Puech [Sill94] use a single square plane face or screen above and very close to patch i, as shown in Fig. 5–96. Using a single plane and ray tracing to probe the scene misses some contributions close to the surface. However, again because of the cosine dependence of the form factor, i.e., $\cos \phi_i \to 0$ as $\phi_i \to \pi/2$, these contributions are negligible. Calculations indicate that if $S/H > 6$, more than 95% of the energy is captured; and if $S/H > 14$, more than 99% of the energy is captured. Here, as shown in Fig. 5–96, S is the length of the side of the square and H is the height of the square above patch i. Sillion and Puech subdivide the plane using edge parallel lines, in an attempt to obtain equal contributions to the form factor. They use a Warnock algorithm in an adaptive subdivision scheme to analyze the projection of patch j onto the plane and solve the occlusion problem. In software, their algorithm is faster than a hemicube using the modified z-buffer (item buffer). However, using a hardware z-buffer eliminates this advantage. Like Sillion and Puech, Recker et al. [Reck90] also use

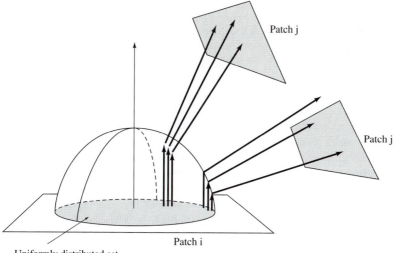

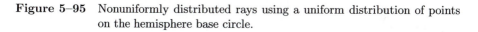

Uniformly distributed set
of jittered points.

Figure 5–95   Nonuniformly distributed rays using a uniform distribution of points
on the hemisphere base circle.

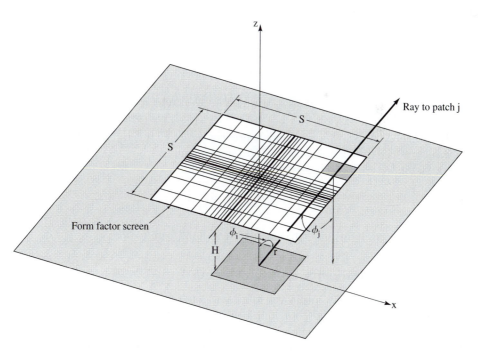

Figure 5–96   Single square plane form factor screen, with equal contribution subdivided proxels.

a uniformly subdivided single plane very close to patch i, but they subdivide it more finely in the center portion of the plane. However, they use the modified z-buffer (item buffer) to determine occlusions.

Spencer [Spen90] used a unit hemisphere erected over patch i to calculate form factors. He subdivided the hemisphere using common latitude and longitude (ϕ, θ) coordinates. Using the common latitude and longitude coordinates yields a nonuniform discretization, which concentrates the number of subdivisions near the axis of symmetry, an advantage for form factor calculation. Spencer projects patch j onto the hemisphere and thence downward to the base of the hemisphere. The resulting delta form factors are stored in an item buffer (modified z-buffer, see Sec. 4–9). He indicates that the algorithm is both faster and more accurate than a hemicube.

Using Renka's method [Renk84], Gatenby [Gate91] initially triangulates the unit hemisphere based on the vertices of a tetrahedron, whose base lies in the $z = 0$ plane with vertices $(0, 0, 1)$, $(1, 0, 0)$, $(-1/2, \sqrt{3}/2, 0)$, $(-1/2, -\sqrt{3}/2, 0)$. Further subdivision results from taking the midpoint of each side of the resulting spherical triangles and connecting them to form four spherical triangles. After four and five Renka subdivisions, the original three spherical triangles yield 768 and 3072 triangles, respectively, with nearly equal areas. The resulting discretization after one subdivision is shown in Fig. 5–97a. Notice that the triangles form 'rows of rings' around the hemisphere. Thus, a Sillion type algorithm that ignores directions that negligibly contribute to the form factor can be implemented by ignoring the ring closest to the base plane. Gatenby casts rays outward through the discretized triangles.

Referring to Fig. 5–97b and recalling that the delta form factor for any location on the base plane is

$$\Delta F_{\text{x,y,z}} = \frac{\cos \phi_i \cos \phi_j}{\pi r^2} \Delta A$$

notice that ϕ_j is always zero and hence $\cos \phi_j = 1$; the radial distance, r, is always one; $\cos \phi_i = z$ and $\Delta A = {}^{2\pi}/_D$ for D equiarea triangles. Thus, the delta form factor for each discretized triangle is simply

$$\Delta F_{\text{x,y,z}} = 2 \frac{z}{D}$$

Gatenby uses an item buffer to calculate the final form factors.

Hierarchical Radiosity and Clustering

As discussed previously, radiosity solutions depend upon adaptive subdivision or meshing to reduce the total number of patches in a scene and hence the computational cost at a given accuracy. However, the computational cost may still be excessive. Adaptive meshing is a 'top-down' approach as is classical hierarchical radiosity [Hanr91, 92]. Classical hierarchical radiosity considers the energy exchange between two surfaces or volumes at various levels-of-detail. At

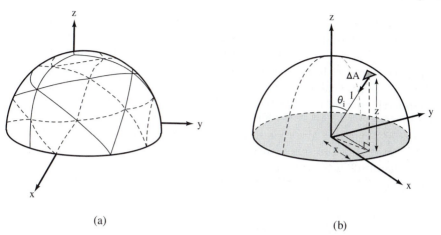

(a)   (b)

Figure 5–97   Triangularization of the unit hemisphere. (a) After one subdivision; (b) geometry for delta form factor calculation.

each level-of-detail the energy exchange between two objects is evaluated. If the energy exchange can be determined to the required accuracy, an energy *link* between the objects is established and the form factor calculated, otherwise one of the objects is subdivided. The algorithm is applied recursively. A quadtree (see Sec. 4–4) or k-d tree [Bent75; Frie77] or similar data structure is used to represent the links. The subdivision decision is typically based on bounding the form factor [Hanr92], the radiosity transfer [Hanr91] or by estimating the energy transfer [Lisc94]. Importance weighting may also be used when evaluating the error bounds [Hanr92].

Once a set of refined energy links is established the energy transfers across the links are computed by gathering the radiosity at each object. After each gather operation, energy at higher levels in the hierarchy is *pushed* downward to the children of that level. Subsequently, the energy at each child level is then *pulled* upward in the hierarchy and averaged. This is the so called *push-pull* operation, which insures the consistency of the solution. The gather and push-pull operations are iterated until no significant changes in radiosity occur. The concept of clustering introduced by Sillion i.e., grouping objects together to determine energy exchanges (see Secs. 4–3, 4–13, 4–20) between groups of objects rather than individual objects, introduces the idea of a bottom-up approach that reduces computational expense [Smit94; Sill94, Sill95a,b,c].

Classical radiosity assumes that the scene is composed of surfaces (polygons). Building on the zonal method [Rush87], which derives from radiosity, hierarchical radiosity is extended to include participating volumes, e.g., fog, smoke, haze, dust, etc. that have varying albedo [Sill94, 95a]. When considering scenes with a mix of surfaces (polygons) and volumes there are four possible types of energy links: surface-surface, surface-volume, volume-surface and volume-volume. Volumes may also exhibit self-links, i.e., one part of a volume may receive or transmit energy to another part of the same volume.

In mixed scenes, which contain both surfaces and volumes, Sillion [Sill95a] uses the idea of the equivalent surface area of a volume which, for isotropic scattering volumes, is proportional to four times the volume, to convert between equivalent surfaces and cluster volumes when performing the energy exchange calculations. In particular, the equivalent volume of a cluster of objects is determined from the sum of the surface areas of the objects in the cluster. Indirectly, the *extinction* (transmission) coefficient used to determine the attenuation of energy passing though an absorbing (or transmitting) volume, e.g., a fog bank or cloud is also obtained in this manner.

An example of an image computed with hierarchical radiosity and clustering is shown on the front cover. The image, computed by Peter Kipfer and François Sillion, incorporates the simple block structure from the first edition to illustrate the vast improvement in computer graphics rendering capability over the last several years.[†] The scene contains 287 initial surfaces which were grouped into 157 clusters. Adaptive subdivision resulted in 1,861,974 links. The back cover image shows an adaptively subdivided mesh superimposed over the front cover image. This image and mesh were created using an error metric 30 times larger than that for the front cover image, resulting in a much coarser mesh than that used to calculate the image on the front cover.

Radiosity for Specular Environments

The radiosity algorithm discussed earlier considers only diffusely reflected light. Immel et al. [Imme86] developed a general radiosity algorithm that considers interreflections for environments with both diffuse and nondiffuse, i.e., specular, reflections. The algorithm extends the concept of the hemicube to a global cube, as shown in Fig. 5–98. If a patch is assumed transparent, light may arrive at the patch, or be reflected from the patch, anywhere on a sphere surrounding the patch. The global cube serves to partition (discretize) space.

When considering a solution encompassing only a nondirectional illumination model, only a single intensity per patch per color sample results. However, for a directional illumination model a solution with one intensity for *each* sample direction of the global cube is required. A global cube with a resolution of 50 along each edge requires $50 \times 50 \times 6 = 15000$ sample points, or $15000 \times 15000 = 2.25 \times 10^8$ coefficients for *each* patch. Thus, the matrix describing the relationships among the patches grows to $N \times 15000 \times N \times 15000$ where N is the number of patches! The storage requirements are prodigious. Immel points out that the resulting solution matrix is very sparse, hence the Gauss-Seidel iteration technique is well suited to solving the matrix.

The illumination model used with the algorithm requires that energy be conserved and that it exhibit reciprocity. Immel used two simple illumination models, a Phong-like model for the bidirectional reflectance given by

---

[†]Calculation time at a resolution of 1800×1200 pixels was approximately 135 minutes on a 195 Mhz MIPS R10000 processor. The software was developed under the direction of François Sillion and George Drettakis.

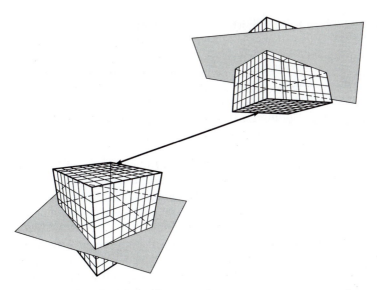

Figure 5–98   A global cube.

$$\rho = \frac{k_d}{S_d} + \frac{k_s}{S_s} \cos^n \phi$$

where k_d and k_s are the fraction of energy diffusely and specularly reflected, respectively, ϕ is the angle between the mirror and reflection directions and S_d and S_s are constant factors included in the energy equation. A mirror reflection illumination model was also used; Hall [Hall89] gives pseudocode for the algorithm. Color Plate 21 was generated[†] using the Phong-like illumination model.

The Rendering Equation

Kajiya [Kaji86] developed a general equation representing the interreflection of light within an enclosure, which he called *The Rendering Equation*. Again, the fundamental basis of the model is derived from radiative heat transfer. The rendering equation fundamentally represents the light energy balance within an enclosure, $\mathcal{R}$. It accounts for all ways that light can reach a point within an enclosure. In computer graphics terms, the equation is

$$I_{\text{out}}(\theta_{\text{out}}) = I_{\text{emit}}(\theta_{\text{out}}) + \int_{\mathcal{R}} \rho(\theta_{\text{out}}, \theta_{\text{in}}) \cos \phi \, d\omega$$

where $I_{\text{out}}(\theta_{\text{out}})$ is the total outgoing light intensity along a direction θ_{out}, $I_{\text{in}}(\theta_{\text{in}})$ is the total incoming light intensity along a direction θ_{in}, $I_{\text{emit}}(\theta_{\text{out}})$ is the total emitted light intensity along a direction θ_{out}, $\rho(\theta_{\text{out}}, \theta_{\text{in}})$ is the bidirectional

---

[†]The solution required approximately 300 hours on a VAX11/750 with a Floating Point Systems FPS264 unit.

reflectance function and ϕ is the angle between the surface normal and the direction of the incoming light.

Kajiya solved the rendering equation using a Monte Carlo Markov chain technique. He used variance reduction techniques in the context of a stochastic ray tracer, to determine whether a single ray shot from an intersection point is a diffuse or specular reflection or a refraction ray. The direction of the ray is determined by stochastic sampling. Because diffuse rays are traced, diffuse interobject reflections are modeled. A single shadow ray is cast toward a point on the light source, again chosen using variance reduction techniques. In his implementation, a fixed number of 40 rays was shot through each pixel for each path corresponding to a point in the probabilistic space used to solve the rendering equation. For complex environments, the computation time for Kajia's technique becomes excessive. For example, one scene took over 20 hours on an IBM 3081, at a resolution of 512×512.

Both Immel's [Imme86] and Kajia's [Kaji86] solutions represent extremes. Immel basically extends the radiosity technique to account for specular interobject reflections, and Kajia extends ray tracing to account for diffuse interobject reflections in a single solution path. The next section considers a more efficient two-pass technique for combined specular and diffuse interobject reflections.

5–18   Combined Ray Tracing and Radiosity

Wallace et al. [Wall87] developed a two-pass solution to the rendering equation that is much more efficient than either Immel's [Imme86] or Kajia's [Kaja86] solution. Their two-pass method divides the solution into view-independent (radiosity) and view-dependent (ray tracing) solutions.

Typical computer graphics illumination models divide the reflection model into two parts: a nondirectional, or diffuse, term and a directional, or specular, term. In essence, the bidirectional reflection is approximated as

$$\rho(\theta_{\text{out}}, \theta_{\text{in}}) = k_s \rho_s(\theta_{\text{out}}, \theta_{\text{in}}) + k_d \rho_d$$

where k_s and k_d are the specular and diffuse reflection fractions, with $k_s + k_d = 1$. Thus, the rendering equation can be rewritten as

$$I_{\text{out}}(\theta_{\text{out}}) = I_{\text{emit}}(\theta_{\text{out}}) + I_{d,\text{out}} + I_{s,\text{out}}(\theta_{\text{out}})$$

where

$$I_{d,\text{out}} = k_d \rho_d \int I_{\text{in}}(\theta_{\text{in}}) \cos \phi \, d\omega$$

$$I_{s,\text{out}}(\theta_{\text{out}}) = k_s \int \rho_s(\theta_{\text{out}}, \theta_{\text{in}}) I_{\text{in}}(\theta_{\text{in}}) \cos \phi \, d\omega$$

Notice that the outgoing intensities depend on the incoming intensities, which are in turn dependent on both outgoing diffuse and specular light intensities from other surfaces. Thus, adding separate diffuse (radiosity) and specular (ray tracing) solutions together is incorrect.

The transfer of light from a surface can be divided into four mechanisms: diffuse to diffuse, specular to diffuse, diffuse to specular and specular to specular, as shown in Fig. 5–99. The standard radiosity solution considers diffuse to diffuse transfers; and the standard ray tracing solution considers the specular to specular and diffuse to specular transfers, although the diffuse to specular transfer is only an approximation. Neither solution handles the critical specular to diffuse transfer of the Immel [Imme86] and Kajiya [Kaji86] solutions, although backward ray tracing [Arvo86] and beam tracing [Heck84] consider it. The two-pass solution accounts for all four transfer mechanisms.

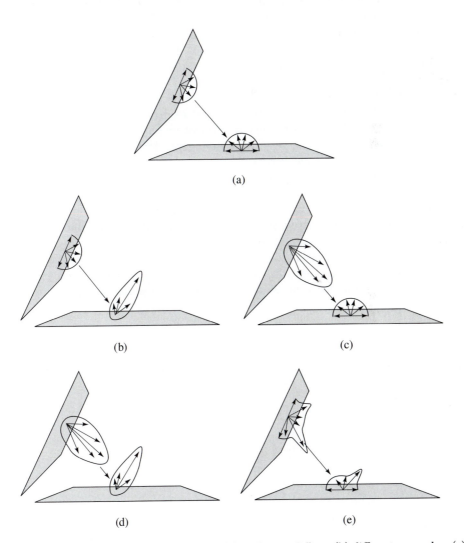

Figure 5–99 Interobject reflections. (a) Diffuse to diffuse; (b) diffuse to specular; (c) specular to diffuse; (d) specular to specular; (e) real.

The first pass is based on a standard radiosity algorithm with extensions to account for diffuse transmission, and to approximate specular reflection and transmission as they affect the diffuse reflection component of all surfaces. Diffuse transmission (translucency) is accounted for by adding a hemicube on the back side of the transmitting surface, in order to calculate *backward form factors* [Rush86, 90]. The backward form factors determine the effect that surfaces seen by the back of a translucent surface have on the intensity of the light on the front of the surface.

Specular to diffuse interreflection, caused by two diffuse surfaces 'seeing' each other via specular reflection from intermediate surfaces, is included in the solution by performing additional work when calculating the form factors. Wallace et al.'s implementation, restricted to perfect planar mirrors or filters, uses the mirror image technique, as shown in Fig. 5–100. This technique is well known in radiative heat transfer. Fundamentally, a virtual enclosure that is a mirror image of the enclosure is created. As shown in Fig. 5–100, patch j receives light from patch i'. Projecting patch i' onto the hemicube is equivalent to projecting patch i onto the hemicube. If ray tracing is used to determine the form factors, then the technique generalizes to curved surfaces including refraction. The final result of the first pass is an accurate view-independent determination of the diffuse intensity at the element vertices.

The second pass adds the view-dependent specular reflection components. It is the view dependence of the specular reflection that allows efficient calculation of the specular component $I_{s,\text{out}}(\theta_{\text{out}})$. The specular component depends on all the intensities arriving at the surface weighted by the specular bidirectional reflectance, $\rho_s(\theta_{\text{in}}, \theta_{\text{out}})$. The bidirectional reflectance function is such that only a limited fraction of the incoming intensities make contributions to the outgoing intensity in the reflected direction. Consequently, an acceptable approximation is obtained even with reduced integration limits confined to a

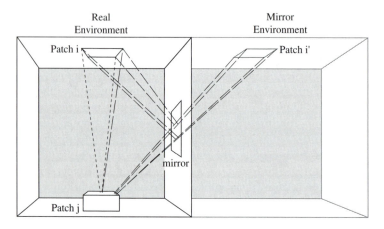

Figure 5–100   Method of images for determining specular to diffuse interreflection form factors.

small volume (solid angle) centered around the mirror directions. Wallace and colleagues' implementation uses a reflection frustum, as shown in Fig. 5–101, with a low resolution z-buffer (10×10 'pixels') to sample the incoming intensity. The incoming intensity may contain both diffuse and specular components. The diffuse component is determined using bilinear interpolation from the vertices using the values obtained during the first pass. The specular component is determined by recursively applying the second pass along the reflected direction, as in a standard ray tracer. Efficiency is increased by adaptively limiting the depth of the ray tree, and by reducing the size of the reflection frustum, as shown in Fig. 5–101. The reflection frustum serves to discretize the integral in the specular intensity equation; thus

$$I_{s,\text{out}}(\theta_{\text{out}}) = k_s \int \rho_s(\theta_{\text{out}}, \theta_{\text{in}}) I_{\text{in}}(\theta_{\text{in}}) \cos \phi \, d\omega$$

$$= k_s \sum_{i=0}^{n} \sum_{j=0}^{n} W_{i,j} I_{\text{in}}(\theta_{i,j}) \cos \theta_{i,j} \, \Delta \omega_{i,j}$$

where the $W_{i,j}$s are weights representing the bidirectional reflectance function, n is the resolution of the reflectance frustum and $\theta_{i,j}$ is the incoming direction corresponding to the 'pixel' i, j in the bidirectional reflectance frustum. The smaller the size of the reflectance frustum, the more mirror-like the reflection. Specular transmission, transparency and refraction are included by defining a bidirectional transmission function and using a transmission frustum centered along the transmission direction.

Antialiasing is efficiently handled by randomly *rotating* the reflectance or transmission frustum about its axis before performing the z-buffer function. Color Plate 22 illustrates the effect of including the specular to diffuse component in the illumination model. Color Plate 22a is a classical ray tracing

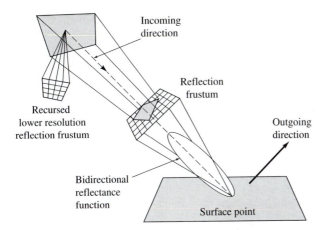

Figure 5–101 Specular reflection frustum.

solution. Color Plate 22b includes the diffuse to diffuse transfer, while Color Plate 22c is the full solution, including specular to diffuse transfers.

The Extended Two-pass Algorithm

Wallace et al.'s algorithm [Wall87] uses the method of images for planar mirrors to determine the specular reflection contributions to the intensity reaching a point. Practically, the depth of the ray tree is limited when determining the specular contribution to the form factors. Shao et al. [Shao88] refine Wallace et al.'s algorithm by introducing directional or extended form factors to account for specular reflections. They also include a Phong-style lighting model.

Sillion and Puech [Sill89] present a more general extension of the two-pass algorithm that includes any number of specular interreflections for patches of any geometry. The first pass in the Sillion and Puech algorithm is a standard radiosity calculation based on standard geometrical diffuse form factors. To account for specular interobject reflections, they extend the form factor definition such that F_{ij} is the fraction of energy leaving surface i and reaching surface j after *any number* of specular reflections or refractions. They use ray tracing to determine the extended form factors. Because of the extended form factor definition, it is necessary to consider the entire tree of reflected and refracted rays. Here it is important to note that the diffuse reflection coefficients are easily changed because they have no effect on the extended form factors. However, the specular coefficients are directly used in the calculation of the extended form factors. Consequently, they cannot be changed without recalculating the extended form factors. Note that if the extended form factors are stored, then the scene can be calculated with new lighting conditions without recalculating the extended form factors; only the classical radiosity solution and the second pass of the algorithm are required. The second pass in their algorithm also uses ray tracing. Note also that in calculating the extended form factors no shadow rays are required. Color Plate 23 illustrates some results, including refraction effects for a simple transparent sphere illuminated by three colored spotlights. Color Plate 23a is a conventional ray tracing solution; note the sharp shadows on the base plane. Color Plate 23b illustrates the results of a conventional radiosity solution; here the shadows are soft. Color Plate 23c illustrates the full solution, using a refraction index of 1.1; note that the character of the shadows is significantly influenced by the refraction of the light through the sphere, and that the shadows take on the colors of the lights.

5–19   Color

Color is casually mentioned throughout this text; it now remains to consider it in some detail. Color is both a psycho*physiological* phenomenon and a psycho*physical* phenomenon. The perception of color depends upon the physics of light considered as electromagnetic energy and its interaction with physical materials, and on the interpretation of the resulting phenomena by the human eye–brain visual system. As such, it is a vast, complex, fascinating subject, the details of which are well beyond the scope of this text. Additional information can be obtained by consulting Wyszecki and Stiles [Wysz82], Judd [Judd75], Hunt [Hunt75] and Hunter [Hntr75]. A short useful tutorial on color science is given by Meyer [Meye86a]. The approach taken here is to develop a basic color vocabulary, a basic understanding of the physical phenomena involved and a basic understanding of color specification systems, the transformations between them, compression (quantization) of color images and the reproduction of color images.

The human visual system interprets electromagnetic energy having wavelengths between approximately 400 and 700 nanometers as visible light. A nanometer (nm) is 10^{-9} meter, or a billionth of a meter. Light is perceived either directly from a source of illumination, e.g., a light bulb, or indirectly by reflection from the surface of an object or refraction through an object.

Chromaticity

When perceived light contains all the visible wavelengths with approximately equal weights, the light source or object is achromatic. An achromatic light source appears white. When the reflected or transmitted light from an object is achromatic, it appears white, black or an intermediate level or shade of gray. Objects that achromatically reflect more than about 80% of the incident light from a white light source appear white. Those that achromatically reflect less than about 3% of the incident light appear black. Intermediate achromatic reflectance levels yield various shades of gray. It is convenient to consider the intensity of the reflected light in a range between 0 and 1, with 0 equated to black and 1 to white. Intermediate values are gray.

Although it is difficult to distinguish between the concepts of lightness and brightness, lightness is most conveniently considered a perceived property of a non-self-luminous or reflecting object (white-black), and brightness a characteristic of the perceived amount of illumination (high-low) present from a self-luminous or emitting object. The perceived lightness or brightness of an object is dependent on the relative sensitivity of the eye to various wavelengths. Figure 5–102 shows that for daylight the eye is most sensitive to light at a wavelength of approximately 550 nm. The eye's sensitivity decreases rapidly at the ends of the visible light range, or spectrum. The curve in Fig. 5–102 is called a luminous efficiency function. It provides a measure of the light energy or intensity corrected for the sensitivity of the eye.

When perceived light contains wavelengths in arbitrary unequal amounts, the color of the light is said to be chromatic.[†] If a single concentration of wavelengths is near the upper end of the visible spectrum, the color of the light is interpreted as red or 'reddish'; i.e., the dominant wavelength is in the red portion of the visible spectrum. If near the lower end of the visible spectrum, the

---

[†]The operative words here are 'perceived' and 'arbitrary.' As shown later, discrete chromatic lights can be combined in specific ways to generate achromatic perceptions.

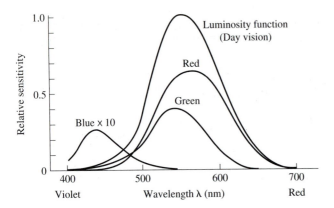

Figure 5–102   Relative sensitivity of the eye.

color is interpreted as blue or 'bluish'; i.e., the dominant wavelength is in the blue portion of the visible spectrum. However, note that electromagnetic energy of a particular wavelength has no color. It is the eye–brain combination that interprets the physical phenomena as the sensation of color. The color of an object depends on both the distribution of wavelengths of the light source and the physical characteristics of the object. If an object reflects or transmits light in only a narrow band of wavelengths, absorbing all others, then the object is perceived as colored. The wavelengths of the reflected or transmitted light determine the color. Interaction of the color of incident and reflected or transmitted light can yield startling results. For example, the reflected light from a green light incident on a normally white object also appears green; i.e., the object is perceived as green. However, a red object illuminated with green light appears black because no light is reflected.

A chromatic color is psychophysiologically defined by its hue, saturation and brightness. Hue is the 'color' of the color. It is the name by which the color is designated. The CIE[‡] defines hue as "the attribute of a visual sensation according to which an area appears to be similar to one of the perceived colours, red, yellow, green and blue or a combination of two of them". Saturation is a measure of the degree to which the pure color is diluted by white. The CIE defines saturation as "the colourfulness of an area judged in proportion to its brightness". A pure color is 100% saturated. As white is added, the degree of saturation decreases; achromatic light is 0% saturated. Brightness is the intensity of the achromatic light. The CIE defines brightness as "the attribute of a visual sensation according to which an area appears to emit more or less light".

The psychophysical equivalents of hue, saturation and brightness are dominant wavelength, purity and luminance. A perceived color generated by electromagnetic energy of a single wavelength in the visible spectrum is monochromatic.

[‡]Commission Internationale de L'Eclairage, the international standards organization dealing with color.

Figure 5–103a shows the energy distribution for such a monochromatic light with a wavelength of 525 nm. Figure 5–103b shows the energy distribution for a low level of 'white' light with energy E_2 and a single dominant wavelength of 525 nm with energy E_1. In Fig. 5–103b, the color of the light is determined by the dominant wavelength, and purity of the color by the relative magnitudes of E_1 and E_2. E_2 represents the amount by which the pure color of wavelength 525 nm is diluted by white light. As the magnitude of E_2 approaches zero, the purity of the color approaches 100%. As the magnitude of E_2 approaches that of E_1, the color of the light approaches white and the purity approaches zero. Luminance is proportional to the energy of the light and is usually considered as intensity per unit area.

Tristimulus Theory of Color

Pure monochromatic light is seldom found in practice; perceived colors are a mixture. The tristimulus theory of color mixing is based on the assumption that three types of color-sensing cones exist in the central portion of the eye. One type of cone senses wavelengths near the middle of the visible light range, which the eye–brain visual system converts into the sensation called green. The other two types sense long and short wavelengths near the upper and lower ends of the visible light range, which are interpreted as the sensations red and blue, respectively. Figure 5–102, which shows the relative sensitivity of the eye, indicates that the eye is most sensitive to green and least sensitive to blue. If all three sets of cones sense equal radiance levels (energy per unit time), the result is interpreted as white light. Natural white light, of course, contains radiance levels for all wavelengths in the visible spectrum. However, because physiologically the eye contains three different types of cones, the sensation of white light is produced by a properly blended combination of any three colors, provided that a mixture of any two of the colors cannot produce the third. These three colors are called primary colors.

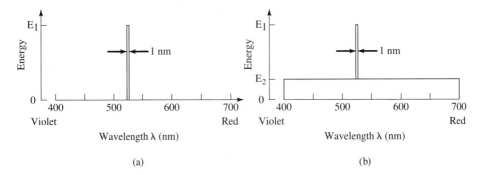

Figure 5–103   Wavelength characteristics of light.   (a) Monochromatic light; (b) 'white' light with a dominant wavelength.

Color Primary Systems

There are two primary color mixing systems of importance in computer graphics: the red, green, blue (RGB) additive color system and the cyan, magenta, yellow (CMY) subtractive color system. The two systems are shown in Fig. 5–104 and in Color Plate 24. The colors in the two systems are complements of each other. Cyan is the complement of red, magenta the complement of green and yellow the complement of blue. A complement is white minus the color. Thus, cyan is white minus red, magenta is white minus green and yellow is white minus blue. Although, technically, red can also be considered the complement of cyan, traditionally red, green and blue are considered the primary colors and cyan, magenta and yellow their complements. It is interesting to note that magenta does not appear in the spectrum of colors created by a rainbow or prism. Hence, it is only a creation of the eye–brain visual system.

For reflective sources, e.g., printing inks and film and non-light-emitting displays, the CMY subtractive system is used. In the subtractive color system, the wavelengths representing the complement of the color are subtracted from the white light spectrum. For example, when light is reflected from or transmitted through a magenta colored object, the green portion of the spectrum is absorbed or subtracted. If the resulting light is then reflected from or transmitted through a yellow object, the blue portion of the spectrum is subtracted. The result is red. Finally, if the remaining light is reflected from or transmitted through a cyan object, the result is black because the entire visible spectrum has been eliminated (see Color Plate 24). Photographic filters work this way.

Color Matching Experiment

For light-emitting sources, e.g., a color CRT display or colored lights, the RGB additive color system is used. A simple experiment illustrates that three mono-chromatic colors is the minimum number required to match or produce almost all colors in the visible spectrum. The experiment involves a single, arbitrary,

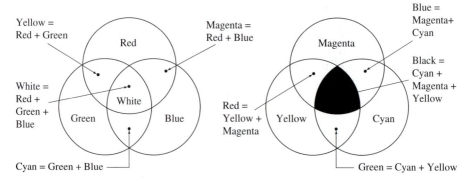

Figure 5–104 Color primary systems. (a) Additive; (b) subtractive.

monochromatic test light incident on a neutral background. An observer attempts to perceptually match (hue, saturation and brightness) the test light by shining a monochromatic light or lights onto the background adjacent to the test light. The intensity of the matching light or lights is variable. If only a single matching light is used, then it must have the same wavelength as the test light in order to match the test light. Thus, only one color can be matched by a single monochromatic matching light. However, if the observer discounts the hue and saturation of the test light, then, for any intensity of the test light, its brightness can be matched. This procedure is called photometry. It leads to gray scale monochromatic reproduction of colored images.

If the observer now uses two superposed monochromatic light sources, more test lights can be matched. However, there are still a large number that cannot be matched. Adding a third matching light allows almost all test lights to be matched, provided that the three matching lights are widely spaced in the visible spectrum, and provided no two of the matching lights can be combined to yield the third; i.e., the colors represented by the lights are primary colors. A good choice of lights is one from the high-wavelength end of the visible spectrum (red), one from the medium wavelengths (green) and one from the low wavelengths (blue). Adding these three lights together to match the perceived color of the monochromatic test light mathematically corresponds to

$$C = rR + gG + bB$$

where C is the color of the test light to be matched, R, G and B correspond to the red, green and blue matching lights, and r, g and b correspond to the relative amounts of the R, G and B lights used, with values in the range 0 to 1.

However, most of the test lights still cannot be matched by adding the three matching lights together. For example, if the test light is blue-green, the observer adds the blue and the green matching lights together, but the result is too light. Adding the red matching light in an attempt to darken the result only makes it lighter, because the energies of the matching lights add. This effect gives the observer an idea: Add the red matching light to the test light to lighten it. It works! The test patches generated by the lights match. Mathematically, adding the red matching light to the test light corresponds to *subtracting* it from the other two matching lights. This is, of course, a physical impossibility, since a negative light intensity is impossible. Mathematically, the result corresponds to

$$C + rR = gG + bB$$

$$C = -rR + gG + bB$$

Figure 5–105 shows the color-matching functions r, g, b for monochromatic lights at wavelengths of 436, 546 and 700 nm required to match all wavelengths in the visible spectrum. Notice that, except for wavelengths near 700 nm, one of these functions is always negative. This corresponds to 'adding' the matching light to the test light. The study of these matching functions is part of colorimetry.

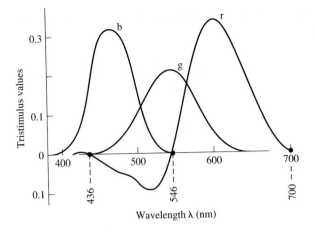

Figure 5–105   Color matching functions.

The observer also discovers that, when the intensity of a test light is doubled, the intensity of each of the matching lights is also doubled, i.e.

$$2C = 2rR + 2gG + 2bB$$

Finally, the observer discovers that, when the same test light is matched in two different sessions, the values of r, g and b are not necessarily the same. The matching colors for the two different sets of values of r, g and b are called metamers of each other. Technically, this means that the test light can be matched by two different composite light sources, each of different spectral energy distribution. In fact, the test light source can be matched by composite light sources with an infinite number of different spectral energy distributions. Figure 5–106 shows two very diverse spectral reflectance distributions that both yield a medium gray.

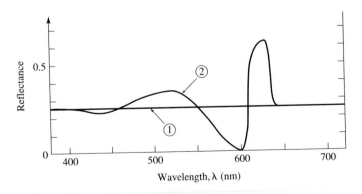

Figure 5–106   Metamers.

These experimental results are embodied in Grassman's laws (see [Wysz82]). Simply stated, Grassman's laws are:

> The eye distinguishes three different stimuli; this establishes the three-dimensional nature of color. The stimuli may, for example, be dominant wavelength (hue), purity (saturation) and luminance (brightness), or red, green and blue.

> Four colors are always linearly related; i.e., $cC = rR + gG + bB$, where $c, r, g, b \neq 0$. Consequently, if two colors $(cC)_1$ and $(cC)_2$ are mixed, then $(cC)_1 + (cC)_2 = (rR)_1 + (rR)_2 + (gG)_1 + (gG)_2 + (bB)_1 + (bB)_2$. If color $C_1 = $ color C and color $C_2 = $ color C, then color $C_1 = $ color C_2 regardless of the spectral energy compositions of $C, C_1,$ and C_2.

> If in a three-color mixture one color is continuously changed while the others are kept constant, the color of the mixture changes continuously; this means that three-dimensional color space is continuous.

Based on experiments similar to these, it is known that the visual system is capable of distinguishing approximately 350,000 colors. When the colors differ only in hue, the visual system can distinguish between colors with dominant wavelengths differing by about 1 nm in the blue-yellow part of the spectrum. However, near the spectrum extremes, approximately a 10 nm separation is required. About 128 distinct hues are distinguishable. If only differences in saturation are present, the visual system's ability to distinguish colors is more limited. Approximately 16 different saturations of yellow and about 23 different saturations of red-violet are distinguishable.

Chromaticity Diagrams

The three-dimensional nature of color suggests plotting the value of each tristimulus component along orthogonal axes as shown in Fig. 5–107a. The result is called tristimulus space. Any color C is represented by the vector from the

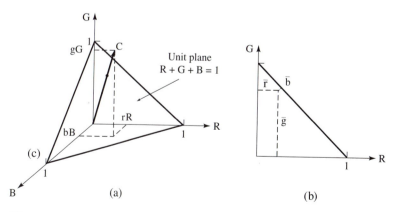

Figure 5–107 Three-dimensional color space. (a) The unit plane; (b) chromaticity diagram.

origin with components rR, gG and bB. Meyer [Meye83] gives a detailed discussion of three-dimensional color space. The intersection of the vector C with the unit plane gives the relative weights of the R, G, B colors required to generate C. The relative weights are called the chromaticity values, or coordinates. They are given by

$$\bar{r} = \frac{r}{r+g+b} \qquad \bar{g} = \frac{g}{r+g+b} \qquad \bar{b} = \frac{b}{r+g+b}$$

Consequently, $\bar{r} + \bar{g} + \bar{b} = 1.0$. Projection of the unit plane onto the $B = 0$ plane, as shown in Fig. 5–107b, yields a chromaticity diagram. The chromaticity diagram directly provides a functional relationship between two colors and indirectly with the third, because, for example, $\bar{b} = 1 - \bar{r} - \bar{g}$. If the color matching functions shown in Fig. 5–105 are plotted in three space, the result does not entirely lie in the positive octant. Projection onto a two-dimensional plane also yields negative values. These negative values are a mathematical nuisance.

The Commission Internationale de L'Eclairage (CIE), at a meeting on international color definition and measurement standards held in England in 1931, adopted a universal two-dimensional chromaticity diagram and a set of standard tristimulus observer functions[†] that not only eliminate the negative values but also exhibit a number of other advantages. The result is known as the 1931 CIE chromaticity diagram. The CIE tristimulus values, or primaries, are derived from the standard observer functions shown in Fig. 5–108 and tabulated in Wyszecki and Stiles [Wysz82]. The three CIE hypothetical primaries are X, Y and Z. The CIE XYZ primaries are hypothetical, because eliminating the negative values makes it impossible for the primaries to correspond to physically real lights. The triangle formed by X, Y and Z was selected to contain the entire spectrum of visible light. The CIE chromaticity values, xyz, are

$$x = \frac{X}{X+Y+Z} \qquad y = \frac{Y}{X+Y+Z} \qquad z = \frac{Z}{X+Y+Z} \qquad (5-18)$$

and $x + y + z = 1$. When the XYZ triangle is projected onto a two-dimensional plane to form the CIE chromaticity diagram, the chromaticity coordinates are selected as x and y. The chromaticity coordinates represent the relative amounts of the three primary XYZ colors required to obtain any color. However, they do not indicate the luminance (intensity) of the resulting color. Luminance is incorporated into the Y value. The X and Z values are then scaled to the Y value. With this convention, both the chromaticity and the luminance are given by (x, y, Y) coordinates. The inverse transformation from chromaticity values to XYZ tristimulus values is

$$X = x\frac{Y}{y} \qquad Y = Y \qquad Z = (1 - x - y)\frac{Y}{y} \qquad (5-19)$$

[†]The 1931 CIE standard observer is based on a $2°$ field of view. In 1964 the CIE defined an additional standard observer based on a $10°$ field of view [Wysz82]. The standard observer functions are slightly different.

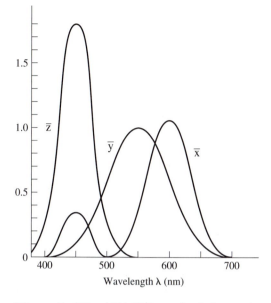

Figure 5–108   1931 CIE standard observer.

The final decision of the commission was to align the XYZ triangle so that equal values of the three hypothetical XYZ primaries produce white.

The 1931 CIE Chromaticity Diagram

The 1931 CIE chromaticity diagram is shown in Fig. 5–109 and in Color Plate 25. The wing-shaped outline represents the locus of all visible wavelengths, i.e., the locus of the visible spectrum. The numbers along the line indicate the wavelength of visible light at that location. Red is at the lower right corner, green at the point and blue in the lower left corner of the diagram. The straight line connecting the ends of the spectrum locus is called the purple line. The curved line labeled the blackbody locus represents the color of a theoretical blackbody as it is heated from approximately $1000°K$ to infinity. The dashed lines indicate the temperature along the blackbody locus and also the direction along which color changes are least discernible to the human eye. The equal energy alignment white is shown as point $E(x = 0.333, y = 0.333)$. The locations of CIE illuminants $A(0.448, 0.408)$, $B(0.349, 0.352)$, $C(0.310, 0.316)$, $D_{6500}(0.313, 0.329)$ are also shown. Illuminant A approximates the warm color of a gas-filled tungsten lamp at $2856°K$; it is much 'redder' than the others. Illuminant B approximates noon sunlight, and illuminant C the light from an overcast sky at midday. Illuminant C is used by the National Television Standards Committee (NTSC) as the alignment white. Illuminant D_{6500}, which corresponds to a blackbody radiating at $6504°K$, is a somewhat 'greener' white used as the alignment white for many television monitors. Illuminant D_{5000} is typically used in the graphic arts.

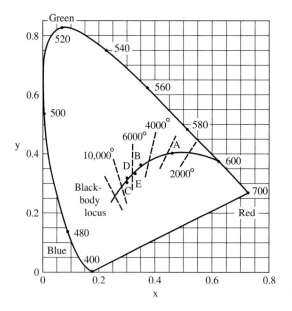

Figure 5–109 CIE diagram showing the blackbody locus, illuminants $A\,B,C,D_{6500}$ (D) and equal-energy white (E).

As Fig. 5–110 illustrates, the chromaticity diagram is quite useful. The complement of a spectrum color is obtained by extending a line from the color, through the alignment white, to the opposite spectrum locus. For example, the complement of the reddish-orange color $C_4(\lambda = 610$ nm) is the blue-green color $C_5(\lambda \approx 491$ nm). A color and its complement added together in the proper proportions yield white. The dominant wavelength for a color is obtained by extending a line from the alignment white, through the color, to the spectrum locus. For example, in Fig. 5–110 the dominant wavelength for color C_6 is 570 nm, a yellow-green. If the extended line intersects the purple line, then the color has no dominant wavelength in the visible spectrum. In this case, the dominant wavelength is specified by the complementary spectrum value for the color with a c suffix. The value is obtained by extending a line backward through the alignment white to the spectrum boundary. For example, the dominant wavelength for color C_7 in Fig. 5–110 is 500c nm.

The pure or fully saturated colors lie on the spectrum locus and are 100% pure. The alignment white is 'fully diluted', with a purity of 0%. The purity of intermediate colors is given by dividing the distance from the alignment white to the color by the distance from the alignment white to the spectrum locus or the purple line. For example, the purity of color C_6 in Fig. 5–110 is $a/(a+b)$ and that of C_7, $c/(c+d)$ expressed as a percentage.

The CIE chromaticity coordinates of a mixture of two colors are obtained, using Grassman's laws, by adding their primary values. For colors $C_1(x_1, y_1, Y_1)$ and $C_2(x_2, y_2, Y_2)$ the mixture of C_1 and C_2 is

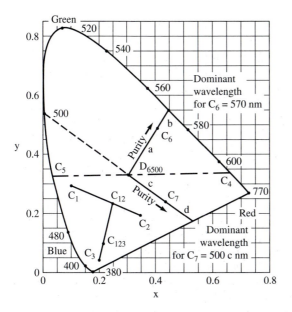

Figure 5–110   Uses of the chromaticity diagram.

$$C_{12} = (X_1 + X_2) + (Y_1 + Y_2) + (Z_1 + Z_2)$$

Recalling Eqs. $(5 - 18)$ and $(5 - 19)$ and defining

$$T_1 = \frac{Y_1}{y_1} \qquad T_2 = \frac{Y_2}{y_2}$$

the chromaticity coordinates of the mixture are

$$x_{12} = \frac{x_1 T_1 + x_2 T_2}{T_1 + T_2} \qquad y_{12} = \frac{y_1 T_1 + y_2 T_2}{T_1 + T_2} \qquad Y_{12} = Y_1 + Y_2$$

These results are applicable to mixtures of more than two colors when applied successively to the mixture and each additional color. An example illustrates the technique.

Example 5–11   Color Mixing

Determine the CIE chromaticity coordinates of the mixture of the colors $C_1(0.1, 0.3, 10)$, $C_2(0.35, 0.2, 10)$ and $C_3(0.2, 0.05, 10)$ shown in Fig. 5–110. Applying the above results successively, the mixture of C_1 and C_2 is first determined. From the specifications

$$T_1 = \frac{Y_1}{y_1} = \frac{10}{0.3} = 33.33 \qquad T_2 = \frac{Y_2}{y_2} = \frac{10}{0.2} = 50$$

and
$$x_{12} = \frac{x_1 T_1 + x_2 T_2}{T_1 + T_2} = \frac{(0.1)(33.33) + (0.35)(50)}{33.33 + 50} = 0.25$$

$$y_{12} = \frac{y_1 T_1 + y_2 T_2}{T_1 + T_2} = \frac{(0.3)(33.33) + (0.2)(50)}{33.33 + 50} = 0.24$$

$$Y_{12} = Y_1 + Y_2 = 10 + 10 = 20$$

Thus, the mixture of C_1 and C_2 is $C_{12}(0.25, 0.24, 20)$. Note that the coordinates for the mixture lie on the line between C_1 and C_2 in the chromaticity diagram. Continuing, the mixture of C_1, C_2 and C_3 is given by the mixture of C_{12} and C_3. Hence

$$T_{12} = \frac{Y_{12}}{y_{12}} = \frac{20}{0.24} = 83.33 \qquad T_3 = \frac{Y_3}{y_3} = \frac{10}{0.05} = 200$$

$$x_{123} = \frac{x_{12} T_{12} + x_3 T_3}{T_{12} + T_3} = \frac{(0.25)(83.33) + (0.2)(200)}{83.33 + 200} = 0.215$$

$$y_{123} = \frac{y_{12} T_{12} + y_3 T_3}{T_{12} + T_3} = \frac{(0.24)(83.33) + (0.05)(200)}{83.33 + 200} = 0.106$$

$$Y_{123} = Y_{12} + Y_3 = 20 + 10 = 30$$

The mixture of C_1, C_2 and C_3 is $C_{123}(0.215, 0.106, 30)$ and lies on the line between C_{12} and C_3 in the chromaticity diagram.

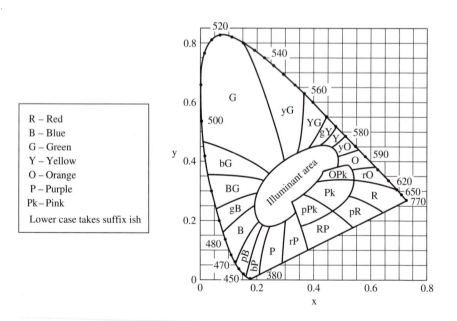

R – Red
B – Blue
G – Green
Y – Yellow
O – Orange
P – Purple
Pk– Pink

Lower case takes suffix ish

Figure 5–111   The 1931 CIE chromaticity diagram with superimposed color names.

Figure 5–111 shows the correspondence between the CIE diagram and common perceptual color names (see [Judd68]). In Fig. 5–111 the abbreviations for the color names beginning with a lowercase letter take an *-ish* suffix; e.g., *yG* is yellow*ish*-green. For each color area, saturation or purity ranges from nearly zero, i.e., a very pastel color near the illuminant area, to a fully saturated, i.e., a vivid, color near the spectrum boundary. Notice that most of the upper area of the diagram is occupied by greenish hues, with the reds and blues crowded into the lower region near the purple line. Consequently, equal areas or distances on the diagram do not represent equal perceptual differences. A number of transformations of the diagram have been proposed to correct this deficiency. These uniform color spaces are discussed in detail in the standard color references (see, e.g., [Hntr75; Hunt75; Judd75; Wysz82].

Uniform Color Spaces

In the CIEXYZ tristimulous color space two colors equally distant from a third color do not exhibit equal perceptual differences, i.e., CIEXYZ tristimulous color space is nonuniform or nonlinear in perceptual color space. This characteristic makes the CIE XYZ color space particularly difficult for users. In 1976, the CIE defined two standard perceptually uniform color spaces: CIE$L^*a^*b^*$ (CIELAB) and CIE$L^*u^*v^*$ (CIELUV) in terms of the CIE XYZ tristimulous values.

The objective was to define the *Just Noticeable Difference* (JND) between two color samples viewed under identical conditions. Figure 5–112 shows the wavelength dependence of the minimum JND in wavelength difference between adjacent samples. The standard is intended for reflective media, hence the color source must also be specified. Both standards use a lightness metric, L^*, proportional to the cube root of the CIE luminance Y. L^* is defined with respect to the reference white, usually one of the CIE reference whites (X_n, Y_n, Z_n). a^* and b^*, or u^* and v^*, define the colorfulness of the color. A convenient method of visualizing these systems uses polar coordinates around the L^* axis, with the

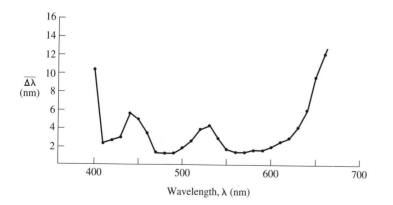

Figure 5–112   Just noticeable color differences. (Data source [Bedf58].)

'hue angle' defined with respect to the a^* or u^* axes, and the 'chroma' defined as the distance from the L^* axis. An example of the CIELAB color space is given in Color Plate 26a. Color Plate 26b shows a slice of the a^*b^* chromaticity diagram through the CIELAB space. The center is achromatic, saturation increases radially outward from the center while hue changes circularly around the center.

The CIELAB color space is defined by

$$L^* = 116 \ \left(\frac{Y}{Y_n} \right)^{1/3} - 16 \qquad\qquad \frac{Y}{Y_n} > 0.008856$$

$$a^* = 500 \left[\left(\frac{X}{X_n} \right)^{1/3} - \left(\frac{Y}{Y_n} \right)^{1/3} \right] \qquad \frac{X}{X_n} > 0.008856$$

$$b^* = 200 \left[\left(\frac{X}{X_n} \right)^{1/3} - \left(\frac{Z}{Z_n} \right)^{1/3} \right] \qquad \frac{Z}{Z_n} > 0.008856$$

The total color difference between two colors is given by

$$\sqrt{(\Delta L^*)^2 + (\Delta a^*)^2 + (\Delta b^*)^2}$$

The CIELUV color space is defined in terms of the three-dimensional CIE XYZ tristimulous values as [Wysz82]

$$u^* = 13L^*(u' - u'_n)$$
$$v^* = 13L^*(v' - v'_n)$$

and

$$u' = \frac{4X}{X + 15Y + 3Z} \qquad u'_n = \frac{4X_n}{X_n + 15Y_n + 3Z_n}$$

$$v' = \frac{9Y}{X + 15Y + 3Z} \qquad v'_n = \frac{9Y_n}{X_n + 15Y_n + 3Z_n}$$

with L^* given above and where the reference white is defined by (X_n, Y_n, Z_n). The total color difference between two colors is given by

$$\sqrt{(\Delta L^*)^2 + (\Delta u^*)^2 + (\Delta v^*)^2}$$

Gamut Limitations

Color television monitors, color film, printing inks, etc., cannot produce the full range or gamut of colors in the visible spectrum. For additive color systems, the reproducible gamut appears as a triangle on the CIE chromaticity diagram. The vertices of the triangle are the chromaticity coordinates of the RGB primaries. Any color within the triangle can be reproduced by the primaries. Figure 5–113

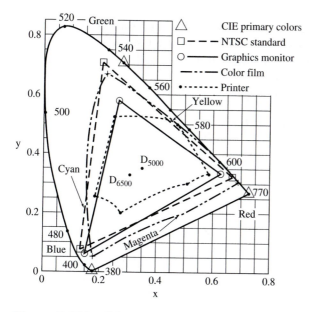

Figure 5–113   Color gamuts.

and Table 5–4 show the gamut of reproducible colors for the RGB primaries of a typical color CRT monitor, and for the NTSC standard RGB primaries. For comparison, the subtractive CMY color system (converted to CIE coordinates) used in a typical color film and a print reproduction process is also shown. Note that these gamuts are not triangular. Note also that the gamut for the color film is larger than the one for the color monitor. Consequently, some film colors cannot be reproduced by the monitor. In addition, the gamut for the print reproduction process is inside the monitor gamut in some areas and is concave (see also Sec. 5–21). Consequently, print media cannot reproduce some monitor colors, particularly a pure blue. The CIE XYZ primary spectrum colors are also

Table 5–4   CIE chromaticity coefficients
for RGB primaries

		x	y
CIE XYZ primaries	Red	0.735	0.265
	Green	0.274	0.717
	Blue	0.167	0.009
NTSC standard	Red	0.670	0.330
	Green	0.210	0.710
	Blue	0.140	0.080
Color CRT monitor	Red	0.628	0.346
	Green	0.268	0.588
	Blue	0.150	0.070

shown. These values lie on the spectrum boundary and correspond to red at 700 nm, green at 543.1 nm and blue at 435.8 nm. These primary spectrum colors are used to produce the matching functions in Fig. 5–105.

Transformations Between Color Systems

The CIE chromaticity coordinates or tristimulus values provide a precise standard specification of a color. However, each industry that uses color employs a unique set of primaries or conventions to specify color. Transferring color information from one industry to another is facilitated by using the CIE chromaticity coordinates. Thus, transformation from CIE values to another set of primary colors, and vice versa, is of interest. For computer graphics, the most common requirement is to transform between CIE XYZ values and the RGB primary system used for television monitors. Consequently, the discussion concentrates on these transformations. More general discussions are given in Wyszecki and Stiles [Wysz82], Judd [Judd75], Hunt [Hunt75] and Meyer [Meye83].

The transformation between two additive color systems is governed by Grassman's laws. The transformation from RGB color space to CIE XYZ color space is given by

$$\begin{bmatrix} X \\ Y \\ Z \end{bmatrix} = \begin{bmatrix} X_r & X_g & X_b \\ Y_r & Y_g & Y_b \\ Z_r & Z_g & Z_b \end{bmatrix} \begin{bmatrix} R \\ G \\ B \end{bmatrix} \qquad (5-20)$$

where X_r, Y_r, Z_r represent the tristimulus values required to produce a unit amount of the R primary, and similarly for X_g, Y_g, Z_g and X_b, Y_b, Z_b. For example, if R = 1, G = 0, B = 0, then from Eq. (5 – 20), $X = X_r$, $Y = Y_r$, $Z = Z_r$. If the CIE chromaticity values $(x(x_r, x_g, x_b), y(y_r, y_g, y_b))$ of the RGB primaries are known, then

$$x_r = \frac{X_r}{X_r + Y_r + Z_r} = \frac{X_r}{C_r}$$

$$y_r = \frac{Y_r}{X_r + Y_r + Z_r} = \frac{Y_r}{C_r}$$

$$z_r = 1 - x_r - y_r = \frac{Z_r}{X_r + Y_r + Z_r} = \frac{Z_r}{C_r} \qquad (5-21)$$

and similarly for x_g, y_g, z_g and x_b, y_b, z_b. With $C_g = X_g + Y_g + Z_g$ and $C_b = X_b + Y_b + Z_b$, Eq. (5 – 20) becomes

$$\begin{bmatrix} X \\ Y \\ Z \end{bmatrix} = \begin{bmatrix} x_r C_r & x_g C_g & x_b C_b \\ y_r C_r & y_g C_g & y_b C_b \\ (1 - x_r - y_r)C_r & (1 - x_g - y_g)C_g & (1 - x_b - y_b)C_b \end{bmatrix} \begin{bmatrix} R \\ G \\ B \end{bmatrix}$$

$$(5-22)$$

or in more compact notation

$$[\mathbf{X}'] = [\mathbf{C}'][\mathbf{R}']$$

C_r, C_g and C_b are required to completely specify the transformations between primary systems. If the luminance Y_r, Y_g and Y_b of the unit amounts of the RGB primaries is known, then

$$C_r = \frac{Y_r}{y_r} \qquad C_g = \frac{Y_g}{y_g} \qquad C_b = \frac{Y_b}{y_b}$$

If the tristimulus values for the alignment white (X_w, Y_w, Z_w) are known, solution of Eq. $(5-22)$, with $[\mathbf{R'}] = [C_r \quad C_g \quad C_b]^T$ and $[\mathbf{X'}] = [X_w \quad Y_w \quad Z_w]^T$, yields the required values. If the chromaticity coordinates and the luminance (x_w, y_w, Y_w) are known instead of the tristimulus values, then (see [Meye83])

$$C_r = \frac{(Y_w/y_w)\left[x_w(y_g - y_b) - y_w(x_g - x_b) + x_g y_b - x_b y_g\right]}{D}$$

$$C_g = \frac{(Y_w/y_w)\left[x_w(y_b - y_r) - y_w(x_b - x_r) - x_r y_b + x_b y_r\right]}{D}$$

$$C_b = \frac{(Y_w/y_w)\left[x_w(y_r - y_g) - y_w(x_r - x_g) + x_r y_g - x_g y_r\right]}{D} \qquad (5-23)$$

and
$$D = x_r(y_g - y_b) + x_g(y_b - y_r) + x_b(y_r - y_g) \qquad (5-24)$$

The inverse transformation from CIE XYZ color space to RGB color space is then given by

$$[\mathbf{R'}] = [\mathbf{C'}]^{-1}[\mathbf{X'}] = [\mathbf{C''}][\mathbf{X'}] \qquad (5-25)$$

where $[\mathbf{C''}] = [\mathbf{C'}]^{-1}$ has components

$$C''_{11} = \frac{\left[(y_g - y_b) - x_b y_g + y_b x_g\right]}{C_r D}$$

$$C''_{12} = \frac{\left[(x_b - x_g) - x_b y_g + x_g y_b\right]}{C_r D}$$

$$C''_{13} = \frac{\left[x_g y_b - x_b y_g\right]}{C_r D}$$

$$C''_{21} = \frac{\left[(y_b - y_r) - y_b x_r + y_r x_b\right]}{C_g D}$$

$$C''_{22} = \frac{\left[(x_r - x_b) - x_r y_b + x_b y_r\right]}{C_g D}$$

$$C''_{23} = \frac{\left[x_b y_r - x_r y_b\right]}{C_g D}$$

$$C''_{31} = \frac{\left[(y_r - y_g) - y_r x_g + y_g x_r\right]}{C_b D}$$

$$C''_{32} = \frac{\left[(x_g - x_r) - x_g y_r + x_r y_g\right]}{C_b D}$$

$$C''_{33} = \frac{\left[x_r y_g - x_g y_r\right]}{C_b D}$$

An example further illustrates the technique.

Example 5–12   CIE to RGB Color Primary Transformations

Transform the color with CIE chromaticity coordinates $x = 0.25$, $y = 0.2$ and luminance $Y = 10.0$ for display on a color monitor with the RGB primary chromaticities given in Table 5–4. The monitor is aligned to D_{6500} white. Consequently, the monitor primary components are

$$x_r = 0.628 \qquad x_g = 0.268 \qquad x_b = 0.150$$
$$y_r = 0.346 \qquad y_g = 0.588 \qquad y_b = 0.070$$

The alignment white components are

$$x_w = 0.313 \qquad y_w = 0.329 \qquad Y_w = 1.0$$

First, calculating D yields

$$D = x_r(y_g - y_b) + x_g(y_b - y_r) + x_b(y_r - y_g)$$
$$= 0.628(0.588 - 0.07) + 0.268(0.07 - 0.346) + 0.15(0.346 - 0.588) = 0.215$$

Now
$$\frac{DC_r}{(Y_w/y_w)} = x_w(y_g - y_b) - y_w(x_g - x_b) + x_g y_b - x_b y_g$$
$$= 0.313(0.588 - 0.07) - 0.329(0.268 - 0.15) + 0.268(0.07)$$
$$- 0.15(0.588) = 0.0539$$

and
$$C_r = \frac{0.0539}{D}\left(\frac{Y_w}{y_w}\right) = \frac{0.0539}{0.215}\left(\frac{1}{0.329}\right) = 0.762$$

Similarly
$$C_g = 1.114 \qquad C_b = 1.164$$

Calculating XYZ tristimulus values from the chromaticity coordinates yields

$$X = x\frac{Y}{y} = 0.25\frac{10}{0.2} = 12.5$$

$$Z = (1 - x - y)\frac{Y}{y} = (1 - 0.25 - 0.2)\frac{10}{0.2} = 27.5$$

The transformation is then given by Eq. $(5 - 22)$

$$[\mathbf{R}'] = [\mathbf{C}''][\mathbf{X}']$$

$$\begin{bmatrix} R \\ G \\ B \end{bmatrix} = \begin{bmatrix} 2.739 & -1.145 & -0.424 \\ -1.119 & 2.029 & 0.033 \\ 0.138 & -0.333 & 1.105 \end{bmatrix} \begin{bmatrix} 12.5 \\ 10.0 \\ 27.5 \end{bmatrix} = \begin{bmatrix} 11.133 \\ 7.209 \\ 28.772 \end{bmatrix}$$

The transformation of RGB coordinates to CIE chromaticity coordinates is accomplished in a similar manner.

Example 5–13   RGB to CIE Color Primary Transformations

Transform the color with RGB components (255, 0, 0), i.e., the maximum red intensity on the monitor, to CIE chromaticity coordinates. The monitor primaries and alignment white are the same as in Ex. 5–12. Consequently, D, C_r, C_g, C_b are also the same. Using Eq. $(5-21)$ yields

$$
\begin{bmatrix} X \\ Y \\ Z \end{bmatrix} = \begin{bmatrix} 0.478 & 0.299 & 0.175 \\ 0.263 & 0.655 & 0.081 \\ 0.020 & 0.160 & 0.908 \end{bmatrix} \begin{bmatrix} 255 \\ 0 \\ 0 \end{bmatrix} = \begin{bmatrix} 121.94 \\ 67.19 \\ 5.05 \end{bmatrix}
$$

The chromaticity values are

$$
x = \frac{X}{X+Y+Z} = \frac{121.94}{121.94 + 67.19 + 5.05} = \frac{121.94}{194.18} = 0.628
$$

$$
y = \frac{Y}{X+Y+Z} = \frac{67.19}{194.18} = 0.346
$$

$$
Y = 67.19
$$

which, of course, are the chromaticity coordinates for the red monitor primary (see Table 5–4).

NTSC Color System

The RGB color primary system used for standard color television broadcasting is dictated by the requirement to confine the broadcast signal to a 0–6 Mhz bandwidth, and by the requirement for compatibility with the standard for black-and-white television. In 1953 the NTSC adopted a standard called the YIQ color primary system. The YIQ color primary system is based on concepts from the CIEXYZ system. Because of bandwidth restrictions, one value, Y (not to be confused with the CIE Y), was chosen to contain the luminance or brightness information. The signal for Y occupies the major portion of the available broadcast bandwidth (0–4 Mhz). The proportions of the NTSC red, green and blue primaries in the Y signal were chosen to yield the standard luminosity curve. Since Y contains the brightness information, only its value or signal is used by a black-and-white monitor. The NTSC alignment white was originally CIE illuminant C, but CIE illuminant D_{6500} is generally used at the present time [Prit77]. The differences are small.

Certain characteristics of the visual system are used to reduce the bandwidth required for the color, i.e., hue and saturation, information transmitted. Specifically, the ability of the eye to sense color decreases with decreasing apparent object size. Below a certain apparent object size, objects are perceived by a two-color vision process. Objects below a certain minimum size produce no perceived color sensation.

The YIQ system uses linear combinations of the differences between the red, green and blue values and the Y value, to contain the hue and saturation 'color' information. The I color value (or in-phase signal) contains orange–cyan color hue information, while Q (the quadrature signal) contains green–magenta hue information. The I value contains hue information that provides the all-important flesh tones, while the Q value contains the remainder. Consequently, a bandwidth of about 1.5 Mhz is used for I, but only about 0.6 Mhz is used for Q. The transformation from RGB to YIQ values is given by

$$\begin{bmatrix} Y \\ I \\ Q \end{bmatrix} = \begin{bmatrix} 0.299 & 0.587 & 0.114 \\ 0.596 & -0.274 & -0.322 \\ 0.211 & -0.522 & 0.311 \end{bmatrix} \begin{bmatrix} R \\ G \\ B \end{bmatrix}$$

I and Q are derived from RGB and Y, using a scale and a rotation by 33° [Blin93]

$$I = \frac{R - Y}{1.14} \cos 33 - \frac{B - Y}{2.03} \sin 33$$

$$Q = \frac{R - Y}{1.14} \sin 33 - \frac{B - Y}{2.03} \cos 33$$

Transforming from YIQ to RGB is accomplished using

$$\begin{bmatrix} R \\ G \\ B \end{bmatrix} = \begin{bmatrix} 1 & 0.956 & 0.623 \\ 1 & -0.272 & -0.648 \\ 1 & -1.105 & 1.705 \end{bmatrix} \begin{bmatrix} Y \\ I \\ Q \end{bmatrix}$$

Transformation from CIE XYZ tristimulus values to YIQ, or vice versa, is accomplished by combining these equations with Eqs. $(5 - 22)$ and $(5 - 25)$. A more detailed description of the YIQ color system characteristics important for computer graphics is given by Blinn [Blin93]. Because of the restricted frequency range, in one sense the YIQ color space can be considered as a lossy color compression scheme. Properly considering the characteristics of the system produces excellent color.

Color Cubes

As with the CIE XYZ tristimulus values, the RGB and CMY color spaces are three-dimensional. Both the RGB and CMY spaces are conveniently represented by three-dimensional color cubes or solids, as shown in Fig. 5–114.

The RGB color cube uses black as the origin, while the CMY color cube uses white. For both models the achromatic colors, i.e., the grays, lie along the diagonal from black to white. The complementary colors lie on opposite corners. The transformation between RGB and CMY color spaces is

$$[R \quad G \quad B] = [1 \quad 1 \quad 1] - [C \quad M \quad Y]$$

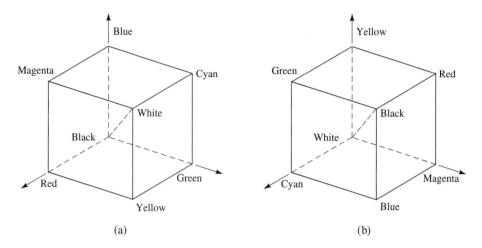

Figure 5–114   Color cubes. (a) RGB; (b) CMY.

and between CMY and RGB color spaces is

$$[C \quad M \quad Y] = [1 \quad 1 \quad 1] - [R \quad G \quad B]$$

The CMYK Color System

An additional color system, much used in printing, is the CMYK system, where K represents black. The fundamental reason for including black is that combining cyan, magenta and yellow inks frequently produces a 'muddy' black, the paper dries faster because one ink wets the paper less than three inks and black ink is less expensive than colored ink. In the CMYK system, black is substituted for equal amounts of cyan, magenta and yellow, i.e.

$$K = \min(C, M, Y)$$
$$C = C - K$$
$$M = M - K$$
$$Y = Y - K$$

This process is referred to as *undercolor removal*. Additional details are given by Stone, Cowan and Beatty [Ston88b].

The Ostwald Color System

Unfortunately, it is difficult for users to specify subjective color concepts in the systems discussed above. For example, what is the CIE, RGB or CMY specification for a pastel reddish-orange (see Fig. 5–111)? Artists specify colors in terms of tints, shades and tones. Given a pure pigment, an artist adds white to obtain a tint, black to obtain a shade, and both to obtain a tone of the color. These ideas are combined into a useful triangular representation, as shown in Fig. 5–115. The triangular representation shown in Fig. 5–115 is for a single color. By arranging triangles for each pure color around a central black-white axis, a useful subjective three-dimensional representation of color is obtained. This basic idea is central to the Ostwald [Ostw31] color system.

The HSV Color System

A useful implementation of a basic subjective color model is the HSV (hue, saturation, value) color solid proposed by Smith [Smit78]. If the RGB color cube shown in Fig. 5–114a is projected onto a plane along the diagonal looking from white to black, a hexagon is formed with the pure RGB primaries and their complements at each vertex. Decreasing the saturation or purity of the primary colors decreases the size of the RGB color cube and the gamut of possible colors. Projection then yields a smaller hexagon. If the projections of the RGB color cube and its subcubes are stacked along the main diagonal representing the value or lightness of the color from black = 0 to white = 1, a three-dimensional hexcone is formed. This is the HSV model shown in Fig. 5–116. Value increases along the axis of the hexcone from 0 at the apex to 1 at the top surface, where the maximum value colors occur. Saturation is given by the distance from the axis, and hue by the angular distance $(0 - 360°)$ measured from red. Here, the projection of the RGB color cube is rotated counterclockwise 120° to place red at 0° . The value of saturation ranges from 0 at the axis to 1 along the outer rim. Notice that saturation is specified relative to the possible gamut of colors, i.e., relative to the distance from the axis to the outer rim for any value of V. The fully saturated primary colors or their complements occur for S = 1. A mixture of three nonzero primaries cannot be fully saturated. If S = 0, the hue, H, is undefined and the color is achromatic, i.e., some shade of gray. The shades of gray occur along the central axis.

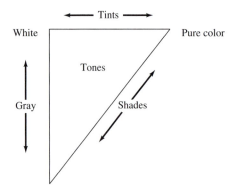

Figure 5–115   Tints, shades and tones of a pure color.

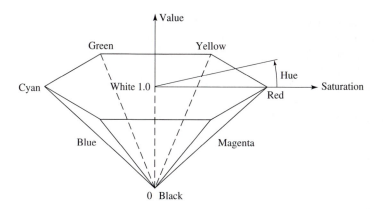

Figure 5–116   HSV hexcone color solid.

The HSV model corresponds to the way artists form colors. The pure pigments are given for V = 1, S = 1. Tints are formed by adding white, i.e., decreasing S. Shades are formed by decreasing V, i.e., adding black, and tones by decreasing both V and S.

Conversion from HSV to RGB color space using geometrical relations between the hexcone and the color cube is straightforward. The pseudocode conversion algorithm adapted from Smith [Smit78] is:

HSV to RGB conversion algorithm

H *is the hue* (0 − 360°) *red at* 0°
S *is the saturation* (0 − 1)
V *is the value* (0 − 1)
RGB *are the red, green, blue primary colors* (0 − 1)
Floor *is the floor function*
    check for the achromatic case
if S = 0 then
    if H = Undefined then
        R = V
        G = V
        B = V
    else
        If H has a value an error has occurred
    end if
else
    chromatic case
    if H = 360 then
        H = 0
    else

$$H = H/60$$
end if
$$I = \text{Floor}(H)$$
$$F = H - I$$
$$M = V*(1 - S)$$
$$N = V*(1 - S*F)$$
$$K = V*(1 - S*(1 - F))$$
$(R, G, B) = (V, K, M)$ *means* $R = V$, $G = K$, $B = M$ *etc.*
if $I = 0$ **then** $(R, G, B) = (V, K, M)$
if $I = 1$ **then** $(R, G, B) = (N, V, M)$
if $I = 2$ **then** $(R, G, B) = (M, V, K)$
if $I = 3$ **then** $(R, G, B) = (M, N, V)$
if $I = 4$ **then** $(R, G, B) = (K, M, V)$
if $I = 5$ **then** $(R, G, B) = (V, M, N)$
end if
finish

Conversion from RGB to HSV color space is given by the following pseudocode algorithm, also adapted from Smith [Smit78].

RGB to HSV conversion algorithm

RGB *are the red, green, blue primary colors* $(0 - 1)$
H *is the hue* $(0 - 360°)$ *red at* $0°$
S *is the saturation* $(0 - 1)$
V *is the value* $(0 - 1)$
Max *is the maximum function*
Min *is the minimum function*

determine the value

$$V = \text{Max}(R, G, B)$$

determine saturation

$$\text{Temp} = \text{Min}(R, G, B)$$
if $V = 0$ **then**
$\quad S = 0$
else
$\quad S = (V - \text{Temp})/V$
end if

determine the hue

if $S = 0$ **then**
$\quad H = \text{Undefined}$
else
$\quad Cr = (V - R)/(V - \text{Temp})$
$\quad Cg = (V - G)/(V - \text{Temp})$
$\quad Cb = (V - B)/(V - \text{Temp})$

the color is between yellow and magenta

if $R = V$ **then** $H = Cb - Cg$

the color is between cyan and yellow

if $G = V$ **then** $H = 2 + Cr - Cb$

the color is between magenta and cyan

if $B = V$ **then** $H = 4 + Cg - Cr$

convert to degrees

$H = 60*H$

prevent negative value

if $H < 0$ **then** $H = H + 360$

    end if

finish

Joblove and Greenberg [Jobl78] discuss an alternate formulation of an HSV color space based on a cylindrical rather than a hexcone representation.

The HLS Color System

An extension of the hexcone model is the HLS (hue, lightness, saturation) double-hexcone model. Since the HLS model applies to self-luminous sources, lightness as used here corresponds to brightness as defined at the beginning of this section. In the HLS model the RGB color cube is projected to yield a double hexcone as shown in Fig. 5–117, with lightness (value) along the axis from black = 0 at one

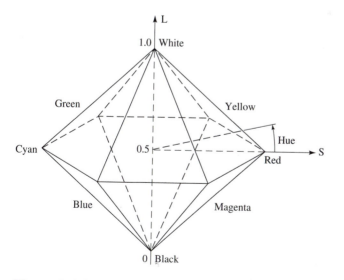

Figure 5–117   HLS double-hexcone color model.

apex to white = 1 at the other. Again, as in the HSV model, saturation is given by the radial distance from the central axis. Here, the fully saturated primary colors and their complements occur at $S = 1$. Again, H is undefined when $S = 0$.

Conversion from HLS to RGB is given here by a pseudocode algorithm adapted from [Stat79] and [Rast80]:

HLS to RGB conversion algorithm

H *is the hue* $(0 - 360°)$ *red at* $0°$
L *is the lightness* $(0 - 1)$
S *is the saturation* $(0 - 1)$
RGB *are the red, green, blue primary colors* $(0 - 1)$

    if $L \leq 0.5$ **then**
        $M2 = L*(1 + S)$
    else
        $M2 = L + S - L*S$
    end if
    $M1 = 2*L - M2$

    check for zero saturation

    if $S = 0$ **then**
        if $H =$ Undefined
            $R = L$
            $G = L$
            $B = L$
        else
            Error because of incorrect data
        end if
    else
        determine RGB values
        call RGB$(H + 120, M1, M2;$ Value$)$
        $R =$ Value
        call RGB$(H, M1, M2;$ Value$)$
        $G =$ Value
        call RGB$(H + 120, M1, M2;$ Value$)$
        $B =$ Value
    end if
finish

subroutine to determine the RGB values
subroutine RGB$(H, M1, M2;$ Value$)$
H *is the hue* $(0 - 360°)$ *red at* $0°$

    adjust the hue to the correct range
    if $H < 0$ **then** $H = H + 360$
    if $H > 360$ **then** $H = H - 360$

determine the value
if $H < 60$ **then**   Value $= M1 + (M2 - M1)*H/60$
if $H \geq 60$ **and** $H < 180$ **then**   Value $= M2$
if $H \geq 180$ **and** $H < 240$ **then**   Value $= M1 + (M2 - M1)*(240 - H)/60$
if $H \geq 240$ **and** $H \leq 360$ **then**   Value $= M1$
return

Conversion from RGB to HLS is given by this pseudocode algorithm:

RGB to HLS conversion algorithm

RGB *are the red, green, blue primary color* $(0 - 1)$
H *is the hue* $(0 - 360°)$ *red at* $0°$
L *is the lightness* $(0 - 1)$
S *is the saturation* $(0 - 1)$
Max *is the maximum function*
Min *is the minimum function*

determine the lightness
$M1 = \text{Max}(R, G, B)$
$M2 = \text{Min}(R, G, B)$
$L = (M1 + M2)/2$

determine the saturation
achromatic case
if $M1 = M2$ **then**
    $S = 0$
    $H = $ Undefined
else

    chromatic case
    if $L \leq 0.5$ **then**
        $S = (M1 - M2)/(M1 + M2)$
    else
        $S = (M1 - M2)/(2 - M1 - M2)$
    end if

    determine the hue
    $Cr = (M1 - R)/(M1 - M2)$
    $Cg = (M1 - G)/(M1 - M2)$
    $Cb = (M1 - B)/(M1 - M2)$
    if $R = M1$ **then** $H = Cb - Cg$
    if $G = M1$ **then** $H = 2 + Cr - Cb$
    if $B = M1$ **then** $H = 4 + Cg - Cr$
    $H = 60*H$
    if $H < 0$ **then** $H = H + 360$
end if
finish

The Munsell Color System

A cylindrical representation is used in the Munsell color system (see [Muns41]). The Munsell system is based on a collection of color samples or swatches, hence it is a reflective standard. In the Munsell system, a color is designated by its Munsell hue, Munsell chroma (purity or saturation) and Munsell value (lightness). The central axis of the cylinder represents values between black at the bottom and white at the top. Increasing radial distance from the central axis represents increasing chroma, or purity, for the color. The color hues are represented by angular positions around the central axis, as shown in Fig. 5–118 and in Color Plate 27. One major advantage of the Munsell system that has resulted in wide industrial acceptance is that equal increments in chroma, hue and value result in equal perceptual changes; because of this characteristic, the entire volume of the cylinder is not filled. Transformation of the subjective Munsell color representation into CIE tristimulus values is available (see, for example, [Keeg58]). Meyer and Greenberg [Meye80] successfully displayed Munsell colors on a color monitor. They used CIE XYZ tristimulus values as an intermediate standard color space. First Munsell color values are transformed to CIE XYZ tristimulus values, and then these values are transformed to the RGB values required for the color monitor. Using this technique, Meyer and Greenberg are able to display some Munsell colors previously known only by extrapolation from existing samples.

The work by Meyer and Greenberg illustrates the practical value of the standard CIE XYZ color space. The use of CIE XYZ tristimulus values to specify colors is particularly important when computer graphics is used to either simulate existing commercially available colorants, e.g., paints or dyestuffs, or to design colors for reproduction using commercially available colorants. As an example, consider selection or simulation of the paint color for the Chevrolet Camaro shown in Color Plate 3. If the paint color is selected from that shown on the monitor, then it is necessary to provide color specifications to the paint manufacturer. Transforming from the display RGB value to CIE XYZ values

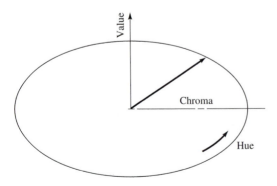

Figure 5–118 Conceptual representation of the Munsell color-ordering system.

and supplying these to the manufacturer accomplishes this. The paint manufacturer converts these values to those used to design the paint, e.g., Munsell hue, chroma and value. Alternately, if the appearance of the Camaro with an existing commercially available paint is to be evaluated, then the paint specifications are converted to CIE XYZ tristimulus values and then to RGB values for display on the monitor. Other applications are apparent.

The Pantone® System

The Pantone® system is based on a system of controlled and calibrated color swatches or samples keyed to standard or proprietary inks. You can specify a specific color by specifying a precise mixture of inks. No translation to CIE is publicly available.

Gamma Correction

The response of the visual system to intensity is decidedly nonlinear. In fact, the response is roughly governed by a power law distribution, where the power is approximately 0.45 ($9/20$). Similarly, the response of a CRTs electron gun to voltage is also nonlinear; again, it is a power law. The intensity of the light produced on the monitor face is proportional to the input voltage to the electron gun(s) raised to a theoretical $5/2$ power. The exponent in these power laws is commonly called gamma, γ. Thus, the intensity at the monitor I is

$$I = \mathrm{constant}(V)^{\gamma}$$

where V is the voltage supplied to the electron guns. Note that the function is a characteristic of the electron gun and not the monitor phosphor. Hence for any desired intensity value I, the voltage supplied to the monitor must be

$$V = \left(\frac{I}{\mathrm{constant}}\right)^{1/\gamma}$$

The process of compensating for the nonlinearity of the electron gun(s) is called gamma correction.

Experience shows that $1 \leq \gamma \leq 4$, with typical values of $2.3 \leq \gamma \leq 2.6$ for the electron guns in a color monitor. Large variations in apparent gamma are caused by the black level, or brightness adjustment, of the monitor [Poyn93] and not by the electron guns. Catmull [Catm79] and Hall [Hall89] discuss detailed procedures for determining both the constant and γ. In computer graphics, the results of the calibration are used as values in a lookup table (see Sec. 1–2); in video, gamma correction occurs *at the video camera*. This process, i.e., the gamma pipeline [Poyn93], is shown in Fig. 5–119.

Implicit in computer graphics is the assumption that realistic images are generated in physical space, thus the generated intensity varies linearly. Consequently, gamma correction to account for the response of the visual system takes

Computer Graphics

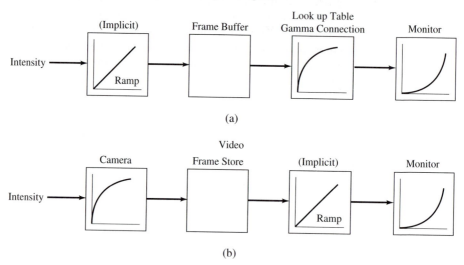

(a)

Video

(b)

Figure 5–119 Comparison of gamma correction in computer graphics and video. (a) Computer graphics; (b) video.

place as the image is displayed. In video, for economic reasons gamma correction occurs as the image is generated (and stored); no gamma correction occurs as the image is displayed.

Notice that the response of the visual system and the response of the electron gun(s) are nearly inverses of each other. Thus, in effect, gamma correction almost exactly compensates for the response of the electron gun(s) to yield a correct visual result.

Gamma correction calibrates only the intensity of the display. Calibrating the color of the display involves determining the CIE chromaticities of the red, green and blue phosphors used in the display as well. Cowan [Cowa83] and Hall [Hall89] discuss detailed calibration procedures for color monitors for both gamma correction and determination of the phosphor chromaticities. Meyer [Meye92] gives a method for setting the monitor white point.

Applying either Gouraud or Phong shading (see Secs. 5–6 and 5–7) to color images can yield startling results. The results depend on the color model used to specify the interpolated shading and the model used to display the results. If the transformation between the two color models is affine, i.e., a straight line transforms into a straight line, then the results are as expected; if not, then visual discontinuities may appear. As already shown, transformations among CIE, RGB, CMY and YIQ color models are affine. However, transformations between these models and either the HSV or HSL color model are not affine. A similar effect occurs when blending colored transparent effects, e.g., in a visible surface algorithm.

Finally, there is the question of color harmony, i.e., how colors are selected for pleasing effects. The literature is vast on this topic alone. A good starting place is Marcus [Marc82] or Judd and Wyszecki [Judd75]. One of the basic principles is to select colors using an orderly plan. An acceptable plan might select the colors from an orderly path in a color model, or confine the colors to a single plane in the color model. It is generally considered best to select colors that differ by equal perceptual distances. Examples of harmonious colors are frequently taken from nature, e.g., a sequence of greens. Another technique is to select colors of constant saturation or hue, i.e., colors that are more or less alike.

5–20   Color Image Quantization

Reducing the number of colors used to represent an image is called color quantization. Color quantization is different and distinct from image compression (see Secs. 2–11 and 2–12). In image compression, the objective is to reduce the electronic storage or transmission requirements for an image or file. This process may or may not result in the loss of data, i.e., it may be either lossless or lossy compression. In contrast, color quantization attempts to reduce the number of colors required to visually represent the image. Color quantization always results in a loss of color information.

The current standard for 'full' color images is 24 bits, i.e., 8 bits of color information for each of the red, green and blue color primaries. Of course, a digital representation of a continuous tone image is a form of quantization; but a 24 bit image is typically used as the standard of comparison. Eight bits of color information translates into 256 'shades' of each of the primary colors, or $2^{24} \approx$ 16.8 million total colors. Interestingly, the typical computer graphics monitor cannot *simultaneously* display *all* 16.8 million colors, because each individual pixel can display *only* a single color. Thus, a typical monitor with a 1280×1024 resolution is capable of displaying only 1,310,720 colors simultaneously, or about 20 bits of color information. To display all 16.8 million colors, a monitor resolution of 4096×4096 is required. The real question is, then, which 1,310,720 colors? The more interesting question is: Can the number of colors be further reduced, e.g., to 15 bits (32,768) or even 8 bits (256) of color information, and still retain an adequate visual representation of the image?

In a classic paper, Paul Heckbert [Heck82] defined color image quantization as the process of determining a set of colors to represent the color gamut (space) of an image, and then determining the mapping from color space to the representative set of colors. Color quantization techniques are generally classified as either uniform or nonuniform (tapered).

In uniform quantization, the variable range is subdivided into equal intervals. Uniform quantization of the color space is computationally faster than nonuniform quantization. However, much of the resulting quantized color space is wasted, because the image might not contain any colors that lie in a given quantized color interval.

In nonuniform quantization, the variable range is subdivided statistically. Because the resulting colors are not uniformly distributed, a color lookup table (LUT) or palette is used (see Sec. 1–2). By using a color lookup table based on image statistics, every color interval in the quantized color space is used. The result is a better visual representation of the image.

Heckbert divides the color quantization process into four steps:

Sample the image to determine color statistics. Generate a color frequency histogram.

Select a lookup table (color map), using the color statistics of the image.

Map the image colors to their nearest neighbor in the lookup table.

Quantize and regenerate the image with, if desired, dither (see Sec. 2–17).

There are a number of color quantization techniques. The most common are: the bit cutting, the popularity, the median cut and the octree algorithms.

The Bit Cutting Algorithm

Bit cutting, or uniform quantization, is conceptually the simplest of the color quantization algorithms. Here, n bits are truncated from each of the three RGB primary components of a full color image. For example, for a 24 bit image if white is represented by

$$R = \begin{bmatrix} 1 & 1 & 1 & 1 & 1 & 1 & 1 & 1 \end{bmatrix}$$
$$G = \begin{bmatrix} 1 & 1 & 1 & 1 & 1 & 1 & 1 & 1 \end{bmatrix}$$
$$B = \begin{bmatrix} 1 & 1 & 1 & 1 & 1 & 1 & 1 & 1 \end{bmatrix}$$

truncating the three right most bits ($n = 5$) yields

$$R_t = \begin{bmatrix} 1 & 1 & 1 & 1 & 1 \end{bmatrix}$$
$$G_t = \begin{bmatrix} 1 & 1 & 1 & 1 & 1 \end{bmatrix}$$
$$B_t = \begin{bmatrix} 1 & 1 & 1 & 1 & 1 \end{bmatrix}$$

which is still white. Similarly, truncating black represented by

$$R = G = B = \begin{bmatrix} 0 & 0 & 0 & 0 & 0 & 0 & 0 & 0 \end{bmatrix} \rightarrow R_t = G_t = B_t = \begin{bmatrix} 0 & 0 & 0 & 0 & 0 \end{bmatrix}$$

which is still black. Intermediate colors are more complex. For example, looking only at a particular red component represented to 8 bits of precision by

$$R = \begin{bmatrix} 0 & 1 & 1 & 1 & 1 & 1 & 1 & 1 \end{bmatrix} = 127_{10}$$

and truncating the right most three bits yields

$$R_t = \begin{bmatrix} 0 & 1 & 1 & 1 & 1 \end{bmatrix} = 15_{10}$$

which is equivalent to

$$R_t = \begin{bmatrix} 0 & 1 & 1 & 1 & 1 & 0 & 0 & 0 \end{bmatrix} = 120_{10}$$

Thus, all shades of red from 120_{10} to 127_{10} are now represented by a single shade. The bit cutting algorithm yields acceptable results for some images but not for others. Contouring, i.e., aliasing in color space, is particularly evident for Phong-shaded, ray traced or similar images.

The Popularity Algorithm

The popularity algorithm, originally developed in 1978 by Tom Boyle and Andy Lippman and independently by Ephraim Cohen, was implemented by Heckbert in 1980 [Heck80]. Fundamentally, the popularity algorithm generates the color lookup table based on the most frequently occurring colors in the original image. If the number of colors in the lookup table is C, then use the C colors with the highest frequencies from the image color histogram. Algorithmically

> Scan the original image, building a list of all the colors in the image while keeping a count of the number of times each color occurs; i.e., generate the color histogram of the image.
>
> Sort the colors in descending order, based on the count.
>
> Generate the color lookup table, using the C highest colors.
>
> Rescan the original image, mapping image colors to the lookup table and using the closest color in the lookup table.
>
> Regenerate the image, using dither if desired.

The popularity algorithm works well on many images but yields poor results for images with a wide range of colors, or when quantizing to a small number of colors. It also neglects colors in sparse regions of color space [Heck82].

A simple example illustrates the technique.

Example 5–14   The Popularity Algorithm

Consider the simple square image shown below and in Fig. 5–120a. The image contains 16 randomly placed shades of gray represented as a percentage of black, as shown by the numbers in each small square. Quantize the image to three bits, i.e., to eight shades of gray, using the popularity algorithm.

Original Image

48	48	90	84	42	72	36	60
12	72	42	66	60	30	48	30
96	12	54	84	54	72	12	6
66	96	78	30	24	84	36	30
30	36	48	60	72	72	18	90
78	36	60	54	18	36	36	96
6	90	72	24	36	48	60	30
36	24	78	12	78	12	6	96

The histogram for the image is

Shade	0	6	12	18	24	30	36	42	48	54	60	66	72	78	84	90	96	
Occurs	0	3	5	2	3	6	8	2	5	3	5	2	6	4	3	3	4	times

or graphically

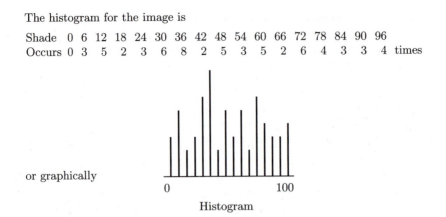

Histogram

The eight most frequent shades are

Shade	12	30	36	48	60	72	78	96	
Occurs	5	6	8	5	5	6	4	4	times

The lookup table is thus

Original image		Quantized image	
Histogram value	% black range	3 bit intensity value	% black value
96	88–100	7	94
78	17–87	6	82
72	67–75	5	71
60	54–66	4	60
48	43–54	3	49
36	33–42	2	38
30	21–33	1	27
12	0–20	0	10

(a)

(b)

Figure 5–120 An 'image' quantized with the popularity algorithm. (a) Original image with 64 shades of gray; (b) the image quantized to 8 shades of gray (see Ex. 5–14).

where the 0–7 intensity values are translated to percentages of black. Notice the somewhat expanded range near the ends of the interval. This expansion takes advantage of the fact that the eye is less sensitive to changes in intensity near the extremes of black and white. Thus, the quantized image is

Quantized Image

49	49	94	81	38	71	38	60
10	71	38	60	60	27	49	27
94	10	49	81	60	71	10	10
60	94	81	27	27	81	38	27
27	38	49	60	71	71	10	94
81	38	60	49	10	38	38	94
10	94	71	27	38	49	60	27
38	27	81	10	81	10	10	94

The original and the quantized images are shown in Fig. 5–120.

Applying the popularity algorithm without prequantization to the 24 bit full color image illustrated in Color Plate 28a results in the image in Color Plate 28b. Notice in particular the significant banding on the face, on the shoulder and in the background.

Although the popularity algorithm can yield acceptable results for computer generated images, the results for natural images are less pleasing. In addition, the popularity algorithm is very sensitive to the choice of prequantizer and to the amount of prequantization. If little or no prequantization of the image is used, then the popularity algorithm does a poor job of clustering and picks a poor color lookup table, as shown by Color Plate 28b. If more prequantization is used, then the popularity algorithm starts to cluster better, but color resolution is lost [Heck96]. The significant banding in the image in Color Plate 28b is a result of poor clustering. Experiments with the image in Color Plate 28a show that increasing prequantization (bit cutting) from RGB = 8:8:8 down to RGB = 3:3:3 results in a decrease in banding with an increase in color shift. Prequantization to RGB = 2:2:2 results in an increase in banding.

The median cut algorithm, discussed next, is only slightly more complex to implement; and it does a much better job of clustering, independent of the prequantizer or the amount of prequantization.

The Median Cut Algorithm

The underlying concept of the median cut algorithm is that each of the colors in the quantized color lookup table represent approximately an equal number of *pixels* in the original image. Starting with a rectangular box in three-dimensional RGB color space that tightly encloses the colors found in the image, the algorithm recursively and adaptively subdivides the box. The colors in the box are sorted along the long dimension of the box; the box is subdivided (cut) at the median point.

The process continues recursively, until the number of boxes equals the number of desired colors, C. Boxes which contain a single color are not subdivided. An attempt to subdivide a box which contains a single color means a spare box is available. The spare box is used to further subdivide the largest remaining box. Heckbert uses a k-d tree data structure [Bent75; Frie77] in implementing the algorithm.

After C boxes are generated, the average of the colors in each box is computed. The resulting list of average colors is used as the color lookup table (color map, or palette).

To limit the storage requirements, a 5:5:5 bit cutting algorithm generally is applied to the original image before applying the median cut algorithm [Heck82]. Cutting the least significant three bits from each of the RGB components of a full color (24 bit) image reduces the resolution of the image to 15 bits.

A simple example serves to further illustrate this algorithm.

Example 5–15   The Median Cut Algorithm

Consider the 10 colors which are represented for simplicity by only their red and green components, given by $C_1(40, 40)$, $C_2(50, 30)$, $C_3(20, 50)$, $C_4(10, 10)$, $C_5(50, 30)$, $C_6(60, 10)$, $C_7(20, 10)$, $C_8(20, 50)$, $C_9(10, 30)$ and $C_{10}(50, 30)$, as shown in Fig. 5–121a. Reduce the number of colors to four, using the median cut algorithm.

The initial 'box' is found using the maximum and minimum of the red (R) and green (G) coordinates, which yields

$$10 \leq R \leq 60 \qquad 10 \leq G \leq 50$$

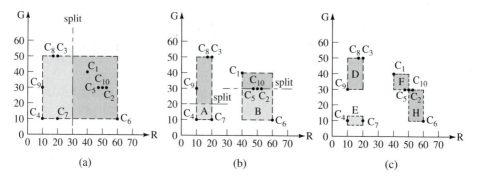

(a)   (b)   (c)

Figure 5–121   Median cut example in RG space. (a) Initial 'box'; (b) first split; (c) final split.

The longest dimension is in the red direction, because

$$R_\ell = 60 - 10 = 50 > G_\ell = 50 - 10 = 40$$

There are a number of algorithms for determining the median of a set of numbers. For simplicity, we determine the total number of colors in the 'box' and sort them in increasing order along the longest axis. If the number of colors is even, count the number of colors while ascending the sequence until the count exceeds half the total number. The median is then the average of the current appropriate color coordinate, R or G, and the previous appropriate color coordinate. The box is split at the median value. If the number is odd, the middle color in the sequence is the median. The box is split halfway between the appropriate middle color coordinate, R or G, and either the previous or next appropriate color coordinate in the sequence.

Sorting the ten colors along the R axis yields

	C_4	C_9	C_3	C_7	C_8	C_1	C_2	C_5	C_{10}	C_6
R	10	10	20	20	20	40	50	50	50	60

Split

The boxes are now shrunk tightly around the included colors, as shown in Fig. 5–121b. Looking first at box A, we see that the longest dimension is along the green axis, G. Sorting the colors in ascending order using the G coordinate yields

	C_4	C_7	C_9	C_3	C_8
G	10	10	30	50	50

Split

The number of colors is odd; the median is C_9. We choose to split the box between C_7 and C_9 at $G = 20$, as shown in Fig. 5–121c.

Looking at box B again, the longest dimension is along the green axis. Sorting the colors into ascending order yields

	C_6	C_2	C_5	C_{10}	C_1
G	10	30	30	30	40

Split

Again, the number of colors is odd; the median is C_5. The box is split between C_2 and C_5 at $G = 30$, as shown in Fig. 5–121c. Notice that C_2 and C_6 are in one box and C_5, C_{10}, C_1 are in the other box, even though the green coordinates, G_{C_2}, G_{C_5} and G_{C_6}, are all equal.

Averaging the colors in each of the four boxes yields the required four entries for the lookup table, i.e.,

$$\text{Box D} \qquad C_D(R, G) = \frac{C_3(20, 50) + C_8(20, 50) + C_9(10, 30)}{3}$$

$$= C_D\left(16\,\frac{2}{3}, 43\,\frac{1}{3}\right)$$

$$= C_D(16, 43)$$

where the color coordinates are truncated. Similarly

$$C_E(R, G) = C_E(15, 10) \quad C_F(R, G) = C_F(46, 33) \quad C_H(R, G) = C_H(55, 20)$$

Color Plate 28c shows the results of applying the median cut algorithm to the original 24 bit full color image of Color Plate 28a. Notice the slight banding on the shoulder, and the slight color change from the original full color image of Color Plate 28a.

Octree Quantization

Both the popularity and the median cut algorithms require sufficient memory to hold index counters for each color in an original image. Gervautz and Purgathofer [Gerv90] developed an algorithm based on octree encoding (see Sec. 4–18) that requires less memory.

Consider the RGB color cube shown in Fig. 5–122. Using octree subdivision, the complete cube is subdivided into eight subcubes. The Left-Down-Front (LDF) subcube is further subdivided. If the subdivision continues for eight levels, at the eighth level each subcube or leaf in the octree data structure represents a single color out of a possible 16.8 million colors ($256 \times 256 \times 256 = 2^8 \times 2^8 \times 2^8$).

Assuming that the number of desired quantized colors, C, is a power of two, then successively averaging the colors in the subcubes at each lower level until the number of remaining subcubes equals C represents a uniform quantization. (See the previous discussion in this section.) However, many of the cubes may be empty; thus, the quantized color space is inefficiently used. The result, as mentioned previously, is banding or aliasing in color space in the resulting quantized image. Gervautz and Purgathofer's algorithm more efficiently derives and uses the resulting quantized color space.

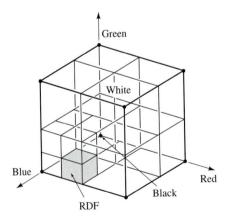

Figure 5–122 Subdivided RGB color cube.

Gervautz and Purgathofer's algorithm incrementally builds the octree while simultaneously quantizing the colors in the image. Thus, only those leaf nodes that represent the quantized colors are stored. For C quantized colors, at most C leaf nodes and $C-1$ intermediate nodes result; thus, the memory requirement is considerably reduced.

The binary encoding of the RGB components of a color directly provides the location of the octree node corresponding to the color. Consider a 24 bit color encoded as three 8 bit bytes, for example

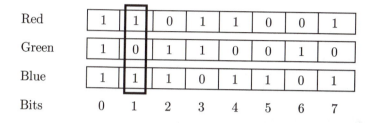

Red	1	1	0	1	1	0	0	1
Green	1	0	1	1	0	0	1	0
Blue	1	1	1	0	1	1	0	1
Bits	0	1	2	3	4	5	6	7

Referring to Fig. 5–122 and assigning $0 =$ Left, $1 =$ Right in the red byte, $0 =$ Down, $1 =$ Up in the green byte and $0 =$ Back, $1 =$ Front in the blue byte, we see that in each case the most significant bit (left-most bit) subdivides the complete color cube into two parts along each axis, i.e., into eight subcubes. Each successive bit from the most significant to the least significant further subdivides the cube. As an example, the boxed RGB bits (101) above represent the color in the Right-Down-Front (RDF, see Sec. 4–18) subcube at the second subdivision level, as shown in Fig. 5–122. Hence, each color specifies a unique path through the octree.

A color is added to the octree by using the RGB encoding to determine its location in the octree or color cube. Only if that leaf node in the octree is empty and the number of desired nodes, C, is not exceeded is the node created. Thus, only nodes that correspond to colors in the image are created.

If an attempt to create a new leaf node results in the number of nodes exceeding the required number of colors, C, the octree is reduced. Octree reduction is accomplished by averaging the colors represented by the child nodes of a parent node and assigning the average color to the parent node. The child nodes are then deleted. The average color in the parent node represents the quantized color for all child nodes of that parent. Thus, the maximum number of leaf nodes is C. However, note that there may be less than C leaf nodes and hence less than C quantized colors.

In order to be a candidate for reduction, a parent node must have two or more child nodes. Note that if octree reduction occurs, the branch of the octree now terminates at the parent node; it cannot grow any farther. Any subsequent color that would result in a child node of the reduced parent node is averaged with the existing color in the parent node.

The node with the greatest depth in the octree represents colors that lie closest together, hence this node is always selected for reduction. If multiple nodes have the same depth, Gervautz and Purgathofer suggest two criteria for selecting the optimal node for reduction:

Select the node with the fewest pixels — this tends to minimize the total image error and to preserve small gradations across large, smoothly shaded areas.

Select the node with the largest number of pixels — this results in some banding in large smooth areas, but preserves fine detail, e.g., antialiasing.

Alternatively, for simplicity the node can be picked arbitrarily, or an heuristic favoring the central area of the image might be useful for animation sequences where the viewer tends to focus on that part of the image [Clar96].

Searching the octree for reducible nodes is time consuming. Gervautz and Purgathofer suggest using eight linear lists, one for each of the octree levels, containing all reducible nodes. Clark [Clar96] implements these lists as linked lists and calls the result a level-linked octree. These lists are easily constructed as the octree is generated.

Example 5–16 Octree Quantization

Consider the two-dimensional analog of the color cube shown in Fig. 5–123. Cubes are addressed by their centers, as shown. For simplicity, only the red and green color components are considered. Given the set of colors in the $16 \times 16 = 256$ color space, as indicated by the $\times$s in Fig. 5–123, reduce the number of colors to 16, using octree quantization. There are potentially 256 leaf nodes in the two-dimensional 'octree', i.e., the quadtree that must be reduced to 16 leaf nodes. Assume that the subdivision proceeds from left to right, bottom to top.

Begin to build the tree by noting that although occupied it is not necessary to store the zeroth level. Subdividing the zeroth level results in four occupied 'subcubes' as indicated by the shading in Fig. 5–124. These are labelled LB, RB, LT, RT for Left-Bottom, Right-Bottom, Left-Top and Right-Top. Because C, the number of nodes, is less than 16, nodes are created for each of the 'subcubes' ($C = 4$). Subdividing the cube at LB-1, where the one indicates the level, shows that only LT-2 is occupied. Thus, only one additional node is created ($C = 5$). Subdividing LT-2 yields four occupied nodes ($C = 9$). Subdividing LB-3 yields four additional occupied nodes ($C = 13$). Returning to RB-3 and subdividing creates leaf nodes for LB-4, RB-4 and LT-4 ($C = 16$). Attempting to create the leaf node for RT-4 yields $C = 17 > 16$, as indicated by the star. The octree must be reduced. Here, if the current number of leaf nodes at this level is equal to the largest number of leaf nodes elsewhere in the tree, the leaf nodes at the current level are reduced. Hence, the colors in the occupied nodes LB-4, RB-4, LT-4 and RT-4 are averaged and are assigned to the node at RB-3 as indicated by the up arrow. The three leaf nodes LB-4, RB-4 and LT-4 are deleted. The node count is reduced by three to $C = 13$.

Subdividing the node at LT-3 results in the creation of leaf nodes LB-4, RB-4 and LT-4 ($C = 16$). Again, an attempt to create the leaf node RT-4 results in $C = 17 > 16$. The octree is again reduced, as shown by the up arrow.

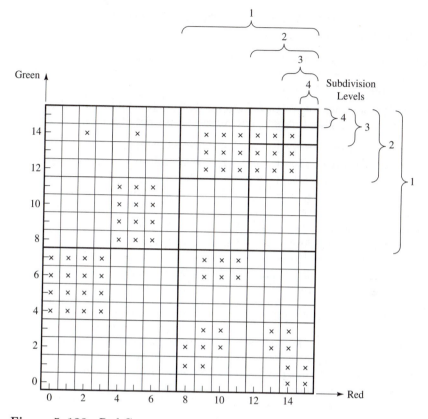

Figure 5–123 Red-Green representation of a color cube.

Subdividing the RT-3 node yields a similar result. The node count is now $C = 13$.

All the current nodes at level 3 have now been processed, There are no additional occupied nodes at level two. Consequently, the node RB-1 is subdivided. Here the LB-2, RB-2 and LT-2 nodes are created ($C = 16$). The RT-2 node is empty. Subdividing the LB-3 node yields $C = 17 > 16$, hence the 'octree' must be reduced. Here the current node with the largest number of colors is LB-1/LT-2/LB-3, where the / is a level separator. Thus, the leaf nodes at LB-1/LT-2/LB-3/LB-4, RB-4, LT-4 and RT-4 are averaged and assigned to node LB-1/LT-2/LB-3. The four leaf nodes are deleted. The node count is now $C = 12$.

The leaf nodes at LB-3, LT-3 and Rt-3 are now created ($C = 15$). Subdivision of LB-3 yields a leaf node at LT-4 ($C = 16$). Attempting to create a leaf node at RT-4 causes further octree reduction at LB-1/LT-2 by combining the leaf nodes at LB-1/LT-2/LB-3, RB-3, LT-3 and RT-3, as shown by the up arrow. The node count is now $C = 12$. Creating the node at RT-4 raises the node count to $C = 13$.

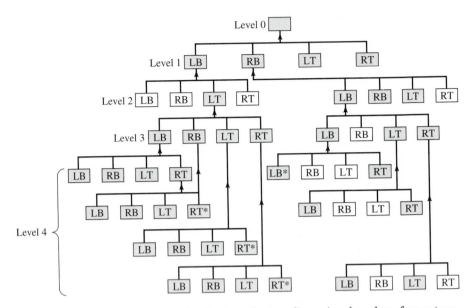

Figure 5–124   Subdivision and reduction of a two-dimensional analog of an octree.

Subdividing LT-3 yields leaf nodes at LB-4, RB-4 and RT-4, with a final node count of $C = 16$. Attempting to create the node at LB-4 causes octree reduction at RB-1/LB-2/LT-3/LB-4, RT-4, as shown by the up arrow.

Octree generation and reduction continues in this manner, until only 16 nodes remain. Completion of the tree is left as an exercise.

Once the reduced octree is complete, the image is scanned a second time. For any color in the original image, the path through the octree ends at a leaf node at some depth. This leaf contains a quantized color representative of the original color. If the index to the color lookup table is also stored in the octree, the search is ended. Because the reduced octree contains only C leaves all the original image colors are mapped to the quantized colors.

Color Plate 28d illustrates the results of applying the octree quantization algorithm to the original 24 bit full color image in Color Plate 28a. Notice the banding on the face and the shoulder.

Sequential Scalar Quantization

The bit cutting, popularity, median cut and octree algorithms yield acceptable results. However, more recent, more mathematically-based algorithms are both faster than the median cut and octree algorithms and yield better results for most images. The sequential scalar quantization (SSQ) algorithm by Balasubramanian et al. [Bala94a] is briefly described here as representative of this class of algorithms. The SSQ algorithm considers a color as a triplet (RGB) or three-dimensional vector. Consequently, color is amenable to quantization using a vector quantization algorithm. However, the scalar components of the vector, i.e., the red, green and blue components of the vector, are also individually amenable to quantization. Sequentially quantizing each of the components is less computationally expensive than quantizing them together, as in vector quantization, hence sequential scalar quantization. In sequential scalar quantization the first scalar is quantized to some number of levels, n_1. Each succeeding scalar is also quantized to some number of levels, n_i *within* the range of the quantization of the previous scalar, e.g., the processes might algorithmically be considered as quant(quant(quant(R),G),B) where quant is the quantization function.

The SSQ algorithm performs the quantization in a luminance-chrominance color space, using luminance-chrominance weighting to account for the visual system's greater sensitivity to errors in luminance than to errors in chrominance. The algorithm also takes advantage of image coherence (activity factor) to reduce quantization errors (banding) in areas of the image with smooth gradations. Figure 5–125a gives an outline of the SSQ algorithm, and Fig. 5–125b illustrates the details of the actual quantization. Briefly, the algorithm is

The image is transformed into SMPTE (see, e.g., [Kass92]) gamma-corrected RGB coordinates and then transformed to the luminance-chrominance YC_rC_b opponent color space given by

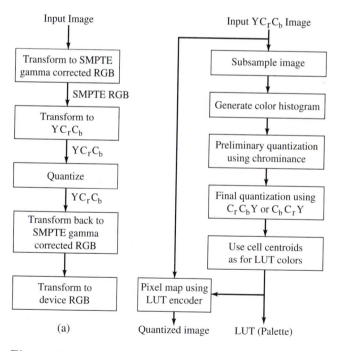

Figure 5–125   The SSQ algorithm.

$$Y = 0.299R + 0.587G + 0.114B$$
$$C_r = 0.713(R - Y) + 128$$
$$C_b = 0.564(B - Y) + 128$$

where the values are scaled to the range 0–255.

An image color histogram using 8 bits for the luminance coordinate Y, but reducing the chrominance coordinates C_r and C_b to 7 bits by dropping the least significant bit (bit cutting) is constructed. Image subsampling by a factor of 2 in each direction is also implemented while constructing the histogram. The resulting linear lists are reformatted into a single linked list to conserve memory.

A practical implementation of the optimal allocation of quantization levels using a density function is achieved by performing an initial approximate quantization on the image and then matching the result to a fixed quantization level. The results yield a near optimal minimum significant quantization error.

The best sequential quantization order is determined by noting that of the six possible quantization orders only four make intuitive sense, i.e., either quantize by luminance component first or last. The SSQ algorithm quantizes the chrominance components first and the luminance component last. Thus, only two possibilities remain, either $C_r C_b Y$ or $C_b C_r Y$. Both possibilities are examined, and the result with the smaller minimum significant quantization error is used.

The sensitivity of the visual system to quantization errors in luminance is compensated for by weighting the calculation of the minimum significant quantization, i.e.

$$Q_3 = d_1 + d_2 + K d_3$$

where Q_3 is the three-dimensional minimum significant quantization error, and d_1, d_2 and d_3 are the errors in each of the scalar coordinates, $C_r(C_b)$, $C_b(C_r)$, Y. K is the weighting factor taken as 4 by Balasubramanian [Bala94a].

The quantization error in smooth regions of color gradation is reduced by computing the average of the luminance gradients in 8 pixel blocks and assigning a block weighting value inversely proportional to the average. Hence, in smooth regions, the weighting factor is larger than in rapidly varying regions of the image. This weighting is incorporated into the SSQ palette (LUT) by allocating the number of quantization levels in luminance proportional to the weighting factor. The result is more quantization levels for colors in smoothly varying regions.

Scanning the image a second time to perform pixel mapping is not required. The SSQ algorithm implements a hierarchical lookup table (LUT). Specifically three LUTs corresponding to the two chrominance color components, C_r and C_b, and the luminance component, Y, are used. The LUTS are actually built during palette design. Hence, color mapping simply consists of indexing into the LUTs; no computation is required.

The SSQ algorithm is faster than, for example, the median cut algorithm and yields better results, as shown by comparing Color Plate 28e with Color Plates 28b, 28c and 28d, and to the original 24 bit full color image in Color Plate 28a. Notice the lack of banding on the smooth shaded area of the shoulder, and note that there is only a very slight degradation in color in the entire image. The implementation details are given by Balasubramanian [Bala94a].

Other Quantization Algorithms

Joy and Xiang [Joy93] present a modification of the median cut algorithm. Instead of selecting the color box with the highest pixel count to cut, they cut the color box with the greatest long dimension. This color box is then cut at its center rather than at the median. Hence, they call it the *center cut algorithm*. Finally a 5:6:4 preliminary bit cutting algorithm is applied rather than the common 5:5:5 bit cutting algorithm. The rationale behind using the 5:6:4 bit cut is that it retains more of the luminance information associated with the green color component and partially compensates for the nonuniformity of RGB color space, as well as the reduced sensitivity of the eye to blue. However, in order to prevent a color shift towards blue they use the full 24 bit color representations for color averaging. The algorithm more accurately renders specular highlights, particularly in synthesized images.

Barkans [Bark97] suggests a technique for recovering a 'true color' image from an 8 bit dithered image called *color recovery*. Fundamentally, color recovery uses a specialized noise filter to de-dither an image. The technique is successful because ordered dither adds known periodic noise to the image. Consequently, applying a noise filter specifically designed to remove the known noise de-dithers the image. The resulting filter is a simple box filter in the spatial domain, with width equal to the periodicity of the dither noise pattern. Using only 8 bit planes, an image of nearly comparable quality to a true color 24 bit image results.

Balasubramanian et al. [Bala94b] give an algorithm based on a modification of the binary splitting algorithm due to Orchard and Bouman [Orch91]. The binary splitting algorithm divides color space along the direction of greatest color variation; hence, it must consider the entire image when performing the division. Consequently, it is quite computationally expensive. Balasubramanian et al. first apply a prequantization step based on 7:8:4 RGB bit cutting, which more closely corresponds to the response of the visual system than the more commonly used 5:5:5 RGB bit cut. The algorithm then generates and performs binary division on a color histogram. Because the histogram contains fewer entries than in the original image, the computational expense is significantly reduced. They further perform a spatial activity weighting which favors splitting color space in those areas represented by smooth areas in the image. The resulting algorithm is generally as fast as or faster than the median cut algorithm; and it yields smaller errors in the image, especially for small color sets.

Xiang and Joy [Xian94] present a modification of the agglomerative clustering algorithm that increases its efficiency. The basic agglomerative clustering algorithm considers N clusters, each containing a single image color. It then hierarchically merges smaller clusters into larger clusters, until the desired number of clusters, C, are obtained. Basically,

n = N
while n > C
      find two clusters, c_i and c_j, such that merging minimizes the
         quantization error for all $1 \leq i \leq j \leq n$

      merge c_i and c_j

      n = n − 1
end while

Xiang and Joy use the smallest bounding box to define each cluster, and they measure the quantization error in terms of the size of the box in each of the RGB color directions. They maintain a proportional size limit on the boxes, using a 6:7:4 bit cut. They chose the 6:7:4 bit cut based on the luminance component of the NTSC YIQ color model where $0.30R + 0.59 \ G + 0.11B$ defines the luminance. Hence, they restrict any shift in the luminance (contrast), which is important in maintaining fine detail and depth information. Their data structure uses a two-dimensional hash table, along with linked lists and trees for efficiency. When scanning the image for the second pass, every 24 bit color corresponds to a node in the hash table, which contains the color lookup table value.

Bragg [Brag92] suggests adding jitter to an image before quantizing the colors to 15 bits (see also [Robe62]). His algorithm divides each of the 256 intensity levels of each of the RGB color components of a 24 bit image into 32 equal regions. Each region is assigned the intensity value of the lowest intensity in the region, e.g., the first region has an intensity of zero. Each RGB component in the original image is divided by eight. The remainder is thus a number between zero and seven. A random number between zero and eight is generated. If the remainder is less than or equal to the random number, the component intensity is increased by eight, i.e., assign it to the next highest intensity. The effect is to vary the intensity but is weighted towards the next highest intensity. Next, random noise is added to the component intensity; noise levels from zero to eight are possible. Bragg recommends a noise level of two; adding noise further eliminates color banding or aliasing in color space. Finally, bit cutting using a 5:5:5 RGB mask is performed. Although the resulting intensities are significantly different from the original 24 bit image, the average intensity is close to that of the original image.

5–21　Color Reproduction

Reproducing high quality computer generated images, normally viewed on a monitor, in a print medium is not easy. It involves both science and art, in particular the graphic arts. It is difficult to quantify those elements that depend upon the graphic arts. There have been a number of studies and experiments, notably by Stone and Cowan and their colleagues [Ston86, 88a, 88b, 90, 91], conducted in an attempt to quantify the necessary procedures. The details are beyond the scope of this text. What follows is an outline of the procedures and a brief discussion of some of the difficulties. For a detailed description, refer to the references [Ston86, 88a, 88b, 90, 91]. Successful reproduction requires knowledge of monitor calibration, printer calibration, screen technology and color transformation, as well as other procedures.

Offset Printing

The print medium most frequently used to generate high quality print images is offset printing. Offset printing is a lithographic process, i.e., the printing plate is flat. Different parts of the plate are treated to either attract or repel ink or water. The image is offset to a rubber sheet, called a blanket, which makes better contact with the paper, hence the name offset printing. The print is made by pressing the blanket against the paper. Offset printing is a bilevel process. Different 'gray' levels are produced by halftoning (see Sec. 2–17). Colors are produced by printing with different inks, one color per impression or run through the printing press. For high quality images typically four impressions are required, one for each of the subtractive primaries cyan, magenta, yellow and black (CMYK see Sec. 5–19). Consequently, the colors in the image must be separated into components, one for each impression. A separate plate is made for each of these *color separations*.

Color Separation

A color separation is a film, one for each color, containing specific halftone patterns. The color separations are used to make a *color proof*. Halftone patterns are specified in dots per inch (dpi), called the screen frequency, and the screen area covered by dots, called the *dot area*, 25%, 50%, 75% etc. Sharpness is defined by dot spacing, with 133–150 dpi screens used for magazine-quality offset printing. In order to minimize interference, the color separations are generated with rotated halftone patterns (see [Holl80]), typically at 105°, 75°, 90° and 45° for cyan, magenta, yellow and black, respectively. The definitive works on color separations are Yule [Yule67] and Southworth [Sout79].

Tone Reproduction

The *tone reproduction* curve defines the mapping from input gray or tone values to device output values. In traditional printing, tone values are related to density, which is a logarithmic function of the media reflectance. For digital images, density values are not available. One approach relates density to dot area. However, the dots produced on the color separations and on the printed media are not idealized circles or squares; thus, it is difficult to precisely determine dot area. An approximation is to visually match a set of gray patches of different intensities, i.e., a gray wedge, on the monitor to those on the printed medium.

Using this technique implies that the halftone patterns of the color separations must be modified to yield the desired dot area.

Gray Balance

On a color monitor, equal amounts of the red, green and blue primaries produce a neutral achromatic gray. In printing, equal amounts of the cyan, magenta and yellow primaries do not, in general, produce a neutral gray. The process of subtly modifying the printing primaries amounts to produce a neutral gray is called *gray balancing*. As an example, a 50% gray might require [C:50% M:47% Y:47%]. Except for the pure primary colors, most colors contain a *gray component* defined as min[CMY]. An obvious, and generally acceptable, technique is to balance the gray component of chromatic colors exactly as for the achromatic colors.

The Black Separation

In four-color printing, the black separation is used to increase contrast in dark areas of the image and to replace some of the cyan, magenta and yellow primary inks for either mechanical (paper wetting) or economic reasons. The process is called *undercolor removal* or *gray component replacement*. The process is nonlinear, e.g., if too much black is used in dark areas these areas can actually appear lighter, because black created from the three primaries is actually darker than the black ink alone. Also, separations are subject to alignment errors, which can produce hue shifts and white or colored gaps in the image. These effects are more noticeable if gray component replacement is incorrectly applied.

Quantization Effects

Full color computer displays typically use 256 levels/shades for each primary. Bilevel displays are restricted by the resolution of the device, because each image halftone dot is created by multiple device dots (see Sec. 2–17). Increasing the number of available shades by increasing the size of the halftone dot decreases the sharpness of the image. Consequently, the total number of levels/shades available to the printer is limited. The result may be banding, i.e., aliasing in color space. (see also Sec. 5–20).

Calibration

To establish the relationship between two output media, each must be calibrated in terms of a known standard, e.g., CIE tristimulus values (see Sec. 5–19). The fundamental calibration procedure measures linearly spaced color samples in device coordinates. The gamut of the device, which is three-dimensional, is divided into cubes. The calibration results are stored in a three-dimensional table. Intermediate values are determined using trilinear interpolation.

Two colors in the device gamut are particularly important: *source black* and *source white*. Source black is the darkest achromatic color in the source gamut, while source white is the brightest achromatic color. These two colors define the black–white, or *gray*, axis.

When transformed to CIE tristimulus coordinates, an ideal monitor gamut yields a parallelepiped with one corner at the origin. The black point is at $(0, 0, 0)$, and the other vertices correspond to red, green, blue, cyan, magenta, yellow and white. The realizable monitor gamut changes with changing viewing conditions; for example, turning on the room lights displaces the black point to a point called *device black*.

A typical printer gamut is not an idealized parallelepiped. The sides of the gamut are more nearly trapezoids than parallelograms, and the black point is off-set. The gamut is typically quite narrow around the black point, indicating that fewer saturated colors are available near black. Also, the edges are curved and frequently concave (see Fig. 5–113). In addition, the entire production process influences the gamut; thus, monitor and printer gamuts are very different.

When transforming between monitor and printer, it is necessary to remember that any saturated monitor color near black may not be reproducible by the printer, that the pure monitor blue is not reproducible by the printer and, except for yellow, the brightness of saturated colors produced by the printer is lower than those generated on a monitor. Finally, the white points, and hence the gray axis, are different.

Gamut Mapping

In reproducing an image from a monitor in a print medium, one of the crucial steps is mapping the monitor gamut to the printer gamut. Because color reproduction seeks to produce a print image that *appears* to be identical to the monitor image, the transformation must be more than just mapping CIE tristimulus values. Stone et al. [Ston88a] provide an example that illustrates this requirement.

A typical monitor has a white point specified by $[X = 23.8\ Y = 25.0\ Z = 27.2]$. The white point, defined as a D_{5000} source illuminating blank white paper, for a typical printer measures $[X = 495\ Y = 526\ Z = 413]$. Using the tristimulus coordinates of the monitor white point directly yields a dark blue, near gray in the printer gamut! Scaling the luminosity, Y, by 526/25 yields $[X = 501\ \ Y = 526\ \ Z = 572]$ for the monitor white point in the printer gamut. But this white point is *outside* the printer gamut! More sophisticated transformations are thus necessary.

Gamut transformations are transformations from one CIE XYZ space to another CIE XYZ space. Stone and colleagues [Ston88b] base the transformations on well-known graphic arts principles. Specifically

> The gray axis of the image is preserved. This means that the gray axis of the monitor image must be aligned with, and scaled to, the gray axis of the printer gamut.

> Maximum luminance contrast is desirable. Contrast or contrast ratio is the ratio of the intensity of the brightest white to the darkest black in

the image. Highlights usually determine the image gray axis. Leaving the highlights slightly out of the printer gamut maximizes luminance contrast.

Only a few colors should lie outside the printer gamut. Out-of-gamut colors are projected onto the three-dimensional surface of the printer gamut. Stone et al. give an appropriate projection transformation.

Hue and saturation shifts should be minimized. However, such shifts must not cause a color to cross a color name boundary, e.g., a lemon yellow on the monitor must not become orange on the print.

It is better to increase rather than decrease saturation, especially for American and Japanese audiences. However, highly saturated monitor colors are often outside the printer gamut.

Stone et al. further comment that colors near black, and the relative shape of the image and printer gamuts in this region, have a profound effect on contrast and saturation. They further comment that it is undesirable to project colors that occupy large areas of the image and lie on or near the boundary of the image gamut onto the surface of the printer gamut, because they may all end up as a single color in the printer gamut. Thus, these colors must be kept inside the printer gamut.

Gray axis alignment is accomplished using the transformation given by Stone and colleagues [Ston88b]

$$[X_d] = [B_d] + csf [X_i - B_i][R]$$

where

$$
\begin{aligned}
[B_d] &= \text{tristimulus coordinates of destination black} \\
[B_i] &= \text{tristimulus coordinates of image black} \\
[R] &= \text{rotation matrix} \\
[X_d] &= \text{tristimulus coordinates of destination pixel} \\
[X_i] &= \text{tristimulus coordinates of image pixel} \\
[W_d] &= \text{tristimulus coordinates of destination white} \\
[W_i] &= \text{tristimulus coordinates of image white} \\
csf &= \text{contrast scale factor}
\end{aligned}
$$

The contrast scale factor is chosen to place the image white just outside the limit of the destination gamut, in order to provide maximum luminance and achromatic contrast.

Once the gray axis is aligned, it is important to bring saturated colors, from the image near the black point, that lie outside the printer gamut back within the gamut. Translating the black point along the gray axis while rescaling the length of the gray axis (adjusting csf) accomplishes this. The transformation is now

$$[X_d] = [B_d] + csf [GA_d] + csf [X_i - B_i][R]$$

where
$$[GA_d] = [W_d - B_d]$$

is the suitably normalized length of the gray axis.

Using only a black point shift to bring the image gamut inside the destination (printer) gamut results in unacceptable contrast loss when images use highly saturated CRT colors. Stone et al. [Ston88b] compensate for this contrast reduction by moving the phosphor chromaticities of the CRT image white point.

Given the original CRT phosphors R_s, G_s, B_s for white point W_s, then an image pixel, r, g, b, is desaturated by moving the phosphors to R_n, G_n, B_n. Thus

$$r[R_s] + g[G_s] + b[B_s]$$

is transformed to a new color

$$r[R_n] + g[G_n] + b[B_n]$$

where $[R_n], [G_n], [B_n]$ define a new white point $[W_n] = [W_s]$, i.e.

$$[R_n] + [G_n] + [B_n] = [R_s] + [G_s] + [B_s]$$

in order for the achromatic image colors to remain achromatic. In addition, to avoid hue shifts, $[R_n], [G_n], [B_n]$ are constrained to lie along the vectors from $[W_s]$ to $[R_s], [G_s], [B_s]$, respectively. The results are shown in Fig. 5–126.

In further work, Stone and Wallace [Ston91] experimented with using the CIEL*a*b* uniform perceptual color space (see Sec. 5–19). Conceptually the process is equivalent in CIEL*a*b* space. Loosely gray balancing corresponds to mapping lightness while mapping out of gamut colors corresponds to chroma compression. They introduce the concept of a *knee function* when compressing chroma from one media gamut to another. A similar function is used in some commercial image scanning and manipulation software.

Stone and colleagues [Ston88b] used an interactive system to define, implement and apply these transformations. Currently, the International Color Consortium is attempting to develop a set of device profiles for input, display

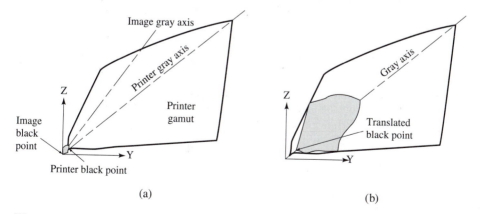

(a)

(b)

Figure 5–126 Gamut mapping. (a) Original image (shaded) and printer gamuts; (b) image gamut after transformation.

and output devices that allow noninteractive *color management systems* to control the reproduction of high quality color images between mediums [ICC96]. For example, Apple's ColorSync [Appl95] system and PostScript Level 2's inclusion of color calibration information are commercial attempts to implement color management systems.

While color reproduction from monitor to printer is emphasized here, similar techniques are required to map a monitor image to either video or film. However, both video and film require special consideration, e.g., in video the color of adjacent pixels influences the perception of an individual pixel color. A full discussion is well beyond the scope of this text.

5–22 Specialty Rendering Techniques

Duotone Printing

The four-color printing process described in Sec. 5–21 typically uses four fixed *process color* inks: cyan, magenta, yellow and black. It is an expensive process. A less expensive two-color process, called *duotone* color reproduction, uses just two inks. Traditionally, the duotone color process has been used to tint monochrome gray-scale images with color. Power et al. [Powe96] extend the duotone process to reproduction of 'full color' images. Formally stated, the duotone process is

> Given a color image C, a paper color P, the set of available printing inks I and a subset of $k = 0$, 1 or 2 inks in I, find the best $2 - k$ additional inks for reproducing the color image, C, on the paper, P, along with the appropriate color separations.

If the paper color is considered [Powe96], then the duotone process is really a combination of four colors:[†] each of the two colors alone, the two colors simultaneously and the paper. Power points out that these four colors define a bilinear surface in color space with a large gamut. In effect, the duotone process is a mapping from a three-dimensional color space to a two-dimensional surface in color space. The paper, of course, does not need to be white, e.g., it could be yellow as in the 'yellow pages' of a telephone directory.

Power uses the Neugebauer equations [Neug37], originally designed for three-color printing, to determine the amount of ink required to reproduce a given color. The Neugebauer equations assume that the color of a small area is the area-weighted average of each of the primary colors. For example, if α_1, α_2 and α_3 are the amounts of cyan, magenta and yellow ink printed, then the contribution of blue is $\alpha_1\alpha_2(1 - \alpha_3)$, because blue is the complement of yellow, i.e., blue is *not* yellow. For three-color printing, the equations are

---

[†]In the same sense, assuming a white paper, the subtractive four-color process is a combination of eight colors: cyan, magenta, yellow, blue (cyan + magenta), green (cyan + yellow), red (magenta + yellow), black (cyan + magenta + yellow) and white (no color).

$$C = \begin{bmatrix} g_0 & g_1 & g_2 & g_3 & g_{12} & g_{23} & g_{123} \end{bmatrix} \begin{bmatrix} (1-\alpha_1)(1-\alpha_2)(1-\alpha_3) \\ \alpha_1(1-\alpha_2)(1-\alpha_3) \\ (1-\alpha_1)\alpha_2(1-\alpha_3) \\ (1-\alpha_1)(1-\alpha_2)\alpha_3 \\ \alpha_1\alpha_2(1-\alpha_3) \\ \alpha_1(1-\alpha_2)\alpha_3 \\ (1-\alpha_1)\alpha_2\alpha_3 \\ \alpha_1\alpha_2\alpha_3 \end{bmatrix}$$

where g_0 is the color of the paper, g_i are the colors of the ink *on the paper*, g_{12} is the color of the inks i and j superimposed *on the paper* and g_{123} is the color of the inks i, j and k superimposed *on the paper*. The inks are described in terms of their CIE *XYZ* coordinates. Specializing to the duotone process yields

$$C = \begin{bmatrix} g_0 & g_1 & g_2 & g_{12} \end{bmatrix} \begin{bmatrix} (1-\alpha_1)(1-\alpha_2) \\ \alpha_1(1-\alpha_2) \\ (1-\alpha_1)\alpha_2 \\ \alpha_1\alpha_2 \end{bmatrix}$$

which again describes a bilinear surface in additive color space.

Power and colleagues found the spectral reflectance for inks and paper using a Colortron™ spectrophotometer, which also provides data for Pantone® inks. Printing primaries were estimated for single and superimposed inks on a selected paper. The spectral reflectance has both an overall reflectance, R, and a Fresnel reflectance, F. They estimated the Fresnel contribution, i.e., the amount of light at each wavelength reflected from the surface without entering the surface (ink) layer. Noting that inks act like filters, while paper acts like an opaque layer, allowed Power to use a simple model for these characteristics. Specifically

$$R_{ij} = (R_i - F_i)(R_j - F_j) + F_i$$
$$F_{ij} = F_i$$

where i and j represent subtractive layers. The Fresnel spectrum of all the inks and the paper was approximated by the spectrum of black ink. To eliminate the contribution of the stock paper to the spectral data, they inverted the equation, that is

$$F_i = F_{ij}$$
$$R_i = \frac{R_{ij} - F_{ij}}{R_j - F_j} + F_i$$

These characteristics determine the duotone gamut.

Once the duotone gamut is determined, it is necessary to map the image colors to the duotone gamut. Power et al. [Powe96] consider it more important to maintain the overall relationships between colors than to map colors exactly. Basically, they define an orthogonal axis system for the duotone gamut, then transform colors along two directions in this axis system and use a parallel projection along the third direction. The CIE Y luminance direction is used as the first transformation; this preserves relative luminance. The second direction preserves the ink spread of the two chosen inks, i.e., the vector $\mathbf{S} = \mathbf{g}_2 - \mathbf{g}_1$ is taken as orthogonal to $\mathbf{Y}$. The orthogonal direction, $\mathbf{P} = \mathbf{Y} \otimes \mathbf{S}$, the average normal of the bilinear duotone gamut surface, is used as the projection direction. $\mathbf{P}$ is the direction of least color variation; projection in this direction sacrifices the least amount of color variation.

The algorithm developed by Power et al. [Powe96] allows selection of an optimal pair of inks for a given image. The algorithm uses an ideal optimization technique, called simulated annealing. It extends the duotone process to include black enhancement (undercolor removal, see Sec. 5–21) and colored paper, as mentioned previously. The algorithm first clusters the image colors, and then it ignores small clusters of colors that lie a large distance from the majority. It seeks to minimize hue differences by mapping unachievable colors to gray. The results are impressive.

Rendering Natural Objects

Rendering naturally occurring objects is difficult, because they are complex, rough, dirty, cracked and otherwise irregular. Examples are fire, smoke, clouds, fog, grass and trees. Considerable work has been done in this area. Selected early references are Blinn [Blin82]; Dungan [Dung79]; Marshal et al. [Mars80]; and Csuri [Csur83].

Particle Systems

Because many natural phenomena are difficult to model with polygons or curved surfaces, Reeves [Reev83] and his co-workers, as well as a number of previous investigators, turned to individual particles as a modeling mechanism. These particles are 'fuzzy'; i.e., , they do not have smooth, well-defined surfaces but rather have irregular, complex surfaces of nonconstant shape. The particles change form and characteristics with time, under the action of physical or stochastic models. Over time, particles are generated or born into the system, move within the system and die or leave the system. The following procedure is used to generate a single frame:

> New particles are generated, assigned individual attributes and introduced into the system.
>
> Old particles in the system that have died are extinguished.
>
> The remaining particles are moved, using an appropriate motion model.
>
> An image of the remaining particles is rendered.

A number of realistic synthetic images have been generated using this technique. An example is shown in Color Plate 29. Reeves [Reev83] also incorporates motion blur within a stochastic particle system by generating special particle shapes.

Problems and Projects

Because computer graphics is very much a learn by doing discipline, a number of problems and programming projects are given. To reduce computational requirements, and also to illustrate effects by exaggeration, using a reduced raster resolution, for example 32 × 32, is sometimes useful. If a raster device with greater resolution is available, this can be accomplished by addressing a group of pixels as a unit. If a single pixel is not square, then the group of pixels should be adjusted to be as nearly square as possible. Suggested projects are grouped by chapter.

Chapter 1

1–1 Develop a subroutine that controls the size of the raster grid, i.e., be able to specify an arbitrary resolution for the display area. Use square pseudopixels containing one or more physical pixels to represent the square pseudopixels.

Chapter 2

2–1 Using both a simple DDA (see Sec. 2–2) and Bresenham's algorithm (see Sec. 2–3), write a program to draw lines from any point to any other point on a pseudo 32 × 32 raster grid. Use a pseudo frame buffer represented by a single vector array to first store the image and then write from this pseudo frame buffer to the display. Demonstrate the program using a test pattern consisting of at least 16 lines from the center of a circle to points equally spaced around its circumferences. Allow for arbitrary location of the center of the circle. Compare the results visually. List the activated pixels for the line from $(0,0)$ to $(-8,-3)$ for both algorithms. How does initialization affect the results? Compare the computational efficiency of the two algorithms by timing the rasterization of 1000 random lines for each algorithm.

2–2 Develop a two-step line rasterization algorithm. Compare the results to the classical Bresenham algorithm.

2–3 Develop a quad-step line rasterization algorithm. Compare the results to the classical Bresenham algorithm.

2–4 Develop a line generation algorithm based on the concepts from the midpoint algorithm of Sec. 2–5.

2–5 A rasterized circle can be generated using the Bresenham circle generation algorithm described in Sec. 2–4. It can also be generated by rasterizing the edges of an inscribed polygon using Bresenham's line rasterization algorithm. Write a program using both techniques to rasterize a circle of radius $R = 15$ on a 32×32 grid. Consider generating only a quarter of the circle and using reflections to generate the remainder. Compare the results for inscribed polygons of $4, 8, 16, 32, 64$ and 128 sides and the Bresenham circle rasterization algorithm. Provide a list of rasterized points using a row-column format for each algorithm. Assume that the origin $(0,0)$ of the pseudo raster is in the lower left corner. Compare the results both visually and computationally.

2–6 Develop a midpoint circle generation algorithm (see Sec. 2–5).

2–7 Implement a space subdivision algorithm for arbitrary cubic curves.

2–8 Implement the simple parity polygon scan conversion algorithm of Sec. 2–11.

2–9 For the polygon with an exterior described by the points $(4, 4)$, $(4, 26)$, $(20, 26)$, $(28, 18)$, $(28, 4)$, $(21, 4)$, $(21, 8)$, $(10, 8)$ and $(10, 4)$, and an interior hole described by $(10, 12)$, $(10, 20)$, $(17, 20)$, $(21, 16)$ and $(21, 12)$ on a 32×32 raster, write a program using the simple ordered edge list algorithm described in Sec. 2–12 to scan convert and display the solid area interior to the polygon. List the filled pixels in scan line order, from top to bottom and left to right, using a row-column format and assuming that $(0, 0)$ is in the lower left hand corner of the raster.

2–10 For the polygon of Project 2–9, write a program using the more efficient ordered edge list algorithm described in Sec. 2–12 to scan convert and display the solid area interior to the polygon. Use an active edge list. Use a linked list to implement the y bucket sort. List the contents of the active edge list for scan line 18 of the 32×32 raster. List the displayed pixels in scan line order. List the contents of the linked list.

2–11 Write programs using the edge fill and fence fill algorithms described in Sec. 2–13 to scan convert the solid area interior to the *exterior only* of the polygon described in Project 2–9. Use a pseudo frame buffer, represented by a two-dimensional array, to store the image; then write to the display from the pseudo frame buffer after scan converting each edge. Compare the results. Compare the computational and input/output efficiencies of the two algorithms. Is it possible to correctly scan convert the entire polygon, including the interior hole, with these algorithms?

2–12 Using the edge flag algorithm described in Sec. 2–14, write a program to scan convert the solid area interior to the *exterior only* of the polygon described in Project 2–9. Use a pseudo frame buffer represented by a two-dimensional array to store the image. Display the frame buffer contents after determining the contour and completing the scan conversion. Compare the results with those of Project 2–11. Is it possible to correctly scan convert the entire polygon, including the interior hole, with this algorithm? If it is, modify the program. If not, why not?

2–13 Write a program using the simple boundary defined seed fill algorithm described in Sec. 2–15 to fill the interior of the polygon given in Project 2–9. Provide a list of the boundary pixels. Generate and provide a filled pixel list as the algorithm progresses for a seed pixel of $(14, 20)$. Be able to show the stack contents at any point. What is the maximum stack depth?

2–14 Do Project 2–13, using the scan line seed fill algorithm described in Sec. 2–15. Compare the results.

2–15 Implement a simple color run-length encoding algorithm. Make sure it switches from RLE to pixel by pixel encoding for efficiency.

2–16 Implement an area image compression scheme using zigzag RLE with progressive display (transmission) capabilities.

2–17 Implement the Bresenham line drawing algorithm with antialiasing described in Sec. 2–16.

2–18 Implement antialiasing of thick lines as discussed in Sec. 2–16.

2–19 Implement the subpixel approximation to polygon edge antialiasing discussed in Sec. 2–16 and Fig. 2–68.

2–20 Using the 2×2 bilevel pattern cells shown in Fig. 2–77, develop a program to show eight 'gray' levels from left to right across a 32×32 raster. Repeat with 64×64 and 128×128 rasters and compare the results. Add ordered dither to the 128×128 raster and compare the results.

2–21 Implement the simple thresholding algorithm of Sec. 2–17.

2–22 Implement the Floyd–Steinberg and simplified Floyd–Steinberg error diffusion algorithms of Sec. 2–17. Compare the results for a variety of images.

2–23 Implement the ordered dither algorithm. Build the dither matrices up from the matrices $[D_2]$ and $[U_n]$ (see Sec. 2–17). Compare the results for different dither matrices.

Chapter 3

3–1 For a two-dimensional rectangular clipping window, implement the Cohen–Sutherland line clipping algorithm described in Sec. 3–2, and the midpoint subdivision line clipping algorithm described in Sec. 3–3; compare their efficiencies. The algorithms should immediately identify and draw totally visible lines and immediately identify and reject totally invisible lines.

3–2 Add Duvanenko's optimizations to the Cohen–Sutherland clipping algorithm as described in Sec. 3–2.

3–3 Write a program to implement the two-dimensional Cyrus–Beck line clipping algorithm of Sec. 3–5 for both interior and exterior clipping to an arbitrary convex polygonal clipping window. The algorithm should identify and reject concave clipping windows. For the special case of a rectangular clipping window compare the results with those of Project 3–1. Vary the number of sides of the polygonal clipping window. Plot the execution time versus number of sides. What is the relationship?

3–4 Extend Project 3–3 to arbitrary three-dimensional convex polyhedral volumes (see Sec. 3–13).

3–5   Implement the Liang–Barsky two-dimensional clipping algorithm (see Sec. 3–6). Compare the results to the Cyrus–Beck algorithm.

3–6   Implement the Nicholl–Lee–Nicholl two-dimensional clipping algorithm for lines in the lower left corner region (see Sec. 3–7).

3–7   Using symmetry, extend Project 3–6 to lines in the upper right corner region.

3–8   Determine if the polygon $V_1(0,0,0)$, $V_2(3,-1,0)$, $V_3(2,2,0)$, $V_4(3,4,0)$, $V_5(0,4,0)$ is concave or convex using the cross product technique and the rotation/translation technique. Find the inner normal for the edge V_2V_3.

3–9   Write a program implementing the Sutherland–Hodgman polygon clipping algorithm described in Sec. 3–19 for arbitrary polygons clipped to rectangular windows. Show the resulting polygon after each clipping stage. In particular, clip the polygon described by vertices $(-4,2)$, $(8,14)$, $(8,2)$, $(12,6)$, $(12,-2)$, $(4,-2)$, $(4,6)$, $(0,2)$ to the window $(0,10,0,10)$.

3–10 Extend Project 3–9 to arbitrary convex windows.

3–11 Using the Cyrus–Beck line clipping algorithm to determine the line end point visibilities and the line surface intersections, extend the Sutherland–Hodgman polygon clipping algorithm to clip the planar polygon defined by the points $P_1(-0.4,0.4,0)$, $P_2(0.1,0.1,0)$, $P_3(0.3,0.3,0)$, $P_4(0.2,0,0)$, $P_5(0.3,-0.2,0)$, $P_6(0.1,-0.1,0)$, $P_7(-0.4,-0.4,0)$, $P_8(-0.2,0,0)$ rotated by $+45$ degrees about the x-axis to the cylinder with axis along the z coordinate direction, a radius of 0.3 and a length along the z-axis of ± 0.3. Do not forget that the cylinder has ends. The cylinder is to be represented by an inscribed polyhedral volume with 32 sides. Display the cylinder and the clipped polygon, using an appropriate viewing transformation. Provide a list of the polygon points after clipping.

3–12 Using the data from Project 3–11, modify the algorithm to clip the polygon to the exterior of the cylinder. Display the cylinder and the clipped polygon using an appropriate viewing transformation. Provide a list of the polygon points after clipping.

3–13 Modify the algorithms developed in Projects 3–11 and 3–12 to clip one cylinder to another. Implement the capability to perform the classical Boolean operations of union and intersection. This project has implications for solids modeling.

3–14 Modify the Liang–Barsky polygon clipping algorithm using special cases to handle vertical and horizontal polygon edges (see Sec. 3–20).

3–15 Complete Ex. 3–25 by using the Liang–Barsky algorithm to clip the line to the physical volume; then transform to the perspective volume. Is the result correct?

3–16 Write a program implementing the Weiler–Atherton concave polygon clipping algorithm described in Sec. 3–21. Show the entering and leaving intersection lists. Show the resulting subject and clip polygon lists. In particular, clip the subject polygon with exterior boundary $(0,0)$, $(20,0)$, $(20,-20)$, $(0,-20)$ and interior hole $(7,-13)$, $(13,-13)$, $(13,-7)$, $(7,-7)$ to the clip polygon with exterior boundary $(-10,-10)$, $(-10,10)$, $(10,10)$, $(10,-10)$, and interior hole $(-5,-5)$, $(5,-5)$, $(5,5)$, $(-5,5)$. See Fig. 3–42c. Show the original clip and subject polygons and the final clipped polygon.

Chapter 4

4–1   Using the floating horizon technique described in Sec. 4–2, develop a computer program that removes the hidden lines for the surface function.

$$F(x,z) = 8\cos\left(\frac{1.2R}{R+1}\right) \qquad R = \sqrt{x^2 + z^2} \qquad 2\pi \le x, \quad z \le 2\pi$$

viewed from a point at infinity on the positive z-axis after having been rotated $25°$ about the x-axis, followed by a $15°$ rotation about the y-axis.

4–2 Using Roberts' technique, by hand, eliminate the hidden lines from the following scene: The scene is viewed using a dimetric transformation, with the observer at infinity on the positive z-axis. A dimetric transformation without projection onto the $z = 0$ plane is given by Rogers and Adams (see [Roge90a]) by the 4×4 homogeneous coordinate transformation

$$\begin{bmatrix} 0.92582 & 0.13363 & -0.35355 & 0 \\ 0 & 0.92541 & 0.35355 & 0 \\ 0.37796 & -0.32732 & 0.86603 & 0 \\ 0 & 0 & 0 & 1 \end{bmatrix}$$

The inverse of the transformation matrix is its transpose. The scene consists of a cube and a rectangular parallelepiped given by

	cube			parallelepiped	
3	1	11	1	2	7
6	1	11	10	2	7
6	4	11	10	3	7
3	4	11	1	3	7
3	1	8	1	2	1
6	1	8	10	2	1
6	4	8	10	3	1
3	4	8	1	3	1

4–3 Complete the solution in Ex. 4–13 for the penetrating lines.

4–4 Write a program to implement Roberts algorithm. Use the scene from Project 4–2 as a test case.

Projects 4–5 to 4–19 use the basic test scene described in Ex. 4–19 plus a modification. This basic test scene consists of a triangle penetrating a rectangle from behind. A 32×32 raster grid is used (see Project 1–1). The corner coordinates of the rectangle are $P_1(10,5,10)$, $P_2(10,25,10)$, $P_3(25,25,10)$, $P_4(25,5,10)$; and the triangular vertices are $P_5(15,15,15)$, $P_6(30,10,5)$, $P_7(25,25,5)$. The modified scene consists of the rectangle and a nonpenetrating triangle with P_5 changed to $P_5(15,15,5)$.

4–5 Write a program to implement the basic Warnock algorithm described in Sec. 4–4. Display the results for both test scenes. Display each window or subwindow as the algorithm processes the scene.

4–6 Increase the efficiency of the algorithm of Project 4–5 by implementing a more sophisticated outsider test. Also add the ability to recognize single surrounder, single contained and single intersector polygons. Add a depth priority sort to the algorithm. Add a list structure to take advantage of prior level information. Add antialiasing to the algorithm (Sec. 2–16). Use more sophisticated scenes to test and compare the algorithms.

4–7 Implement the haloed line algorithm in the context of a classical two- or three-dimensional plotting program (see Fig. 4–48).

4-8 Write a program to implement the Weiler–Atherton algorithm (see Sec. 4–7) for the test scenes described above.

4-9 Implement a z-buffer algorithm (see Sec. 4–9). Use the two scenes described above to test it. Display the contents of the frame and the z-buffer after each polygon is processed. What is the effect of truncating the z value to correspond to $32, 16, 8, 4$ bits of precision for the z-buffer?

4-10 Implement the A-buffer algorithm (see Sec. 4–10). Use the two scenes described above to test it.

4-11 Write a program to implement the Newell–Newell–Sancha list priority algorithm which is described in Sec. 4–12. Add a diamond with vertices $P_8(15, 20, 20)$, $P_9(20, 25, 20)$, $P_{10}(25, 20, 20)$, $P_{11}(20, 15, 20)$ to the test scenes described above. Display the contents of the frame buffer after each polygon is processed.

4-12 Implement a BSP algorithm. Use the polygons in Fig. 4–68 to test it.

4-13 Implement the scan line z-buffer algorithm described in Sec. 4–15. Use the two scenes described above to test it. Display the result scan line by scan line. Be able to display the active polygon and edge lists for each scan line.

4-14 Implement the spanning scan line algorithm (Watkins) described in Sec. 4–16. Use the two scenes described above to test it. Display the result scan line by scan line. Be able to display the active edge list and intersection stack at any scan line.

4-15 Modify the spanning scan line visible surface algorithm of Sec. 4–16 to take advantage of depth priority coherence [Romn68].

4-16 Modify the spanning scan line algorithm with penetrating polygons to incorporate a z priority sort to determine if intersecting span segments are visible (see p. 412).

4-17 Implement an octree visible surface algorithm for a simple scene (see Sec. 4–18).

4-18 Implement the marching cubes algorithm.

4-19 Implement the opaque visible surface ray tracing algorithm described in Sec. 4–20. Use the two scenes described above to test it. Assume the observer is at infinity on the positive z-axis. Display the result pixel by pixel as it is generated. Be able to display the active object list as each pixel is processed. Improve the efficiency of the algorithm by defining a bounding box for the entire scene and projecting it onto the image plane. Any pixel outside the projected area need not be traced. Compare the results with and without this addition.

Chapter 5

The following projects are most conveniently implemented with a raster display having at least 256 intensity levels or colors. More intensity levels or colors will yield more aesthetically pleasing results.

5-1 Consider an n-sided polygonal representation of an opaque cylinder of radius R, with its axis normal to the view direction. For $n = 8, 16, 32$, a simple Lambertian ambient illumination model (see Eq. $5 - 1$) and a suitable visible surface algorithm, write a program to display a cylinder of radius $R = 15$ (see Fig. 5–3). Assume that a single point light source is located at infinity on the positive z-axis, as is the observer. Rotate the cylinder $90°$ about the z-axis, and compare the results.

5–2 Add Gouraud shading (see Sec. 5–6) to the cylinder of Project 5–1 using the simple illumination model. Compare the results. Add specular reflection to the illumination model (see Eq. $5 - 7$). Vary the parameter n.

5–3 Add Phong shading (see Sec. 5–7) to the cylinder of Project 5–1 using the simple illumination model. Compare the results to those of Projects 5–1 and 5–2. Add specular reflection to the illumination model (see Eq. $5 - 7$); compare the results, in particular the shape of the specular reflection, to those for Gouraud shading.

5–4 Using the rectangle plus triangle test scene described earlier for Projects 4–5 to 4–19, write a program to display a transparent triangle (see Sec. 5–10) and an opaque rectangle using the Newell–Newell–Sancha (see Sec. 4–12) or the spanning scan line hidden surface algorithm (see Sec. 4–16). Ignore refraction effects. Use a linear combination of the intensity of the visible transparent surface and the opaque surface immediately behind it to represent the intensity of the combined surface. Vary the transparency factor and observe the effects. Make the rectangle transparent and the triangle opaque, and compare the results.

5–5 Add shadows to the spanning scan line algorithm implemented in Project 4–14. Assume both the triangle and the rectangle are opaque. The observer is located at infinity on the positive z-axis, and the single point light source is located at $x = 30$, $z = 40$. How would you handle the shadow from a transparent triangle?

5–6 Add shadows to the opaque visible surface ray tracing algorithm implemented in Project 4–19. Assume the triangle and the rectangle are opaque, the observer is at positive infinity on the z-axis and the single point light source is at $x = 30$, $z = 40$. How would you handle the shadow from a transparent triangle?

5–7 Write a program to add a black and white texture pattern to an octant of the sphere using the patch subdivision technique and mipmapping. Display the results on a 32×32 raster grid. Use a 64×64 raster grid and compare the results.

5–8 Add shadows to the z-buffer algorithm of Project 4–9.

5–9 Implement a simple program to show umbra and penumbra shadows, using an area light source. Use a scene composed of two planes, as shown in Fig. 5–36.

5–10 Generate a stochastic mountain starting from a simple pyramid.

5–11 Construct the image in Fig. 5–63.

5–12 Implement the global illumination model with the ray tracing algorithm described in Sec. 5–14. Use the simple test scene described in Ex. 5–9 to test the program.

5–13 Write a program to draw simple variable-sized colored squares on a color monitor. Modify the program to allow the color of the current square to be added to, subtracted from, or to replace the color of the previous square. Use the program to verify the additive color system (see Sec. 5–19), e.g., Red + Blue = Magenta. Experiment with the effects of simultaneous contrast by drawing a small purple square inside both a bright red and a bright blue square.

5–14 Implement the median cut color quantization algorithm. Apply it to several images. Comment on the results for various levels of quantization.

5–15 Complete the generational reduction of the octree of Ex. 5–16.

REFERENCES

[Abra85] Abram, G., Westover, L., and Whitted, T., Efficient alias-free rendering using bit-masks and look-up tables, *Comput. Graph.*, Vol. 19, pp. 53–59, 1985 (SIGGRAPH 85).

[Ackl80] Ackland, B., and Weste, N., Real time animation on a frame store display system, *Comput. Graph.*, Vol. 14, pp. 182–188, 1980 (SIGGRAPH 80).

[Ackl81] Ackland, B., and Weste, N., The edge flag algorithm—a fill method for raster scan displays, *IEEE Trans. on Comput.*, Vol. C-30, pp. 41–48, 1981.

[Adob85] Adobe Systems, *PostScript language reference manual*, Reading, MA: Addison-Wesley, 1985.

[Aman84] Amanatides, J., Ray tracing with cones, *Comput. Graph.*, Vol. 18, pp. 129–135, 1984 (SIGGRAPH 84).

[Aman87] Amanatides, J,. and Woo, A., A fast voxel traversal algorithm for ray tracing, *Eurographics 87*, Marechal, G., Ed., pp. 3–10, North Holland, 1987.

[Appe67] Appel, A., The notion of quantitative invisibility and the machine rendering of solids, *Proc. ACM Nat. Conf.*, pp. 387–393, Washington, DC: Thompson Books, 1967; see also [Free80].

[Appe68] Appel, A., Some techniques for shading machine rendering of solids, *SJCC 1968*, pp. 37–45, Washington, DC: Thompson Books, 1968.

[Appe79] Appel, A., Rohlf, F.J., and Stein, A.J., The haloed line effect for hidden line elimination, *Comput. Graph.*, Vol. 13, pp. 151–157, 1979 (SIGGRAPH 79).

[Appl92] Apple Computers, *Macintosh Human Interface Guidelines*, Reading, MA: Addison-Wesley, 1992.

[Appl95] Apple Computers, *Advanced Color Imaging on the Mac OS*, Reading, MA: Addison-Wesley, 1995.

665

666   References

[Arch72]   Archuleta, M., Hidden surface line drawing algorithm, University of Utah Comp. Sci. Dept., Tech. Rep. UTEC-CSc-72-121, June 1972.

[Arna87]   Arnalldi, B., Priol, T., and Bouatouch, K., A new space subdivision method for ray tracing CSG modelled scenes, *The Visual Computer*, Vol. 3, pp. 98–108, 1987.

[Arvo86]   Arvo, J., Backward ray tracing, *Developments in Ray Tracing*, Course Notes 12 for (SIGGRAPH 86), Dallas, TX, 18–22 August 1986.

[Athe78a]   Atherton, P.R., "Polygon Shadow Generation with Application to Solar Rights", Master's thesis, Cornell University, 1978.

[Athe78b]   Atherton, P.R., Weiler, K., and Greenberg, D., Polygon shadow generation, *Comput. Graph.*, Vol. 12, pp. 275–281, 1978 (SIGGRAPH 78).

[Athe81]   Atherton, P.R., A method of interactive visualization of CAD surface models on a color video display, *Comput. Graph.*, Vol. 15, pp. 279–296, 1981 (SIGGRAPH 81).

[Athe83]   Atherton, P.R., A scan-line hidden surface removal procedure for constructive solid geometry, *Comput. Graph.*, Vol. 17, pp. 73–82, 1983 (SIGGRAPH 83).

[Badl77]   Badler, N.I., Disk generator for a raster display device, *Comput. Graph. and Image Process.*, Vol. 6., pp. 589–593, 1977.

[Baec79]   Baecker, R., Digital video display systems and dynamic graphics, *Comput. Graph.*, Vol. 13, pp. 48–56, 1979 (SIGGRAPH 79).

[Bala94a]   Balasubramanian, R., Bouman, C.A., and Allebach, J.P., Sequential scalar quantization of color images, *Jour. of Elect. Imag.*, Vol. 3, No. 1, pp. 45–59, 1994.

[Bala94b]   Balasubramanian, R., Allebach, J.P., and Bouman, C.A., Color-image quantization with use of a fast binary splitting technique, *Jour. Opt. Soc. of America*, Series A, Vol. 11, pp. 2777–2786, 1994.

[Barb93]   Barber, C.B., Dobkin, D.P., and Huhdanpaa, H., The quickhull algorithm for convex hull, TR GCG53, The Geometry Center, University of Minnesota, July 1993.

[Bark97]   Barkans, A.C., Color recovery: True-color 8-bit interactive graphics, *IEEE Comput. Graph. and Appl.*, Vol. 17, No. 1, pp. 67–77, 1997.

[Barr74]   Barrett, R.C., and Jordan, B.W., Scan conversion algorithms for a cell organized raster display, *CACM*, Vol. 17, pp. 157–163, 1974.

[Barr84]   Barr, A.H., private communication, 1984.

[Baum89]   Baum, D.R., Rushmeier, H.E., and Winget, J.M., Improving radiosity solutions through the use of analytically determined form-factors, *Comput. Graph.*, Vol. 23, pp. 325–344, 1989 (SIGGRAPH 89).

[Baye73] Bayer, B.E., An optimum method for two-level rendition of continuous-tone pictures, *Int. Conf. Commun. Conf. Rec.*, pp. (26-11)–(26-15), 1973.

[Beat81] Beatty, J.C., Booth, K.S., and Matthies, L.H., Revisiting Watkins algorithm, CMCCS'81, *Proc. 7th Canadian Man-Computer Communications Conference*, pp. 359–370, June 1981.

[Beat82] Beatty, J.C., and Booth, K.S., Eds., Tutorial on computer graphics, 2nd ed., Silver Spring, MD: IEEE Computer Society Press, 1982.

[Beck63] Beckmann, P., and Spizzichino, A., *Scattering of Electromagnetic Waves from Rough Surfaces*, New York: MacMillan, pp. 1–33, 70–98, 1963.

[Bedf58] Bedford, R.E., and Wyszecki, G.W., Wavelength discrimination for point sources, *Jour. Opt. Soc. of America*, Vol. 48, Series A, pp. 129–135, 1958.

[Bels76] Belser, K., Comment on "An improved algorithm for the generation of nonparametric curves", *IEEE Trans. on Comput.*, Vol. C-25, pp. 103, 1976.

[Bent75] Bentley, J.L., Multidimensional binary search trees used for associative searching, *CACM*, Vol. 18, pp. 509–517, 1975.

[Berg78] Bergeron, R.D., Bono, P.R., and Foley, J.D., Graphics programming using the core system, *Computing Surveys*, Vol. 10, pp. 389–443, 1978.

[Berg86] Bergeron, P., A general version of Crow's shadow volumes, *IEEE Comput. Graph. and Appl.*, Vol. 6, No. 9, pp. 17–28, 1986.

[Besi37] Besicovitch, A.S., and Ursell, H.D., Sets of fractional dimensions (V): On dimensional numbers of some continuous curves, *Jour. of the Lon. Math. Soc.*, Vol. 12, pp. 18–25, 1937.

[Bier86] Bier, E.A., and Sloan, K.R., Jr., Two-part texture mappings, *IEEE Comput. Graph. and Appl.*, Vol. 6, No. 9, pp. 40–53, 1986.

[Bish86] Bishop, G., and Weimer, D.M., Fast Phong shading, *Comput. Graph.*, Vol. 20, pp. 103–106, 1986 (SIGGRAPH 86).

[Blin76] Blinn, J.F., and Newell, M.E., Texture and reflection in computer generated images, *CACM*, Vol. 19, pp. 542–547, 1976.

[Blin77] Blinn, J.F., Models of light reflection for computer synthesized pictures, *Comput. Graph.*, Vol. 11, pp. 192–198, 1977 (SIGGRAPH 77).

[Blin78a] Blinn, J.F., and Newell, M.E., Clipping using homogeneous coordinates, *Comput. Graph.*, Vol. 12, pp. 245–251, 1978 (SIGGRAPH 78).

[Blin78b] Blinn, J.F., Simulation of wrinkled surfaces, *Comput. Graph.*, Vol. 12, pp. 286–292, 1978 (SIGGRAPH 78).

[Blin78c] Blinn, J.F., A scan line algorithm for the computer display of parametrically defined surfaces, *Comput. Graph.*, Vol. 12, 1978 (supplement (SIGGRAPH 78)); see also [Lane80].

[Blin82] Blinn, J.F., Light reflection functions for simulation of clouds and dusty surfaces, *Comput. Graph.*, Vol. 16, pp. 21–29, 1982 (SIGGRAPH 82).

[Blin93] Blinn, J.F., NTSC: Nice technology, super color, *IEEE Comput. Graph. and Appl.*, Vol. 13, No. 2, pp. 17–23, 1993.

[Bloo88] Bloomenthal, J., Polygonalization of implicit surface, *Comput. Aid. Geom. Des.*, Vol. 5, pp. 341–355, 1988.

[Bouk69] Bouknight, W.J., An improved procedure for generation of half-tone computer graphics representations, University of Illinois Coordinated Science Lab. Tech. Rep. R-432, September 1969.

[Bouk70a] Bouknight, W.J., and Kelly, K.C., An algorithm for producing half-tone computer graphics presentations with shadows and movable light sources, *SJCC 1970*, Montvale, NJ: AFIPS Press, pp. 1–10, 1970.

[Bouk70b] Bouknight, W.J., A procedure for generation of three-dimensional half-toned computer graphics representations, *CACM*, Vol. 13, pp. 527–536, 1970.

[Bouv85] Bouville, C., Bounding ellipsoids for ray-fractal intersection, *Comput. Graphics*, Vol. 19, pp. 45–52, 1985 (SIGGRAPH 85).

[Brag92] Bragg, D., A simple color reduction filter, in *Graphic Gems III*, Kirk, D., Ed., San Diego: Academic Press, pp. 20–22, 429–431, 1992.

[Bres65] Bresenham, J.E., Algorithm for computer control of a digital plotter, *IBM System Journal*, Vol. 4, pp. 25–30, 1965.

[Bres77] Bresenham, J.E., A linear algorithm for incremental digital display of circular arcs, *CACM*, Vol. 20, pp. 100–106, 1977.

[Bres90] Bresenham, J.E., Attribute considerations in raster graphics, in *Computer Graphics Techniques—Theory and Practice*, Rogers, D.F., and Earnshaw, R.A., Eds., New York: Springer-Verlag, pp. 9–41, 1990.

[Brig74] Brigham, E.O., *The Fast Fourier Transform*, Englewood Cliffs, NJ: Prentice-Hall, 1974.

[Brot84] Brotman, L.S., and Badler, N.I., Generating soft shadows with a depth buffer algorithm, *IEEE Comput. Graph. and Appl.*, Vol. 4, No. 10, pp. 5–12, 1984.

[Brow89] Brown, J.R., and Cunningham, S., *Programming the User Interface*, New York: John Wiley & Sons, 1989.

[Butl79] Butland, J., Surface drawing made simple, *CAD*, Vol. 11, pp. 19–22, 1979.

[Carp80] Carpenter, L.C., Computer rendering of fractal curves and surfaces, pp. 1–8, 1980, suppl. to *Proc. SIGGRAPH 80* .

[Carp84] Carpenter, L., The A-buffer, an antialiased hidden surface method, *Comput. Graph.*, Vol. 18, pp. 103–107, 1984 (SIGGRAPH 84).

[Catm74] Catmull, E., "A Subdivision Algorithm for Computer Display of Curved Surfaces", Ph.D. dissertation, University of Utah, 1974. Also as UTEC-CSc-74-133 and NTIS A004968.

[Catm75] Catmull, E., Computer display of curved surfaces, *Proc. IEEE Conf. Comput. Graphics Pattern Recognition Data Struct.*, p. 11, May 1975.

[Catm78] Catmull, E., A hidden-surface algorithm with anti-aliasing, *Comput. Graph.*, Vol. 12, pp. 6–11, 1978 (SIGGRAPH 78).

[Catm79] Catmull, E., Tutorial on compensation tables, *Comput. Graph.*, Vol. 13, pp. 1–7, 1979 (SIGGRAPH 79).

[Catm80] Catmull, E., and Smith, A.R., 3-D transformations of images in scanline order, *Comput. Graph.*, Vol. 14, pp. 279–285, 1980 (SIGGRAPH 80).

[Chin89] Chin, N., and Feiner, S., Near real-time shadow generation using BSP trees, *Comput. Graph.*, Vol. 23, pp. 99–106, 1989 (SIGGRAPH 89).

[Chin90] Chin, N., "Near Real-time Object-precision Shadow Generation Using BSP Trees", Master's thesis, Computer Science Department, Columbia University, New York, 1990.

[Chin92] Chin, N., and Feiner, S., Fast object-precision shadow generation for area light sources using BSP trees, *Comput. Graph.*, Vol. 25, No. 2, pp. 21–30, 1992 (1992 Symp. on Inter. 3D Graphics).

[Chin95] Chin, N., A walk through BSP trees, in *Graphics Gems V*, Paeth, A.W., Ed., Boston: Academic Press, pp. 121–138, 1995.

[Clar79] Clark, J.H., A fast scan-line algorithm for rendering parametric surfaces, *Comput. Graph.*, Vol. 13, 1979 suppl. to *Proc. SIGGRAPH 79*.

[Clar82] Clark, J.H., The geometry engine: A VLSI geometry system for graphics, *Comput. Graph.*, Vol. 16, pp. 127–133, 1982 (SIGGRAPH 82).

[Clar96] Clark, D., Color quantization using octrees, *Dr. Dobb's Journal*, pp. 54–57, 102–104, January 1996.

[Clea88] Cleary J.G., and Wyvill, G., Analysis of and algorithm for fast ray tracing using uniform space subdivision, *The Visual Computer*, Vol. 4, pp. 65–83, 1988.

[Clin87] Cline, H.E., and Lorensen, W.E., System and method for the display of surface structure contained within the interior region of a solid body, U. S. Patent No. 4,710,876, 1 December 1987.

[Cohe80] Cohen, E., Lyche, T., and Riesenfeld, R.F., Discrete B-splines and subdivision techniques in computer-aided geometric design and computer graphics, *Comput. Graph. and Image Process.*, Vol. 14, pp. 87–111, 1980. Also University of Utah, Comp. Sci. Dept. Rep. UUCS-79-117, October 1979.

[Cohe85] Cohen, M.F., and Greenberg, D.P., The hemi-cube, a radiosity solution for complex environments, *Comput. Graph.*, Vol. 19, pp. 31–40, 1985 (SIG-GRAPH 85).

[Cohe86] Cohen, M.F., Greenberg, D.P., Immel, D.S., and Brock, P.J., An efficient radiosity approach for realistic image synthesis, *IEEE Comput. Graph. and Appl.*, Vol. 6, No. 2, pp. 26–35, 1986.

[Cook82a] Cook, R.L., "A Reflection Model for Realistic Image Synthesis", Master's thesis, Cornell University, 1982.

[Cook82b] Cook, R.L., and Torrance, K.E., A reflectance model for computer graphics, *ACM TOG*, Vol. 1, pp. 7–24, 1982.

[Cook84] Cook, R.L., Porter, T., and Carpenter, L., Distributed ray tracing, *Comput. Graph.*, Vol. 18, pp. 137–145, 1984 (SIGGRAPH 84).

[Cook86] Cook, R.L., Stochastic sampling in computer graphics, *ACM TOG*, Vol. 5, pp. 51–72, 1986.

[Cook87] Cook, R.L., Carpenter, L., and Catmull, E., The Reyes image rendering architecture, *Comput. Graph.*, Vol. 21, pp. 95–102, 1987 (SIGGRAPH 87).

[Cook89] Cook, R.L., Stochastic sampling and distributed ray tracing, in *An introduction to Ray Tracing*, Glassner, A.S., Ed., pp. 161–199, San Diego: Academic Press, 1989.

[Corn70] Cornsweet, T.N., *Visual Perception*, New York: Academic Press, 1970.

[Cowa83] Cowan, W.B., An inexpensive scheme for calibration of a colour monitor in terms of CIE standard coordinates, *Comput. Graph.*, Vol. 17, pp. 315–321, 1983 (SIGGRAPH 83).

[Croc84] Crocker, G.A., Invisibility coherence for faster scan-line hidden surface algorithms, *Comput. Graph.*, Vol. 18, pp. 95–102, 1984 (SIGGRAPH 84).

[Crow77a] Crow, F.C., The aliasing problem in computer-generated shaded images, *CACM*, Vol. 20, pp. 799–805, 1977.

[Crow77b] Crow, F.C., Shadow algorithms for computer graphics, *Comput. Graph.*, Vol. 11, pp. 242–248, 1977 (SIGGRAPH 77).

[Crow81] Crow, F.C., A comparison of antialiasing techniques, *IEEE Comp. Graph. and Appl.*, Vol. 1, pp. 40–47, 1981.

[Crow84] Crow, F.C., Summed-area tables for texture mapping, *Comput. Graph.*, Vol. 18, pp. 207–212, 1984 (SIGGRAPH 84).

[Csur83] Csuri, C.A., Panel: The simulation of natural phenomena, *Comput. Graph.*, Vol. 17, pp. 137–139, 1983 (SIGGRAPH 83).

[Cyru78] Cyrus, M., and Beck, J., Generalized two- and three-dimensional clipping, *Computers & Graphics*, Vol. 3, pp. 23–28, 1978.

[DaSi89] Da Silva, D., "Raster algorithms for 2D primitives", Master's thesis, Brown University, Computer Science Department (CS-89-M6), 1989.

[Davi64] Davis, M.R., and Ellis, T.O., The RAND Tablet: A man-machine graphical communication device, *AFIPS Conf. Proc.*, Vol. 26, pp. 325–332, Part I, 1964 FJCC.

[Dipp85] Dippe, M.A.Z., and Wold, E.H., Antialiasing through stochastic sampling, *Comput. Graph.*, Vol. 19, pp. 69–78, 1985 (SIGGRAPH 85).

[Doct81] Doctor, L.J., and Torborg, J.G., Display techniques for octree-encoded objects, *IEEE Comput. Graph. and Appl.*, Vol. 1, No. 3, pp. 29–38, 1981.

[Doro79] Doros, M., Algorithms for generation of discrete circles, rings, and disks, *Comput. Graph. and Image Process.*, Vol. 10, pp. 366–371, 1979.

[Duff79] Duff, T., Smooth shaded renderings of polyhedral objects on raster displays, *Comput. Graph.*, Vol. 13, pp. 270–275, 1979 (SIGGRAPH 79).

[Duff92] Duff, T., Interval arithmetic and recursive subdivision for implicit functions and constructive solid geometry, *Comput. Graph.*, Vol. 26, No. 2, pp. 131–138, 1994 (SIGGRAPH 92).

[Dung79] Dungan, W., A terrain and cloud computer image generation model, *Comput. Graph.*, Vol. 13, pp. 143–150, 1979 (SIGGRAPH 79).

[Dunl83] Dunlavey, M.R., Efficient polygon-filling algorithms for raster displays, *ACM TOG*, Vol. 2, pp. 264–273, 1983.

[Durs88] Durst, M.J., Additional reference to "Marching cubes", *Comput. Graph.*, Vol. 22, No. 2, pp. 72–73, 1988.

[Duva90a] Duvanenko, V.J., Simple and efficient 2D and 3D span clipping algorithms, Master's thesis, North Carolina State University, December 1990.

[Duva90b] Duvanenko, V.J., Gyurcsik, R.S., and Robbins, W.E., Improving line segment clipping, *Dr. Dobb's Journal*, pp. 36–45, 98, July 1990.

[Duva93] Duvanenko, V.J., Gyurcsik, R.S., and Robbins, W.E., Simple and efficient 2D and 3D span clipping algorithms, *Computers & Graphics*, Vol. 17, pp. 39–54, 1993.

[Eber94] Ebert, D.S., Musgrave, F.K., Peachey, D., Perlin, K., and Worley, S., *Texturing and Modeling, A Procedural Approach*, Ebert, D.S., Ed., Boston: Academic Press, 1994.

[Elbe95] Elber, G., Line Illustrations ϵ computer graphics, *The Visual Computer*, Vol. 11, pp. 290–296, 1995.

[Feib80] Feibush, E.A., Levoy, M., and Cook, R.L., Synthetic texturing using digital filters, *Comput. Graph.*, Vol. 14, pp. 294–301, 1980 (SIGGRAPH 80).

[Fell93] Fellner, D.W., and Helmberg, C., Robust rendering of general ellipses and elliptical arcs, *ACM TOG*, Vol. 12, pp. 251–276, 1993.

[Fiel86] Field, D., Algorithms for drawing antialiased circles and ellipses, *Comput. Vis., Graph. and Image Process.*, Vol. 33, pp. 1–15, 1986.

[Fish85] Fishkin, K.P., and Barsky, B.A., An analysis and algorithm for fill propagation, *Proc. Graph. Interface '85*, pp. 203–212, 1985.

[Fish90] Fishkin, K.P., Filling a region in a frame buffer, in *Graphic Gems*, Glassner, A.S., Ed., San Diego: Academic Press, pp. 278–286, 1990.

[Floy75] Floyd, R., and Steinberg, L., An adaptive algorithm for spatial gray scale, Soc. for Infor. Disp. 1975, *Int. Symp. Dig. Tech. Pap.*, pp. 36–37, 1975.

[Fole74] Foley, J.D., and Wallace, V.L., The art of natural man-machine conversation, *Proc. IEEE*, Vol. 62, pp. 462–471, 1974.

[Fole82] Foley, J.D., and Van Dam, A., *Fundamentals of Interactive Computer Graphics*, Reading, MA: Addison-Wesley, 1982.

[Fole90] Foley, J., van Dam, A., Feiner, S., and Hughes, J., *Computer Graphics: Principles and Practice*, Reading, MA: Addison-Wesley, 1990.

[Forr85] Forrest, A.R., Computational geometry in practice, in Earnshaw, R.E., Ed., *Fundamental Algorithms for Computer Graphics*, pp. 707–724, Berlin: Springer-Verlag, 1985.

[Four80] Fournier, A., and Fussell, D., Stochastic modeling in computer graphics, pp. 9–15, 1980, suppl. to *Proc. SIGGRAPH 80* .

[Four82] Fournier, A., Fussell, D., and Carpenter, L., Computer rendering of stochastic models, *CACM*, Vol. 25, pp. 371–384, 1982.

[Four88] Fournier, A., and Fussell, D., On the power of the frame buffer, *ACM TOG*, Vol. 7, pp. 103–128, 1988.

[Fran80a] Franklin, W.R., Efficiently computing the haloed line effect for hidden line elimination., Rensselaer Polytechnic Institute, Image Processing Laboratory Report IPL-81-004, December 1980.

[Fran80b] Franklin, W.R., A linear time exact hidden surface algorithm, *Comput. Graph.*, Vol. 14, pp. 117-123, 1980 (SIGGRAPH 80).

[Fran81] Franklin, W.R., An exact hidden sphere algorithm that operates in linear time, *Comput. Graph. and Image Process.*, Vol. 15, pp. 364-379, 1981.

[Fran87] Franklin, W.R., and Akman, V., A simple and efficient haloed line effect for hidden line elimination, *Comp. Graph. Forum.*, Vol. 6, pp. 103-110, 1987.

[Free80] Freeman, H., Ed., *Tutorial and selected readings in interactive computer graphics*, Silver Spring, MD: IEEE Computer Society Press, 1980.

[Frie77] Friedman, J.J., Bentley, J.L., and Finkel, R.A., An algorithm for finding best matches in logarithmic expected time, ACM Trans. Math. Software, Vol. 3, pp. 209–226, 1977.

[Frie85] Frieder, G., Gordon, D., and Reynolds, R., Back-to-front display of voxel-based objects, *IEEE Comput. Graph. and Appl.*, Vol. 5, No. 1, pp. 52–60, 1985.

[Fuch80] Fuchs, H., Kedem, Z.M., and Naylor, B.F., On visible surface generation by a priori tree structures, *Comput. Graph.*, Vol. 14, pp. 124–133, 1980 (SIGGRAPH 80).

[Fuch83] Fuchs, H., Abram, G.D., and Grant, E.D., Near real-time shaded display of rigid objects, *Comput. Graph.*, Vol. 17, pp. 65–72, 1983 (SIGGRAPH 83).

[Fuji86] Fujimoto, A., Tanaka, T., and Iwata, K., ARTS: Accelerated ray-tracing systems, *IEEE Comput. Graph. and Appl.*, Vol. 6, No. 4, pp. 16–26, 1986.

[Gang82] Gangnet, M., Perny, D., and Coueignous, P., Perspective mapping of planar textures, *Eurographics 82*, pp. 57–71. Also in *Comput. Graph.*, Vol. 16, No. 1, May 1982.

[Gard84] Gardner, G.Y., Simulation of natural scenes using textured quadric surfaces, *Comput. Graph.*, Vol. 18, pp. 11–20, 1984 (SIGGRAPH 84).

[Gard85] Gardner, G.Y., Visual simulation of clouds, *Comput. Graph.*, Vol. 19, pp. 297–303, 1985 (SIGGRAPH 85).

[Garg82a] Gargantini, I., Linear octrees for fast processing of three-dimensional objects, *Comput. Graph. and Image Process.*, Vol. 20, pp. 365–374, 1982.

[Garg82b] Gargantini, I., An effective way to represent quadtrees, *CACM*, Vol. 25, pp. 905–910, 1982.

[Garg86] Gargantini, I., Walsh, T.R., and Wu, O.L., Viewing transformations of voxel-based objects via linear octrees, *IEEE Comput. Graph. and Appl.*, Vol. 6, No. 10, pp. 12–21, 1986.

[Gate91] Gatenby, N., "Radiosity in Computer Graphics: A Proposed Alternative to the Hemi-cube Algorithm", Master's thesis, University of Manchester, 1991; also in *Photorealistic Rendering in Computer Graphics*, (Proc. of Second Eurographics Workshop on Rendering), Brunet, P., and Jansen, F.W., Eds., New York: Springer-Verlag, pp. 104–111, 1994.

[Gerv90] Gervautz, M., and Purgathofer, W., A simple method for color quantization: Octree quantization, in *Graphic Gems*, Glassner, A.S., Ed., San Diego: Academic Press, pp. 287–293, 1990.

[Gill94] Gill, G.W., N-step incremental straight-line algorithms, *IEEE Comput. Graph. and Appl.*, Vol. 14, No. 3, pp. 66–72, 1994.

[Glas84] Glassner, A.S., Space subdivision for fast ray tracing, *IEEE Comput. Graph. and Appl.*, Vol. 4, No. 10, pp. 15–22, 1984.

[Glas86] Glassner, A.S., Adaptive precision in texture mapping, *Comput. Graph.*, Vol. 20, pp. 297–306, 1986 (SIGGRAPH 86).

[Glas91] Glassner, A.S., Adaptive run-length encoding, in *Graphic Gems II*, Arvo, J., Ed., San Diego: Academic Press, pp. 89–92, 1991.

[Gold71] Goldstein, R.A., and Nagel, R., 3-D visual simulation, *Simulation*, pp. 25–31, January 1971.

[Gold87] Goldsmith, J., and Salmon, J., Automatic creation of object hierarchies for ray tracing, *IEEE Comput. Graph. and Appl.*, Vol. 7, No. 5, pp. 14–20, 1987.

[Gold96] Goldsmith, J., and Jacobson, A.S., Marching cubes in cylindrical and spherical coordinates, *Jour. of Graph. Tools*, Vol. 1, pp. 21–31, 1996.

[Gora84] Goral, C., Torrance, K.E., Greenberg, D.P., and Battaile, B., Modeling the interaction of light between diffuse surfaces, *Comput. Graph.*, Vol. 18, pp. 213–222, 1984 (SIGGRAPH 84).

[Gord91] Gordon, D., and Chen, S., Front-to-back display of BSP trees, *IEEE Comput. Graph. and Appl.*, Vol. 11, No. 5, pp. 79–85, 1991.

[Gots93] Gotsman, C., Halftoning of image sequences, *The Visual Computer*, Vol. 9, pp. 255–266, 1993.

[Gott78] Gottlieb, M., Hidden line subroutines for three dimensional plotting, *Byte*, Vol. 3, No. 5, pp. 49–58, 1978.

[Gour71] Gouraud, H., "Computer Display of Curved Surfaces", Ph.D. dissertation, University of Utah, 1971. Also as Comp. Sci. Dept. Rep. UTEC-CSc-71-113 and NTIS AD 762 018. A condensed version is given in *IEEE Trans. on Comput.*, C-20, pp. 623–628, 1971.

[Gree86] Greene, N., Environment mapping and other applications of world projections, *IEEE Comput. Graph. and Appl.*, Vol. 6, No. 11, pp. 21–29, 1986.

[Gree93] Greene, N., Kass, M., and Miller, Gavin, Hierarchical z-buffer visibility, *Comput. Graph.*, Vol. 18, pp. 231–238, 1993 (SIGGRAPH 93).

[Gupt81] Gupta, S., and Sproull, R.F., Filtering edges for gray-scale displays, *Comput. Graph.*, Vol. 15, pp. 1–6, 1981 (SIGGRAPH 81).

[Hain89] Haines, E., Essential ray tracing algorithms, in *An Introduction to Ray Tracing*, Glassner, A.S., Ed., pp. 33–77, London: Academic Press, 1989.

[Hain97] Haines, E., private communication, 1997. See also *Ray Tracing News*, 15 January 1988.

[Hall83a] Hall, R.A., "A Methodology for Realistic Image Synthesis", Master's thesis, Cornell University, 1983.

[Hall83b] Hall, R.A., and Greenberg, D., A testbed for realistic image synthesis, *IEEE Comput. Graph. and Appl.*, Vol. 3, pp. 10–20, 1983.

[Hall89] Hall, R.A., *Illumination and Color in Computer Generated Imagery*, New York: Springer-Verlag, 1989.

[Haml77] Hamlin, G., and Gear, C., Raster-scan hidden surface algorithm techniques, *Comput. Graph.*, Vol. 11, pp. 206–213, 1977 (SIGGRAPH 77).

[Hanr89] Hanrahan, P., A survey of ray-surface intersection algorithms, in *An Introduction to Ray Tracing*, Glassner, A.S., Ed., pp. 79–119, London: Academic Press, 1989.

[Hanr91] Hanrahan, P., Saltzman, D., and Aupperle, L., A rapid hierarchical radiosity algorithm, *Comput. Graph.*, Vol. 25, pp. 197–206, 1991 (SIGGRAPH 91).

[Hanr92] Hanrahan, P., and Saltzman, D., A rapid hierarchical radiosity algorithm for unoccluded environments, in *Photorealism in Computer Graphics*, Bouville, C., and Bouatouch, K., Eds., Berlin: Springer-Verlag, 1992.

[Hart78] Hartke, D.H., Sterling, W.M., and Shemer, J.E., Design of a raster display processor for office applications, *IEEE Trans. on Comput.*, Vol. C-27, pp. 337–348, 1978.

[Heck80] Heckbert, P.S., "Color Image Quantization For Frame Buffer Display", BS thesis, Architecture Machine Group, MIT, Cambridge, MA, 1980.

[Heck82] Heckbert, P.S., Color image quantization for frame buffer display, *Comput. Graph.*, Vol. 16, pp. 297–307, 1982 (SIGGRAPH 82).

[Heck83] Heckbert, P.S., Texture mapping polygons in perspective, Tech. Memo No. 13, Comp. Graph. Lab. NYIT, 28 April 1983.

[Heck84] Heckbert, P.S., and Hanrahan, P., Beam tracing polygon objects, *Comput. Graph.*, Vol. 18, pp. 119–128, 1984 (SIGGRAPH 84).

[Heck86] Heckbert, P.S., Survey of texture mapping, *IEEE Comput. Graph. and Appl.*, Vol. 6, No. 11, pp. 56–67, 1986.

[Heck89] Heckbert, P.S., "Fundamentals of Texture Mapping and Image Warping", Master's thesis, Computer Science Division (EECS), University of California, Berkeley, CA, Rept. No. UCB/CSD 89/516, 17 June 1989.

[Heck90a] Heckbert, P.S., Concave polygon scan conversion, in *Graphic Gems*, Glassner, A.S., Ed., San Diego: Academic Press, pp. 87–91; 681, 1990.

[Heck90b] Heckbert, P.S., A seed fill algorithm, in *Graphic Gems*, Glassner, A.S., Ed., San Diego: Academic Press, pp. 275–277, 1990.

[Heck91] Heckbert, P.S., and Moreton, H.P., Interpolation for polygon texture mapping and shading, in *State of the Art in Computer Graphics: Visualization and Modeling*, Rogers, D.F., and Earnshaw, R.A., Eds., pp. 101–111, New York: Springer-Verlag, 1991.

[Heck96] Heckbert, P.S., Letter to the editor, A popular algorithm, *Dr. Dobb's Journal*, p. 10, February 1996.

[Hect74] Hect, E., and Zajac, A., *Optics*, Reading, MA: Addison-Wesley, 1974.

[Hedg82] Hedgley, D.R., Jr., A general solution to the hidden-line problem, NASA Ref. Pub. 1085, March 1982.

[Hntr75] Hunter, R.S., *The Measurement of Appearance*, New York: John Wiley & Sons, 1975.

[Hodg85] Hodges, L.F., and McAllister, D., Stereo and alternating-pair techniques for display of computer-generated images, *IEEE Comput. Graphics and Appl.*, Vol. 5, No. 9, pp. 38–45, 1985.

[Hodg92] Hodges, L.F., Time-multiplexed stereoscopic computer graphics, *IEEE Comput. Graph. and Appl.*, Vol. 12, No. 2, pp. 20–30, 1992.

[Holl80] Holladay, T.M., An optimum algorithm for halftone generation for displays and hard copies, *Proc. of the Society for Information Display*, Vol. 21, No. 2, Playa del Rey, CA: Society for Information Display, pp. 185–192, 1980.

[Horn76] Horn, B.K.P., Circle generators for display devices, *Comput. Graph. and Image Process.*, Vol. 5, pp. 280–288, 1976.

[Hour83] Hourcade, J.C., and Nicolas, A., Inverse perspective mapping in scanline order onto non-planar quadrilaterals, in *Eurographics 83*, ten Hagen, P.J.W., Ed., pp. 309–319, North-Holland, 1983.

[Howe82] Howell, J.R., *A Catalog of Radiation Configuration Factors*, New York: McGraw-Hill, 1982.

[Hunt75] Hunt, R.W.G., *The Reproduction of Color*, 3d ed., New York: John Wiley & Sons, 1975.

[ICC96] International Color Consortium, ICC Profile Format Specification, Version 3.3, Nov. 11, (available from http://www.color.org), 1996.

[IES87] Illumination Engineering Society Nomenclature Committee, ANSI/IES RP-16-1986, Amer. Nat. Stand. Nomenclature and Definitions for Illumination Engineering Society of North America, New York, 1987.

[Imme86] Immel, D.S., Cohen, M.F., and Greenberg, D.P., A radiosity method for non-diffuse environments, *Comput. Graph.*, Vol. 20, pp. 133–142, 1986 (SIGGRAPH 86).

[Jack80a] Jackins, C.L., and Tanimoto, S.L., Oct-trees and their use in representing three-dimensional objects, *Comput. Graph. and Image Process.*, Vol. 14, pp. 249–270, 1980.

[Jack80b] Jackson, J.H., Dynamic scan-converted images with a frame buffer display device, Vol. 14, *Comput. Graph.*, pp. 163–169, 1980 (SIGGRAPH 80).

[Jans86] Jansen, F.W., Data structures for ray tracing, in *Data Structures for Raster Graphics, Proceedings Workshop*, Kessener, L.R.A., Peters, F.J., and Lierop, M.L.P., Eds., pp. 57–73, Eurographics Seminars, 1986, Berlin: Springer-Verlag.

[Jarv76] Jarvis, J.F., Judice, C.N., and Ninke, W.H., A survey of techniques for the display of continuous tone pictures on bilevel displays, *Comput. Graph. and Image Process.*, Vol. 5, pp. 13–40, 1976.

[Jenk76] Jenkins, F.A., and White, H.E., *Fundamentals of Optics*, New York: McGraw-Hill, 1976.

[Jobl78] Joblove, G.H., and Greenberg, D.P., Color spaces for computer graphics, *Comput. Graph.*, Vol. 12, pp. 20–25, 1978 (SIGGRAPH 78).

[Jord73] Jordon, B.W., Jr., Lennon, W.J., and Holm, B.D., An improved algorithm for the generation of nonparametric curves, *IEEE Trans. on Comput.*, Vol. C-22, pp. 1052–1060, 1973.

[Jord74] Jordan, B.W., and Barrett, R.C., A cell organized raster display for line drawings, *CACM*, Vol. 17, pp. 70–77, 1974.

[Joy86] Joy, K.I., A dissection of Fujimoto's algorithm, Div. of Comp. Sci., Dept. of Elec. and Comp. Eng., University of CA: Davis, CSE-86-6, October 1986.

[Joy93] Joy, G., and Xiang, Z., Center-cut for color-image quantization, *The Visual Computer*, Vol. 10, pp. 62–66, 1993.

[Judd68] Judd, D.B., *Colorimetry*, National Bureau of Standards Circular 478, 1950. Updated in Nimerof, I., *Colorimetry*, NBS monograph 104, 1968.

[Judd75] Judd, D.B., and Wyszecki, G., *Color in Business, Science and Industry*, New York: John Wiley & Sons, 1975.

[Kaan91] Kaandorp, J.A., Modelling growth forms of sponges with fractal techniques, in *Fractals and Chaos*, Crilly, A.J., Earnshaw, R.A., and Jones, H., Eds., pp. 71–88, New York: Springer-Verlag, 1991.

[Kaan93] Kaandorp, J.A., 2D and 3D modelling of marine sessile organisms, in *Applications of Fractals and Chaos*, Crilly, A.J., Earnshaw, R.A., and Jones, H., Eds., pp. 41–61, New York: Springer-Verlag, 1993.

[Kaji82] Kajiya, J.T., Ray tracing parametric patches, *Comput. Graph.*, Vol. 16, pp. 245–254, 1982 (SIGGRAPH 82).

[Kaji83] Kajiya, J.T., New technique for ray tracing procedurally defined objects, *Comput. Graph.*, Vol. 17, pp. 91–102, 1983 (SIGGRAPH 83). Also in *ACM TOG*, Vol. 2, pp. 161–181, 1983.

[Kaji86] Kajiya, J.T., The rendering equation, *Comput. Graph.*, Vol. 20, pp. 143-150, 1986 (SIGGRAPH 86).

[Kapl87] Kaplan, M.R., The use of spatial coherence in ray tracing, in *Techniques for Computer Graphics*, Rogers, D.F., and Earnshaw, R.A., Eds., pp. 173–193, New York: Spring-Verlag, 1987.

[Kapp85] Kappel, M.R., An ellipse-drawing algorithm for raster displays, in *Fundamental Algorithms for Computer Graphics* Earnshaw, R.A., Ed, Vol. 17 of NATO ASI Series F., Berlin: Springer-Verlag, pp. 257–280, 1985.

[Kass92] Kasson, J.M., and Plouffe, W., An analysis of selected computer interchange color spaces, *ACM TOG*, Vol. 11, pp. 373–405, 1992.

[Kay79a] Kay, D.S., "Transparency, Refraction and Ray Tracing for Computer Synthesized Images", Master's thesis, Cornell University, 1979.

[Kay79b] Kay, D.S., and Greenberg, D., Transparency for Computer Synthesized Images, *Comput. Graph.*, Vol. 13, pp. 158–164, 1979 (SIGGRAPH 79).

[Kay86] Kay, T.L., and Kajiya, J.T., Ray tracing complex scenes, *Comput. Graph.*, Vol 20, pp. 269–278, 1986 (SIGGRAPH 20).

[Keeg58] Keegan, H.J., Rheinboldt, W.C., Schleter, J.C., Menard, J.P., and Judd, D.B., Digital reduction of spectrophotometric data to Munsell renotations, *Jour. Opt. Soc. of America*, Vol. 48, p. 863, 1958.

[Kell70] Kelley, K.C., "A Computer Graphics Program for the Generation of Halftone Images with Shadows", Master's thesis, Univ. of Illinois, 1970.

[Kirk87] Kirk, D.B., The simulation of natural features using cone tracing, *The Visual Computer*, Vol. 3, pp. 63–71, 1987.

[Klas93] Klassen, R.V., Increasing the apparent addressability of supersampling grids, *IEEE Comput. Graph. and Appl.*, Vol. 13, No. 5, pp. 74–77, 1993.

[Klim94] Klimaszewski, K.S., "Faster Ray Tracing Using Adaptive Grids and Area Sampling", Ph.D. dissertation, Dept. of Civil Engineering, Brigham Young University, Provo, Utah, 1994.

[Knut73] Knuth, D.E., *The Art of Computer Programming* Vol. 3, *Sorting and Searching*, Reading, MA: Addison-Wesley, 1973.

[Knut87a] Knuth, D.E., Digital halftones by dot diffusion, *ACM TOG* pp. 245–273, 1987.

[Knut87b] Knuth, D.E., Fonts for digital halftones, TUGboat, Vol. 8, pp. 135–160, 1987.

[Koda82] *Halftone Methods for the Graphic Arts*, (Q3), 3d ed., Eastman Kodak, Rochester, NY, 1982.

[Kore83] Korein, J., and Badler, V.R., Temporal anti-aliasing in computer generated animation, *Comput. Graph.*, Vol. 17, pp. 377–388, 1983 (SIGGRAPH 83).

[Kubo84] Kubo, S., Continuous color presentation using a low-cost ink jet printer, *Proc. Comput. Graphics Tokyo 84*, pp. 24–27, April 1984, Tokyo, Japan.

[Kunz57] Kunz, K.S., *Numerical Analysis*, New York: McGraw-Hill, 1957.

[Lane79] Lane, J.M., and Carpenter, L.C., A generalized scan line algorithm for the computer display of parametrically defined surfaces, *Comput. Graph. and Image Process.*, Vol. 11, pp. 290–297, 1979.

[Lane80] Lane, J.M., Carpenter, L.C., Whitted, T., and Blinn, J.F., Scan line methods for displaying parametrically defined surfaces, *CACM*, Vol. 23, pp. 23–34, 1980.

[Lang94] Lange, B., The simulation of radiant light transfer with stochastic ray-tracing, in *Photorealistic Rendering in Computer Graphics*, (Proc. of Second Eurographics Workshop on Rendering, Barcelona, Spain, 13–15 May 1991), Brunet, P., and Jansen, F.W., Eds., pp. 30–44, New York: Springer-Verlag, 1994.

[Laws75] Laws, B.A., A gray-scale graphic processor using run-length encoding, *Proc. IEEE Conf. Comput. Graph., Pattern Recognition, Data Struct.*, pp. 7–10, May 1975.

[Lian83] Liang, Y., and Barsky, B., An analysis and algorithm for polygon clipping, *CACM*, Vol. 26, pp. 868–877, 1983.

[Lian84] Liang, Y., and Barsky, B., A new concept and method for line clipping, *ACM TOG*, Vol. 3, pp. 1–22, 1984.

[Limb69] Limb, J.O., Design of dither waveforms for quantized visual signals, *Bell System Tech. Jour.*, Vol. 48, pp. 2555–2582, 1969.

[Lisc94] Lischinski, D., Smits, B., and Greenberg, D.P., Bounds and error estimates for radiosity, *Comput. Graph.*, Vol. 28, pp. 67–74, 1994 (SIGGRAPH 94).

[Lore87] Lorensen, W.E., and Cline, H.E., Marching cubes: A high resolution 3D surface construction algorithm, *Comput. Graph.*, Vol. 21, pp. 163–169, 1987 (SIGGRAPH 87).

[MAGI68] Mathematical Applications Group, Inc., 3-D simulated graphics offered by service bureau, *Datamation*, Vol. 13, p. 69, February 1968.

[Magn70] Magnan, G.A., *Using Technical Art: An Industry Guide*, New York: John Wiley & Sons, 1970.

[Mall88] Malley, T.J.V., "A Shading Method for Computer Generated Images", Master's thesis, University of Utah, 1988.

[Mand77] Mandelbrot, B., *Fractals: Form, Chance, and Dimension*, San Francisco: W.H. Freeman, 1977.

[Mand82] Mandelbrot, B., Comment on computer rendering of fractal stochastic models , *CACM*, Vol. 25, No. 8, pp. 582–584, 1982 (see also [Four82]).

[Marc82] Marcus, A., Color—A tool for computer graphics communication, *Close-up*, Vol. 13, pp. 1–9, August 1982.

680 References

[Mars80] Marshall, R., Wilson, R., and Carlson, W., Procedural models for generating three-dimensional terrain, *Comput. Graph.*, Vol. 14, pp. 154–162, 1980 (SIGGRAPH 80).

[Maxw79] Maxwell, P.C., and Baker, P.W., The generation of polygons representing circles, ellipses and hyperbolas, *Comput. Graph. and Image Process.*, Vol. 10, pp. 84–93, 1979.

[McCr75] McCracken, T.E., Sherman, B.W., and Dwyer, S.J., III, An economical tonal display for interactive graphics and image analysis data, *Computers & Graphics*, Vol. 1, pp. 79–94, 1975.

[McIl83] McIlroy, M.D., Best approximate circles on integer grids, *ACM TOG*, Vol. 2, pp. 237–263, 1983.

[McIl92] McIlroy, M.D., Getting raster ellipses right, *ACM TOG*, Vol. 11, pp. 259–275, 1992.

[Meag82a] Meagher, D., Geometric modeling using octree encoding, *Comput. Graph. and Image Process.*, Vol. 19, pp. 129–147, 1982.

[Meag82b] Meagher, D., Efficient image generation of arbitrary 3-D objects, in *Proc. of the IEEE Computer Society Conf. on Pattern Recognition and Image Processing*, Washington, DC: IEEE Computer Society Press, 1982.

[Mete74] Metelli, F., The perception of transparency, *Scientific American*, Vol. 230, No. 4, pp. 90–98, April, 1974.

[Meye80] Meyer, G.W., and Greenberg, D.P, Perceptual color spaces for computer graphics, *Comput. Graph.*, Vol. 14, pp. 254–261, 1980 (SIGGRAPH 80).

[Meye83] Meyer, G.W., Colorimetry and computer graphics, Prog. of Computer Graphics, Report Number 83-1, Cornell University, April 1983.

[Meye86a] Meyer, G.W., Tutorial on color science, *The Visual Computer*, Vol. 2, pp. 278–290, 1986.

[Meye86b] Meyer, G.W., An experimental evaluation of computer graphics imagery, *ACM TOG*, Vol. 5, pp. 30–50, 1986.

[Meye88] Meyer, G.W., Wavelength selection for synthetic image generation, *Comput. Graph. and Image Process.*, Vol. 41, pp. 57–79, 1988.

[Meye92] Meyer, G.W., An inexpensive method of setting the monitor white point, in *Graphic Gems III*, Kirk, D., Ed., San Diego: Academic Press, pp. 159–163, 1992.

[Mill86] Miller, G.S.P., The definition and rendering of terrain maps, *Comput. Graph.*, Vol. 20, pp. 39–48, 1986 (SIGGRAPH 86).

[Mitc87] Mitchell, D.P., Generating antialiased images at low sampling densities, *Comput. Graph.*, Vol. 21, pp. 65–69, 1987 (SIGGRAPH 87).

[Mitc96] Mitchell, D.P., Consequences of stratified sampling in graphics, *Comput. Graph.*, Vol. 30, pp. 277–280, 1996 (SIGGRAPH 96).

[Miya90] Miyata, K., A method of generating stone wall patterns, *Comput. Graph.*, Vol. 24, pp. 387–394, 1990 (SIGGRAPH 90).

[Moor79] Moore, R.E., Methods and Applications of interval Analysis, Soc. for Indust. and App. Math. (SIAM), Philadelphia, 1979.

[Mora81] Moravec, H.P., 3D graphics and the wave theory, *Comput. Graph.*, Vol. 15, pp. 289–296, 1981 (SIGGRAPH 81).

[Muns41] Munsell, A.H., *A Color Notation*, 9th ed., Munsell Color Company, Baltimore, 1941. The latest *Book of Color* is available from Munsell Color Company, 2441 North Calvert Street, Baltimore, Maryland 21218.

[Musg89] Musgrave, F.K., Kolb, C.E., and Mace, R.S., The synthesis and rendering of eroded fractal terrains, *Comput. Graph.*, Vol. 23, pp. 41–50, 1989 (SIGGRAPH 89).

[Myer75] Myers, A.J., An efficient visible surface program, Rep. to NSF, Div. of Math. and Comp. Sci., Computer Graphics Res. Group, Ohio State University, July 1975.

[Nayl86] Naylor, B.F., and Thibault, W.C., Application of BSP trees to ray tracing and CSG evaluation. Tech. Rep. GIT-ICS 86/03, School of Infor. and Comp. Sci., Georgia Institute of Technology, Atlanta, GA, February 1986.

[Negr77] Negroponte, N., Raster scan approaches to computer graphics, *Computers & Graphics*, Vol. 2, pp. 179–193, 1977.

[Neid93] Neider, J., Davis, T., and Woo, Mason, *Open GL Programming Guide*, Reading, MA: Addison-Wesley, 1993.

[Nels92] Nelson, M., *The Data Compression Book*, San Mateo, CA: M&T Publishing, pp. 347–408, 1992.

[Neug37] Neugebauer, H.E.J., Die Theoretischen Grundlagen des Mehrfarbenedruckes (The Theoretical Foundation for Multicolor Printing), *Z. Wiss Photogr.*, pp. 73–89, 1937 (reprinted in *Neugebauer Memorial Seminar on Color Reproduction*, Sayanai, K., Ed., Vol. 1184, *SPIE Proc.*, Bellingham, WA: SPIE, 1990).

[Newe72] Newell, M.E., Newell, R.G., and Sancha, T.L., A solution to the hidden surface problem, *Proc. ACM Annual Conf.*, pp. 443–450, Boston, August 1972.

[Newe74] Newell, M.E., "The Utilization of Procedure Models in Digital Image Synthesis", Ph.D. dissertation, University of Utah, 1974. Also UTEC-CSc-76-218 and NTIS AD/A 039 008/LL.

[Newm73] Newman, W.M., and Sproull, R.F., *Principles of Interactive Computer Graphics*, 1st ed., New York: McGraw-Hill, 1973.

[Newm79] Newman, W.M., and Sproull, R.F., *Principles of Interactive Computer Graphics*, 2d ed., New York: McGraw-Hill, 1979.

[Nico77] Nicodemus, F.E., Richmond, F.C., Hsia, J.J., Ginsberg, I.W., and Limperis, T., Geometrical considerations and nomenclature for reflectance, NBS Monograph 160, U.S. Dept. of Commerce, Washington, DC, October 1977.

[Niel91] Nielson, G.M., and Hamann, B., Resolving the ambiguity in marching cubes, *IEEE Visualization 91*, pp. 83–91, San Diego, CA, 21-25 October 1991.

[Nish83] Nishita, T., and Nakamae, E., Half-tone representation of 3-D objects illuminated by area sources or polyhedron sources, in *Proc. of IEEE Comput. Soc. International Comput. Software and Applic. Conf. (COMPAC83)*, pp. 237–242, Chicago, IL, November 1983.

[Nish85a] Nishita, T., Okamura, I., and Nakamae, E., Shading models for point and linear sources, *ACM TOG*, Vol. 4, pp. 124–146, 1985.

[Nish85b] Nishita, T., and Nakamae, E., Continuous tone representation of three-dimensional objects taking account of shadows and interreflection, *Comput. Graph.*, Vol. 19, pp. 23–30, 1985 (SIGGRAPH 85).

[Ohls78] Ohlson, M., System design considerations for graphics input devices, *Computer*, pp. 9–18, November 1978.

[Oliv84] Oliver, M.A., Two Display Algorithms for Octrees, in *Eurographics 84*, Bo, K., and Tucker, H.A., Eds., pp. 251–264, North-Holland, 1984.

[Oppe75] Oppenheim, A.V., and Shafer, R.W., *Digital Signal Processing*, Engelwood Cliffs, NJ: Prentice Hall, 1975.

[Oppe86] Oppenheimer, P.E., Real time design and animation of fractal plants and trees, *Comput. Graph.*, Vol. 20, pp. 55–64, 1986 (SIGGRAPH 86).

[Orch91] Orchard, M.T., and Bouman, C.A., Color quantization of images, *IEEE Trans. Signal Process.*, Vol. 39, pp. 2677–2690, 1991.

[ORou94] O'Rourke, J., *Computational Geometry in C*, New York: Cambridge University Press, 1994.

[Ostr94] Ostromoukhov, V., Hersch, R.D., and Amidror, Isaac, Rotated dispersed dither: A new technique for digital halftoning, *Comput. Graph.*, Vol. 28, pp. 123–130, 1994 (SIGGRAPH 94).

[Ostw31] Ostwald, N., *Colour Science*, Vols. I, II; London: Winsor & Winsor, 1931.

[Pavl82] Pavlidis, T., *Algorithms for Graphics and Image Processing,*, Rockville, MD: Computer Science Press, 1982.

[Peac85] Peachey, D.R., Solid texturing of complex surfaces, *Comput. Graph.*,

Vol. 19, pp. 279–286, 1985 (SIGGRAPH 85).

[Perl85] Perlin, K., An image synthesizer, *Comput. Graph.*, Vol. 19, pp. 287–296, 1985 (SIGGRAPH 85).

[Pete86] Peterson, J.W., Bogart, R.G., and Thomas, S.W., The Utah raster toolkit, Dept. of Comp. Sci., University of Utah, Salt Lake City, UT, 1986.

[Pett77] Petty, J.S., and Mach, K.D., Contouring and hidden-line algorithms for vector graphic displays, Air Force Applied Physics Lab. Rep., AFAPL-TR-77-3, January 1977, ADA 040 530.

[Phon75] Phong, B.T., "Illumination for Computer Generated Images", Ph.D. dissertation, University of Utah, 1973; also as Comp. Sci. Dept. Rep. UTEC-CSc-73-129, NTIS ADA 008 786. A condensed version is given in *CACM*, Vol. 18, pp. 311–317, 1975.

[Pirs83] Pirsch, P., and Netravali, A.N., Transmission of gray level images by multilevel dither techniques, *Computers & Graphics*, Vol. 7, pp. 31–44, 1983.

[Pitt67] Pitteway, M.L.V., Algorithm for drawing ellipses or hyperbolas with a digital plotter, *Comput. Jour.*, Vol. 10, pp. 282–289, 1967.

[Pitt80] Pitteway, M.L.V., and Watkinson, D.J., Bresenham's Algorithm with Gray Scale, *CACM*, Vol. 23, pp. 625–626, 1980.

[Port78] Porter, T., Spherical shading, *Comput. Graph.*, Vol. 12, pp. 282–285, 1978 (SIGGRAPH 78).

[Port79] Porter, T., The shaded surface display of large molecules, *Comput. Graph.*, Vol. 13, pp. 234–236, 1979 (SIGGRAPH 79).

[Potm81] Potmesil, M., and Chakravarty, I., A lens and aperture camera model for synthetic image generation, *Comput. Graph.*, Vol. 15, pp. 297–305, 1981 (SIGGRAPH 81).

[Potm82] Potmesil, M., and Chakravarty, I., Synthetic image generation with a lens and aperture camera model, *ACM TOG*, Vol. 1, pp. 85–108, 1982.

[Potm83] Potmesil, M., and Chakravarty, I., Modeling motion blur in computer-generated images, *Comput. Graph.*, Vol. 17, pp. 389–399, 1983 (SIGGRAPH 83).

[Poul90] Poulin, P., and Fournier, A., A model for anisotropic reflection, *Comput. Graph.*, Vol. 19, pp. 273–282, 1990, (SIGGRAPH 90).

[Powe96] Power, J.L., West, B.S., Stollnitz, E.J., and Salesin, D.H., Reproducing color images as duotones, *Comput. Graph.*, Vol. 30, pp. 237–248, 1996 (SIGGRAPH 96).

[Poyn93] Poynton, C.A., Gamma and it disguises: The nonlinear mappings of intensity in perception, CRTs, film and video, *Jour. SMPTE*, Vol. 102, pp. 1099–1102, 1993.

[Prit77] Pritchard, D.H., US color television fundamentals—a review, *IEEE Trans. on Consumer Electronics*, Vol. CE-23, pp. 467–478, 1977.

[Prus86] Prusinkiewicz, P., Graphical applications of L-systems, *Proc. Graph. Interface '86*, pp. 247–253, Toronto, Ont.: Canadian Inform. Proc. Soc., 1986.

[Prus93] Prusinkiewicz, P., and Hammel, M., A fractal model of mountains and rivers, *Proc. Graph. Interface '93*, pp. 174–180, Toronto, Ont.: Canadian Inform. Proc. Soc., 1993.

[Ramo76] Ramot, J., Nonparametric curves, *IEEE Trans. on Comput.*, Vol. C-25, pp. 103–104, 1976.

[Rast80] *Raster Graphics Handbook*, Conrac Division, Conrac Corporation, 600 N. Rimsdale Ave., Covina, CA 91722, 1980.

[Ratl72] Ratliff, F., Contour and contrast, *Scientific American*, Vol. 226, No. 6, pp. 91–101, June 1972. Also in [Beat82], pp. 364–375.

[Reck90] Recker, R.J., George, D.W., and Greenberg, D.P., Acceleration techniques for progressive refinement radiosity, *Comput. Graph.*, Vol. 24, pp. 59–66, 1990 (SIGGRAPH 90).

[Reev83] Reeves, W.T., Particle systems—A technique for modeling a class of fuzzy objects, *Comput. Graph.*, Vol. 17, pp. 359–376, 1983 (SIGGRAPH 83). Also in *ACM TOG*, Vol. 2, pp. 91–108, 1983.

[Renk84] Renka, R.J., Interpolation of data on the surface of a sphere, *ACM Trans. on Math. Software*, Vol. 10, pp 417-436, 1984.

[Robe62] Roberts, L.G., Picture coding using pseudo-random noise, *IRE Trans. on Info. Theory*, Vol. IT-8, pp. 145–154, 1962.

[Robe63] Roberts, L.G., Machine perception of three-dimensional solids, MIT Lincoln Lab. Rep., TR 315, May 1963. Also in *Optical and Electro-Optical Information Processing*, Tippet, J.T., et al., Eds., Cambridge, MA: MIT Press, pp. 159–197, 1964.

[Roge76] Rogers, D.F., and Adams, J.A., *Mathematical Elements for Computer Graphics*, New York: McGraw-Hill, 1976.

[Roge77] Rogers, D.F., B-spline curves and surfaces for ship hull design, *Proc. of SNAME, SCAHD 77*, First International Symposium on Computer Aided Hull Surface Definition, Annapolis, MD, 26–27 September 1977.

[Roge79] Rogers, D.F., Rodriguez, F., and Satterfield, S.G., Computer aided ship design and the numerically controlled production of towing tank models, *Proc. of 16th Design Automation Conf.*, pp. 24–27, San Diego, CA, June 1979.

[Roge80a] Rogers, D.F., and Satterfield, S.G., B-spline surfaces for ship hull design, *Comput. Graph.*, Vol. 14, pp. 211–217, 1980 (SIGGRAPH 80).

[Roge80b] Rogers, D.F., Rodriguez, F., and Satterfield, S.G., A simple CADCAM system for the design and construction of towing tank models, *Proc. of Numerical Control Society 17th Annual Meeting and Technical Conf.*, Hartford, CT, 27–30 April 1980.

[Roge80c] Rogers, D.F., Interactive graphics and numerical control, *CAD*, Vol. 12, No. 5, pp. 153–159, 1980.

[Roge82] Rogers, D.F., Meier, W., and Adlum, L., Roberts algorithm, U.S. Naval Academy, Computer Aided Design/Interactive Graphics Group Study, 1982, unpublished.

[Roge83a] Rogers, D.F., and Satterfield, S.G, Dynamic B-spline surfaces, *Proc. of Int. Conf. on Computer Applications in the Automation of Shipyard Operation and Ship Design IV* (ICCAS '82), Annapolis, MD, 7–10 June 1982, North-Holland, 1983.

[Roge83b] Rogers, D.F., Satterfield, S.G., and Rodriquez, F.A., Ship hulls, B-spline surfaces, and CADCAM, *IEEE Comput. Graph. and Appl.*, Vol. 3, No. 9, pp. 37–45, 1983.

[Roge85] Rogers, D.F., *Procedural Elements for Computer Graphics*, New York: McGraw-Hill, 1985.

[Roge90a] Rogers, D.F., and Adams, J.A., *Mathematical Elements for Computer Graphics*, 2nd ed., New York: McGraw-Hill, 1990.

[Roge90b] Rogers, D.F., and Adlum, L., Dynamic rational and nonrational B-spline surface for display and manipulation, *CAD*, Vol. 22, pp. 609–616, 1990.

[Rokn90] Rokne, J.G., Wyvill, B., and Wu, X., Fast line scan conversion, *ACM TOG*, Vol. 9, pp. 376–388, 1990.

[Romn68] Romney, G.W., Watkins, G.S., and Evans, D.C., Real time display of computer generated half-tone perspective pictures, *IFIP 1968*, Amsterdam: North-Holland, pp. 973–978, 1968.

[Romn69a] Romney, G.W., Watkins, G.S., and Evans, D.C., Real-time display of computer generated half-tone perspective pictures, *Inform. Process.*, Vol. 68, pp. 973–978, 1969.

[Romn69] Romney, G.W., "Computer Assisted Assembly and Rendering of Solids", Ph.D. dissertation, Dept. of Elec. Engr., University of Utah, Salt Lake City, Utah, 1969.

[Roth82] Roth, S.D., Ray casting for modeling solids, *Comput. Graph. and Image Process.*, Vol. 18, pp. 109–144, 1982.

[Rubi80] Rubin, S.M., and Whitted, T., A 3-dimensional representation for fast rendering of complex scenes, *Comput. Graph.*, Vol. 14, pp. 110-116, 1980 (SIGGRAPH 80).

[Rush86] Rushmeier, H.E., "Extending the Radiosity Method to Transmitting and

Specularly Reflecting Surfaces", Master's thesis, Sibley School of Mech. and Aero. Engnrg., Cornell University, Ithaca, NY, January 1986.

[Rush87] Rushmeier, H.E., and Torrance, K.E., The zonal method for calculating light intensities in the presence of a participating medium, *Comput. Graph.*, Vol. 21, pp. 293–302, 1987 (SIGGRAPH 87).

[Rush90] Rushmeier, H.E., and Torrance, K.E., Extending the radiosity method to include specularly reflecting and translucent materials, *ACM TOG*, Vol. 9, pp. 1–27, 1990.

[Saka93] Sakas, G., Schroder, F., and Koppert, H., Pseudo-satellitefilm: Using fractal clouds to enhance animated weather forecasting, in *Eurographics '93*, Hubbold, R.J., and Juan, R., Eds., pp. 330–338, Blackwell Publishers, 1993.

[Same89a] Samet, H., Neighbor finding in images represented by octrees, *Comput. Vis., Graph. and Image Process.*, Vol. 46, pp. 367–386, 1989.

[Same89b] Samet, H., Implementing ray tracing with octrees and neighbor finding, *Computers & Graphics*, Vol. 13, pp. 445–460, 1989.

[Same90a] Samet, H., *Design and Analysis of Spatial Data Structures*, Reading, MA: Addison-Wesley, 1990.

[Same90b] Samet, H., *Applications of Spatial Data Structures: Computer Graphics, Image Processing and GIS*, Reading, MA: Addison-Wesley, 1990.

[Sand85] Sandor, J., Octree data structures and perspective imagery, *Computers & Graphics*, Vol. 9, pp. 393–405, 1985.

[Scha80] Schacter, B.J., Long-crested wave models, *Comput. Graph. and Image Process.*, Vol. 12, pp. 187–201, 1980.

[Scha83] Schacter, B.J., *Computer Image Generation*, New York: John Wiley & Sons, 1983.

[Schi91] Schilling, A., A new simple and efficient antialiasing with subpixel masks, *Comput. Graph.*, Vol. 25, No. 4, pp. 133–141, 1991 (SIGGRAPH 91).

[Schl94] Schlick, C., A fast alternative to Phong's specular model, in *Graphic Gems IV*, Heckbert, P.S., Ed., San Diego: Academic Press, pp. 385–387, 1994.

[Schu69] Schumacker, R.A., Brand, B., Gilliland, M., and Sharp, W., Study for applying computer-generated images to visual simulation, U.S. Air Force Human Resources Lab. Tech. Rep., AFHRL-TR-69-14, September 1969, NTIS AD 700 375.

[Schu91] Schumacher, D.A., A comparison of digital halftoning techniques, in *Graphic Gems*, Glassner, A.S., Ed., San Diego: Academic Press pp. 57–71, 1991.

[Shan80] Shani, U., Filling regions in binary raster images: A graph-theoretic approach, *Comput. Graph.*, Vol. 14, pp. 321–327, 1980, (SIGGRAPH 80).

[Shao88] Shao, M., Peng, Q., and Liang, Y., A new radiosity approach by procedural refinements for realistic image synthesis, *Comput. Graph.*, Vol. 22, pp. 93–101, 1988 (SIGGRAPH 88).

[Shap60] Shapiro, H.S., and Silverman, R.A., Alias-free sampling of random noise, *SIAM Jour.*, Vol. 8, No. 2, pp. 225–248, 1960.

[Shin87] Shinya, M., Takahashi, T., and Naito, S., Principles and applications of pencil tracing, *Comput. Graph.*, Vol. 21, pp. 45–54, 1987 (SIGGRAPH 87).

[Shu95] Shu, R., Zhou, C., and Kankanhalli, M.S., Adaptive marching cubes, *The Visual Computer*, Vol. 11, pp. 202–217, 1995.

[Sieg81] Siegel, R., and Howell, J., *Thermal Radiation Heat Transfer*, 2nd ed., Washington, DC: Hemisphere, 1981.

[Sill89] Sillion, F., and Puech, C., A general two-pass method integrating specular and diffuse reflection, *Comput. Graph.*, Vol. 23, pp. 335–344, 1989 (SIGGRAPH 89).

[Sill94a] Sillion, F., Clustering and volume scattering for hierarchical radiosity calculations, in *Proc. of Fifth Eurographics Workshop on Rendering*, Darmstadt, Germany, June 1994.

[Sill94b] Sillion, F., and Puech, C., *Radiosity and Global Illumination*, San Francisco: Morgan Kaufman, 1994.

[Sill95a] Sillion, F., A unified hierarchical algorithm for global illumination with scattering volumes and object clusters, *IEEE Trans. Visual. and Comp. Graph.*, Vol. 1, pp. 240–254, 1995.

[Sill95b] Sillion, F., Drettakis, G., and Soler, C., A clustering algorithm for radiance calculation in general environments, *Proc. of Sixth Eurographics Workshop on Rendering*, Dublin, Ireland, June 1995.

[Sill95c] Sillion, F., and Drettakis, G., Feature-based control of visibility error: A multiresolution clustering algorithm for global illumination, *Comput. Graph.*, Vol. 29, pp. 145–152, 1995 (SIGGRAPH 95).

[Smit78] Smith, A.R., Color gamut transformation pairs, *Comput. Graph.*, Vol. 12, pp. 12–19, 1978 (SIGGRAPH 78).

[Smit79] Smith, A.R., Tint fill, *Comput. Graph.*, Vol. 13, pp. 276–283, 1979 (SIGGRAPH 79).

[Smit94] Smits, B.E., Arvo, J.R., and Greenberg, D.G., A clustering algorithm for radiosity in complex environments, *Comput. Graph.*, Vol. 28, pp. 435–442, 1994 (SIGGRAPH 94).

[Snyd87] Snyder, J.M., and Barr, A.H, Ray tracing complex models containing surface tessellations, *Comput. Graph.*, Vol. 21, pp. 119–128, 1987 (SIGGRAPH 87).

[Sout79] Southworth, M., Color separation techniques, 2nd ed., *Graphics Arts*, Livonia, MI, 1979.

[Spar78] Sparrow, E.M., and Cess, R.D., Radiation heat transfer, *Hemisphere*, Washington, DC, 1978.

[Spen90] Spencer, S.N., The hemisphere radiosity method: A tale of two algorithms, in *Workshop on Photosimulation, Realism and Physics in Comput. Graph.*, Bouatouch, K., and Bouville, C., Eds., pp. 127–135, 1990: Berlin: Springer-Verlag, 1992.

[Spro68] Sproull, R.F., and Sutherland, I.E., A Clipping Divider, 1968 Fall Joint Comput. Conf., Washington, DC: Thompson Books, pp. 765–775, 1968.

[Spro82] Sproull, R.F., Using program transformations to derive line-drawing algorithms, *ACM TOG*, Vol. 1, pp. 259–273, 1982.

[Stam91] Stam, J., and Fiume, E., A multiple-scale stochastic modelling primitive, *Proc. of Graph. Interface '91*, pp. 24–31, 1991.

[Stan80] Standish, T.A., *Data Structures Techniques*, Reading, MA: Addison-Wesley., 1980.

[Stat79] Status report of the graphics standards committee, *Comput. Graph.*, Vol. 13, August 1979.

[Stau78] Staudhammer, J., On the display of space filling atomic models in real time, *Comput. Graph.*, Vol. 12, pp. 167–172, 1978, (SIGGRAPH 78).

[Ston86] Stone, M., Cowan, W., and Beatty, J.C., A description of the reproduction methods used for the color pictures in this issue of color research and application, *Color Res. Appl.*, Vol. 11, suppl. (June 1986), pp. S83–S88, 1986.

[Ston88a] Stone, M., Color Printing for Computer Graphics, Tech. Rep. EDL-88-5, Xerox PARC, Dec. 1988.

[Ston88b] Stone, M., Cowan, W., and Beatty, J.C., Color gamut mapping and the print of digital color images, *ACM TOG*, Vol. 7, pp. 249–292, 1988.

[Ston91] Stone, M., and Wallace, W.E., Gamut mapping computer generated imagery, *Proc. Graph. Interface '91*, Calgary, Alberta, pp. 32–39, 3–7 June 1991.

[Stuc81] Stucki, P., MECCA—a multiple-error correcting computation algorithm for bilevel image hardcopy reproduction, Res. Rept. RZ1060, IBM Research Laboratory, Zurich, Switzerland, 1981.

[Suen79] Suenaga, Y., Kamae, T., and Kobayashi, T., A high-speed algorithm for the generation of straight lines and circular arcs, *IEEE Trans. on Comput.*, Vol. C-28, pp. 728–736, 1979.

[Sung92] Sung, K., and Shirley, P., Ray tracing with the BSP tree, in *Graphics Gems III*, Kirk, D., Ed., pp. 271–274, San Diego: Academic Press, 1992.

[Suth74a] Sutherland, I.E., Sproull, R.F., and Schumacker, R.A., A characterization of ten hidden-surface algorithms, *Computing Surveys*, Vol. 6, pp. 1–55, 1974.

[Suth74b] Sutherland, I.E., and Hodgman, G.W., Reentrant Polygon Clipping, *CACM*, Vol. 17, pp. 32–42, 1974. Also see Sutherland, Ivan E., and Hodgman, G.W., U.S. Patent No. 3 816 726, dated 11 June 1974.

[Szel89] Szeliski, R., and Terzopoulos, D., From splines to fractals, *Comput. Graph.*, Vol. 23, pp. 51–60, 1989 (SIGGRAPH 89).

[Taub94a] Taubin, G., Distance approximations for rasterizing implicit curves, *ACM TOG*, Vol. 13, No. 1, pp. 3–42, 1994.

[Taub94b] Taubin, G., Rasterizing algebraic curves and surfaces, *IEEE Comp. Graph. and Appl.*, Vol. 14, No. 2, pp. 14–23, 1994.

[Thib87] Thibault, W.C., and Naylor, B.F., Set operations on polyhedra using BSP trees, *Comput. Graph.*, Vol. 21, pp. 153–162, 1987 (SIGGRAPH 87).

[Thom68] Thomas, T.A., *Technical Illustration*, 2nd ed., New York: McGraw-Hill, 1968.

[Thom91] Thomas, S.W., and Bogart, R.G., Color dithering, in *Graphic Gems II*, Arvo, J., Ed., San Diego: Academic Press, pp. 72–77; pp. 509–513, 1991.

[Tilo80] Tilove, R.B., Set membership classification: A unified approach to geometric intersection problems, *IEEE Trans. on Comput.*, C-29, Vol. 10, pp. 847–883, 1980.

[Torr66] Torrance, K.E., Sparrow, E.M., and Birkebak, R.C., *Polarization, Directional Distribution, and Off-Specular Peak Phenomena in Light Reflected from Roughened Surfaces*, Vol. 56, pp. 916–925, 1966.

[Torr67] Torrance, K.E., and Sparrow, E.M., Theory for off-specular reflection from roughened surfaces, *Jour. Opt. Soc. of America*, Vol. 57, pp. 1105–1114, 1967.

[Toth85] Toth, D.L., On ray tracing parametric surfaces, *Comput. Graph.*, Vol. 19, pp. 171–179, 1985 (SIGGRAPH 85).

[Toul70] Touloukian, Y.S., and DeWitt, D.P., Eds., Purdue University, "Thermophysical Properties of Matter: The TPRC Data Series", Vol. 7: *Thermal Radiative Properties: Metallic Elements and Alloys*, New York: Plenum Press, 1970.

[Toul72a] Touloukian, Y.S., and DeWitt, D.P., Eds., Purdue University, "Thermophysical Properties of Matter: The TPRC Data Series", Vol. 8: *Thermal Radiative Properties: Nonmetallic Solids*, New York: Plenum Press, 1972.

[Toul72b] Touloukian, Y.S., and DeWitt, D.P., Eds., Purdue University, "Thermophysical Properties of Matter: The TPRC Data Series", Vol. 9: *Thermal Radiative Properties: Coatings*, New York: Plenum Press, 1972.

[Trow75] Trowbridge, T.S., and Reitz, K.P., Average irregularity representation of a rough surface for ray reflection, *Jour. Opt. Soc. of America*, Vol. 65, pp. 531–536, 1975.

[Tumb93] Tumblin, J., and Rushmeier, H., Tone reproduction for realistic images, *IEEE Comput. Graph. and Appl.*, Vol. 13, No. 6, pp. 42–48, 1993.

[Ulic87] Ulichney, R., *Digital Halftoning*, Cambridge, MA: MIT Press, 1987.

[VanA84] Van Aken, J., An efficient ellipse-drawing algorithm, *IEEE Comput. Graph. and Appl.*, Vol. 4, No. 9, pp. 24–35, 1984.

[VanA85] Van Aken, J., and Novak, M., Curve drawing algorithms for raster displays, *ACM TOG*, Vol. 4, pp. 147–169, 1985.

[Veen88] Veenstra, J., and Ahuja, N., Line drawings of octree-represented objects, *ACM TOG*, Vol. 7, pp. 61–75, 1988.

[Velh91] Velho, L., and Gomes, J.de M., Digital halftoning with space filling curves, *Comput. Graph.*, Vol. 25, pp. 81–90, 1991 (SIGGRAPH 91).

[Verb84] Verbeck, C.P., and Greenberg, D.P., A comprehensive light-source description for computer graphics, *IEEE Comput. Graph. and Appl.*, Vol. 4, No. 7, pp. 66–75, 1984.

[Vien89] Viennot, X.G., Eyrolles, G., Janey, N., and Arqués, D., Combinatorial analysis of ramified patterns and computer imagery of trees, *Comput. Graph.*, Vol. 23, pp. 31–40, 1989 (SIGGRAPH 89).

[Wall76] Wallace, V.L., The semantics of graphic input devices, *Comput. Graph.*, Vol. 10, pp. 61–65, 1976.

[Wall87] Wallace, J.R., Cohen, M.F., and Greenberg, D.P., A two-pass solution to the rendering equation: A synthesis of ray tracing and radiosity methods, *Comput. Graph.*, Vol. 21, pp. 311–320, 1987 (SIGGRAPH 87).

[Wall89] Wallace, J.R., Kells, A., Elmquist, K.A., and Haines, E.A., A ray tracing algorithm for progressive radiosity, *Comput. Graph.*, Vol. 23, pp. 315–324, 1989 (SIGGRAPH 89).

[Walt87] Walton, G.N., Algorithm for calculating radiation view factors between plane convex polygons with obstructions, in *Fundamentals and Applications of Radiation Heat Transfer*, 24th National Heat Transfer Conference and Exhibition, HTD-Vol. 72, pp. 45–52, 1987.

[Warn68] Warnock, J.E., A hidden line algorithm for halftone picture representation University of Utah Computer Science Dept. Rep. TR 4-5, May 1968, NTIS AD 761 995.

[Warn69a] Warnock, J.E., A hidden-surface algorithm for computer generated half-tone pictures, University of Utah Computer Science Dept. Rep. TR 4-15, June 1969, NTIS AD 753 671.

[Warn69b] Warnock, J.E., "A Hidden Surface Algorithm for Halftone Picture Representation", Ph.D. dissertation, Dept. of Comp. Sci., University of Utah, Salt Lake City, 1969.

[Warn80] Warnock, J.E., The display of characters using gray level sample arrays, *Comput. Graph.*, Vol. 14, pp. 302–307, 1980 (SIGGRAPH 80).

[Warn83] Warn, D.R., Lighting controls for synthetic images, *Comput. Graph.*, Vol. 17, pp. 13–21, 1983 (SIGGRAPH 83).

[Watk70] Watkins, G.S., A real-time visible surface algorithm, University of Utah Computer Science Dept. Tech. Rep. UTEC-CSC-70-101, June 1970, NTIS AD 762 004.

[Watk74] Watkins, S.L., Algorithm 483, masked three-dimensional plot program with rotations, *CACM*, Vol. 17, pp. 520–523, 1974.

[Wegh84] Weghorst, H., Hooper, G., and Greenberg, D., Improved computational methods for ray tracing, *ACM TOG*, Vol. 3, pp. 223-237, 1984.

[Weil77] Weiler, K., and Atherton, P., Hidden surface removal using polygon area sorting, *Comput. Graph.*, Vol. 11, pp. 214–222, 1977 (SIGGRAPH 77).

[Weil78] Weiler, K., "Hidden Surface Removal Using Polygon Area Sorting", Master's thesis, Program of Computer Graphics, Cornell University, January 1978.

[Weil80] Weiler, K., Polygon comparison using a graph representation, *Comput. Graph.*, Vol. 14, pp. 10–18, 1980 (SIGGRAPH 80).

[Well91] Wells, S.C., Grant, J.W., and Carrie, S.E., Dithering for 12-bit true-color graphics, *IEEE Comput. Graph. and Appl.*, Vol. 11, No. 5, pp. 18–29, 1991.

[Welz91] Welzl, E., Smallest enclosed disks (balls and ellipsoids), Fachbereich Mathematrik, Vol. B 91-09, Freie Universität Berlin, 1991.

[Whit78] Whitted, J.T., A scan-line algorithm for computer display of curved surfaces, *Comput. Graph.*, Vol. 12, 1978 (supplement to (SIGGRAPH 78); see also [Lane80].

[Whit79] Whitted, J.T., An improved illumination model for shaded display, *CACM*, Vol. 23, pp. 343–349, 1979 (SIGGRAPH 79).

[Whit80] Whitted, J.T., An improved illumination model for shaded display, *CACM*, Vol. 23, pp. 343–349, 1980.

[Whit81] Whitted, J.T., A software test-bed for the development of 3-D raster graphics systems, *Comput. Graph.*, Vol. 15, pp. 271–277, 1981 (SIGGRAPH 81).

[Whit82] Whitted, J.T., and Weimer, D.M., A software testbed for the development of 3D raster graphics systems, *ACM TOG*, Vol. 1, pp. 43–58, 1982.

[Whit84] Whitten, M., Memory design for raster graphics displays, *IEEE Comput. Graph. and Appl.*, Vol. 4, No. 3, pp. 48–65, 1984.

[Whit91] Whitted, J.T., Evolution of 3D graphics architectures, in *State of the Art in Computer Graphics: Visualization and Modeling*, Rogers, D.F., and Earnshaw, R.A., Eds., pp. 33–56, New York: Springer-Verlag, 1991.

[Whit94] Whitted, J.T., Architectures for 3D Graphics Display Hardware, in *State of the Art in Computer Graphics: Aspects of Visualization*, Rogers, D.F., and Earnshaw, R.A., Eds., pp. 197–232, New York: Springer-Verlag, 1994.

[Wilh90] Wilhelms, J., and Van Gelder, A., Topological considerations in isosurface generation, *Comput. Graph.*, Vol. 24, No. 5, pp. 79–86, 1990, Workshop on Volume Visualization.

[Will72] Williams, H., Algorithm 420, hidden-line plotting program, *CACM*, Vol. 15, pp. 100–103, 1972.

[Will78a] Williams, L., Casting curved shadows on curved surfaces, *Comput. Graph.*, Vol. 12, pp. 270–274, 1978 (SIGGRAPH 78).

[Will78b] Willett, K., The 4027—Adding a color dimension to graphics, *Tekscope*, Vol. 10, pp. 3–6, 1978.

[Will83] Williams, L., Pyramidal parametrics, *Comput. Graph.*, Vol. 17, pp. 1–11, 1983 (SIGGRAPH 83).

[Witt82] Witten, I.H., and Neal, M., Using Peano curves for bilevel display of continuous tone images, *IEEE Comput. Graph. and Appl.*, Vol. 2, No. 2, pp. 47–52, 1982.

[Wrig73] Wright, T.J, A two-space solution to the hidden line problem for plotting functions of two variables, *IEEE Trans. on Comput.*, Vol. C–22, pp. 28–33, 1973.

[Wu87] Wu, X., and Rokne, J.G., Double-step incremental generation of lines and circles, *Comput. Vis., Graph. and Image Process.*, Vol. 37, pp. 331–344, 1987.

[Wu89a] Wu, X., and Rokne, J.G., Double-step incremental generation of canonical ellipses, *IEEE Comput. Graph. and Appl.*, Vol. 9, No. 3, pp. 56–69, 1989.

[Wu89b] Wu, X., and Rokne, J.G., On properties of discretized convex curves, *IEEE Trans. Patt. Anal. Mach. Intell.*, Vol. 11, pp. 217–223, 1989.

[Wu94] Wu, X., Digital halftoning by iterative isotropic error feedback, *The Visual Computer*, Vol. 11, pp. 69–81, 1994.

[Wyli67] Wylie, C., Romney, G.W., Evans, D.C., and Erdahl, A.C., Halftone perspective drawings by computer, FJCC 1967, Washington, DC: Thompson Books, pp. 49–58, 1967.

[Wysz82] Wyszecki, G., and Stiles, W.S., *Color Science*, 2nd ed., New York: John Wiley & Sons, 1982.

[Wyvi86] Wyvill, G., McPheeters, C., and Wyvill, B., Data structure for soft objects, *The Visual Computer*, Vol. 2, pp. 227–234, 1986.

[Wyvi90] Wyvill, B., Symmetric double step line algorithm, in *Graphic Gems*, Glassner, A.S., Ed., San Diego: Academic Press, pp. 101–104, 686–689; 1990.

[Xian94] Xiang, Z., and Joy, G., Color image quantization by agglomerative clustering, *IEEE Comput. Graph. and Appl.*, Vol. 1, No. 3, pp. 44–48, 1994.

[Yell83] Yellott, J.I., Jr., Spectral consequences of photoreceptor sampling in the Rhesus retina, *Science*, Vol. 221, pp. 382–385, 22 July 1983.

[Yule67] Yule, J.A.C., *Principles of Color Reproduction*, New York: John Wiley & Sons, 1967.

[Zhan96] Zhang, Y., Line diffusion: A parallel error diffusion algorithm for digital halftoning, *The Visual Computer*, Vol. 12, pp. 40–46, 1996.

[Zhao91] Zhao, J., and Davis, W.A., Fast display of octree representations of 3D objects, *Proc. of Graphics Interface '91*, Calgary, Alberta, Canada, 3–7 June 1991.

[Zhou94] Zhou, C., Shu, R., and Kankanhalli, M.S., Handling small features in isosurface generation using marching cubes, *Computers & Graphics*, Vol. 18, pp. 845–848, 1994.

WITHDRAWN
LIBRARY OF MOUNT ST. MARY'S COLLEGE EMMITSBURG, MA